FUZZY AUTOMATA
AND DECISION PROCESSES

T M

FUZZY AUTOMATA AND DECISION PROCESSES

Edited by

Madan M. Gupta
University of Saskatchewan

with Associate Editors

George N. Saridis
Purdue University

Brian R. Gaines
University of Essex

NORTH-HOLLAND·NEW YORK
NEW YORK · AMSTERDAM · OXFORD

Elsevier North-Holland, Inc.
52 Vanderbilt Avenue, New York, New York 10017

North-Holland Publishing Company
P.O. Box 211
Amsterdam, The Netherlands

Library of Congress Cataloging in Publication Data

Main entry under title:
Fuzzy automata and decision processes.
  Bibliography: p.
  Includes index.
  1. Set theory.   2. Machine theory.   3. Automata.
4. Decision-making.   I. Gupta, Madan M.   II. Saridis,
George N. 1931-   III. Gaines, Brian R.
QA248.F85   511'.3   77-534
ISBN 0-444-00231-6

Manufactured in the United States of America

This volume is dedicated to

PROFESSOR LOTFI A. ZADEH

who, during the past decade, believing in the power of fuzzy thinking created an environment of certainty thus making this work possible.

CONTENTS

FOREWORD

The natural world in which we live is a world of imprecision and inexactitude. It is a pervasive, nonquantitative world in which there are few sharp boundaries; one in which the transition from membership in one set to another is gradual rather than abrupt. It is a world in which fuzziness is the rule rather than the exception. The human brain has been accustomed to think and to reason in such an environment with varying degrees of success for a long time. However, in dealing with this real world, whether by means of analytical models or actual systems, engineers, scientists, mathematicians, and others have largely ignored this fact. Far too frequently they tried to apply the precision of classical mathematics to this imprecise, nonquantitative pervasive world of ours; when failure resulted, they wondered what went wrong. Many still try.

Obviously, a new approach is needed in this type of work—an approach in which fuzziness is accepted as an essential reality, a reality that cannot be overlooked or ignored. It is especially gratifying, therefore, to acknowledge the work of the researchers in this publication for their valuable contributions to this very important and rapidly developing field. It is also gratifying to acknowledge the devotion of many individuals that has helped to explore the new areas of applications, to stimulate the exchange of scientific information, and to reinforce international cooperation in this important field of *Fuzzy Automata and Decision Processes*.

P.N. NIKIFORUK
Dean of Engineering
University of Saskatchewan

PREFACE

The problem of control and decision-making in a fuzzy environment presents one of the most fundamental and challenging issues in the design and analysis of man-machine systems. At present, the behavior of such systems is usually analyzed by the use of methods rooted in classical mathematics. It is becoming increasingly clear, however, that classical mathematics, with a conceptual structure that rests on two-valued logic, is not well-suited for dealing with systems that manifest a high degree of fuzziness—as all man-machine systems do. To deal with fuzziness effectively, we must be prepared to lower our standards of precision and be tolerant of approaches that are approximate in nature. This is the essence of fuzzy logic and is the spirit in which one should apply the theory of fuzzy sets to the analysis of man-machine systems much too complex to be susceptible of description in numerical terms.

Commenting on this issue in some of his papers, Zadeh writes:

> In a large measure, our inability to design such machines stems from a fundamental difference between human intelligence, on the one hand, and machine intelligence on the other. The difference lies in the ability of the human brain—an ability which present day digital computers do not possess—to think and reason in imprecise, nonquantitative, fuzzy terms. It is this ability that makes it possible for humans to decipher sloppy handwriting, understand distorted speech, and focus on that information which is relevant to a decision. It is the lack of this ability that makes even the most sophisticated large scale computers incapable of communicating with humans in natural—rather than artificially-constructed—languages.

> Fuzzy set theory rests on the notion that the key elements in human thinking and human decision-making are based not on numbers but on fuzzy sets—classes of objects in which transition from membership to nonmembership is gradual rather than abrupt. The pervasiveness of fuzziness in human thought processes suggests that much of the logic behind human reasoning is not the traditional two-valued or multivalued logic, but a logic with fuzzy truths, fuzzy connectives, and fuzzy rules of inference.

> The theory of 'fuzzy sets' (or subsets) is, in effect a step toward a rapprochement between the precision of classical mathematics and the pervasive imprecision of the real world—a rapprochement born of the incessant human quest for a better understanding of mental processes and cognition.

Today, the theory initiated by Zadeh is slightly more than a decade old. Although still in its formative stages, it is clear that the theory of fuzzy sets offers a new and highly promising direction for the study of the behavior of complex man-machine systems and, more generally, human decision processes and cognition. In growing numbers, investigators in many countries are exploring possible applications of the theory and are contributing new concepts and techniques both to the theory proper and its uses in various fields. Thus, the coming decade is likely to witness a rapid growth in the literature of fuzzy set theory and its evolution into an important field of scientific methodology.

To become familiar with the theory of fuzzy sets and develop an understanding of its applications is not, at present, an easy task. The papers collected in this volume are intended to provide the reader with a broad view of the field and expose him/her to a representative collection of concrete problems to which the theory of fuzzy sets has been applied.

More specifically, in Part I of the volume, the introductory papers provide a broad perspective view, while the survey papers present an overview of fuzzy mathematics, fuzzy measures and fuzzy integrals, with applications to control systems and fuzzy reasoning.

The papers in Part II are addressed, for the most part, to the basic aspects of the theory and recent theoretical developments, while the papers in Part III are given over to applications in such fields as process control, pattern classification, cluster detection, group consensus formation and decision-making in prosthetic devices. To aid the reader in furthering his/her study of the theory and its applications, an annotated bibliography of the literature since 1965 is included in the volume.

The contributors to this volume will feel that their efforts have been rewarded if their papers provide a stimulus to others to contribute to the theory of fuzzy sets and extend its applications in various directions.

MADAN M. GUPTA
Editor

PROLOGUE

Fuzzy set theory originated in the work of Lotfi A. Zadeh about a dozen years ago. Since then, it has blossomed into a many-faceted field of scientific inquiry, drawing on and contributing to a wide spectrum of areas ranging from pure mathematics and physics to medicine, linguistics and philosophy.

The papers appearing in this volume were contributed in part by participants in a round table discussion on Fuzzy Automata and Decision Processes, held at the Sixth IFAC World Congress at MIT, Cambridge, in August 1975; and in part by other leading workers in the theory of fuzzy sets and its applications, both in the United States and abroad.

The wide ranging nature of the theory of fuzzy sets, the diversity of its applications and the geographical dispersion of contributors made the task of organizing and editing this volume a rather difficult undertaking. As editors, we have attempted to provide the reader with a broad exposure both to the basic theory of fuzzy sets and a representative selection of its applications. To this end, the volume presents a review of fuzzy set theory, including expositions of fuzzy algebra, fuzzy measures and fuzzy integrals; surveys applications of the theory to decision processes, control systems, fuzzy reasoning, fuzzy algorithms, medical diagnosis and related fields; and provides an up-to-date annotated bibliography covering the pèriod 1965 to the present.

The material in this volume is of particular relevance to those fields in which human judgment, perception and reasoning play an important role. This includes systems analysis, especially of socioeconomic systems, psychology, sociology, law, management science, operations research, medicine, linguistics, artificial intelligence and related areas.

In the years ahead, the theory of fuzzy sets is likely to gain increasing recognition as an effective tool for the analysis of systems too complex or too ill-defined to be susceptible to analysis by conventional quantitative techniques. We hope that this volume will serve to introduce the reader to the basic concepts and techniques of fuzzy set theory and acquaint him/her with some of its more important applications.

The task of organizing and editing a collection of papers on a subject as new and as diverse as the theory of fuzzy sets has not been an easy one to accomplish. We are deeply appreciative of the spirit of cooperation and understanding manifested by all of the contributors to this volume and especially those who participated in the round table discussion at the IFAC World Congress. In particular, R. G. Lex of the IFAC Advisory

Committee deserves special mention for his interest and support during and after the IFAC World Congress.

Finally, We wish to express my heartfelt appreciation to Elsevier North-Holland for undertaking the publication of this volume.

MADAN M. GUPTA
GEORGE N. SARIDIS
BRIAN R. GAINES

PART ONE
INTRODUCTION

FUZZY SET THEORY—A PERSPECTIVE 1

L. A. Zadeh

Fuzziness, vagueness and imprecision are terms with pejorative connotations. We accord respect to what is precise, logical and clear and we look with disdain upon reasoning that is fuzzy or lacking in mathematical discipline. And yet, as we learn more about human cognition, we may well arrive at the realization that man's ability to manipulate fuzzy concepts is a major asset rather than a liability, and it is this ability, above all, that constitutes a key to the understanding of the profound difference between human intelligence, on the one hand, and machine intelligence, on the other.

To some, fuzziness is a disguised form of randomness. This is a misconception—a deep-seated misconception that has retarded the development of a conceptual framework for dealing with fuzziness as a basic and distinct facet of reality. Indeed, fuzziness is more than a facet of reality; it is one of its most pervasive characteristics—a characteristic rooted in the bounded capacity of the human mind to process and store information.

More specifically, fuzziness relates not to the uncertainty concerning the membership of a point in a set, but to the graduality of progression from membership to nonmembership. Thus, the pervasiveness of fuzziness derives from the fact that, in most of the classes of objects that we form in our perception of reality, the transition from membership to nonmembership is gradual rather than abrupt. This is true of the classes of tall men, beautiful women and large numbers. And it is true of the meaning of such concepts as meaning, intelligence, truth, democracy, and love. In fact, the only domain of human knowledge in which nonfuzzy concepts play the dominant role is that of classical mathematics. On the one hand, this endows mathematics with a beauty, power and universality unmatched by any other field. On the other, it severely restricts its applicability in fields in which fuzziness is pervasive—as is true, in particular, of humanistic systems, that is, systems in which human judgment, perceptions and emotions play a central role.

Since its inception about a dozen years ago, the theory of fuzzy sets has evolved in various directions and is finding applications in a wide variety of fields—as is evidenced by the papers appearing in this volume. What is important to recognize, however, is that there are two distinct directions in which the evolution of the theory of fuzzy sets is likely to progress in the years ahead. In one, fuzzy sets are treated as precisely defined mathematical objects subject to the rules of classical logic. In another and more recent development associated with the linguistic approach, the underlying logic is not the classical two-valued logic, but a fuzzy logic in which the truth-values themselves are fuzzy sets and the rules of inference are approximate rather than exact. In this case, it is not only the assertions about fuzzy sets that are fuzzy in nature, but also their truth-values and the rules of inference by which the consequent assertions are derived.

It is my belief that, in the years to come, approximate reasoning and fuzzy logic will evolve into an important field in its own right, providing a basis for new approaches to problems in philosophy, linguistics, psychology, sociology, management science, medical diagnosis, decision analysis and other fields. At the same time, we shall also witness many important developments in the mathematical theory of fuzzy sets based on classical logic—developments that will rank as significant contributions to pure as well as applied mathematics. Needless to say, what will happen during the next decade can be foreseen only dimly at this early stage of the development of the theory of fuzzy sets. But what is certain is that, with many new and talented investigators joining the ranks of fuzzy set theorists and users, the theory of fuzzy sets will grow rapidly in importance, influence and applicability and, eventually, will be accorded recognition as one of the basic areas of human knowledge and scientific methodolgy.

"FUZZY-ISM", THE FIRST DECADE   2

Madan M. Gupta

"Fuzzy-ism" is a body of concepts and techniques aimed at providing a systematic framework for dealing with the vagueness and imprecision inherent in human thought processes. In particular, it enables one to give a precise mathematical description of what are normally vague statements. Thus, it is an attempt to remove "linguistic" barriers between humans, who think in fuzzy terms, and machines that accept only precise instructions.

"Fuzzy-ism" is young [44] and has just entered into the second decade of its existence, but its doctrine is having a profound impact on the development of the theory of decision-making. In recent years, fuzzy set theory has been applied to a wide range of problems. In many applications, conventional quantitative mathematics has been replaced by fuzzy mathematics. At the same time, researchers have developed many new mathematical concepts in fuzzy theory applicable to humanistic processes [1,27,35,47].

"FUZZY-ISM" AND DECISION-MAKING

The stimulus for advances in fuzzy set theory may be summarized by a principle—Zadeh [46] calls it "the principle of incompatibility",—which may be stated as follows:

> The closer one looks at a 'real world' problem, the fuzzier becomes its solution. Stated informally, the essence of this principle is that as the complexity of a system increases, our ability to make precise and yet significant statements about its behavior diminishes until a threshold is reached beyond which precision and significance (or relevance) become almost mutually exclusive characteristics.

Advances in science and technology have made our modern society very complex, and with this our decision processes have become increasingly fuzzy and hard to analyze. The human brain possesses some special characteristics that enable it to learn and reason in a vague and fuzzy environment. It has the *ability* to arrive at decisions based on imprecise, qualitative data in contrast to formal mathematics and formal logic which demand precise and quantitative data. Modern computers possess capacity

5

but lack the human ability. Undoubtedly, in many areas of cognition, human intelligence far excells the computer 'intelligence' of today, and the development of fuzzy concepts is a step forward toward the development of tools capable of handling humanistic types of problems [15–19].

We do have sufficient mathematical tools and computer-based techniques for analyzing and solving the problems embodied in deterministic and uncertain (probabilistic) environment [4–6, 36, 37, 41–43]. Here uncertainity may arise from the probabilistic behavior of certain physical phenomena in mechanistic systems.[1] We knew the important role that vagueness and inexactitude play in human decision-making, but we did not know until 1965 how the vagueness arising from subjectivity (which is inherent in human thought processes) can be modeled or analyzed [44].

In 1965, Professor Zadeh laid the foundation of 'fuzzy-ism' by introducing what he called "fuzzy Sets." In effect, fuzzy set theory is a body of concepts and techniques that laid a form of mathematical precision to human thought processes that in many ways are imprecise and ambiguious by the standards of classical mathematics. Today, these concepts are gaining a growing acceptability among engineers, scientists, mathematicians, linguists, and philosophers.

EXPOSURE TO 'FUZZY-ISM'

I was, and still am a member of the school of 'determinism' and 'stochasticism.' It was in the summer of 1968 that I had an opportunity to listen to Professor Zadeh, the founder of 'Fuzzy-ism,' at the IFAC Symposium on Adaptivity and Sensitivity held at Dubrovnic, Yugoslavia. There I heard his lucid exposition of his ideas and was impressed by his break with the traditional modes of thinking. These concepts were just three years old at that time and it was difficult to assign any certainty to the growth and acceptibility of 'fuzzy mathematics' in mathematical and technological circles.

I continued a casual interest in the field by occasionally reading the literature but without much excitement. It was in 1972 that I came across some very interesting and convincing papers [12, 14, 31, 45] which re-awakened my interest in the field.

I was invited to organize a special Round-Table Discussion session on 'Estimation and Control in a Fuzzy Environment' at the Third IFAC Symposium on Identification and Parameter Estimation held at The Hague in June 1973. Panel members of international repute were invited to

---

[1]Mechanistic systems are those which, in the main, are governed by the laws of mechanics, electromagnetism, and thermodynamics.

present their views on the subject, followed by a long discussion. Although most of the work presented there was theoretical in nature, the discussion did help to remove some misconceptions and open challenging opportunities for further theoretical development and applied research in the field [21,23]. The discussion inspired the interest of many more researchers. In particular, it was found that there was a great deal of interest in Japan and that Japanese researchers were contributing significantly to the field.

Following this, a very successful U.S.—Japan Seminar on 'Fuzzy Set Theory' was held at the University of California, Berkeley, in July 1974. The seminar was marked by many interesting applications of Fuzzy Set Theory to Cognitive and Decision Processes. The important papers have appeared in a volume edited by Zadeh, Fu, Tanaka, and Shimura [47].

Following the success of the discussion session at The Hague, I was invited to organize and chair the Second IFAC Round-Table Discussion session on 'Fuzzy Automata and Decision Processes' at MIT during the Sixth Trienniel World IFAC Congress, Boston/Cambridge, August 24–30, 1975 [24]. A panel of researchers from various institutions were invited to present their work. The presentation had an integrated and balanced mixture of theory and applications. A detailed report appears in the IFAC Proceedings as well as in *Automatica* [32], and a number of selected papers appear in this volume.

GROWTH OF FUZZY-ISM

The first decade of 'Fuzzy-ism' is exhibiting an exponential growth: from two publications in 1965, the year it was founded, to about 100 by 1973, the year the first IFAC Round-Table Discussion session was held, to about 450 by the time of the second IFAC Round-Table Diccussion, to over 600 by the end of May 1976 (see the annotated bibliography at the end of this volume).

Aizerman [1] has rightly pointed out: "The boldness of this (fuzzification) idea combined with not only a scientific talent but also a missionary zest and great energy of Professor Zadeh, have led to the adoption of his ideas by many scientists."

Undoubtedly, impressive progress has been achieved. In the first place, we have a better understanding of the need to abandon many of the traditional conceptions associated with the construction of mathematical models of real-world phenomena. Actually, we were confronted with this type of problem all along in the past, but now the problem has become more pressing because of the increasing complexity of our social and scientific environment and the inability of conventional computers to model the behavior of ill-defined, large-scale systems.

THE FUTURE

The growth of the first decade has convinced me that man's intuitive thinking can be modeled much more effectively via the concepts of fuzzy set theory rather than with conventional precise mathematics. In effect, fuzzy set theory provides us with a different conception of precision and allows us to solve problems that are beyond the reach of classical methods.

At this time there can be no doubt that 'Fuzzy-ism' has made, and will continue to make, a strong impact on theoretical thinking. However, it will have its greatest value only if we could apply it, with equal zest, to practical 'real-world' decision problems.

REFERENCES

1. Aizerman, M.A. (1975). Fuzzy sets, fuzzy proofs and some unsolved problems in the theory of automatic control. *Special Interest Discussion Session Fuzzy Automata and Decision Processes*. 6th IFAC World Congress, Boston, MA.
2. Albin, M. (1975). Fuzzy sets and their application to medical diagnosis. Ph.D. Thesis. Department of Mathematics, University of California, Berkeley.
3. Arbib, M.A., and Manes, E.G. (1975). A category-theoretic approach to systems in a fuzzy world. *Synthese, 30*, 381–406.
4. Bellman, R.E. (1957). *Dynamic Programming*. Princeton University Press, Princeton, N.J.
5. Bellman, R.E. (1961). *Adaptive Control Processes*. Princeton University Press, Princeton, N.J.
6. Bellamn, R. E., and Zadeh, L.A. (1970). Decision making in a fuzzy environment. *Management Science, 17*, B.141–B.164.
7. Bellman, R.E., and Giertz, M. (1973). On the analytic formalism of the theory of fuzzy sets. *Information Sciences, 5*, 149–156.
8. Bellman, R.E., and Zadeh, L.A. (1976). Local and Fuzzy Logics. ERL Memorandum M–584. University of California, Berkeley. To appear in *Modern Uses of Multiple-Valued Logic* (D. Epstein, ed.). D. Reidel, Dordrecht, 1976.
9. Bezdek, J.C. (1974). Numerical taxonomy with fuzzy sets. *J. Math. Biology, 1*, 57–71.
10. Brown, J.G. (1971). A note on fuzzy sets. *Inf. Control, 18*, 32–39.
11. Chang, S.S.L. (1961). *Synthesis of Optimal Control Systems*. McGraw Hill, New York.
12. Change, S.S.L. (1972). Fuzzy mathematics, man and his environment. *IEEE Trans. on Systems Man and Cybernatics, SMC–2*, 30–34.
13. Chang, C.L. (1968). Fuzzy topological spaces. *J. Math. Anal. Appln., 24*, 182–190.
14. DeLuca, A., and Termini, S. (1972). Algebraic properties of fuzzy sets. *J. Math Anal. and Applns., 40*, 373–386.

15. Fellinger, W.L. (1974). Specifications for a fuzzy systems modelling language. Ph.D. Thesis. Oregon State University, Corvallis.
16. Fine, K. (1975). Vagueness, truth and logic. *Synthese*, **30**, 265–300.
17. Gaines, B.R. (1976). Stochastic and fuzzy logics. *Electronics Letters*, **11**, 444–445.
18. Gaines, B.R. (1976). General fuzzy logics. *Proc. 3rd European Meeting on Cybernetics and Systems Research*, Vienna.
19. Gaines, B.R. (1976). Fuzzy reasoning and the logic of uncertainty. *Proc. 6th Int. Sump. Multiple-values logic*, Utah, IEEE 76CH 1111–4C, pp. 179–188.
20. Goguen, J.A. (1969). The logic of inexact concepts. *Synthese*, **19**, 325–373.
21. Gupta, M.M., Nikiforuk, P.N., and Kanai, K. (1973). Decision and Control in a fuzzy environment: a rationale. *Proc. 3rd IFAC Symp. on Identification and System Parameter Estimation* (The Hague), pp. 1048–1049, June 12–15.
22. Gupta, M.M. (1974). Introduction to fuzzy control. *Proceedings of the Computer and Electronics* and *Control Symposium*. Calgary, May 22–25, VI 3.1–3.8.
23. Gupta, M.M. (1975). IFAC Report: Round table discussion on the estimation and control in a fuzzy environment. *Automatica*, **11**, 209–212.
24. Gupta, M.M. (1975). Fuzzy automata and decision processes: The first decade. *Sixth Trienniel World IFAC Congress*. Boston/Cambridge, August 24–30.
25. Hamacher, H. (1976). On logical connectives of fuzzy statements and their affiliated truth functions. *Proc. 3rd European Meeting on Cybernetics and Systems Research*, Vienna.
26. Hutton, B. (1975). Normality in fuzzy topological spaces. *J. Math. Anal. Appln.*, **50**, 74–79.
27. Kaufmann, A. (1975). *Introduction to the theory of fuzzy subsets*, vol. 1. Academic Press, New York.
28. Kling, R. (1974). Fuzzy Planner: Reasoning with inexact concepts in a procedural problem-solving language. *J. Cybernetics*, **4**, 105–122.
29. Kochen, M., and Badre, A.N. (1974). On the precision of adjectives which denote fuzzy sets. *J. Cybernetics*, **4**, 49–59.
30. Kohout, L.J., and Gaines, B.R. (1976). Protection as a general systems problem. *Int. J. Gen. Syst.*, **3**, 3–23.
31. Lee, E.T., and Chang, C.L. (1971). Some properties of fuzzy logic. *Information and Control*, **19**, 417–431.
32. Mamdani, E.H., and Gupta, M.M. (1975). IFAC Report on the second IFAC Round Table Discussion on fuzzy automata and decision processes, held at the *Sixth Trienniel IFAC World Congress*. Boston/Cambride, August. Also in *Automatica*, **12**, pp. 241–296.
33. Mamdani, E.H. (1976). Application of fuzzy logic to approximate reasoning using linguistic synthesis. *Proc. 6th Int. Sump. Multiple-values logic*, Utah. IEEE 76CH 1111–4C, 192–202.
34. Maydole, R.E. (1972). Many-Valued Logic as a Basis for Set Theory. Ph.D. Thesis. Boston University, Boston, MA.
35. Negoita, C.V. (1975). *Introduction to Fuzzy Set Theory for Systems Analysis.*

Wiley, New York.

36. Pratt, S.W., Raiffa, H., and Schlaifer, R. (1965). *Introduction to Statistical Decision Theory*. McGraw-Hill, New York.

37. Raiffa, H. (1968). *Decision Analysis—Introductory Lectures on Choices Under Uncertainty*. Addison-Wesley, Reading, MA.

38. Ragade, R.K. (1976). Fuzzy sets in communication systems and in consensus formation systems. To appear in *Journal of Cybernetics*.

39. Ragade, R.K. (1976). Profile Transformation Algebra and Group Consensus Formation through Fuzzy Set Theory. *this volume*, part III.

40. Russell, B. (1923). Vagueness. *Australian J. Philos.*, **1**, 84–92.

41. Tsypkin, Ya.Z. (1968). Is there a theory of optimal adaptive systems? *Automat. Remote Control* (USSR), **29** (1).

42. Zadeh, L.A. (1958). What is optimal? *IRE Trans. Inform. Theory*, IT–4 (1), 3.

43. Zadeh, L.A. (1963). On the definition of adaptivity. *Proc. IEEE*, **51**, 469.

44. Zadeh, L.A. (1965). Fuzzy sets. *Information and Control*, **8**, 338–353.

45. Zadeh, L.A. (1972). A new approach to system analysis. In *Man and Computer* (Marois, M., ed.), pp. 55–94. North Holland, Amsterdam.

46. Zadeh, L.A. (1973). Outline of a new approach to the analysis of complex systems and decision processes. *IEEE Trans. Syst. Man Cybern.*, **SMC–1**, 28–44.

47. Zadeh, L.A., Fu, K.S., Tanaka, K., and Shimura, M. (1975). *Fuzzy Sets and their Application to Cognitive and Decision Processes*. Academic Press, New York.

48. Zadeh, L.A. (1975). Fuzzy logic and approximate reasoning (In memory of Grigore Moisil). *Synthese*, **30**, 407–428.

49. Zadeh, L.A. (1975). The concept of a linguistic variable and its application to approximate reasoning. *Inf. Sci.*, **8**, 199–249; **8**, 301–357; **9**, 43–80.

50. Zadeh, L.A. (1976). The Linguistic Approach and Its Application to Decision Analysis. In *Directions in Large Scale Systems* (Y.C. Ho and S.K. Mitter, eds.), pp. 339–370. Plenum, New York.

51. Zadeh, L.A. (1976). A fuzzy algorithmic approach to the definition of complex or imprecise concepts. *Inter. J. Man-Machine Studies*, **8**, 249–291.

52. Zadeh, L.A. (1976). Semantic Inference from Fuzzy Premises, *Proc. 6th Inter. Symp. on Multiple-Valued Logic*, Utah State University, Logan, pp. 217–218.

PROGRESS IN MODELING OF HUMAN REASONING BY FUZZY LOGIC $\qquad$ 3

A. Kaufmann

During the past dozen years, the seminal work of Zadeh has stirred widespread interest in the modeling of human reasoning through the use of fuzzy logic, leading to many important contributions from a worldwide community of scholars and scientists. In growing numbers, investigators in a wide variety of fields—ranging from psychology, sociology, philosophy and economics to natural sciences and engineering—are exploring this new path to the understanding of human reasoning and cognition, and are developing novel methods for dealing with systems that are too complex for analysis by conventional quantitative techniques.

In retrospect, it is evident that the trend toward the use of fuzzy logic—a logic that is much closer in spirit to human thought and language than the conventional logical systems— could have been anticipated during the past century. What held back the development of fuzzy logic was the attitudes from the mechanistic era of the nineteenth century and, more recently, the habits of programmatic reasoning fostered by the rapidly widening use of machine computation.

But, the goal of science and objective knowledge is to construct models that are closer and closer approximations to reality. Considering that human thinking is articulated by an internal language that is implicit and an external language that is explicit in nature, why should we turn away from the semantics associated with natural languages and thereby reduce the power of human expression and communication to the formalistic rudiments employed in the dialog between humans and machines? In the interest of scientific universality, informaticians tend to employ languages of greatest possible generality which are shorn of individual semantics to a point of being completely user-independent. With such languages, the user has to adapt to the language rather than the other way around. Is this not the way to lose the great richness of individual thinking, and is this not also, in the long run, a way of standardizing the human approach to problem solving? In opposition to this simplistic attitude of the majority of informaticians, there is now a strong counterinfluence of those who subscribe to the view that one should not avoid what is naturally vague or fuzzy, and are permissive of the use of words that might be equivocal in information-theoretic sense.

In man—machine communication, a word is usually an instruction with one and only one meaning. By contrast, in communication between humans, this is rarely the case. Thus, normally, to each word corresponds a universe of concrete or abstract objects, with the phrases composed of words having variable meaning and differing connotations. Could or should we follow the same pattern in our logical systems? In effect, those who argue in favor of the use of fuzzy logic are answering this question in the affirmative.

In taking as the point of departure the conventional Boolean logic (which we also refer to as informational or formal logic), the introduction of fuzziness into such a logic may be accomplished in a number of different ways. What is important, however, is that any fuzziness in our state of knowledge should be modeled in such logic in a consistent fashion. In this connection, it should be remarked that it makes no difference as to whether one talks about fuzzy logic or the theory of fuzzy subsets. Parenthetically, we shall employ the term *fuzzy subsets* in preference to *fuzzy sets* because it places in evidence the fact that the reference space of which a fuzzy set is a subset is always assumed to be nonfuzzy.

The first way in which fuzziness can be introduced into set theory is to remove the basic assumption that the question of whether or not an element of a space belongs to a subset of it admits of only two answers: "yes" or "no." Instead, we allow the characteristic function (or, equivalently, the membership function) of a set to take values in the interval $[0, 1]$. In this way, one is led to an n-ary logic in which n may be arbitrarily large or, more generally, the characteristic function may take any value in $[0, 1]$.

This "fuzzification" in the sense of Zadeh is rich enough for many applications, containing as it does the potential for a wide variety of modes of semantical interpretation. On examining this conception, some make the mistake of assuming that, since the membership function takes values in the interval $[0, 1]$, the theory of fuzzy subsets is a variant of probability theory. In fact, this is not the case. Probability theory may be viewed as a part of a general theory of measure. By contrast, Zadeh's conception falls within the theory of "valuation" (which is improperly referred to by some as "fuzzy measure"). Thus, a basic property of measure is its additivity. A valuation, on the other hand, exhibits a weaker property of monotonicity with respect to inclusion and thus is a more general notion than that of measure. Indeed, no matter what the form of a probability might be (*a priori, a posteriori, subjective,* etc.), it is always assumed to posses the property of additivity. The same is not true of valuations, which, in addition to the monotonicity with respect to inclusion, are usually assumed to satisfy certain axioms that are close to and yet distinct from that of probability theory, with the result that the concept of a valuation differs in important ways from that of a measure. In this perspective, Zadeh's theory of fuzzy subsets may be viewed as a very significant generalization of earlier work of Post, Lukasiewicz, Moisil and many others who have anticipated the need for a logic that does not exclude intermediate truth-values or degrees of membership in a set.

Another and more general way of introducing fuzziness is to allow the characteristic function of a set to take values not in [0, 1] but in a finite or infinite distributive lattice. The properties of such lattices make it possible to model human reasoning without imposing a total ordering on the valuations. Furthermore, many of the basic operations of a fuzzy logic with truth-values in [0, 1] can be extended quite readily as well as naturally to truth-values in a distributive lattice. We shall refer to this generalization as "fuzzy subsets in the sense of Goguen". Clearly, the same idea can be applied to valuations in a semilattice, modular lattice, preordering, etc. Needless to say, by giving up the property of distributivity, we lose some of the operational richness of the theory of fuzzy subsets which is associated with valuations in a distributive lattice. On the other hand, such theories may fit more closely certain forms of human thinking.

Another generalization is that of "P-fuzzy subsets". In this generalization, each element of the reference space is associated not with a point in [0, 1], but a subset (or a part) of this interval. Such P-fuzzy valuations (with P standing for "part") provide an appropriate model for many types of human reasoning, especially in decision-making—as in medical diagnosis. The algebra of P-fuzzy subsets may be reduced to an algebra of classes.

Another very interesting generalization is that associated with *heterogeneous fuzzy subsets*. In this case, each element of the reference space takes its values in a distributive lattice which is particular to that element (and may be the interval [0, 1]). Thus, in this model each element may be associated with a valuation that fits it best. The great variety and richness of distributive lattices might make it possible to select valuations which could model human thinking very closely.

One can also consider valuations that are fuzzy in the sense that an element in the reference space takes values in a distributive lattice L_1, which in turn is mapped into a distributive lattice L_2. In this way, one is led to fuzzy subsets of order 2 and, more generally, of order n. It may well be the case that some concepts related to human cognition could, and perhaps should, be treated in such a framework.

Valuations may be restricted to subsets of the reference space, as it is done in measure theory in connection with the notion of Borel fields. In effect, in this case valuations are defined on the reference space which form a structure that is convenient to use with the given operation. Such an approach to theory of fuzzy subsets has recently been described in a highly significant work by Sugeno. In this connection, it should be noted that the transition from the theory of valuations to the more restricted theory of measure could be achieved directly via the notion of λ-*subvaluation*. In effect, this involves the use of a weakened form of additivity expressed by

$$v(A \cup B) = v(A) + v(B) + \lambda v(A)v(B)$$

when A and B are disjoint sets and $0 \leqslant \lambda \leqslant 1$. Other types of λ-valuations may also be employed and are useful in some cases. It is worthy of note that this approach to valuations may be used in combination with others.

In the case of fuzzy subsets in the sense of Zadeh, that is, when the reference space E is mapped by a membership function μ into $L = [0, 1]$, the central part of L is the neutral point $\frac{1}{2}$. Thus, and valuation above $\frac{1}{2}$ may be regarded as "high", while that below $\frac{1}{2}$ would be regarded as "low." However, where needed, this neutral point may be shifted up or down. In this way, the position of the neutral point may be employed as a parameter—a possibility which may be of use in the study of some aspects of human cognition. It should be noted that the concept of a neutral point and its shifting property may be generalized to distributive lattices.

There does not appear to be a limit to the ways in which the theory of fuzzy subsets may be extended in various directions. Thus, it is reasonable to believe that in the years ahead new subtheories of fuzzy subsets will be developed to model more closely the cognitive, associative and logical processes of human thinking.

A very important notion related to the theory of fuzzy subsets is nonprobabilistic entropy—an entropy that serves as a measure of the fuzziness of a fuzzy subset. Some aspects of this notion were studied in detail by DeLuca and Termini, and some by the present writer. In brief, the entropy of a nonfuzzy set is zero, and it becomes positive when the valuation of an element is a number other than 0 or 1. Thus, the positiveness of this entropy may be interpreted as a manifestation of fuzziness or—to use a term that is commonly employed in physics and system theory—disorder. This disorder or, equivalently, positive entropy, may be an intrinsic part of the abstract or concrete phenomenon which is the object of modeling and observation. However, it is important to recognize that the entropy in question is not the classical probabilistic entropy which has its roots in measure and information theories. Rather, it is a more general concept that is susceptible of different definitions. My personal preference is to call it *index of fuzziness*, which is both suggestive and has the virtue of avoiding an infringement on the terminologies of physics and information theory. In any case, the concept of entropy in the sense described above appears to have considerable relevance to many other concepts arising in the theory of fuzzy subsets. For example, the making of a decision is associated with a certain strategy for reducing the entropy—a reduction which is not necessarily monotone in nature. The same applies, more generally, to the process of cognition, pattern recognition, and, in interesting ways, to innovation and creativity. The innovation appears in a zone of entropy whose lower and upper bounds are, respectively, neither too low nor too high. What is necessary, in addition, is the existence of an alternation of entropy in the zone in question. Thus, it appears that the notion of entropy in the theory of fuzzy subsets relates in a natural way to some of the basic aspects of human decision-making and creativity.

We know the fundamental role which the concept of implication or—as it should be more properly called—meta-implication plays in human thinking. The operator, or rather the meta-operator, "if...then...", is widely used in computer and information sciences, even though its meaning is not always well defined, especially in applications involving the use of decision tables. This operator has been extended to fuzzy subsets by Zadeh, leading to the concepts of "conditioned" fuzzy subsets and fuzzy causal relations. What is involved in such relations are equations of the form

$$A \circ B = C$$

where A, B and C are fuzzy relations, and $\circ$ is the operation of composition. Thus, if A is the cause and C is the effect, then B is the relation of causality. When representing meta-implications, such causality relations may be generated sequentially and have interesting interpretations in terms of chains of logical implications.

A method for the inverse of fuzzy relations has been developed by Sanchez. His method casts much light on the utilization and manipulation of inverse fuzzy relations as well as inverse "meta-implications" which are meaningful in the context of fuzzy subsets but not otherwise. In this connection, it should be noted that the use of the operators "max" and "min" in the composition of fuzzy relations may be justified on the basis of maximization of the valuation of the information yielded by the composition. However, there is nothing to prevent the use of other operators to define the composition of fuzzy relations—operators such as max-product or, more generally, max-star, where star denotes a particular operator which is chosen to fit the needs of a specific application. What we observe in this area of research is that the theory of fuzzy relations is undergoing a process of generalization and elaboration similar to that which took place in matrix calculus during the past century. Indeed, there are many parallelisms between the two theories, with the operations of max and min in the theory of fuzzy relations corresponding to those of sum and product in matrix calculus. It appears very likely that the recently initiated studies of fuzzy relations will lead to many results of both theoretical and practical interest.

As was pointed out earlier, the theory of fuzzy subsets provides a basis for the explanation of many phenomena relating to cognitive processes and, in particular, pattern recognotion. We know that such processes are, for the most part, of the parallel-series type, in the sense that the receptors of information act, in the main, in parallel, while their outputs are processed serially by rules which, though highly variable and complex, are susceptible of analysis by methods derived from the theory of fuzzy subsets. As an illustration, consider a fuzzy subset G, of the Cartesian product $E_1 \times E_2$. We shall refer to G as a "graph" or, preferably, as an "image". Using Zadeh's characterization of fuzzy subsets, the fuzzy graph or image G assumes the form of a matrix whose entries are the numbers in the interval $[0, 1]$. What is of great interest in connection with such graphs is the family of non-fuzzy graphs which correspond to the α-level sets of G. The latter graphs form a nested collection of sets which exhibit many interesting properties and might be of use in the modeling of mechanisms of acquisition of information and cognition. In particular, the fuzzy graphs in the product $E \times E$ appear to have a wide field of applications, especially in the modeling of relations of resemblance (characterized by symmetry and reflexivity)—relations which have many remarkable properties and wide-ranging implications. In particualr, their decomposition, for a given α-level, into maximal similarity subrelations (which are symmetric, reflexive, and transitive), yields a hierarchical structure which may provide a basis for explaining various phenomena relating to form perception and pattern recognition.

Although the theory of fuzzy subsets is distinct from the theory of probabilities, there are areas of interaction between the two. Thus, there are states of nature which are perceived fuzzily and yet have measure in the sense of probability theory. By adapting the axiomatic Borel-Kolmogorov foundations of probability theory, one can then speak of "fuzzy events". What must be taken with consideration, however, is that, in the case of fuzzy subsets, a subset has a pseudo-complement rather than a Boolean complement. With this modification in the axiomatic structure of probability theory, one can construct a calculus of probabilities that is adapted to fuzzy subsets and is applicable to both *a priori* and *a posteriori* (Bayesian) probabilities. Similarly, many statistical techniques may be adapted to deal with fuzzy data which are not well-defined in the conventional sense. This applies, in particular, to factorial analysis, which may be extended quite naturally to deal with fuzzy, overlapping subsets. What this suggests, in turn, is that we should not force disjointness upon clusters of points if, in reality, they do not have this property.

Decision theory, econometrics and economic planning—all deal with data which, in large measure, are fuzzy in nature. Many investigations which are now in progress should make it possible to manipulate fuzzy data in economic analyses and thereby render the conclusions arrived at through such analyses more realistic and hence more reliable. What this implies, however, is that the notion of optimality in economics will have to undergo a significant revision. Thus, in the presense of fuzzy data, one can no longer define a point or a region where a function is optimal; rather, one should treat economic preferences as a problem of optimization under multiple criteria. This is, in fact, the sense in which operations research is evolving at present, mainly in response to the pressure for greater realism in the solution of problems within its field. Subjectivity is no longer rejected; it must be dealt with if it exists. Furthermore, it need not be measurable in quantitative terms; all that is needed is that it be susceptible of valuation in the sense defined above. What is evident is that the notion of fuzzy optimality, in the sense defined by Zadeh and other investigators, makes it possible to gain much better insight into the complexities of human preference relations. Thus, it is quite likely, as was anticipated by Bergson more than fifty years ago, that a mathematical structure that is adapted to the needs of humanistic sciences would be effective in the modeling of human systems. In this connection, it should be noted that the powerful techniques of dynamic programming in the sense of Bellman-Pontryagin can readily be adapted to fuzzy concepts, since the basic principles remain the same, with only the notion of strategy requiring an appropriate extension.

It is my belief that in system theory, in the theory of languages, in all that is concerned with automata and Turing machines, in machines with parallel processing as in Rosenblatt's perceptrons, in such abstract areas as topology as well as in the much more concrete areas relating to pattern recognition, in quantum physics and geophysics, and many other areas too numerous to cite, the theory of fuzzy subsets offers new and powerful tools for the analysis, synthesis and systematic study. Its influence in science has been felt already and is certain to grow in the years to come.

Like others, I have encountered antagonistic attitudes toward the theory of fuzzy subsets, but it did not take me long to realize that such attitudes were a reflection of prior prejudice, professed by those who did not want or did not have the time to study the theory or its ramifications. But I have yet to meet anyone who remained opposed to the theory of fuzzy subsets after becoming familiar with its substance. Needless to say, whatever can be explained by the theory of fuzzy subsets can also be explained in other ways. But is this not also true of all mathematical theories? The *raison d'etre* for mathematics is its power and fertility. The same can be said about the theory of fuzzy subsets, a part of modern mathematics.

FOUNDATIONS OF FUZZY REASONING $\quad$ 4

B. R. Gaines

Models of human reasoning are clearly relevant to a wide variety of subject areas such as sociology, economics, psychology, artificial intelligence and man–machine systems. Broadly there are two types: psychological models of what people actually do; and formal models of what logicians and philosophers feel a rational individual would, or should, do. The main problem with the former is that it is extremely difficult to monitor thought processes—the behaviorist approach is perhaps reasonable with rats but a ridiculously inadequate source of data on man; while the introspectionist approach is far more successful (e.g. in analysing human chess strategy [117], but the data obtained is still incomplete and may not reflect the actual thought processes involved.

Formal models of reasoning avoid these psychological problems and have the attractions of completeness and mathematical rigor, hopefully proving a normative model for human reasoning. However, despite tremendous technical advances in recent years that have greatly increased the scope of formal logic, particularly modal logic [146], the applications of formal logic to the imprecise situations of real life are very limited. Some 50 years ago, Bertrand Russell [131] noted *"All traditional logic habitually assumes that precise symbols are being employed. It is therefore not applicable to this terrestial life but only to an imagined celestial existence...logic takes us nearer to heaven than other studies."*

The attempts of logicians to rectify this situation and broaden the scope of logic to cover various real-world problems has been surveyed recently by Haack [62a], and the role of modern developments in philosophical logic in artificial intelligence has been excellently presented by McCarthy and Hayes [103]. The current paper is concerned with an area of massive recent development not covered by either of these references, that of *fuzzy set theory* and *approximate reasoning* initiated by Zadeh.

It is no coincidence that Zadeh's previous work had been concerned

Acknowledgments: I have Joe Goguen and Abe Mamdani to thank for wakening my interest in this area by their stimulating studies and conversations. Ladislav Kohout has for many years been a close collaborator in foundational studies of system theory and I am grateful for his help and advice. Animated discussions with Susan Haack at MVL '76 influenced the presentation of this material. Finally, I am grateful to Lofti Zadeh for conversations at Berkely in May 1975 that triggered off these studies and for his continued interest and encouragement.

with successively improved refinement in the definitions of such terms as "state" [173, 166] and "adaptive" [165] in systems engineering. It was dissatisfaction with the decreasing semantic content of such increasingly refined concepts that lead to his [168] remarks that

> In general, complexity and precision bear an inverse relation to one another in the sense that, as the complexity of a problem increases, the possibility of analysing it in precise terms diminishes. Thus 'fuzzy thinking' may not be deplorable, after all, if it makes possible the solution of problems which are much too complex for precise analysis.

An independent development of the same conclusions in the context of control engineering has recently been given in [4]. They are probably valid in most scientific disciplines where the development of formal theory has had sufficient time to expand way beyond the reach of practice—journals of '*X*-theory' are often renowned for their irrelevance to '*X*-practice'!

The interaction of over-precision with lengthy chains of reasoning to produce dubious or nonsensical results is not a new phenomenon. It had been noted by Greek philosophers in such paradoxes [19] as those of *sorites* (the "heap" that remains one even if an object is removed) or *falakros* (the "bald man" who remains so even if he grows one additional hair). In the more modern context of control theory and practice cited above, consider a study in "control engineering." It clearly remains one if we replace the actual plant controlled with a computer model of that plant. It clearly remains so if we consider the plant model as a set of numeric equations. It continues to remain so if we consider the general algebraic form of those equations. And so on—each step in itself is a small enough change that we agree that the content of the paper cannot have crossed a borderline between "control engineering" and "not control engineering." Yet when the final paper appears (called "residues of contraction mappings in Banach spaces"!), few control engineers will recognize it as belonging to their discipline.

The *sorites* paradox and its variants may be seen as arising from our introducing artificial precision into naturally vague (but usable) concepts. Ultimately the motivation for such precision seems to come from a requirement for truth itself to be bivalent: "Either it is true that this is a paper on control engineering, or it is false. Which do you assert?." Whilst many may feel that the logic of science requires such bivalency, and the associated precision, there can be little doubt that we reason quite capably in everyday life without it. For example, the classical syllogism:

Socrates is a man.
All men are mortal.
Socrates is mortal.

has no classical counterpart for:

Socrates is very healthy.
Healthy men live a long time.
Socrates will live a very long time.

and yet would we wish to distinguish the validity of these two argument forms in everyday reasoning?

It was both the paradoxes introduced by over-precision, and the loss of powerful argument forms involving imprecise predicates, that led Zadeh to question the direction taken by methodologies of science that reject the *fuzziness* of concepts in natural use and replace them with non-fuzzy scientific *explicata* by a process of *precisiation*. During recent years (see bibliography) Zadeh has developed in detail a model for approximate reasoning with vague data. Rather than regard human reasoning processes as themselves 'approximating' to some more refined and exact logical process that could be carried out perfectly with mathematical precision, he has suggested that the essence and power of human reasoning is in its capability to grasp and use inexact concepts directly. Zadeh argues that attempts to model, or emulate, it by formal systems of increasing precision will lead to decreasing validity and relevance. Most human reasoning is essentially "shallow" in nature and does not rely on long chains of inference unsupported by intermediate data—it requires, rather than merely allows, redundancy of data and paths of reasoning—it accepts minor contradictions and contains their effects so that universal inferences may not be derived from their presence.

The insights that these arguments give into the nature of human thought processes and, in particular, to their modelling and replication in the computer, are of major importance to a wide range of theoretical and applied disciplines—particularly to the role of formalism in the epistemology of science. The arguments have become associated with "fuzzy sets theory" [167], and this does indeed provide a mathematical foundation for the explication of approximate reasoning. However, it is important to note that Zadeh's analysis of human reasoning processes and his exposition of fuzzy set theory are not one and the same—indeed they are quite distinct developments that must be separated, at least conceptually, if a full appreciation is to be had of either. As analogies one may conceive of fuzzy sets being to approximate reasoning what Lebesgue integration is to probability theory; what matrix algebra is to systems theory; or what lattice theory is to a propositional calculus; i.e., vital mathematical tools for certain approaches to the theory but not the theory itself.

Figure 1 was compiled from an up-to-date bibliography on fuzzy systems containing some 600 references [53] and demonstrates the epidemic

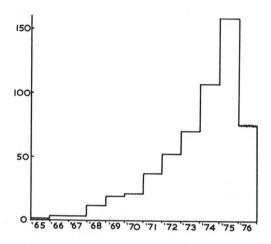

Figure 1.   Histogram of papers on fuzzy systems against year of publication.

growth of such work in recent years. The practical relevance of these studies is illustrated by such applications as pattern recognition [143]; clustering [14]; political geography [54]; decision making [10]; robot planning [61,81,99]; chromosome classification [96]; medical diagnosis [5]; engineering design [11]; systems modelling [37]; process control [109,108]; social interaction systems [159]; and structural semantics [126].

The best introduction to fuzzy reasoning is undoubtedly Zadeh's work [167,171,174,13]; this article is intended as an overview to fuzzy reasoning rather than as an introduction. There are relationships between fuzzy set theory and the studies of the paradoxes of naive set theory [23,27,113]; to studies of the concept of "truth" in formal systems and everyday language [151,95,106,36]; to previous studies of vagueness [131,15,41], inexact measurement [2,89], and the psychology of inexact expression [139]; to the work of the Polish logic school of 1920–1939 [102] devastated by the war, to many aspects of work on multivalued logics [125] where fuzzy reasoning provides a new semantics; to work on modal logics of entailment [7], possibility and necessity [73,146], quantity [6], knowledge and belief [69], and time [122]; to the many aspects of probability theory [42] particularly that concerned with "subjective" foundations [135,43] and belief [62]; to studies of the foundations of science [92,55,68,39] particularly inductive reasoning [78,91,70]; and to studies of human linguistics, reasoning and rhetoric [40,28,71,142].

In the following sections, a brief outline of fuzzy set theory, fuzzy reasoning, and their relationship to these other areas of study are presented, and an attempt to give some feeling for why the subject area has developed so rapidly at this time and where it is going. The section entitled

"Fuzzy Set Theory" introduces the problem of *borderline* cases in set theory and the two classical approaches of *precisifying* them out of or admitting them as a *third case*. The problems of either approach leading to Zadeh's suggestion of continuous degrees of set membership, and the Kalman–Zadeh debate, are then discussed. The section entitled "Operations on Fuzzy Sets" extends the basic set operations to continuous degrees of membership, presenting the fundamental Bellman and Giertz results. The section entitled "Some Alternative Formulations" introduces other derivations of multivalued logical foundations for set theory and variants on Zadeh's operations. The section entitled "Fuzzification of Mathematical Structures" describes the *fuzzification* of mathematical structures and illustrates this with the propositional calculus. The section entitled "Fuzzy Logics and Inference" develops the concepts of *fuzzy logics and inference*, paying particular attention to *implication*, and giving an axiom schema for $Ł_1^1$ as a base logic for fuzzy reasoning. The section entitled "Analysis of Some Paradoxes" illustrates some basic aspects of fuzzy reasoning by showing the different ways in which the paradoxes of the barber, and of sorites, are resolved in fuzzy logic. The section entitled "Fuzzy Reasoning, Hedges, and Truth" develops Zadeh's theory of *hedges* and *truth* and gives examples of tautologies in fuzzy reasoning involving these concepts, and of non-tautologous fuzzy reasoning. The section entitled "Logical, Psychological and Other Models for Truth Values" is concerned with the role of numerical degrees of membership, and truth values, in fuzzy reasoning, and demonstrate how they may be derived from; the logic in axiomatic form; various intuitively meaningful models; and psychological studies. The last section concludes this paper, and is particularly concerned with the reasons for current interest in human linguistic reasoning with imprecise concepts.

FUZZY SET THEORY

Set theory forms the foundations of arithmetic, logic, and indeed the major part of mathematics and formal reasoning. We tend to move naturally from the classifications of everyday language to the mathematical formulation of a set. A person may be tall—consider the set of tall people; an object may be red—consider the set of red objects; a system may be stable—consider the set of stable systems. The move from a predicate to a set satisfying it, from an intension to an extension [20], is a powerful tool in mathematics [161] and a powerful, albeit dangerous, procedure in everyday reasoning [88].

---

[1] $Ł_1$ is used throughout as an abreviation for $Ł_{\aleph_1}$, the infinite valued form of Łukasiewicz logic [125].

However, in all three examples given above the step from predicate to set is a dubious one. Membership of a set is a very precise concept: either a potential element is a member, or it is not. Whilst there may be many people, objects and systems that we can unreservedly declare tall or not tall, red or not red, stable or not stable, respectively; do we actually possess a decision procedure that enables us to classify in this binary fashion any appropriate entity? If we do not, then what is the status of the unclassified entities, the *borderline cases* [104].

One way out of the dilemma is to have no borderline cases. Carnap [21] puts forward a process of "precisiation" in which everyday concepts are given precise scientific explicata which do not necessarily coincide with their explicanda but which are to be, firstly: "Similar...in such a way that, in most cases in which the explicandum has so far been used, the explicatum can be used; however, close similarity is not required, and considerable differences are permitted", and secondly: "useful for the formulation of many universal statements". This process of precisiation has always been an important component in the development of a "science", but it is its universal applicability and utility that Zadeh, for one, now questions. Now, however, that Carnap's formulation is quite deliberately explicit about the deviation of the explicandum, justifying this cost in terms of the benefit of being able to obtain universal laws. Thus the criticism of classic methodologies quoted from Russell and Zadeh in the beginning section; more crudely, that science does indeed "say more and more about less and less" is seen by Carnap not as a source of contradiction but rather as a trade-off. There is a continuous spectrum with isolated, but "real", phenomena at one extreme and universal, but "unreal", laws at the other.

However, if one takes "precisiation" in its narrow sense to be a process of explicating out the borderline cases, then there is an alternative approach that has its attractions and that is to treat them separately as distinct class. Each entity is regarded as a member, a non-member, or a borderline member, of a set. We have a ternary rather than a binary distinction, rather like that of future contingents in logic where an event may be, as yet, neither true nor false but has to be ascribed a third truth value, "possible" [101]. In developing arguments we can concentrate on the definite cases and leave borderline exemplars outside the debate, e.g., the universal law that, "all birds can fly" is not falsified by the ostrich which is "not quite a bird", a borderline case. There is no doubt that we use this kind of logic in everyday reasoning and are prepared to claim that, "the exception proves the rule." However, it still leaves open the question of where the borderline actually is, giving rise to the secondary phenomenon of entities that are borderline "borderline" cases, and so on!

It is between the thesis of no borderline cases and the antithesis of definite borderline cases that Zadeh [167] creates the dialectical synthesis of continuously graded degree of membership to a set. This is a natural generalization of the characteristic function, $A : S \rightarrow \{0, 1\}$, of a subset A of a set, S. For any $x \in S$, $A\mathbf{x} = 1$ if $x \in S$, whereas $A\mathbf{x} = 0$ otherwise.[2] Zadeh [167] suggests that $A\mathbf{x}$ not be restricted to the binary endpoints of the interval [0, 1], but instead be allowed to range continuously throughout the interval. The semantics of intermediate values of $A\mathbf{x}$ are not tightly defined but are to be consistent with the natural order relation on the unit interval, e.g. that $A\mathbf{x} = 0.6$ denotes a greater degree of membership of $\mathbf{x}$ to A than does $A\mathbf{x} = 0.4$. Sets with such a graded characteristic function Zadeh calls *fuzzy sets* and proposes that such predicates as tall, red, and stable, do not define classical sets with a binary membership function but instead fuzzy sets with graded membership.

The concept of a fuzzy set has advantages relative to either of the possible approaches to borderline cases so far considered. The deviation that Carnap saw as necessarily introduced in replacing the explicandum by the explicatum is minimized because no artificial precision need be introduced to avoid borderline cases—we do not have to say that, "a tall man has a height greater than 1.82755 m", or that, "a red object is one indistinguishable in hue from a uniformly reflecting surface illuminated with monochromatic light of wavelength between 580.27 and 702.35 nm", and so on. As height decreases so does degree of membership to the (fuzzy) set of tall men—as the wavelength of the matching hue decreases so does degree of membership to the (fuzzy) set of red objects.

On the other hand, we do not have to introduce a clearcut distinction between borderline and definite membership; this would involve the same type of arbitrary numeric threshold but now at the metalevel of degrees of membership. It is interesting to compare Łukasiewicz's [101] logic of future

[2]In fuzzy set theory and logic there is a danger of typographical obscurity with elementary concepts being expressed through a mixture of subscripts and parentheses: $\mu_s(x)$ for the degree of membership of the fuzzy variable x to the fuzzy set s. When the designation of s is itself a complex expression then the typography becomes very messy, e.g., $\mu_{((p \cup q) \cap r)}(x)$, etc. In this paper the convention is adopted that fuzzy variables are in a bold typeface, and that the set to which they are a member is placed to their left to indicate degree of membership, i.e. if $\mathbf{x}$ is a fuzzy variable belonging to fuzzy set s, the $s\mathbf{x}$ is the degree of membership of $\mathbf{x}$ to s. In addition parentheses are dropped whenever there is no ambiguity, e.g., $(p \cup q)\mathbf{x}$ is written $p \cup q\mathbf{x}$ since the expression may be resolved only in one way. Concatenation of letters in the same typeface is taken to bind them into a single symbol, so that "sleek" is the name of a fuzzy set *not* the result of implied operations on five variables. Degrees of membership will always be assumed at least partially ordered so that expressions such as $s\mathbf{x} < p\mathbf{x}$ may be used without further definition. If arithmetic operations are used on them then a mapping into the unit interval is being assumed. Finally, for **MVL**s the roman form of a logical variable will be used for its truth value, e.g., x is the truth value of **x**.

contingents in which he introduces a third truth value, $\frac{1}{2}$ (possible), between 0 (false) and 1 (true). We could do this for set theory with $\frac{1}{2}$ being the value of the characteristic function for a borderline element. Zadeh can then be seen to have extended the ternary membership values of a "borderline" set theory, $\{0, 0.5, 1\}$ to an infinite range of values.

Thus the concept of a "fuzzy set" may be seen as providing a new tool, more appropriate than that of classical set theory, for a program of precisiation. It allows the inherent imprecision of the concepts that we actually use, and wish to use, to be neither discarded nor introduced explicitly in the explicatum, but rather to be subsumed in the (universal) concept of a degree of membership to a fuzzy set centered on that explicatum. There is thus no conflict between either the objectives of the methodology of Carnap's approach and that of Zadeh; instead, the latter may be seen as a logical extension of the former.

This is an important point to make because there has been misunderstanding of the objectives of work on "fuzzy" systems theory; perhaps, that normal standards of scientific method are to be dropped, or at least relaxed. Kalman in the discussion following Zadeh [169] states:

> The most serious objection of 'fuzzification' of system analysis is that lack of methods of system analysis is not the principle scientific problem in the 'systems' field. That problem is one of developing basic concepts and deep insight into the nature of 'systems', perhaps trying to find something akin to the 'laws' of Newton.

This division of opinion is of interest because Kalman and Zadeh have in the past adopted very similar approaches to systems theory, both with great, and related, success. As noted previously, a key feature of this work has been the definition with ever increasing precision of terms such as "controllable", "stable", "adaptive", etc. [166, 77]. Zadeh now feels that new tools and methodologies are necessary for the furtherance of this work. At least part of the reason for this may be seen in the explosive growth of definitions of apparently simple concepts, such as stability, as system theory attempts to cope with the more subtle features of complex systems. For example, Habets and Peifer [63] report some 184,320 [sic!] formally different concepts of stability based on variants of those in the literature, and Gaines [44, 45] reports a wide variety of concepts of adaptivity arising out of Zadeh's [165] original definition. The ultimate precisiation is to treat every event in the world as different from every other—which it is!

Kalman feels that the classical tools and methodologies are adequate, or at least have not proved to be inadequate, for the continued pursuit of "universal" laws of system theory. It would clearly be unfruitful to deliberately "fuzzify" a situation unnecessarily, and there is also the obvious danger of becoming engrossed in a fascinating methodology that has little relevance to the problems it purports to solve. Conversely, however, it would seem equally misleading to pretend to clarity, and to develop methodologies dependent on this pretence, in situations where clarity is inherently impossible except at the expense of losing the very nature of the concept to be clarified. The debate is not about the intrinsic value of fuzzy reasoning, but about whether the imprecision of our knowledge of the real world is inherent, and an essential component of any theory, or whether it can be removed by continuing effort. That is, Kalman is affirming the basic doctrine of the theology of science—if we have no clear and precise model of a phenomenom that we should not rest content with out imperfect knowledge but must continue to search for a better model and continue to have faith that it is there. He quotes Hilbert's, "*Wir wollen wissen: wir werden wissen*".

A continuing search for ever-increasing precision does not in itself appear to be a bad thing. It would certainly seem reasonable to suppose that it is undecidable when we have achieved the maximum possible precision. However, a similar debate has taken place about the role of randomness in system theory [163]. Many eminent scientists, including Darwin, Freud and Einstein, have regarded randomness as a sign of our ignorance rather than as a phenomenom in its own right. As Hume [75] notes: "it is commonly allowed by philosophers that what the vulgar will call chance is nothing but a secret and concealed cause". This attitude to randomness persists today as is shown by Suppes [150] vehement attack on the "*new theology*" that holds such tenets as "every event must have a sufficient determinant cause".

It might be supposed that to hold such a view could be erroneous but that, in itself, it cannot do any harm, and, as Kalman has suggested, it is important to continue to act as if there were precise universal laws. However, Gaines [47] has shown that a modeller assuming causality faced with a sequence generated by a system having the slightest acausal component forms a model that is not just incorrect but totally meaningless. Whereas a probabilistic modeller [50,51] can acquire an accurate, if uncertain, model of the actual system generating the behavior. Thus it is dangerous to assume certain forms of precision when they do not exist in the world. Interesting results may be obtained but they stem from the mismatch between presupposition and observation, not from the nature of the observed system itself.

Comparable examples in terms of fuzzy, rather than probabilistic, uncertainty may be found in such statements as "the number of trees in Canada is even", which was used by Putnam [123] as an example of a sentence to which Tarski's criterion of truth cannot be applied. The statement is well-formed in all the obvious ways and looks superficially open to an operational decision procedure for empirical verification. However, on deeper inspection of the requirements the effect of the fuzziness of both the Canadian boundary and the nature of a tree upon the determination of eveness becomes apparent, and the sentence appears nonsensical. Indeed one can see that 'eveness' of a quantity is more precise than the concept of a quantity itself—large numbers become fuzzily represented in everyday language, and the exact cardinality required to determine evenesss would be unusual.

Much has been written about truth and vagueness and it is impossible to review all of it here. To round off this survey it seems appropriate to give the last word to Popper whose "unended quest" has been for a theory of knowledge that mirrors "reality." In his autobiography [120] he notes:

> both precision and certainty are false ideals. They are impossible to attain, and therefore dangerously misleading if they are uncritically accepted as guides. The quest for precision is analogous to the quest for certainty, and both should be abandoned. I do not suggest, of course, that an increase in the precision of, say, a prediction, or even a formulation, may not sometimes be highly desirable. What I do suggest is that it is always undesirable to make an effort to increase precision for its own sake—especially linguistic precision—since this usually leads to lack of clarity, and to a waste of time and effort on preliminaries which often turn out to be useless, because they are bypassed by the real advance of the subject: one should never try to be more precise than the problem situation demands.

The key point in Popper's argument is that linguistic precision should grow *ad hoc* to meet the demands of the "problem to be solved." *Clarity* of explanation stems from the naturalness and simplicity of the concepts and vocabulary used. The complexity of additional precision should only be introduced when, of necessity, we are forced to "make new distinctions —ad hoc, for the purpose in hand." This emphasis on the primacy of natural, 'fuzzy' concepts, and the need to justify and motivate increased (linguistic) precision seems to epitomize the attitudes of those attracted to Zadeh's fuzzy set theory. The distinction that Popper draws between *linguistic* precision and *problem* precision seems also to point to a source of confusion between proponents and opponents of fuzzy reasoning. It may well be a meaningless distinction in certain approaches to epistemology, but it is one that will make sense to the majority of practising scientists and engineers.

Thus the two contrasting points of view arising out of the Kalman–Zadeh debate both have their merits and their dangers. If we assume and accept fuzziness in the world to cloak our own ignorance than we may never make the necessary effort to discern possible precise underlying phenomena. If, however, we refuse to allow that certain concepts are inherently imprecise and yet still useful then we may generate a multitude of alternatives of increasing precision yet decreasing application. Fuzzy set theory in itself is neutral since it allows for 'crisp', or precise, concepts as well as fuzzy ones. The only advantages and dangers are in the way that we use it, and the applications already noted are beginning to demonstrate that it can be used effectively.

OPERATIONS ON FUZZY SETS

Whilst the concept of a characteristic function allowing the degree of membership of an element to a set to range continuously through the interval $[0, 1]$ is itself appealing in developing explicata for certain concepts, it requires further extension if a fuzzy set thus defined is to assume a role comparable to that of a classical set. What do we mean by the complement of a fuzzy set, or by the union, or intersection of two fuzzy sets? If a car x belongs 0.7 to the (fuzzy) set of sleek cars (we write sleek $x = 0.7$) and 0.9 to the set of fast cars (fastx $= 0.9$), then what degree of membership to the sets of not-sleek, sleek-or-fast, or sleek-and-fast cars does it have? These questions become particularly interesting when we have defined new concepts in linguistic terms as combinations of the others, e.g., swish $=$ (sleek-and-fast).

One legitimate answer would be that we cannot tell—the degrees of membership $A x$, $B x$ of an element x to sets A, B may not be sufficient information to determine its membership to the complements $\bar{A}$, $\bar{B}$ the union $A \cup B$, or intersection, $A \cap B$. For example, we may need to know more of the structures of A and B and their relationships, and even this may not be enough. However, in any theory of fuzzy set operations that is to reduce to classical set theory when degrees of membership are restricted to the binary values $\{0, 1\}$, we must have at least the constraints

$$A x = 0 \rightarrow \bar{A} x = 1 \tag{1}$$

$$A x = 1 \rightarrow \bar{A} x = 0 \tag{2}$$

$$A x = 0, \quad B x = 0 \rightarrow A \cup B x = 0, \quad A \cap B x = 0 \tag{3}$$

$$A x = 0, \quad B x = 1 \rightarrow A \cup B x = 1, \quad A \cap B x = 0 \tag{4}$$

$$A x = 1, \quad B x = 1 \rightarrow A \cap B x = 1, \quad A \cup B x = 1 \tag{5}$$

There are further constraints if the natural numerical order relation of degrees of membership is to be consistent with our concepts of union and intersection. We must have that the degree of membership in the union of A and B (member of either) is not less than membership in either

$$A \cup B\mathbf{x} \geqslant A\mathbf{x} \quad \text{and} \quad A \cup B\mathbf{x} \geqslant B\mathbf{x}$$

which may be expressed

$$A \cup B\mathbf{x} \geqslant \max(A\mathbf{x}, B\mathbf{x}) \tag{6}$$

and degree of membership in the intersection of A and B (member of both) is not more than membership in either

$$A \cap B\mathbf{x} \leqslant A\mathbf{x} \quad \text{and} \quad A \cap B\mathbf{x} \leqslant B\mathbf{x}$$

which may be expressed

$$A \cap B\mathbf{x} \leqslant \min(A\mathbf{x}, B\mathbf{x}) \tag{7}$$

Similarly, for consistency between the semantics of a small change in degree of membership and a small numerical change in characteristic function, it is reasonable to require that as $A\mathbf{x}$ increases continuously from 0 to 1, then $A \cup B\mathbf{x}$ and $A \cap B\mathbf{x}$ should, for constant $B\mathbf{x}$, neither decrease nor jump discontinouusly, i.e.,

$$A \cup B\mathbf{x}, A \cap B\mathbf{x} \quad \text{are continuous, nondecreasing in} \quad A\mathbf{x}, B\mathbf{x} \tag{8}$$

In addition, for consistency with the algebraic framework of ordinary set theory, one may require the normal constraints of associativity, commutativity, idempotency and distributivity on the union and the intersection

$$(A \cup B) \cup C\mathbf{x} = A \cup (B \cup C)\mathbf{x}, (A \cap B) \cap C\mathbf{x} = A \cap (B \cap C)\mathbf{x} \tag{9}$$

$$A \cup B\mathbf{x} = B \cup A\mathbf{x}, A \cap B\mathbf{x} = B \cap A\mathbf{x} \tag{10}$$

$$A \cup A\mathbf{x} = A\mathbf{x}, A \cap A\mathbf{x} = A\mathbf{x} \tag{11}$$

$$(A \cup B) \cap C\mathbf{x} = (A \cap C) \cup (B \cap C)\mathbf{x}, (A \cap B) \cup C\mathbf{x}$$

$$= (A \cup C) \cap (B \cup C)\mathbf{x} \tag{12}$$

In a classic paper, Bellman and Giertz [12] show that relations (3) through (12) are consistent with one another and sufficient to constrain the inequalities of (6) and (7) to be equalities, that is,

$$A \cup B\mathbf{x} = \max(A\mathbf{x}, B\mathbf{x}), \quad A \cap B\mathbf{x} = \min(A\mathbf{x}, B\mathbf{x}) \tag{13}$$

Since all we have required is existence, continuity, semantic consistency with the natural order on the unit interval, and algebraic consistency with standard set theory, this result shows that the use of a max function to compute the union of two fuzzy sets and of a min function to compute the intersection of two fuzzy sets (as proposed by Zadeh [167] in his original paper) is a standard extension of set theory and, in some sense, natural and necessary if the characteristic function of a set is to be extended to range throughout the interval [0,1].

Figure 2 illustrates how the standard and fuzzy set unions and intersections relate to one another: the top diagram shows two standard sets A and B intersecting and gives the values of the characteristic functions for A, B, $A \cup B$, $A \cap B$, in various regions; the four plots in the center show how the characteristic functions vary along the line drawn through the sets; the bottom show the same variations for fuzzy sets A' and B' similar to A and B but with a graded characteristic function. Clearly the ellipses delimiting the boundaries of the nonfuzzy sets A and B would have to be replaced by mounds coming out of the paper in order to show the fuzzy sets A' and B' in a comparable fashion.

What of complementation? Again the semantics of the numerical order

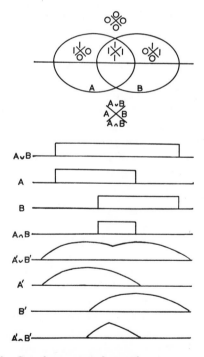

Figure 2.   Sets, fuzzy sets and operations.
Top: Binary characteristic function of two sets A and B,
their union and intersection.
Center 4 graphs: Variation of characteristic functions along
center line for A, B, classical sets.

may be considered and clearly require that complementation be order-reversing:

$$A\mathbf{x} > B\mathbf{x} \rightarrow \overline{A}\mathbf{x} < \overline{B}\mathbf{x} \qquad (14)$$

Bellman and Giertz [12] suggest that in addition to this order reversal complementation should be such that

$$\overline{\overline{A}}\mathbf{x} = A\mathbf{x} \qquad (15)$$

so that the complement of the complement of a fuzzy set is the original set. But, as they point out, these two constraints are still insufficient to determine a unique function for complementation. However, it is readily shown that if we add a symmetry requirement, essentially that the effect of complementation on a deviation of membership function from unity is the same as on a deviation from zero, so that

$$A\mathbf{y} = 1 - A\mathbf{x} \rightarrow \overline{A}\mathbf{y} = 1 - \overline{A}\mathbf{x} \qquad (16)$$

then relations (14), (15) and (16) taken together imply

$$\overline{A}\mathbf{x} = 1 - A\mathbf{x} \qquad (17)$$

which is Zadeh's original definition for the membership function of the complement of a fuzzy set.

The computations of the membership function of an element in the complement of a fuzzy set, or in the union or intersection of two fuzzy sets, given by relations (17) and (13), are by far the most widely used in the literature both in theoretical and applied studies. Complementation is the most weakly constrained and subject to variation, but, as I shall illustrate in the section entitled "Fuzzification of Mathematical Structures", it is not used in some important developments such as the "fuzzification" of other mathematical structures.

SOME ALTERNATIVE FORMULATIONS

Whilst Zadeh's fuzzy set theory arose from the semantics of applied system analysis, there have been developments of a rather more formal nature that closely parallel it [125], p. 13. The delightful story of Russell's discovery of a paradox in Frege's "Grundsetze der Arithmetik", and Frege's reactions to it are well-known (for translations of the original correspondence see Heijenoort [65], pp. 124—128). Russell attempted to resolve it through his "theory of types" which, together with the original paradox and its variants [80], has been a massive stimulation to a variety of developments in mathematics ever since [65]. One of these has been the application of multivalued logic (MVL) to set theory.

Russell's original version of the paradox [27] depends on the principle of bivalence in the form of the "law of the excluded middle" (LEM), that either p or $\sim p$ must be asserted. Shaw-Kwei [138] noted that certain multivalued logics, notably Łukasiewicz $Ł_3$, in which LEM does not hold do not show this paradox, nor the variant of it not involving negation developed by Curry [29]. However, he also demonstrated that other forms of inconsistency leading to paradoxes can still arise.

These paradoxes arise from the axiom schema of "comprehension" (COM), in naieve set theory, by which every "well-defined property" determines a set. It has the general form

$$\forall z_1, z_n, x, y, x \in y \Leftrightarrow P(x, z_1, \ldots, z_n)$$

where P is any property-defining expression. Skolem [144] noted that COM may be inconsistent if P is an expression in a bivalent logic, even if quantifier-free, whereas it is then consistent in the infinite-valued Łukasiewicz logic, $Ł_1$ (and $Ł_3$ [145]). Chang [22, 23] and Fenstad [38] extended this result to allow for various restricted forms of quantification in P.

Recently Maydole [113] has tidied up and extended these developments using a concise methodology for proving COM inconsistent for arbitrary logics underlying P. He demonstrates that the paradoxes that arise will also arise with quantified versions of various well-established, nonstandard logics, and probability logic. Only a few infinite-valued logics (including those of Łukasiewicz and Post) cannot be shown to lead to inconsistency in COM by Maydole's technique, and he argues that it is plausible that consistent versions of naieve set theory could be developed based on them.[3]

That work on the paradoxes of naieve set theory, and that on fuzzy set theory, should result in a common advocation of a switch to underlying multivalued logic, is not surprising in retrospect. Both the paradoxes of Russell *et al*; and those of borderline cases, arise from bivalency, or more subtle logical constraints on P the property-defining predicate. The standard counterexample for non-fuzzy theories of vague predicates is the sorites paradox and this involves a long chain of iteration closely resembling those generated in Maydole's method. Thus, there are close links between Zadeh's very practical arguments in terms of the applications of systems theory, and the apparently far more abstract and fundamental studies of set theory and the foundations of arithmetic.

A difficulty in fuzzy set theory that becomes a major problem in multivalued logical foundations for set theory is that "the numbers are not

---

[3]Maydole's [112] doctoral dissertation can be recommended as a comprehensive introduction to the role of MVLs in the foundations of set theory. His later paper is very much condensed and the full thesis is more readily assimilated.

available early enough", i.e., set theory is a necessary foundation to the arithmetic that allows us to talk in terms of a "degree of membership" of 0.3. Formally, this may be overcome by using an axiomatic form of the multivalued logic rather than introducing it in terms of truth-values. However, there have also been some recent studies of more fundamental derivations. Varela [154] has extended Brown's [16] calculus of "distinctions" to include the paradoxical cases as a basis for an analysis of "self-reference". Chapin [25,26] is developing a "set-valued set theory" in which the degree of membership of one "set" to another is itself a "set," and is axiomatizing this through to arithmetic in close correspondence with the classical Zermelo–Fraenkel theory. Goguen [59] has established a category-theoretic framework for fuzzy set theory, and has linked the axioms for the category very closely to a phenomenological analysis of human "concepts."

At a more specific level, it is possible to accept Zadeh's extension of the characteristic function to range over the whole unit interval, to require that the theory reduce to the standard set theory in the $0/1$ case, and to accept many of the constraints defined in the previous section, but, by rejecting others, to generate different functions for the union, etc. Various authors have suggested alternative functions, often within the framework of fuzzy logic rather than fuzzy set theory, but it is convenient to consider them at this stage and relate the alternative functions to the constraints dropped.

For example, Zadeh ([172], appendix) suggests the functions

$$A \cup B\mathbf{x} = A\mathbf{x} + B\mathbf{x} - A\mathbf{x} \times B\mathbf{x} \tag{18}$$

$$A \cap B\mathbf{x} = A\mathbf{x} \times B\mathbf{x} \tag{19}$$

somewhat akin to the rules for the calculation of the measures of unions and intersections of Borel sets of independent events in probability theory. These satisfy (1) through (5) reducing to classical results in the binary case. They also satisfy (6) through (8) preserving the order semantics and (9) through (10) preserving associativity and commutativity. However, neither function gives the idempotency of (11) and taken together, they do not give the distributivity of (12).

Despite their algebraic weakness these functions, together with the complementation of (17), have been suggested as more appropriate in their semantics than the max/min operations of (13) by several authors. Koczy and Hajnal [85] develop them axiomatically from semantic considerations that include a deliberate exclusion of idempotency: "The repeated reference to a statement in a disjunctive or conjunctive connection ... causes an increase and decrease of the acceptance, respectively".

Giles [57] has also argued that lack of idempotency may be desirable in a logic reflecting the semantics of natural language. Goguen [58] uses (19) on a similar basis that a chain of links in an argument, each with the same degree of membership to "truth" should over-all have a lesser degree of truth that decreases with the length of the chain. Rödder [127] presents data from human decision-making indicating that this predicted decrease does actually occur (it would be expected to do so on a Bayesian model of information acquisition as investigated by Edwards *et al.* [35]). Hamacher [64] has followed this result by developing a two-paramenter variant of (18) and (19) based on Bellman and Giertz's arguments but dropping idempotency and distributivity, and strengthening (8) to require that union and intersection be strictly increasing functions of their arguments.

In terms of the chain analogy the min/max connectives may be viewed as assuming that a chain of elements in series is as strong as its weakest link, whilst a set of elements in parallel is as strong as the strongest. These concepts are also intuitively appealing and the debate on the "correct" forms of function for fuzzy unions and intersections is likely to continue with different outcomes for different semantic constraints and intuitions. Gaines [46] has compared the functions of (18) and (19) with those of (13) in a re-analysis of the very successful fuzzy linguistic controller of Mamdani and Assilian [109] and reports no significant variation in the over-all control policy with the different forms of fuzzy connective. It may well be that in real-world applications where there is essential redundancy and robustness in the problem formulation that the precise form of fuzzy function does not matter, i.e., the operations may be fuzzy as well as the data.

Sanford [132], again in the context of vague reasoning, presents various intuitive arguments that rule out the simple max/min functions and goes on to develop his own "borderline" logic. This has the property, unique among current variants, of dropping the continuity requirement of (8). For example, when a and b are two atomic propositions such that $a+b<1$ then, if $c = a \vee b, c = \max (a,b)$, but otherwise it is 1. Thus, if $a=0.49$, $b=0.50$ then $c=0.50$, but if $a=0.51$, $b=0.50$ then $c=1$, a discontinuous jump. Sanford's paper is particularly interesting both for its innovative approach and for its illustration of the variety of phenomena that can arise in logics of vagueness.

Gaines [48,49] has attempted to integrate together many variants of logics of vagueness, including those based on min/max connectives, probability logic and (18)/(19) above, by dropping the functionality of the union and intersection. He requires only that

$$A \cup Bx + A \cap Bx = Ax + Bx \tag{20}$$

plus the algebraic constraint that $\cup$ and $\cap$ act as lattice operators in expressions. This gives a common foundation for many variants of fuzzy set theory and fuzzy logic from which many key results may be derived. Particular variants then arise through additional constraints which may be based on specific semantic requirements. The min/max function proposed by Zadeh assumes a key role, as suggested by the Bellman and Giertz result, that they are uniquely *strongly* truth-functional, i.e., to ascertain the truth values of connectives between compound propositions it is necessary to know only the truth values of these propositions, not their structures in terms of atomic propositions. This strong truth-functionality substantially reduces the memory requirements of an information processing system, and would be an advantage to a limited capacity decision maker such as the human being.

Thus there is rich ground underlying the particular choice of nonbivalent logic with which to extend classical set theory. The framework established by Bellman and Giertz is useful in comparing variants. However, only the semantics of particular applications can determine which is the appropriate choice. In many practical situations these semantics are themselves so "fuzzy" that the choice does not matter over a wide range of possibilities. Developments of the mathematical foundations of vague reasoning need to take this into account and *not* attempt to introduce a new level of arbitrary precision in the metalanguage—detailed and specific arguments as to what are the "right" functions seem singularly inappropriate to the subject area. We need integrative, broadly-based theories with strong intuitive appeal.

FUZZIFICATION OF MATHEMATICAL STRUCTURES

Given the concept of a fuzzy set and the definition of union and intersection in (13), it is possible to *fuzzify* any domain of mathematical reasoning based on set theory. The fundamental change is to replace the precise concept that a variable has a *value* with the fuzzy concept that a variable has a *degree of membership to each possible value*, i.e., instead of having a sharp value each variable is fuzzily restricted to a domain of values. Sharp values then consist of one particular form of restriction, i.e., a singleton having degree of membership unity with all other degrees zero. A conventional "set-valued" variable consists of a number of values with degree of membership unity and all other degrees zero. Other forms of restriction may be imposed to constrain the relationship between the fuzzy structure and additional mathematical structures, e.g., that the fuzzy set is *normalized* in the sense that at least one value has degree of membership unity.

In terms of notation of the earlier Section entitled "Operations on Fuzzy Set" it is natural to write $v\mathbf{x}$ for the degree of membership of the fuzzy variable $\mathbf{x}$ to the value v, i.e., values themselves now appear to play the role of functions. Hence, non-fuzzy functions become *functionals* mapping function to function when fuzzified. Consider a (non-fuzzy) function g of n variables y_1 through y_n. Before fuzzification we write as usual

$$v = g(y_1, y_2, \ldots, y_n) = g(Y) \tag{21}$$

A natural extension to $v(x)$, the degree of membership of the fuzzy variable x to each value v, is

$$vx = \begin{cases} \max_{Y} (\min(y_1 x, y_2 x, \ldots, y_n x)) & \text{where } v = g(Y) \\ 0 & \text{if there is no } Y \text{ such that } v = g(Y) \end{cases}$$

$$\tag{22}$$

That is, with each possible value of the argument of the function is associated a degree of membership that is the lowest of the degrees of membership of each of its components; and with each possible value of a result of the function is associated a degree of membership that is the highest of those of all the arguments giving the value. We are taking the union of the fuzzy sets of results arising from the intersection of the fuzzy sets of values of components. Note that fuzzification does *not* involve the complementation of a fuzzy set, which is advantageous since we have noted that this operation is not as well-defined as those of union and intersection.

Many fuzzified mathematical structures have now been studied and basic results extended from the original structures to the fuzzy ones replacing them, e.g., fuzzy topological spaces [24, 60, 164, 76]; groups [128]; graphs [129]; automata [134, 115, 52, 156]; algorithms [133]; languages [152, 72]; and logics [97, 48, 49]. In the context of fuzzy reasoning the fuzzification of logic is of particular interest and I shall devote the remainder of this section to the application of formula (22) to the standard propositional calculus (PC).

Any logical structure may be fuzzified by considering propositions not to have a single truth value, but instead to have fuzzy degrees of membership to each possible truth value. Conventional propositional calculus PC has two truth values F and T, so that after fuzzification each proposition x will be represented by a pair of values (Fx, Tx). These may be regarded as representing its degree of membership to falsity, and to truth, respectively. The logical connectives of PC are truth-functional and hence may be represented as functions of their arguments and fuzzified. For example, the truth table for implication $\supset$ is

if $c = a \supset b$

	$a = F$	$a = T$
$b = F$	$c = T$	$c = F$
$b = T$	$c = T$	$c = T$

which gives, with the application of (22)

$$(Fc, Tc) = \big(\min(Ta, Fb), \max(\min(Fa, Fb)), \min(Fa, Tb), \min(Ta, Tb)\big)$$

$$(23)$$

Similar expressions may be derived by fuzzifying the truth tables for negation $\sim$ disjunction $\vee$, conjunction $\wedge$ and equivalence $\equiv$, but they are more simply obtained by noting that fuzzification preserves the interdefinability of the connectives of PC. That is, if f is any false proposition such that $(Ff, Tf) = (1, 0)$, then we may write

$$\sim a \qquad \text{for} \qquad a \supset f \qquad\qquad (24)$$

$$a \vee b \qquad \text{for} \qquad \sim a \supset b \qquad\qquad (25)$$

$$a \wedge b \qquad \text{for} \qquad \sim(\sim a \vee \sim b) \qquad\qquad (26)$$

$$a \equiv b \qquad \text{for} \qquad (a \supset b) \wedge (b \supset a) \qquad\qquad (27)$$

For example, (24) when substituted in (23) yields

$$\text{if } b = \sim a \text{ then } (Fb, Tb) = (Ta, Fa) \qquad\qquad (28)$$

and, similarly, expressions may be derived for the other connectives.

This fuzzified PC may be shown related to a well-known MVL under a simple transformation. If we assume the fuzzy truth values are *normalized* to have only one nonunity component, there is a 1–1 correspondence between them and the unit interval that simplifies the above expressions. Let

$$a = (1 - Fa + Ta)/2 \qquad\qquad (29)$$

and so on for the other variables (this transformation can be inverted given that one of Fa and Ta must be 1). Then the equations for the new variables under the different connectives become

$$c = a \supset b \rightarrow c = \max(1 - a, b) \qquad\qquad (30)$$

$$b = \sim a \quad\ \rightarrow b = 1 - a \qquad\qquad (31)$$

$$c = a \vee b \rightarrow c = \max(a, b) \qquad\qquad (32)$$

$$c = a \wedge b \rightarrow c = \min(a, b) \qquad\qquad (33)$$

$$c = a \equiv b \rightarrow c = \min(\max(1 - a, b), \max(1 - b, a)) \qquad\qquad (34)$$

This system of equations gives an MVL that Rescher ([125], p. 50) calls the infinite valued form of a variant standard sequence (VSS). It was first developed by Dienes [33] who actually obtains it by replacing Lukasiewicz implication with the material implication of PC. Hence it is not too surprising that normalized, fuzzified PC turns out to be Dienes' VSS. Note that $1 - a$ definition of negation arises naturally from our transformation and was *not* introduced through a fuzzy complement operation.

FUZZY LOGIC AND INFERENCE

To use fuzzy set theory as a basis for reasoning with imprecise concepts one needs to develop the notion of a *fuzzy logic* in greater depth and determine what are valid forms of inference with such logics. This is the area of much current research and it is worth noting initially that there are differences in terminology in the literature leading to at least three distinct denotations for the term "fuzzy logic."

(a) *Basis for Reasoning with Vague or Imprecise Statements*: This very general definition is consistent with the colloquial use of the term "fuzzy" and its use in technical senses different from that of Zadeh (e.g., [121,30]), or in more general formulations (e.g., [59,9]). "Fuzzy" become a modern term replacing previous usage in the literature of terms such as "inexact" or "vague." One may give the term a reasonable definition by noting that it is applicable to predicates defining concepts that have no well-defined borderline and are such that "hedges" such as "very" may be applied to them, e.g., "very tall," "very beautiful," but not "very pregnant" or "very dead."[4] Imprecision gives rise to fuzziness because it blurs the borderline, and vagueness usually has a connotation of excessive fuzziness that makes a definition difficult to use.

(b) *Basis for Reasoning with Imprecise Statements using Fuzzy Sets Theory for Fuzzification of Logical Structures*: This more restricted form of definition (a) comes closest to being the intensive form of that given extensively by Zadeh's own papers. However, it is only the more recent of these papers that consider fuzzy reasoning as such and come to use the term "fuzzy logic" [174,13]. In earlier papers Zadeh fuzzifies a variety of mathematical structures to provide models of their use in approximate, linguistic reasoning by people, and does not treat linguistic terms denoting truth, such as "very true" any differently from terms denoting other, less abstract concepts, such as "very hot." However, the development of complete logical structure for fuzzy reasoning has been the prime long-term objective [168,171]:

> much of the logic behind human reasoning is not the traditional two-valued or even multi-valued logic, but a logic with fuzzy truths, fuzzy connectives and fuzzy rules of inference...

[4]I am dubious about the reality of this distinction. As we come to define a concept more closely it is invariably found to be fuzzy. For example, with modern studies of "heart death," "brain death," etc., it is clear that the actual occurrence of death is fuzzy. One can well envisage a clinician stating, "He is almost dead. He is now very dead!"

and his most recent papers cited above have gone far to develop just such a logic.

(c) *Multivalued Logic in Which Truth Values are in Interval* [0,1], *and Valuation of Disjunction is the Maximum of Those Disjuncts, and Valuation of Conjunction is Minimum of Conjuncts*: This restricted definition has been widely used [110,97,96] but it applies to most MVL's that have been studied in detail [125] and may be regarded as defining a family of infinite valued MVL's differing only in their implication functions. The definition may be generalized to truth values in a lattice [58,17,32] or ordered semiring [136,8,59,52] or specialized to include the truth value of negation as being one minus the truth value of the statement negated. However, all variants of this definition require statements to have truth values in an ordered structure, and define the logical connectives in terms of the order relation.

Clearly definitions (a) and (b) are compatible, differing only in generality. However, there is scope for some confusion, particularly between definitions (b) and (c), because

(1) Some "fuzzy logics" in sense (c) have no derivation in sense (b) or application in sense (a);
(2) However, as shown in Section 5, some fuzzified logics in sense (b) are also MVL's in sense (c);
(3) Zadeh fuzzifies in terms of (b) logics which are already fuzzy in sense (c).

In retrospect, it would be very much better if the term "fuzzy logic" had been used consistently in the sense of (b), with the term MVL used generically for logic satisfying (c) and the standard names applied, such as VSS, to those whose implication functions are sufficiently well-specified for their classical counterparts to be determined. Hopefully, the literature will move towards this more consistent terminology in the future.

Given the representation of imprecise concepts in terms of fuzzy sets described in previous sections, what would constitute a logic for fuzzy reasoning? Clearly some definition of *truth* and a basis for inferring the *consequences* of true statements is required. By the very nature of the imprecise concepts involved one cannot expect a clear-cut distinction between a statement being true, and its not being true. It is natural to take the truth value of a statement expressing the membership of a particular individual to a fuzzy set to be the *degree of membership* to that set, i.e., the truth-value of "this snow is white" is the degree of membership of *this snow* to the fuzzy set of *white objects*. A valid inference will then be one that takes us from a premise to a consequence of at least equal truth value. Note that both these concepts are consistent with the non-fuzzy case: the truth value of the predicate, P, in an axiom of the general form shown in the beginning of the earlier section entitled "Some Alternative Formulations" may be taken as the 'degree of membership' of x to y, and the definition of material implication $\supset$ in PC is completely equivalent to saying that $x \supset y$ is true if and only if the truth value of y is at least equal to that of x.

Unfortunately, fuzzified PC, or VSS, does not have this property for its implication function. For example, substituting $c = 1$ in (30) gives us, $a = 0$ or $b = 1$, and not the simple inference rule $b \geqslant a$, ie., VSS allows an inference to be precisely true only if the premise is precisely false or the consequent precisely true—it essentially forces us back to a non-fuzzy logic. Many other MVL's *do* satisfy the more useful condition that

$$\text{if } c = a \supset b, \qquad \text{then } c = 1 \rightarrow b \geqslant a \qquad (35)$$

Note that the converse does not necessarily hold, though it may do in some MVL's.

In terms of Zadeh's exposition of fuzzy reasoning, and in virtually all application of fuzzy reasoning, it seems that the rules for disjunction conjunction, and negation of (32), (33) and (31), respectively, together with the inference role of (35) are an adequate definition of a base MVL to be fuzzified. In essence, implication is being used only metalinguistically, e.g., in Mamdani's (1976) fuzzy linguistic controller a *linguistic rule*, such as "*if* preasure error is negative small and the change in preasure error is posivitve small *then* heater control change should be positive medium" is formalized as rule$_n$

$$(\text{condition belongs to condition}_n) \quad \text{and} \quad (\text{input belongs to input}_n)$$
$$\text{implies} \quad (\text{input belongs to actual input}) \qquad (36)$$

where "condition$_n$" is a fuzzy predicate specifying the plant conditions for the rule to be applied ("pressure error negative small and change positive small"), and "input$_n$" is a fuzzy predicate specifying the input constraint called for by the rule ("heater control change positive medium"), "actual input" is a fuzzy predicate restricting the control action to be applied to the plant, and "condition" and "input" are fuzzy variables specifying the actual plant condition and input, respectively. More formally (36) may be expressed as

$$(\textbf{condition} \in \text{condition}_n) \wedge (\textbf{input} \in \text{input}_n) \supset (\textbf{input} \in \text{input}) \qquad (37)$$

where the implication expressed by the rule is taken to be precise so that we have, from (35)

$$\text{input } \mathbf{input} \geqslant \min(\text{condition}_n \, \mathbf{condition}, \, \text{input}_n \, \mathbf{input}) \qquad (38)$$

If there are a number of rules of this type, rule_1 to rule_n, we can infer

$$\text{input } \mathbf{input} \geqslant \max_n \, (\min(\text{condition}_n \, \mathbf{condition}, \, \text{input}_n \, \mathbf{input})) \qquad (39)$$

which is the basis of inference used in the fuzzy linguistic controller [109].

If implication is to be used in the object language as well as the metalanguage then the truth value of $a \supset b$ itself needs definition. Several are possible that have reasonable interpretations and conform with (35), e.g., if $c = a \supset b$

$$c = \begin{cases} 1 & \text{if } a \leqslant b \\ 0 & \text{otherwise} \end{cases} \qquad (40)$$

$$c = \begin{cases} 1 & \text{if } a \leqslant b \\ b & \text{otherwise} \end{cases} \qquad (41)$$

$$c = \min(1, 1 - a + b) \qquad (42)$$

$$c = \min(1, b/a) \qquad (43)$$

Taking these forms of implication with the connectives of (31), (32), (33), and (27), gives [125] the infinite valued forms of the sequence $\mathbf{S}_n$, (40); the sequence $\mathbf{S}_n{}^*$, (41); and Łukasiewicz $\mathbf{Ł}_1$, (42). The implication function of (43) does not seem to have been studied in conjunction with the other connectives, but it is closely related to conditional probability. Indeed [48, 49] shows that (42) can be derived from

$$p(a \supset b) = 1 - p(a) + p(a \wedge b) \qquad (44)$$

and (43) from

$$p(a \rightarrow b) = p(a \wedge b)/p(a) \qquad (45)$$

that are the standard definitions for implication in a probability logic, and a conditional probability logic, respectively.

Zadeh [174, 172] has suggested that Łukasiewicz $\mathbf{Ł}_1$ be taken as the base logic for fuzzification in modeling linguistic truth values. However, it is worth emphasizing that whilst this is an important possibility, particularly in view of the wealth of study of this particular MVL, there is inadequate evidence from either theory or practice as yet to discriminate between the different possibilities given above. Maydole [43] generates paradoxes for $\mathbf{S}_n$ and $\mathbf{S}_n{}^*$ which indicate grounds for ruling out (40) and (41) as implication functions. Both (44) and (45), leading to (42) and (43) have their intuitive attractions and need further investigation in practical situations. In the examples in the following section it will be found, in general, that either will suffice and, indeed, for most examples the common inference rule (35) is adequate without further specification.

It is interesting now to consider cases in which the implication itself is not precise. Suppose $c = a \supset b$ but $c \neq 1$, $c = 1 - \epsilon$ say. What can we infer about the relationship between a and b? Here again the defects of (40) and (41) become apparent because (40) will not allow this case and (41) will not allow it if $a \leqslant c$. Definitions (42) and (43) however give us freedom to fix c and a without constraint and then infer an inequality for b. From (42) we obtain

$$b \geqslant a - (1 - \epsilon) \qquad (46)$$

and from (43)

$$b \geqslant a \times (1 - \epsilon) \qquad (47)$$

We can actually derive the stronger result that these inequalities become equalities when $\epsilon \neq 1$. This seems rather too strong, however, allowing us to infer the truth value of b from those of a and $(a \supset b)$, and Gaines [48,49] uses the rather weaker result that (46) and (47) may be derived from the general forms (44) and (45), respectively, and the general result that if $x = a \wedge b, x \leqslant a$, i.e., the min/max connectives for conjunction/disjunction are not assumed. Alternatively we might assume that the truth value for a second-order concept of implication is known only itself as an inequality, $c \geqslant 1 - \epsilon$, which would again make the inequalities of (46) and (47) proper under all conditions.

Various other operations may be defined, or introduced, in the logic e.g., if we take the *PC* disjunction of (25) but use the implication of (42) we obtain

$$d = {}^{\sim}a \vee b \rightarrow d = \min(1, a + b) \qquad (48)$$

an operation which Zadeh calls the "*bounded sum.*" If we take the negation of the implication of (42) we obtain

$$c = {}^{\sim}(a \supset b) \rightarrow c = 1 - \min(1, 1 - a + b) = \max(0, a - b) \qquad (49)$$

which Zadeh calls the "bounded difference."

Whilst "bounded sum" and "bounded difference" are definable within the framework of Lukasiewicz $Ł_1$, Zadeh also makes extensive use of a new unary operation (written here as γ) to represent the hedge "very." This is additional to L_1 and has the form

$$b = \gamma a \rightarrow b = a^2 \qquad (50)$$

we clearly have

$$\gamma x \supset x \qquad (51)$$

which may be read that the truth value of something being 'x' is at least that of its being 'very x.' However, γ may also be read formally as an unary operation extending $Ł_1$.

In summary, a logic may be developed based on fuzzy set theory in which the degree of membership of an element to a set is taken to be the truth value of the statement that the element belongs to the set. The appropriate connectives and inference rules for the logic then depend on the definition of union, intersection, and complementation of fuzzy sets, and the inequality of (35) which is a form of *modus ponens* for MVL's. If implication is to be allowed in statements then its valuation must be defined consistent with (35), for example, by (44) or (45).

It is interesting to move outside the arithmetic context for fuzzy logic established so far and consider their axiomatic forms. Many classical logics do *not* have representations as truth-functional, many-valued logics, and it is easier to see their relationship to fuzzy logic from the relative axiom schemes. It may also be a more intuitively satisfying foundation for the fuzzy logic to develop them nonnumerically as patterns of reasoning and then reintroduce "degrees of membership" as a mathematical (or computational) device using Wajsberg's technique [155].

Zadeh's standard connectives for fuzzy sets together with the implication of (44) give Łukasiewicz infinite valued logic $Ł_1$. For comparison purposes, this is best axiomatized by a scheme involving only implication

$$\frac{a \quad a \supset b}{b} \qquad \textit{modus ponens} \qquad (52)$$

$$\frac{\dagger}{a} \qquad \text{contradiction} \qquad (53)$$

$$\frac{*}{a \supset (b \supset a)} \qquad \text{"paradox"} \qquad (54)$$

$$\frac{*}{((a \supset b) \supset a) \supset ((b \supset a) \supset a)} \qquad \text{disjunction} \qquad (55)$$

$$\frac{*}{(a \supset b) \supset ((b \supset c) \supset (a \supset c))} \qquad \begin{array}{c}\text{transitivity,} \\ \text{second syllogism}\end{array} \qquad (56)$$

$$\frac{*}{\forall x\, Fx \supset Fa} \qquad \text{instantiation} \qquad (57)$$

$$\frac{a \supset Fx}{a \supset \forall x\, Fx} \qquad \text{generalization} \qquad (58)$$

where a and b are propositions, F is a propositional function, and x is an individual variable that does not occur free in a. In this scheme [82] an '*' denotes that the null proposition may be replaced by that below the line, and '†' is a false, or contradictory, proposition. Quantification has been introduced for convenience at this stage as it fits naturally in the axiom scheme and will be needed later. The remaining logical connectives for quantified L_1, QL_1, may be introduced by the definitions:

$\sim a$	for	$a \supset \dagger$	negation	(59)
$a \lor b$	for	$(a \supset b) \supset b$	disjunction	(60)
$a \land b$	for	$\sim(\sim a \lor \sim b)$	conjunction	(61)
$a \equiv b$	for	$(a \supset b) \land (b \supset a)$	equivalence	(62)
$\exists xa$	for	$\sim(\forall x)\sim a$	existence	(63)

All the definitions and inference rules of this schema are valid in the standard lower predicate calculus LPC so that L_1 may be regarded as a weakened form of PC and quantified L_1, QL_1, as a weakened form of LPC. The missing rule for LPC is

$$\frac{*}{((a \supset b) \supset a) \supset a} \qquad (64)$$

and addition of this to (52)–(56) gives PC or, with (57)–(58) LPC. It is probably more familiar as *consequentia mirabilis* with $\dagger$ replacing b

$$\frac{*}{(\sim a \supset a) \supset a} \qquad \text{\textit{consequentia mirabilis}} \qquad (65)$$

Which from definition (60) may be written

$$\frac{*}{(\sim a \lor a)} \qquad \text{excluded middle} \qquad (66)$$

which is definately not part of L_1. Note that (55) may be regarded as a weakened form of (64), particularly if written

$$\frac{*}{((a \supset b) \supset a) \supset (a \lor b)} \qquad (67)$$

Ackerman [1] notes that one consequence of the lack of (64) is that a common deduction theorem is missing

$$(a \supset (a \supset b)) \supset (a \supset b) \qquad (68)$$

which would allow the deduction of $a \supset b$ from the hypothesis of a to allow us to drop the hypothesis of a and still retain $a \supset b$. This highlights the care needed with L_1 and QL_1 to avoid importing results of PC and LPC which are no longer valid. It is the same problem that exists when working within the axiom scheme of other variants such as the intuitionistic positional calculus (IPC) or the Lewis–Langford modal logic.

Whilst the addition of (64) or LEM to L_1 takes us back to PC, there are other alternative logics that do *not* contain LEM also.[5] It is interesting to

[5]Note that the modal logics considered here do not contain 'LEM' as defined here because the implication used in its definition is the *strict* form, i.e., necessary implication.

establish the relationship of these to $\mathbf{Ł}_1$. If one compares (54)–(56) with the implication fragments of the modal logics **S2** through **S5** [100], then (54) is regarded as a "paradox" of strict implication but (68) is a theorem of the modal logics. This deduction theorem is available in IPC also stemming from the axiom

$$(a \supset (b \supset c)) \supset ((a \supset b) \supset (a \supset c)) \tag{69}$$

which is the *only* one of the ten (Łukasiewicz) IPC axioms [125] that is not a theorem of $\mathbf{Ł}_1$. Conversely from (55)–(56), we can derive

$$((a \supset \dagger) \supset \dagger) \supset a \tag{70}$$

that is,

$$\sim(\sim a) \supset a \tag{71}$$

which is a key non-thesis of IPC.

Thus in terms of the stocks of tautologies **S2–S5**, IPC and $\mathbf{Ł}_1$ each contain *different* fragments of PC. The lack of (68) in $\mathbf{Ł}_1$ compared with the others illustrates the wider role of implication in a system with graded truth values. The hypothesis a may be at a low enough level of truth to derive $a \supset b$ does not allow us to assert unconditionally $a \supset b$, e.g., $a = 0.5, b = 0.4$, gives $(a \supset (a \supset b))$ a truth value of 1, but $a \supset b$ a truth value 0.9. It is interesting to recall Mostowski's remarks ([116], p. 17) to the effect that only IPC so far satisfied Łukasiewicz's program of developing alternative logic that would actually be *used* by working scientists. Developments in recent years in modal logics and their applications, and now in fuzzy logics and their applications, indicate that the use of alternative logics (a key factor is evaluating their utilities!) is now spreading.

So far as I am aware no axioms characterizing γ or the alternative form of implication $\rightarrow\!\!\!\!3$, (45), have been given.[6] Several authors have studied conditional probability-like valuations as measures of implication [3, 31, 147]; these are interesting open questions. A multivalued interpretation of the quantifiers may be introduced, consistent with (57) and (35), that

$$a = \forall x b \quad \rightarrow \quad a \quad = \quad \inf(b') \tag{72}$$

$$a = \exists x b \quad \rightarrow \quad a \quad = \quad \sup(b') \tag{73}$$

where b' is any substitution instance of b. Modalities are also readily

---

[6] It appears quite feasible to axiomatize γ and $\rightarrow\!\!\!\!3$ within the framework of $\mathbf{Ł}_1$. For example,

$$\gamma(\sim a \supset b) \supset (\sim \gamma a \supset \gamma b) \equiv (\sim \gamma a \supset \gamma b) \supset \gamma \sim (a \supset b)$$

catches the essence of γ. Whilst,

$$a \rightarrow\!\!\!\!3 (\sim b \supset c) \equiv \sim (a \rightarrow\!\!\!\!3 b) \supset (a \rightarrow\!\!\!\!3 c)$$

$$\gamma(a \rightarrow\!\!\!\!3 b) \equiv (\gamma a \rightarrow\!\!\!\!3 \gamma b)$$

do the same for $\rightarrow\!\!\!\!3$.

introduced into the $\mathbf{QL}_1$ schema using a conventional "possible worlds" model [146]. Since much of fuzzy reasoning is concerned with sequential structures, automata [52] and sociodynamic systems [159, 86], the possible worlds have natural and important interpretations as "reachable" or "potential" states of affairs. In particular, the stability theory of fuzzy linguistic controllers needs the fuzzy tense logic equivalent to Prior's [122] interpretations of **S4**. However, this is again an area of great practical importance that appears to be undeveloped as yet.

ANALYSIS OF SOME PARADOXES

Before moving on to the linguistic aspects of fuzzy reasoning, particularly the linguistic correlates of logical terms, it is worthwhile analyzing how some of the classical 'paradoxes' of logic and set theory may be resolved using logic based on fuzzy set theory. Russell's paradox and that of sorites illustrate different aspects of the use of a multivalued logic as a basis for set theory and reasoning.[7]

Consider Russell's well-loved barber who performs the (very socially desirable) duty of shaving those people who do not shave themselves, but becomes very puzzled when he tries to work out whether to shave himself or not.[8] Let *bshav* be the (fuzzy) set of people who are shaved by the barber and *sshav* be the (fuzzy) set of those who shave themselves. That the barber shaves those who do not shave themselves (not shaving implies barber shaves) gives us

$$\overline{sshav}\ \mathbf{x} \leqslant bshav\,\mathbf{x} \tag{74}$$

so that

$$1 - sshav\,\mathbf{x} \leqslant bshav\,\mathbf{x} \tag{75}$$

That those who shave themselves are not shaved by the barber gives us

$$sshav\,\mathbf{x} \leqslant 1 - bshav\,\mathbf{x} \tag{76}$$

Taking inequalities (75) and (76) together, we have

$$sshav\,\mathbf{x} + bshav\,\mathbf{x} = 1 \tag{77}$$

However, now consider the barber: his membership to the set of those who shave themselves is clearly the same as that to the set of those shaved by the barber (because that is himself; those who feel this step is dubious can

---

[7]The analysis of paradoxes is a fruitful test of techniques for formalizing imprecise reasoning. Several authors [111, 157, 74] have written interesting discussions of suitable paradoxes.

[8]The actual barber on whom the anecdote is based did not cut his throat as is often reported, but lived to a peaceful old age when, becoming bald of face, he lost interest in the problem.

go away and invent a theory of types to forbid it!) Hence, for the barber **b**

$$bshav\,\mathbf{b} = sshav\,\mathbf{b} = \frac{1}{2} \qquad (78)$$

This value $\frac{1}{2}$ is a third truth value that is not available in a bivalent logic, but becomes so in an appropriate trivalent logic as noted by Shaw–Kwei [138], Skolem [144], Varela [154], in the context of classical set theory, and by Hendry [67] in the context of fuzzy set theory.

The analysis of the barber paradox shows us that the barber is a different *type* of individual from the others, in fact a midrange case at exactly the *borderline* between the two degrees of membership (0 and 1) previously allowed. It is interesting to note that the logical argument has forced us to *generate* a new truth value, i.e., the possibility of $\frac{1}{2}$ has not been introduced through an arbitrary extension to a ternary logic, but forced from the inequalities of implication (75) and (76). It is the natural way in which new truth values are generated as needed that makes this approach so attractive.[9]

The solution to the paradoxes of sorites, falakros, etc., is of a rather different nature. Let us consider what it is to be a bald man.[10] Most bald men are not completely hairless yet we would still claim them bald. Suppose a stranger comes along with only one more hair than one of our bald men. We would clearly call him bald also (although this may be dangerous with strangers). But then another stranger comes along with one more hair than this one, and so on. There is no reasonable way in which our criterion for baldness can depend on the possession of one additional hair and yet, before you can say hello to the ten-millionenth man, you are calling very shaggy men bald.

Let $\mathbf{hair}_n$ designate a person with n hairs on his head (the boundaries of heads and the enumerability of hairs will be here taken to be precise, not fuzzy) who has a degree of membership, bald $\mathbf{hair}_n$, to the fuzzy set of bald people. The key inference is that a person with only one more hair than a bald man is still bald, so that

$$\forall n, (\mathbf{hair}_{n-1} \text{ is bald}) \supset (\mathbf{hair}_n \text{ is bald}) \qquad (79)$$

Thus, using (35), we have

$$\forall n, \text{bald } \mathbf{hair}_n \geqslant \text{bald } \mathbf{hair}_{n-1} \qquad (80)$$

which gives us, by induction on n

$$\forall n, \text{bald } \mathbf{hair}_n \geqslant \text{bald } \mathbf{hair}_0 \qquad (81)$$

---

[9] I am grateful to Francisco Varela for this insight.

[10] It may well have been the same barber, in deciding who needed shaving at all, who came up with this problem also. Debate on this point would be fruitless, or at least only a matter of splitting hairs.

This, remembering that we take the truth value of a statement such as, "a man with n hairs on his head is bald" to be the degree of membership of the man to the (fuzzy) set of bald men, bald hair$_n$, may be read as: "it is at least as true that a man with an arbitrarily large number of hairs is bald as that a man with no hairs is bald"—certainly a paradox! Whence is it derived?

The weakness is in the transition from (79) to (80) since this is derived from (35) which is valid only if the implication of (79) is itself precise, i.e., absolutely true. When asked to agree to the statement that, "a man with only one more hair than a bald man is still bald," we must surely have our doubts–it is an argument "in the wrong direction," but not by much. We might answer, "Well, we suppose so", and feel that it would be somewhat pedantic to express too strong a doubt. If now told that truth is bivalent, "Be more precise. Is it true or not?", we are forced to make a choice. We cannot say that the statement is not true - it is far more reasonable to suppose it true than false, and, if these are the only possible choices, then we must say it is true.

Thus the demand for precision and bivalency of truth forces us to a choice and to a paradox. What we really wish to say is, "Yes, that is true", "Yes, that is quite true", or even "Yes, that is very true." "Truth" is itself a fuzzy concept that we *hedge* in everyday usage. I will discuss this further in the following section, but let us for the moment take it that truth is *not* bivalent and that the implication of (79) has itself a truth value of less than 1. Then the proper inference from (79) is not (80) but one based on (46) or (47) according to which implication function we are using, i.e., if the truth values of implication in (79) is $1 - \varepsilon$

$$\forall n, \text{bald hair}_n \geqslant \text{bald hair}_{n-1} - \varepsilon \qquad (82)$$

or

$$\forall n, \text{bald hair}_n \geqslant \text{bald hair}_{n-1} \times (1 - \varepsilon) \qquad (83)$$

which by induction on n gives us

$$\forall n, \text{bald hair}_n \geqslant \text{bald hair}_0 - n \times \varepsilon \qquad (84)$$

or

$$\forall n, \text{bald hair}_n \geqslant \text{bald hair}_0 \times (1 - \varepsilon)^n \qquad (85)$$

Note the interesting forms of inequalities (84) and (85): the right-hand side goes to zero with n, either linearly or exponentially; however, the right-hand side is greater than or equal to this decreasing quantity. We can no longer infer that the truth value of a man with an arbitrarily large number of hairs being bald is at least that of a man with none. However, neither can we infer that the truth value tends to zero, only that the lower bound on it obtained through our long chain or reasoning is zero and hence non-informative. It is the long chain of reasoning that is worthless (one is tempted to say invalid—however, it is the false inference of (81) that is invalid). If we are to say anything about the baldness of a man with n hairs on his head it is certainly not through this chain of reasoning.

This analysis of falakros raises many interesting points. It may be contrasted with that of Lake [93] who finds no satisfactory analysis in terms of fuzzy set theory but is still looking for a definite criterion of baldness—the argument chain does not break at some definite point— rather its information content peters out as it becomes longer. And this, in terms of the discussion at the beginning of this article, is just what we hope an adequate account of reasoning with imprecise concepts will do with sorites, falakros, etc.: defuse them rather than use them as a source of further artificial precisiation. The paper does not suddenly become irrelevant to control engineering, rather its relevance drops to a point where it is no longer robust against the random actions of referees, editors and readers, and it disappears quietly rather than through a dramatic application of new and precise criteria!

The point that the implication of (79) is not itself to be assigned a truth value of 1 is highly significant. I believe that this will be found to be of key importance in all aspects of practical reasoning. Each step we take in the chain of reasoning downgrades our estimate of the truth value of the result. The form of *modus ponens* in fuzzy reasoning is always like (46) or (47) and not the precise step of (35). This raises a methodological point for studies of human reasoning. If we have two premeises a and b of given truth value then inferring the truth value of $c = a \lor b$ is not just a matter of using a rule such as

$$c = \max(a, b) \qquad (86)$$

but rather one of using the *inferences*

$$a \supset c, b \supset c \qquad (87)$$

and hence involves a chain of reasoning and a potential downgrading of the truth value of the result. In fuzzy reasoning we 'pay' for each application of *modus ponens*. The long chain of argument eventually peters out even if every premise is known to be precisely true; we have a small, but not negligible, mistrust of each step. This gives a very tangible significance to the, otherwise, only aesthetic principle in logic that shorter proofs are to be preferred to longer ones (a principle long accepted, with little justification, by referees and commentators!).

FUZZY REASONING: HEDGES AND TRUTH

The analysis of the paradoxes in the previous section shows how they can be avoided in natural, and constructive ways, using reasoning based on a multivalued logic. This, in itself, may be viewed as illustrating only how the "classical" nonstandard approaches to these paradoxes may be regarded as part of fuzzy reasoning. To go beyond this we need to develop further the *linguistic* aspects of membership in fuzzy sets, *hedges*, and Zadeh's theory of *truth*.

First of all, we will formally adopt the conventions previously suggested that: expressions of properties in the form '*x* is *y*' may be translated into logical statements of the form '**x** is a member of the fuzzy set *y*'; and hence the degree of membership of **x** to *y*, *y***x** is meaningful and corresponds to the truth value of the original statement '*x* is *y*'. This relationship between linguistic forms and fuzzy sets is important because it enables us to go on to consider linguistic extensions such as '*x* is *y if u* is *v*', '*x* is *very y*', '"*x* is *y*" is true', etc.

It is customary in exposition of fuzzy reasoning to introduce at this stage some 'examples' of fuzzy sets, such as the set of *tall men*, and to do so by prescribing *a* a degree of membership to this set for a particular man as a function of his height. For illustrative purposes, in that it allows one to draw diagrams of fuzzy sets and their modifications, this procedure is useful. However, it has a danger of putting the ontological cart before the phenomenological horse—the concept, the perception, of 'tallness' exists in a more primitive sense than does the measurement of 'height'—to derive, even for illlustrative purposes, the concept *tall* from measurements of the physical variable *height* can be misleading. We are able to generate and follow arguments involving 'tallness' without having any concept of inches, centimeters, or any other metric scales. To introduce the former in terms of the latter reverses the actual process of derivation and, in particular, leads to a false distinction between these concepts, such as 'tallness,' that have a well-defined, single-parameter, physical metric, and those, such as 'beautiful' which do not.

Thus, whilst a 'scientific' analysis might conclude that there is a wide and ill-defined range of physical phenomena that combine in an extremely complex fashion to produce the subjective impression of beauty, in everyday reasoning it is as primitive a term as, the more simply explicable, tallness. We certainly do not distinguish between them in arguments such as:

He likes girls that are tall and beautiful.
Mary is not very tall but very beautiful.
He will probably like Mary.

or

This ladder is too tall to put in the kitchen.
This vase is too beautiful to put in the kitchen.

I emphasize this point at this stage because it is rather easier to illustrate fuzzy reasoning with linguistic variables that do have a simple physical interpretation—it is possible then to validate the results by comparing them with a more scientific argument. However, there is a definite tutorial danger that the reasoning patterns thus exhibited become associated with such variables, "tall", "heavy", "wide", etc., and terms such as "beautiful", "angry", "peaceful" are seen as less amenable to formal inference. Such an association would be very wrong—it is the main motivation of studying and formalizing fuzzy reasoning that it allows equal facility of inference with such 'non-physical' and 'ill-defined' terms as one normally has with those more amenable to precisiation.

Thus the concept of degree of membership to a fuzzy set is primitive. If we are able to go beyond this and define an operational procedure leading to a number that, over a population, is isotonically related to the degree of membership all well and good. We then have a physical measure that corresponds to the concept and which may itself have further properties that make the measuring scale more tractable [89]. It is the isotone relationship between measurement and degree of membership that makes for 'pretty' diagrams, but it is also this same factor which makes the measurement useful in explicating the concept, not vice versa. This may be seen clearly, for example, in multidimensional scaling techniques [140] where the computation is constrained to force data into the lowest dimensions of physical measurement that enable the order relationship between distances between points to be maintained, i.e., the fuzzy concept of "degree of similarity" is the *primitive from which measures are derived*.

In the light of these arguments I shall develop Zadeh's theories of *hedges*, and of *truth*, in rather more formal terms than usual, and examplify them initially without introducing actual, numerically-defined fuzzy sets. This approach also serves to distinguish those patterns of fuzzy reasoning that are tautologous properties of the definitions, and those which depend on the empirical properties of actual fuzzy sets.

In the same way that PC may be seen as an attempt to formalize colloquial linguistic usage of terms such as "and" and "or", and various modal logics as attempts to formalize "possible" and "necessary" or "permissible" and "obligatory", so can much of the current work on fuzzy logic be seen as formalizing linquistic usage of certain *hedges* applied to imprecise concepts, such as "very", "more or less", "slightly", etc.[11] [94, 170]. Before launching into technical detail it is worth re-issuing the usual disclaimer [170] that must be made when attempting to parallel the colloquial use of language in a logical formalism:

> It is useful to attempt to concretize the meaning of a hedge such as very even if the postulated meaning does not have universal validity

[11]For a variety of linguistic approaches to hedges see [77].

and is merely a fixed approximation to a variety of shades of meaning which very can assume in different contexts

Note, in passing, that this disclaimer is itself a fuzzy metalinguistic statement. When it comes to precisiation there is a sense in which fuzzy logic is the *only* one that can provide its own metalanguage!

Zadeh [170] suggests that the hedge *very* is interpreted as the operator γ introduced in an earlier section entitled "Fuzzy Logic and Inference". Thus if a is the statement
"The vase is beautiful"   (vase $\in$ beautiful objects)
then γa is the statement:
"The vase is very beautiful"   (vase $\in$ very beautiful objects).

This new unary operator can combine with the normal "and", "or", "not", operations, to produce very complex predicates. The statement b
"The vase is very beautiful but not very very beautiful" is

$$b = \gamma a \wedge {}^{\sim}\gamma\gamma a \tag{88}$$

so that, from (31), (33), and (50)

$$b = \min(a^2, 1 - a^4) \tag{89}$$

Clearly, particularly when compounded with further statements, such as "the vase is green", to give "the vase is not very green, but very very beautiful", very complex numerical relationships between truth values can develop. Zadeh points out the way in which language develops to give short forms of the commonly used compound hedges. "Very not beautiful" is ungrammatical and we replace "not beautiful" with "ugly": allowing "very ugly." A compound such as "the vase is beautiful but not very beautiful" may be condensed to "the vase is *slightly* beautiful", i.e if we represent "slightly" by the unary operator σ, then:

$$\sigma a = a \wedge {}^{\sim}\gamma a \tag{90}$$

To deal with other hedges, Zadeh introduces a range of other operators that may be defined in terms of γ. Since γ itself decreases the degree of membership most for those elements that already have a low degree of membership he calls it "*concentration.*" "*Dilation*" δ has the opposite effect and is used to express the hedge "more or less." It can be defined implicitly as

$$a = \delta b \Leftrightarrow b = \gamma a \tag{91}$$

we clearly have

$$a = b^{0.5} \tag{92}$$

"*Intensification*" ι pushes values above 0.5 towards 1 and values below 0.5 towards 0, i.e., it decreases the "fuzziness" of the set. It may be defined as

$$a = \iota b \Leftrightarrow a = (({}^{\sim}\gamma b \supset \gamma b) \wedge b) \vee (\gamma {}^{\sim} b \supset {}^{\sim}\gamma {}^{\sim} b) \tag{93}$$

so that

$$a = \begin{cases} 2 \times b^2 \text{ if } b \leqslant 0.5 \\ 1 - 2 \times (1 - b)^2 \quad \text{ if } b \geqslant 0.5 \end{cases} \tag{94}$$

Thus "concentration" and "dilation" are essentially compound hedges defined in terms of the connectives of $\mathbf{L}_1$ with the added operator γ. Zadeh also finds it useful to introduce a "normalization" operator ν that may be used to ensure that a fuzzy set is normalized; i.e., attains a maximum degree of membership of 1. In terms of the connective $\dashv$ of (45) we may define

$$a = \nu b \Leftrightarrow a = (\exists x \, b) \dashv b \tag{95}$$

so that

$$a = b / (\sup b') \tag{96}$$

where b' is any substitution instance of b.

The hedge "sort of" can be defined in terms of ν and δ as

$$a = \nu(\gamma\gamma b \wedge \delta b) \tag{97}$$

where a might be "the dog is sort of fierce" and b "the dog is fierce". Lakoff and Zadeh define many other hedges in this way, "pretty", "rather", "highly", etc. An important feature of their approach is that the hedges serve to derive new fuzzy sets in a standard fashion from those originally defined. If we know what is meant by "beautiful" then we also know what is meant by "very beautiful", "slightly beautiful", "not beautiful", and soon. The hedges clearly represent a way of deriving new fuzzy predicates in a standard fashion, independent of the structure of the particular fuzzy sets to which they are applied.

In general, a chain of reasoning results in some fuzzy predicate that is often expressible linguistically in terms of standard hedges. For example, we can finally assert $\sim\gamma\gamma b \wedge \delta b$, then if b is "my hair is wet", we can state "my hair is sort of wet". However, there are far more combinations of connectives possible than there are standard linguistic hedges in our vocabulary, and Zadeh [174] introduces the notion of "*linguistic approximation*", in which the function expressed by linguistic hedge does not precisely correspond to that resulting from some reasoning but is a good approximation to it. Linguistic approximation may be expressed axiomatically as a binary predicate λ between two fuzzy predicates a and b, which are themselves functions of the free variable x

$$\lambda(a,b) = \forall x \, (a \equiv b) \tag{98}$$

so that the degrees of membership of a and b to the fuzzy set of linguistic approximations is 1 minus the maximum difference between them over the domain of the fuzzy set on which they act.

The concept of *linguistic approximation* provides a clear example of the phenomenon mentioned earlier whereby fuzzy logic acts as its own metalanguage. The statement that *"very but not very very* is a linguistic approximation to *rather"* is itself imprecise and requires formalization in terms of fuzzy reasoning. The expression in (98) shows that this formalization is available within the framework already developed, and enables us immediately to formulate metalinguistic arguments about fuzzy reasoning such as: *"rather* is not a very good linguistic approximation to *very but not very very."* This metalinguistic completeness is one of the most satisfying features of the theory of fuzzy reasoning development by Zadeh. It is a *de facto* rejoinder to those who argue that bivalent logics must be foundational because we use them to argue about multivalued logics—in reality this is just false—'precisiation' itself is most naturally discussed and analyzed in a fuzzy metalanguage.

This is a natural point at which to discuss Zadeh's theory of truth [13] which takes *truth* itself to be a hedgeable linguistic concept, *not* an absolute, bivalent entity. I have already suggested in connection with the *falakros* type of paradox that our answer to the question, "Is a man with one more hair than a bald man still bald", might be, "yes, that is very true". Zadeh treats such a statement as expressing a relationship between the truth value of the first statement and the (fuzzy) set of truth statements. Thus the truth value of the second statement is the degree of membership of the truth value of the first statement to the set of true statements.

This concept is very clear and elegant; it enables us to analyze immediately statements of the form: *"'a'* is true" (*"'a'* is true" is a more or less true statement), "it is not true that 'rather' is a linguistic approximation to very more or less'", and so on. By placing appropriate constraints upon the function between the value of a statement, a, and its degree of membership to the set of true statements $\tau(a)$ we can infer some powerful metalinguistic results. For example, it is reasonable to constrain $\tau(a)$ to be such that

$$\tau(a) \leqslant a \qquad (99)$$

in effect, that the truth value does not increase when we say "is true." We then have

$$\text{"}a \text{ is true"} \supset a \qquad (100)$$

which is reminiscent of Tarski's convention T [151]. We also have, however

$$\text{"'}a \text{ is } b\text{' is very true"} \supset \text{"}a \text{ is very } b\text{"} \qquad (101)$$

because

$$(\tau(ba))^2 \leqslant (ba)^2 \qquad (102)$$

which is a new type of result in which the hedge of a statement about truth *transfers* to become a hedge of the primary statement, i.e., a hedge in the metalanguage induces one in the object language.

Zadeh gives numerical examples using functions for $\tau(a)$ in terms of a in which the inequality of (99) is proper. We do not then have the inverse inference that: $a \supset \text{'}a\text{'}$ is true, and it seems reasonable that this should be lacking. However, it is interesting also to consider $\tau(a)$ to be identical to a

$$\tau(a) = a \tag{103}$$

in which case

$$a \equiv \text{'}a\text{'} \text{ is true} \tag{104}$$

This particular function has the advantage that one can do without the numeric values in many cases and deal with arguments involving statements about truth in linguistic terms. This itself is significant because the old problem of the meaning of intermediate truth values still persists. "'Jack is tall' is 0.9 true" raises complications that "'Jack is tall' is very true" does not.

As in any analysis of reasoning in colloquial language there are bound to be counterexamples to the straightforward analysis of hedges and truth so far proposed, both Lakoff and Zadeh give examples where the analysis of this section breaks down. However, there is also a very wide variety of examples of reasoning with imprecise concepts that can now be formalized and understood using their models of hedges and truth. In particular such imprecise reasoning may now be automated in computer programs dealing with the everyday concepts of natural language and decisionmaking. Logicians who object to inferences of the form: "'Socrates is healthy' is very true, so 'Socrates is very healthy'", had better demolish the basis for them very rapidly. Tomorrow, they will be faced by computer terminals that use such patterns of reasoning in deciding what articles they should read; whether their credit is sound; and whether their divorce requests should be allowed!

I will conclude this section with two examples of fuzzy reasoning in action, the first dependent upon, and the second independent of, actual numeric truth values. Consider the well-known children's poem[12]:

Fuzzy Wuzzy was a bear
Fuzzy Wuzzy had no hair
Fuzzy Wuzzy wasn't very fuzzy, was he?

Let Fuzzy Wuzzy be represented as **fw**. The intention of the first line is not

[12]Whilst everyone seems to know it, the origins of this masterpiece are obscure (see Louis Untermeyer (Ed.), *Golden Treasury of Poetry*, Golden Press, 1959).

clear but it probably introduces the concept of a degree of membership i.e.,

$$\text{bear } \mathbf{fw} \approx 1 \tag{105}$$

The second line is clearly a contraction of some longer statement (we say someone has *no* sense, or *no* taste, meaning they have very little) and is probably best precisiated as if it were **fw** *had very little hair* (which does not scan[13]) or *was very bald* (which does not rhyme), i.e.,

$$\text{very-bald } \mathbf{fw} = 1 - \epsilon \tag{106}$$

so that

$$(\text{bald } \mathbf{fw})^2 = 1 - \epsilon \tag{107}$$

The final line questions the truth value of very-fuzzy **fw**. It is clear in this context that *fuzzy* is to be taken as *hairy* and hence as *very not bald* Hence, we have

$$\text{very-fuzzy } \mathbf{fw} = (\text{fuzzy } \mathbf{fw})^2 = (1 - \text{bald } \mathbf{fw})^4 \leqslant (\epsilon/2)^4 \tag{108}$$

Thus, finally,

$$\text{not-very-fuzzy } \mathbf{fw} \geqslant 1 - (\epsilon/2)^4 \geqslant 1 - \epsilon = \text{very-bald } \mathbf{fw} \tag{109}$$

so that the inference that Fuzzy Wuzzy was not very fuzzy from his lack of hair is valid with a substantial margin, indeed *very valid*. We would be entitled to answer, "yes, that is most certainly correct.."

Note that argument is independent of ϵ. I could have presented it in terms of order relationships only. The original assertion that Fuzzy Wuzzy has no hair does *not* have to be asserted with truth value 1. In essence, our reply is, "Whatever degree of certainty you have in the first assertion will most certainly be more than guaranteed in the last." Thus, the argument is in essence a theorem of fuzzy logic reflecting the meanings of the hedges used and not dependent on empirical tests of bald and hairy bears. Most nursery rhymes have a moral and it seems reasonable to suggest that this one introduces an important theorem of fuzzy reasoning to a child at an early age.

As a second example, let us examine the concept of height. In the same way that having "no hair" is used conversationally as a term meaning "very little hair", so an apparently precise description of height such as "six feet tall" is used conversationally to mean a fairly tightly constrained degree of membership peaking at 6 feet. If we wish to express more precision we would say, "exactly six feet", and less would be expressed by "about six feet" with still less by "roughly six feet." Figure 3(a)–(d) illustrates the form of plots of degree of membership to each of these terms

---

[13]I am grateful to Susan Haack for noting this.

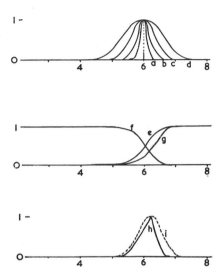

Figure 3. **Variation of membership to various fuzzy sets relating to "tall" against height (in feet): a—"Exactly six feet tall"; b—"Six feet tall"; c—"About six feet tall"; d—"Roughly six feet tall"; e—"Tall"; f—"Not tall"; g—"Very tall"; h—"Tall but not very tall"; i—"About six feet three."**

of objects of various heights. Note that we can interpret these curves in terms of truth values by saying that if John is 5 ft. 9 ins. tall than "John is 6 feet tall" has a truth value of 0.7, whereas "John is exactly six feet tall" has a truth value of 0.1, and "John is roughly six feet tall" has a truth value of 0.95.

Thus one feature of our normal linguistic expressions of measurement is that they carry with them a connotation of precision as well as one of expected value. They are expressions in *two dimensions*, the *central tendency* and the *degree of precision*, rather than just one. Similar considerations apply to statements about height that do not mention measurements. Figure 3(e) shows the type of variation of degree of membership with height for the fuzzy set specified by "is tall." The exact form of this graph is not likely to be well-specified. However, once one is given then the rules of fuzzy logic expressed so far specify how it will change under modification by logical operators and hedges. For example, Fig. 3(f) and (g) show the graphs for "is not tall" and "is very tall" obtained by $1 - a$ and a^2 rules, respectively. Now consider a statement such as "John is tall but not very tall." The normalized combination of logical operators and hedges produces a degree of membership graph, shown in Fig. 3(h). This is similar to the dotted graph, Fig. 3(i), for "about six feet three" being a linguistic approximation to it with

$$\lambda \text{ (about six feet three, tall but not very tall)} = 0.8 \qquad (110)$$

Thus, we can infer that "John is tall but not very tall" means he is about six feet three tall. This is a further example of fuzzy reasoning, but one that is now crucially dependent on the forms of degree of membership plots.

It would clearly be unreasonable to suppose that terms such as "tall" could be analyzed entirely independent of their context; "tall" amongst a tribe of pygmies would not be the same as in a football team! However, in this example, the use of the term would at least be consistent with "tall" for the human race, and it is possible that the membership function within the tribe might be derived from that over the race by taking the normalization function, v of (95), over the tribe. This derivability of membership function *relative to subsets* is an important feature of the order relation of degree of membership, e.g., "young" people in a geriatric population will be "old" in normal terms, but "young" relative to the population and this will appear when their degree of membership is normalized relative to the population.

Another effect one has to take into account is that statements made in conversation do not stand alone but are intended to affect the recipient.[14] Unless one takes this into account, and hypothesizes that statements are normally made to *convey the maximum information to the recipient*, anomolies can arise. For example, I say "John is tall", when he appears, you look at him and complain: "You misinformed me. John is nearly 7 feet. He is not just tall but *very tall*." The principle here seems to be that one chooses the most reasonable description. However, "most reasonable" is *not* the same as "most true"—"John is tall" has a truth value that is substantially higher than "John is very tall." Perhaps the anomaly can be resolved by noting that "John is tall" is very true, but "John is very tall" is just true—we make fuzzy statements at a certain conventional level of truth. It is just as misleading to make them exceptionally true as exceptionally false!

It is clear that a principle of maximum truth is, in any case, inadequate to select amongst statements, we need *relevance* also. The connectives of QL_1 are *not* those of a relevance logic in their current form, g., $a \supset b$ is precisely true if and only if $b \geqslant a$, regardless of the relevance of a to b. We have not noticed this defect so far because, as usual, we avoid fallacies of relevance in the way we use the logic. It would be very worthwhile to apply the program developed by [7] to QL_1 to ensure formally that fallacies of relevance and modality are avoided, particularly in computational forms of the logic.

---

[14]See, for example, Grice's theory of meaning [105].

Thus, there is much to be done before the formal theory of fuzzy reasoning is adequate and complete. However, the concepts developed and examples given do seem to provide a substantial step forward in understanding, and more importantly, emulating human reasoning with imprecise concepts. One important conclusion intended to be drawn from these last two sections is that Zadeh's analysis of fuzzy reasoning, hedges and truth, including such notions as "linguistic approximations," is completely formalizable within a logical framework that is nonstandard, but related to classical logic and rigorously expressible. This framework also provides the formal *fuzzy metalanguage* necessary to any discussion of precisiation and vital to the formulation of Zadeh's general arguments about linguistic hedges and truth.

LOGICAL, PSYCHOLOGICAL AND OTHER MODELS FOR TRUTH VALUES

One of the key methodological questions posed to proponents of fuzzy reasoning is, "where do the numbers come from?" One appears to be replacing fairly simple natural language inferences with complex operations on fuzzy sets that are themselves defined in terms of fairly complex numeric relationships between degrees of membership and physical properties. Clearly, from the previous sections, one possible answer is that, "we can do without the numbers." Fuzzy set theory and logic may be treated axiomatically as a set of inference rules that may be applied to logical expressions in extended $\mathbf{QL}_1$. The fact that connectives in $\mathbf{QL}_1$ can be characterized by operations on numeric "truth-values", by infinite-valued matrices, is then of secondary interest. It enables fuzzy reasoning to be carried out using numeric computation rather than symbolic processing, an important practical advantage but without foundational significance. This lack of fundamental reliance on numerical operations and intermediate truth values is itself important, and I attempted to illustrate and clarify it in previous sections.

However, from a practical point of view the underlying numeric matrices are an important feature of fuzzy logic, and this section surveys some aspects of the generation of these numbers, logically, psychologically and through intuitively meaningful models.

First, let us derive the numbers from the axioms. Consider a series of propositions that I shall call *primitive paradoxes*,[15] p_i for $i = 0, 1 \ldots$, defined recursively by

$$(\tilde{p}_{i+1} \supset p_{i+1}) = p_i, \qquad i > 0 \tag{111}$$

---

[15]These are clearly related to Rosser and Turquette's *J-functions* for axiomatizing the finite-valued versions of Lukasiewicz logic.

with $p_0 = † ⊃ †$,

$$p_1 = {}^\sim p_0 \equiv p_0 \tag{112}$$

In terms of truth values it can be seen that

$$p_i = (0.5)^i \tag{113}$$

so that we have generated an (infinite) sequence of propositional constants with truth values being the binary fractional powers. Now the truth value of any arbitrary proposition may be expressed as a fractional binary expression, e.g., 0.75 decimal = 0.11 binary, that may, or may not terminate. Consider expressions of the form

$$p = \left({}^\sim p_i \supset \left({}^\sim p_j \supset \left({}^\sim p_j \supset \left({}^\sim p_k \supset (\ldots)\right)\right)\right)\right) \tag{114}$$

where $i < j < k < \ldots$. The truth value of this expression is

$$p = p_i + p_j + p_k + \cdots$$

Hence, if the proposition p_i occurs in the definition of p (114) if and only if there is a 1 in the ith place of the fractional binary expansion of the truth value of a proposition a, then we have $p = a$. Thus, we can express the truth value of any proposition not as a number but as expression in primitive propositional constants that are themselves directly introduced from our axiom schema for $\mathbf{QL}_1$.

The argument above is readily turned into a formal derivation of a binary numbering system for arbitrary propositional constants that serve to *introduce* the numbers into the system. That is we can prove that if two sequences of the form of (114) p and p' are such that they commence with the same sequence of primitive paradoxes and then first differ by one being absent from p, we have $p \supset p'$. This enables us to insert arbitrarily long sequences of propositions of the form of (114) between p and a, and a and p', in relations of the form $p \supset a \supset p'$, and hence to approximate the truth value of a by a Dedekind section of standard sequences of arbitrarily high accuracy. Thus, we are able to both do without the numbers in fuzzy reasoning and also to introduce them if required, not on an arbitrary basis, but directly from the axiom schema of (52)–(58).

Rather different approaches to the numerical truth values have been taken by Giles [57] and Gaines [47, 49] in their models of fuzzy logic in terms of *dialogs* and *population responses*, respectively. Giles models $\mathbf{QL}_1$ as a *game* between two players who engage in a *dialog* to establish a *payoff* for a compound proposition that may be used to define its truth value. The connectives are defined by rules such as

(a) He who asserts $a \vee b$ undertakes to assert either a or b at his own choice;

(b) He who asserts $a \wedge b$ undertakes to assert either a or b at his opponent's choice;

(c) He who asserts $a \supset b$ undertakes to assert b if his opponent will assert a;

(d) He who asserts $\exists x \, a$ undertakes to assert some instance of a at his own choice;

(e) He who asserts $\forall x \, a$ undertakes to assert some instance of a at his opponent's choice;

(f) He who asserts † promises to pay his opponent $1.

This model can be seen as a set of rules for generating sequences expressed in game theoretic form. The dialog representation is particularly attractive in some situations, however, and Giles [56] uses it very effectively to model some of the observational problems of particle physics. In particular, he is able to give integrated model-theoretic interpretations of probabilistic and fuzzy decision-making.

This integrated derivation of probabilistic and fuzzy logics is also an important feature of Gaines' [48, 49] model in terms of the *responses of a population*. He considers a population each member of which can respond to certain questions with a binary, yes or no, reply. The forms of question involve evaluating some proposition a e.g. "is this propostion a true or false, reasonable or unreasonable, believed or not believed" etc. The value of a is defined to be the proportion of the population answering "yes." A conjunction of propositions $a \wedge b$ is given a truth value in terms of the proportion answering "yes" to both a and b,, whilst that for $a \vee b$ is the proportion answering "yes" for either.

Values for implication are defined as in (44) or (45) and values for equivalence and negation are defined in terms of these. The model is in essence a simple topological one, and its real interest is in terms of interpretation rather than theory:

(a) If we interpret the population as one of physical events and the "questions" as experiments then we have a model of frequentist probability:

(b) If we interpret the population as one of people expressing opinions then the model is a socio-linguistic one of the use of terms by the population-a very reasonable interpretation in terms of "fuzzy reasoning";

(c) If we interpret the population as a population of individual decision-making elements, e.g. "neurons", then the model is one of "subjective probability" or "belief".

Text analysis studies such as those of Rieger [126] of fuzzy semantic relations in a "population" of documents, fall naturally into this form of interpretation.

The population model so far described gives a non-truth-functional, multivalued logic. Gaines [48,49] shows that requiring it to be *strongly truth functional*, so that the value of a compound propostion can be expressed in terms of those of its components regardless of their structure, is sufficient to constrain the logic to be L_1. He also shows that, alternatively, the law of the excluded middle gives a non-truth-functional logic that is precisely *probability logic* [125] and goes on to generate a variety of logics by making this truth-functional in different ways. For example, addition of the constraints that, for two atomic propositions a and b

(i) $c = a \wedge b \to c = a \times b$,   gives a logic of *statistical independence*;
(ii) $c = a \wedge b \to c = 0$,   gives a logic of *mutual exclusion*;
(iii) $c = a \wedge b \to c = \min(a,b)$,   gives a logic of *mutual dependence*.

Gaines suggests that in any particular population different propositions will be found to be related in different ways, e.g. by a fuzzy logic or by statistical independence. If this relationship persists in all relevant variants of the population (possible worlds) then it is a structural constraint and can be expressed in a suitable modal logic. These are the interesting objects to study: the modal logics of fuzziness, independence, exclusion, etc.

One obvious question in terms of the population model is how the constraints leading to a fuzzy logic might arise. Those leading to statistical independence seem somehow more natural and usual. Here there is some interesting psychological evidence relating to interpretation (b) in terms of a population of people. L_1 would be obtained if members of the population each evaluated the evidence relating to a question in the same way but applied differing thresholds of acceptance when deciding whether to answer "yes." The member with the lowest threshold would then always answer "yes" if any other member did, and so on up the scale of thresholds. This gives a relationship of implication between propostions that generates the min/max connectives of L_1. This model, although unusual, has its intuitive attractions, e.g., Reason [124] has shown that the threshold applied by human beings in coming to a binary decision on an essentially analog variable seems to be associated with personality factors and a trait of the individual. If so, human populations would tend to show more a fuzzy, than a probabilistic logic in their decision-making.

There have now also been a number of studies of human decision-making to determine whether "degree of membership" graphs may be obtained consistently from people; what their form is [107,84,83,34]; what the effect of hedges is [107]; and what the effect of logical connectives is [127]. The results of these early studies are encouraging, indicating that the concept of a "degree of membership" is one that can be understood by subjects in a natural way and measured empirically, but they are not yet extensive to give definitive answers to questions about the "psycholinguistic reality" of fuzzy sets.

These experiments are reminiscent of those in the psychological literature of *semantic differentials* [118] the use of *everyday quantitative expressions* [139]; subjective decision-making and the elicitation of *subjective probabilities* [135,141]; *inter-sensory scaling* [148]; and other techniques for obtaining numeric estimates of subjective qualities from human beings. Stevens, [148] results are particularly interesting because he had subjects give estimates of the intensity of a wide variety of different sensations by the single output of exerting force on a handgrip. The consistency and coherency of his results for a wide range of sensations: shock, warmth, weight, vibration, noise, light, etc. demonstrate that people have no problem transferring qualitative appreciation from one dimension to another, and hence makes it plausible that there may be some high level 'logic' of imprecise estimation. Certainly there is much worthwhile work to be done in bringing together these various psychological studies within the framework by fuzzy reasoning. It might well be, for example, that results, such as those of Edwards, Phillips, Hayes and Goodman [35] that show human subjects as remarkably wasteful of information in a Bayesian decision-making situation, become explicable if people use fuzzy, rather than probabilistic, decision-making logics.

There are also links from fuzzy reasoning to linguistic studies. Wilks [162] *preference grammars* and *preference semantics* depend on an order relationship of preference between diffferent possible structures and interpretations, a relationship that arises naturally in fuzzy semantics. His approach is extremely powerful in resolving ambiguous, vague and unlikely constructions, for example, in metaphor and poetry. Thorne's [153] parser depends on the distinction between a comparatively small and known, set of *closed-class* words, and a potentially infinite and unknown set of *open-class* words. The parts of speech of (unrecognizable) open-class words in a sentence are allocated with reference to the closed-class key-words that are recognized in that sentence. Fuzzy *hedges* fall into the closed class and enable one to recognize that the hedged word is an imprecise predicate. Thereafter, one can manipulate it in a reasonable fashion even though one cannot understand it. For example, an ELIZA-type program [158], could recognize the key word "very" and have reconstruction rules that allowed

Person:	*I am very unhappy*
Computer:	*It is true that you are unhappy?*
Person:	*I dream I am very sad*
Computer:	*Do you dream you are more or less sad?*

Which enriches the conversation somewhat!

Thus the formal approach to fuzzy reasoning adopted in previous sections may be given a variety of less formal semantic models and links to human psychology and linguistics. In particular, the numerical values that belong to the multivalued logics underlying fuzzy reasoning may be derived from a number of different sources, ranging from the purely logical to the completely psychological, with a variety of interesting models in between. There is a *plurality* of derivations and which one is appropriate clearly depends on the semantics of the intended application.

CONCLUSION

I am acutely conscious in reading back through this material what a superficial presentation of the subject area it actually gives. What I have been able to do is to give some impression of how developments in fuzzy reasoning might be logically underpinned, not what *are* the foundations, but what *might be* the foundations. This is largely due to the lack of developments in logic such as QL_1 comparable to those in the classical predicate calculus.[16] Sanford [132] quotes Peirce [119]:

"Logicians have been at fault in giving Vagueness the go-by':

and Kripke [90]:

"Logicians have not developed a logic of vagueness"

Future historians will some day undoubtedly puzzle over this lack of interest, and certainly will need to explain the explosion exhibited in Fig. 1 triggered off by Zadeh's seminal paper of 1965.

Why the lack of interest in vagueness? Logical positivism is blamed for so much nowadays that chalking up another black mark will scarcely be noticed. Part of the drive of that movement was undoubtedly to greater precision [120]. However, there is nothing in the formal presentation of the positivist approach to scientific theories that precludes the standard predicate calculus in the *Received View* [149], p.16) being replaced with a weaker logic such as QL_1. It was presumably the influence of Whitehead and Russell's *Principia* [160] that made the choice of logic obvious. Hopefully now the need to develop weaker underlying logics for set theory, coupled with the need to avoid artefacts of precisiation, coupled with the need to model natural language reasoning, is focusing the attention of philosophers and logicians of mathematics, science and language in the same direction and will lead to rapid progress.

[16]Scott (1975) are the best modern discussions of QL_1 are [112, 137].

This still does not explain the growth of interest in fuzzy reasoning amongst engineers and social scientists. Suppe ([1974)], p. 19) has the wry footnote:

> It seems to be characteristic, but unfortunate, of science to continue holding philosophical positions long after they are discredited...

and that may be a sufficient explanation. Certainly precisiation has preceeded apace, and still proceeds, in systems engineering, linguisitcs, psychology and sociology, where the development of fuzzy reasoning has been most welcomed. These are the new sciences, post von Neumann and the computer, post Norbert Wiener and cybernetics, but they have tended to model themselves on the established, and highly successful, physical sciences, just at the point when these sciences themselves were entering an era of self-doubt and review of foundations [87].

What is particularly interesting in applied studies of fuzzy reasoning, such as those as diverse as Mamdani and Assilian's [108] of process control and Wenstop's [159] of social dynamics, is the emphasis on reasoning in natural language. This is taken to be, not just a remote model, but instead an almost directly manipulable representation of data. One is taken back to the debate about the role of formal logic in relation to language about which John Stuart Mill remarks in his *System of Logic* (1843):

> Since reasoning, or inference, the principal subject of logic, is an operation which usually takes place by means of words, and in complicated cases can take place in no other way: those who have not a thorough insight into both the signification and purpose of words, will be under chances, amounting almost to certainty, of reasoning or inferring incorrectly.

One may speculate that the growth of formal logic, despite its poverty in relationship to natural language, was *not* due to any deep philosophical developments but rather to the lack of computers. As an analogy, we have developed and used linear systems theory not because it works but because it is the *most powerful theory that we could utilize before computers were available*. Similar considerations apply to the classical propositional calculus, its value is largely computational due to its characteristic bivalent matrices. $\mathbf{QL}_1$ and similar logics without such a simple representation are too difficult to formalize by hand, see, for example, Prior [122], Chap. 2) to get some feeling for the type of effort involved. Synder [146], p.12) remarks on the dramatic change that the computer has made to such studies:

> The high adventure of seeking clever strategies for deductive proofs ...lost to us in the present set of formal systems. Instead, the

adventure...lies in the development of a variety of systems of logic for a variety of tasks.

Given a computer, we no longer need the simplicity, uniformity and analyticity, that is vital to paper and pencil implementation of formal reasoning. We can, in fact, take natural language at its face value and implement its diverse patterns as they are. This seems far closer to Leibniz's goal ([18]), p. 299):

> if we could find characters or signs appropriate for expressing all our thoughts as definitely and as exactly as arithmetic expresses numbers or geometric analysis expresses lines, we could in all subjects in so far as they are amenable to reasoning accomplish what is done in arithmetic and geometry.

rather more than his own *universal language* of numbers. Natural language is not precise in itself but it does "exactly express our thoughts"!

A further attraction of taking the reasoning patterns of natural language as our model is that the (strange) distinction between deductive and inductive logic disappears. A variety of qualitative differences between patterns of reasoning may still be distinguished encompassing this one distinction, but it no longer has its unique prominence. Again, for the engineer and scientist, the stark presentation of deductive reasoning as vacuous but valid, and inductive reasoning as fertile but unjustifiable, is disconcerting to say the least. Pragmatically one turns to the reasoning patterns of natural language and says, "we may never know how they work, but they *do* work, and we will use them."

Clearly, in practice as shown in this paper, formal techniques can, to a large extent, catch up with the pragmatic successs of applications of fuzzy reasoning and give a rationalization for it in the classical style. Formalisms have virtues of clarity, communicability and universality, that are valuable provided they do not constrain us unduly. Having used quotations so freely in this paper, I feel inclined to give the last words to an aphorism by a man (Lazarus Long, quoted in Heinlein [66]) who has had more experience than any other philosopher (he lived for some 2,000 years!):

> The difference between science and the fuzzy subjects is that science requires reasoning whilst those other subjects merely require scholarship

Hopefully, the direction of the work described in these notes indicates that the scholarship of multivalued logic has a part to play both in science of reasoning about (rather fuzzy) human linguisitic behavior and in the foundations of science itself.

REFERENCES

1. Ackermann, R. (1967) *Introduction to Many Valued Logics* London: Routledge and Kegan Paul.
2. Adams, E. W. (1965) Elements of a Theory of Inexact Measurement, *Philos. Sci.* 32, 205–228.
3. Adams, E. W. (1966) Probability and the logic of conditionals, in Hintikka, J. and Suppes, P. (Eds.) *Aspects of Inductive Logic*, 265–316.
4. Aizermann, M. A. (1975) Fuzzy sets, fuzzy proofs and some unsolved problems in the theory of automatic control, *Special Interest Discussion Session Fuzzy Automata and Decision Processes*, 6th IFAC World Congress, Boston, Mass.
5. Albin, M. (1975) Fuzzy sets and their application to medical diagnosis, Ph. D. Thesis, Department of Mathematics, University of California, Berkeley.
6. Altham, J. E. J. (1971) *The Logic of Plurality*. Methuen, London.
7. Anderson, A. R. and Belnap, N. D. (1975) *Entailment Vol. 1.* Princeton U. Press.
8. Arbib, M. A. (1970) Semiring languages. Electrical Engineering Depart., Stanford U. Calif.
9. Arbib, M. A. and Manes, E. G. (1975) A category-theoretic approach to systems in a fuzzy world. *Synthese* 30, 381–406.
10. Baas, S. M. and Kwakernaak, H. (1976) Rating and ranking of multiple-aspect alternatives using fuzzy sets, *Automatica* 12.
11. Becker, J. M. (1973) A structural design process: philosophy and methodology, PhD Thesis, Structural Engineering Laboratory, U. Calif., Berkeley.
12. Bellman, R. E. and Giertz, M. (1973) On the analytic formalism of the theory of fuzzy sets, *Infor. Sci.* 5, 149–156.
13. Bellman. R. E. and Zadeh, L. A. (1976) Local and fuzzy logics, ERL–M584 Electronics Research Laboratory, College of Engineering, U. of Calif., Berkeley.
14. Bezdek, J. C. (1974) Numerical taxonomy with fuzzy sets, *J. Math. Biology* 1, 57–71.
15. Black, M. (1937) Vagueness, *Phil. Sci.* 4, 427–455.
16. Brown, G. S. (1969) *Laws of Form*. London: Allen and Unwin.
17. Brown, J. G. (1971) A note on fuzzy sets. *Inf. Control* 18, 32–39.
18. Burks, A. W. (1975) Logic, biology and automata-some historical reflections. *Int. J. Man-Machine Studies* 7, 297–312.
19. Cargile, J. (1969). The sorites paradox, *Brit. J. Philos. Sci.* 20, 198–202.
20. Carnap, R. (1947) *Meaning and Necessity*. U. Chi. Press, Ill.
21. Carnap, R. (1950) *Logical Foundations of Probability*. U. Chi. Press, Ill.
22. Chang, C. C. (1963) The axiom of comprehension in infinite valued logic, *Math.Scand.* 13, 9–30.
23. Chang, C. C. (1965) Infinite valued logic as a basis for set theory, in Bar-Hillel (Ed.), *Proceedings of 1964 International Congress for Logic Methodology and Philosophy of Science*. North-Holland, Amsterdam, 93–100.

24. Chang, C. L. (1968) Fuzzy topological spaces, *J. Math. Anal. Appl.* **24**, 182–190.

25. Chapin, E. W. (1974) Set-valued set theory: Part One, *Notre Dame J. Formal Logic* **15**, 619–634.

26. Chapin, E. W. (1975) Set-valued set theory: Part Two, *Notre Dame J. Formal Logic* **16**, 255–267.

27. Chihara, C. S. (1973) *Ontology and the Vicious Circle Principle.* Cornell U. Press, N.Y.

28. Cresswell, M. J. (1973) *Logics and Languages.* Methuen, London.

29. Curry, H. B. (1942) The inconsistency of certain formal logics. *J. Sym. Logic* **7**, 115–117.

30. Dal Cin, M. (1973) Fuzzy-state automata, their stability and fault-tolerance, University of Tublingen, Germany.

31. Danielsson. S. (1967) Modal logic based on probability theory, *Theoria* **33**, 189–197.

32. DeLuca, A., and Termini, S. (1972) Alegbraic properties of fuzzy sets. *J. Math. Anal. and Applns.* **40**, 373–386.

33. Dienes, Z. P. (1949) On an implication function in many-valued systems of logic, *J. Sym. Logic* **14**, 95–97.

34. Dreyfuss, G. R., Kochen, M., Robinson, J., and Badre, A. N. (1975). On the psycholinguistic reality of fuzzy sets, in Grossman, R. E., San, L.J., and Vance, T. J. (Eds.), *Functionalism*, U. Chi. Press, Ill.

35. Edwards, W., Phillips, L. D., Hayes, W. L., and Goodman, B. C. (1968) Probabilistic information processing systems: design and evaluation, *IEEE Trans. Syst. Man Cybern* **SSC–4**, 248–265.

36. Evans, G. and McDowell, J. (1976) *Truth and Meaning*, Clarendon Press, Oxford.

37. Fellinger, W. L (1974) Specifications for a fuzzy systems modelling language, PhD Thesis, Ore. State U, Corvallis.

38. Fenstad, J. E. (1964) On the consistency of the axiom of comprehension in the Lukasiowicz infinite valued logic, *Math Scand.* **14**, 65–74.

39. Feyerabend, P. (1975) *Against Method.* NLB, London.

40. Fillmore, C. J. and Langendoen, (Eds.) (1971) *Studies in Linguistic Semantics.* Holt, Rinehart & Winston, New York.

41. Fine, K. (1975) Vagueness, truth and logic *Synthese* **30**, 265–300.

42. Fine. T. L. (1973) *Theories of Probability.* Academic press, N. Y.

43. Finetti. B. de (1972) *Probability, Induction and Statistics.* John Wiley, N. Y.

44. Gaines, B. R. (1972) Axioms for adaptive behaviour. *Int. J. Man-Machine Studies* **4**, 169–199.

45. Gaines, B. R. (1974) Training, stability and control, *Instr. Sci.* **3**, 151–176.

46. Gaines, B. R. (1975) Stochastic and Fuzzy logics. *Electronics Letters* **11**, 444–445.

47. Gaines, B. R. (1976a) On the Complexity of causal models, *IEEE Trans. Syst. Man Cybern.* **SMC-6**, 56–59.

48. Gaines, B. R. (1976b) General fuzzy logics, *Proc. Third Eur. Meeting Cybernetics and Systems Research*, Vienna.

49. Gaines, B. R. (1976c) Fuzzy reasoning and the logic of uncertainty, *Proc. 6th. Int. Symp. Multiple-Valued logic* Utah, *IEEE* **76CH 1111-4C**, 179–188.

50. Gaines, B. R. (1976d) Behavior/structure transformations under uncertainty. *Int. J. Man-Machine Studies* **8**, 337–365.

51. Gaines, B R. (1976e) System identification, approximation and complexity, *Int. J. Gen. Syst.* **3**,

52. Gaines, B. R. and Kohout, L. J. (1975) The logic of automata, *Int. J. Gen. Syst.* **2**, 191–208.

53. Gaines, B. R. and Kohout, L. J. (1977) The fuzzy decade: a bibliography of fuzzy systems and closely related topics, *Int. J. Man-Machine Studies* **9**.

54. Gale, S. (1975) Conjectures on many-valued logic, regions and criteria for conflict resolution, *Proc. 1975 Int. Symp. Multiple-Values Logic*, Indiana, IEEE 75 CH0959-7C, 212–225.

55. Gellner, E. (1974) *Legitimation of Belief.* Cambridge U. Press, Cambridge.

56. Giles, R. (1975) Formal languages and the foundations of physics. Queen's Math. Preprint No. 1975–32, Queen's University, Kingston, Ontario, Canada.

57. Giles, R. (1976) Łukasiewicz logic and fuzzy set theory, *Int. J. Man–Machine Studies* **8**, 313–327.

58. Goguen, J. A. (1969) The logic of inexact concepts, *Synthese* **19**, 325–373.

59. Goguen, J. A. (1974a) Concept representation in natural and artificial languages: axioms, extensions and applications for fuzzy sets, *Int. J. Man-Machine Studies* **6**, 513–561.

60. Goguen, J. A. (1974b) The fuzzy Tychonoff theorem, *J. Math. Anal. Appl.* **43**, 734–742.

61. Goguen. J. A. (1975) On fuzzy robot planning, in Zadeh *et al.* (1975), 429–447.

62. Grofman, B. and Hyman, G. (1973) Probability and logic in belief systems, *Theory and Decision* **4**, 179–195.

62a. Haack, S. (1974). *Deviant Logic*, Cambridge University Press.

63. Habets, P. and Peiffer, K. (1973) Classification of stability-like concepts and their study using vector Lyapunov functions, *J. Math. Anal. App.* **44**, 537–570.

64. Hamacher, H. (1976) On logical connectives of fuzzy statements and their affiliated truth functions, *Proc. Third Eur. Meeting Cybernetics and Systems Res.*, Vienna.

65. Heijenoort, J. van (1967) *From Frege to Gödel.* Harvard U. Press, Cambridge.

66. Heinlein, R. (1974) *Time Enough for Love.* NEL.

67. Hendry, W. L. (1972) Fuzzy sets and Russell's paradox, Los Alomos Scientific Laboratory, N. M.

68. Hesse, M. (1974) *The Structure of Scientific Inference*, Macmillan, London.

69. Hintikka, J. (1962) *Knowledge and Belief.* Cornell U. Press, N.Y.

70. Hintikka, J. and Suppes, P. (eds) (1970) *Information and Inference.* Reidel, Holland.

71.	Hockney, D., Harper, W., and Freed, B. (1975) *Contemporary Research in Philosophical Logic and Linguistic Semantics.* Reidel, Holland.
72.	Honda, N. and Nasu, M. (1975) Recognition of fuzzy languages, in Zadeh *et al.* (1975). 279–299.
73.	Hughes, G. E. and Resswell, M. J. (1968) *An Introduction to Modal Logic.* Methuen, London.
74.	Hughes, P., and Brecht, G. (1976) *Viscious Circles and Infinity* Jonathan Cape, London.
75.	Hume, D. (1739) *A treatise of human nature,* London.
76.	Hutton. B. (1975) Normality in fuzzy topological spaces. *J. Math. Anal. Appl.* **50**, 74–79.
77.	Kalman, R. E. Falb, P. L. and Arbib, M. A. (1969) *Topics in Mathemtical Systems Theory* McGraw-hill, New York.
78.	Katz, J. J. (1962) *The Problem of Induction and Its Solution.* U. of Chi. Press, Ill.
79.	Kimball, J. P., Cole, P, and Morgan, J. L. (1972–75) *Syntax and Semantics,* Vols. 1–4. Academic Press, N. Y.
80.	Kleene, S. C. (1952) *Introduction to Metamathematics.* Van Nostrand, N. Y.
81.	Kling, R. (1974) Fuzzy PLANNER: reasoning with inexact concepts in a procedural problem-solving language, *J. Cybernetics* **4**, 105–122.
82.	Kneale, W. and Kneale, M. (1962) *The Development of Logic.* Clarendon Press, Oxford.
83.	Kochen, M. (1975) Applications of fuzzy sets in psychology, in Zadeh *et al.* (1975), 395–408.
84.	Kochen, M. and Badre, A. N. (1974) On the precision of adjectives which denote fuzzy sets. *J. Cybernetics* **4**, 49–59.
85.	Koczy, L. T. and Hajnal, M. (1975) A new fuzzy calculus and its application as a pattern recognition technique, *Proc. Third Inter. Congr. Cybern. Syst.,* Rumania.
86.	Kohout, L. J. and Gaines, B. R. (1976) Protection as a general systems problem. *Int. J. Gen. Syst.* **3**, 3–23
87.	Körner, S. (Ed.) (1957) *Observation and Interpretation in the Philosophy of Physics.* Dover Publications, N. Y.
88.	Korzybski, A. (1958) *Science and Sanity.* International Non-Aristotelian Library.
89.	Krantz, D. H. Luce, R. D., Suppes, P, and Twersky, A. (1971) *Foundations of Measurement Vol. 1.* Academic Press, N. Y.
90.	Kripke, S. (1970) Naming and necessity, in Harman, G., and Davidson, D. (Eds). *Semantics of Natural Language.* D. Reidel, Dordrecht, 345.
91.	Kyburg, H. E. (1970) Probability and Inductive Logic. Macmillan, London.
92.	Lakatos, I. and Musgrave, A. (1970) *Criticism and the Growth of Knowledge* Cambridge U. Press, Cambridge.
93.	Lake, J. (1974) Fuzzy sets and bald men, Department of Mathematics, Polytechnic of the South Bank, London, U. K.
94.	Lakoff, G. (1975) Hedges: a study in meaning criteria and the logic of fuzzy

concepts, in Hockney *et al.* (1975), 221–271.

95. Leblanc, H. (Ed.) (1973) *Truth, Syntax and Modality.* North Holland, Amsterdam.

96. Lee. E. T. (1975) Shape-oriented chromosome classification, *IEEE Trans. Syst. Man Cybern., SMC-5,* 629–682.

97. Lee, E. T. and Chang, C. L. (1971) Some properties of fuzzy logic, *Information and Control* 19, 417–431.

98. Lee, R. C. T. (1972) Fuzzy logic and the resolution principle. *J. Assn. Comput. Mach.* 19, 1099–119

99. LeFaivre, R. A (1974) The representation of fuzzy knowledge, *J. Cybernetics* 4, 57–66.

100. Lemmon, E. J., Meredith, C. A., Meredith, D., Prior, A. N., and Thomas, I. (1969). Calculi of pure strict implication, in Davis, J. W., Hockney, D. J. and Wilson, W. K. (Eds.). *Philosophical Logic.* D. Reidel, Dordrecht, 215–250.

101. Łukasiewicz, J. (1930) Philosophical remarks on many-valued systems of propositional logic, in McCall (1967), 40–65.

102. McCall, S. (1967) *Polish Logic* 1920–1939. Clarendon Press, Oxford.

103. McCarthy, J. and Hayes, P. J. (1969) Some philosophical problems from the standpoint of machine intelligence, in Meltzer, B. and Michie, D. (Eds.). *Machine Intelligence* 4. Edinburgh University Press, 463–502.

104. Machina, K. F. (1972) Vague predicates. *Am. Philos. Quart.* 9, 225–233.

105. Mackay, A. F. (1972) Professor Grice's theory of meaning, *Mind* 81, 57–66.

106. Mackie, J. L. (1973) *Truth, Probability and Paradox.* Oxford U. Press, Oxford.

107. MacVicar-Whelan, P. J. (1974) Fuzzy sets, the concept of height, and the hedge very. Tech. Memo. 1, Physics Dept., Grand Valley State College, Allendale, Mich.

108. Mamdani, E. H. (1976) Application of fuzzy logic to approximate reasoning using linguistic synthesis, *Proc. Sixth Inter. Symp. Multiple-Valued Logic,* Utah, *IEEE* 76 CH1111–4C, 196–202.

109. Mamdani, E. H. and Assilian, S. (1975) An experiment in linguistic synthesis with a fuzzy logic controller. *Int. J. Man–Machine Studies* 7, 1–13.

110. Marinos, P. N. (1969) Fuzzy logic and its application to switching systems. *IEEE Trans. Electron. Comp.* EC-18, 343–348.

111. Martin, R. L. (Ed.) (1970) *The Paradox of the Liar.* Yale U. Press, New Haven.

112. Maydole, R. E. (1972) *Many-valued Logic as a Basis for Set Theory.* PhD. Thesis, Boston University, Boston, Mass.

113. Maydole, R. E. (1975) Paradoxes and many-valued set theory, *J. Philos. Logic* 4, 269–291.

114. Mill, J. S. (1843) *A System of Logic.* Longmans, London.

115. Mizumoto, M., Toyoda, J., and Tanaka, K. (1969) Some considerations on fuzzy automata, *J. Computer Syst. Sci.* 3, 409–422.

116. Mostowski, A. (1966) *Thirty Years of Foundational Studies.* Basil Blackwell, Oxford.

117. Newell, A. and Simon, M. A. (1972) *Human Problem Solving*. Prentice-Hall, N. J.

118. Osgood, C. E., Suci, G. J. and Tannenbaum, P. H. (1957) *The Measurement of Meaning*. U. Ill. Press, Urbana.

119. Pierce, C. S. (1931) *Collected Papers*. Cambridge U. Press, Cambridge.

120. Popper, K. (1976) *Unended Quest*. Fontana/Collins, London.

121. Poston, T. (1971) Fuzzy Geometry. PhD Thesis. U. Warwick, England.

122. Prior, A. (1967) *Past, Present and Future*. Clarendon Press, Oxford.

123. Putnam, H. (1976) Meaning and Truth, Sherman Lectures, February, University College, London.

124. Reason, J. T. (1969) Motion sickness-some theoretical considerations, *Inter. J. Man-Machine Studies* 1, 21–28.

125. Rescher, N. (1969) *Many-Valued Logic*. McGraw-Hill, N. Y.

126. Rieger, B. (1976) Fuzzy structural semantics, *Proc. Third European Meeting on Cybernetics and Systems Research*, Vienna.

127. Rödder, W. (1975) On 'and' and 'or' connectives in fuzzy logic. EURO I, RWTH Aachen, Germany.

128. Rosenfeld, A. (1971) Fuzzy groups. *J. Math. Anal. Appl.* **35**, 512–517.

129. Rosenfeld, A. (1975) Fuzzy graphs, in Zadeh *et al.* (1975), 77–95.

130. Rosser, J. B. and Turquette, A. R. (1952) *Many-valued Logics*. North-Holland, Amsterdam.

131. Russell, B. (1923) Vagueness, *Australian J. Philos.* **1**, 84–92.

132. Sanford, D. H. (1975) Borderline Logic. *Am. Philos. Quart.* **12**, 29–39.

133. Santos, E. S. (1970) Fuzzy algorithms. *Information and Control* **17**, 236–339.

134. Santos, E. S. and Wee, W. G. (1968) General formulation of sequential machines, *Information and Control* **12**, 5–10.

135. Savage, L. J. (1971) Elicitation of personal probabilities and expectations, *J. Amer. Stat. Assn.* **66**, 783–801.

136. Schützenberger, M. P. (1962) On a theorem of R. Jungen, *Proc. Amer. Math. Soc.* **13**, 885–890.

137. Scott, D. (1974) Completeness and axiomatizability in many-valued logic, in Henkin, L. (Ed.) *Proceedings of the Tarski Symposium*, Am. Math. Soc., R. I., 412–435.

138. Shaw-Kwei, M. (1954) Logical paradoxes for many-valued systems, J. Sym. Logic **19**, 37–41.

139. Sheppard, D. (1954) The adequacy of everyday quantitative expressions as measurements of qualities, *Brit. J. Psychol.* **45**, 40–50.

140. Shepard, R. N., Romney, A. K. and Nerlove, S. B. (1972) *Multidimensional Scaling*. Seminar Press, N. Y.

141. Shuford, E., and Brown, T. A. (1975) Elicitation of personal probabilities and their assessment, *Inst. Sci.* **4**, 137–188.

142. Simons, H. W. (1976) *Persuasion*. Addison-Wesley, Mass.

143. Siy, P. and Chen, C. S. (1974) Fuzzy logic for handwritten numerical character recognition, *IEEE Trans. Syst. Man Cybern.* **SMC-4**, 570–575.

144. Skolem, Th. (1957) Bemerkungen zum Komprehensionsaxiom, *Z. Math. Logik Grandlagen Math.* **3**, 1–17

145. Skolem, Th. (1960) A set theory based on a certain 3-valued logic, *Math. Scand.* **8**, 127–136.
146. Snyder, D. P. (1971) *Modal Logic and its Applications.* Van Nostrand, N. Y.
147. Stalnaker, R. (1970) Probability and conditionals, *Philos. Sci.* **37**, 64–80.
148. Stevens, S. S. (1961) To honor Fechner and repeal his law. *Science* **133**, 80–86.
149. Suppe. F. (1974) *The Structure of Scientific Theories* U. Ill. Press. Urbana, Ill.
150. Suppes, P. (1974) *Probabilistic Metaphysics*, Filofiska Studier nr. 22, Uppsala University, Sweden.
151. Tarski, A. (1956) *Logic, Semantics, Metamathematics.* Clarendon Press, Oxford.
152. Thomason, M. G. and Marinos, P. N. (1974) Deterministic acceptors of regular fuzzy languages, *IEEE Trans. Syst. Man Cybern.* **SMC-4**, 228–230.
153. Thorne, J. P. (1969) A program for the syntactic analysis of English sentences. *Comm. Assn. Comput. Mach.* **12**, 476–478.
154. Varela, F. J. (1975) A calculus for self-reference, *Int. J. Gen. Syst.* **2**, 5–24.
155. Wajsberg, M. (1931) Axiomatization of the three-valued propositional calculus, in McCall, S. (1967), 265–284.
156. Wechler, W. (1975) *R*-fuzzy automata with a time-variant structure, in Goos, G. and Hartmanis, J. (Eds.), *Mathematical Foundations of Computer Science.* Springer-Verlag, Berlin, 73–76.
157. Weiss, S. E. (1973) The Sorites Antinomy-A Study in the Logic of Vagueness and Measurement. PhD. Thesis, U. N. C., Chapel Hill, N. C.
158. Weizenbaum, J. (1967) Contextual understanding by computers. *Comm. Assn. Comput. Mach.* **10**, 474–480.
159. Wenstop, F. (1976) Deductive verbal models of organizations, *Int. J. Man-Machine Studies* **8**, 293–311.
160. Whitehead, A. N., and Russell, B. (1910–1913) *Principia Mathematics.* Cambridge University Press, Cambridge.
161. Wiener, N. (1914) A simplification of the logic of relations. *Proc. Cambridge Philosophical Society* **17**, 387–390.
162. Wilks, Y. (1975) Preference semantics, in Keenan, E. L., *Formal Semantics of Natural Language*, Cambridge University Press, 320–348.
163. Witten, I. H. and Gaines, B. R. (1976) The Role of randomness in system theory. *Proc. Third Eur. Meeting on Cybernetics and Systems Research*, Vienna.
164. Wong, C. K. (1975) Fuzzy topology, in Zadeh *et al.* (1975). 171–190.
165. Zadeh, L. A. (1963) On the definition of adaptivity. *Proc. IEEE* **51**, 469.
166. Zadeh, L. A. (1964) The concept of state in system theory. In Mesarovic, M. D. (Ed.) *Trends in General Systems Theory*, John Wiley, N. Y., 39–50.
167. Zadeh, L. A. (1965) Fuzzy sets. *Information and Control* **8**, 338–353.
168. Zadeh, L. A. (1972a) Fuzzy languages and their relation to human intelligence. *Proc. Int. Conf. Man and Computer*, Bordeaux, France. S. Karger, Basel, 130–165.

169. Zadeh, L. A. (1972b) A new approach to system analysis. In Marois, M. (Ed.) *Man and Computer*, North-Holland, Amsterdam, 55–94.
170. Zadeh, L. A. (1972c) A fuzzy-set-theoretic interpretation of linguistic hedges, *J. Cybernetics* **2**, 4–34.
171. Zadeh, L. A. (1973) Outline of a new approach to the analysis of complex systems and decision processes, *IEEE Trans. Syst. Man Cybern.* **SMC–1**, 28–44.
172. Zadeh, L. A. (1976) A fuzzy-algorithmic approach to the definition of complex or imprecise concepts, *Int. J. Man-Machine Studies* **8**, 249–291.
173. Zadeh, L. A. and Desoer (1963) *Linear System Theory*. McGraw-Hill, N. Y.
174. Zadeh, L. A., Fu, K. S., Tanaka, K., and Shimura, M. (1975) *Fuzzy Sets and their Application to Cognitive and Decision Processes*. Academic Press, N. Y.

APPLICATIONS OF FUZZY SET THEORY TO CONTROL SYSTEMS: A SURVEY

5

E. H. Mamdani

This paper surveys the field of application of fuzzy logic in designing controllers for industrial plants. It should be noted that fuzzy logic is a minor aspect of the whole field of fuzzy mathematics and perhaps little related to the majority of the rest of the literature on the subject. The true antecedent of the work described here is an outstanding paper by Zadeh [21], which lays the foundation of what we have termed linguistic synthesis [11], and which has also been described by Zadeh as Approximate Reasoning (AR). In the 1973 paper referred to above Zadeh shows how vague logical statements can be used to construct computational algorithms which may be used to derive inferences (also vague) from vague data. The paper suggests that this method is useful in the treatment of complex humanistic systems. However, it was realized that this method could equally be applied to 'hard' systems such as industrial plant controllers. In such cases where a linguistic control protocol can be obtained from a skilled operator of a plant, fuzzy logic, following the approach described by Zadeh can be used to synthesis this protocol.

This method was first applied to control a pilot scale steam-engine using fuzzy logic to interpret linguistic rules which qualitatively express the control strategy. The reader is referred to [11] for a fuller description of this work. Prior to that the same steam engine had been used as a vehicle to investigate the practical applicability of artificial intelligence and learning control techniques. However, the results of such techniques did not seem to recommend themselves for industrial applications, see Assilian and Mamdani [1]. A lucid account of this background is given in the doctorate thesis by Assilian [1]. Such artificial intelligence and pattern recognition methods are principally characterized by a great deal of heuristics that is incorporated in them. It was easy to see that fuzzy logic was the most appropriate tool to implement heuristics. This then was what originally led to the use of fuzzy logic in controller design, even though the first controller did not possess learning ability but was merely a straight description of what should be done to control the plant. To summarize,

77

therefore, the approach was not from a control engineering point of view but from an artificial intelligence (AI) viewpoint.

This method was of course nonanalytic and the results were consequently presented as a single case study showing what could be done using fuzzy logic. Since then the full potential of this method has gradually become more apparent as more results are obtained by various other researchers applying this method. A great deal of additional analysis and discussion has taken place during the past year or so. Much of this is yet unpublished and exists at present in the form of internal reports and research memoranda. It is the purpose of this article to survey the results and the ongoing work at various places devoted to fuzzy mathematics. However, it may first be necessary to present a brief outline of the method.

SYNTHESIS OF "FUZZY CONTROLLER"

The purpose of any plant controller is first to relate the state variables to action variables, i.e., to periodically look at the values of the state variables and from the expressed relationships to compute the value of the action variable. Now the controller of a physical system need not itself be physical but may be purely logical. Furthermore where the known relationships are vague and qualitative a fuzzy logic based controller may be constructed to implement the known heuristics. Thus in such a controller the variables are equated to non-fuzzy universes giving the possible range of measurement or action magnitudes. These variables, however, take on linguistic values which are expressed as fuzzy subsets of the universes.

A fuzzy subset F of a universe of discourse $U = \{x\}$ is defined as a mapping $\mu_F(x): U \rightarrow [0, 1]$ by which each x is assigned a number in $[0, 1]$ indicating the extent to which x has the attribute F. Thus, if x is the magnitude of pressure say, then "small" may be considered as a particular fuzzy value of the variable pressure and each x is assigned a number $\mu_{SMALL}(x) \in [0, 1]$ which indicates the extent to which that x is considered to be small.

Given the fuzzy sets A, B of U, the basic operations on A, B are
1. The complement $\bar{A}$ of A, defined by
$$\mu_{\bar{A}}(x) = 1 - \mu_A(x)$$
2. The union $A \cup B$ of A and B, defined by
$$\mu_{A \cup B}(x) = \max\{\mu_A(x), \mu_B(x)\}$$
3. The intersection $A \cap B$ of A and B, defined by
$$\mu_{A \cap B}(x) = \min\{\mu_A(x), \mu_B(x)\}$$

A fuzzy relation R from $U = \{x\}$ to $V = \{y\}$ is a fuzzy set on the Cartesian product $U \times V$, characterized by a function $\mu_R(x,y)$, by which each pair (x,y) is assigned a number in $[0,1]$ indicating the extent to which the relation R is true for (x,y). There are several ways of constructing $\mu_R(x,y)$. The one used here will be seen later.

Finally given a fuzzy relation R from U to V and a fuzzy subset A of U, a fuzzy subset B of V is inferred, given by the compositional rule of inference:

$$B = A \circ R,$$

or

$$\mu_B(y) = \max_x \left\{ \min\{ \mu_R(x,y), \mu_A(x) \} \right\}.$$

A heuristic approach to the control problem was employed, which resulted in a set of linguistic control statement. The above basic ideas of the theory of fuzzy subsets were used for the quantitative interpretation of these instructions as well as the decision-making process.

The fuzzy control instructions for the heat-pressure loop of the steam engine are shown in Fig. 1[1] and are of the form

---

IF PE = (NB or NM) THEN IF CPE = NS THEN HC = PM
OR
IF PE = NS THEN IF CPE = PS THEN HC = PM
OR
IF PE = NO THEN IF CPE = (PB or PM) THEN HC = PM
OR
IF PE = NO THEN IF CPE = (NB or NM) THEN HC = NM
OR
IF PE = (PO or NO) THEN IF CPE = NO THEN HC = NO
OR
IF PE = PO THEN IF CPE = (NB or NM) THEN HC = PM
OR
IF PE = PO THEN IF CPE = (PB or PM) THEN HC = NM
OR
IF PE = PS THEN IF CPE = (PS or NO) THEN HC = NM
OR
IF PE = (PB or PM) THEN IF CPE = NS THEN HC = NM

Figure 1. Fuzzy control instructions for the heat-pressure loop of the steam engine. (Pressure Error = PE, Change in Pressure Error = CPE, and Heat Input Change = HC.)

[1]The abbreviations used for the linguistic values in Fig. 1 are ZE = zero; PZ = positive zero; PS = positive small; PM = positive medium; PB positive big and the same for negative values NZ, NS, NM, and NB. Change in error negative is taken as movement set point and positive as away from set point.

if $E = -ve$ big OR $-ve$ medium
and if $R = -ve$ small
then $H = +ve$ medium
else if $E = -ve$ small
and if $R = +ve$ small
then $H = +ve$ medium
else etc....

Now there are several such rules employed in the control. Each rule is a fuzzy relation between the measurements E, R and the action H. Thus,

$$E = -ve \text{ small}; \qquad R = +ve \text{ small}$$

is a fuzzy phrase P on the inverse of discourse $E \times R$ with grade of membership function

$$\mu_P(e,r) = \min\{ \mu_{-ve \text{ small}}(e), \mu_{+ve \text{ small}}(r)\}$$

The implication "if P then $H = +ve$ medium" is also a fuzzy phrase Q defined on $E \times R \times H$ with grades of membership function:

$$\mu_Q(e,r,h) = \min\{ \mu_P(e,r), \mu_{+ve \text{ medium}}(h)\}$$

Finally, two or more fuzzy phrases Q_1, Q_2 connected by "else" form a fuzzy clause C defined as $E \times R \times H$ with grades of membership function:

$$\mu_C(e,r,h) = \max\{ \varrho_1(e,r,h), \mu_{Q_2}(e,r,h) \ldots \text{etc.}\}.$$

The control action, as derived from the implementation of a fuzzy clause (i.e., a set of fuzzy implications forming an algorithm) is determined according to the compositional rule of inference as given above. That is, given the set of the actual inputs x and the fuzzy algorithm C, the resultant output is the max-min product $x \circ C$. The whole procedure for deciding the control action is explicitly described in Mamdani and Assilian [11]. This work also describes the results that were obtained on the steam engine trials.

Two main conclusions were drawn from this early study using the steam-engine. First, that the results vindicated the approach advocated by Zadeh and demonstrate its potential. The significant nature of this approach is that fuzzy logic can be used to implement heuristics in a fairly straightforward manner. There are other ways of implementing heuristics as well. In particular Gaines [5] has reanalyzed the steam-engine control rules using a form of probability logic obtaining results substantially similar to those obtained using fuzzy logic. The nature of this relationship between stochastic logic, multiple valued logics and fuzzy logic has been investigated at great length by Gaines [6][2].

---

[2]The Workshop on Discrete Systems and Fuzzy Reasoning at which this work was reported also had many contributions on fuzzy and multiple-valued logic. Interested readers are referred to the proceedings of this Workshop.

Case	Condition	Action to be Taken
1	BZ low	When BZ is drastically low
	OX low	a. Reduce kiln speed
	BE low	b. Reduce fuel
		When BZ is slightly low
		c. Increase I.D. fan speed
		d. Increase fuel rate
2	BZ low	a. Reduce kiln speed
	OX low	b. Reduce fuel rate
	BE ok	c. Reduce I.D. fan speed
3	BZ low	a. Reduce kiln speed
	OX low	b. Reduce fuel rate
	BE high	c. Reduce I.D. fan speed
(Total of 27 rules)		

Figure 2. Three examples of rules for controlling a kiln. (Back-end temperature = BE, burning zone temperature = BZ, percentage of oxygen gas in the kiln exit gas = OX).

Secondly, it was asserted that the method can easily be applied to many practical industrial situations. This assertion is supported by considering the instance of cement kiln operation. In a book on the subject Peray and Waddell [16] list a collection of rules for controlling a kiln. A few examples of these rules are shown in Fig. 2. On comparing this with the steam-engine rules in Fig. 1 it is clear how fuzzy logic can be employed in cement kiln control. This potential of employing fuzzy logic to implement control heuristics has been further investigated. In the following section all known investigations on this topic are briefly described.

FURTHER TRIALS WITH "FUZZY CONTROLLER"

Below are some brief accounts of further trials with the fuzzy logic control scheme undertaken by other groups working in the area.

Delft Technical High School, Delft, Holland

The work was conducted by Professor Van Nauta Lemke and W.J.M. Kickert in the Control Engineering Laboratory DTH. In this research project the control of a warm water plant was investigated. This plant, which was a form of heat exchanger, had poor control properties and so was considered suitable on which to try out a fuzzy controller. The linguistic control algorithm was derived from the experience of a human operator. The results were satisfactory and compared favorably with an optimally tuned PI controller. The fuzzy controller had a faster rise time and after rule modification it was able to achieve a steady-state accuracy equal to that of the PI controller. These results are reported in detail in Kickert and Van Nauta Lemke [9].

Danish Technical High School, Lyngby, Denmark

Shortly afterwards Professor P.M. Larsen and Dr. J.J. Østergaard began experiments on fuzzy logic control of a pilot exchanger process of their own. Apart from different plant characteristics and non-linearities the control problem differed in that it was a two input–two output type with strong cross-coupling.

A particularly interesting subject of this work was the software implementation of the controller using APL on an IBM/1800 machine. The grammatical structure of APL made it particularly suitable for calculations involving fuzzy sets producing clear and compact programs.

The linguistic protocol was originally derived from common sense and then tuned after successive runs. Although it differed in its finer details from Mamdani and Van Nauta Lemke it gave good results which can be examined in detail in J.J. Østergaard [22].

McMaster University, Canada

Work is being done by Professor N.K. Sinha and the research group in simulation, optimization and control in the Faculty of Engineering, again on a heat exchanger. The findings are not as yet published but the broad conclusions seem to be the same as in most other studies.

UMIST, Manchester, England

This work is being carried out by D.A. Rutherford of Control Systems Centre, UMIST (see [18]). This is an interesting study as the method, without major modifications, is the first one to be tried on an industrial plant. In cooperation with G.A. Carter and M.J. Hague the controller has been implemented for a sinter making plant at the British Steel Corporation, Middlesborough.

The control problem was to obtain the most efficient sintering by control of the moisture of the initial raw mix. The efficiency and uniformity of the sintering is monitored by the standard deviation of the permeability of the pre-sintered mix.

The fuzzy algorithm used was a slightly modified version of the one used by Mamdani and Assilian. The results showed about a 40% reduction in standard deviation over that for manual control. The controller was comparable if not slightly better than a conventional two-term controller. Carter and Hague conclude that the method is particularly useful "where the requirement for little or no plant tuning is matched by a poor knowledge of the plant...".

British Steel Corporation, Battersea, England

The interest here is the investigation of useful methods for the automatic control of a Basic Oxygen steel making process. This investigation is being undertaken by R. Tong, who is at present working as a research associate at Control and Management Systems group, University Engineering Department, Cambridge. The possibilities of using a fuzzy logic controller for such a process are reported in [20].

Warren Spring Laboratory, Stevenage, England

The work was done by P.J. King jointly with W.J.M. Kickert and E.H. Mamdani of Queen Mary College. A pilot scale batch chemical process was used in this study and the controller designed for the temperature control of the process.

Summary of Results

A characteristic feature of this process was the large time lag in the response leading to instability when the loop was closed. A model predictor scheme using a fuzzy model of the plant was devised to eliminate this with success. The model was a very crude one consisting of only a few rules supporting the fact that quite satisfactory results can be obtained without having to resort to exact mathematics. The findings are reported in detail in [10] and [7].

All these studies have been carried out from a control engineering point of view and the main conclusion from all this is that the method, though unorthodox, merits serious consideration for application to certain difficult plants. The main point to be made here is that the merit of the method does not rest on the use of fuzzy logic but rather the use purely of heuristics for designing a controller. This means that the controller is not deduced from an available model of the plant but is explicitly stated in the form of heuristics. Thus the method is useful for plants which are difficult in the sense that they are difficult to model accurately. Fuzzy logic is suggested as the best tool for implementing these heuristics. The instance of the cement kiln control and the experience with the sinter plant cited above supports this below.

These studies have also indicated two other characteristics of the heuristic controller. One is that in most studies, rules exactly as those illustrated in Fig. 1 are applied. This is because the heuristics continue to maintain the 'proportional plus integral' nature of the classical controller only rendering it more flexible (a control engineer might say 'making it nonlinear'). Second, many studies have found that this type of a controller is more robust to plant parameter changes than a classical controller. The reasons have not been analyzed but as suggested by Mamdani [10] this is merely the consequence of using heuristics. Human experience which these heuristics amount to is by nature robust.

QUESTION OF STABILITY

What concerns many control engineers is how to predict that such a heuristic controller will be stable. Many of those who are investigating this method have not taken the matter seriously or commented on it. This is very likely due to the fact they have assumed that the fuzzy control method is not an alternative to classical design techniques and that this would be obvious to everyone concerned. However, such apparently is not the case. Control engineering orthodoxy imposes a certain rigid design approach which must include stability analysis. This is assumed to have an important, perhaps sole, bearing in the reliability of the controller. Nevertheless, it should be a simple matter to realize that stability analysis relies on the availability of the mathematical model of the plant but if this were the case then one could possibly deduce the controller in a classical way. As mentioned above, the main advantage of the heuristic controller is that it can be used for plants that are difficult to model.

There is one study, however, which has attempted to investigate this problem. Kickert [8] has shown that under certain restrictive assumptions the fuzzy controller can be viewed as a multidimensional (multi-input single output) multi-level relay. Under such conditions one can use describing functions to model the controller. Then along with the model of the system, a frequency domain stability analysis can be carried out. Theoretical results of such an analysis accord well with the practical results. However, the method is applicable under very rigid conditions and only with low order systems using low dimensional relay. Thus its practical use is very limited.

A fuzzy controller can be analyzed qualitatively to gain assurance that a runaway instability will not occur. The concern of control engineers, on the other hand, is a rigorous analysis of oscillatory form of instability. Now the best way to do this is to carry out the analysis in the frequency domain and this is what Kickert's work mentioned above amounts to. The conclusion of this work is that frequency domain analysis of fuzzy controllers is not applicable in practical cases. It is the view of this author that the desire for rigorous stability analysis in the frequency domain even if it were possible runs counter to the main advantages of the approach which is that it can be used with plants that are difficult to model. A confidence in the quality of control can always be obtained by running it in open-loop with the human operator present to make any changes in its structure to improve its performance. The discussion on stability is irrelevant because it implies that no attempt be made to control difficult processes unless a rigorous theory can be found to design controllers. Thus the main source of discomfort with fuzzy controllers, it may be suggested, is that it elevates heuristics to control plants which some feel ought not be so controlled.

QUESTION OF DERIVATION OF PROTOCOL

The quality of control obtained using the scheme under discussion here is dependent entirely on the clause C (see previous section entitled "Synthesis of 'Fuzzy Controller' "), assuming, of course, that the sampling rate has been fixed as some rational basis. Hence the various factors affecting C can be used to tune the controller. C is constructed by assuming three more or less arbitrary factors. In fact the choice involved in these factors is governed by the experience of the designer.

In the first place it is necessary to choose appropriate membership functions for the fuzzy subsets involved such as medium, small and so on. An assertion in the steam-engine study and unchallenged since then is that these functions are not arbitrary and indeed that there is a great deal of objective concensus about the subsets defining these linguistic terms. Thus these subsets should be kept fixed and any change in the membership functions is not the proper way of tuning the controller.

The second arbitrary factor involved is the range of values in the various universes. In all the studies cited a finite set of quantised values is used as the universe. If the universe is formed by quantising into the same number of levels 0–50 units of measurements instead 0–100 units say, then this is equivalent to making the controller twice as sensitive to that measured variable. This form of 'gain control' is bound to have a substantial effect on the performance of the controller. It does not affect the linguistic nature of the clause C itself in any way, thus it does not amount to a structural change in the controller. In the classical form of a PI controller this is the only form of tuning that a designer can do.

However, there is a third arbitrary factor which allows a designer to carry out a structural form of tuning in the clause C of a fuzzy controller. This is done by altering the set of rules themselves in the control protocol. Unfortunately this raises the important question of how to derive the best or effective set of control rules. The cement kiln rules of Peray and Waddell notwithstanding, it is the conclusion of most industrial psychologists that a great deal of effort is required to arrive at the protocol used by a skilled operator (see for example, Bainbridge [3]). Future attempts at practical applications of fuzzy control will no doubt have to recognize that human factors research has an important bearing on controller design.

The difficulties of obtaining a good protocol to start with can nevertheless be alleviated to some extent in various ways. Firstly it has been realized by most workers that it is not necessary to close the loop with a fuzzy controller nor is it the aim of fuzzy control method to replace the human controller. The use of a fuzzy controller in an advisory capacity can itself be a great help in the control of difficult plants. It is then possible to write the software implementing a fuzzy control algorithm such that the rules can be modified on-line. An example of such a program is the one by Marks [14]. Through such a modification procedure the controller can be made more and more reliable. As confidence increases in the action recommended by it, the result can lead to a more consistent control being applied to the plant than is possible by a human operator. In many industrial plants this consistency is important because it leads to a consistent product obtained from the process.

A second approach being studied by Mamdani and Baaklini [12] is to automate the modification of rules by introducing a form of adaptive behavior into the controller. Noting that in a control situation the goal of regulating the plant output about the set-point can be easily stated and assuming that plant input and output are monotonically related, then a fuzzy algorithm can be developed which effectively says that if the output is higher than required, too much input was applied and vice versa. In trials this scheme has worked well and is capable of deriving control policy even when initially started without any rules. Further details of this are also given in [13] and [17].

CONCLUSION

This article has concentrated on the various studies relating to industrial applications of fuzzy control. As is apparent here all workers have approached this method from a very practical view and indeed there is a concensus of opinion among them that the method is practically viable. There have of course been critics of the approach. Although the main discussion has been about the prediction of stability of such a controller, it has been suggested here that the underlying question is whether heuristics should be formally used for controlling certain types of industrial plants.

There is no doubt that heuristics are the best, perhaps only, form of control in humanistic systems. Pappis and Mamdani [15] have applied fuzzy controller for the control of road traffic junction. It is apparent that fuzzy controller is essentially an extension of decision tables based on fuzzy logic instead of binary-valued logic. Thus in numerous humanistic systems decision making is achieved with a great degree of reliability by implementing heuristics, often using decision tables. There seems little doubt that industrial systems may be similarly controlled using fuzzy decision tables which is what a fuzzy controller amounts to.

There has already been considerable work done in obtaining such heuristics for difficult process plants by human factors researchers and industrial psychologists. In this work fuzzy control methods can have definite applications. Furthermore, with software aids as suggested above, and the use of hierarchic adaptive controllers the job of implementing heuristics is further simplified.

REFERENCES

1. Assilian S., and Mamdani, E.H. (1974). Learning Control Algorithms in Real Dynamic Systems. *Proc 4th Int. IFAC/IFIP Conf. on Digital Computer Applications to Process Control*, Zurich, March 1974.
2. Assilian (1974). Artificial Intelligence in the Control of Real Dynamic Systems. Ph.D. Thesis. London University.
3. Bainbridge, L. (1975). The Process Controller. In *The Study of Real Skills* (W.T. Singleton, ed.), Academic, New York.
4. Carter, G.A., and Hague, M.J. (1976). Fuzzy Control of Raw Mix Permeability at a Sinter Plant. *Proc. Workshop on Discrete Systems and Fuzzy Reasoning.* Queen Mary College, London.
5. Gaines, B.R. (1975). Stochastic and fuzzy logics. *Electronics Letters*, **11**, 188–189.
6. Gaines, B.R. (1976). Understanding Uncertainity. *Proc. Workshop on Discrete Systems and Fuzzy Reasoning.* Queen Mary College, London.
7. Kickert, W.J.M. (1975a). Analysis of a Fuzzy Logic Controller. Internal Report. Queen Mary College, London.
8. Kickert, W.J.M. (1975b). Further Analysis and Application of Fuzzy Logic Control. Internal Report. Queen Mary College, London.
9. Kickert, W.J.M., and Van Nauta Lemke (1976). Application of fuzzy controller in a warm water plant. *Automatica*, **12**, 301 – 308.
10. King, P.J., and Mamdani, E.H. (1976). The Application of Fuzzy Control Systems to Industrial Processes. *Proc. Workshop on Discrete Systems and Fuzzy Reasoning.* Queen Mary College, London.

11. Mamdani, E.H. and Assilian, S. (1975). An experiment in linguistic synthesis with a fuzzy logic controller. *Int. J. Man-Machine Studies*, **7**, 1–13.
12. Mamdani, E.H., and Baaklini, N. (1975). Prescriptive method for deriving control policy in a fuzzy-logic controller. *Electronics Letters*, **11**, 625.
13. Mamdani, E.H., Procyk, T.J., and Baaklini, N. (1976). Application of Fuzzy Logic Controller Design Based on Linguistic Protocol. *Proc. Workshop on Discrete Systems and Fuzzy Reasoning.* Queen Mary College, London.
14. Marks, P. (1976). A Fuzzy Logic Control Software. Internal Report. Queen Mary College, London.
15. Pappis, C.P., and Mamdani, E.H. (1976). A Fuzzy Logic Controller for a Traffic Junction. *Research Report.* Department of Electrical Engineering, Queen Mary College, London.
16. Peray, K.E., and Waddell, J.J. (1972). *The Rotary Cement Kiln.* The Chemical Publishing Co., New York.
17. Procyk, T.J. (1976). A Proposal for a Learning System. Internal Report. Queen Mary College, London.
18. Rutherford, D.A., and Bloore, G.C. (1975). The Implementation of Fuzzy Algorithm for Control. Control System Centre Report No. 279. UMIST, Manchester.
19. Rutherford, D.A. (1976) The Implementation and Evaluation of a Fuzzy Control Algorithm for a Sinter Plant. *Proc. Workshop on Discrete Systems and Fuzzy Reasoning.* Queen Mary College, London.
20. Tong, R.M. (1976). An Assessment of a Fuzzy Control Algorithm for a Nonlinear Multivariable System. *Proc. Workshop on Discrete Systems and Fuzzy Reasoning.* Queen Mary College, London.
21. Zadeh, L.A. (1973). Outline of a new approach to the analysis of complex systems and decision processes. *IEE Trans.*, **SMC-3**, 28.
22. Østergaard, J.J. (1976). Fuzzy Logic Control of a Heat Exchanger Process, Internal Report. Electric Power Engineering Department, Danish Technical High School, Lyngby, Denmark.

FUZZY MEASURES AND FUZZY INTEGRALS—A SURVEY

6

M. Sugeno

As is well-known in recent years, there are two kinds of uncertainities, randomness and fuzziness, which can be both dealt with from a mathematical point of view. We know the concept of probabilities with respect to randomness and also that of fuzzy sets with respect to fuzziness.

This fact tempts us to discuss fuzzy sets in comparison with probabilities. However, such a direct comparison must fail. The concept of fuzzy sets (precisely speaking, fuzzy subsets of an ordinary set) is nothing but an extended concept of ordinary sets. We have to notice that the concept of probabilities is absolutely different from that of sets.

To discuss our problem in detail, let us consider probabilities for the time being. There are a number of interpretations for probabilities: classical probabilities (originated by Laplace); measure theoretical probabilities (by Kolmogorov); subjective probabilities in Bayesian statistics; probabilities as logics and so on.

Among these, probabilities as measures are the most widely used from a mathematical point of view since all the aspects of probabilities can be explained by the concept of probability measures (including the essential concept of conditional probability measures). Therefore it is proper to pick up a probability measure as a mathematical model of probabilities.

Let $(X, \mathscr{B}, P)$ be a probability space. Here $\mathscr{B}$ is a Borel field of X, and P is a probability measure

$$P: \mathscr{B} \to [0, 1]$$

On the other hand, a fuzzy subset of X can be conveniently described by its membership function

$$h: X \to [0, 1]$$

From the viewpoint of mappings, P and h are usually distinguished from each other: P defined on $\mathscr{B}$ is particularly called a set function, while h defined on X is an ordinary function. Therefore we cannot compare P with h at the same level.

When X is a finite set, it seems to be able to compare $P(\{x\})$ with $h(x)$: $\Sigma_{x \in X} P(\{x\}) = 1$ and $\Sigma_{x \in X} h(x) \neq 1$, etc. However in an infinite case, say

$X = R^1$, we shall unfortunately face the following difficulty. We have for $(a,b] \subset R^1$ that $P((a,b]) = \int_a^b \rho(x)\,dx$, where $\rho(x)$ is a probability density, not a probability itself. From this it follows that $P(\{x\}) = 0$, $\forall x \in R^1$ even if $\rho(x) \neq 0$, $\forall x \in R^1$ (see $P(\{x\}) \neq \rho(x)$), while $h(x) \neq 0$.

It may still seem that a probability density $\rho(x)$ and a membership function $h(x)$ are mutually comparable. But $\rho(x)$ has no practical meaning except the fact that $\rho(x) = dP((-\infty, x])/dx$.

There is only one point of contact between probabilities and fuzzy sets, that is, we have the concept of fuzzy events presented by Zadeh[17].

Apart from such unfruitful and unsuccessful efforts to the comparison as stated above, two significant and mathematical comparisons between randomness and fuzziness have been performed. One of them is a comparison from the viewpoint of logics[1]: probability logic and fuzzy logic. The other is from that of measures: probability measures and fuzzy measures.

The purpose of this paper is to give an introductory survey on the concept of fuzzy measures and fuzzy integrals.

There might be another way to the comparison. We have known in the past ten years the algorithm definition of randomness: randomness (or complexity) of a string $a_1 a_2 \ldots a_n$ is defined in terms of Turing machines. It may be possible for us to define fuzziness in an analogous way.

FUZZY MEASURES, FUZZY INTEGRALS AND THEIR SEMANTICS

As mentioned, we have probability measures as scales for randomness from the measure theoretical point of view. In contrast with this, fuzzy measures [6,7] are generally considered as subjective scales for fuzziness. Those are set functions with monotonicity but do not necessarily possess additivity.

Fuzzy integrals [6,7] are functionals defined by using fuzzy measures, which correspond to probability expectations. We shall only briefly mention their definitions since their properties are described in [14].

Let X be an arbitrary set and $\mathscr{B}$ a Borel field of X. An element of X is denoted by x.

Definition 1 A set function defined on $\mathscr{B}$ which has the following properties is called a fuzzy measure.

(1) $g(\varnothing) = 0$, $g(X) = 1$

(2) If $A, B \in \mathscr{B}$ and $A \subset B$, then $g(A) \leqslant g(B)$.

(3) If $F_n \in \mathscr{B}$ for $1 \leqslant n < \infty$ and a sequence $\{F_n\}$ is monotone (in the sense of inclusion), then $\lim_{n \to \infty} g(F_n) = g(\lim_{n \to \infty} F_n)$.

A triplet $(X, \mathcal{B}, g)$ is called a fuzzy measure space, and g is called a fuzzy measure of $(X, \mathcal{B})$.

Definition 2 Let $h: X \rightarrow [0, 1]$ be a $\mathcal{B}$-measurable function. A fuzzy integral over $A \in \mathcal{B}$ of a function $h(x)$ with respect to a fuzzy measure g is defined as follows:

$$\int_A h(x) \circ g(\cdot) = \sup_{\alpha \in [0, 1]} \left[\alpha \wedge g(A \cap F_\alpha) \right] \qquad (1)$$

where $F_\alpha = \{ x \mid h(x) \geq \alpha \}$.

As is easily seen, it is sufficient to define a fuzzy integral that $F_\alpha \in \mathcal{B}$ for all $\alpha \in [0, 1]$. By $\tilde{\mathcal{B}}$, denote a family of all fuzzy subsets of X with $\mathcal{B}$-measurable membership functions. We have $\tilde{\mathcal{B}} \supset \mathcal{B}$ since the concept of fuzzy subsets includes that of ordinary (non-fuzzy) subsets. $\tilde{\mathcal{B}}$ is called the fuzzy extension of $\mathcal{B}$, which preserves all the properties of $\mathcal{B}$.

Hereafter, we shall write a fuzzy set A as $\tilde{A}$ when we wish to distinguish it from a non-fuzzy set. As for a membership function, it will be written as h_A, not as $h_{\tilde{A}}$.

Definition 3 A set function $\tilde{g}[6]$ defined by

$$\tilde{g}(\tilde{A}) = \int_X h_A(x) \circ g \qquad (2)$$

for $\tilde{A} \in \tilde{\mathcal{B}}$ is called the extension of g onto $\tilde{\mathcal{B}}$.

We have $\tilde{g} = g$ on $\mathcal{B}$. Further, $\tilde{g}$ holds all the properties of g on $\tilde{\mathcal{B}}$. For example, if $\tilde{A} \subset \tilde{B}$, then $\tilde{g}(\tilde{A}) \leq \tilde{g}(\tilde{B})$. Therefore we may write $\tilde{g}$ merely as g.

Definition 4 A fuzzy integral over $\tilde{A} \in \tilde{\mathcal{B}}$ is defined by

$$\int_{\tilde{A}} h(x) \circ g(\cdot) = \int_X \left[h_A(x) \wedge h(x) \right] \circ g(\cdot). \qquad (3)$$

In fuzzy measures theory, the concept of "grade of fuzziness" is generally used. This general concept includes, for example, "grade of importance", "grade of charmness" and, as a special case, "grade of membership" in the fuzzy sets theory. Fuzzy measures as subjective scales for grade of fuzziness can be interpreted in a number of ways in the applications. Here let us show an example of fuzzy measures.

Assume that a person picks up an element x out of X, but he does not exactly know which one he has picked up. Given a subset E of X, let us consider the problem in which one subjectively guesses if x is within E. Define $\mathrm{Gr}(x \in E)$ by the grade of fuzziness of the statement "$x \in E$".

As natural assumptions, we may state that $\mathrm{Gr}(x \in \varnothing) = 0$ and $\mathrm{Gr}(x \in X) = 1$. We can also conclude under reasonable considerations, that if $E \subset F$, then $\mathrm{Gr}(x \in E) \leqslant \mathrm{Gr}(x \in F)$. From this, we have a fuzzy measure g by defining $g(E) = \mathrm{Gr}(x \in E)$. We can interpret g as a subjective measure for the fuzziness surrounding E in the sense of "$x \in E$". Speaking in the terms of probabilities, $\mathrm{Pr}(x \in E)$, probability of "$x \in E$", is expressed by a probability measure P as $P(E) = \mathrm{Pr}(x \in E)$.

Now assume that x is known, say x_0. It is clear that $\mathrm{Gr}(x_0 \in E) = \chi_E(x_0)$ where χ_E is the characteristic function of E. Let us define in this special case $g(x_0, E) = \mathrm{Gr}(x_0 \in E)$. When E is a given fuzzy set $\tilde{A}$, $g(x_0, \tilde{A})$ can be written according to Definition 3 as follows.

$$g(x_0, \tilde{A}) = \int_X h_A(x) \circ g(x_0, \cdot)$$
$$= h_A(x_0) \tag{4}$$

This implies that the grade of fuzziness of the statement "$x_0 \in \tilde{A}$" is just equal to the grade of membership of x_0 in a fuzzy set $\tilde{A}$. Thus it can be said that the concept of grade of fuzziness in fuzzy measures theory includes as a special case the concept of grade of membership in fuzzy sets theory. A more concrete example of grade of fuzziness will be discussed later.

As can be readily seen from their definition, fuzzy measures formally include probability measures as a special case. However, the concept of fuzzy measures is not used in a probabilistic environment but in a fuzzy environment where human subjectivity particularly plays an important role.

Let us now discuss the semantics of fuzzy integrals. Fuzzy integrals are interpreted as subjective evaluation of objects in their applications where subjectivity is grasped by fuzzy measures. There are of course a number of ways to interpret fuzzy integrals. For example, we may call them fuzzy expectations in comparison with probability expectations. When fuzzy integrals are compared with ordinary (Lebesque) integrals, they could be called nonlinear integrals or something similar. More generally discussing from the viewpoint of functionals, fuzzy integrals are merely a kind of nonlinear functionals (precisely speaking, monotonous functionals), while Lebesque integrals are linear ones. Anyway, the semantics of fuzzy integrals lies in an extended concept of integrals since fuzzy integrals are defined by using "measures". Fuzzy integrals are very similar to Lebesque integrals in their definition. Both qualitative and quantitative comparisons between them are discussed in [2, 6].

Monotonicity is the fundamental feature of fuzzy integrals, which comes from the property of fuzzy measures. That is, we have

$$(1) \quad \text{If } A \subset B, \text{ then } \int_A h(x) \circ g \leqslant \int_B h(x) \circ g \qquad (5)$$

$$(2) \quad \text{If } h_1 \leqslant h_2, \text{ then } \int_X h_1(x) \circ g \leqslant \int_X h_2(x) \circ g \qquad (6)$$

On the other hand, the characteristics of Lebesque integrals are seen by their additivity. Let μ be a Lebesque measure, then it follows that

$$(1) \quad \text{If } A \cap B = \phi,$$

$$\text{then } \int_{A \cup B} h(x)\,d\mu = \int_A h(x)\,d\mu + \int_B h(x)\,d\mu \qquad (7)$$

$$(2) \quad \int_X (h_1(x) + h_2(x))\,d\mu = \int_X h_1(x)\,d\mu + \int_X h_2(x)\,d\mu \qquad (8)$$

These properties are deeply connected with additivity of Lebesque measures. In an abstracted sense, a quantity obtained by integration could be said something endowed with additivity, e.g., area, average, probability expectations. This quantity can be suitably measured by measures with additivity. Thus we may presumably expect that a quantity with only monotonicity, provided that it exists, can be measured by measures with monotonicity, i.e., fuzzy measures.

As is well-known, there are two important theorems, Fubini's and Radon–Nikodym's, in Lebesque integrals theory. Two theorems corresponding to those are also proved in fuzzy integrals theory [7]. A Radon–Nikodym-like theorem is used to define conditional fuzzy measures, as Radon–Nikodym's theorem was used to define conditional probabilities by Kolmogorov.

Conditional fuzzy measures are similar to conditional probabilities and have the following properties. Let $(X, \mathcal{B}_X, g_X)$ be a fuzzy measure space and $(Y, \mathcal{B}_Y)$ a measurable space. A conditional fuzzy measure with respect to X is written $\sigma_Y(\cdot|x)$, which has the following properties:

(1)   For a fixed $F \in \mathcal{B}_Y$, $\sigma_Y(F|x)$ is, as a function of x, a $\mathcal{B}_X$-measurable function.

(2)   For a fixed $x \in X$, $\sigma_Y(\cdot|x)$ is a fuzzy measure of $(Y, \mathcal{B}_Y)$.

From g_X and $\sigma_Y(\cdot|x)$, a fuzzy measure g_Y of $(Y, \mathcal{B}_Y)$ is induced as

$$g_Y(\cdot) = \int_X \sigma_Y(\cdot|x) \circ g_X \tag{9}$$

Given $g_X, \sigma_Y(\cdot|x)$, and g_Y, there exists $\sigma_X(\cdot|y)$ and it follows

$$\int_E \sigma_Y(F|x) \circ g_X = \int_F \sigma_X(E|y) \circ g_Y \tag{10}$$

This relation corresponds to Bayes' formula used to obtain a posteriori probability. In this sense, $\sigma_X(\cdot|y)$ is called a posteriori fuzzy measure, while g_X is called the a priori fuzzy measure.

Now let us consider how to construct fuzzy measures. The problem is described as "How is $g(E \cup F)$, where $E \cap F = \phi$, constructed from $g(E)$ and $g(F)$?" A fuzzy measure satisfying the next relation is written g_λ.

When $E \cap F = \phi$,

$$g(E \cup F) = g(E) + g(F) + \lambda g(E)g(F), \qquad -1 < \lambda < \infty \tag{11}$$

Equation (11) is called λ-rule. We have that

(1) If $\lambda \geqslant 0$, $g_\lambda(E \cup F) \geqslant g_\lambda(E) + g_\lambda(F)$;

(2) If $\lambda < 0$, $g_\lambda(E \cup F) < g_\lambda(E) + g_\lambda(F)$.

Taking into account that $g_\lambda(X) = 1$, it follows from (11) that

$$g_\lambda(E^c) = \frac{1 - g_\lambda(E)}{1 + \lambda g_\lambda(E)} \tag{12}$$

where E^c is the complement of E.

Let X be R^1. Then g_λ on $(R^1, \mathcal{B})$ is easily constructed from a function $H(x)$ such that (1) if $x \leqslant y$, then $H(x) \leqslant H(y)$; (2) $\lim_{x \uparrow a} H(x) = H(a)$; (3) $\lim_{x \to -\infty} H(x) = 0$; and (4) $\lim_{x \to +\infty} H(x) = 1$. $H(x)$, just the same as a probability distribution function, is also called an F-distribution function.

Define for $(a, b] \subset R^1$

$$g_\lambda((a,b]) = \frac{H(b) - H(a)}{1 + \lambda H(a)} \tag{13}$$

It is easily shown that the above defined g_λ satisfies λ-rule. In particular, we have

$$g_\lambda((-\infty, x]) = H(x) \qquad \text{for } -1 < \lambda < \infty \tag{14}$$

Next assume that X is a finite set $K = \{s_1, s_2, \ldots, s_n\}$. A fuzzy measure g_λ on $(K, 2^K)$ is constructed as follows. Let

$$0 \leqslant g^i \leqslant 1, \qquad 1 \leqslant i \leqslant n, \tag{15}$$

$$\frac{1}{\lambda}\left[\prod_{i=1}^{n}(1 + \lambda g^i) - 1\right] = 1, \qquad -1 < \lambda < \infty \tag{16}$$

Define for $K' \subset K$

$$g_\lambda(K') = \frac{1}{\lambda} \left[\prod_{s_i \in K'} (1 + \lambda g^i) - 1 \right] \tag{17}$$

Then this also satisfies λ-rule. It particularly follows that

$$g_\lambda(\{s_i\}) = g^i, \tag{18}$$

$$g_\lambda(\{s_i, s_j\}) = g^i + g^j + \lambda g^i g^j, \quad i \neq j \tag{19}$$

Therefore g^i is called a fuzzy density of g_λ.

After obtaining a construction rule of g, fuzzy integrals on $(K, 2^K)$ are easily calculated as follows. Let $h: K \to [0, 1]$ and assume $h(s_1) \leqslant h(s_2) \leqslant \cdots \leqslant h(s_n)$, if not, rearrange $h(s)$ in an increasing order. Then we have

$$\int_K h(s) \circ g = \bigvee_{i=1}^{n} \left[h(s_i) \wedge g(K_i) \right] \tag{20}$$

where

$$K_i = \{s_i, s_{i+1}, \ldots, s_n\}$$

Tsukamoto [15] suggested another construction rule of g on $(K, 2^K)$. Using the same g^i, let

$$(1 - \mu) \bigvee_{i=1}^{n} g^i + \mu \sum_{i=1}^{n} g^i = 1, \quad 0 \leqslant \mu \leqslant 1 \tag{21}$$

Define for $K' \subset K$

$$g^*(K') = (1 - \mu) \bigvee_{s_i \in K'} g^i + \mu \sum_{s_i \in K'} g^i \tag{22}$$

Let $K' \cap K'' = \phi$, then

$$g_\mu^*(K') \vee g_\mu^*(K'') \leqslant g_\mu^*(K' \cup K'') \leqslant g_\mu^*(K') + g_\mu^*(K'')$$

Although g_λ is a special type of fuzzy measures, it is useful to express approximately a general g. As for the λ-complement of a fuzzy set [7], $\tilde{g}_\lambda$ preserves the property of g_λ (12). The λ-complement of a fuzzy set $\tilde{A}$, written $\tilde{A}^{c_\lambda}$, is a fuzzy set with the next membership function

$$h_A c_\lambda(x) = \frac{1 - h_A(x)}{1 + \lambda h_A(x)}, \quad -1 < \lambda < \infty \tag{23}$$

It is clear that for a non-fuzzy set E, $E^{c_\lambda} = E^c$ for $-1 < \lambda < \infty$. We have for $-1 < \lambda < \infty$ that

$$\tilde{A}^{c_\lambda} \supset \tilde{B}^{c_\lambda} \quad \text{iff } \tilde{A} \subset \tilde{B} \tag{24}$$

$$(\tilde{A}^{c_\lambda})^{c_\lambda} = \tilde{A} \tag{25}$$

$$(\tilde{A} \cup \tilde{B})^{c_\lambda} = \tilde{A}^{c_\lambda} \cap \tilde{B}^{c_\lambda} \tag{26}$$

$$(\tilde{A} \cap \tilde{B})^{c_\lambda} = \tilde{A}^{c_\lambda} \cup \tilde{B}^{c_\lambda} \tag{27}$$

For a fuzzy set $\tilde{A} \in \tilde{\mathfrak{B}}$, it follows that

$$g_\lambda(A^{c_\lambda}) = \frac{1 - g_\lambda(A)}{1 + \lambda g_\lambda(\tilde{A})} \tag{28}$$

Fuzzy integrals are now being extended onto L-fuzzy sets and Phi-fuzzy sets (introduced by Sambuc in 1975) by Kaufmann [14].

APPLICATIONS

Since the idea of fuzzy integrals was proposed [6], it has been applied in a variety of problems. These applications are mainly classified into (1) subjective evaluation process, (2) decision-making process, and (3) learning process and so on.

Throughout the applications, one of the most essential problems is the identification of a person's (or generally, human) fuzzy measure. It is very important to identify experimentally one's fuzzy measure since a fuzzy measure is considered as an individual's subjective measure. There are two, indirect and direct, methods for the identification. In the both methods, a fuzzy measure g_λ is usually used as a mathematical model of subjective measures.

Subjective Evaluation Process

Let us consider a problem where a person subjectively evaluates an object, e.g., a house, a face, according to his preference. Assume that the object in the problem can be divided into n elements or it has n attributes. Let $K = \{s_1, s_2, \ldots, s_n\}$ be a set of such elements or attributes. For example, we may have $s_1 =$ area, $s_2 =$ facilities, etc. for a house and $s_1 =$ eyes, $s_2 =$ nose, etc., for a face. Generally speaking, K is not necessarily a set of physical elements but it could be a set points of view or a set of criteria.

Now let $h: K \to [0, 1]$ be a partial evaluation of the object. That is, $h(s)$ implies a partial evaluation of the object from the viewpoint of an element s. If we think of pattern recognition, $h(s)$ can be regarded as the characteristic function of a pattern. In the applications, a partial evaluation $h(s)$ can be determined either objectively or subjectively. For example, when the object is a house, we may have objectively $h(\text{area}) = 800$ m^2, which must be of course normalized in $[0, 1]$. On the other hand when it is a face, we have, for example, $h(\text{eyes}) = 0.8$, which may be subjectively determined by an individual.

Next assume that a fuzzy measure of $(K, 2^K)$ is a subjective measure expressing grade of importance of a subset of K. For example, $g(\{s_1\})$

expresses to what extend a viewpoint of s_1 is important to evaluate an object, and $g(\{s_1, s_2\})$ similarly implies the grade of importance of s_1 and s_2. It is necessary to assume that grade of importance of K is unity. From the meaning of grade of importance, it is a reasonable assumption that g has monotonicity.

Taking a fuzzy integral of h with respect to g, we have

$$e \triangleq \int_K h(s) \circ g \tag{29}$$

Equation (29) represents the aggregation of n partial evaluations; where e can be considered as the over-all evaluation of the object.

A linear aggregation model is usually used in a case where the elements of the object are mutually independent. On the other hand, a fuzzy integral model is said to be suitable when the elements are not perfectly independent. Actually, those are often, more or less, dependent on each other.

Identification of Fuzzy Measures

Let us first show an indirect method for the identification of fuzzy measures. Assume that there are m objects. Let $h_j: K \to [0, 1]$ be a partial evaluation of jth object and e_j the overall one obtained from (29).

Showing a person the objects and their partial evaluations, ask him/her to express his/her subjective over-all evaluations d_j's for $1 \leq j \leq m$ in $[0, 1]$. Define $\bar{e} = \max\{e_j\}$, $\underline{e} = \min_j \{e_j\}$ and similarly $\bar{d}$, $\underline{d}$. By normalizing e_j so that $\bar{e} = \bar{d}$ and $\underline{e} = \underline{d}$, we have for $1 \leq j \leq m$

$$\omega_j = \frac{\bar{d} - \underline{d}}{\bar{e} - \underline{e}} e_j + \frac{\underline{d}\bar{e} - \bar{d}\underline{e}}{\bar{e} - \underline{e}} \tag{30}$$

Define

$$J = \sqrt{\frac{1}{m} \sum_{j=1}^{m} (d_j - \omega_j)^2} \tag{31}$$

We can identify a person's fuzzy measure by finding g which minimizes J, where g is for simplicity assumed to satisfy λ-rule.

The first application of fuzzy integrals to subjective evaluation process appeared in [9], which deals with the evaluation of similarity of one dimensional patterns. In this case, the identified fuzzy measure is not an individual's one but the average of several persons.

Tsukamoto [15] considered a problem of evaluating houses. In his application, a house has five attributes, i.e., area, facilities and furniture, natural environment, circumstance for life and time required to go to office. The values $h(s_i)$, $1 \leqslant i \leqslant 5$, are objectively determined. He also compared a fuzzy integral model with an ordinary linear model.

Sugeno [12] dealt with a problem where the niceness of female faces is subjectively evaluated by a person (male). Here a face is also divided into five elements, i.e., eyes, nose, mouth, chin and the remains. The partial evaluations of a face are subjectively determined according to a subject's preference.

In the both applications, the identified g is an individual's subjective measure and $\min J$ is approximately 0.1.

As a more concrete application, Tsukamoto [16] reported on the evaluation of attractivity of sightseeing zones, where a sightseeing zone is attached several attributes such as beauty of nature, traditional buildings, etc. The sightseers are classified into some classes according to their ages and a fuzzy measure is considered to be different from class to class. Therefore, we can know through the identified fuzzy measures the difference of subjectivities in the age of sightseers. The results were used for the prediction of the increase of sightseers in the next ten years.

Two other types of applications are being carried out. One of them is to social systems by Sekita [4] and the other to information retrieval by Negoita [3].

Let us next discuss the direct method for the identification of fuzzy measures. Ask directly a subject about his grade of importance for all subsets of K and then we have d: $2^K \rightarrow [0, 1]$.

Assume that $d(\cdot)$ satisfies the properties of fuzzy measures. Define

$$J = \sqrt{\frac{1}{2^n} \sum_{E \in 2^K} (d(E) - g_\lambda(E))^2} \tag{32}$$

By minimizing J with respect to fuzzy densities $g^1, \ldots, g^n$ and a parameter λ, we can approximate $d(\cdot)$ by a model $g_\lambda(\cdot)$.

In [8], fuzzy measures of subjects were identified by the direct method. It is shown that fuzzy measures are superior to ordinary additive measures. Generally, the value of λ is different from person to person depending on one's subjectivity.

Both negative and positive values of λ have been obtained in experiments, while a value regarded approximately as zero has not been reported. The additivity of subjective measures is assumed in subjective probabilities. Additivity is, however, considered a very severe condition for an actual person. We are free from such a severe condition so long as we use the concept of fuzzy measures.

Sekita [5] considered the minimizing problem of J by SUMT method which would save a subject's labor since in the direct method a subject is required to answer more values of $d(E)$, $E \in 2^K$ as the number of elements of k increases.

Decision-Making Process

Let us next discuss the applications of conditional fuzzy measures. We can apply the concept of conditional fuzzy measures to many practical problems since the concept is very similar to that of conditional probabilities.

Terano [13] showed two different models on the transition of fuzzy phenomena (subjectivities) by using conditional fuzzy measures. As is seen in the preceding chapter, we have

$$g_Y(\cdot) = \int_X \sigma_Y(\cdot | x) \circ g_X \qquad (33)$$

Regarding g_X and g_Y as an input–output pair, we have a transition process of fuzzy measures where the characteristic of the process is described by $\sigma_Y(\cdot | x)$ as in a Markov process.

On the other hand, if we pick up a $g_X - \sigma_X(\cdot | y)$ pair (*a priori–a posteriori* fuzzy measure) we have an improvement process of *a priori* fuzzy measure, where $\sigma_X(\cdot | y)$ is calculated from (10). A *posteriori* fuzzy measure $\sigma_X(\cdot | y)$ is interpreted to represent the refinement of *a priori* fuzzy measure g_X after obtaining an information y.

Now, let us briefly show the outline of fuzzy decision-making problems (FDP) [8]. FDP is 6-tuples as follows:

$$\langle \Theta, \quad X, \quad A, \quad g_\Theta(\cdot), \quad \sigma_X(\cdot | \theta), \quad \ell \rangle$$

where Θ is a finite set of states of nature; X, a finite set of samples; A, a finite set of actions; g_Θ, a fuzzy measure for states of nature; $\sigma_X(\cdot | \theta)$, a conditional fuzzy measure for samples under the condition that a state of nature is θ; ℓ, the membership function of a fuzzy relation in $\Theta \times A$ which implies fuzzy loss when an action $a \in A$ is taken for $\theta \in \Theta$.

The problem is to find a fuzzy action or a fuzzy strategy which minimizes the fuzzy expectation of loss. Here a fuzzy action $\tilde{a}$ is a fuzzy subset of A with a membership function $h_{\tilde{a}} : A \rightarrow [0,1]$ and a fuzzy strategy $\tilde{t}$ is a fuzzy relation in $X \times A$ with a membership function $h_{\tilde{t}} : X \times A \rightarrow [0,1]$. A fuzzy action $\tilde{t}(x)$ based on a fuzzy strategy $\tilde{t}$ is defined by $h_{\tilde{t}(x)}(a) = h_{\tilde{t}}(x,a)$.

The fuzzy loss ℓ is extended for a fuzzy action as

$$\ell(\theta, \tilde{a}) \triangleq 1 - \max_{a \in A} \left[h_{\tilde{a}}(a) \wedge (1 - \ell(\theta, a)) \right] \qquad (34)$$

When a decision-maker takes a fuzzy strategy $\tilde{t}$, the expected fuzzy loss can be written as

$$\langle \ell \rangle_{\tilde{i}} = \int_\Theta \left[\int_X \ell(\theta, \tilde{i}\,(x)) \circ \sigma_X(\cdot | \theta) \right] \circ g_\Theta \tag{35}$$

The solution of FDP is given by

$$h_{\tilde{i}_\circ}^-(x, a) = \int_\Theta (1 - \ell(\theta, a)) \circ \sigma_\Theta(\cdot | x) \tag{36}$$

where $\sigma_\Theta(\cdot | x)$ is *a posteriori* fuzzy measure. The fuzzy strategy $\tilde{i}\circ$ of (36) is called a likely-good strategy.

We applied FDP to a problem of how one should buy a house fuzzily advertised in a newspaper. In the problem, Θ is regarded as a set of attributes of houses, X a set of advertised houses, g_X a fuzzy measure for grade of importance of attributes and $\sigma_X(\cdot | \theta)$ is interpreted to be a fuzzy measure for grade of charmness of houses when the houses are evaluated from the viewpoint of an attribute θ.

The ability of FDP was experimentally tested by using some subjects in this application. The idea of FDP is applicable to many subjective decision problems in a nonprobabilistic environment.

Learning Process

One of the most remarkable features of human learning is his ability to learn in a fuzzy environment. In other words, a human being can learn something through a fuzzy information. Actually, most of available informations are fuzzy ones. Further there are many occasions in the real world where only fuzzy information is available.

In the field of psychology, a stochastic learning model has been usually used as a model of human learning. However, learning ability in a probabilistic environment does not seem to be essential for a human being.

From the above point of view, it is especially important to develop a learning model which works in a fuzzy environment. Terano and Sugeno [14, 11] suggested a learning model based on a fuzzy information, which is structurally similar to a Bayesian learning model.

The model is built by using conditional fuzzy measures and is applied to a problem of finding an extremum of an unknown multimodal function.

The comparison of the presented model with Bayesian learning is discussed in [11]. Let $X = \{x_1, \ldots, x_n\}$ be a set of causes, $Y = \{y_1, \ldots, y_m\}$ a set of results, g_x a fuzzy measure of X and $\sigma_Y(\cdot | x)$ a conditional fuzzy measure with respect to X. Define a fuzzy information $\tilde{A}$ by a fuzzy subset of Y which implies that an element y has fuzzily resulted in the sense of its grade of membership $h_A(y)$.

Then *a priori* fuzzy measure g_X is improved by a fuzzy information $\tilde{A}$ [14, Chapter 13]. On the other hand, a Bayesian learning model can be modified for a fuzzy information by using the concept of probabilities of fuzzy events.

Let $P_X(x_i)$, $1 \leqslant i \leqslant n$, be a probability density of X and $\rho_Y(Y_j|x_i)$, $1 \leqslant j \leqslant m$, $1 \leqslant i \leqslant n$, conditional probability densities of Y. By generalizing Bayes' formula, we have *a posteriori* probability after obtaining a fuzzy information as follows

$$\rho_X(x_i|\tilde{A}) = \frac{\rho_Y(\tilde{A}|x_i)P_X(x_i)}{\sum\limits_{i=1}^{n} \rho_Y(\tilde{A}|x_i)P_X(x_i)} \tag{37}$$

where

$$\rho_Y(\tilde{A}|x_i) \triangleq \sum\limits_{j=1}^{m} h_A(y_j)\rho_Y(y_j|x_i)$$

It is reported that the present model works with fuzzy information better than a Bayesian model. For example, let $\tilde{A}$ be a strictly fuzzy information such that $h_A(y) = C$ (constant). As can be readily seen from (37), we have $\rho_X(x_i|\tilde{A}) = P_X(x_i)$, $1 \leqslant i \leqslant n$, in this case. This implies that *a priori* probability remains unchanged, while in the presented model the fuzzy density $g_X(\{x_i\})$ of *a priori* fuzzy measure is changed tending to C for $1 \leqslant i \leqslant n$.

REFERENCES

1. B.R. Gaines, "Fuzzy Reasoning and the Logics of Uncertainty," Tech. Rep. EES-MMS-UNC-75, Depart. Electrical Engineering Sci., U. of Essex, Colchester, England, 1975.
2. A. Kaufmann, "Introduction à la Théorie des Sous-Ensembles Flous," 5, Masson (to appear).
3. C.U. Negoita and P. Flandor, "On Fuzziness in Information Retrieval," *J. ACM* (to appear).
4. Y. Sekita, "A Consideration on Fuzzy Evaluation of Complex Social Systems," *Osaka U. Eco.* **25**, No. 2, 1975.
5. Y. Sekita, "A Note on the Identification of Fuzzy Measures," *Osaka U. Eco.* **25**, No. 4, 1976.
6. M. Sugeno, "Fuzzy Measures and Fuzzy Integrals," *Trans. S.I.C.E.* **8**, No. 2 (1972).
7. M. Sugeno, "Theory of Fuzzy Integrals and Its Applications," Ph.D Thesis, Tokyo Institute of Technology, 1974.
8. M. Sugeno, "Fuzzy Decision-Making Problems," *Trans. S.I.C.E.* **11**, No. 6, 1975.

9. M. Sugeno and T. Terano, "An Approach to the Identification of Human Characteristics by Applying Fuzzy Integrals," *Proc. Third IFAC Symp. Identification and System Parameter Estimation*, The Hague, 1973.
10. M. Sugeno and T. Terano, "Analytical Representation of Fuzzy Systems", chapter 11, this volume.
11. M. Sugeno and T. Terano, "A Model of Learning Based on Fuzzy Information," *Proc. Third Eur. Meeting Cybern. and Systems Res.*, Vienna, 1976 (to appear).
12. M. Sugeno *et al.*, "Subjective Evaluation of Fuzzy Objects," *Proc. IFAC Symp. Stochastic Control*, Budapest, 1974.
13. T. Terano and M. Sugeno, "Conditional Fuzzy Measures and Their Applications," *Fuzzy Sets and Their Applications to Cognitive and Decision Processes*. Academic Press, N.Y., 1975.
14. T. Terano and M. Sugeno, "Macroscopic Optimization by Using Conditional Fuzzy Measures", chapter 13, this volume.
15. Y. Tsukamoto, "Identification of Preference Measure by Means of Fuzzy Integrals," *Ann. Conf. of JORS*, 1972.
16. Y. Tsukamoto, "Attractivity of Sightseeing Zones," *Summary of Papers on General Fuzzy Systems, Rep. No. 1*, Working Group on Fuzzy Systems, Tokyo, Japan, 1975.
17. L.A. Zadeh, "Probability Measures of Fuzzy Events," *J. Math. Anal. Appl.* **23**, 1972, 421–427.

PART TWO
THEORY

FUZZY SET THEORY: INTRODUCTION 7

Rammohan K. Ragade and Madan M. Gupta

Decision-making in the real world of human intereaction and in socio-technological design, planning and management processes with humanistic intervention is very often vague and imprecise. It is equally imprecise in legal, medical and enviromental contexts. Conventional precise mathematics has not helped us in the understanding of human decision processes in such tasks as speech recognition and understanding, abstraction, conceptualization and informative summarization. In design and policy formation areas, imprecison may even be a strategic necessity. Politicians are often attributed with making vague and imprecise promises. Imprecision enters in problems of classification and pattern recognition, a task at which humans far excel machines.

An underlying philosophy of the theory of fuzzy sets is to provide a strict mathematical framework, where these imprecise conceptual phenomena in decision-making may be precisely and rigorously studied. It provides for a gradual transition from the realm of rigorous, quantitative and precise phenomena to that of vague, qualitative and imprecise conceptions. This theory enables one to characterize imprecision in terms of 'fuzziness', a concept to which one can assign many meanings: for example, ambiguity, a problem of the collective, reasoning with 'ball-park' figures, an abstraction, and as a characteristic of ill-formed problems.

In aggregation problems, some information and hence precision is lost. The précis may have what seemed to be the most needed and relevant information, yet some other aspects are lost in such summarization. Partitions and clusters that may be formed on data sets are not precise. Abstraction loses some details on relations and hence is a fuzzy process.

Human ability to recognize fuzzy speech, sloppy writing, give meaning to abstract pictures, to communicate and interchange ideas between cultural groups, translate languages is as yet not well-understood for machine implementation. Humans can work out a fuzzy plan, and interact in a fuzzy environment.

For very highly precise complicated and detailed models, one needs equally an elaborate system or measurements. In many industrial processes, this is difficult to achieve. Supervisory control by human beings with a set of linguistically described rules (or a rule book) can achieve successful control in problem situations. Supervisory personnel with years of experience can express their control processes effectively in linguistic terms, but not so effectively in mathematical terms.

Thus fuzziness is pervasive in human attempts to conceptualize, categorize, classify and relate all perceived phenomena. Objectivity in science is attempted on the basis of representations and models, on empirical observations, on observed laws; in other words, on the perception of the collective of scientists and practitioners.

One aspect is definite. It is not synonymous with probability, although the latter may serve as a meaning of 'fuzziness' in a very restricted sense and context. It is also not an attempt to establish continuity for essentially discontinuous variables and functions. Here again one may conceive of fuzziness, as providing a topological space in a restricted sense.

Thus without intending to restrict the meaning of fuzziness to other existing well-known mathematical structures one may examine the properties of fuzzy sets. This is the intent of this paper. The subject itself has been originated by Zadeh [9, 10, 11, 13, 14], who has contributed much to the development of the theory and of the applications. Many others have made important contributions. In this paper, some specific properties of fuzzy set theory are examined. (Readers who seek more details of the theory are referred to a selected bibliography given in this book and the references at the end of this chapter.)

ORDINARY FINITE SET THEORY

This section considers properties of ordinary finite sets useful for relating to fuzzy sets. Ordinary finite sets may be illustrated by the following collections of objects

(1) Set of all integers up to 100.
(2) Set of all symbols on the typewriter.
(3) Set of (finite) attributes or features characterizing Roman print alphabets .
(4) Set of all finger positions in sign language.
(5) Set of all regular facial expressions.
(6) Set of all states of a machine.

One may represent a set of any *finite* number of objects by X, an object x in X is called an element. In mathematics these concepts are undefined and are only illustrated and exemplified.

A subset B of X is another set, every element of which is also a member of X. One writes this in the following way

$$x \in B \rightarrow x \in X$$

as well as

$$B \subseteq X$$

where x is any arbitrary element. The symbol '$\in$' may be read as "is an element of" or "is present in." An example is $X = \{a, b, *, \$, @ \}$. A subset B of X may be a set $B = \{a, @\}$. One may also write a subset in the following notations

(1) $B = \{(1|a), (0|b), (0|*), (0|\$), (1|@)\}$
(2)

$$B = \begin{array}{cc}
a & \boxed{1} \\
b & \boxed{0} \\
* & \boxed{0} \\
\$ & \boxed{0} \\
@ & \boxed{1}
\end{array}$$

where 1 is entered in the vector if the element is present in the set B and 0 is entered if it is absent. One can proceed further and write the row vector 10001 for B bearing in mind that each element appears in an ordered manner. Let $\mu(x)$ denote, in general, the presence or absence of x in a subset. Then one may write

$$B = \int_{x \in X} (\mu(x)|x) \tag{2}$$

In this form, we are considering a function $\mu : X \to \{0, 1\}$, which associates a value of 1 if $x \in B$ and a value 0 if x is not in B. This function is called the characteristic function of the set B. If $B = \int_{x \in X}(0|x)$ then B is called the *empty* set and denoted by $\varnothing$, or as the **0** vector. If $B = \int_{x \in X}(1|x)$ then B is the whole set X and can be written as the vector **1**. The set X is also referred to as the *universal* set under consideration.

With these notations one can summarize the basic operators of ordinary set theory:

(1)   The *union* of two sets A, B; $A \subseteq X, B \subseteq X$ is written $A \cup B$ and is the set

$$A \cup B = \int_{x \in X} \left(\max(\mu_A(x), \mu_B(x)|x) \right) \tag{3}$$

i.e., the characteristic function $\mu_{A \cup B}$ assigns the maximum of the values $\mu_A(x)$ and $\mu_B(x)$ to x. In other words, it records the presence of x in either subset.

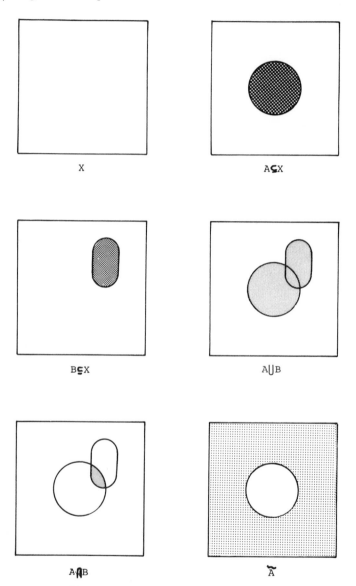

Figure 1. Venn diagram for ordinary set theory.

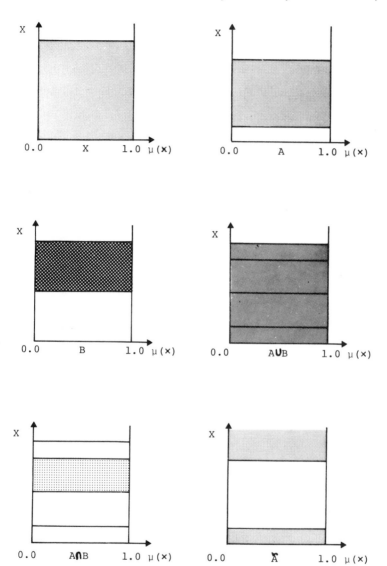

Figure 2. Profile format Venn diagram.

(2) The *intersection* of two sets A, B; $A \subseteq X, B \subseteq X$ is written $A \cap B$ and is the set

$$A \cap B = \int_{x \in X} \left(\min(\mu_A(x), \mu_B(x)|x) \right) \tag{4}$$

i.e., the characteristic function $\mu_{A \cap B}$ assigns the minimum of the values $\mu_A(x)$ and $\mu_B(x)$ to x. In other words, it records joint presence.

(3) The complement of $A \subseteq X$ is the set $\tilde{A}$,

$$\tilde{A} = \int_{x \in X} \left(1 - \mu_A(x)|x \right) \tag{5}$$

i.e., in it, a presence of x is changed to its absence and viceversa.

Traditionally the union, intersection, and complementation are also written in the form

$$A \cup B = \{ x | (x \in A) \text{ or } (x \in B), \forall x \in X \} \tag{6}$$

$$A \cup B = \{ x | (x \in A) \text{ and } (x \in B), \forall x \in X \} \tag{7}$$

$$\tilde{A} = \{ x | x \notin A, \forall x \in X \} \tag{8}$$

The forms given earlier are suitable when considering fuzzy sets.

We use the concept of Venn diagrams to show these operations that are usually displayed as in Fig. 1. For fuzzy set theory application, it is proposed to represent these in an alternative format as shown in Fig. 2. The elements of X are listed on the left along the vertical axis in some order. The characteristic function of a set A is evaluated at each element. This generates a graphic representation of a set very similar to the column vector notation used earlier. In this case $\mu(x) = 1$ or 0. This shall be termed a *profile format*.

With this basic review, we can discuss the properties of fuzzy sets. Other extensions of ordinary set theory may be explained as special cases of fuzzy set theory.

FUZZY SETS OF FINITE UNIVERSE

Imprecision in characterizing the presence or absence of properties in a concept leads to a fuzzy set. Suppose we consider the character recognition problem of a faded typescript; we are aware of the character set available on the typewriter. Suppose a compound symbol such as 'D' appears on the typescript. It is easily identifiable as being made up of the characters 'L' and 'O'. We would then say that 'D' is associated with the subset {O, L} of the character set on the typewriter.

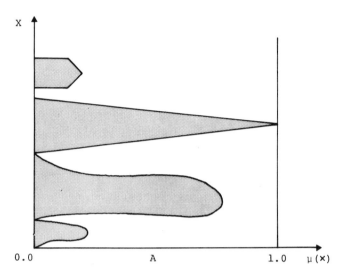

Figure 3. Profile of a fuzzy subset *A*.

Suppose instead a compound symbol such as '**Q**' appears. On a first glance we think we recognize a 'Q', but on a closer examination we find it as a superimposed 'Q','G','O' and possibly 'C'. We are not sure as to the presence or absence of 'C' in '**Q**'. Thus, if this symbol has to be represented as a subset of the symbols on the typewriter, then we either assign a 'doubtful' label to 'C' or decide that maybe it is present. How do we represent a partial presence?

Such examples may be multiplied. How is one to measure beauty? The marks assigned to a student in a course represents the degree to which his/her teacher measures his/her ability or performance in that subject. These marks may range from 0 to 100% or graded from A to F. A *fuzzy concept* of his/her over-all perforannce is obtained by his/her mark list for the term. Thus, instead of treating presence or absence in a binary manner, as in ordinary fuzzy set theory, one deals with presence in a graded manner, from 0 to 100% or from 0 to 1.

A subset *A* of *X* with a membership function $\mu(x)$ which takes any value in the interval $[0, 1]$ is called a fuzzy set.

$$A = \int_{x \in X} (\mu_A(x)|x) \tag{9}$$

where $\mu_A : X \rightarrow [0, 1]$; Fig. 3 shows the profile representation.

We can define the *union* of two fuzzy sets A, B with membership functions μ_A, μ_B as

$$A \cup B \triangleq \int_{x \in X} \max(\mu_A(x), \mu_B(x) | x) \qquad (10)$$

The *intersection* A and B is the set

$$A \cap B \triangleq \int_{x \in X} \min(\mu_A(x), \mu_B(x) | x) \qquad (11)$$

The *complement* of a set A is the set $\tilde{A}$

$$\tilde{A} \triangleq \int_{x \in X} (1 - \mu_A(x) | x) \qquad (12)$$

The profile diagrams of these operations on fuzzy sets are given in Fig. 4.

Example

$$X = \{x_1, x_2, x_3, x_4, x_5, x_6\}$$
$$A = \{(0.6|x_1), (0.4|x_2), (0.3|x_3), (0.8|x_4), (0.5|x_5), (1|x_6)\}$$
$$B = \{(0.8|x_1), (0.3|x_2), (1|x_3), (1|x_4), (0.4|x_5), (0.9|x_6)\}$$

Then

$$A \cup B = \{(0.8|x_1), (0.4|s_2), (1|x_3), (1|x_4), (0.5|x_5), (1|x_6)\}$$
$$A \cap B = \{(0.6|x_1), (0.3|x_2)(0.3|x_3), (0.8|x_4), (0.4|x_5), (0.9|x_6)\}$$
$$\tilde{A} = \{(0.4|x_1), (0.6|x_2), (0.7|x_3), (0.2|x_4), (0.5|x_5), (0|x_6)\}$$

Note that unlike in ordinary set theory,

$$A \cup \tilde{A} \neq X \qquad (13)$$
$$A \cap \tilde{A} \neq \emptyset$$

necessarily. Also note that an ordinary set is a special case of a fuzzy set where membership is either 0 or 1.

A fuzzy set A with memberhsip function $\mu_A(\cdot)$ is said to be a subset of a fuzzy set B with membershp function $\mu_B(\cdot)$ if $\mu_A(x) \leqslant \mu_B(x)$ for all $x \in X$. In this case, we write $A \subseteq B$.

Let $m_A = \max_{x \in X} \mu_A(x)$ be called the height of the fuzzy set. If $m_A = 1$ the fuzzy set is called a normal fuzzy set; for $m_A < 1$ it is a *subnormal fuzzy set*.

Let $B = \alpha A$ denote a fuzzy set obtained by changing memberships proportionately; $\mu_B(x) = \alpha \mu_A(x)$. For normal fuzzy sets $\alpha \leqslant 1$; while for subnormal fuzzy sets $\alpha \leqslant 1/m_A$. It is understood that $\alpha > 0$. The partial

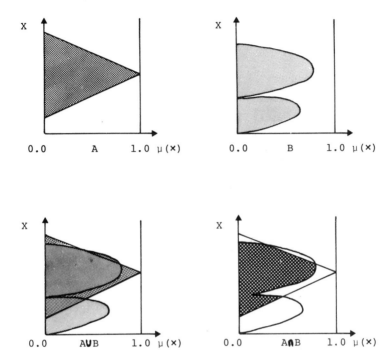

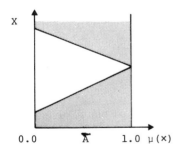

Figure 4. Profile diagrams of fuzzy operations $A \cup B$, $A \cap B$ **and** $\tilde{A}$.

113

presence indicated by $\mu(x)$ is also called the *degree* of membership of x in A or its *fuzziness level*. This level may be measured in a number of ways.

(1) A *cover* K of an ordinary set X is any collection of ordinary subsets $\{A_1, A_2, \ldots, A_k\}$ of X, such that $A_i \neq \varnothing$ and

$$A_1 \cup A_2 \cdots \cup A_k = X \tag{14}$$

An extreme case is when for any $A_1 \neq A_j$

$$A_i \cap A_j = \varnothing$$

This case is termed a *partition* of X. Suppose one has a subset $B \subseteq X$, then B may be considered a fuzzy subset of K, with $\mu_B(A_i)$ given by

$$\mu_B(A_i) = \frac{|A_i \cap B|}{|A_i \cup B|} \tag{15}$$

where the notation $|A|$ stands for the number of elements in A.

Example
Let

$$X = \{1, 2, 3, 4, 5, 6, 7, 8, 9\}$$

and

$$K = \{\{1, 3, 5\}, \{3, 6, 9\}, \{2, 4, 8,\}, \{1, 3, 7\}, \{2, 3, 8\}\}$$
$$= \{A_1, A_2, A_3, A_4, A_5\}$$

Let

$$B = \{2, 3, 5, 9, 8\}$$

Then considering B as a fuzzy subset of K it may be written as

$$B = \left\{ \left(\frac{1}{3}|A_1\right), \left(\frac{1}{3}|A_2\right), \left(\frac{1}{3}|A_3\right), \left(\frac{1}{7}|A_4\right), \left(\frac{3}{5}|A_5\right) \right\}$$

or as the 5-tuple of partial membership

$$\mu_B = \left[\frac{1}{3}, \frac{1}{3}, \frac{1}{3}, \frac{1}{7}, \frac{3}{5} \right]$$

(2) Consider an optimization problem with 'r' objective functions $f_1, \ldots, f_r$ where

$$f_i : \Re^n \to \Re \tag{16}$$

and each of the objective functions are to be maximized. Any solution x may be considered a fuzzy subset of the set of objectives in the following way: Let f^*_i denote the maximum value disregarding other objective functions assuming $f^*_i < \infty$. Then for any arbitrary x in the feasible region

$$f_i(x) \leqslant f^*_i \qquad (17)$$

Let $C = \{f_1,\ldots,f_r\}$ be the set of objective functions. Then any x may be considered as a fuzzy set of C with membership vector $\mu_x = \{\mu_1,\ldots,\mu_r\}$ where

$$\mu_i = (f^*_i - f_i(x))|f^*_i \qquad (18)$$

(3) Consider the set of objects shown in Fig. 5(a). All of these have resemblances to the label "five." Thus "five" may be considered to be the fuzzy set shown in Fig. 5(b). To some readers the figure in Fig. 5(c) may be given the label "four" while to some others it may be given the lable "five." The object is a handwritten form of the Hindi numeral "five." In this case 'membership' is identified by individual perception.

(4) *Method of Semantic Differential*: Osgoode and his coworkers [4,8] developed the concept of the semantic differential to measure the 'meaning' of a concept. It is widely used in many social science applications in management science, in marketing, in health care, in fact, wherever one can obtain a set of evaluation scales. The basic procedure consists of three steps:

(a) identify the list of properties by which to evaluate the concept or product,

(b) seek in this list polar properites and set up a polar scale,

(c) on each polar scale the concept is evaluated as to how much of the positive property is possessed.

Human respondents are naturally imprecise. Many schemes have evolved to yield some quasi-numeric information. In the original scheme numbers ranging from -3 to $+3$ or from 1 to 7 were used. A range of 0 to 100% or from 0 to 10 is also in use (Ragade [5]). The collection of values for each scale is called a *profile* of the

a. 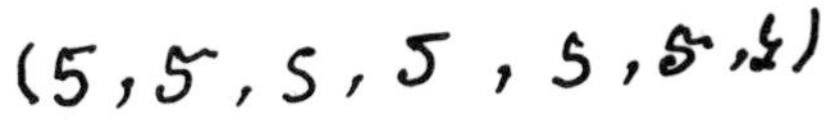 $(5, 5, 5, 5, 5, 5, 4)$

b. $\mu_{FIVE} = (1, \cdot 9, \cdot 6, \cdot 4, \cdot 2, \cdot 5., \cdot 5)$

c.  γ

Figure 5. Fuzzy five and membership of perception.

concept. Hence the vector with entries ranging from 0 to 1 is also called a profile. It is a fuzzy subset of the positive list of properties or scales. Thus a profile is a fuzzy set identified on a set of polar scales.

Example In face-identification problems one may set up scales such as:

x_1 Forehead:	_____Narrow	_____Broad
x_2 Nose:	_____Upturned	_____Hooked
x_3	_____Long	_____Hooked
x_3:	_____Long	_____Short
x_4 Eyes:	_____Narrow	_____Wide
x_5	_____Dark	_____Light
x_6 Chin:	_____Square	_____Pointed
x_7 Lips:	_____Narrow	_____Broad
x_8 Color:	_____Dark	_____Fair
x_9 Shape:	_____Oval	_____Square

A face that has an extremely broad forehead, an extremely hooked, short nose, with extremely wide eyes, an extremely pointed chin, with extremely large eyes, an extremely fair color, and a square face may be identified with the fuzzy set

$$\{(1|x_1),(1|x_2),(1|x_3),(1|x_4),(1|x_5),(1|x_6),(1|x_7),(1|x_8),(1|x_9)\}$$

or equivalently identified with the vector

$$111\ 111\ 111$$

A face identified by the vector 000 000 000 is just the polar opposite. All other face descriptions are fuzzy sets in between these two.

Example A physical enviroment is characterized by a list of polar scales with 100% for total q and 0% for no q

q_1: roominess	55%
q_2: clean	90%
q_3: light	70%
q_4: chaotic	60%
q_5: exciting	70%
q_6: casual	80%
q_7: interesting	65%

Since fuzziness connotes ambiguity, imprecision, vagueness, it is quite likely that the scales set up above are not orthogonal, but are just the natural scales that would be set up.

We can take advantage of partial membership to consider other operations on fuzzy sets not available in ordinary set theory. For this we consider a fuzzy set as a "representational picture" obtained by a set of evaluations and criteria. This permits concepts of picture processing to be applied to a fuzzy set. Such an approach yields a new meaning to the membership of an element $x \in X$. In this one sets up a "gray scale" of memberhip between full memberhsip to nonmembership. A (black and white) television picture is a fuzzy subset of the white screen (or the black screen). Thus, one can think of *focusing* a fuzzy set, of *concentrating*, of *dilating, of contrast intensifying*, of *blurring*, etc.

Let A be a fuzzy set of X with membership function $\mu_A(\cdot)$. Then its concentration, written $\text{CON}(A)$, is the set

$$\text{CON}(A) = \int_{x \in X} \left(\mu_A^{\,2}(x) | x \right) \tag{19}$$

while its dilation is written $\text{DIL}(A)$ and is the set

$$\text{DIL}(A) = \int_{x \in X} \left(\mu_A^{\,0.5}(x) | x \right) \tag{20}$$

The set A^α is defined

$$A^\alpha = \int_{x \in X} \left(\mu_A^{\,\alpha}(x) | x \right) \tag{21}$$

of which the CON and DIL are special cases for $\alpha = 2$ and $\alpha = 0.5$, respectively.

We may build other operations from the above operations.

The *contrast intensification* of a fuzzy set A is written $\text{INT}(A)$ and is the set defined as

$$\text{INT}(A) = \begin{cases} \text{CON}(A) & \text{for all } x \text{ such that } \mu_A(x) < 0.5 \\ \text{DIL}(A) & \text{for all } x \text{ such that } \mu_A(x) \geqslant 0.5 \end{cases} \tag{22}$$

This has the property of increasing membership if greater than 0.5 and decreasing it if less than 0.5.

The *blurring* of a fuzzy set A, written $\text{BLR}(A)$, is the set defined as

$$\text{BLR}(A) = \begin{cases} \text{DIL}(A) & \text{for all } x \text{ such that } \mu_A(x) < 0.5 \\ \text{CON}(A) & \text{for all } x \text{ such that } \mu_A(x) \geqslant 0.5 \end{cases} \tag{23}$$

This has the property of decreasing membership if greater than 0.5, and increasing it if less than 0.5. The level 0.5 is chosen arbitrarily.

We may define some further compositions of two fuzzy sets A and B on X. Their *convex combination* is defined as the fuzzy set

$$\alpha A + (1 - \alpha)B = \int_{x \in X} \left(\alpha \mu_A(x) + (1 - \alpha) \mu_B(x) \right) | x \quad 0 \leqslant \alpha \leqslant 1. \tag{24}$$

Their *product* is defined as the fuzzy set

$$AB = \int_{x \in X} \mu_A(x)\,\mu_B(x)|x \tag{25}$$

Their *algebraic sum* is defined as the fuzzy set

$$A \oplus B = \int_{x \in X} (\mu_A(x) + \mu_B(x) - \mu_A(x)\,\mu_B(x)|x) \tag{26}$$

This last definition is clearly related to the additive set concept in measure theoretic terms.

However, we can see it as a special case of a k-sum of two fuzzy sets A and B where $k_* \leqslant k \leqslant k^*$ and

$$k^* = \frac{\min\limits_x (\mu_A(x) + \mu_B(x))}{\mu_A(x) \cdot \mu_B(x)} \tag{27}$$

and

$$k_* = \frac{\max\limits_x (\mu_A(x) + \mu_B(x) - 1)}{\mu_A(x) \cdot \mu_B(x)} \tag{28}$$

provided $\mu_A(x) \neq 0 \neq \mu_B(x)$.

A k-sum ensures the resulting fuzzy set to have a proper characteristic function. It follows that $k = 1$ always satisfies any arbitrary k-sum of fuzzy sets. If fuzzy sets are restricted to a particular family then (k_*, k^*) is chosen to characterize the family.

Example Consider the fuzzy sets A and B of an earlier Example. Their characteristic vectors are

$$\mu_A = [0.6, 0.4, 0.3, 0.8, 0.5, 1]$$
$$\mu_B = [0.8, 0.3, 1, 1, 0.4, 0.9]$$

Thus, we have

$$\mu_{\text{CON}(A)} = [0.36, 0.16, 0.09, 0.64, 0.25, 1]$$
$$\mu_{\text{DIL}(A)} = [0.77, 0.63, 0.54, 0.89, 0.71, 1]$$
$$\mu_{\text{INT}(A)} = [0.77, 0.16, 0.98, 0.89, 0.71, 1]$$
$$\mu_{\text{BLR}(A)} = [0.36, 0.63, 0.54, 0.64, 0.25, 1]$$

For a convex combination with $\alpha = 0.2$

$$\mu_{\alpha A + (1-\alpha)B} = [0.76, 0.32, 0.86, 0.96, 0.42, 0.92]$$
$$\mu_{AB} = [0.48, 0.12, 0.3, 0.8, 0.2, 0.9]$$
$$\mu_{A \oplus B} = [0.92, 0.58, 1, 1, 0.7, 1]$$

For a k-sum, $k_* = 1 \leqslant k \leqslant 1 \ 2/7 = k^*$. In this case the k-sum has a limited range. It may happen $k^* = \infty$.

MEMBERSHIP FUNCTIONS WHEN X IS NOT FINITE

In this case X may either be having a countable infinity of elements or is uncountable. In the former case the membership functions may be represetned by an infinite series. In the latter, we can develop some standard functions in case X admits a continuous parameter.

Example Let X be the infinite series of integers $1, 2, 3, \ldots$. Then a membership function may be set up for a fuzzy set A with $\mu_A(i) = 1/i$, $i \in X$.

Example Let X be the positive real line $\mathfrak{R}^+$. Then a membership function can be given as $\mu(\lambda) = e^{-\lambda}, \lambda \geqslant 0$. In fact, this example suggests some standard functions; these are given below.

For a statement such as "λ is small" we have the following membership functions

(1) Delta membership:
$$\mu(\lambda) = 1, \qquad \lambda = 0$$
$$= 0, \qquad \lambda > 0 \qquad (29)$$

(2) Step membership:
$$\mu(\lambda) = 1, \qquad 0 \leqslant \lambda \leqslant \epsilon$$
$$= 0, \qquad \lambda > \epsilon \qquad (30)$$

(3) Ramp membership:
$$\mu(\lambda) = 1 - t\lambda, \qquad 0 \leqslant \lambda \leqslant 1/t$$
$$= 0, \qquad \lambda \geqslant 1/t (t > 0) \qquad (31)$$

(4) Exponential membership:
$$\mu(\lambda) = e^{-t\lambda}, \qquad \lambda \geqslant 0 \qquad (32)$$

(5) S-function membership:
$$\mu(\lambda) = \frac{1}{1 + t\lambda^2}, \qquad t \geqslant 0 \qquad (33)$$

For the statement "λ is large", we have

(1) Delta membership:
$$\mu(\lambda) = 0, \quad 0 < \lambda < \infty$$
$$\mu(\infty) = 1 \quad 0 < \lambda < L \qquad (34)$$

(2) Step membership:
$$\mu(\lambda) = 0, \quad L < \lambda$$
$$\mu(\lambda) = 1, \quad 0 < \lambda \leqslant L_1 \qquad (35)$$

(3) Ramp membership:
$$\mu(\lambda) = 0,$$
$$\mu(\lambda) = (\lambda - L_1)/(L_2 - L_1), \quad L_1 \leqslant \lambda < L_2$$
$$= 1, \quad \lambda \geqslant \lambda_2 \qquad (36)$$

(4) Exponential membership: $\mu(\lambda) = 0, \quad 0 \leqslant \lambda \leqslant L$

$$= 1 - e^{-t(\lambda - L)}, \quad \lambda > L, t > 0 \qquad (37)$$

For the statement "λ is around M"

(1) Delta membership: $\quad \mu(\lambda) = 1, \qquad \lambda = M$

$\qquad\qquad\qquad\qquad\qquad\;\; = 0, \qquad$ otherwise $\qquad (38)$

(2) Step membership: $\quad \mu(\lambda) = 1, \qquad M - M_1 \leqslant \lambda \leqslant M + M_1$

$\qquad\qquad\qquad\qquad\qquad\;\; = 0, \qquad$ otherwise $\qquad (39)$

(3) Ramp or triangular
membership: $\quad \mu(\lambda) = 0, \qquad \lambda < M - M_1$ or
$\qquad\qquad\qquad\qquad\qquad\qquad\qquad\qquad \lambda > M + M_1 \qquad (40)$

$$= \frac{\lambda - M_1}{M - M_1} \qquad M - M_1 \leqslant \lambda \leqslant M$$

$$= 1 - \frac{\lambda - M}{M_1} \qquad M \leqslant \lambda \leqslant M + M_1$$

(4) Exponential membership: $\quad \mu(\lambda) = e^{-t|\lambda - M|} \qquad t > 0 \qquad (41)$

(5) Gaussian membership: $\quad \mu(\lambda) = e^{-t(\lambda - M)^2} \qquad\qquad\qquad (42)$

Many other membership functions may be developed, and will be left to the reader's imagination. We need not consider the entire positive real line as the set X. Suppose one considers an interval $[a,b]$. The standard membership functions given above can be modified appropriately.

Example Let N be the set of numerical ages from 0 to 100 of a population P in a region obtained from census data. Let $y(x)$ be the number of people who claim to be young given the age x. Let $n(x)$ be the actual number of people given the age x. Then we have

$$P = \int_0^{100} dn(x) \qquad\qquad (43)$$

where $dn(x)$ is the total differential of $n(x)$ at x. The label *young* may be regarded as describing a fuzzy subset of N with a membership function

$$\mu(x) = \frac{y(x)}{n(x)} \qquad\qquad (44)$$

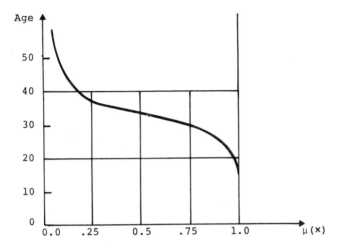

Figure 6. Profile of the label 'young'.

It is likely that for lower numerical ages, 0 to 20 say, $y(x) = n(x)$. Hence, $\mu(x) = 1$. However, while not all of $n(35)$ would consider themselves young some do. Hence, $y(x) < n(x)$. After $x = 80$, $y(x)$ could be very, very small. The profile of the function $\mu(x)$ is shown in Fig. 6.

Likewise, profiles for "middle aged", "old", "not so young", etc., may be developed.

Example Consider the problem of stopping a car at a traffic light. A traffic sign says "When the light is red, stop here." A driver recognizes three boundaries: the white line in front, the interlane boundary to the left, and the curb at the right. Somewhere in the center between the left boundary and the curb he is in a correct position. Likewise, at a distance of x feet away from the cross street boundary he is also in a correct position (see Fig. 7). The driver judges correctness based on his perception of the distance of point L from the left lane and of the distance of point R from the curb. In either case, he perceives a distance of x meters from the front line. Let the width of the lane be $2a$ and of the car $2b, b < a$. The perception of a distance z meters from the right lane translates also into an evaluation of correctness. The values of y and z are obviously related. Let $\mu^{f}(x)$ stand for the perceived correctness of stopping x meters away from the cross street line, y meters from the left lane, and z meters from the right curb. We can define a profile of correctness for each position of the car as given by the distances x, y and z.

Now although y and z are physically along the same direction a slight distortion can take place due to the angle of vision, the shape of the

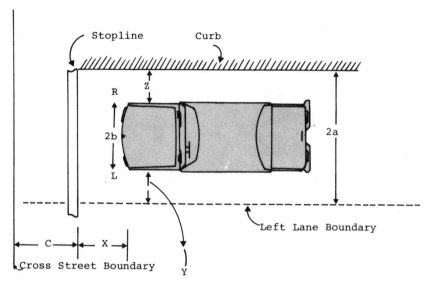

Figure 7. Perception of distance in car stopping.

windshield, the driver's posture, etc. Thus, the profile

$$
\begin{bmatrix}
\mu^{f}(x) \\
\mu^{l}(y) \\
\mu^{r}(z)
\end{bmatrix}
$$

gives the meaning of correct position to the driver in terms of the membership functions $\mu^{f}(x), \mu^{l}(y), \mu^{r}(z)$.

For example, one may consider a sample of drivers and estimate their correctness perception for each point (x, y, z). From this sample, we may hypothesize the functions $\mu^{f}, \mu^{l}, \mu^{r}$ for a population. Alternatively we may choose *a priori* a standard function such as the ramp or exponential memberships as given above and estimate the parameters of $\mu^{f}, \mu^{l}, \mu^{r}$. Suppose we choose ramp membership for front perception and Gaussian for the side perceptions. Assuming no distortion on the side, we can reduce the coordinates to two (x, y). Then

$$
\mu^{f}(x) = \frac{x}{c} \qquad x < c
$$
$$
= 1 \qquad x \geqslant c \tag{45}
$$

while

$$
\mu^{l}(y) = e^{-k(y + b - a)^{2}} \qquad k > 0 \tag{46}
$$

DISTANCE AND ENTROPY CONCEPTS IN FUZZY SETS

The profile of a fuzzy set may be considered a point in a unit n-cube. One may define both a norm and a distance concept. One defines the *distance* between two fuzzy sets A and B on a finite universe X, with membership functions $\mu_A(\cdot)$ and $\mu_B(\cdot)$ in the following way

$$d_p(A,B) = \left\{ \sum_{x \in X} |\mu_A(x) - \mu_B(x)|^p \right\}^{1/p} \quad p \geqslant 1 \qquad (47)$$

For $p = 1$, we obtain a generalized Hamming distance between A and B. For $p = 2$, we obtain a root-square distance, or Euclidean distance. For $p > 2$, we have an l_p distance between A and B. It is easy to show that $d_p(A, B)$ satisfies the necessary properties of a distance function

$$d_p(A, B) \geqslant 0 \qquad \text{non-negativity}$$
$$d_p(A, B) = d_p(B, A) \qquad \text{symmetry}$$
$$d_p(A, B) + d_p(B, C) \geqslant d_p(A, C) \qquad \text{triangle inequality}$$

for

$$A \neq B \neq C \qquad (48)$$

By setting $B = \varnothing$ one has $\mu_B(x) = 0$ for all $x \in B$. This yields all distances of fuzzy sets $A, A \neq B$, with respect to $\varnothing$. The distances are termed the *norm* or *length* of the fuzzy set, which we write

$$\|A\|_p = d_p(A, \varnothing)$$
$$= \left(\sum_{x \in X} |\mu_A(x)|^p \right)^{1/p} \quad p \geqslant 1 \qquad (49)$$

In the case of ordinary sets the Hamming distance between two sets is the number of elements in which they differ while the norm is the number of elements in a set.

Example Consider the fuzzy sets of an earlier example with

$$\mu_A = [0.6, 0.4, 0.3, 0.8, 0.5, 1]$$
$$\mu_B = [0.8, 0.3, 1, 1, 0.4, 0.9]$$

The Hamming distance ($p = 1$) written $d_H(A, B)$ is given by

$$d_H(A, B) = |0.8 - 0.6| + |0.4 - 0.3| + |0.3 - 1| + |0.8 - 1| + |0.5 - 0.4| + |1 - 0.9|$$
$$= 1.4$$

Likewise the Hamming lengths of A and B are

$$\|A\|_1 = 3.6$$

$$\|B\|_1 = 4.4$$

The *focus* of a fuzzy set A on a fuzzy set B is the set $\mathrm{FCS}(A) = A^{\alpha^*}$

$$\mathrm{FCS}(A) = A^{\alpha^*}$$

where

$$d_p(A^{\alpha^*}, B) = \min_\alpha d_p(A^\alpha, B) \tag{50}$$

This has the property of altering a set A by taking its powers and bringing it close to B. When X has a countable infinity of elements then the summation in the definition for the Hamming length can be determined if the series is convergent. Likewise for X, an uncountable point set, a convergent integral must be considered.

Consider the interpretation of a fuzzy set as a profile determined on a set of polar scales. It would be a very unclear evaluation if each scale response is right in the middle. On the other hand, if each evaluation is to one extreme or the other then the evaluation is very clear. For example, a "maybe" response is unclear whereas a response "yes" or "no" is clear. Likewise, saying a picture is extremely beautiful makes the evaluation more clear then saying it is "average". A measure of this *incertitude* of evaluation is provided by the entropy concept first developed by DeLuca and Termini [1]. The entropy of a fuzzy set A on a universe X, with membership function $\mu_A(\cdot)$, is given by

$$H_L(A) = \frac{1}{N} \sum_{x \in X} \mathrm{In}(x) \tag{51}$$

where N is the number of elements in x, X being finite, and $\mathrm{In}(x)$ is the *incertitude* of the evaluation along scale x given by

$$\mathrm{In}(x) = -\left(\mu_A(x) \log_2 \mu_A(x) + (1 - \mu_A(x)) \log_2 \mu_A(x) \right) \tag{52}$$

The incertitude of a scale is 1 if $\mu_A(x) = 0.5$ and is 0 if $\mu_A(x) = 1$ or 0. Likewise, the entropy of a set A is 1 if for every $x, \mu_A(x) = 0.5$ and is 0 if for every $x, \mu_A(x) = 1$ or 0.

This notion of entropy is obtained in a nonprobabilistic setting. An interesting property left to the reader to prove is the following: Given a fuzzy set A then

$$H_L(A) \geqslant H_L(\mathrm{INT}(A)) \tag{53}$$

i.e., intensifying a set reduces its incertitude, see Ragade [6].

A natural question is the relation between this concept of incertitude and the more well-known concept of (probabilistic) uncertainty. A later section considers their interrelationship. In the following section a very useful concept of a fuzzy relation is introduced. This forms the basis of many studies in pattern recognition and communications.

FUZZY RELATIONS, MATRICES AND GRAPHS

In a similar spirit to defining relations and graphs in ordinary set theory, we can consider their fuzzy version [7]. Let X and Y be two sets countable or otherwise.

A fuzzy relation R between X and Y is a fuzzy subset of their Cartesian product $X \times Y$

$$R = \int_{(x,y) \in X \times Y} (\mu(x,y)|(x,y)) \tag{54}$$

with $\mu(x,y)$ as their membership functions. When X and Y are finite R may be represented by a matrix T_R and a graph Γ_R, respectively. The matrix T_R has entries $\mu(x,y)$ yielding the membership of cell (x,y) and the graph Γ_R yields a weighted bipartite graph whose nodes are the elements of the sets X and Y and whose arc-weights correspond to entries $\mu(x,y)$.

Example

Let

$$X = \{x_1, x_2, x_3, x_4, x_5\}$$
$$Y = \{y_1, y_2, y_3\}$$

then

		y_1	y_2	y_3
	x_1	1	0.8	0.6
	x_2	0.2	1	0.4
$T_R \quad =$	x_3	0.0	1	0.7
	x_4	0.2	0.9	0.5
	x_5	0.3	0.4	1

and the corresponding graph is shown as a weighted bipartite graph in Fig. 8.

Consider two fuzzy relations R on $X \times Y$ and S on $Y \times Z$. Then these

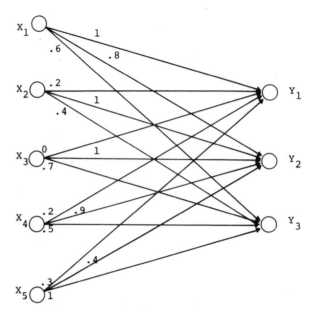

Figure 8. Fuzzy graph for the example.

may be composed in various ways. Their composition is denoted $R \circ S$ and is a fuzzy relation on $X \times Z$.

(1) max-min composition:

$$R \circ S = \int_{(x,z) \in X \times Z} \max_{y \in Y} \min \left(\mu(x,y), \mu(y,z) \right) | (x,z) \qquad (55)$$

(2) max-product composition:

$$R \circ S = \int_{(\alpha,z) \in X \times Z} \max_{y \in Y} \left(\mu(x,y) \cdot \mu(y,z) \right) | (x,z) \qquad (56)$$

Other compositions may likewise be defined. In case X, Y, Z are finite sets, these compositions may be written in terms of the T_R, T_S matrices

$$T_{R \circ S} = T_R \circ T_S \qquad (57)$$

where $\circ$ denotes the corresponding composition for matrices.

In particular, we may consider a fuzzy relation between elements of X. For finite X, the matrices are square, and the resulting graph is defined on

the node set X. It is a complete graph with weights for every arc ranging from 0 to 1, reflecting the membership of the pair of nodes joined in R.
A relation R is said to be:

reflexive: if $\mu(x,x)=1$ and $\mu(x,y)<1, y\neq x$, $\forall x \in X$

symmetric: if $\mu(x,y)=\mu(y,x)$, $\forall(x,y)\in X$

antisymmetric: if $\mu(x,y)\neq\mu(y,x)$, $\forall(x,y)\in X$

antireflexive: if $\mu(x,x)=0$, $\forall x \in X$

max-min
transitivity: if $\mu(x,z)\geqslant \max \min(\mu(x,y),\mu(y,z))$, $\forall x,y,z \in Xy \in X$

min-max
transitivity: if $\mu(x,z)\geqslant \min \max(\mu(x,y),\mu(y,z))$, $\forall x,y,z \in Xy \in X$

A fuzzy relation is said to be a *pre-order* if it is reflexive and has max-min transitivity. It is a *similarity relation* if it is reflexive, symmetric and has max-min transitivity. It is a *resemblance relation* if it is reflexive and symmetric.

The reader is directed to Kaufmann [2] for a full discussion on fuzzy relations. We can extend the entropy measure H_L to fuzzy relations and graphs. Let R be a fuzzy relation on X with $\mu_R(\cdots)$ as its membership function. Then, its incertitude is given by

$$H_L(R)=-\frac{1}{n^2}\sum_x\sum_y \text{In}(x,y) \tag{58}$$

$$\text{In}(x,y)=-(\mu\log\mu+(1-\mu)\log(1-\mu)) \tag{59}$$

$$\mu=\mu_R(x,y) \tag{60}$$

TOPOLOGICAL AND PROBABILISTIC CONNECTIONS

We return to the question of incertitude and uncertainty. Fuzziness has been given the interpretation of subjective probability. It seems to be an unnecessary restriction as we might rightly point to the existence of literature dealing with subjective probability and its use in Bayesian methods of decision analysis. There are many other properties of fuzziness such as the incertitude caused by vague language, ambiguity, persistent and deliberate. These may be studied by interpretations other than that of subjective probability. There are many interrelations between fuzziness and probability as may be seen in this section.

Let X have n elements. Let A be a fuzzy set on X with membership function $\mu_A(\cdot)$. Then, one can associate a finite dimensional probability vector with A. Let this vector be denoted by $\mathbf{p}_A$. Then one has

$$) = 1 \tag{61}$$

Now each $p_A(x)$ can be found from the memberships $\mu_A(\cdot)$. We proceed thus: Define

$$l = d_1(A) = \sum_{x \in X} \mu_A(x) \tag{62}$$

This gives the Hamming norm of A. Then

$$p_A(x) = \mu_A(x)|l \qquad \text{for } l \neq 0 \tag{63}$$

and set

$$p_A(x) = 0 \qquad \text{for } A = \phi \tag{64}$$

In fact, this association is not unique. The family

$$A = \left\{ A \left| \begin{array}{ll} A & \text{is a fuzzy set} \\ p_A & \text{is a fixed vector} \end{array} \right. \right\} \tag{65}$$

where $p_A = \mu_A(x)|l$ defines a collection of fuzzy sets all having the same probability vectors.

Sometimes it is possible to confuse a fuzzy set with a finite probability vector. A strange reasoning prevails in that any vector dealing with incertitude and imprecision, with numbers ranging from 0 to 1, must be a probability vector. It is an erroneous reasoning as the reader must have by now come to realize. *Fuzziness is not probability.*

Suppose one has n normalized random variables, $x_i(\omega)$, $i = 1, \ldots, n$, where $\omega \in \Omega$ is a random parameter with an associated distribution function $dp_i(\omega)$ and the joint distribution function $dp_{ij}(\omega)$. Then one can set up a variance-covarancne matrix of size $n \times n$ with the ijth entry,

$$\xi_{ij} = \text{Exp}(x_i x_j) \tag{66}$$

This matrix has $\xi_{ii} = 1$ for all i and $|\xi_{ij}| \leq 1$. Define a transformation

$$\mu_{ij} = \frac{1 + \xi_{ij}}{2} \tag{67}$$

This yields a fuzzy matrix with entries between 0 and 1. From this we can consider a similarity relation on the set of random variables $1, \ldots, n$, or that the ith random variable is a fuzzy set of the variables $x_1, \ldots, x_n$.

We can think of many other ways of combining and treating probabilistic and fuzzy concepts jointly; keeping their intrinsic characterizations of event uncertainty and event labeling ambiguity separate.

Again, consider a finite set X and the set of all its fuzzy sets denoted $\mathcal{F}(X)$. A topology may be described on $\mathcal{F}(X)$ since

(1) The fuzzy set theoretic union of an arbitrary number of fuzzy sets in $\mathcal{F}(X)$ is still in $\mathcal{F}(X)$.
(2) The fuzzy set theoretic intersection of a finite number of fuzzy sets in $\mathcal{F}(X)$ is also in $\mathcal{F}(X)$.

Thus, $(X, \mathcal{F}(X))$ forms a natural topology. (In fact, any collection $\mathcal{F}$ of fuzzy sets of $\mathcal{F}(X)$ that obey (i) and (ii) define a topology $(X, \mathcal{F})$.) With the distance concept $d_p(A, B)$ between two fuzzy sets A a metric topology can be defined on X. The usual consideration is that $\mathcal{F}(X)$ has a lattice structure under the union operator $\cup$ and intersection operator $\cap$.

Since fuzziness is a concept dealing with many linguistic issues, in the next section are considered semantic hedges and ways of representing them.

HEDGES AND OPERATORS REPRESENTING THEM

In constructing the semantic differential, responses have been arbitrarily sought on a numerical scale. Suppose, on the other hand, various subsets of the interval $[0, 1]$ (or the traditional scale -3 to $+3$ or a scale 0 to 10), are assigned labels such as very bright, moderately bright, not quite bright. Such adjectival modifiers of the positive end of the scale may be called *hedges*. Zadeh [12] identifies two types of hedges. Type I has hedges that may be represented as operators acting on fuzzy sets, e.g., "very", "more or less", "much", "slightly", "highly". Type II has more complicated hedges, which are approached algorithmically. Such hedges are *actually, in a sense, essentially*, etc.

For a Type I hedge represented as an operator consider the meaning of "very A" given by $\mathrm{INT}(A)$, i.e., it concentrates the membership if it is less than 0.5 bringing it closer to 0 and dilates the membership if it is greater than 0.5 bringing it closer to 1. For example, on the polar scale bad–good, very good brings the membership closer to 1, very bad closer to 0. Thus, the hedge "very" is represented by INT.

To illustrate a Type II hedge consider representing the hedge *essentially* that acts on a composite fuzzy set G that is a convex combination of four basic fuzzy sets A, B, C, D. This combination may be indicated thus

$$\mu_G = \omega_1 \mu_A + \omega_2 \mu_B + \omega_3 \mu_C + \omega_4 \mu_D \tag{68}$$

with

$$1 = \omega_1 + \omega_2 + \omega_3 + \omega_4 \tag{69}$$

The weights ω_i ascribe a measure of importance to the associated fuzzy set. The hedge "essentially" acts on these weights to increase the importance of the more important ones and decrease those of the less important ones.

Let W denote the vector of weights. Consider it as a fuzzy set. It can be normalized by dividing each weight by $\max \omega_i$. From this obtain the concentration of norm (W), i.e., the fuzzy vector $y = \mathrm{CON}(\mathrm{norm}(W))$. Let $l = \|y\|_1$, i.e., its Hamming length. Then the vector $y^* = y/l$ yields weights that can now be used to combine the fuzzy sets A, B, C, D.

Thus, *essentially*,

$$\mu_G = y_1{}^* \mu_A + y_2{}^* \mu_B + y_3{}^* \mu_C + y_3{}^* \mu_D \tag{70}$$

It is possible to develop many "quasi-quantitative representations of linguistic operators. It is, however, not the intent of this chapter to develop these details. The reader is also directed to Negoita [3] for applications.

CONCLUSION

A subject in its early developmental stages has many ramifications. Some of these have been introduced to the reader. Many other candidate topics have been left out. The authors hope that novice readers having obtained a flavor of the theory of fuzzy sets may on their own discover new interpretations.

In this chapter, an interpretation of fuzzy set theory in terms of the semantic differential concept has been given. This interpretation has many practical implications. In many areas of decision and information sciences the semantic differential has been successfully used as an "instrument': of measuring the meaning of a concept. Fuzzy set theory provides an excellent framework within which such measurements can be used in conjunction with theoretical studies.

APPENDIX

Herein are listed some important properties of the set of all fuzzy sets of a set x, $\mathcal{F}(x)$.

Commutativity:
$$A \cup B = B \cup A$$
$$A \cap B = B \cap A$$

Associativity:
$$(A \cap B) \cap C = A \cap (B \cap C)$$
$$(A \cup B) \cup C = A \cup (B \cup C)$$

Distributivity:
$$A \cap (B \cup C) = (A \cap B) \cup (A \cap C)$$
$$A \cup (B \cap C) = (A \cup B) \cap (A \cup C)$$

$$A \cup \phi = A \qquad A \cap \phi = \phi$$
$$A \cup X = X \qquad A \cap X = A$$

Idempotence:

$A \cap A = A$

$A \cup A = A$

DeMorgan's laws:

$\sim(A \cap B) = \tilde{A} \cup \tilde{B}$

$\sim(A \cup B) = \tilde{A} \cap \tilde{B}$

Fuzzy subsets, in general, do not obey the following

$A \cap \tilde{A} = \phi$ $A \cup \tilde{A} = X$

REFERENCES

1. A. DeLuca and S. Termini, "A Definition of a Non-Probabilistic Entropy in a Setting of Fuzzy Sets Theory," *Info. Control* **20** (1972), 301–312.

2. A. Kaufmann, *Introduction to the Theory of Fuzzy Subsets, Vol.* 1. Academic Press, N. Y., 1975.

3. C. V. Negoita, *Introduction to Fuzzy Set Theory for Systems Analysis*. John Wiley, N. Y., 1975.

4. C. E. Osgoode, G. J. Suci, and P. H. Tannenbaum, *Measurement and Meaning*, U. Ill. Press, Urbana, Ill., 1957.

5. R. K. Ragade, "Profile Transformation Algebra and Group Consensus Formation through Fuzzy Set Theory", chapter 21, this volume.

6. R. K. Ragade, "Fuzzy Sets in Communication Systems and in Consensus Formation Systems," *J. Cybernetics* **6** (1976), 21–38.

7. A. Rosenfeld, "Fuzzy Graphs," *Fuzzy Sets and their Application to Cognitive and Decision Processes* L. A. Zadeh, K. S. Fu, K. Tanaka, and M. Shimura, Eds.) Academic Press, N. Y. 1975.

8. J. G. Snider and C. E Osgoode, *Semantic Differential Techniques, A Source Book*. Aldine Publishing Co., Chicago, 1969.

9. L. A. Zadeh, "Fuzzy Sets," *Infor. Control* **8** (1965), 338–353.

10. L. A. Zadeh, "Quantitative Fuzzy Semantics," *Infor. Sci.* **3** (1970), 159–176.

11. L. A. Zadeh, "Similarity Relations and Fuzzy Orderings," *Infor. Sci.* **3** (1970), 177–200.

12. L. A. Zadeh, "A Fuzzy Set Theoretic Interpretation of Linguistic Hedges," E. R. C. Memo—M335, U. Calif., Berkeley, April,1972. [Also in *J. of Cybernetics* **2** (1972), 4–34.]

13. Zadeh, L. A. "Outline of a New Approach to the Analysis of Complex Systems and Decision Processes," *IEEE Trans. Sys., Man and Cybernetics* **SMC-3** (January 1973), 22–44.

14. Zadeh, L. A. "The Concept of a Linguistic Variable and its Application to Approximate Reasoning, I–III," *Infor. Sci.* **8** (1975), 199–249, 301–357; **9** (1975), 43–80.

FUZZY AND PROBABILISTIC PROGRAMS

8

Eugene S. Santos

Many important notions, fuzzy in nature, may be assigned a precise meaning using the concept of the membership function of a fuzzy set [12] and thereby making them amenable to mathematical analysis. One such example is the notion of fuzzy programs or fuzzy algorithms introduced in [13]. Intuitively, a fuzzy program or algorithm is a way of imprecisely specifying a course of action. We encounter many such situations in our daily life. Familiar examples include cooking recipes, driving instructions, etc. Two equivalent formulations of fuzzy programs or algorithms were introduced in [6] corresponding to the conventional Turing algorithms and Markŏv algorithms. These formulations provide a solid foundation for the study of fuzzy programs and algorithms. However, like their conventional counterparts, these formulations cannot be conveniently applied to most problems of practical interest. Another formulation of fuzzy programs or algorithms was introduced in [1], and generalizations of this formulation were given in [4, 11]. Although this formulation and its generalizations are satisfactory in dealing with certain practical problems, it is shown in the present paper that they are very restrictive in nature.

The main objective of the present paper is to provide a formulation of fuzzy programs or algorithms general enough to encompass all existing formulations and yet suitable enough for dealing with problems of practical interest. The basic ideas behind this formulation are similar to those given in [8, 10].

The main contents of the present paper are contained in the next four sections. In the next section, the basic formulation of fuzzy programs is introduced. There are many interesting models of fuzzy programs, including probabilistic programs, maximin programs [5], max-product programs [5], nondeterministic programs [3], etc. In order to provide a uniform definition for these and other models of fuzzy programs, the concepts of ordered semiring W and W-machine are introduced. The various models of fuzzy programs are then obtained by choosing the appropriate ordered semiring W.

In the sections entitled "Generalized Fuzzy Machines" and "Turing Fuzzy Algorithms", the relationship between the formulation of fuzzy programs given in the next section and those given in [1,4,6,7,11] are examined. It is shown, among other things, that the formulations given in [1,4,11] are programs computable on a finite *W*-automaton, and the formulations given in [6,7] are programs computable on a Turing *W*-machines.

An example of fuzzy programs is given in the last section. This same example was also considered in [1,11]. It is chosen to enable the readers to compare the various formulations involved.

FUZZY PROGRAMS

In this section, a mathematical formulation of fuzzy programs is introduced. Relationships between this formulation and the existing ones [1,4,6,7,11] are discussed in subsequent sections.

Definition   An instruction is a string of one of the following forms:

   Start: go to L
      L: do F; go to L_1
      L: if P then go to $(L_1, L_2, \ldots, L_n)$
      L: halt

where $n = 1, 2, 3, \ldots$; $L, L_1, L_2, \ldots, L_n \in \mathcal{L}$ (the labels); $F \in \mathcal{F}$ (the function or operation symbols); and $P \in \mathcal{P}_n$ (the *n*-valued predicate or test symbols). The four types of instructions are called, respectively, start, operation, test and halt instructions. If an instruction start with the label *L*, then *L* is called the label of the instruction. A program is a finite set π of instruction containing exactly one start instruction and no two instructions in π have the same label.

Except for the concept of test instructions, the definition of the various concepts introduced above are essentially the same as those given in [8,10], and the readers are referred there for further details and motivations. The idea behind the concept of test instructions as defined above is as follows: in the deterministic case, the symbol *P* is to represent an *n*-valued predicate, i.e., *P* is a function which assumes values in the set $\{1, 2, 3, \ldots, n\}$, and if the value of *P* is *k*, then the next instruction to be executed has label L_k. Clearly, if $n = 2$, then the concept of test instructions defined above reduces to the corresponding concept given in [8,10].

In the above definition, *F* and *P* are merely symbols and no meaning have yet been given to them. The problem of giving meaning to these symbols and the various concepts defined above will be the main concern of the rest of this section.

There are many interesting models of fuzzy programs. The following concept will enable us to give a uniform definition for these models, as well as other models, of fuzzy programs.

Definition An ordered semiring is a quadruple $(W, \oplus, \otimes, \prec)$ where W is a nonempty set, $\oplus$ and $\otimes$ are binary operations on W, and $\prec$ is a partial ordering relation on W satisfying the following conditions:

(1) For every $a,b,c \in W$, $a \oplus b = b \oplus a$, $a \otimes b = b \otimes a$, $a \oplus (b \oplus c) = (a \oplus b) \oplus c$, $a \otimes (b \otimes c) = (a \otimes b) \otimes c$, and $a \otimes (b \oplus c) = (a \otimes b) + (a \otimes c)$;

(2) There exists $0, 1 \in W$ such that $a \oplus 0 = a = 0 \oplus a$ and $a \otimes 1 = a = 1 \otimes a$ for all $a \in W$;

(3) For every $a, b \in W$, $a \prec a \oplus b$

The concept of semiring was introduced in [9] to serve as a unifying concept for the various existing models of finite automata. However, the structure of a semiring alone is not sufficient for our present endeavor, since we are often faced with the problem of applying the $\oplus$ operator to an infinite set. A simple solution to the problem is the concept of ordered semiring introduced above. Unfortunately, condition (3) of the definition of ordered semiring rules out such semiring as the semiring associated with generalized automata [9]. However, this is a small price to pay since it is difficult, if not impossible, to extend addition to an infinite set of real numbers.

Examples of ordered semiring that yield interesting models of fuzzy programs include: $W_W = (R_+, +, \times, \leqslant)$, $W_X = ([0,1], \max, \min, \leqslant)$, $W_I = ([0,1], \min, \max, \geqslant)$, $W_T = ([0,1], \max, \times, \leqslant)$, and $W_N = (\{0,1\}, \max, \min, \leqslant)$, where R_+ is the set of all nonnegative real numbers.

Definition Let $(W, \oplus, \otimes, \prec)$ be an ordered semiring, $a \in W$ and $W_0 \subseteq W$. The symbol a is an upper bound of W_0 if and only if $b \prec a$ for all $b \in W_0$. The symbol a is the least upper bound of W_0, in symbols, $a = \operatorname{lub} W_0$, if and only if a is an upper bound of W_0 and for every upper bound b of W_0, $a \prec b$. The symbol a is the sum of all elements in W_0, in symbols, $a = \Sigma W_0$, if and only if $a = \operatorname{lub}\{a_1 + a_2 + \cdots + a_n | a_i \in W_0, i = 1, 2, \ldots, n$ and $n = 1, 2, 3, \ldots\}$.

Proposition *Let $(W, \oplus, \otimes, \prec)$ be an ordered semiring.*

(a) $0 \prec a$ for all $a \in W$

(b) $\Sigma\{a_1, a_2, \ldots, a_n\} = a_1 \oplus a_2 \oplus \cdots \oplus a_n$ for all $a_i \in W$, $i = 1, 2, \ldots, n$, and $n = 1, 2, 3, \ldots$.

In what follows, if no confusion is likely to arise, then we shall write W for the ordered semiring $(W, \oplus, \otimes, \prec)$.

Definition Let W be an ordered semiring, and let U and V be nonempty sets. A W-function f from U into V is a function from $V \times U$ into W.

Remark $f(v|u)$ is the weight or grade that the value of the function at u is v.

Definition Let W be an ordered semiring. A W-machine is a function $\mathfrak{M}$ defined on the set $\{I\} \cup \mathfrak{F} \cup \mathfrak{P} \cup \{O\}$ for which there exist sets X (the input set), M (the memory set and Y (the output set) such that:

(1) $\mathfrak{M}_I$ is a W-function from X into M;

(2) for every $F \in \mathfrak{F}$, $\mathfrak{M}_F$ is a W-function from M into M;

(3) for every $P \in \mathfrak{P}$, there exists a positive integer n such that $\mathfrak{M}_P$ is a W-function from M into $\{1, 2, \ldots, n\}$; and

(4) $\mathfrak{M}_O$ is a W-function from M into Y.

The four kinds of functions given in (1)–(4) are called, respectively, input, operation, test and output functions.

In the above definition, we assume the symbols I and O (standing for input and output, respectively) are identifiers not belonging to either the sets $\mathfrak{F}$ or $\mathfrak{P}$. Moreover, we used the subscript notation $\mathfrak{M}_I$ as an alternate to the functional value notation $\mathfrak{M}(I)$.

If W is taken to be W_W, W_X, W_I, W_T or W_N, then the corresponding W-machine will be referred to, respectively, as weighted, maximin, minimax, maxproduct, or nondeterministic machines. Besides these machines, there are two other interesting types of machines, namely, the probabilistic and the deterministic machines. A probabilistic machine is a weighted machine in which the input, operation, test and output functions are all probabilistic. A W_W-function f from U into V is probabilistic if and only if for all $u \in U$, $\Sigma \{f(v|u): v \in V\}$ exists and is less than or equal to 1. A deterministic machine is any W-machine in which the input, operation, test and output functions are all deterministic. A W-function f from U into V is deterministic if and only if for every $u \in U$, there exists a $v_0 \in V$ such that $f(v_0|u) = 1$ and $f(v|u) = 0$ for all $v \neq v_0$. The concept of deterministic machines coincides with the concept of machines defined in [8, 10].

Notation Let $\mathfrak{M}$ be a W-machine and $n = 1, 2, 3, \ldots$. $\mathfrak{P}_n$ is the subset of $\mathfrak{P}$ consisting of all $P \in \mathfrak{P}$ such that $\mathfrak{M}_P$ is a W-function from M into $\{1, 2, \ldots, n\}$.

Definition Let $P \in \mathcal{P}_n$. If $\mathfrak{M}_P(k|m) = \mathfrak{M}_P(k|m')$ for all m, $m' \in M$ and $k = 1, 2, \ldots, n$, then P is said to be unconditional. A test instruction L: if P then go to $(L_1, L_2, \ldots, L_n)$ where P is unconditional is called an unconditional test instruction.

Remark In the deterministic case, an unconditional test instruction corresponds to an unconditional GO TO statement. These unconditional test instructions make it unnecessary to consider programs in which a weight is assigned for the next instruction to be executed.

Definition Let π be a program and $\mathfrak{M}$ a W-machine. π is admissible on $\mathfrak{M}$, or $\mathfrak{M}$ admits π, if and only if (i) for every operation instruction of the form L: do F; go to L', $F \in \mathcal{F}$, and (ii) for every test instruction of the form L: if P, then go to $(L_1, L_2, \ldots, L_n)$, $P \in \mathcal{P}_n$.

Notation Let π be a program and $\mathfrak{M}$ a W-machine which admits π. For every $L_1, L_2 \in \mathcal{L}$, $m_1, m_2 \in M$, and $w \in W$, we write $(L', m_1) \overset{w}{\to} (L'', m_2)$ if and only if we have either an instruction of the form

$$L': \text{do F; go to L}$$

belonging to π, in which case $L'' = L$ and $w = \mathfrak{M}_F(m_2|m_1)$, or an instruction of the form

$$L': \text{if P then go to } (L_1, L_2, \ldots, L_n)$$

belonging to π, in which case $m_1 = m_2$, $L'' = L_k$ for some $k = 1, 2, \ldots, n$, and $w = \mathfrak{M}_P(k|m)$. Otherwise, $(L', m_1) \overset{0}{\to} (L'', m_2)$, where 0 is the additive identity of W.

Definition A computation by the program π on the W-machine $\mathfrak{M}$ which admits π is a finite sequence

$$x, L_0, m_0, L_1, m_1, \ldots, L_n, m_n, y \tag{1}$$

where $x \in X$, $y \in Y$, $L_i \in \mathcal{L}$, $m_i \in M$, $i = 0, 1, \ldots, n$, in which L_0 is the label contained in the start instruction of π, and L_n is the label of some halt instruction in π. The weight associated with (1) is an element $w \in W$ such that $w = w_0 \otimes w_1 \otimes w_2 \otimes \cdots \otimes w_{n+1}$, where $w_i \in W$, $i = 0, 1, 2, \ldots, n+1$, $w_0 = \mathfrak{M}_I(m_0|x)$, $w_{n+1} = \mathfrak{M}_0(y|m_n)$, and for every $i = 1, 2, \ldots, n$, $(L_{i-1}, m_{i-1}) \overset{w_i}{\to} (L_i, m_i)$. The computation (1) is feasible if and only if its weight $w \neq 0$. The x and y in (1) are called, respectively, the input and output of the computation (1).

Definition Let π be a program and $\mathfrak{M}$ a W-machine which admits π. For each $x \in X$ and $y \in Y$, define $\mathfrak{M}_\pi(y|x)$ to be ΣW_0, if ΣW_0 exists, where

W_0 is the set of weights associated with some computation by π on $\mathfrak{M}$ with input x and output y.

In general, $\mathfrak{M}_\pi(y|x)$ is not always defined. If $\mathfrak{M}_\pi(y|x)$ is defined, then it represents the weight that the program π computed on the machine $\mathfrak{M}$ yields output y given input x.

It is easy to verify that for $W = W_X$, W_I, W_P, or W_N, $\mathfrak{M}_\pi(y|x)$ is defined for all $x \in X$ and $y \in Y$. Thus $\mathfrak{M}_\pi$ is a W-function from X into Y. In addition, if $\mathfrak{M}$ is a probabilistic machine and π is a program admissible on $\mathfrak{M}$, then $\mathfrak{M}_\pi(y|x)$ is also defined for all $x \in X$ and $y \in V$. Moreover, in this case, $\mathfrak{M}$ is a probabilistic function from X into Y.

Definition A program π together with a W-machine that admits π is called a W-program. In general, any W-program is referred to as a fuzzy program. Moreover, if $\mathfrak{M}$ is a so-and-so machine and π is a program admissible on $\mathfrak{M}$, then we shall call the pair $(\pi, \mathfrak{M})$ a so-and-so program.

The above discussion gives a precise formulation of the concepts of maximin programs, probabilistic programs, max-product programs, nondeterministic programs, deterministic programs and other types of fuzzy programs. It is clear that a deterministic program behaves in exactly the same manner as a program defined in [8, 10]. Moreover, except for the role of input/output, a deterministic program is essentially an ordered pair $(S, \mathcal{I})$, where S is a program schema and $\mathcal{I}$ is an interpretation of S, as defined in [14].

GENERALIZED FUZZY MACHINES

Another formulation of fuzzy programs was introduced in [1], and generalizations of this formulation were discussed in [4, 11]. Although this formulation and its generalizations are satisfactory in dealing with certain practical problems, it will be shown in this section that this formulation of fuzzy programs together with its generalizations are very special cases of the fuzzy programs defined in the previous section, and hence are very restrictive.

Definition A generalized machine is a 6-tuple $A = (K, S, \Psi, s_0, T, W)$ where K and S are finite nonempty sets, W is an ordered semiring, Ψ is a W-function from $K \times S$ into S, $s_0 \in S$ and $T \subseteq S$.

In the above definition, K is the set of machine instructions, S is the set of internal states, W is a weight space, Ψ is the state-transition function, s_0 is the initial state, and T is the set of final states. In the definition of generalized machine given in [11], W is assumed to be a lattice ordered semigroup. It is clear that every lattice ordered semigroup with identity is an ordered semiring. Since all lattice ordered semigroups which are of interest in the theory of fuzzy programs have identity, therefore the above definition of generalized machines is a generalization of the corresponding concept defined in [11]. This generalization enables us to consider the probabilistic case by taking $W = W_W$ and imposing certain constraints on Ψ. (Observe that it is impossible to obtain the probabilistic case from the definition given in [11] with W being a lattice ordered semigroup.)

Notation Let C be a nonempty set. C^* is the free semigroup generated by C with identity e. If $\mu \in C^*$, then $\lg(\mu)$ will denote the length on μ.

Definition Let $A = (K, S, \Psi, s_0, T, W)$ be a generalized machine. The W-function Ψ will be extended to a W-function from $K^* \times S$ into S as follows by induction on $\lg(\bar{\mu})$, $\bar{\mu} \in K^*$:

$$\Psi(s'' | e, s') = \begin{cases} 1 & \text{if } s' = s'' \\ 0 & \text{if } s' \neq s'' \end{cases}$$

and

$$\Psi(s'' | \mu\mu_0, s') = \sum \left\{ \Psi(s'' | \mu, s) \otimes \Psi(s' | \mu_0, s) : s \in S \right\}$$

where $s', s'' \in S$, $\bar{\mu} \in K^*$ and $\mu_0 \in K$.

In [11], the extension of Ψ is done by using the operation $\vee$ of a lattice instead of the sum Σ defined above. The former method of definition rules out probabilistic machines as a type of generalized machines.

Definition A generalized fuzzy machine is an ordered pair (A, Σ) where $A = (K, S, \Psi, s_0, T, W)$ is a generalized machine and Σ is a finite set of fuzzy instructions and each fuzzy instruction $\sigma \in \Sigma$ is a W-function from S into K.

In the definition of generalized fuzzy machines given in [11], the generalized fuzzy machine may have a weight space different from the weight space of its generalized machine. Although this is mathematically possible, it is rather unnatural as we shall see in the sequel. For this reason, we shall consider only generalized fuzzy machines whose weight space is the same as the weight space of its generalized machines.

Definition Let (A, Σ) be a generalized fuzzy machine where $A = (K, S, \Psi, s_0, T, W)$. Any element $\bar{\sigma}$ of Σ^* is called an elementary fuzzy program, and any function from Σ^* into W is called a fuzzy program.

In [1, 11], a fuzzy program is defined to be a regular expression over Σ. Clearly, it is a special case of the above definition.

Definition Let (A, Σ) be a generalized fuzzy machine where $A = (K, S, \Psi, s_0, T, W)$ and let $\bar{\sigma} = \sigma_1 \sigma_2 \cdots \sigma_n \in \Sigma^*$ where $\sigma_i \in \Sigma$ for all $i = 1, 2, \ldots, n$. An execution of $\bar{\sigma}$ on A is a sequence

$$s_0, \mu_1, s_1, \mu_2, \ldots, \mu_n, s_n \tag{2}$$

where $s_i \in S$ and $\mu_i \in K$ for all $i = 1, 2, \ldots, n$ and $s_n \in T$. The weight associated with execution (2) is an element $w \in W$ such that $w = w_1 \otimes w_1' \otimes w_2 \otimes w_2' \otimes \cdots \otimes w_n \otimes w_n'$ where for every $i = 1, 2, \ldots, n$, $w_i = \sigma_i(\mu_i | s_{i-1})$ and $w_i' = \Psi(s_i | \mu_i, s_{i-1})$. The execution (2) is feasible if and only if $w \neq 0$. The s_n in expression (2) is called the final state of the execution.

Definition Let (A, Σ) be a generalized fuzzy machine where $A = (K, S, \Psi, s_0, T, W)$. For every $\bar{\sigma} \in \Sigma^*$ and $s \in S$, define $A(s | \bar{\sigma})$ to be ΣW_0 where W_0 is the set of weights associated with some execution of $\bar{\sigma}$ on A with final state s, if $s \in T$, and define $A(s | \bar{\sigma}) = 0$ if $s \notin T$.

Theorem *There exists a W-machine $\mathfrak{M}$ where $X = Y = U^*$ for some set U, such that for every generalized fuzzy machine (A, Σ) where $A = (K, S, \Psi, s_0, T, W)$, $\Sigma \subseteq U$ and $S \subseteq U$, there exists a program π which is admissible on $\mathfrak{M}$ for which $\mathfrak{M}_\pi(s | \bar{\sigma}) = A(s | \bar{\sigma})$ for all $s \in S$ and $\bar{\sigma} \in \Sigma^*$.*

Proof Let $\mathfrak{M}$ be a W-machine with $X = Y = U^*$ for some set U, $M = U^* \times U^*$, $\mathfrak{F} = \{F_0\} \cup \{F_u : u \in U\}$ and $\mathfrak{P} = \{P_u : u \in U\} \cup \mathfrak{P}_0$, where for every $\alpha, \beta, \gamma, \delta \in U^*$, and $k = 1, 2$,

$$\mathfrak{M}_I((\alpha, \beta) | \gamma) = \begin{cases} 1 & \text{if } \alpha = e \text{ and } \beta = \gamma \\ 0 & \text{otherwise} \end{cases}$$

$$\mathfrak{M}_0(\alpha | (\beta, \gamma)) = \begin{cases} 1 & \text{if } \alpha = \beta \\ 0 & \text{otherwise} \end{cases}$$

$$\mathfrak{M}_{F_0}((\alpha, \beta) | (\gamma, \delta)) = \begin{cases} 1 & \text{if } \alpha = \gamma \text{ and } \delta = u\beta \text{ for some } u \in U \\ 0 & \text{otherwise} \end{cases}$$

$$\mathfrak{M}_{F_u}((\alpha, \beta) | (\gamma, \delta)) = \begin{cases} 1 & \text{if } \beta = \delta \text{ and } \alpha = \gamma u \\ 0 & \text{otherwise} \end{cases}$$

$$\mathfrak{M}_{P_u}(k | (\alpha, \beta)) = \begin{cases} 1 & \text{if } k = 1 \text{ and } \beta = u\tau \text{ for some } \tau \in U^* \\ & \text{or } k = 2 \text{ and } \beta \neq u\tau \text{ for all } \tau \in U^* \\ 0 & \text{otherwise} \end{cases}$$

and $\mathscr{P}_0$ is the collection of all unconditional test functions. Observe that $\mathfrak{M}$, except for the unconditional test functions, is essentially the one-way finite automaton defined in [8, 10]. Let $\Sigma = \{\sigma_1, \sigma_2, \ldots, \sigma_n\}$, $K = \{\mu_1, \mu_2, \ldots, \mu_r\}$ and $S = \{s_0, s_1, \ldots, s_t\}$. Define π to be the program consisting of the following instructions

Start: go to $L_0{}^1$

  $L_j{}^i$:   if P_i then go to $(L_j{}^{i0}, L_j{}^{i+1})$

  $L_j{}^{i0}$:   do F_0; go to $L_j{}^{i1}$

  $L_j{}^{i1}$:   if P_j^i then go to $(L_{1j}, L_{2j}, \ldots, L_{rj})$

  $L_{\mathscr{K}j}$:   if $P_{\mathscr{K}j}$ then go to $(L_0{}^1, L_1{}^1, \ldots, L_m{}^1)$

$L_\ell{}^{n+1}$:   do F_{s_ℓ}; go to L

    L: halt

where $i = 1, 2, \ldots, n$; $j = 0, 1, 2, \ldots, t$; $\mathscr{K} = 1, 2, \ldots, r$; $L \in \{\ell : s_\ell \in T\}$; $\mathfrak{M}_{P_i}$ is a W-function from M into $\{1, 2, \ldots, r\}$ such that $\mathfrak{M}_{P_i}(q|m) = \sigma_i(\mu_q|s_j)$ for all $m \in M$ and $q = 1, 2, \ldots, r$; and $\mathfrak{M}_{P_{kj}}$ is a W-function from M into $\{1, 2, \ldots, n+1\}$ such that $\mathfrak{M}_{P_{kj}}(q|m) = \Psi(s_{q-1}|\mu_k, s_j)$ for all $m \in M$ and $q = 1, 2, \ldots, n+1$. Observe that the instruction with label $L_j{}^{i1}$ and L_{kj} simulate, respectively, the action of σ_i and Ψ. Thus, it is easy to verify that $\mathfrak{M}_\pi(s|\bar{\sigma}) = A(s|\bar{\sigma})$ for all $s \in S$ and $\sigma \in \Sigma^*$.

It follows from the above proof that the formulations of Chang [1], Tawaka and Mizumoto [11], etc., are very restrictive since finite automaton has very limited computational capability.

TURING FUZZY ALGORITHMS

A natural way to formalize the concept of fuzzy algorithms is via the concept of Turing fuzzy machines. A brief discussion of Turing fuzzy machines was given in [13] and detail formulation of this concept for the maximin and probabilistic cases can be found in [6] and [7], respectively. In this section, we shall examine the relationship between Turing fuzzy machines and fuzzy programs.

Definition Let W be an ordered semiring. A Turing W-machine is specified by a sextuple $Z = (U, S, V, C, p, s_0)$ where U, S, V, and C are finite nonempty sets, $U \cup V \subseteq C$, $S \cap C = \phi$ (empty set); p is a W-function from $T \times S$ into $S \times (C \cup \{+, -, \cdot\})$, $+, -, \cdot \notin C$; and $s_0 \in S$. Moreover, for every $c \in C$, $p(s', \cdot | c, s) = 0$ for $s \neq s'$.

In the above definition, U, V and C are, respectively, the set of input, output and tape symbols; S is the state set and s_0 is the initial state; $p(s',z|c,s)$ is the weight of the "next act" of the Turing W-machine given that its present state is s and the tape symbol c is scanned. Like the conventional Turing machines [2], the "next act" of the Turing W-machine may be one of the following:

(1) $z \in C^*$:   replace c by z and go to state s'.
(2) $z = +$:   move one square to the right and go to state s'.
(3) $z = -$:   move one square to the left and go to state s'
(4) $z = \cdot$:   stop.

In what follows, if $Z = (U, S, V, C, p, s_0)$ is a Turing W-machine, then we shall assume that $b \in C$ and $b \notin U \cup V$. The symbol b stands for blank.

Definition   Let $Z = (U, S, V, C, p, s_0)$ be a Turing W-machine and $\alpha \in (C \cup S)^*$; α is an instantaneous description of Z if and only if (i) α contains exactly one $s \in S$ and s is not the rightmost symbol of α, (ii) the leftmost symbol of α is not b, and (iii) the rightmost symbol of α is not b unless it is the symbol immediately to the right of s. The collection of all instantaneous descriptions of Z will be denoted by $D(Z)$.

Definition   Let $Z = (U, S, V, C, p, s_0)$ be a Turing W-machine; p^Z is the W-function from $D(Z)$ into $D(Z)$ such that for every $\alpha, \beta \in D(Z)$,

$$
p^Z(\beta\,\alpha) = \begin{cases}
p(s', c'|c,s) & \text{if} \begin{cases} \alpha = \zeta sc\delta,\ \beta = \zeta s'c'\delta,\ c'\delta \neq e \\ \alpha = \zeta sc,\ \beta = \zeta s'b,\ c' = e \end{cases} \\[2em]
p(s', +|c,s) & \text{if} \begin{cases} \alpha = \zeta scc'\delta,\ \beta = \zeta cs'c'\delta,\ \zeta c \neq b \\ \alpha = scc'\delta,\ \beta = s'c'\delta,\ c = b \\ \alpha = \zeta sc,\ \beta = \zeta cs'b,\ \zeta c \neq b \\ \alpha = sc,\ \beta = s'b,\ c = b \end{cases} \\[3em]
p(s', -|c,s) & \text{if} \begin{cases} \alpha = \zeta c'sc\delta,\ \beta = \zeta s'c'c\delta,\ c\delta \neq b \\ \alpha = \zeta c'sc,\ \beta = \zeta s'c',\ c = b \\ \alpha = sc\delta,\ \beta = s'bc\delta,\ c\delta \neq b \\ \alpha = sc,\ \beta = s'b,\ c = b \end{cases} \\[3em]
0 & \text{otherwise}
\end{cases}
$$

where $\zeta, \delta \in C^*$, $s, s' \in S$, $c, c' \in C$ and $z \in C$.

Definition Let $Z = (U, S, V, C, p, s_0)$ be a Turing W-machine. A computation of Z with input $x \in U^*$ and output $y \in V^*$ is a finite sequence

$$\alpha_0, \alpha_1, \alpha_2, \ldots, \alpha_n \tag{3}$$

of elements of $D(Z)$ where $\alpha_0 = s_0 x$ and $\alpha_n = \beta s \gamma$ where $\beta \gamma = y$, $s \in S$. The weight associated with computation (3) is

$$\omega = p^Z(\alpha_1 | \alpha_0) \otimes p^Z(\alpha_2 | \alpha_1) \otimes \cdots \otimes p^Z(\alpha_n | \alpha_{n-1}) \otimes p(s, \cdot | c, s)$$

where c is the symbol contained in α_n which is immediately to the right of s,

Definition Let $Z = (U, S, V, C, p, s_0)$ be a Turing W-machine. For every $x \in U^*$ and $y \in V^*$, define $Z(y | x)$ to be ΣW_0, if it exists, where W_0 is the set of weights associated with some computation of Z with input x and output y.

We shall refer to the Turing W-machine where W is W_W, W_X, W_I, W_T or W_N as Turing weighted machines, Turing maximin machines, Turing minimax machines, Turing max-product machines, or Turing nondeterministic machines, respectively. In addition, a Turing weighted machine in which p is probabilistic will be referred to as a Turing probabilistic machine, and any Turing W-machine in which p is deterministic will be referred to as a Turing deterministic machine.

It is clear that Turing deterministic machines behave in exactly the same manner as conventional Turing machines [2]. Moreover, despite the differences in definitions, the behavior of Turing maximin machines and Turing probabilistic machines are essentially the same as Turing fuzzy algorithms [6] and simple probabilistic Turing machines [7].

Theorem *There exists a W-machine with $X \subseteq \Sigma^*$ and $Y \subseteq \Sigma^*$ for some set Σ such that for every Turing W-machine $Z = (U, S, V, C, p, s_0)$ with $C \subseteq \Sigma$, there exists a program π which is admissible on $\mathfrak{M}$ with the property that for every $x \in U^*$ and $y \in U^*$, $\mathfrak{M}_\pi(y | x)$ and $Z(y | x)$ are either both defined or both undefined, and if both are defined, then $\mathfrak{M}_\pi(y | x) = Z(y | x)$.*

Proof Let $\mathfrak{M}$ be a W-machine with $M = (\Sigma \cup \{\uparrow\})^*$, $\uparrow$ is a pointer which does not belong to Σ, $X \subseteq \Sigma$, $Y \subseteq \Sigma$, $\mathfrak{F} = \{MR, ML\} \cup \{F_a : a \in \Sigma\}$ and $\mathfrak{P} = \{P_a : a \in \Sigma\} \cup \mathfrak{P}_0$, where for every $x \in X$, $y \in Y$, $a \in \Sigma$, $\alpha, \beta \in M$ and

$k = 1, 2,$

$$\mathfrak{M}_I(\alpha|x) = \begin{cases} 1 & \text{if } \alpha = \uparrow x \\ 0 & \text{otherwise} \end{cases}$$

$$\mathfrak{M}_O(y|\alpha) = \begin{cases} 1 & \text{if } y \text{ is obtained from } \alpha \text{ by omitting } \uparrow \\ 0 & \text{otherwise} \end{cases}$$

$$\mathfrak{M}_{F_a}(\beta|\alpha) = \begin{cases} 1 & \text{if } \alpha = \gamma\uparrow c\delta, \beta = \gamma\uparrow a\delta \text{ for some } \gamma, \delta \in \Sigma^* \text{ and } c \in \Sigma \\ 0 & \text{otherwise} \end{cases}$$

$$\mathfrak{M}_{MR}(\beta|\alpha) = \begin{cases} 1 & \text{if } \alpha = \gamma\uparrow c\delta, \beta = \gamma c\uparrow\delta \text{ for some } \gamma, \delta \in \Sigma^* \text{ and } c \in \Sigma \\ 0 & \text{otherwise} \end{cases}$$

$$\mathfrak{M}_{ML}(\beta|\alpha) = \begin{cases} 1 & \text{if } \alpha = \gamma c\uparrow c'\delta, \beta = \gamma\uparrow cc'\delta \text{ for some } \gamma, \delta \in \Sigma^* \text{ and} \\ 0 & \text{otherwise} \end{cases}$$

$$\mathfrak{M}_{P_a}(k|\alpha) = \begin{cases} 1 & \text{if } k = 1 \text{ and } \alpha = \gamma\uparrow a\delta \text{ for some } \gamma, \delta \in \Sigma^* \\ & \text{or } k = 2 \text{ and } \alpha \neq \gamma\uparrow a\delta \text{ for all } \gamma, \delta \in \Sigma^* \\ 0 & \text{otherwise} \end{cases}$$

and $\mathfrak{P}_0$ is the collection of all unconditional test functions. Observe that $\mathfrak{M}$, except for the unconditional test functions, behaves essentially in the same manner as the Turing machine defined in [10]. Let $S = \{s_0, s_1, \ldots, s_n\}$, $C = \{c_1, c_2, \ldots, c_m\}$, $c_{m+1} = +$, $c_{m+2} = -$, and $c_{m+3} = \cdot$. Define π to be the program consisting of the following instructions:

Start: go to L_{01}

L_{ij}: if P_{c_j} then go to $(L_{i0}{}^j, L_{i,j+1})$

$L_{i0}{}^j$: if $P_i{}^j$ then go to
$(L0^1, L_0{}^2, \ldots, L_0{}^{m+3}, L1^1, L_1{}^2, \ldots, L_1{}^{m+3}, \ldots, L_n{}^1, L_n{}^2, \ldots, L_n{}^{m+3})$

$L_i{}^4$: do F_{c_j}; go to L_{i1}

$L_i{}^{m+1}$: do F_{MR}; go to L_{i1}

$L_i{}^{m+2}$: do F_{ML}; go to L_{i1}

$L_i{}^{m+3}$: halt

where $i = 0, 1, 2, \ldots, n$; $j = 1, 2, \ldots, m$; and $\mathfrak{M}_{Pj}$ is a W-function from M into $\{1, 2, \ldots, (n+1)(m+3)\}$ such that

$$\mathfrak{M}_{Pj}(\mathcal{Q}|\alpha) = \begin{cases} p(s_k, c_\ell|c_j, s_i) & \begin{cases} \text{if } \alpha = \gamma\uparrow c_j\delta, \mathcal{Q} = \ell + k(m+3), \\ k = 0, 1, 2, \ldots, n, \text{ and } \ell = 1, 2, \ldots, m+3 \end{cases} \\ 0 & \text{otherwise} \end{cases}$$

It is easy to verify that $\mathfrak{M}$ and π have the desired properties.

Definition   Let f be a W-function from X into Y. f is computable if and only if there exists a Turing W-machine $Z = (U, S, V, C, p, s_0)$ such that $X = U^*$, $Y = V^*$ and $f(y|x) = Z(y|x)$ for all $x \in X$ and $y \in Y$. In this case, we say that f is computable by Z or Z computes f.

Definition   A W-machine $\mathfrak{M}$ is computable if and only if the input, operation, test and output functions are all computable.

Observe that if $\mathfrak{M}$ is computable, then the sets X, Y and M are at most countable. Moreover, it is easy to construct a Turing W-machine to simulate the computations of a program which is admissible on a computable W-machine. More precisely, we have the following theorem.

Theorem   *Let $\mathfrak{M}$ be a computable W-machine with input set X and output set Y, and π a program admissible on $\mathfrak{M}$. There exists a Turing W-machine $Z = (U, S, V, C, p, s_0)$ such that $X = U^*$, $Y = V^*$ and for every $x \in X$ and $y \in Y$, $\mathfrak{M}_\pi(y|x)$ and $Z(y|x)$ are either both defined or both undefined, and if both are defined, then $\mathfrak{M}_\pi(y|x) = Z(y|x)$.*

EXAMPLE OF FUZZY PROGRAMS

Several examples of fuzzy programs were given in [1, 11]. In order to illustrate how to fit these examples into the formulation given in the first section, we shall discuss briefly in this section one of these examples.

In this example, a sequence of driving instructions and a map is given. A driver is supposed to use this information to find his destination. For simplicity, we shall assume that the map is digitized and hence it could be represented by a set of points on the plane whose coordinates are integers, where each point in the set represents a point on the road. Typical driving instructions include "go straight about n unit distances", "turn left", "turn right", "go straight until the nth landmark", etc., where the "landmark" could be a street light, a gasoline station, etc.

In order to fit the above problem into the formulation given in the first section, we will have to construct an appropriate W-machine $\mathfrak{M}$. The W-machine $\mathfrak{M}$ has memory set M consisting of triples (a, b, v) where (a, b) is a point on the plane with integral coordinates which represents the location of the car, and v is a unit vector which represents the direction in which the car is headed. The input set $X = M$ and the output set Y consists of ordered pairs (a, b) where a and b are integers. The input function $\mathfrak{M}_I$ corresponds to the identity function and the output function $\mathfrak{M}_O$ corresponds to the function which maps every (a, b, v) into (a, b). Moreover, $\mathfrak{M}$ does not have any test functions but has several operation functions, one for each type of driving instructions. Using these operation functions, the ith driving instruction in a sequence of driving instructions can be translated into an operation instruction of the form L_{i-1}: do F_i; go to L_i. The collection of all such operation instructions together with the instructions "Start: go to L_0" and "L_n: halt", where n is the length of the sequence, forms a program π. The computation by π on $\mathfrak{M}$ behaves in a manner specified by the sequence of driving instructions and the map.

It remains to show how to construct the corresponding operation function for each driving instruction. For simplicity, we shall consider only the driving instruction "go straight about n unit distances." The corresponding operation function $\mathfrak{M}_{F_n}$ may be defined as follows

$$\mathfrak{M}_{F_n}((a_2,b_2,v_2)|(a_1,b_1,v_1)) = f_n\left(\sqrt{(a_2-a_1)^2+(b_2-b_1)^2}\right)$$
$$\times G\left((a_2,b_2,v_2)|(a_1,b_1,v_1)\right)$$

where $f_n(d)$ is the weight associated with the distance d and $G_n((a_2,b_2,v_2)|(a_1,b_1,v_1))$ is the weight associated with the statement "the location (a_2,b_2) and the direction v_2" can be attained by going "straight from the location (a_1,b_1) and headed in the v_1 direction." Typical examples of f_n and G_n for the maximin case are

$$f_n(d) = \frac{1}{1+\left(\dfrac{n-d}{c}\right)^2}$$

where c is a parameter, and G is a deterministic function where $G_n((a_2,b_2,v_2)(a_1,b_1,v_1)) = 1$ if and only if $v_1 = v_2$, the vector from (a_1,b_1) to (a_2,b_2) is parallel to v_1, and every point on the line segment joining (a_1,b_1) and (a_2,b_2) having integral coordinates is a point on the map. Observe that the function f_n depends only on n while G depends only on the map. Operation functions of other driving instructions can be constructed in a similar manner.

For practical purposes, the fuzzy program $(\pi,\mathfrak{M})$ obtained above is applicable only to a given input (a,b,v) where (a,b) and v denotes the original location and direction of the car. However, theoretically, $(\pi,\mathfrak{M})$ may accept any input from the input set S, and $\mathfrak{M}_\pi((a_2,b_2)|(a_1,b_1,v))$ gives the weight that the car will arrive at location (a_2,b_2) given that its original location and direction are (a_1,b_1) and v, respectively.

REFERENCES

1. S.K. Chang, "On the Execution of Fuzzy Programs using Finite-State Machines," *IEEE Trans. Computer* **21** (1972), 241–253.

2. M. Davis, *Computability and Unsolvability*. McGraw-Hill, New York, 1958.
3. R.W. Floyd, "Nondeterministic Algorithms," *J. Assoc. Comput. Mach.* **14** (1967), 636–644.
4. R. Jakwbowski and A. Kasprzak, "Application of Fuzzy Programs to the Design of Matching Technology," *Bull. L'Acad. Pol. Sci.* **11** (1973).
5. E.S. Santos, "Maximin Sequential-Like Machines and Chains," *Math. Systems Theory* **3** (1969), 300–309.
6. E.S. Santos, "Fuzzy Algorithms," *Inform. Control* **17** (1970), 326–339.
7. E.S. Santos, "Computability by Probabilistic Turing Machines," *Trans. Am. Math. Soc.* **159** (1971), 165–184.
8. E.S. Santos, "Machines, Programs, and Languages, *J. Cybernetics* (to appear).
9. E.S. Santos, "Finite Automata over a Semiring." Computer Science Conf., Detroit, Michigan.
10. D. Scott, "Some Definitional Suggestions for Automata Theory, *J. Comp. Sys. Theory* **1** (1967), 187–212.
11. K. Tanaka and M. Mizumoto, "Fuzzy Programs and Their Executions," *Proc. U.S.–Japan Sem. on Fuzzy Sets and Their Appl.* (to appear).
12. L.A. Zadeh, "Fuzzy Sets," *Infor. Control* **8** (1965), 338–353.
13. L.A. Zadeh, "Fuzzy Algorithms," *Infor. Control* **12** (1968), 94–102.
14. M. Zohar, "Program Schemas," *Currents in the Theory of Computing* (A. H. Aho, Ed.). Prentice-Hall, N.J., 1973, 90–142.

F-RECOGNITION OF FUZZY LANGUAGES 9

Namio Honda, Masakazu Nasu and Sadaki Hirose

Recently the concept of *f*-recognition of fuzzy languages by machines was proposed in [3]. This paper is an extended version of [3] and includes the content of [3] in a revised form. In addition, it gives an application of the theory of *f*-recognition to the theory of probabilistic automata and discusses the closure properties of some fuzzy language classes corresponding to machine classes.

In the formal language theory, languages are classified by the complexities of machines that recognize them. The most typical ones of such machines are finite automata, push-down automata, linear bounded automata and Turing machines. As for fuzzy languages, it is also interesting to develop the theory of recognition of fuzzy languages by machines and their classification by the complexities of machines that recognize them. Of course, the theory should be a reasonable extension of the ordinary language recognition theory. In the ordinary language recognition theory, a machine is said to recognize a language L if and only if for every word in L the machine decides that it is a member of L, and for any word not in L, the machine either decides that it is not a member of L or loops forever. In other words, a machine may be said to recognize a language if and only if the machine computes the characteristic function of the language. So it is natural to define a machine to recognize a fuzzy language if and only if the machine computes its fuzzy membership function. But what does it mean that a machine computes a fuzzy membership function? In the ordinary language theory, it is defined that for a given input word a machine computes the characteristic function value at 1, if and only if it takes one of special memory-configurations, such as configurations with a final state and configurations with the empty stack for cases where the machine has pushdown stacks. Therefore it is a straightforward extension to define each fuzzy membership function value (which is an element of some lattice) to be represented by some memory configuration of the machine. That is to

The authors wish to thank the members of their research group for their helpful discussions.

say, we require that the memory configuration which the machine moves into after a sequence of moves for a given input word should be uniquely associated with the membership function value of the word.

However, even though the machine has obtained a configuration uniquely associated with the membership function value of the word, can we say that the machine has computed the membership function value of the word? How can we assure that the machine certainly knows the value? We think that for the machine to know the value is to be able to answer exactly any question about the value. Furthermore, we consider that it is essential that the values represented by memory configurations of the machine are lattice elements. Thus, we require that the machine should potentially be able to compare the fuzzy membership function value of a given word, which is stored in its memory, with any lattice element when the latter is given to the machine as a question. A lattice element which is given to the machine as a question will be called a cutpoint. It is reasonable to assume that a cutpoint will be represented by an infinite sequence of symbols in a finite alphabet, following the infinite expansions of decimals. We require that for any cutpoint λ the machine having the memory configuration associated with the fuzzy membership function value $f(w)$ of a given input word w should be able to read, as a subsequent input, the infinite sequence corresponding to the cutpoint λ sequentially, and after a finite step of deterministic moves, it can determine which of the following four cases is valid, (i) $f(w) > \lambda$, (ii) $f(w) < \lambda$, (iii) $f(w) = \lambda$, and (iv) $f(w)$ and λ are incomparable.

In this paper, a first step will be given toward the fuzzy language recognition theory on the line stated above.

FUZZY LANGUAGES

Let Σ be a finite set of symbols called an alphabet. The set of all strings of symbols in Σ including the null string ϵ will be denoted by Σ^*. An element of Σ^* will be called a word over Σ. A subset of Σ^* will be called a language over Σ. Let L be a lattice with minimum element 0. An L-fuzzy language over Σ is defined to be a mapping from Σ^* to L (following Goguen [2]). The symbol L will be often omitted if we are not confused. Let f be an L-fuzzy language over Σ, then $f(x)$ for x in Σ^* represents the grade for x to be a member of the fuzzy language.

CUTPOINTS AND THEIR REPRESENTATION

Let L be a lattice with minimum element 0. Usually a value in L is specified and is used as a cutpoint. It is interesting to consider languages associated with an L-fuzzy language f and a cutpoint λ such as

$$L_G(f,\lambda) = \{x \in \Sigma^* | f(x) > \lambda\}$$

$$L_{GE}(f,\lambda) = \{x \in \Sigma^* | f(x) \geqslant \lambda\}$$

Such languages will be called cutpoint languages for f and λ.

Let Δ be a finite alphabet. Let Δ^∞ be the set of all infinite sequences of symbols in Δ extending infinitely to the right. We will define a representation of L over Δ. A one-to-one mapping r from L to Δ^∞ is a representation of L over Δ if there exists a mapping d which assigns to any distinct two elements $r(l)$ and $r(m)$ in $r(L)$ a positive integer $d(r(l),r(m))$ $(= d(r(m),r(l)))$ so that the following (i) and (ii) are satisfied.

(i) Let $l \neq m$ for $l,m \in L$. Then for the prefix w_l of $r(l)$ and the prefix w_m of $r(m)$ of length $d(r(l),r(m))$, respectively, and for any $\alpha',\beta' \in \Delta^\infty$, either following (a) or (b) holds:

    (a)   Either $w_l\alpha'$ or $w_m\beta'$ is not in $r(L)$.
    (b)   Both $w_l\alpha'$ and $w_m\beta'$ are in $r(L)$, and

$$r^{-1}(w_l\alpha') > r^{-1}(w_m\beta') \qquad \text{if } l > m$$

$$r^{-1}(w_l\alpha') < r^{-1}(w_m\beta') \qquad \text{if } l < m$$

and $r^{-1}(w_l\alpha')$ and $r^{-1}(w_m\beta')$ are incomparable if l and m are incomparable, where $r^{-1}(\alpha)$ denotes the element in L such that $r(r^{-1}(\alpha)) = \alpha$ for $\alpha \in r(L)$.

(ii) For any l, m and n in L with $l > m > n$, $d(r(l),r(n)) \leqslant \min\{d(r(l),r(m)), d(r(m),r(n))\}$.

For $\alpha,\beta \in r(L)$, $d(\alpha,\beta)$ is called the D-length of α and β. We will say that for $l \in L$, $r(l)$ is the representation of l with respect to r. A lattice cannot always have its representation. We will consider from now on only lattices that can have a representation over some finite alphabet. Condition (ii) means that representations of lattices are restricted to the type of one such as decimal expansions of real numbers. However, there may be many representations for a lattice.

Example Let L be a lattice with finite elements. If L has elements $l_1,\ldots,l_k$, let $\Delta = \{l_1,\ldots,l_k\}$ and $r(l_i) = l_i l_i l_i \ldots$ for $1 \leqslant i \leqslant k$, then r is a representation of L over Δ.

Example Let $L_{[0,1]}$ be the set of all real numbers in $[0,1]$ with the ordinary ordering. A representation r_1 is given as follows: $\Delta = \{0,1,\dot{0},\dot{1}\}$. Let $e(l)$ for

$l \in L_{[0,1]}$ be the binary expansion of l not of the form $w111\ldots$ with $w \in \{0,1\}^*0$. For any rational number l in $[0,1]$, we set $e(l) = w_0 w_1 w_1 w_1 \ldots$ such that if $e(l) = w_0' w_1' w_1' w_1' \ldots$, then $|w_0| \leqslant |w_0'|^\dagger$ and $|w_1| \leqslant |w_1'|$. Let $\dot{e}(l) = w_0 \dot{w}_1 w_1 w_1 \ldots$ where $\dot{w}_1 = \dot{a}_1 \dot{a}_2 \ldots \dot{a}_k$ for $w_1 = a_1 a_2 \ldots a_k$ with $a_i \in \{0,1\}$ $(1 \leqslant i \leqslant d)$.

$$r_1(l) = e(l) \qquad \text{if } l \text{ is irrational}$$

$$r_1(l) = \dot{e}(l) \qquad \text{if } l \text{ is rational}$$

Example Let $L_{[0,1]_R}$ be the set of all rational numbers in $[0,1]$ with the usual ordering. A representation r_2: $L_{[0,1]_R} \to \Delta^\infty$ is defined as follows: $\Delta = \{0,1,\dot{0},\dot{1}\}$. $r_2(0) = \dot{0}\dot{0}\dot{0}\ldots$, $r_2(1) = \dot{1}\dot{1}\dot{1}\ldots$, for l such that $e(l) = w000\ldots$ with $w \in \{0,1\}^*1$, $r_2(l) = w\dot{0}\dot{0}\dot{0}\ldots$ and for other l in $L_{[0,1]_R}$, $r_2(l) = e(l)$.

F-RECOGNITIONS BY MACHINES

Machines treated hereafter may be finite automata, pushdown automata, linear bounded automata and Turing machines, which can generally be represented for convenience as follows:

A machine has an input terminal that reads input symbols and ϵ sequentially, a memory storing and processing device and an output terminal. Formally, a machine is given by 8-tuple $M = \langle \Phi, \Gamma, \Psi, \theta, \delta, \Omega, \kappa, \gamma_0 \rangle$ where

Φ : a finite set of input symbols
Γ : a finite set of memory-configuration symbols
Ψ : a finite set of output symbols
Ω : a finite set of partial function $\{\omega_i\}$ from Γ^* to Γ^*
θ : a partial function from Γ^* to Γ^n, for some $n \geqslant 1$

(For a memory configuration $\gamma \in \Gamma^*$, $\theta(\gamma)$ designates the instantaneously accessible information of γ by M.)

δ : a partial function from $(\Phi \cup \{\epsilon\}) \times \Gamma^n$ to 2^Ω
κ : a partial function from Γ^n to $\Psi \cup \{\epsilon\}$
γ_0 : an element in Γ^* (called the initial memory configuration)

A memory configuration ξ is said to be derived from a memory configuration γ by $\sigma \in \Phi \cup \{\epsilon\}$ and is denoted by $\gamma \Rightarrow^\sigma \xi$, if and only if there exists $\rho = \theta(\gamma)$ and $\omega_i \in \delta(\sigma, \rho)$ such that $\omega_i(\gamma) = \xi$. For a word $w \in \Phi^*$, a memory

---

$\dagger |w|$ represents the length of a word w.

configuration ξ is said to be derived from a memory configuration γ by w and is denoted by $\gamma \underset{w}{\Rightarrow} \xi$ if and only if there exist $\sigma_1, \sigma_2, \ldots, \sigma_l$ with σ_i in $\Phi \cup \{\epsilon\}$ such that $w = \sigma_1 \sigma_2 \ldots \sigma_l$, and there exist $\gamma_0, \gamma_1, \ldots, \gamma_l$ with $\gamma_i \in \Gamma^*$ such that $\gamma_0 = \gamma$, $\gamma_l = \xi$ and $\gamma_i \underset{\sigma_{i+1}}{\Rightarrow} \gamma_{i+1}$ for all $0 \leqslant i \leqslant l - 1$. ($\gamma \underset{\epsilon}{\Rightarrow} \gamma$ is valid for all $\gamma \in \Gamma^*$.) Given an input word $w \in \Phi^*$ and having the initial memory configuration γ_0 first, M reads input symbols or ϵ sequentially along w, changes step by step memory configurations possibly in a nondeterministic way and reaches into γ such that $\gamma_0 \underset{w}{\Rightarrow} \gamma$, emitting output $\kappa(\theta(\gamma))$.

Obviously a machine $M = \langle \Phi, \Gamma, \Psi, \theta, \delta, \Omega, \kappa, \gamma_0 \rangle$ can be restricted to a specified family of automata such as Turing machines, pushdown automata, finite automata for appropriate choices of $\Gamma, \theta, \delta, \Omega, \kappa$, and γ_0.

Furthermore, we will define a deterministic machine. A machine $M = \langle \Phi, \Gamma, \Psi, \theta, \delta, \Omega, \kappa, \gamma_0 \rangle$ will be called a deterministic machine if for any memory configuration γ such that $\gamma_0 \underset{x}{\Rightarrow} \gamma$ for some x in Φ^*, if $\delta(\epsilon, \theta(\gamma)) \neq \phi$, then $\delta(\epsilon, \theta(\gamma))$ contains at most one element and $\delta(\sigma, \theta(\gamma)) = \phi$ for any $\sigma \in \Phi$, and if $\delta(\epsilon, \theta(\gamma)) = \phi$, then for any $\sigma \in \Phi$, $\delta(\sigma, \theta(\gamma))$ contains at most one element.

Now we will define recognition of a fuzzy language by a machine. Let L be a lattice with a minimum element 0 and $f: \Sigma^* \to L$ be a fuzzy language over an alphabet Σ. Let r be a representation of L over an alphabet Δ. A machine $M = \langle \Phi, \Gamma, \Psi, \theta, \delta, \Omega, \kappa, \gamma_0 \rangle$ is said to f-recognize f with r if and only if the following conditions hold

(1) $\Phi = \Sigma \cup \Delta \cup \{c\}$, where c is an element not in $\Sigma \cup \Delta$

(2) $\Psi = \{ >, <, =, ! \}$

(3) There exists a partial function ν from Γ^* to L which satisfies the following conditions (i)–(iv):

    (i) Let $S_x = \{ \gamma | \gamma_0 \underset{xc}{\Rightarrow} \gamma \}$ for all $x \in \Sigma^*$. Then for all $x \in \Sigma^*$ such that $S_x \neq \phi$, $S_x \subset \mathrm{dom}\, \nu$[1] and $\nu_x = \max\{ \nu(\gamma) | \gamma \in S_x \}$ exists. If $S_x = \phi$, ν_x is undefined.

    (ii) Let γ be any memory configuration in S_x. Let a machine M_γ be $\langle \Delta, \Gamma, \Psi, \theta, \delta', \Omega, \kappa, \gamma \rangle$, where δ' is the restriction of δ over $(\Delta \cup \{\epsilon\}) \times \Gamma^n$. Then M_γ is a deterministic machine.

    (iii) For any memory configuration $\gamma \in \Gamma^*$, if $\kappa(\theta(\gamma))$ is in Ψ, that is, $\kappa(\theta(\gamma)) \neq \epsilon$, then for any $\sigma \in \Phi \cup \{\epsilon\}$, $\delta(\sigma, \theta(\gamma))$ is empty. And $\kappa(\theta(\gamma))$ is in Ψ only if $\gamma_0 \underset{xcy}{\Rightarrow} \gamma$ for some $x \in \Sigma^*$ and y in $\mathrm{PRE}\gamma(L)$.[2]

---

[1] $\mathrm{dom}\, \nu = \{ \gamma \in \Gamma^* | \nu(\gamma)$ is defined$\}$.

[2] w_1 will be called a prefix of a word or an infinite sequence α if $\alpha = w_1 \beta$ for some β. Let Π be either a set of words or a set of infinite sequences. PRE Π is the set of all prefixes of elements in Π.

(iv) Let γ be any element in dom ν. For any $l \in L$, there exists a prefix v of $r(l)$ and γ' in Γ such that

$$\gamma \underset{v}{\Rightarrow} \gamma'$$

and the following hold

$\kappa(\theta(\gamma'))$ is $>$, if $\nu(\gamma) > l$,
$\kappa(\theta(\gamma'))$ is $=$, if $\nu(\gamma) = l$,
$\kappa(\theta(\gamma'))$ is $<$, if $\nu(\gamma) < l$,
$\kappa(\theta(\gamma'))$ is!, if $\nu(\gamma)$ and l are incomparable.

Given an input sequence xc in Σ^*c where c indicates the end of the input sequence, a machine M moves possibly nondeterministically into some memory configuration γ such that $\nu(\gamma)$ is defined. S_x is the set of all such γ's. We consider the maximum value ν_x of $\{\nu(\gamma)|\gamma \in S_x\}$ as the value of x computed by M. If $S_x = \phi$, we consider that the value of x cannot be computed by M. A sequence of moves from the initial memory configuration to a memory configuration in S_x is called a value computation for x.

When the machine M completes the value computation for $x \in \Sigma^*$, that is, when M has a configuration $\gamma \in S_x$, M is required to have the following potential ability. Let γ be any memory configuration in S_x. Then M_γ should be able to compare $\nu(\gamma)$ with any element l in L if the representation $r(l)$ of l is given to M_γ as a question. That is, when $r(l)$ is given to M_γ, M_γ moves deterministically reading input symbols in $\{\epsilon\} \cup \Delta$ along the infinite sequence $r(l)$ and emits one of $>$, $<$, $=$ and ! following the order of $\nu(\gamma)$ and l in L after reading a finite length of prefix of $r(l)$, and halts (see (iv)). A sequence of moves of M from $\gamma \in \text{dom} \nu$ to a halting configuration is called an order-comparing computation for γ.

If a fuzzy language $f: \Sigma^* \to L$ is the function such that

$$f(x) = \nu_x \qquad \text{if } \nu_x \text{ is defined}$$
$$f(x) = 0 \qquad \text{otherwise}$$

then f is said to be f-recognized by the machine M with the representation r.

Note that, by the condition (iii), if M reads a word in Δ^* which is not any prefix of $r(l)$ for any $l \in L$, M does not emit any of $>$, $<$, $=$ and !. That is, if M is given an illegal question, M does not answer.

Let T_0, T_1, T_2 and T_3 be the classes of Turing machines, linear bounded automata, pushdown automata and finite automata, respectively. Let DT_0, DT_1, DT_2 and DT_3 be the classes of deterministic Turing machines, deterministic linear bounded automata, deterministic pushdown automata and deterministic finite automata, respectively. A fuzzy language f is said to be f-recognized by a machine in $T_i(DT_i)$ if and only if f is f-recognized by a machine in $T_i(DT_i)$ with some representation r, for $i = 0, 2$ and 3. And we will say that a fuzzy language $f: \Sigma^* \to L$ is f-recognized by a (deterministic) linear bounded automaton if and only if f is f-recognized by a (deterministic) Turing machine M with some representation r as follows: For any $x \in \Sigma^*$ and $l \in L$, if

$$\gamma_0 \underset{y_1}{\Rightarrow} \gamma$$

for some prefix y_1 of xc, or

$$\gamma_0 \underset{xcy}{\Rightarrow} \gamma$$

for some y in $\text{PRE}\,\gamma(L)$, then $|\gamma| \leqslant c|x|$ for some constant c, where γ_0 is the initial configuration of M. (This means that length of memory configurations in M for any $x \in \Sigma^*$ are always not greater than some constant time of $|x|$ throughout the value computation and the order-comparing computation of x with any cutpoint in L.)

Example Let $\Sigma = \{a,b\}$. For $w \in \Sigma^*$, let $n_a(w)$ and $n_b(w)$ be the numbers of occurrences of a and b in w respectively. A fuzzy language

$$f_1 : \Sigma^* \to L_{[0,1]_R}$$

defined by

$$f_1(w) = \frac{1}{2} + \left(\frac{1}{2}\right)^{|n_a(w) - n_b(w)| + 1} \qquad (w \in \Sigma^*)$$

is f-recognized by a deterministic pushdown automaton.

A pushdown automaton $M = \langle \Phi, \Gamma, \Psi, \theta, \delta, \Omega, \kappa, \sigma_0 \rangle$ with γ_2 in the previous example f-recognizes f_1, where $\Phi = \Sigma \cup \Delta \cup \{c\}$ with $\Sigma = \{a,b\}$ and $\Delta = \{0, 1, \dot{0}, \dot{1}\}$, $\Gamma = Q \cup \{z_0, a, b, 1\}$ where $Q = \{q_0, q_1, q_>, q_<, q_=\}$, $\Psi = \{>, <, =\}$, θ is a partial function from $\Gamma^* \to \Gamma^2$ such that $\theta(qx\sigma) = (q, \sigma)$ for all $q \in Q$, $x \in \{\epsilon\} \cup z_0\{ab\}^*$ and $\sigma \in \{z_0, a, b, 1, \dot{1}\}$,

$$\Omega = \{\omega_{1a}, \omega_{1b}, \omega_a, \omega_b, \omega_-, \omega_1, \omega_i, \omega_>, \omega_<, \omega_=\}$$

where

$$\gamma_0 = q_0 z_0$$

$$\omega_{1a}(x) = x1\sigma, \qquad \text{for } x \in \Gamma^* \text{ and } \sigma \in \{a,b\}$$

$$\omega_\sigma(x) = x\sigma, \qquad \text{for } x \in \Gamma^* \text{ and } \sigma \in \{a,b\}$$

$$\omega_-(x\sigma) = x, \qquad \text{for } x \in \Gamma^* \text{ and } \sigma \in \Gamma$$

$$\omega_1(q_0 1 x\sigma) = q_0 1 x 1, \qquad \text{for } \sigma \in \{a,b\}$$

$$\omega_i(q_0 z_0) = \omega_i(q_0 z_0 1) = q_1 z_0 \dot{1}$$

$$\omega_>(q_1 x) = q_> x$$

$$\omega_<(q_1 x) = q_< x$$

$$\omega_=(q_1 x) = q_= x, \qquad \text{for } x \in \Gamma^*$$

$\delta : \Phi \times \Gamma^2 \to 2^\Omega$ is defined as follows

$$\delta\left(c, (q_0, z_0)\right) = \{\omega_{\dot{\imath}}\}$$

$$\delta\left(\sigma, (q_0, z_0)\right) = \{\omega_{1\sigma}\}, \qquad \text{for } \sigma \in \{a, b\}$$

$$\delta\left(\sigma, (q_0, \sigma)\right) = \delta\left(\sigma, (q_0, 1)\right) = \{\omega_\sigma\}, \qquad \text{for } \sigma \in \{a, b\}$$

$$\delta\left(a, (q_0, b)\right) = \delta\left(b, (q_0, a)\right) = \{\omega_-\}$$

$$\delta\left(c, (q_0, \sigma)\right) = \{\omega_1\}, \qquad \text{for } \sigma \in \{a, b\}$$

$$\delta\left(c, (q_0, 1)\right) = \{\omega_{\dot{\imath}}\}$$

$$\delta\left(1, (q_1, 1)\right) = \delta\left(0, (q_1, \sigma)\right) = \{\omega_-\}, \qquad \text{for } \sigma \in \{a, b\}$$

$$\delta\left(0, (q_1, 1)\right) = \{\omega_>\}$$

$$\delta\left(1, (q_1, \sigma)\right) = \{\omega_<\}, \qquad \text{for } \sigma \in \{a, b\}$$

$$\delta\left(\dot{0}, (q_1, z_0)\right) = \{\omega_=\}$$

$$\delta\left(\sigma, (q_1, z_0)\right) = \{\omega_<\}, \qquad \text{for } \sigma \in \{0, 1\}$$

$$\delta\left(\sigma, (q_1, \dot{\imath})\right) = \{\omega_>\}, \qquad \text{for } \sigma \in \{0, 1, \dot{0}\}$$

$$\delta\left(\dot{\imath}, (q_1, \dot{\imath})\right) = \{\omega_=\}$$

$\kappa(q_\eta, \sigma) = \eta$ for $\eta \in \Psi$ and $\sigma \in \{z_0, a, b, 1, \dot{\imath}\}$. We set $\nu \colon \Gamma^* \to [0, 1]_R$ defined by

$$\nu\left(q_1 z_0 \dot{\imath}\right) = 1$$

and

$$\nu(q_1 z_0 1 \sigma^n 1) = \frac{1}{2} + \left(\frac{1}{2}\right)^{n+1}, \qquad \text{for } \sigma \in \{a, b\} \text{ and } n \geqslant 1$$

Let $f_1' \colon \Sigma^* \to L_{[0,1]}$ such that $f_1'(w) = f_1(w)$ for $w \in \Sigma^*$. Then it is easily seen that f_1' is f-recognized by a deterministic pushdown automaton with the representation r_1 of an earlier example.

CUTPOINT LANGUAGES

Isolated Cutpoints

Let f be an L-fuzzy language over Σ, where L is a lattice with a minimum element 0. Then $l \in L$ will be called an isolated cutpoint of f if one of the following (i), (ii), and (iii) hold

(i) There exist l_1 and l_2 in L such that $l_1 < l < l_2$ and for any $f(x)$ $(x \in \Sigma^*)$ with $f(x) \neq l$, either $f(x) \leqslant l_1$ or $f(x) \geqslant l_2$.

(ii) l is a maximum element of L and there exists $l_1 \neq l$ in L such that for any $f(x)$ $(x \in \Sigma^*)$ with $f(x) \neq l$, $f(x) \leqslant l_1$ holds.

(iii) $l = 0$ and there exists $l_2 \neq 0$ in L such that for any $f(x)$ $(x \in \Sigma^*)$ with $f(x) \neq 0$, $f(x) \geqslant l_2$ holds.

Theorem *Let L be a lattice with minimum element 0. Let $f: \Sigma^* \to L$ be a fuzzy language and let l be an isolated cutpoint of f. Then, for $0 \leqslant i \leqslant 3$, it holds that if f is f-recognized by a machine in T_i, each of $L_{GE}(f,l)$ and $L_G(f,l)$ is recognized by a machine in T_i.*

Proof Assume that f is f-recognized by a machine $M = \langle \Sigma \cup \Delta \cup \{c\}$, $\Gamma, \Psi, \theta, \delta, \Omega, \kappa, \gamma_0 \rangle$ in T_i with a representation r over Δ. Since l is an isolated cutpoint of f, either (i), (ii) or (iii) holds. We will only prove the case where (i) holds. (Proofs for other cases are similar.) Let l_1 and l_2 in L be such that $l_1 < l < l_2$ and for any $f(x)$ $(x \in \Sigma^*)$ with $f(x) \neq l$, either $f(x) \geqslant l_2$ or $f(x) \leqslant l_1$ holds. Let d_1 and d_2 be the D-length of $r(l_1)$ and $r(l)$ and that of $r(l)$ and $r(l_2)$, respectively. Let $d_3 = \max(d_1, d_2)$ and let $w \in \Delta^*$ be the prefix of $r(l)$ of length d_3. From the definition of f-recognition, the set $L[M, \geqslant]$ is recognized by a machine in T_i, where $L[M, \geqslant]$ is the set of all words of the form xcy with $x \in \Sigma^*$ and $y \in \Delta^*$ such that $\gamma_0 \underset{xcy}{\Rightarrow} \gamma$ and $\kappa(\theta(\gamma))$ is $=$ or $>$. Furthermore, it holds that

$$\{x \in \Sigma^* | f(x) \geqslant l\} = \{x \in \Sigma^* | xcy \in L[M, \geqslant] \text{ for some } y \text{ in PRE } w\Delta^*\}$$

This is proved as follows. If $f(x) \geqslant l$, there exists $\gamma \in \Gamma^*$ and $y \in \text{PRE}\{r(l)\} \subset \text{PRE } w\Delta^*$ such that $\gamma_0 \Rightarrow \gamma$ and $\kappa(\theta(\gamma))$ is $=$ or $>$. Conversely, assume that $\gamma_0 \underset{xcy}{\Rightarrow} \gamma$ and $\kappa(\theta(\gamma))$ is $=$ or $>$ for $x \in \Sigma^*$, $y \in \text{PRE } w\Delta^*$ and $\gamma \in \Gamma^*$. If $y \in \text{PRE } r(l)$, then obviously $f(x) \geqslant l$. Otherwise, there exists $l' \in L$ such that $f(x) \geqslant l'$ and for some $w' \in \Delta^*$ and $\alpha \in \Delta^\infty$, $r(l') = y\alpha = ww'\alpha$. From the definition of D-length, neither l' and l_1 nor l' and l_2 are incomparable, and also neither $l' < l_1$ nor $l_2 < l'$ is valid. Therefore, $l_1 \leqslant l' \leqslant l_2$, and hence $f(x) = l$ or $f(x) \geqslant l_2$. Thus $f(x) \geqslant l$. It is obvious that there exists a gsm-mapping G such that

$$L_{GE}(f,l) = G(L[M, \geqslant] \cap \Sigma^* c\text{PRE} w\Delta^*)$$

Since classes of recursively enumerable sets, context-free languages and regular sets are closed under a gsm-mapping operation, respectively, it holds for $i = 0$, 2 and 3 that $L_{GE}(f,l)$ is recognized by a machine in T_i.

For the case of $i = 1$, the machine M is a Turing machine such that for some constant c, $|\gamma| \leqslant c|x|$ for any $x \in \Sigma^*$ and for any memory configuration γ such that $\gamma_0 \underset{xcy}{\Rightarrow} \gamma$ for some $y \in \mathrm{PRE}\{r(l)|l \in L\}$. A machine M' is a modification of M as follows, M' moves reading $xc(x \in \Sigma^*)$ in the same way as M reading xc. After reading xc, M' continues to read ϵ and changes sequentially memory configurations in the same way as M reads some y in $\mathrm{PRE}w\Delta^*$. In order to move in this way, M' has an autonomous finite state machine as a submachine that generates any y in $\mathrm{PRE}w\Delta^*$ nondeterministically. Obviously M' is in T_1 and hence the set $\mathrm{L}(M')$ of all words xc ($x \in \Sigma^*$) for which M' emits $>$ or $=$ is recognized by a machine in T_1. It holds that $\mathrm{L}(M') = \{xc|x \in \Sigma^*, y \in \mathrm{PRE}w\Delta^* \text{ and } xcy \in \mathrm{L}(M, \geqslant)\}$. Therefore $\mathrm{L}(M') = \mathrm{L}_{GE}(f,l)c$. Hence $\mathrm{L}_{GE}(f,l)$ is recognized by a machine in T_1.

As for $\mathrm{L}_G(f,l)$, the proof is similar.

Corollary *Let L be a finite lattice and let $f: \Sigma^* \to L$ be a fuzzy language. Then, for $0 \leqslant i \leqslant 3$, it holds that if f is f-recognized by a machine in T_i, then for any $l \in L$, each of $\mathrm{L}_{GE}(f,l)$ and $\mathrm{L}_G(f,l)$ is recognized by a machine in T_i.*

Proof Assume that f is f-recognized by a machine

$$M = \langle \Sigma \cup \Delta \cup \{c\}, \Gamma, \Psi, \theta, \delta, \Omega, \kappa, \gamma_0 \rangle$$

in T_i. Let $L = \{l_1, l_2, \ldots, l_s\}$. Then there exists w_j's in Δ^* such that $r(l_j)$ is in $w_j\Delta^\infty$ but is not in $w_k\Delta^\infty$ for $1 \leqslant j < k \leqslant s$. Let $\mathrm{L}[M, \geqslant]$ be the set of all words of the form xcy with $x \in \Sigma^*$ and $y \in \Delta^*$ such that $\gamma_0 \underset{xcy}{\Rightarrow} \gamma$ and $\kappa(\theta(\gamma))$ is $=$ or $>$. Then, from the definition of f-recognition, $\mathrm{L}[M, \geqslant]$ is recognized by a machine in T_i. Clearly it holds that

$$\{x \in \Sigma^*|f(x) \geqslant l_j\} = \{x \in \Sigma^*|xcy \in \mathrm{L}[M, \geqslant] \text{ for some } y \text{ in } \mathrm{PRE}\ w_j\Delta^\infty\}$$

for $1 \leqslant j \leqslant s$ such that l_j is not the minimum element of L. And if l_j is the minimum element of L, $\{x \in \Sigma^*|f(x) \geqslant l_j\} = \Sigma^*$ is obviously recognized by a machine in T_i. The rest of the proof is the same as in the proof of the theorem.

Theorem *Let L be a lattice with minimum element 0 which has a representation r_0 over Δ_0. Let $f: \Sigma^* \to L$ be a fuzzy language such that*

$$f(\Sigma^*) = \{f(x)|x \in \Sigma^*\}$$

is finite. Then it holds for $0 \leqslant i \leqslant 3$ that if $\mathrm{L}_{GE}(f,f(x))$ is recognized by a machine in T_i for any $f(x)$ $(x \in \Sigma^*)$, then f is f-recognized by a machine in T_i.

Proof Assume that $f(\Sigma^*) = \{l_1, l_2, \ldots, l_s\}$. Let M_j be a machine recognizing $\mathrm{L}_{GE}(f,l_j)$ for $1 \leqslant j \leqslant s$. A machine M which f-recognizes f with a representation r over Δ is given as follows: Let $\Delta = \Delta_0 \cup \Delta_1 \cup \Delta_2$ where $\Delta_1 = \{l_1', l_2', \dots, l_s'\}$ (l_i' is a new symbol corresponding uniquely to l_i for $1 \leqslant j \leqslant s$) $\Delta_2 = 2^{\Delta_1} \times 2^{\Delta_1}$. We define r as

$$r(l_j) = l_j' r_0(l_j) \qquad \text{for } 1 \leqslant j \leqslant s$$

$$r(l) = (A_l, B_l) r_0(l) \qquad \text{if } l \in \overline{f(\Sigma^*)}$$

where

$$A_l = \{l_j' \mid l_j > l\} \text{ and } B_l = \{l_j' \mid l_j < l\}$$

M contains M_i for $1 \leqslant i \leqslant s$ as submachines. For any word xc with $x \in \Sigma^*$, M reads first ϵ and chooses nondeterministically the initial configuration of any one of M_j's say M_k, and hereafter M_k moves reading x as an input word. Let Γ_j be the set of all configurations of M corresponding to accepting configurations of M_j ($1 \leqslant j \leqslant s$). From any configuration $\gamma_t^j \in \Gamma_j$ ($1 \leqslant j \leqslant s$), M moves into the new memory configuration $\tilde{\gamma}_t^j$ by the input symbol c. No transition into $\tilde{\gamma}_t^j$ other than the above one is not permitted in M. And M with the configuration $\tilde{\gamma}_t^j$, say $M(\tilde{\gamma}_t^j)$, moves deterministically as follows: By an input symbol l_k', $M(\tilde{\gamma}_t^j)$ emits respectively $=$, $>$, $<$ and ! according to the cases (i) $l_j = l_k$, (ii) $l_j > l_k$, (iii) $l_j < l_k$ and (iv) l_j and l_k are incomparable, and then halts. Reading (A_l, B_l), $M(\tilde{\gamma}_t^j)$ emits, respectively, $>$, $<$ and ! according to the cases (i) $l_j' \in A_l$, (ii) $l_j' \in B_l$ (iii) $l_j' \in A_l \cup B_l$, and then halts. Let $\tilde{\Gamma}_j = \{\tilde{\gamma}_t^j \mid \gamma_t^j \in \Gamma_j\}$ and we set ν as $\nu(\tilde{\gamma}_t^j) = l_j$ for all $\tilde{\gamma}_t^j \in \tilde{\Gamma}_j$ and for all $1 \leqslant j \leqslant s$. If $f(x) = l_k$, then $S_x = \bigcup_{l_j < l_k} \tilde{\Gamma}_j$. Therefore $f(x) = \nu(\tilde{\gamma}_t^k) = \max\{\nu(\gamma) \mid \gamma \in S_x\}$. Thus, f is f-recognized by M.

We obtain the following corollaries directly from the first theorem and its corollary and the second theorem.

Corollary *Let L be a totally ordered set with a minimum element and has some representation or L be a finite lattice. If f is an L-fuzzy language over some alphabet Σ such that $f(\Sigma^*)$ is finite, then for $0 \leqslant i \leqslant 3$, a necessary and sufficient condition for f to be f-recognized by a machine in T_i is that for any $f(x)$ ($x \in \Sigma^*$) $L_{GE}(f, f(x))$ is recognized by a machine in T_i.*

Corollary *Let L be a language over Σ and let $f_L : \Sigma^* \to B$ be the characteristic function of L, where B is the Boolian lattice with two elements. For $0 \leqslant i \leqslant 3$, L is recognized by a machine in T_i if and only if f_L is f-recognized by a machine in T_i.*

The above corollary shows that the recognition concept for fuzzy languages introduced in this paper is a fairly good extension of the one for ordinary languages.

Example Let L be a lattice with a minimum element 0 and a maximum element 1. An L-fuzzy context-free grammar is defined as a quadruple $G = (V, \Sigma, P, S)$ where V is a finite set of symbols, $\Sigma \subset V$ is the set of terminal symbols, $V - \Sigma$ is the set of nonterminal symbols, S is in $V - \Sigma$ and P is a finite set of production rules of the form

$$A \xrightarrow{l} \alpha$$

with $A \in V - \Sigma$, $\alpha \in V^*$ and $l \in L$. For β, γ in V^*, we write

$$\beta \xrightarrow{l} \gamma$$

if there exists δ, η in V^* and $A \xrightarrow{l} \gamma$ in P such that $\beta = \delta A \eta$ and $\gamma = \delta \alpha \eta$. We will write

$$\beta \overset{1}{\underset{*}{\Rightarrow}} \beta$$

$$\beta \overset{0}{\underset{*}{\Rightarrow}} \gamma$$

for all β, $\gamma \in V^*$, and

$$\beta \overset{m}{\underset{*}{\Rightarrow}} \gamma$$

if and only if there exists a sequence of elements in $V^*, \beta_0, \beta_1, \ldots, \beta_t$ such that $\beta_0 = \beta$, $\beta_t = \gamma$, $\beta_{i-1} \overset{l_i}{\Rightarrow} \beta_i$ for $1 \leqslant i \leqslant t$ and $\bigwedge_{i=1}^{t} l_i = m$, where $\bigwedge_{i=1}^{t} l_i$ denotes the greatest lower bounds of l_i's. For any x in Σ^*, let l_x be the least upper bound of $\{l \in L | S \overset{l}{\underset{*}{\Rightarrow}} x\}$. The L-fuzzy language f defined by

$$f(x) = l_x, \qquad \text{for all } x \in \Sigma^*$$

is said to be generated by G. An L-fuzzy language generated by some L-fuzzy context free grammar is called an L-fuzzy context free language. (L-fuzzy phrase structure, L-fuzzy context sensitive, L-fuzzy regular grammars and languages are similarly defined respectively.) $L_{[0,1]}$-fuzzy context free languages were studied by Lee and Zadeh [5]. From Proposition 18 in [10] and the second theorem, it follows that any $L_{[0,1]}$-fuzzy context free language is f-recognized by a pushdown automaton.

Example Let $\Sigma = \{a, b, c\}$ and let f_2 be an $L_{[0,1]}$-fuzzy language over Σ defined by

$$f_2(a^i b^j c^k) = \left(\frac{1}{2}\right)^{|i-j|+1} + \left(\frac{1}{2}\right)^{|j-k|+1}$$

$$f_2(w) = 0, \qquad \text{if } w \overline{\in} a^* b^* c^*$$

Then 1 is an isolated cutpoint of f_2 and $\mathbf{L_{GE}}(f_2, 1) = \{a^i b^i c^i | i \geqslant 0\}$ is not recognized by any pushdown automaton. Hence from the first theorem, f_2 is not f-recognized by any pushdown automaton. It can be seen that f_2 is f-recognized by some deterministic linear bounded automaton with the representation r_1 of the second example.

Regular Representations

The following theorem is clear from the proof of the first theorem.

Theorem *Let L be a lattice with a minimum element. If an L-fuzzy language f is f-recognized by a machine in $T_i(DT_i)$ with a representation r, and if $r(l)$ with $l \in L$ is generated by an autonomous finite automaton sequentially, then each of $\mathbf{L_G}(f, l)$ and $\mathbf{L_{GE}}(f, l)$ is recognized by a machine in $T_i(DT_i)$, where $i = 0, 1, 2$ and 3.*

Thus, we introduce the concept of a regular representation. Let L be a lattice with a minimum element. A representation r of L is said to be regular if for all $l \in L$, $r(l)$ is generated sequentially by some autonomous finite automaton.

The following corollary follows from the third theorem.

Corollary *Let L be a lattice with a minimum element. For any $1 \leqslant i \leqslant 3$, it holds that if an L-fuzzy language f is f-recognized by a machine in $T_i(DT_i)$ with a regular representation, then for all $l \in L$, each of $\mathbf{L_G}(f, l)$ and $\mathbf{L_{GE}}(f, l)$ is recognized by a machine in $T_i(DT_i)$.*

The representation r_2 of $L_{[0, 1]_R}$ shown in the third example is regular. Hence, for the fuzzy language f_1 of the fourth example and for any $l \in L_{[0, 1]_R}$, $\mathbf{L_G}(f, l)$ and $\mathbf{L_{GE}}(f, l)$ are context-free languages. It is clear that only lattices of restricted type have regular representations. For example, $L_{[0, 1]}$ cannot have any regular representation. However, f-recognition of a fuzzy language with a regular representation is interesting because, due to the above corollary, it gives a property independent of cutpoints of the fuzzy language with respect to recognition of its cutpoint languages.

FUZZY LANGUAGE NOT *F*-RECOGNIZED BY MACHINE IN DT_2

Considering the first theorem and its corollary, it is easy to find fuzzy languages not f-recognized by a machine in T_i for $0 \leqslant i \leqslant 3$. But we can not use the first theorem and the first corollary to find an L-fuzzy language whose membership function-values distribute densely over L and which is not f-recognized by a machine in T_i for $0 \leqslant i \leqslant 2$. Hence, it is interesting to find such a language. But only the following result has been obtained.

Example   Let $\Sigma = \{0, 1\}$ and let f_3 be an $L_{[0, 1]_R}$-fuzzy language over Σ such that for $a_i \in \Sigma \, (1 \leqslant i \leqslant k)$,

$$f_3(a_1 a_2 \ldots a_k) = a_1 2^{-1} + a_2 2^{-2} + \cdots + a_k 2^{-k}$$

(binary expansion), and

$$f_3(\epsilon) = 0$$

Then f_3 is not f-recognized by any deterministic pushdown automaton.

Proof   Assume that f_3 is f-recognized by a deterministic pushdown automaton $M = \langle \Sigma \cup \Delta \cup \{c\}, \Gamma, \{<, =, >\}, \theta, \delta, \Omega, \kappa, \gamma_0 \rangle$ with a representation r over Δ. Let

$$L_1 = \left\{ xcy \, | \, \gamma_0 \underset{xcy}{\Rightarrow} \gamma \quad \text{and} \quad \kappa(\theta(\gamma)) = (=) \right\}$$

then L_1 is a context-free language included in $\Sigma^* c \Delta^*$. Let $L_2 = L_1 \cap 0^* 1^* c \Delta^*$; L_2 is also a context-free language. Since M is deterministic, for any xcy in L_1, there exists α in Δ^∞ such that $r(f_3(x)) = y\alpha$. Due to the pumping lemma of the theory of context-free languages, it holds that there exists a constant K such that if $|z| \geqslant K$ and $z \in L_2$, then we can write $z = uvwxy$ such that $vx \neq \epsilon$, $|vwx| \leqslant K$, and for all i, $uv^i wx^i y$ is in L_2. Let $m \geqslant K$ and let z_p be an element in L_2 of the form $0^p 1^m cg_p (g_p \in \Delta^*)$ for any $p \geqslant 0$. We can write $z_p = u_p v_p w_p x_p y_p$ such that $v_p x_p \neq \epsilon$, $|v_p w_p x_p| \leqslant K$, and for all $i \geqslant 0$, $u_p v_p^i w_p x_p^i y_p$ in L_2. Since M is deterministic and halts immediately after it emits $(=)$, there exist no x in Σ^* and y and y' in Δ^* with $y \neq y'$ such that both xcy and xcy' are in L_2. Since $f_3(x) \neq f_3(x')$ for distinct x and x' in $0^* 1^m$, there exist no x and x' in $0^* 1^m$ with $x \neq x'$ and y in Δ^* such that both xcy and $x'cy$ are in L_2. Thus, for all p neither u_p nor y_p contains c. Since c cannot occur in either v_p or x_p, w_p contains c for all p. And clearly, each of v_p and x_p are not ϵ for all $p \geqslant 0$, so that for all $p \geqslant 0$ we can write $v_p = 1^{s_p}$ for some $s_p \geqslant 1$ and $w_p = 1^{t_p} c W_p$ for some $t_p \geqslant 0$ and W_p in Δ^*. Since $|v_p w_p x_p| \leqslant K$ for all p, there exist non-negative integers p and q, and W and $x \neq \epsilon$ in Δ^* such that $p < q$, $W_p = W_q = W$, $s_p = s_q = s$ and $x_p = x_q = x$. Hence

$$z_p = 0^p 1^m c W x y_p$$

$$z_q = 0^q 1^m c W x y_q$$

and for all $i \geqslant 0$

$$0^p 1^{m-s} 1^{si} c W x^i y_p \in L_2$$

$$0^q 1^{m-s} 1^{si} c W x^i y_q \in L_2$$

For some α_0 and α_1 in Δ^∞, it holds that

$$r^{-1}(Wy_p\alpha_0) = f_3(0^p1^{m-s}) < f_3(0^p1^m) = r^{-1}(Wxy_p\alpha_1)$$

Let d_0 be the D-length of $Wy_p\alpha_0$ and $Wxy_p\alpha_1$, and let $j > d_0$, then for some α_2 in Δ^∞,

$$r^{-1}(Wx^jy_p\alpha_2) = f_3(0^p1^{m-s}1^{sj}) > f_3(0^p1^m)$$

Hence the D-length d_1 of $Wy_p\alpha_0$ and $Wx^jy_p\alpha_2$ is not greater than d_0. Since $j > d_0$, it holds that $j > d_1$. But for some α_3 in Δ^∞,

$$r^{-1}(Wx^jy_q\alpha_3) = f_3(0^q1^{m-s}1^{sj}) < f_3(0^p1^{m-s}) = r^{-1}(Wy_p\alpha_0),$$

which contradicts the definition of a representation. Thus f_3 cannot be f-recognized by any deterministic pushdown automaton.

It is a well-known result in the theory of probabilistic automata [7] that $L_{GE}(f,l)$ and $L_G(f,l)$ are regular sets for any l in $L_{[0,1]_R}$. Thus, it is noted that generally a fuzzy language is not f-recognized by a machine in T_3 (even in DT_2) even if all its cutpoint languages are recognized by machines in T_3. This implies that the converse of the corollary of the third theorem does not hold.

RATIONAL PROBABILISTIC EVENTS

In this section, we show that any rational probabilistic event is f-recognized by a deterministic linear bounded automaton with a regular representation. A rational probabilistic automaton A with n ($\geqslant 1$) states over a finite alphabet Σ is given by $A = \langle \pi, \{A(\delta)|\delta \in \Sigma\}, \eta \rangle$ where π is a $1 \times n$ matrix $(\pi_1, \ldots, \pi_n)$ with $\pi_i \in [0,1]_R$ for $0 \leqslant i \leqslant n$ such that $\sum_{i=1}^n \pi_i = 1$, for all $\sigma \in \Sigma$, $A(\sigma)$ is an $n \times n$ stochastic matrix such that all components of $A(\sigma)$ are in $[0,1]_R$, and η is an $n \times 1$ matrix whose components are in $[0,1]_R$. A fuzzy language $p: \Sigma^* \to L_{[0,1]_R}$ is said to be realized or accepted by a rational probabilistic automaton A if $p(\epsilon) = \pi\eta$ and for any $m \geqslant 1$ and $\sigma_i \in \Sigma$ for $1 \leqslant i \leqslant m$

$$p(\sigma_1\sigma_2\cdots\sigma_m) = \pi A(\sigma_1)A(\sigma_2)\cdots A(\sigma_m)\eta$$

A fuzzy language p is called a rational probabilistic event if p is realized by some rational probabilistic automaton. (Details about probabilistic automata are found in [7].)

Theorem *Any rational probabilistic event is f-recognized by a machine in DT_1 with a regular representation.*

Proof Assume that $p: \Sigma^* \to L_{[0,1]_R}$ is any rational probabilistic event, and assume that p is realized by a rational probabilistic automaton $A = \langle \pi, \{A(\sigma) | \sigma \in \Sigma\}, \eta \rangle$ with n states. Let all components of $\pi, A(\sigma)$'s $(\sigma \in \Sigma)$ and η be represented in the form v/U for non-negative integers v and U such that U is common to all of them. For any word $x = \sigma_1 \ldots \sigma_m$ of length $m \geqslant 1$, let $\pi(x) = (\pi_1(x), \pi_2(x), \ldots, \pi_n(x))$ be $\pi A(\sigma_1) A(\sigma_2) \ldots A(\sigma_m)$, and let $\pi(\epsilon) = \pi$. Then for any word x of length m, $\pi_i(x)$ is represented in the form $v_i(x)/U^{m+1}$ with $0 \leqslant v_i(x) \leqslant U^{m+1}$, for $1 \leqslant i \leqslant n$, and $p(x)$ is represented in the form $w(x)/U^{m+2}$ with $0 \leqslant w(x) \leqslant U^{m+2}$. We denote the binary expansion of a non-negative integer u by $b(u)$ and we denote the length of $b(u)$ by $|b(u)|$. Then we can construct a Turing machine z such that when z reads an input word $x \in \Sigma^*$, z gives the output string

$$T(x) = b(v_1(x)) \# b(v_2(x)) \# \cdots \# b(v_n(x)) \# b(w(x)) \# b(U^{|x|+2})$$

on its tape using at most $d|x|$ working spaces, where d is a constant independent of x. It is easily seen that by a Turing machine, $T(x\sigma)$ with $\sigma \in \Sigma$ can be computed from $T(x)$ at most a constant multiple of $|b(U^{|x\sigma|+1})|$ spaces and that for any non-negative integer s, $|b(U^s)| \leqslant d's$ for some constant d'. Thus, by induction on the length of an input word, we can show the existence of the Turing machine z that computes $T(x)$ for $x \in \Sigma^*$ using at most $d|x|$ spaces.

Furthermore, we define subsequent moves of z as follows: If z with a memory configuration $T(x)$ reads c as its next input symbol, then z transforms $T(x)$ into $b(s(x)) \# b(t(x))$ on its tape where $s(x)/t(x) = w(x)/U^{|x|+2}$ and $s(x)$ and $t(x)$ are relatively prime. (If $w(x) = 0$, z prints 0, and if $w(x) = U^{|x|+2}$, z prints 1 on its tape.) Since division by a binary number not greater than $b(U^{|x|+2})$ can be done with at most a constant multiple of $|b(U^{|x|+2})|$ spaces, z can give $b(s(x)) \# b(t(x))$ on its tape using $d|x|$ spaces after it reads xc.

Now we define a representation $r: L_{[0,1]_R} \to \Delta'^\infty$ as follows, where $\Delta' = \{0,1\} \times \{0,1,\#\}$: Define $\tau_1: \Delta'^\infty \to \{0,1,\#\}^\infty$ and $\tau_2: \Delta'^\infty \to \{0,1\}^\infty$ as $\tau_i((\sigma_1, \sigma_2)) = \sigma_i$ for $(\sigma_1, \sigma_2) \in \Delta'$ and $\tau_i(\alpha) = \tau_i(\sigma_1)\tau_i(\sigma_2)\tau_i(\sigma_3) \cdots$ for $\alpha = \sigma_1\sigma_2\sigma_3 \cdots$ with $\sigma_j \in \Sigma (j \geqslant 1)$, for $i = 1$ or 2. For any $0 < l < 1$ in $L_{[0,1]_R}$, let $l = s/t$, where s and t be relatively prime positive integers. Then $r(l)$ is the element in Δ'^∞ such that $\tau_1(r(l)) = b(s) \# t(s) \# \# \# \cdots$ and $\tau_2(r(l)) = e(l)$ where $e(l)$ was given in the second example. Then $r(0) = (0,0)(\#,0)(\#,0)(\#,0)\ldots$ and $r(1) = (1,1)(\#,1)(\#,1)(\#,1)\ldots$. Clearly, r is a representation because D-length of $r(l)$ and $r(m)$ with $l \neq m$ may be defined as the positive integer p such that $\tau_2(r(l))$ and $\tau_2(r(m))$ differ first at the pth digit. It is also clear that r is a regular representation. If z with $b(s(x)) \# b(t(x))$ on its tape is given a representation $r(l)$ of $l \in L_{[0,1]_R}$ as an input sequence succeeding xc for $x \in \Sigma^*$, z computes the binary expansion of $s(x)/t(x)$, digit by digit, and compares it with $\tau_2(r(l))$. In parallel with this computation, z compares sequentially $b(s(x)) \# b(t(x))$ with $\tau_1(r(l))$. Then, either z emits $=$ and halts if $b(s(x)) \# b(t(x)) = b(s) \# b(t)$, where $\tau_1(r(l)) = b(s) \# b(t) \# \# \# \dots$, or z emits $>$ or $<$ and halts according to the comparison of the first distinguished digit of $\tau_2(r(l))$ and binary expansion of $s(x)/t(x)$. Since the digit by digit generation of the binary expansion of $s(x)/t(x)$ can be made using at most a constant multiple of $|b(t(x))|$ spaces, z can do the above value comparing computation for $x \in \Sigma^*$ using at most $d|x|$ spaces. Thus, p is f-recognized by z in DT_1 with the regular representation r.

The following result, which was already proved in [8], is a direct consequence of corollary and theorem.

Corollary Let $p: \Sigma^* \to L_{[0,1]_R}$ be a rational probabilistic event. Then for all $l \in L_{[0,1]_R}$, each of $\mathbf{L_G}(f,l)$ and $\mathbf{L_{GE}}(f,l)$ is recognized by a machine in DT_1.

RECURSIVE FUZZY LANGUAGES

The relation between deterministic machines and nondeterministic machines with respect to the f-recognizability of fuzzy languages is somewhat different from that of ordinary languages. It will be shown that in the f-recognition of fuzzy languages nondeterministic Turing machines are more powerful than deterministic Turing machines. Let $\{t_0, t_1, t_2, \dots\}$ be an enumeration of deterministic Turing machines. Let L_3 be a lattice with three elements 0, a and 1 such that $0 < a < 1$. Let $\Sigma = \{\sigma\}$. f_4 and f_5 are L_3-fuzzy languages over Σ defined as follows: For $n \geqslant 0$

$$f_4(\sigma^n) = \begin{cases} 1 & \text{if } t_n \text{ with the blank tape eventually halts} \\ 0 & \text{otherwise} \end{cases}$$

$$f_5(\sigma^n) = \begin{cases} 1 & \text{if } t_n \text{ with the blank tape eventually halts} \\ a & \text{otherwise} \end{cases}$$

Then the following lemma holds.

Lemma f_4 is f-recognized by a deterministic Turing machine. f_5 is f-recognized by a nondeterministic Turing machine, but it is not f-recognized by any deterministic Turing machine.

Proof It is easily seen that there exists a deterministic Turing machine that f-recognizes f_4. Since $\mathbf{L_{GE}}(f_5, 1)$ and $\mathbf{L_{GE}}(f_5, a)$ are recursively enumerable languages, it follows from the second theorem that f_5 is f-recognized by a Turing machine. Assume that f_5 is f-recognized by a deterministic Turing machine. Then, it is easily shown that the language $\{\sigma^n|f_5(\sigma^n)=a\}$ is recursively enumerable. Hence, the halting problem of Turing machines is solvable, which is not valid. Thus f_5 is not f-recognized by any deterministic Turing machine.

Let $\mathcal{L}(T_i)$ and $\mathcal{L}(DT_i)$ be the families of fuzzy languages f-recognized by a machine in T_i and DT_i, respectively, for $i=0$, 1, 2 and 3.

Theorem

   (i) $\mathcal{L}(T_0) \underset{+}{\supsetneq} \mathcal{L}(DT_0)$ ♦

   (ii) $\mathcal{L}(T_2) \underset{+}{\supsetneq} \mathcal{L}(DT_2)$

   (iii) $\mathcal{L}(T_3) = \mathcal{L}(DT_3)$

(i) is a direct consequence of the lemma. (ii) follows from the corollary of the second theorem. The proof of (iii) is easy. But it is not known whether $\mathcal{L}(T_1) \underset{+}{\supsetneq} \mathcal{L}(DT_1)$ or not.

Considering the lemma, it seems reasonable to define recursive fuzzy languages as follows: A fuzzy language f over Σ is recursive if and only if f is f-recognized by some machine $M=\langle\Sigma\cup\Delta\cup\{c\},\Gamma,\Psi,\theta,\delta,\Omega,\kappa,\gamma_0\rangle$ in DT_0 with some representation r over Δ with the condition that $S_x\neq\phi$ for any $x\in\Sigma^*$, where S_x is $\{\gamma\in\Gamma^*|\gamma_0\underset{xc}{\Rightarrow}\gamma\}$.

Obviously any fuzzy language in $\mathcal{L}(T_3)$ is recursive; the following proposition is easily proved.

Proposition *A fuzzy language in $\mathcal{L}(DT_2)\cup\mathcal{L}(T_1)$ is a recursive fuzzy language.*

CLOSURE PROPERTIES

In this section, we discuss some closure properties of the classes of fuzzy languages corresponding to machine classes T_i's under fuzzy set operations. It will be seen that these properties are the extensions of some closure properties of ordinary languages such as regular sets, context free languages, context sensitive languages and, recursively enumerable sets. Following Zadeh [9], we consider $L_{[0,1]}$ fuzzy languages and the most basic operations, i.e., union and intersection.

Let f and g be $L_{[0,1]}$ fuzzy languages over an alphabet Σ. The union of f and g denoted by $f\vee g$ is defined as $f\vee g(x)=\max\{f(x),g(x)\}$ for all

$x \in \Sigma^*$, and the intersection of f and g denoted by $f \wedge g$ is defined as $f \wedge g(x) = \min\{f(x), g(x)\}$ for all $x \in \Sigma^*$.

Theorem *Let f and g be $L_{[0,1]}$-fuzzy languages over Σ. If each of f and g is f-recognized by a machine in T_i ($i = 0$, 1, 2 and 3), then $f \vee g$ is f-recognized by a machine in T_i.*

Proof Assume that f and g is f-recognized by a machine M_1 with a representation $r_1: L_{[0,1]} \to \Delta_1^\infty$ and a machine M_2 with a representation $r_2: L_{[0,1]} \to \Delta_2^\infty$, respectively. Let $\Delta = \Delta_1 \times \Delta_2$. And for $j = 1, 2$ define $\tau_j: \Delta^\infty \to \Delta_j^\infty$ as follows: $\tau_j((a_1, a_2)) = a_j$ with $a_j \in \Delta_j$ and for $\alpha = b_1 b_2 b_3 \cdots$ with $b_k \in \Delta(k \geqslant 1)$, $\tau_j(\alpha) = \tau_j(b_1)\tau_j(b_2)\tau_j(b_3)\cdots$. Let $r: L_{[0,1]} \to \Delta^\infty$ be such that for any $l \in L_{[0,1]}$ $\tau_1(r(l)) = r_1(l)$ and $\tau_2(r(l)) = r_2(l)$. Then r is a representation of $L_{[0,1]}$ over Δ because D-length $d(r(l), r(m))$ of $r(l)$ and $r(m)$ for any distinct $l, m \in L_{[0,1]}$ can be defined as $d(r(l), r(m)) = d(r_1(l), r_1(m))$. A machine M which f-recognizes $f \vee g$ with the representation r is given as follows: M has M_1 and M_2 as submachines. For any word xc with $x \in \Sigma^*$, M reads first ϵ, chooses nondeterministically M_1 or M_2 and simulates the choosed machine hereafter reading xc. If M reads through xc simulating M_j ($j = 1, 2$) and if M is given $r(l)$ ($l \in L_{[0,1]}$), then M moves as M_j does if it is given $\tau_j(r(l)) = r_j(l)$. It is clear that M f-recognizes $f \vee g$.

Theorem *Let i be any one of 0, 1 and 3 for T_i. Let f and g be $L_{[0,1]}$-fuzzy languages over Σ. If each of f and g is f-recognized by a machine in T_i, then $f \wedge g$ is f-recognized by a machine in T_i.*

Proof A proof is given for $i = 1$. For $i = 0$ and 3, proofs are similar. Assume that f and g are f-recognized by a machine M_1 in T_1 with a representation $r_1: L_{[0,1]} \to \Delta_1^\infty$ and a machine M_2 in T_1 with a representation $r_2: L_{[0,1]} \to \Delta_2^\infty$, respectively. Let $\Delta = \Delta_1 \times \Delta_2$ and define a representation $r: L_{[0,1]} \to \Delta^\infty$ as defined in the proof of the previous theorem. We give a machine M in T_1 which f-recognizes $f \wedge g$ with the representation r. M has M_1 and M_2 as submachines. When M is given xc with $x \in \Sigma^*$ as an input word, submachines M_1 and M_2 of M moves in parallel reading xc, and M reaches the configuration γ corresponding to the pair of configurations γ_1 of M_1 and γ_2 of M_2 which they reach after reading xc, respectively. Note that for this computation of M, at most a constant multiple of $|x|$ spaces is necessary. If M with the configuration γ is given $r(l)$ with $l \in L_{[0,1]}$ as a subsequent input, then M makes M_1 with the configuration γ_1 read $\tau_1(r(l)) = r_1(l)$ and in parallel makes M_2 with the configuration γ_2 read $\tau_2(r(l)) = r_2(l)$. When one of M_1 and M_2 emits an output, i.e., one of $>$, $<$ and $=$, M remembers it in a state and then continues to make another submachine move until it emits an output. If both of M_1 and M_2 emit $>$, then M emits $>$, if one of them emits $=$ and another emits $>$ or $=$, then M emits $=$, and if either one of them emits $<$, then M emits $<$. M halts immediately after M emits an output. Since M_1 and M_2 are machines in T_1, M needs at most a constant multiple of $|x|$ spaces in order to do the above value comparing computation for $x \in \Sigma^*$. Thus, it is shown that M in T_1 f-recognizes $f \wedge g$.

Since for two context-free languages L_1 and L_2, $L_1 \cap L_2$ is not necessarily a context-free language, it follows from the corollary of the second theorem that for two fuzzy languages f and g each of which is f-recognized by a machine in T_2, $f \wedge g$ is not necessarily f-recognized by a machine in T_2. However, similar proof to that of the above theorem shows that if f is f-recognized by a machine in T_2 and g is f-recognized by a machine in T_3, then $f \wedge g$ is f-recognized by a machine in T_2.

REFERENCES

1. A.V. Aho and J.D. Ullman, *The Theory of Parsing, Translation, and Compiling, vol. 1.* Prentice-Hall, N. J., 1972.
2. J. A. Goguen, "*L*-Fuzzy Sets," *J. Math. Anal. Appl.* **18** (1967), 145–174.
3. N. Honda and M. Nasu, "Recognition of Fuzzy Languages," *Fuzzy Sets and Their Applications to Cognitive and Decision Processes* (L. A. Zadeh, K. S. Fu, K. Tanaka and M. Shimura, Eds.). Academic Press, N. J., 1975, 279–299.
4. H. H. Kim, M. Mizumoto, J. Toyoda, and K. Tanaka, "Lattice Grammars," *Trans. Inst. Elect. Commun. Engrs. Japan* **57-D**, No. 5, 253–260 (in Japanese).
5. E. T. Lee and L. A. Zadeh, "Note on Fuzzy Languages," *Info. Sci.* **1** (1969) 421–434.
6. M. Mizumoto, J. Toyoda and K. Tanaka, "Examples of Formal Grammars With Weights," *Info. Proc. Letters* **2** (1973), 74–78.
7. A. Paz, *Introduction to Probabilistic Automata.* Academic Press, N. Y. 1971.
8. N. Tokura, M. Fujii and T. Kasami, "Some Considerations on Linear Automata," *Records Natl. Convention, IECE, Japan* **S8-2** (1968) (in Japanese).
9. L. A. Zadeh, "Fuzzy Sets," *Info. Control* **8** (1965), 338–353.
10. L. A. Zadeh, "Fuzzy Languages and Their Relation to Human and Machine Intelligence," *Man And Computer, Proc. Int. Conf. Bordeaux—1970.* Karger, Basel, 1972, 130–165.

REGULAR FUZZY EXPRESSIONS 10

Eugene S. Santos

In the theory of deterministic finite automata [1], the concept of regular expressions was introduced for the express purpose of representing the languages accepted by finite automata. This is necessary in the analysis and synthesis of finite automata since the languages accepted by finite automata are usually infinite.

Various models of fuzzy automata are studied in the literature, including maximin and max-product automata [2]. In the present paper, we introduce the concept of regular fuzzy expressions. This concept provides not only the necessary tool for the analysis and synthesis of fuzzy automata, but it also provides a means for recursively generating the family of fuzzy languages accepted by fuzzy automata from certain simple fuzzy languages. Since the families of fuzzy languages accepted by the various models of fuzzy automata is, in general, nondenumerable, the concept of regular fuzzy expressions could provide the necessary insights to the study of the structure of such families.

In order to present a concept of regular fuzzy expressions applicable to the various existing and other models of fuzzy automata, we first introduce the concept of ordered semigroup.

Definition A linearly ordered set is an ordered pair $(R, <)$ where R is a nonempty set and $<$ is a relation on R such that for every $a, b, c \in R$:

(i) $a < a$
(ii) $a < b, b < a$ implies $a = b$
(iii) $a < b, b < c$ implies $a < c$
(iv) either $a < b$ or $b < a$

Definition Let $(R, <)$ be a linearly ordered set, $R_0 \subseteq R$ and $a_0 \in R$. Then a_0 is an upper bound of R_0 if and only if $a < a_0$ for all $a \in R$. Moreover, $a_0 = \text{lub} \, R_0$ if and only if (i) a_0 is an upper bound of R_0, and (ii) for every upper bound b of R_0, $a_0 < b$.

Clearly, if $(R, <)$ is a linearly ordered set and $R_0 \subseteq R$, then lub R_0 is unique if it exists. We also write $a_1 \vee a_2$ for lub $\{a_1, a_2\}$, and $\bigvee_{i \in I} a_i$ for lub $\{a_i : i \in I\}$.

Definition An ordered semigroup is a triple $(R, \otimes, <)$ where $(R, <)$ is a linearly ordered set with minimal element 0, and $(R, \otimes)$ is a commutative semigroup with identity 1 such that for every $R_0 \subseteq R$ and $a_0 \in R$, $a_0 \otimes 0 = 0$ and lub $\{a_0 \otimes a : a \in R_0\} = a_0 \otimes$ lub R_0.

Clearly, for every $a, b \in R$, if $a < b$, then $a \otimes c < b \otimes c$ for all $c \in R$.

In what follows, unless otherwise stated, R will always stand for an ordered semigroup with minimal element 0 and identity 1 for $\otimes$.

Notation Let Σ be a nonempty set. Σ^* is the free semigroup generated by Σ with identity Λ.

Definition Let Σ be a nonempty set. An R-language over Σ is a function f from Σ^* into R.

Remark If f is an R-language over Σ, then for each $\alpha \in \Sigma^*$, $f(\alpha)$ is the grade of membership [5] that α is a member of the language.

Definition Let Σ be a finite nonempty set. An R-automaton over Σ is a 4-tuple $A = (S, p, h, g)$, where S is a finite nonempty set, p is a function from $S \times \Sigma \times S$ into R, and h and g are functions from S into R.

Definition Let $A = (S, p, h, g)$ be an R-automaton over Σ.

(1) p^* is the function from $s \times \Sigma^* \times S$ into R defined inductively as follows:

$$p^*(s'|e,s) = \begin{cases} 1 & \text{if } s = s' \\ 0 & \text{if } s \neq s' \end{cases}$$

$$p^*(s'|\sigma\alpha,s) = \bigvee_{s'' \in S} p(s''|\sigma,s) \otimes p^*(s'|\alpha,s'')$$

where $s, s' \in S$, $\sigma \in \Sigma$ and $\alpha \in \Sigma^*$.

(2) f^A is the function from Σ^* into R such that for every $\alpha \in \Sigma^*$

$$f^A(\alpha) = \bigvee_{s \in S} \bigvee_{s' \in S} h(s) \otimes p^*(s'|\alpha,s) \otimes g(s')$$

In the above definitions, Σ is the set of input symbols, S is the set of states, $p(s'|\sigma,s)$ is the grade of membership that the next state is s' given that the present state is s and input σ is applied, $h(s)$ is the grade of membership that s is the initial state and $g(s)$ is the grade of membership that s is an accepting state. Moreover, f^A is the R-language over Σ accepted by A.

The above definition of R-automata includes the various existing models of fuzzy automata. These models may be obtained by appropriate choices of R, e.g.,

(1) Max-product automata [4]: $R_p = (R, \otimes, <)$, where R is the set of all nonnegative real numbers, $a \otimes b = ab$ and $a < b$ means $a \leqslant b$.

(2) Strict max-product automata [4]: $R_s = (R, \otimes, <)$ where $R = [0, 1]$, the closed unit interval, $a \otimes b = ab$ and $a < b$ means $a \leqslant b$.

(3) Nondeterministic automata [1]: $R_N = (R, x, <)$ where $R = \{0, 1\}$, and $\otimes$ and $<$ are same as above.

(4) Maximin automata [2]: $R_M = (R, \otimes, <)$ where R is a subset of the real number system, usually $[0, 1]$, $a \otimes b = \min\{a, b\}$, and $a < b$ means $a \leqslant b$.

Definition An R-language f over Σ is regular if and only if $f = f^A$ for some R-automaton $A = (S, p, h, g)$ over Σ.

Notation Let f, f_1 and f_2 be T-languages over Σ and $a \in R$.

(1) $f_1 \vee f_2$ is the R-language over Σ such that for every $\alpha \in \Sigma^*$,

$$\left(f_1 \vee f_2\right)(\alpha) = f_1(\alpha) \vee f_2(\alpha)$$

In general, if $f_1, f_2, \ldots, f_n$ are R-languages over Σ, then

$$\bigvee_{i=1}^{n} f_i = \left(f_1 \vee f_2 \vee \cdots \vee f_{n-1}\right) \vee f_n$$

(2) $f_1 \circ f_2$ is the R-languages over Σ such that for every $\alpha \in \Sigma^*$

$$(f_1 \circ f_2)(\alpha) = \mathrm{lub}\{f_1(\beta_1) \otimes f_2(\beta_2) : \alpha = \beta_1 \beta_2\}.$$

(3) af is the R-language over Σ such that for every $\alpha \in \Sigma^*$, $(af)(\alpha) = a \otimes f(\alpha)$

(4) f^* is the R-language over Σ such that for every $\alpha \in \Sigma^*$

$$f^*(\alpha) = \begin{cases} f(e) & \text{if } \alpha = e \\ \mathrm{lub}\{f(\beta_1) \otimes f(\beta_2) \otimes \cdots \otimes f(\beta_n) : \alpha = \beta_1 \beta_2 \cdots \beta_n, \end{cases}$$

$$\beta_i \neq e \quad \text{for } i = 1, 2, \ldots, n \quad \text{and} \quad n = 1, 2, \ldots\} \quad \text{if } \alpha \neq e$$

Theorem *If $a \in R$ and f is a regular R-language over Σ, then af is a regular R-language over Σ.*

Proof Let $f=f^A$ where $A=(S,p,h,g)$ is an R-automaton over Σ. Let $A'=(S,p,h,g')$ be an R-automaton over Σ where $g'(s)=a\otimes g(s)$ for all $s\in S$. It can be verified that $af=f^{A'}$.

Theorem *If f_1 and f_2 are regular R-languages over Σ, then $f_1\vee f_2$ is a regular R-language over Σ.*

Proof For $i=1,2$, let $f_i=f^{A_i}$, where $A_i=(S_i,p_i,h_i,g_i)$ is an R-automaton over Σ. Without loss of generality, assume $S_1\cap S_2=\varnothing$ (empty set), let $A=(S,p,h,g)$ be an R-automaton over Σ where $S=S_1\cup S_2$ and for each s, $s'\in S$ and $\sigma\in\Sigma$,

$$p(s'|\sigma,s)=\begin{cases} p_1(s'|\sigma,s) & \text{if } s,s'\in S_1 \\ p_2(s'|\sigma,s) & \text{if } s,s'\in S_2 \\ 0 & \text{otherwise} \end{cases}$$

$$h(s)=\begin{cases} h_1(s) & \text{if } s\in S_1 \\ h_2(s) & \text{if } s\in S_2 \end{cases}$$

$$g(s)=\begin{cases} g_1(s) & \text{if } s\in S_1 \\ g_2(s) & \text{if } s\in S_2 \end{cases}$$

It can be verified that $f_1\vee f_2=f^A$.

Theorem *If f_1 and f_2 are regular R-languages over Σ, then $f_1\circ f_2$ is a regular R-language over Σ.*

Proof For $i=1,2$, let $f_i=f^{A_i}$ where $A_i=(S_i,p_i,h_i,g_i)$ is an R-automaton over Σ. Without loss of generality, assume that $S_1\cap S_2=\varnothing$. Let $A=(S,p,h,g)$ be an R-automaton over Σ where $S=S_1\cup S_2\cup\{s_0\}$, $s_0\notin S_1\cup S_2$, and for each s', $s''\in S$ and $\sigma\in\Sigma$,

$$p(s''|\sigma,s')=\begin{cases} p_1(s''|\sigma,s') & \text{if } s',s''\in S_1 \\ p_2(s''|\sigma,s') & \text{if } s',s''\in S_2 \\ \displaystyle\bigvee_{s\in S_1}\left[h_1(s)\otimes p_1(s''|\sigma,s)\right] & \text{if } s'=s_0, s''\in S_1 \\ f_1(e)\otimes\left\{\displaystyle\bigvee_{s\in S_2}\left[h_2(s)\otimes p_2(s''|\sigma,s)\right]\right\} & \text{if } s'=s_0, s''\in S_2 \\ g_1(s')\otimes\left\{\displaystyle\bigvee_{s\in S_2}\left[h_2(s)\otimes f_2(s''|\sigma,s)\right]\right\} & \text{if } s'\in S_1, s''\in S_2 \\ 0 & \text{otherwise} \end{cases}$$

$$h(s') = \begin{cases} 1 & \text{if } s' = s_0 \\ 0 & \text{otherwise} \end{cases}$$

$$g(s') = \begin{cases} f_1(e) \otimes f_2(e) & \text{if } s' = s_0 \\ f_2(e) \otimes g_1(s') & \text{if } s' \in S_1 \\ g_2(s') & \text{if } s' \in S_2 \end{cases}$$

It can be verified that $f_1 \circ f_2 = f^A$.

Theorem *If f is a regular R-language over Σ, then f^* is a regular R-language over Σ.*

Proof Let $f = f^A$ where $A = (S, p, h, g)$ is an R-automaton over Σ. Let $A' = (S', p', h', g')$ be an R-automaton over Σ where $S' = S \cup \{s_0\}$, $s_0 \notin S$, and for every s', $s'' \in S'$ and $\sigma \in \Sigma$.

$p'(s''|\sigma, s')$

$$= \begin{cases} p(s''|\sigma, s') \bigvee \left\{ g(s') \times \left[\bigvee_{s \in S} \{ h(s) \otimes p(x''|\sigma, s) \} \right] \right\} & \text{if } s', s'' \in S \\ \bigvee_{s \in S} \left[h(s) \otimes p(s''|\sigma, s) \right] & \text{if } s' = s_0, s'' \in S \\ 0 & \text{otherwise} \end{cases}$$

$$h'(s') = \begin{cases} 1 & \text{if } s' = s_0 \\ 0 & \text{if } s' \neq s_0 \end{cases}$$

$$g'(s') = \begin{cases} g(s') & \text{if } s \in S \\ f(e) & \text{if } s = s_0 \end{cases}$$

It can be verified that $f^* = f^{A'}$.

Notation

(1) If $\alpha \in \Sigma^*$, then f_α is the R-language over Σ where $f_\alpha(\alpha) = 1$ and $f_\alpha(\alpha) = 0$ for all $\gamma \neq \alpha$.

(2) $f_\varnothing$ is the R-language over Σ where $f_\varnothing(\alpha) = 0$ for all $\alpha \in \Sigma^*$.

Definition Let Σ be a finite nonempty set. The family $\mathcal{R}$ of regular R-expressions over Σ is defined inductively as follows

(1) $\varnothing \in \mathcal{R}$
(2) $\wedge \in \mathcal{R}$

(3) $\sigma \in \mathcal{R}$, for all $\mathcal{R} \in \Sigma$

(4) $a\alpha \in \mathcal{R}$, for all $a \in R$ and $\alpha \in \mathcal{R}$

(5) $\alpha_1 \vee \alpha_2 \in \mathcal{R}$, for all $\alpha_1, \alpha_2 \in \mathcal{R}$

(6) $\alpha_1 \circ \alpha_2 \in \mathcal{R}$, for all $\alpha_1, \alpha_2 \in \mathcal{R}$

(7) $\alpha^* \in \mathcal{R}$, for all $\alpha \in \mathcal{R}$

(8) There are no other regular R-expressions other than those given in steps (1) to (7).

Definition For every $\alpha \in \mathcal{R}, |\alpha|$ is the R-language over Σ defined recursively as follows:

(1) $|\alpha| = f_\alpha$, for all $\alpha \in \Sigma \cup \{\varnothing, \Lambda\}$

(2) $|a\alpha| = a|\alpha|$, for all $a \in R$ and $\alpha \in \mathcal{R}$.

(3) $|\alpha_1 \vee \alpha_2| = |\alpha_1| \vee |\alpha_2|$, for all $\alpha_1, \alpha_2 \in \mathcal{R}$.

(4) $|\alpha_1 \circ \alpha_2| = |\alpha_1| \circ |\alpha_2|$, for all $\alpha_1, \alpha_2 \in \mathcal{R}$.

(5) $|\alpha^*| = |\alpha|^*$ for all $\alpha \in \mathcal{R}$.

Theorem *If $\alpha \in R$, then $|\alpha|$ is a regular R-language over Σ.*

Proof Follows from the other theorems and the fact that for each $\alpha \in \Sigma \cup \{\varnothing, \Lambda\}, f_\alpha$ is a regular R-language over Σ.

Theorem *If f is a regular R-language over Σ, then $f = |\alpha|$ for some $\alpha \in R$.*

Proof Let $f = f^A$, where $A = (S, p, h, g)$ is an R-automaton over Σ, with $S = \{s_1, s_2, \ldots, s_n\}$ and $\Sigma = \{\sigma_1, \sigma_2, \ldots, \sigma_m\}$. For each $i, j = 1, 2, \ldots, n$, let $\alpha_{ij}{}^0 = (s_{ij}\Lambda) \vee [\vee_{t=1}{}^p (s_j | \sigma_t, s_i)\sigma_t]$ and $\alpha_{ij}{}^k = \alpha_{ij}{}^{k-1} \vee [\alpha_{ik}{}^{k-1} \circ (\alpha_{kk}{}^{k-1})^* \circ \alpha_{kj}{}^{k-1}]$, $k = 1, 2, \ldots, n$, where $\sigma_{ij} = 1$, if $i = j$ and $\sigma_{ij} = 0$ if $i \neq j$. It can be shown by induction on k that $|\alpha_{ij}{}^k|(e) = \sigma_{ij}$, $|\alpha_{ij}{}^k|(\sigma) = p(s_j | \sigma, s_i)$ for all $\sigma \in \Sigma$, and for $r \geqslant 1$:

$$|\alpha_{ij}{}^k|(\sigma_{i_0}\sigma_{i_1}\ldots\sigma_{i_r}) = \bigvee_{i_1 \leqslant k} \bigvee_{i_2 \leqslant k} \cdots \bigvee_{i_r \leqslant k} p(s_{i_1} | \sigma_{i_0}, s_i) \otimes$$
$$\times p(s_{i_2} | \sigma_{i_1}, s_{i_1}) \otimes \ldots \otimes p(s_j | \sigma_{i_r}, s_{i_r}).$$

Thus, for every $\sigma \in \Sigma^*$, $|\alpha_{ij}{}^n|(\sigma) = p^*(s_j | \sigma, s_i)$. Let $\alpha = \bigvee_{i=1}^{n} \bigvee_{j=1}^{n} [h(s_i) \otimes g(s_j)]\alpha_{ij}{}^n$. It can be shown that $|\alpha| = f$.

These last two theorems present solutions to the synthesis and analysis problem of R-automata, respectively. Together, they provide a generalization of Kleene's theorem for fuzzy automata.

REFERENCES

1. M.A. Harrison, *Introduction to Switching and Automata Theory*. McGraw-Hill, New York, 1965.
2. E.S. Santos, "Realization of Fuzzy Languages by Probabilistic, Max-Product and Maximin Automata," *Info. Sci.* **8** (1975), 39–53.
3. E.S. Santos, "Fuzzy Sequential Functions," *J. Cybernetics* **3** (1973), 15–31.
4. E.S. Santos, "Fuzzy Automata and Languages," *Info. Sci.* (to appear).
5. L.A. Zadeh, "Fuzzy Sets," *Information Control* **9** (1965), 338–353.

ANALYTICAL REPRESENTATION OF FUZZY SYSTEMS

11

M. Sugeno and T. Terano

In general, systems which have been dealt with in systems theory can be divided into three classes: nondeterministic systems, stochastic ones, and deterministic ones. In the above, nondeterministic systems have the largest amount of uncertainty. It is well-known that we have the probabilistic representation of systems when uncertainty is caused by random phenomena. Deterministic systems have, of course, no uncertainty.

The fuzzy systems discussed in this paper are those in which uncertainty is caused by fuzzy phenomena. That is, our fuzzy systems are placed between nondeterministic ones and deterministic ones, at the same level with stochastic systems, because the concept of fuzziness corresponds to that of randomness.

Fuzzy systems studied so far are those derived by replacing merely a deterministic input–output relation or a transition of states by a fuzzy relation. These fuzzy systems are, therefore, algebraic ones, a fuzzy automation is a typical example. If we look at this derivation, however, from the point of view of describing actual systems, it is a question whether algebraic systems can have "reality" or not.

We shall attempt, in this paper, to derive the representation of fuzzy systems, assuming that "fuzzy disturbance" inputs are put into deterministic systems. This method is the same as used for the derivation of stochastic systems when probabilistic disturbance inputs are put into the systems.

Here fuzziness of disturbance is subjectively measured by a fuzzy measure. Using fuzzy measures, fuzzy integrals are defined that take the place of probabilistic expectations. Fuzzy measures are set functions with monotonicity that have not necessarily additivity. Fuzzy integrals are the functionals with monotonicity and may be considered as the extended Lebesgue integrals.

Algebraic methods have been mainly used to approach fuzziness so far, while analytical methods have been seldom explored. Fuzzy measures and fuzzy integrals belong to analytical methods that make it possible to deal with fuzziness qualitatively and quantitatively.

A simple example of the derivation of a fuzzy system is shown in the final part of this paper.

FUZZY MEASURES AND FUZZY INTEGRALS

The concept of fuzzy measures and fuzzy integrals has been presented by one of the authors [1]. Here let us briefly explain about fuzzy measures and fuzzy integrals which are used in the next section.

Let X be an arbitrary set and $\mathscr{B}$ be a Borel field of X.

Definition A set function g defined on $\mathscr{B}$ that has the following properties is called a fuzzy measure:

(1) $g(\phi) = 0$, $g(X) = 1$
(2) If A, $B \in \mathscr{B}$ and $A \subset B$, then $g(A) \leqslant g(B)$
(3) If $F_n \in \mathscr{B}$ and $\{F_n\}$ is monotone, the $\lim_{n \to \infty} g(F_n) = g(\lim_{n \to \infty} F_n)$

In the definition, if further g has finite additivity, then g becomes a probability measure. Fuzzy measure can be interpreted in several ways. Here let us interpret it abstractly as follows. A more concrete interpretation is seen in [4].

First, suppose that a person picks up an element x out of X, but does not know which one he has picked up. Next, suppose that he guesses if x belongs to a given subset A. It is uncertain and fuzzy for him whether $x \in A$ or not. His guess would become subjective when there are few clues for guessing.

Assume, in general, that a human being has a subjective quantity called the grade of fuzziness measuring fuzziness such as stated above. If it is assumed in this case that he can consider a quantity $\mathrm{gr}(x \in A)$ which expresses the grade of fuzziness of a statement "$x \in A$", then $g(A)$ is interpreted as $\mathrm{gr}(x \in A)$. It will be easily accepted that if $A \subset B$, then $\mathrm{gr}(x \in A) \leqslant \mathrm{gr}(x \in B)$. If x is known, say x_0, it is clear that $\mathrm{gr}(x_0 \in A) = 0$ if $x_0 \notin A$ and $\mathrm{gr}(x_0 \in A) = 1$ if $x_0 \in A$. Therefore, we have $g(A) = \chi_A(x_0)$ where $\chi_A(x_0)$ is the characteristic function of A.

Let $h : X \to [0, 1]$ be a $\mathscr{B}$-measurable function.

Definition A fuzzy integral of h over A with respect to g is defined as follows:

$$\int_A h(x) \circ g(\cdot) = \sup_{\alpha \in [0, 1]} \left[\alpha \bigwedge g(A \cap F_\alpha) \right], \tag{1}$$

where $F_\alpha = \{ x \mid h(x) \geqslant \alpha \}$.

Fuzzy integrals correspond to probabilistic expectations and are also called fuzzy expectations. A triplet $(X, \mathscr{B}, g)$ is called an F-measure space. Here g is called a fuzzy measure of the measurable space $(X, \mathscr{B})$ or merely that of X. In the above definition, the symbol f is an integral with a small bar and also shows a symbol of the letter f. The small circle is the symbol of the composition used in the fuzzy sets theory.

Hereafter, it is assumed that all the integrands including constants, have the range $[0,1]$. For simplification, a fuzzy integral is written as $\int_A h \circ g(\cdot)$ or $\int_A h \partial g$. In the case of $A = X$, it is written briefly as $\int h \circ g$.

By using fuzzy integrals, it is possible to express one's subjective evaluation of fuzzy objects. A couple of applications [2, 3, 1] have been presented. Fuzzy integrals have the following properties. Let $a \in [0, 1]$, then

$$\int a \circ g(\cdot) = a \tag{2}$$

$$\int (a \wedge h) \circ g(\cdot) = a \wedge \int h \circ g(\cdot) \tag{3}$$

$$\int (a \vee h) \circ g(\cdot) = a \vee \int h \circ g(\cdot) \tag{4}$$

If $h \leqslant h'$, there holds

$$\int h \circ g(\cdot) \leqslant \int h' \circ g(\cdot) \tag{5}$$

If $A \subset B$, then there holds

$$\int_A h \circ g(\cdot) \leqslant \int_B h \circ g(\cdot) \tag{6}$$

If $\{h_n\}$ is a monotone sequence of $\mathscr{B}$-measurable functions, then

$$\int \lim_{n \to \infty} h_n \circ g = \lim_{n \to \infty} \int h_n \circ g \tag{7}$$

If $\{h_n\}$ is a monotone decreasing (increasing) sequence of $\mathscr{B}$-measurable functions and $\{a_n\}$ is a monotone increasing (decreasing) sequence of real numbers, then

$$\int \left[\bigvee_{n=1}^{\infty} (a_n \wedge h_n) \right] \circ g = \bigvee_{n=1}^{\infty} \left[a_n \wedge \int h_n \circ g \right] \tag{8}$$

There holds $\int_A h \circ g = M$ if and only if $g(A \cap F_M) \geqslant M \geqslant g(A \cap F_{M+0})$, where $F_M = \{x | h \geqslant M\}$ and $F_{M+0} = \{x | h > M\}$.

The fuzzy integrals are very similar to the Lebesque integrals in their definition. Let $h(x)$ be a simple function such that[1]

$$h(x) = \sum_{i=1}^{n} \alpha_i \chi_{E_i}(x) \tag{9}$$

[1]$\chi_E(x) = 1$ if $x \in E$ and $\chi_E = 0$ if $x \notin E$.

where

$$X = \sum_{i=1}^{n} E_i, \quad E_i \in \mathfrak{B} \quad \text{and} \quad E_i \cap E_j = \phi \quad (i \neq j)$$

Let μ be a Lebesque measure. In the measure space $(X, \mathfrak{B}, \mu)$, the Lebesgue integral of h over A is defined as

$$\int_A h \, d\mu = \sum_{i=1}^{n} \alpha_i \mu(A \cap E_i) \tag{10}$$

Here assume $0 \leqslant \alpha_i \leqslant 1$ $(1 \leqslant i \leqslant n)$ and $\alpha_1 \leqslant \alpha_2 \leqslant \ldots \leqslant \alpha_n$. Further, let $F_i = E_i + E_{i+1} + \cdots + E_n$ $(1 \leqslant i \leqslant n)$. Then a simple function $h(x)$ can also be written as

$$h(x) = \bigvee_{i=1}^{n} \left[\alpha_i \wedge \chi_{F_i}(x) \right] \tag{11}$$

and two expressions are identical. With respect to a simple function h on X, there holds

$$\int_A h \circ g(\cdot) = \bigvee_{i=1}^{n} \left[\alpha_i \wedge g(A \cap F_i) \right] \tag{12}$$

The similarity of Lebesque and fuzzy integrals is clarified by comparing (9) with (11) and (10) with (12), respectively.

Next a quantitative comparison is tried. Let h be a $\mathfrak{B}$-measurable function. Then both integrals, fuzzy and Lebesque, with respect to a probability measure P can be defined and the following inequality is obtained. Let $(X, \mathfrak{B}, P)$ be a probability space and $h: X \rightarrow [0, 1]$ be a $\mathfrak{B}$-measurable function, then there holds

$$\left| \int_X h(x) \, dP - \int_X h(x) \circ P(\cdot) \right| \leqslant \frac{1}{4} \tag{13}$$

Since the operations of fuzzy integrals include only comparisons of grades, the above inequality implies that using only $\vee$ and $\wedge$, a value different by at most $\frac{1}{4}$ from a probabilistic expectation can be obtained.

Now let $\phi: X \rightarrow Y$, then both the Borel field $\mathfrak{B}^{(\phi)}$ and the fuzzy measure $g^{(\phi)}$ are induced from X into Y. That is:

$$F \in \mathfrak{B}^{(\phi)} \quad \text{if and only if} \quad \phi^{-1}(F) \in \mathfrak{B}$$

$$g^{(\phi)}(F) = g\left(\phi^{-1}(F)\right)$$

A fuzzy measure space $(y, \mathfrak{B}^{(\phi)}, g^{(\phi)})$ is interpreted in the following way. If Y is related to X by a mapping ϕ, then a fuzzy measure of Y by which grade of fuzziness in Y is measured should be also related to that of X.

Definition   Let $E \in \mathfrak{B}$ and $F \in \mathfrak{B}^{(\phi)}$. By $\rho(E|\phi=y)$, denote the representative of all functions equivalent[2] to $h(y)$ with respect to g such that

$$g\big(E \cap \phi^{-1}(F)\big) = \int_F h(y) \circ g^{(\phi)}(\cdot)$$ (14)

Here $\rho(\cdot|\phi=y)$ is called a conditional fuzzy measure under the condition of $\phi=y$.

Let $F = Y$ in the definition, then we obtain

$$g(E) = \int_Y \rho(E|\phi=y) \circ g^{(\phi)}(\cdot)$$ (15)

Conditional fuzzy measures have the following properties:

(1)   For a fixed $E \in \mathfrak{B}$, $\rho(E|\phi=y)$ is, as a function of y, a $\mathfrak{B}^{(\phi)}$-measurable function.
(2)   For fixed y, $\rho(\cdot|\phi=y)$ is a fuzzy measure of $(X, \mathfrak{B})$ in the sense of $g^{(\phi)} - \text{a.e.}$[3]

Even if two fuzzy measure spaces $(X, \mathfrak{B}_X, g_X)$ and $(Y, \mathfrak{B}_Y, g_Y)$ are related to each other, a mapping ϕ may not be explicit in general. We then write $\rho(\cdot|\phi=y)$ as $\rho_X(\cdot|y)$ which is called a conditional fuzzy measure from Y to X. In this case, there must hold similarly

$$g_X(\cdot) = \int_Y \rho_X(\cdot|y) \circ g_Y$$ (15')

Under the above consideration, it is possible to give first $\rho_X(\cdot|y)$ and g_Y instead of g_Y and g_X.

REPRESENTATION OF FUZZY SYSTEMS

First, we show a simple way for obtaining the representation of fuzzy systems by using fuzzy measures. It will be useful for clarifying the difference between stochastic systems and fuzzy ones.

Let us consider a nondeterministic automation. Let K be a finite set of states and Σ a finite set of inputs. State transitions are described by δ such that $\delta: K \times \Sigma \to 2^K$. Define $K' = \delta(s, u)$ where $s \in K$ and $u \in \Sigma$. The state s changes to a certain state s' in K' ($\subset K$).

[2]If $\int_A h(x) \circ g = \int_A h'(x) \circ g$ for any $A \in \mathfrak{B}$, then $h(x)$ is said to be equivalent to h' with respect to g.
[3]When a proposition holds except on a null set E such that $g(E)=0$, it is said to hold almost everywhere with respect to g. We write this statement as $g - \text{a.e.}$

The statement "the next state s' exists in K'''" shows uncertainty since s' is not specified. This uncertainty may be said to be that of $x' \in K'$, which can be decreased as follows. Let us interpret the uncertainty of $x' \in K'$ as the probability of $s' \in K'$ by introducing a probability measure.

Let

$$0 \le p(s,u,s') \le 1 \qquad \text{for all } s' \in K \tag{16}$$

$$\sum_{s' \in K} p(s,u,s') = 1 \tag{17}$$

Then the probability of $s' \in K'$ is expressed by

$$P(s,u,K') = \sum_{s' \in K'} p(s,u,s') \tag{18}$$

On the other hand, if a fuzzy measure $g(s,u,\cdot)$ is introduced, then the grade of $s' \in K'$ is expressed similarly by $g(s,u,K')$. It is clear that the uncertainty is decreased by both the methods. Because $P(s,u,K'')$ and $g(s,u,K'')$ can be defined for any $K'' \subset K'$.

Further, we can assume arbitrary properties as for the uncertainty of $s' \in K'$. These properties are nothing but the properties of a certain set function defined on 2^K. However, if we derive fuzzy systems, so to speak, by an artificial method, we must assume *a priori* without any proof, the property of state transitions corresponding to Chapman-Kolmogoroff's equation as shown later. Thus, this method becomes unrealistic.

Now, we return to the main argument. When we consider on fuzzy systems, it is necessary to find where fuzziness is in the system and where it is not. It is particularly important for us to make clear in what manner subjectivity is involved in an actual and objective system.

The matter described above has seldom been discussed in dealing with fuzzy systems. Hereafter, we say that a system is fuzzy, when objectivity is associated with subjectivity in the system. It does not imply that the system has merely uncertainty. Subjectivity is a kind of uncertainty, but this uncertainty would not disappear even if we study more on it. That is, it seems that as for subjectivity, there exists something like the "principle of uncertainty" as in quantum mechanics.

Now let U and Ω be sets of inputs of a system, X a set of state variable, and Y a set of outputs. Assume that the elements of U can be controlled and those of Ω are disturbance inputs that are uncontrollable. For taking notice of $\omega \in \Omega$, we regard $u \in U$ as a parameter. Let $\phi_{u_{tt'}}$ be a state transition function and ψ_{u_t} an output function.

Then a dynamical system can be expressed as follows:

$$x_{t'} = \phi_{u_{tt'}}(x_t, \omega_{tt'}) \qquad \text{for } t' \ge t \tag{19}$$

$$y_t = \psi_{u_t}(x_t, \omega_t) \tag{20}$$

where it is assumed that

$$\phi_{u_{tt''}}(x_t, \omega_{tt''}) = \phi_{u_{t't''}}\left(\phi_{u_{tt'}}(x_t, \omega_{tt'}), \omega_{t't''}\right) \qquad \text{for } t'' \geqslant t' \geqslant t \qquad (21)$$

Now we make the necessary assumptions:

(1) Ω is a fuzzy measure space $(\Omega, \mathcal{B}, g)$.
(2) The fuzzy measure g is independent of time, i.e., stationary.

Let us call ω a fuzzy disturbance input. If Ω is a probability space, then ω becomes a stochastic disturbance input. Our problem is to show in what manner fuzziness in Ω is transmitted to the states and outputs of the system. For simplification of the following discussions, time is regarded discrete and the matters concerned with outputs are omitted.

For discrete times t_1 and t_2 that are denoted simply by 1 and 2, we rewrite (19):

$$x_1 = \phi_{u_1}(x_0, \omega_1) \qquad (22)$$

$$x_2 = \phi_{u_2}(x_1, \omega_2) = \phi_{u_1 u_2}(x_0, \omega_1 \omega_2) \qquad (23)$$

where x_0 is an initial state of the system.

Equation (21) is also rewritten as

$$\phi_{u_1 u_2}(x_0, \omega_1 \omega_2) = \phi_{u_2}\left(\phi_{u_1}(x_0, \omega_1), \omega_2\right). \qquad (24)$$

Here ϕ_{u_1}, ϕ_{u_2}, and $\phi_{u_1 u_2}$ can be considered as the following mappings:

$$\phi_{u_1} : X_0 \times \Omega_1 \rightarrow X_1$$
$$\phi_{u_2} : X_1 \times \Omega_2 \rightarrow X_2$$
$$\phi_{u_1 u_2} : X_0 \times \Omega_1 \times \Omega_2 \rightarrow X_2$$

From the assumptions, Ω_1 and Ω_2 are spaces with the common fuzzy measure g.

We attempt to induce fuzzy measures into X_1 and X_2 in an analogous way as in the previous section. For this purpose, it is necessary to define a fuzzy measure of X_0, i.e., the set of initial states. Assuming that an initial state x_0 is known, a fuzzy measure is naturally defined as has been also showed in the previous section.

Let

$$X_0 = \left(X, \mathcal{B}^{(\phi_e)}, g^{(\phi_e)}\right)$$

where $g^{(\phi_e)}(A) = \chi_A(x_0)$ for $A \in \mathcal{B}^{(\phi_e)}$.

Here, e implies the empty input and ϕ_e is a one-to-one mapping such that $\phi_e : X \rightarrow X$.

What is necessary next is to consider the fuzzy product measure space:

$$X_0 \times \Omega_1 = \left(X \times \Omega, \mathcal{B}^{(\phi_e)} \times \mathcal{B}, g^{(\phi_e)} \times g \right).$$

If $g^{(\phi_e)} \times g$ can be defined, a fuzzy measure is induced into X_1. Consequently, we have

$$X_1 = \left(X, \mathcal{B}^{(\phi_{u_1})}, g^{(\phi_{u_1})} \right)$$

Here $\mathcal{B}^{(\phi_e)} \times \mathcal{B}$ can be defined in an ordinary way. We define $g^{(\phi_e)} \times g$ on $\mathcal{B}^{(\phi_e)} \times \mathcal{B}$ as follows:

$$\left(g^{(\phi_e)} \times g \right)(F) = \int_{X_0} \left[\int_{\Omega_1} \chi_F(x_0, \omega_1) \circ g \right] \circ g^{(\phi_e)} \tag{25}$$

where $F \subset X_0 \times \Omega_1$ and $F \in \mathcal{B}^{(\phi_e)} \times \mathcal{B}$.

Now let us construct the fuzzy measure space $(X_1, \mathcal{B}^{(\phi_{u_1})}, g^{(\phi_{u_1})})$:

(1) $E \in \mathcal{B}^{(\phi_{u_1})}$ if and only if $\phi_{u_1}^{-1}(E) \in \mathcal{B}^{(\phi_e)} \times \mathcal{B}$,

(2) $g^{(\phi_{u_1})}(E) = (g^{(\phi_e)} \times g)(F)$,
     where $F = \{(x_0, \omega_1) | \phi_{u_1}(x_0, \omega_1) \in E\}$

Define for $E \in \mathcal{B}^{(\phi_{u_1})}$

$$\rho^{(\phi_{u_1})}(E|x_0) = \int_{\Omega_1} \chi_F(x_0, \omega_1) \circ g \tag{26}$$

Then we obtain

$$g^{(\phi_{u_1})}(E) = \int_{x_0} \rho^{(\phi_{u_1})}(E|x_0) \circ g^{(\phi_e)} \tag{27}$$

It is clear that $\rho^{(\phi_{u_1})}(\cdot | x_0)$ satisfies the properties of a conditional fuzzy measure. We omit the proof.

In an analogous way, we obtain

$$X_2 = \left(X, \mathcal{B}^{(\phi_{u_2})}, g^{(\phi_{u_2})} \right)$$

For $H \in \mathcal{B}^{(\phi_{u_2})}$

$$g^{(\phi_{u_2})}(H) = \int_{X_1} \left[\int_{\Omega_2} \chi_G(x_1, \omega_2) \circ g \right] \circ g^{(\phi_{u_1})} \tag{28}$$

here

$$G = \left\{ (x_1, \omega_2) | \phi_{u_2}(x_1, \omega_2) \in H \right\}$$

Further define

$$\rho^{(\phi_{u_2})}(H|x_1) = \int_{\Omega_2} \chi_K(x_1, \omega_2) \circ g \qquad (29)$$

From (28) follows

$$g^{(\phi_{u_2})}(H) = \int_{X_1} \rho^{(\phi_{u_2})}(H|x_1) \circ g^{(\phi_{u_1})} \qquad (30)$$

Now, another fuzzy measure is induced into X_2 also by the mapping

$$\phi_{u_1 u_2} : X_0 \times \Omega_1 \times \Omega_2 \to X_2$$

Define

$$X_2' = \left(X, \mathcal{B}^{(\phi_{u_1 u_2})}, g^{(\phi_{u_1 u_2})} \right)$$

For $H \in \mathcal{B}^{(\phi_{u_1 u_2})}$, $g^{(\phi_{u_1 u_2})}(H)$ can be defined as follows:

$$g^{(\phi_{u_1 u_2})}(H) = \int_{X_0 \times \Omega_1} \left[\int_{\Omega_2} \chi_K(x_0, \omega_1, \omega_2) \circ g \right] \circ g^{(\phi_e)} \times g$$

$$= \int_{X_0} \left[\int_{\Omega_1} \left[\int_{\Omega_2} \chi_K(x_0, \omega_1, \omega_2) \circ g \right] \circ g \right] \circ g^{(\phi_e)} \qquad (31)$$

where

$$K = \left\{ (x_0, \omega_1, \omega_2) | \phi_{u_1 u_2}(x_0, \omega_1, \omega_2) \in H \right\}$$

Define

$$\rho^{(\phi_{u_1 u_2})}(H|x_0) = \int_{\Omega_1} \left[\int_{\Omega_2} \chi_K(x_0, \omega_1, \omega_2) \circ g \right] \circ g \qquad (32)$$

Then we obtain

$$g^{(\phi_{u_1 u_2})}(H) = \int_{X_0} \rho^{(\phi_{u_1 u_2})}(H|x_0) \circ g^{(\phi_e)} \qquad (33)$$

From the property of the mapping ϕ_u in (24), X_2 and X_2' must be the same measure space. We have the next theorem.

Theorem *(After Theorem 7.2 of* [1].)

(1) $\mathcal{B}^{(\phi_{u_1 u_2})} = \mathcal{B}^{(\phi_{u_2})}$

(2) $\rho^{(\phi_{u_1 u_2})}(H|x_0) = \int_{X_1} \rho^{(\phi_{u_2})}(H|x_1) \circ \rho^{(\phi_{u_1})}(\cdot|x_0) \qquad (34)$

Lemma

$$g^{(\phi_{u_1 u_2})}(\cdot) = g^{(\phi_{u_2})}(\cdot) \tag{35}$$

Our purpose has been now accomplished. From the above lemma it follows

$$g^{(\phi_{u_1 u_2})}(H) = \int_{X_0} \left[\int_{X_1} \rho^{(\phi_{u_2})}(H|x_1) \circ \rho^{(\phi_{u_1})}(\cdot|x_0) \right] \circ g^{(\phi_e)} \tag{36}$$

Equation (34) corresponds to Chapman–Kolmogoroff's equation.

Now, let us use the following notations:

$$\sigma_X(\cdot|u_1 u_2 \ldots u_n, x_0) = \rho^{(\phi_{u_1 u_2 \cdots u_n})}(\cdot|x_0) \tag{37}$$

$$g_X^n(\cdot) = g^{(\phi_{u_1 u_2 \cdots u_n})}(\cdot) \tag{38}$$

By generalizing (36), we obtain that

$$g_X^n(H) = \int_{X_{n-1}} \sigma_X(H|u_n, x_{n-1}) \circ g_X^{n-1}(\cdot)$$

$$= \int_{X_0} \sigma_X(H|u_1 u_2 \ldots u_n, x_0) \circ g_X^0(\cdot) \tag{39}$$

where

$$\sigma_X(H|u_1 u_2 \ldots u_n, x_0) = \int_{X_k} \sigma_X(H|u_{k+1} \ldots u_n, x_k) \circ \sigma_X(\cdot|u_1 u_2 \ldots u_k, x_0) \tag{40}$$

In general, we can assume that an initial state x_0 is unknown, though it was assumed at first to be known. In this case $g_X^0(\cdot)$ can be considered as a fuzzy measure for fuzziness of initial states. It corresponds to an initial distribution of a stochastic system.

Further, the conditional fuzzy measure $\sigma_Y(K|u_n, x_n)$ can be derived as for outputs of the system. The fuzzy measure with respect to the output y_n can be obtained as

$$g_Y^n(K) = \int_{X_n} \sigma_Y(K|u_n, x_n) \circ g_X^n(\cdot) \tag{41}$$

Now, $g_X^n(H)$ expresses the grade of fuzziness of "$x_n \in H$." On the other hand, $\sigma_X(\cdot|u_1 u_2 \ldots u_n, x_0)$ can be interpreted as a fuzzy measure for the fuzzy transition of states as a result that the input sequence $u_1 u_2 \ldots u_n$ is put into the system under the condition that the initial state is x_0.

We have now obtained the representation of a fuzzy system under the condition that fuzzy disturbance inputs are put into a deterministic system.

Note: if a time sequence $t_1 t_2 \ldots t_n$ is substituted for $u_1 u_2 \ldots u_n$ in (39), then we obtain a system equation corresponding to a Marköff chain.

EXAMPLE

Let us consider the following dynamical system.

$$x_n = \phi_n(x_{n-1}, \omega_n)$$
$$= a x_{n-1} + \omega_n, \quad a > 0 \tag{42}$$

Here X and Ω are both assumed to be R^1 and U is omitted. In the above case, the F-distribution function of $g_X{}''(\cdot)$ can be analytically obtained. Let $g(\cdot)$ be the fuzzy measure of Ω. Define $H(\omega)$ as $H(\omega) = g((-\infty, \omega])$, then $H(\omega)$ is called the F-distribution function of $g(\cdot)$. $H(\omega)$ has the same properties as the distribution function of a probability measure; $\lim_{\omega \to -\infty} H(\omega) = 0$, $\lim_{\omega \to +\infty} H(\omega) = 1$ and $H(\omega)$ is monotonously increasing.

Generalizing (26), let $E = (-\infty, x_n]$, $F = \{(x_{n-1}, \omega_n) | a x_{n-1} + \omega_n \in (-\infty, x_n]\}$ and further define

$$F(x_{n-1}) = \{\omega_n | a x_{n-1} + \omega_n \in (-\infty, x_n]\}$$
$$= \{\omega_n | \omega_n \in (-\infty, x_n - a x_{n-1}]\},$$

then it is obtained from (27) that

$$\rho^{(\phi_n)}\big((-\infty, x_n] | x_{n-1}\big) = \int_{\Omega_n} \chi_{F(x_{n-1})}(\omega_n) \circ g$$
$$= H(x_n - a x_{n-1}), \quad 1 \leqslant n < \infty \tag{43}$$

From (34)

$$\rho^{(\phi_{n-1,n})}\big((-\infty, x_n] | x_{n-2}\big) = \int_{X_{n-1}} H(x_n - a x_{n-1}) \circ \rho^{(\phi_{n-1})}(\cdot | x_{n-2}) \tag{44}$$

Taking into account that $a > 0$ and $H(\omega)$ is monotonously increasing, (44) is, using (1) and (43), rewritten as

$$\rho^{(\phi_{n-1,n})}\big((-\infty, x_n] | x_{n-2}\big) = \sup_{\alpha \in [0,1]} \big[\alpha \wedge H(\beta - a x_{n-2})\big], \quad \alpha = H(x_n - a\beta)$$
$$= \sup_{\beta \in (-\infty, \infty)} \big[H(x_n - a\beta) \wedge H(\beta - a x_{n-2})\big]$$
$$= H\left(\frac{1}{1+a} x_n - \frac{a^2}{1+a} x_{n-2}\right) \tag{45}$$

Repeating the above procedure, it follows generally that

$$\rho^{(\phi_{1,2,\ldots,n})}\big((-\infty, x_n]\,|\,x_0\big) = H\left[\frac{x_n - a^n x_0}{\sum_{k=0}^{n-1} a^k}\right] \tag{46}$$

Now let $H_X{}^n(x)$ be the F-distribution function of $g_X{}^n$ and let x_n be x in (46) since x_n is a dummy variable, then it is obtained from (39) that

$$H_X{}^n(x) = \int_{X_0} H\left[\frac{x - a^n x_0}{\sum_{k=0}^{n-1} a^k}\right] \circ g_X{}^0 \tag{47}$$

In (47), $\lim_{n \to \infty}$ and f are commutative [1]. Therefore taking the limit of $H_X{}^n(x)$, we have

$$\lim_{n \to \infty} H_X{}^n(x) = \begin{cases} H\big((1-a)x\big), & 1 > a > 0 \\ H(0), & a = 1 \\ \int_{X_0} H\big((1-a)x_0\big) \circ g_X{}^0, & a > 1 \end{cases} \tag{48}$$

As is seen in (48), if $a \leqslant 1$, then the limit distribution does not depend on the initial distribution $g_X{}^0$ and if $a \geqslant 1$, then it becomes a constant; any clue for the location of x is lost. The case of $a = 1$ is the critical case.

CONCLUSION

In this paper, it has been tried to derive an analytical representation of a fuzzy system. It is assumed that "fuzzy disturbance" inputs are put into a deterministic system. Here fuzziness of disturbance is measured by a fuzzy measure. The approach to fuzzy systems discussed in the paper seems to be more realistic than an algebraic one does.

A simple example has been also shown. The subject for a future study would be to examine the ability of our model of a fuzzy system by applying it to actual fuzzy systems.

REFERENCES

1. M. Sugeno, "Theory of Fuzzy Integrals and its Applications," Ph.D. Thesis, Tokyo Institute of Technology, 1974.

2. M. Sugeno and T. Terano, "An Approach to the Identification of Human Characteristics by Applying Fuzzy Integrals," *Proc. Third IFAC Symp. Identification and System Parameter Estimation*, 1973.
3. M. Sugeno *et al.*, "Subjective Evaluation of Fuzzy Objects," *IFAC Symp. on Stochastic Control*, 1974.
4. T. Terano and M. Sugeno, "Macroscopic Optimization Using Conditional Fuzzy Measures," Chapter 13, this volume.

ON FUZZY ALGORITHM AND MAPPING

12

Sheldon S. L. Chang

Zadeh's original paper [7] on fuzzy algorithms gave the following rationale:

> It is a truism that precision is respectable and fuzziness is not. However, in our quest for ever greater degree of precision in pure and applied science, we have perhaps tended to lose sight of one basic fact, namely, that the class of nontrivial problems for which one can find precise algorithmic solutions is quite limited. Unfortunately, most realistic problems tend to be complex, and many complex problems are either algorithmically unsolvable or, if solvable in principle, are computationally infeasible.

Many examples of complex systems were given including parking a car, and playing chess.

In studying the instructions in fuzzy algorithms, one distinction can be made between two types of instructions:

(i)   non-fuzzy instructions on a fuzzy systems
(ii) fuzzy instructions on a fuzzy or non-fuzzy system

Class (i) instructions are not intentionally fuzzy. The system is not equipped to carry out a precise instruction or it can do so only at additional cost. Class (ii) instructions are true fuzzy instructions. Algorithms containing class (ii) instructions will be called a *true fuzzy algorithm*.

To illustrate the difference between the two types of instructions, the car–driver system is not equipped to measure the turning angular speed, turning angle, or the exact distance from the curb. The system itself is a fuzzy system. Zadeh gave the following fuzzy algorithm:

> First, while the car is moving forward, the wheels are turned to the right and then to the left; and second, the direction of motion is reversed and the wheels are turned first to the right and then to the

Acknowledgment: This work was sponsored by the National Science Foundation under Grant No. ENG69-00643A04.

left. By repeating this maneuver as many times as necessary, the car can be moved in a lateral direction by any desired amount.

Is the algorithm a *true* fuzzy algorithm? The answer is "yes", because (a) some approximate turning angle can be specified but is not specified, and (b) no specification is made in the timing "*then* to the left," etc.

Example   A baseball manager gave the batter signal to bunt. The bunting operation is fuzzy, but the instruction to bunt is a non-fuzzy instruction on a fuzzy system.

Example   If x is large, increase y by several units. This is a fuzzy instruction on a non-fuzzy system.

The distinction between the two types of "fuzzy" instructions is important from a system theoretical point of view because one important unanswered question is "when a fuzzy algorithm is called for ?" Obviously if a system itself is fuzzy, the least fuzzy instruction one can give is of type (i). A meaningful reformulation of the question is then "when is a *true* fuzzy algorithm is called for ?"

It seems that one unnecessary and insufficient, but highly plausible, condition for a true fuzzy algorithm is distributed intelligence: that is, that both the designer and the executor of the algorithm are intelligent. Take Zadeh's example of fuzzy algorithms in everyday experience (a) cooking recipes, (b) directions for repairing a TV set, (c) instructions on how to treat a disease, (d) instructions on how to park a car, etc. Is there any *mechanical* way of carrying out any of these instructions? A fuzzy algorithm in the above category is no more than a general outline. Its successful execution depends very much on the executor's observation, learning and intelligence to fill out the details in view of the current situation.

An alternative condition for fuzzy algorithm is irrelevence. Consider the example of parking a car. The speed of turning the front wheel and the speed of moving forward or backward are irrelevent as long as they belong to the fuzzy set *slow*.

It is difficult to think of a true fuzzy algorithm where neither the condition of distributed intelligence nor the condition of irrelevence is present. However, the above observations do not constitute anything definite. In the following sections, the concept of "optimum" or "non-inferior" is defined for fuzzy systems, and a proof will be given that in the absence of distributed intelligence, true fuzzy instructions do not do better than non-fuzzy instructions.

OPTIMUM, OR NON-INFERIOR, SET

We begin this section with a definition.

Definition Let S denote a set of intervals I_ν, with $I_\nu' = \inf I_\nu$ and $I_\nu'' = \sup I_\nu$. An interval I_1 is said to be *inferior* to I_2 if

$$I_1' \leqslant I_2' \quad \text{and} \quad I_1'' < I_2''$$

or

$$I_2' < I_2' \quad \text{and} \quad I_1'' \leqslant I_2''$$

The inferior relation is denoted by

$$I_1 < I_2 \quad \text{or} \quad I_2 > I_1 \tag{2}$$

An interval I_0 is said to be *optimum* (non-inferior) if there does not exist a $I_\nu \in S$ such that $I_\nu > I_0$. The set of optimum intervals is denoted by OS. It is a subset of S, and will be called the *optimum subset* of S. Let S^* denote the set of intervals obtained by finite numbers of union and intersection operations of member of S, $S \subset S^*$.

Theorem $OS \subset OS^*$

The theorem states that an optimum interval I_0 in S remains optimum in the larger set S^*.

Proof If $I_\mu \in S$, $I_\nu \in S$, and $I_1 = I_\mu \cup I_\nu$, then

$$I_1' = I_\mu' \bigwedge I_\nu'$$

$$I_1'' = I_\mu'' \bigvee I_\nu'' \tag{3}$$

If $I_1'' > I_0''$, then one of the two I_μ'' or I_ν'' must be greater than I_0''. Without loss of generality let it be assumed

$$I_\mu'' > I_0'' \tag{4}$$

Since $I_0 \in OS$, (3) and (4) imply that $I_1' \leqslant I_\mu' < I_0'$. Therefore, I_0 is not inferior to I_1.

Similarly, let $I_2 = I_\mu \cap I_\nu$. Then

$$I_2' = I_\mu' \bigvee I_\nu'$$

$$I_2'' = I_\mu'' \bigwedge I_\nu'' \tag{5}$$

Without loss of generality, assume I_μ' to be the larger of the two: I_μ' and I_ν'. Then $I_2' > I_0' \Rightarrow I_\mu' > I_0' \Rightarrow I_\mu'' < I_0''$. From (5)

$$I_2'' \leqslant I_\mu'' < I_0''$$

Therefore, I_0 is not inferior to I_2. The above proves that optimality is preserved for any number of union and intersection operations of members of S.

Definition   Let Σ denote a set of fuzzy sets A_ν on the real line. Let $A_\nu(m)$ denote the level set of A_ν for membership m.

Let $\Sigma(m)$ denote the set of level sets $A_\nu(m), \nu = 1, 2, \ldots$, and $0\Sigma(m)$ the optimum subset of $\Sigma(m)$. Then $A_0 \in \Sigma$ is said to be an *optimum* fuzzy set if $A_0(m) \in 0\Sigma(m)$ for every m:

$$A_0 \in 0\Sigma \Leftrightarrow \forall_m, A_0(m) \in 0\Sigma(m) \tag{6}$$

Let Σ^* denote the set of fuzzy sets obtained by union and intersection operations of members of Σ. The following theorem can be stated:

Theorem   *If A_0 is optimum in Σ, it is optimum in Σ^*.*

$$0\Sigma \subset 0\Sigma^* \tag{7}$$

Proof   It is easy to show that

$$\Sigma^*(m) = \left[\Sigma(m) \right]^* \tag{8}$$

Since $A_0(m)$ is optimum in $\Sigma(m)$, it is optimum in $[\Sigma(m)]^*$ by the first theorem . From (8), $A_0(m)$ is optimum in $\Sigma^*(m)$ for every m.

DECISION PROCESSES

Zadeh described fuzzy algorithm in terms of a fuzzy Turing machine [7], which is identical with his fuzzy system description. The same description was also used later in a paper by Chang and Zadeh for a multistage decision processes [4]:

$$x(t+1) = f(x(t), u(t)) \tag{9}$$

For a fuzzy system, f is defined by a membership function $\mu_f(x(t+1, x(t), u(t))$, on $X \times X \times U$. Value function $V(x)$ maps X into the real line. The problem is to maximize $V(x(N))$ by choosing $u(\cdot): u(0), u(1) \ldots u(N-1)$. A nonfuzzy algorithm as defined at the beginning means that each $u(i), i = 0, 1, 2 \ldots$ is a point in U ($u(\cdot)$ is a point in U^N). A *true* fuzzy algorithm means that some $u(i)$ is a fuzzy set in U ($u(\cdot)$ is a fuzzy set in U^N).

If any of f, u, or $X(0)$ is fuzzy, then $V(x(N))$ is a fuzzy set on the real line. Let $V(x(N)/u(\cdot))$ denote the $V(x(N))$ resulting from $u(\cdot)$. Optimality may be defined for m-level set of $V(x(N))$ or $V(x(N))$ itself in the non-inferior sense of the first section II. A decision $u(\cdot)$ is said to be m-optimum if the m-level set of $V(x(N)/u(\cdot))$ is optimum. A decision $u(\cdot)$ is said to be optimum if $V(x(N)/u(\cdot))$ is an optimum fuzzy set.

Let L denote a finite lattice in U^N. A fuzzy lattice decision $u(\cdot)$ has finite membership for each lattice point and zero membership elsewhere. Assuming that f has continuous partial derivatives of u (or some fuzzy equivalent of such an assumption) it can be shown that each fuzzy decision can be approximated by a fuzzy lattice decision.

Theorem *If a non-fuzzy decision $u(\cdot)$ is m-optimum (optimum) among all non-fuzzy decisions, then it is m-optimum (optimum) among all fuzzy lattice decisions.*

Proof An N-stage decision is equivalent to a single-stage decision in U^N space:

$$\mu(x(N)) = \sup_{(x(0)),u(\cdot)} \mu_F(x(N),x(0),u(\cdot))\,\mu_d(u(\cdot)),\mu_0(x(0)) \quad (10)$$

where

$$\mu_F(x(N),x(0),u(\cdot))$$
$$= \sup_{x(1),x(2)\ldots x(N-1)} \inf_{n=0,1,\ldots,N-1} \mu_f(x(n+1),x(n),u(n)) \quad (11)$$

and

$$\mu_d(u(\cdot)) = \min_{n=0,1,\ldots,N-1} \mu_{dn}(u(n)) \quad (12)$$

Equation (11) defines the fuzzy function $F(x(0),u(\cdot))$ that maps $X \times U^N$ into X. The function $V(F(x(0),u(\cdot))$ in turn maps X into the real line. Considering $x(0)$ as given $\phi(u(\cdot)) \triangleq V(F(x(0),u(\cdot)))$ is a mapping of U^N into the real line. Then [4]

$$\phi(u_1(\cdot) \cup u_2(\cdot)) = \phi(u_1(\cdot)) \cup \phi(u_2(\cdot))$$

From the above relation and the first two theorems the theorem is proved.

Definition A fuzzy set is said to be *compact* if for each given nonvanishing m, its m-level set is compact. A decision $u(\cdot)$ is said to be a *compact fuzzy decision* if $u(\cdot)$ is a compact fuzzy set in U^N. The third theorem can be improved as follows: If $\mu_f(x(t+1),x(t),u(t))$ is continuous in $u(t)$, and a non-fuzzy decision $u(\cdot)$ is m-optimum (optimum) among all non-fuzzy decisions, then it is m-optimum (optimum) among all compact fuzzy decisions.

CONCLUSION

The last theorem can be interpreted (fuzzily) as showing that in the absence of distributed intelligence a non-fuzzy algorithm is at least as good as the best of the fuzzy algorithms for a fuzzy or non-fuzzy system.

The above conclusion throws some light on the important problem of how to execute a fuzzy algorithm. If intelligence is assumed to exist in the algorithm executor, this intelligence must be allowed to take part. To execute the algorithm either on a membership or a probability basis would not represent the actual situation.

If the "fuzzy algorithm" is a non-fuzzy algorithm in a fuzzy system, the problem is then not how to execute the algorithm but how to simulate the system itself.

REFERENCES

1. R. E. Bellman and L. A. Zadeh, "Decision-Making in a Fuzzy Environment," *Management Sci.* **17** (1970), B-141–B-164.
2. S. S. L. Chang, "On Risk and Decision Making in a Fuzzy Environment," NSF Workshop on Fuzzy Systems and Applications, Berkeley, Calif., July 1974.
3. S. S. L. Chang and P. E. Barry, "Optimal Control of Systems with Uncertain Parameters," *Fifth IFAC Congr.*, Paris, 1972.
4. S. S. L. Chang and L. A. Zadeh, "Fuzzy Mapping and Control," *IEEE Trans. Syst., Man, Cybern.* **SMC-2** (Jan. 1962), 30–34.
5. E. Santos, "Fuzzy Algorithms," *Inform. Contr.* **12** (1970), 326–339.
6. L. A. Zadeh, "Fuzzy Sets," *Inform. Contr.* **8** (1965), 338–353.
7. L. A. Zadeh, "Fuzzy Algorithms," *Inform. Contr.* **12** (1968), 94–102.

MACROSCOPIC OPTIMIZATION USING CONDITIONAL FUZZY MEASURES 13

T. Terano and M. Sugeno

Many papers have been published related to the method of optimum seeking of multimodal functions. In most of them they suggest heuristic searches that combine random searches and logical decisions. This problem can be considered as decision making under uncertainty. For instance, if random search is carried out, we face two kinds of uncertainties that come from the lack of knowledge of the objective function J as shown in Fig. 1. One of them is concerned with the value of J between the examined points. This is quite vague as the marked area A in Fig. 1 shows, even if we assume the continuity of J. We had better choose the next search point in the area where this vagueness is vast, because the possibility of finding the extremum is large. The other uncertainty comes from the fact that we cannot say the maximum value of all the examined points is really extremum of J. This is shown as B in Fig. 1. This uncertainty is related to the economics of search, because we can stop the search in the minimum number of trials if we know B is small.

Both uncertainties are, of course, decreased in proportion to the number of the past trials. But the purpose of heuristic search is to reduce the trials more quickly. In this paper, we suggest a decision modle, that is similar to the learning process of humans, and apply it to the optimization problems of multimodal unknown functions.

Before we enter the discussion in detail, we must point out that the exact value and the precise position of an extremum point are not always needed in most of the engineering problems, but it is more important to get the macroscopic map of J covering the whole area and the approximate value of extremum quickly. Some experiments of the optimum seeking by a human operator [1] show us that he never tries to search in detail before getting the general idea about J. For this purpose, we have divided, the whole area of J into some blocks and, after a few trials, evaluated the grade of fuzziness of the statement "they include the true maximum point." This grade of fuzziness is conveniently expressed by fuzzy integrals [2] and the learning process is simulated by the improvement of *a priori* weights of the criteria that measure the grade of fuzziness.

Consequently, we do not use any fuzzy automata but use a fuzzy

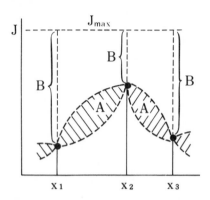

Figure 1.   Uncertainty in search problem.

integral for the evaluation of the blocks; the new search points are assigned to each block in accordance with the evaluation.

LEARNING PROCESS BY FUZZY INFORMATION

Let us consider the problem of estimating the causes from fuzzy information when there are many results and causes. Let X be a set of causes and Y a set of results of which fuzzy measures [2] are denoted by g_X and g_Y, respectively. Now we assume that g_Y is expressed by the fuzzy integral of $\sigma_Y(\cdot|x)$ with respect to g_X

$$g_Y(\cdot) = \int_X \sigma_Y(\cdot|x) \circ g_X \qquad (1)$$

where $\sigma_Y(\cdot|x)$ is a conditional fuzzy measure [3] of Y with respect to X.

The physical meaning of this equation is similar to that of the probability of y (with $y \in Y$) when the conditional probability $p(\cdot|x)$ and the probability measure $p(x)$ (with $x \in X$) are given. But their mathematical definitions and properties are quite different from those in probability theory. The fuzzy measure g_X can be considered as a subjective weight of x that the decision maker holds *a priori*.

Next we consider the information by which g_X is improved. This information is also given as a set E (with $E \subset Y$), which means that one of the elements of E has happened. If E has only a single element, the information is deterministic. It is uncertain (non-deterministic) when E consists of some elements. Further, it is fuzzy when E is a fuzzy set A.

In the optimum seeking problems, the information obtained from the past trials are fuzzy as shown in Fig. 1. Therefore, we consider only the last case. The grade of fuzziness of the whole informations is expressed by a fuzzy integral

$$g_Y(A) = \int_Y h_A(y) \circ g_Y \tag{2}$$

where $h_A(y)$ is the membership function of a fuzzy set A. In (2), g_Y expresses the grade of fuzziness of the statement "y really results," and $h_A(Y)$ represents the accuracy of the information objectively.

From (1) and (2), we obtain

$$g_Y(A) = \int_Y h_A(y) \circ \left[\int_X \sigma_Y(\cdot|x) \circ g_X \right]$$

$$= \int_X \sigma_Y(A|x) \circ g_X \tag{3}$$

where

$$\sigma_Y(A|x) \triangleq \int_Y h_A(y) \circ \sigma_Y(\cdot|x) \tag{4}$$

The correction of g_X should be done so as to increase $g_Y(A)$, that is, to decrease the grade of fuzziness.

Here $g_X(\cdot)$ and $\sigma_Y(\cdot|x)$ are assumed to satisfy λ-rule.[1] Assuming that $\sigma_Y(A|x_i)$ is arranged decreasingly, we have

$$g_Y(A) = \bigvee_{i=1}^{n} \left[\sigma_Y(A|x_i) \wedge g_X(\{x_1, x_2, \ldots, x_i\}) \right] \tag{3'}$$

Let the range of x, which contribute the fuzzy integral in (3'), be F_l.

$$F_l \triangleq \{x_1, x_2, \ldots, x_l\}$$

In (3'), x_l is the intersection of $\sigma_Y(A|x_i)$ and $g_X(\{x_1, x_2, \ldots, x_i\})$.

Let $g_X{}^i$ denote the fuzzy density of g_X, corresponding to x_i. When we choose $g_X{}^i$ large for $i = 1, 2, \ldots, l$ and small for $i = l+1, \ldots, n$, the value of $g_Y(A)$ becomes large. Therefore, we can improve the accuracy of evaluation, that is $g_Y(A)$, by using such learning rules as follows:

$$
\begin{aligned}
(g_X{}^i)' &= \alpha g_X{}^i + (1-\alpha)\sigma_Y(A|x_i), &&\text{for } i = 1, 2, \ldots, l \\
(g_X{}^i)' &= \alpha g_X{}^i &&\text{for } i = l+1, l+2, \ldots, n
\end{aligned}
\tag{5}
$$

where $0 < \alpha < 1$. In the above equations, $g_X{}^i$ never exceeds $\sigma_Y(A|x_i)$. Because $g_Y(A)$ is not improved, even if $g_X{}^i$ is increased more than $\sigma_Y(A|x_i)$ for $i = 1, 2, \ldots, l$.

Now, let us examine the effects of learning process with some numerical

---

[1] Denote $g_X(\{x_i\})$ by $g_X{}^i$; this is called the fuzzy density of g_X. If $g_X{}^i$ and $g_X(\cdot)$ satisfy the following equation for a given value of λ, the calculation of fuzzy integrals becomes very easy.

$$\prod_{i=1}^{n} (1 + \lambda g_X{}^i) - 1 = \lambda, \qquad -1 < \lambda < \infty$$

$$g_X(E) = \frac{1}{\lambda} \left[\prod_{x_i \in E} (1 + \lambda g_X{}^i) - 1 \right]$$

examples. In these examples, $\sigma_Y(\{y_j\}|x_i)$ is given in Table 1, α from (5) is fixed at 0.8, and the density of *a priori* fuzzy measures is given by $g_X{}^i = 0.5$, 0.3, 0.1, 0.3, 0.5, for $i = 1, 2, \ldots, 5$, respectively. Three kinds of informations, which are shown in Table 2, are given repeatedly to the decision maker until g_X converges.

Table 1

$\sigma_Y(\{y_j\}|x_i)$

	y_1	y_2	y_3	y_4	y_5
x_1	0.70	0.23	0.16	0.08	0.39
x_2	0.40	0.64	0.32	0.16	0.08
x_3	0.16	0.49	0.57	0.24	0.16
x_4	0.08	0.16	0.40	0.64	0.32
x_5	0.17	0.34	0.25	0.42	0.50

$\lambda = -0.8$

Table 2

$h_A(y)$

	y_1	y_2	y_3	y_4	y_5
Case (1)	0	0	1	0	0
Case (2)	0.3	0.5	0.8	0.5	0.3
Case (3)	0.6	0.6	0.6	0.6	0.6

The learning processes of g_X, in these cases, are shown in Figs. 2, 3, and 4, where m are the number of repetitions. From these calculations, we get the following conclusions:

(1)   When the information is deterministic, the settling time is short as shown in Fig. 2. However, if it is fuzzy, the speed of convergence is not so rapid.

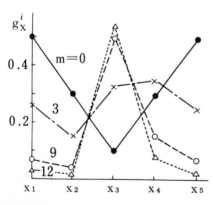

Figure 2. Learning through deterministic information.

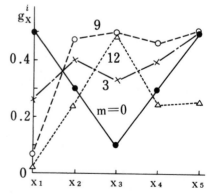

Figure 3. Learning through fuzzy information (1),

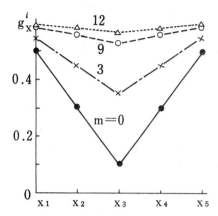

Figure 4. Learning through fuzzy information (2).

(2) The final values of $g_X{}^i$ do not depend on *a priori* values, but are equal to $\sigma_Y(A|x)$ for x which makes $\sigma_Y(A|x)$ a maximum value and equal to zero for other x.

(3) If the information is constant, that is $h_A(y) = C$, $g_X{}^i$ also converges to C as shown in Fig. 4. This implies that *a posteriori* weights of evaluation become fuzzy because the given information is so fuzzy.

(4) Another interesting result, which is not shown here, is that the speed of convergence is faster for the fuzzy information than that for the non-deterministic information when two kinds of informations are given alternatively.

ALGORITHM OF MACROSCOPIC SEARCH

In this article, the above mentioned learning model is applied to obtain a scheme of unknown objective functions. It is reasonable to search preponderantly the region where the possibility of finding the maximum is large. For this reason, the whole area is divided into some blocks denoted by y_j. The possibility of finding maximum in the block y_j is expressed by $g_Y(\{y_j\})$. Two basic factors are necessary for the estimation of g_y. One of them is the objective evaluation of jth block $\sigma_y(\{y_j\}|x_i)$ obtained by referencing the criteria x_i. The other is the subjective weights $g_X{}^i$ of these criteria.

We can consider many criteria from such viewpoints as the amount of information, the average value of past searches, the number of points belonging to the best ten, the amplitude, and the slope of the objective functions. The formulas of the evaluation are as follows:

(1) $c_j(x_1) = \exp[-m/3]$, where m is the number of the past searched points in the jth block. If m is small, the possibility of finding the maximum in this block may become large.

(2) $c_j(x_2) = [\tan^{-1}\{6(M_j - M)/M\}]/\pi + 0.5$, where M_j and M are the mean values of the past searches in jth block and in the whole area, respectively.

(3) $c_j(x_3) = 0.3\sqrt{N} + 0.1$, where N is the number of the searched points in jth block that are classified into the best ten of the past searches in the whole area.

(4) $c_j(x_4) = 2[\tan^{-1}(3Q_j/M_j]/\pi, \qquad Q_j \triangleq M_j + (P_j - R_j)$, where P_j and R_j are the maximum and minimum values of the past searches in jth block. The term Q_j means the estimated maximum value from the past variance of the objective function.

(5) $c_j(x_5) = [\tan^{-1}\{6(P_j - M_j)/M_j\}]/\pi + 0.5$. This is the criterion related to the slope of the objective function.

From these $c_j(x_i)$, the density of $\sigma_Y(\cdot|x_i)$ is obtained as follows: Choose β_i so that

$$\prod_j \left[1 + \lambda\beta_i c_j(x_i)\right] - 1 = \lambda, \qquad -1 < \lambda < \infty \tag{6}$$

where λ is a given constant, and $\sigma_Y(\{y_j\}|x_i)$ is defined such that

$$\sigma_Y(\{y_j\}|x_i) \triangleq \beta_j c_j(x_i) \tag{7}$$

Here $\sigma_Y(\{y_j\}|x_i)$ means the grade of fuzziness of the statement "the true optimum seems to lie in jth block" which is guessed from the viewpoint of criterion x_i. When *a priori* weights $g_X{}^i$ are given for each x_i, the evaluation of any block is calculated from (1) and (7).

Next, we consider the information h_A that is necessary for the learning. Of course, g_Y is a kind of powerful information, but it is an accumulation of the past experience. The improvement of *a priori* weight $g_X{}^i$ must be done by the current information. We define the information $h_A(y_j)$ as follows:

$$h_A(y_j) \triangleq \left(P_j - \min_j R_j\right) / \left(\max_j P_j - \min_j R_j\right) \tag{8}$$

Thus, the value of $h_A(y_j)$ of the block that includes the maximum value obtained by the past searches is equal to 1, and decreases according with the value of P_j. In other words, $h_A(y_j)$ expresses the fuzzy information "jth block seems to include the extremum" and it can be considered as a membership function of a fuzzy set.

The physical meaning of the learning process which changes $g_X{}^i$ so as to increase $g_Y(A)$ is as follows. The value of the fuzzy integral of (2) is large, only when $g_Y(\{y\})$ is large for the block of which $h_A(y)$ is large and also $g_Y(\{y\})$ is small[2] for the block of small $h_A(y)$. This corresponds to the case when the maximum point is really found in the block of which the decision-maker made much account. In this case, *a priori* weights $g_X{}^i$ of the criteria are justified and their effects are strengthened further by learning, that is, by increasing the large $g_X{}^i$ and decreasing the small $g_X{}^i$ together. On the other hand, when $h_A(y)$ is small for large $g_Y(\{y\})$ and large for small $g_Y(\{y\})$, $g_Y(A)$ is small and the prediction is not exact. This is because *a priori* weights $g_X{}^i$ are wrong. In this case $g_X{}^i$ should be corrected so that large $g_X{}^i$ is decreased and small one is increased.

It is easily seen that (5) satisfies the above rules of correction. The effect of correction is larger if the value of α is smaller.

NUMERICAL EXAMPLES

As an objective function with two variables, we use the next equation which has four peaks:

$$J = 15\exp\left[-20(z_1 - 0.22)^2 - 22(z_2 - 0.24)^2\right] + 17\exp\left[-19(z_1 - 0.4)^2 - 15(z_2 - 0.85)^2\right]$$
$$+ 14\exp\left[-23(z_1 - 0.87)^2 - 18(z_2 - 0.15)^2\right] + 16\exp\left[-20(z_1 - 0.85)^2 - 20(z_2 - 0.85)^2\right]$$

This is shown in Fig. 5; of course, this is unknown for the decision-maker.

The whole area is divided into nine blocks denoted by $y_1, y_2, \ldots, y_9$. At the first trial, some number of searched points are assigned to each block equally, but thereafter more points are assigned to the block of which $g_Y(\{y\})$ is larger. The procedure of search is as follows.

Step (1) In each block, two points are chosen at random and $\sigma_Y(\{y_j\}|x_i)$ are calculated from (7). The terms $g_Y(\{y_j\})$ are also calculated from (1), where $g_X{}^i$ are given *a priori*. Next the information $h_A(y_j)$ are calculated from (8). The grade of fuzziness $g_Y(A)$ of total information can be known from (2), and $g_X{}^i$ is corrected according to the learning rule (5).

Step (2) In proportion to $g_Y(\{y_j\})$, another eighteen search points are newly assigned as follows. Three points are assigned to each three blocks of top class and two points to each three of middle class, and one point to each three of lowest. Then random search is done as same as step (1) and σ_Y, g_X,

---

[2] The terms $g_Y(\{y\})$ and $g_X{}^i$ satisfy the λ-rule. Therefore, if some of $g_Y(\{y\})$, $y \in Y$ are large, the others must be small.

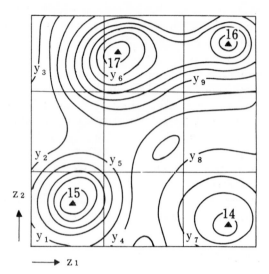

Figure 5. $J(z_1, z_2)$.

$g_Y(\{y_j\})$, $g_Y(A)$ are calculated. The terms g_X^i are corrected again according to the results.

Step (3) Step (2) is repeated until $g_Y(\{y_j\})$ converges. In our examples, the repetition is stopped when $m = 4$, because the total number of search points reaches 72.

Some results of the above examples are shown in the following figures and tables. Figures 6, 7, and 8 show the process of the convergence of g_X^i

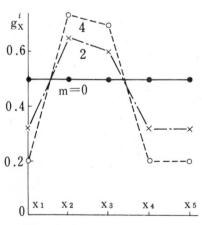

Figure 6. Improvement of g_x^i (case A).

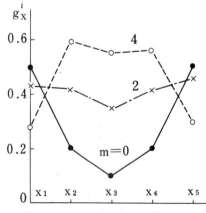

Figure 7. Improvement of g_x^i (case B).

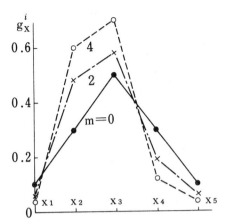

Figure 8.   Improvement of $g_x{}^i$ (case C).

on the different initial conditions (*a priori* weights). Tables 3, 4, and 5 show the change of macroscopic evaluation $g_Y(\{y_j\})$ of each block in each step. From these figures, we can see the speed of convergence is most rapid in the case (C). In Figs. 6 and 7, the $g_X{}^i$ are not settled yet, but they will soon converge because the form of $g_X{}^i$ are becoming similar to those of Fig. 8.

The locations of the real extrema are y_6, y_9, y_1, y_7 as shown in Fig. 5. The evaluation $g_Y(\{y_j\})$ of each block does not always indicate the correct order, but the results are acceptable as a rough map of J as shown in Tables 3, 4, and 5. We also understand from these figures that, among the

Table 3

$g_Y(\{y_j\})$—Fuzzy Information, Case (A)

m \ y_j	y_1	y_2	y_3	y_4	y_5	y_6	y_7	y_8	y_9
1	0.36	0.41	0.38	0.25	0.36	0.50	0.27	0.31	0.50
2	0.30	0.38	0.39	0.33	0.26	0.57	0.33	0.33	0.59
3	0.31	0.32	0.32	0.32	0.31	0.60	0.31	0.31	0.65
4	0.26	0.26	0.32	0.27	0.30	0.57	0.26	0.26	0.67

Table 4

$g_Y(\{y_j\})$—Fuzzy Information, Case (B)

m \ y_j	y_1	y_2	y_3	y_4	y_5	y_6	y_7	y_8	y_9
1	0.33	0.26	0.50	0.25	0.36	0.27	0.31	0.38	0.30
2	0.44	0.40	0.40	0.33	0.23	0.33	0.38	0.22	0.44
3	0.44	0.42	0.36	0.43	0.27	0.42	0.42	0.23	0.42
4	0.45	0.34	0.33	0.37	0.32	0.50	0.34	0.32	0.51

Table 5
$g_Y(\{y_j\})$—**Fuzzy Information, Case (C)**

m \ y_j	y_1	y_2	y_3	y_4	y_5	y_6	y_7	y_8	y_9
1	0.36	0.27	0.17	0.28	0.16	0.36	0.36	0.22	0.36
2	0.30	0.24	0.15	0.26	0.18	0.53	0.30	0.21	0.53
3	0.39	0.24	0.19	0.25	0.16	0.48	0.39	0.19	0.53
4	0.30	0.20	0.19	0.20	0.21	0.59	0.30	0.20	0.56

many criteria, x_3 is most important and x_2 is next. It may be better to eliminate other criteria in this example.

For comparison, the block evaluation $g_Y(\{y_j\})$ without learning (g_X^i are fixed as shown in Table 6) are shown in Tables 7 and 8, which correspond to cases (B) and (C) of Table 6. The convergence looks more rapid in these cases. But, from the viewpoint of the detection of extrema, it is clear that in Tables 7 and 8 that the accuracy is inferior to that shown in Tables 3, 4,

Table 6
A Priori **Fuzzy Density of** g_X

g_X^i Case	g_X^1	g_X^2	g_X^3	g_X^4	g_X^5
(B)	0.5	0.2	0.1	0.2	0.5
(C)	0.1	0.3	0.5	0.3	0.1

Table 7
$g_Y(\{y_j\})$—**Deterministic Information, Case (B)**

m \ y_j	y_1	y_2	y_3	y_4	y_5	y_6	y_7	y_8	y_9
1	0.30	0.22	0.20	0.41	0.20	0.30	0.22	0.25	0.30
2	0.30	0.24	0.24	0.23	0.26	0.38	0.30	0.25	0.38
3	0.34	0.29	0.29	0.27	0.25	0.34	0.34	0.25	0.35
4	0.34	0.28	0.28	0.27	0.28	0.35	0.30	0.23	0.35

Table 8
$g_Y(\{y_j\})$—**Deterministic Information, Case (C)**

m \ y_j	y_1	y_2	y_3	y_4	y_5	y_6	y_7	y_8	y_9
1	0.30	0.19	0.38	0.12	0.19	0.30	0.30	0.23	0.30
2	0.31	0.19	0.30	0.10	0.19	0.32	0.32	0.19	0.37
3	0.34	0.19	0.30	0.19	0.19	0.41	0.30	0.18	0.46
4	0.38	0.19	0.28	0.19	0.19	0.44	0.28	0.19	0.50

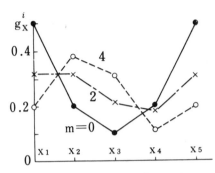

Figure 9. Improvement of g_x^i through deterministic information (case B).

Figure 10. Improvement of g_x^i through deterministic information (case C).

and 5. Because, there are no remarkable differences among the values of $g_Y(\{y_j\})$ in Tables 7 and 8.

Next we consider a case when the information is deterministic, that is, $h_A(y)$ is equal to 1 for the block which contains the maximum of the past searches and equal to zero for other blocks. In this case, some results are shown in Figs. 9 and 10 and in Tables 9 and 10. Comparing Tables 9 and 10 with Tables 4 and 5, it is interesting to know that both the convergence speed and the accuracy are inferior to the case when the fuzzy information is given.

The maximum values obtained in each block are not shown here,

Table 9
$g_Y(\{y_j\})$—Without learning, Case (B)

m\\y_j	y_1	y_2	y_3	y_4	y_5	y_6	y_7	y_8	y_9
1	0.33	0.25	0.50	0.25	0.36	0.27	0.31	0.38	0.30
2	0.39	0.40	0.40	0.33	0.23	0.33	0.38	0.22	0.39
3	0.37	0.32	0.37	0.32	0.28	0.37	0.37	0.23	0.37
4	0.30	0.31	0.29	0.26	0.29	0.54	0.25	0.26	0.54

Table 10
$g_Y(\{y_j\})$—Without Learning, Case (C)

m\\y_j	y_1	y_2	y_3	y_4	y_5	y_6	y_7	y_8	y_9
1	0.36	0.27	0.17	0.28	0.16	0.36	0.36	0.22	0.36
2	0.30	0.24	0.15	0.26	0.18	0.53	0.30	0.21	0.53
3	0.39	0.24	0.19	0.25	0.16	0.43	0.39	0.19	0.53
4	0.30	0.20	0.19	0.20	0.21	0.59	0.30	0.20	0.47

because Monte Carlo method must be used for the detail discussion. Roughly speaking, the final values are neither so different regardless of the kind of information nor the learning. But we can say that the learning is effective because the maximum value in each block is improved very rapidly in the case when the g_x^i are corrected.

CONCLUSION

The optimization of multimodal functions is a typical problem that contains many fuzzy points. The decision-maker, who faces it, utilizes all the past experiences and the information in order to find the extrema efficiently. But the way of utilization looks not so strict but rather vague. Sometimes it is called the sixth sense.

The authors try to apply the fuzzy measures and the fuzzy integrals to express this kind of vagueness, and also apply the conditional fuzzy measures to simulate the learning process. They cannot conclude from the few examples that this attempt is completely successful. But some interesting results are obtained, for instance, fuzzy information is sometimes more useful than deterministic information, *a priori* weights of criteria are automatically corrected with experiences, macroscopic map of objective function is easily calculated, and so on.

The authors hope the method, suggested in this paper, is not only effective for optimum seeking but also has wider applications as a decision model.

REFERENCES

1. K. Nakamura and M. Oda. "Heuristics and Learning Control," *Pattern Recognition and Machine Learning* (K. S. Fu, ed.), Plenum Press, N. Y., 1971, 297.
2. M. Sugeno. "Theory of Fuzzy Integrals and Its Applications," PhD Thesis, Tokyo Institute of Technology, 1974.
3. M. Sugeno and T. Terano. "Conditional Fuzzy Measures and Their Applications," *U.S.–Japan Seminar on Fuzzy Sets and Their Appl.*, U. Calif., Berkeley, July, 1974.

CHARACTERIZATION OF A CLASS OF FUZZY OPTIMAL CONTROL PROBLEMS 14

L. W. Fung and K. S. Fu

Consider a dynamic system[†] described by the ordinary differential equation

$$\dot{x}(t) = A(t)x(t) + B(t)u(t) \tag{1}$$

where x is an n-dimensional state vector, u is an r-dimensional control vector, $A(t)$ and $B(t)$ are $n \times n$ and $n \times r$ matrices, respectively, which are continuous in t. We shall assume that initial time t_0 and initial state $x(t_0)$ are given. We are interested in giving a formal characterization of the type of performance function that defines a large class of optimal control problems. The formulation is based on the notion of fuzzy sets [7].

Let I be the set of membership values which is a connected order topology induced by some linear order $\gtrsim$. If D denotes the universal set that contains all elements of interest, then a fuzzy set A in D is defined as a set of ordered pairs $A = \{(a, \mu_A(a)) : a \in D\}$ where $\mu_A : D \to I$. In our problems both the final time t_f and control $\{u(t), t \geq t_0\}$ are unknown. The design objective is to find a pair (u^*, t_f^*) that maximizes some performance function characterized below. Let $U = \{u : u \text{ is a bounded and measurable function defined on } [t_0, \infty)\}$ and let $V = U \times [t_0, \infty)$. Then V is our universal space, every element $v = (u, t_f)$ of which represents a control u such that the process terminates at time t_f. Let C_t, S_t, T and F be fuzzy constraint sets in V where, with $v = (u, t_f) \in V$, $t_0 \leq t \leq t_f$,

$\mu_{C_t}(v)$ is the membership of the control u at time t, (hence depends inversely on the magnitude of $u(t)$);

$\mu_{S_t}(v)$ is the membership of the state $x(t)$ which is reached at time t with the application of control u through (1) (hence depends only on $x(t)$);

$\mu_T(v)$ is the membership of the final time t_f (hence is a strictly decreasing function of t_f)

$\mu_F(v)$ is the membership of the final state $x(t_f)$ (F is called a fuzzy target set).

[†]This work was supported by the National Science Foundation Grant GK-36721.

209

Here memberships take values in I and are ordered by $\gtrsim$ such that in any fuzzy set A if $\mu_A(a_1) \lesssim \mu_A(a_2)$, then a_2 is *preferred* to a_1.

Introduce a binary operation $\oplus: \tilde{V} \times \tilde{V} \to \tilde{V}$ which is called a *fuzzy aggregate*,[1] with the well-known fuzzy union and fuzzy intersection as special cases [7]. It will be assumed that if A_1, $A_2 \in \tilde{V}$, then $A_1 \oplus A_2$ is defined as the set $\{(v, \mu_{A_1}(v)*\mu_{A_2}(v)): v \in V\}$ where $*$ is some mapping from $I \times I$ to I. We can regard the fuzzy constraint sets C_t, S_t, T and F as a collection of optimality criteria for v and the fuzzy goal set J defined below gives an *over-all evaluation* of every v in V as a result of amalgamating the whole collection of criteria. (Such a view of fuzzy operations is studied in details by Fung and Fu [3]. Formally, we define the fuzzy goal set $J: V \to I$ as

$$J_m = T \oplus F \oplus \left[\sum_{\substack{\oplus \\ t \in K_m}} C_t\right] \oplus \left[\sum_{\substack{\oplus \\ t \in K_m}} S_t\right]$$

where m is a positive integer, and $K_m = \{t_1, t_2, \ldots, t_m: t_0 \leqslant t_i, i = 1, 2, \ldots, m\}$, which is a set of time points at which the performance of the control process is evaluated. This definition implies that for any $v = (u, t_f) \in V$, the membership of v in J_m is given by

$$\mu_{J_m}(v) = \mu_T(v)*\mu_F(v)*\left(\mu_{C_{t_1}}(v)* \cdots *\mu_{C_{t_m}}(v)\right)*\left(\mu_{S_{t_1}}(v)* \cdots *\mu_{S_{t_m}}(v)\right)$$

with the understanding that $\mu_{C_t}(v)$ and $\mu_{S_t}(v)$ are deleted from the expression if $t \geqslant t_f$. v^* is an *optimal control* if it maximizes the performance function $\mu_{J_m}(v)$ over all $v \in V$.

The following conditions are imposed on $\oplus$:

(i)   Idempotent law: For all $A \in \tilde{V}$, $A \oplus A = A$.

(ii) Commutative law: For all A_1, $A_2 \in \tilde{V}$, $A_1 \oplus A_2 = A_2 \oplus A_1$.

(iii) Inductive Definition: For $m \geqslant 3$, $A_1, A_2, \ldots, A_m \in \tilde{V}$,

$$A_1 \oplus A_2 \oplus \cdots \oplus A_m = (A_1 \oplus \cdots \oplus A_{m-1}) \oplus A_m$$

(iv) Associative law: For all $A_1, A_2, A_3 \in \tilde{V}$,

$$(A_1 \oplus A_2) \oplus A_3 = A_1 \oplus (A_2 \oplus A_3)$$

(v)   Non-decreasingness of $\oplus$: For any $v \in \tilde{V}$ and any $B, C_1, C_2 \in \tilde{V}$ with $A_1 = B \oplus C_1$ and $A_2 = B \oplus C_2$, if $\mu_{C_1}(v) > \mu_{C_2}(v)$, then $\mu_{A_1}(v) \geqslant \mu_{A_2}(v)$.

The idempotent law states that amalgamating two identical criteria gives the original criterion. The commutative law states that the amalgamation of two criteria is independent of the order in which they are considered.

---

[1] $\tilde{V}$ be the collection of all fuzzy sets in V, where the membership space is I. We do not put any restriction on the membership functions for these fuzzy sets.

The inductive definition makes it possible to define the over-all performance using m criteria as the result of the overall performance of $(m-1)$ criteria amalgamated with the remaining criterion. The associative law assumes that amalgamation of two criteria is independent of the order in which they are considered. The inductive definition makes it possible to define the over-all performance using m criteria as the result of the over-all performance of $(m-1)$ criteria amalgamated with the remaining criterion. The associative law assumes that amalgamation of the two criteria followed by a third criterion is the same as amalgamating the last two criteria followed by the first. The law of non-decreasingness of $\oplus$ states that if any control v has a better performance with respect to criterion C_1 than to criterion C_2, then this control has a better over-all performance with respect to the amalgamated criterion $B \oplus C_1$ than to the amalgamated criterion $B \oplus C_2$. Note that in these two cases, C_1 and C_2 are amalgamated with the same criterion B, respectively.

These axioms have reasonable interpretations as in ordinary set theory and are shown [3] to be *necessary and sufficient* for either one of the following three types of performance function:

(1) Optimistic criterion:

$$\mu_{J_m}(v) = \max\left\{ \mu_T(v), \mu_F(v), \mu_{C_{t_1}}(v), \ldots, \mu_{C_{t_m}}(v), \mu_{S_{t_1}}(v), \ldots, \mu_{S_{t_m}}(v) \right\}$$

(2) Pessimistic criterion:

$$\mu_{J_m}(v) = \min\left\{ \mu_T(v), \mu_F(v), \mu_{C_{t_1}}(v), \ldots, \mu_{C_{t_m}}(v), \mu_{S_{t_1}}(v), \ldots, \mu_{S_{t_m}}(v) \right\}$$

(3) Mixed criterion: Let θ be any element in I. If every argument $\mu_T(v), \ldots, \mu_{S_{t_m}}(v) > \theta$, then $\mu_{J_m}(v)$

is given by (2); and if every argument $\mu_T(v), \ldots, \mu_{S_{t_m}}(v) < \theta$, then $\mu_{J_m}(v)$ is given by (1). Moreover, if *some* arguments are $\lesssim \theta$ and *some* are $\gtrsim \theta$, $\mu_{J_m}(v) = \theta$. (We make the usual assumption that $\mu_{C_t}(v)$ and $\mu_{S_t}(v)$ are deleted from the expressions if $t \geqslant t_f$.)

The first two types of operations for fuzzy sets described above are generalized to the situation where the memberships take on values in a connected order topological space I rather than the real interval $[0,1]$ originally proposed by Zadeh. The third type is a very interesting case that has not been considered previously. Fung and Fu [3] also studied alternative conditions that imply that $\oplus$ can only be one of the first two types. The optimistic criterion (1) (also called high-risk policy) has been considered by [2] while the pessimistic criterion (2) (also, called guaranteed-risk policy) is a generalized version of the criterion used for fuzzy decision and control[1].

SPECIAL PROBLEMS USING THE PESSIMISTIC CRITERION

For continuous dynamic systems as in (1), it is natural to consider the case where $K_m = [t_0, \infty)$ with m informally set to ∞. As a consequence the performance function (2) becomes

$$\mu_J(v) = \mu_T(v) \bigwedge \mu_F(v) \bigwedge \left(\inf_{t_0 \leq t < t_f} \mu_{C_t}(v) \right) \bigwedge \left(\inf_{t_0 \leq t < t_f} \mu_{S_t}(v) \right)$$

where $v = (\{u(t), t_0 \leq t \leq t_f\}, t_f)$ (and $\bigwedge$ denotes taking minimum value of the two sides). If we further *assume* that $\mu_{C_t} = \mu_C$ and $\mu_{S_t} = \mu_S$ for all $t \geq t_0$, i.e., the control and state constraint sets C_t and S_t are time-independent, and use the more explicit notation $\mu_T(v) = \mu_T(t_f)$ and $\mu_F(v) = \mu_F(x(t_f))$, then the performance function can be written as

$$\mu_J(u, t_f) = \mu_T(t_f) \bigwedge \mu_F(x(t_f)) \bigwedge \left(\inf_{t_0 \leq t < t_f} \mu_C(u) \right) \bigwedge \left(\inf_{t_0 \leq t < t_f} \mu_S(x(t)) \right)$$

$$(2)$$

An optimal control u^* with terminal time t_f^* satisfies the condition

$$\mu_J(u^*, t_f^*) = \sup_{\substack{u \in U \\ t_f \in [t_0, \infty)}} \mu_J(u, t_f) \tag{3}$$

A general solution to (3) is still unknown, but we shall discuss briefly some techniques which we can use to solve a number of particular cases. The membership space I will be assumed to be the usual real interval $[0, 1]$ and every membership function in (2) be differentiable. We can readily identify four subcases:

Subcase (A) t_f and $x(t_f)$ are given; $\mu_S(x(t)) = 1$ for every $x(t)$; $\inf_{t_0 \leq t < t_f}$ $\mu_C(u) = \inf_{t_0 \leq t < t_f} \max_{1 \leq j \leq r} \mu_C(|u^j(t)|)$. Since μ_C is strictly decreasing in $|u^j(t)|$, criterion (3) is equivalent to minimizing the performance function $\xi(u(t)) = \max_{1 \leq j \leq r} \sup_{t_0 \leq t < t_f} |u^j(t)|$. This class of *mimimum effort* control problems are studied in detail [5].

Subcase (B) t_f given, $\mu_F(x(t_f)) = 1$ for $x(t_f)$ in some target set described by $\mathcal{J}(x(t_f)) = 0$, and $\mu_C(u) \mathcal{J} 1$ for u in some control constraint set, and 0 otherwise. Then criterion (3) is equivalent to minimizing the functional $J(u) = \sup_{t_0 \leq t < t_f} g(x(t))$. This class of *minimax control* problems are studied in detail [5].

Subcase (C) For t_f given, $\mu_S(x(t)) = 1$ for all $x(t)$ and u is 1-dimensional. The performance function is then

$$\mu_J(u) = \mu_F(x(t_f)) \bigwedge \inf_{t_0 \leq t < t_f} \mu_C(u(t))$$

which is the membership of control $\{u(t), t_0 \leqslant t < t_f\}$ in the fuzzy goal set J. The particular choice of u^* having maximal membership in J is the optimal control. This is a class of *fuzzy control* problems studied by Bellman and Zadeh [1].

Subcase (D) $\mu_F(x(t_f)) = 1$ for $x(t_f) = z(t_f)$ where $z(t)$ is a given time-dependent moving target, and 0 otherwise; $\mu_S(x(t)) = 1$ for all $x(t)$; and u is a 1-dimensional control. Then the performance function is simply

$$\mu_J(u, t_f) = \mu_T(t_f) \bigwedge \inf_{t_0 \leqslant t < t_f} \mu_C(u(t))$$

which is to be maximized for some choice of (u^*, t_f^*).

METHODS OF SOLUTION

In general, we use the symbol $h(v)$ to denote $\mu_F(x(t_f))$ in subcase (C) or $\mu_T(t_f)$ in subcase (D). Then the performance function for these two subcases is $\mu_J(v) = h(v) \bigwedge \inf_{t_0 \leqslant t < t_f} \mu_C(u(t))$, $v = (u, t_f)$ and the optimality criterion is to find $v^* = (u^*, t_f^*)$ which maximizes $\mu_J(v)$ over V. It is easy to prove the following propositions which can be used to solve subcases such as (C) and (D):

Proposition *For all $\theta \in I$, using V_θ to denote $\{v \in V: \inf_{t_0 \leqslant t < t_f} \mu_C(u(t)) = \theta\}$,*

$$\sup_{v \in V} \left\{ h(v) \bigwedge \inf_{t_0 \leqslant t < t_f} \mu_C(u(t)) \right\} \geqslant \left[\sup_{v \in V_\theta} h(v) \right] \bigwedge \theta.$$

The optimal v^* can be obtained from

(i) θ^* which maximizes $[\sup_{v \in V_\theta} h(v)] \bigwedge \theta$
(ii) v^* which maximizes $h(v)$ over V_{θ^*}.

Proposition *For all $\psi \in I$, using V_ψ to denote $\{v \in V: h(v) = \psi\}$,*

$$\sup_{v \in V_\psi} \left\{ h(v) \bigwedge \inf_{t_0 \leqslant t < t_f} \mu_C(u(t)) \right\} \geqslant \psi \bigwedge \sup_{v \in V_\psi} \left\{ \inf_{t_0 \leqslant t < t_f} \mu_C(u(t)) \right\}$$

The optimal v^* can be obtained from

(i) ψ^* which maximizes $\psi \bigwedge \sup_{v \in V_\psi} [\inf_{t_0 \leqslant t < t_f} \mu_C(u(t))]$,
(ii) v^* which maximizes $[\inf_t \mu_C(u(t))]$ over V_{ψ^*}.

These propositions represent two different views of looking at the same problem. For example in Subcase (D), the first proposition reduces the original problems to the case where magnitude of the control is bounded by $\mu_C^{-1}(\theta)$ (note that μ_C is strictly decreasing with $|u(t)|$), for every $\theta \in I$, and hence we can treat them as a sequence of time-optimal control problems (e.g., [4]. The second proposition however, reduces the original problems to the case where the final time t_f is fixed, for every $t_f \geqslant t_0$, and hence we can treat them as a sequence of minimum-effort control problems (Subcase (A)). Let us study the former situation in more detail.

PROPERTIES OF THE OPTIMAL FUZZY CONTROL IN SUBCASE (D)

When the first proposition is applied to subcase (D) where $h(v) = \mu_T(t_f)$ and μ_T is a decreasing function of t_f, our problem is equivalent to solving for:

Step (i) θ^* which maximizes $[\sup_{v \in V_\theta} \mu_T(t_f)] \bigwedge \theta$

Step (ii) v^* which maximizes $\mu_T(t_f)$ over V_{θ^*}

Let us first fix some $\theta \in [0,1]$, and make the assumption that Z is a fixed and closed target set in R^n. Then $[\sup_{v \in V_\theta} \mu_T(t_f)]$ is equivalent to solving the time-optimal control problem with target set Z (i.e., we want to bring the system from its given initial state to $x(t_f) \in Z$ in the minimal time t_f), where the control satisfies the constraint $|u(t)| \leqslant \mu_C^{-1}(\theta)$ for all $t \geqslant t_0$. Hermes and LaSalle [4] presents a thorough study of this class of problems. The following discussion will be based on the terminology used in their book.

Consider a normal system $\dot{x} = Ax + bu$, where x is an n-dimensional state vector, u a scalar control, A a constant matrix and b a constant n-vector. Here condition of normality is equivalent to the condition that the vectors $b, Ab, \ldots, A^{n-1}b$ are linearly independent. Let Z be a closed target set in R^n and let $x(t; u)$ denote the absolutely continuous solution the system satisfying $x(t_0) = x^0$, which is a fixed initial state. The time-optimal control problem is to determine a control u^*, subject to its constraints, in such a way that the solution $x(t; u^*)$ reaches the target set Z in minimal time $t^* \geqslant t_0$. Such a control u^* will be called time-optimal and t^* the minimal time (to hit the target Z).

Let θ be a number in $[0,1]$, which is a parameter for the attainable set

$$A_\theta(t) \triangleq \left\{ x(t; u): u \text{ measurable}, u(t) \leqslant \mu_C^{-1}(\theta) \text{ for } t \in [0,t] \right\}$$

where μ_C is the membership function of the fuzzy control constraint set C, and is a decreasing function of the absolute value of its arrangement as described in the previous sections. The set $\mathcal{Q}_\theta^{(t)}$ is called the attainable set at time t with parameter θ, and consists of *all* possible values that solutions of the normal systems can assume using all admissible controls constrained by the condition $u(\tau) \leqslant \mu_C^{-1}(\theta)$ for $\tau \in [0, t]$, i.e., $u \in V_\theta$. Hitting the target set Z at time t is equivalent to the situation that $Z \cap \mathcal{C}_\theta(t) \neq \phi$. Throughout our discussions, we shall assume that the system is controllable, i.e., there is some value of $t_\theta \geqslant t_0$ for which $Z \cap \mathcal{C}_\theta(t_\theta) \neq \phi$ for every parameter θ in $[0, 1]$. If this is the case, then

$$t_f^*(\theta) \triangleq \inf\{t : Z \cap \mathcal{C}_\theta(t) \neq \phi\} \tag{4}$$

will be the minimal time, and an admissible control u_θ^* such that $x(t_f^*(\theta); u_\theta^*) \cap Z \neq \phi$ will be the time-optimal control (with respect to θ).

It can be shown [4] that if the system is controllable, then there is a time-optimal control u_θ^*, and furthermore if the system is normal, the optimal control is unique and bang-bang, determined by the form

$$u_\theta^*(t) = \mu_C^{-1}(\theta)\operatorname{sgn}\big[\eta' Y(t)\big], t \in \big[0, t_f^*(\theta)\big] \tag{5}$$

for some nonzero vector η, where $t_f^*(\theta)$ is the minimal time, $Y(t) = X^{-1}(t)b$ with $X(t)$ being the principal matrix solution of the homogeneous system $\dot{x} = Ax$, and

$$\operatorname{sgn}[w] = \begin{cases} 1, & \text{if } w > 0 \\ \text{arbitrary}, & \text{if } w = 0 \\ -1, & \text{if } w < 0 \end{cases}$$

Proposition *The parameter θ^* that maximizes*

$$\left[\sup_{v \in V_\theta} \mu_T(t_f)\right] \wedge \theta \tag{6}$$

In step (i) of this section is the (unique) solution to the equation

$$\mu_T(t_f^*(\theta)) = \theta \tag{7}$$

If the system is normal. Such θ^* can be obtained numerically by computing t_f^* as a function of θ and solving (7) for θ^*.

Proof Suppose θ_1 and θ_2 are two parameters in $[0, 1]$ and let $\theta_2 < \theta_1$. Then for all $t \geqslant t_0$, since μ_C is a decreasing function, we have $\mu_C^{-1}(\theta_1) \leqslant \mu_C^{-1}(\theta_2)$,

$$\mathcal{C}_{\theta_1}(t) \subseteq \mathcal{C}_{\theta_2}(t) \tag{8}$$

by the definition of $\mathcal{C}_\theta(t)$. At time $t_f^*(\theta_1)$, we have $Z \cap a_{\theta_1}(t_f^*(\theta_1)) \neq \phi$. Let $y \in Z \cap \mathcal{C}_{\theta_1}(t_f^*(\theta_1))$.

If $\mathcal{C}_{\theta_1}(t_f^*(\theta_1)) = \mathcal{C}_{\theta_2}(t_f^*(\theta_1))$, we can immediately conclude that since

$Z \cap \mathcal{Q}_{\alpha_1}(t_f{}^*(\theta_1)) = Z \cap \mathcal{Q}_{\theta_2}(t_f{}^*(\theta_1)) \neq \phi$, the minimal time with respect to parameter θ_2 satisfies the inequality:

$$t_f{}^*(\theta_2) \triangleq \inf\{t : Z \cap \mathcal{Q}_{\theta_2}(t) \neq \phi\} \leqslant t_f{}^*(\theta_1) \tag{9}$$

Now suppose $\mathcal{Q}_{\theta_1}(t_f{}^*(\theta_1)) \subset \mathcal{Q}_{\theta_2}(t_f{}^*(\theta_1))$. We shall prove $t_f{}^*(\theta_2) < t_f{}^*(\theta_1)$ by invoking the following lemma.

Lemma (*After lemma 12.3, [4].*) *If y is in the interior of $\mathcal{Q}_{(t^*)}$ for some $t^* > 0$, then y is an interior point of $\mathcal{Q}(t)$ for some $0 < t < t^*$. (Note that $\mathcal{Q}(t)$ is closed if t_f^* and u^* exist.)*

Proof (continued) Now we can pick $y \in Z \cap \mathcal{Q}_{\theta_1}(t_f{}^*)(\theta_1))$ such that y is an interior point of $\mathcal{Q}_{\theta_2}(t_f{}^*(\theta_1))$ since $\mathcal{Q}_{\theta_1}(t_f{}^*(\theta_1)) \subset \mathcal{Q}_{\theta_2}(t_f{}^*(\theta_1))$ and so every point in $\mathcal{Q}_{\theta_1}(t_f{}^*(\theta_1))$ is an interior point of $\mathcal{Q}_{\theta_2}(teb_f{}^*(\theta_1))$. Applying the above lemma repeatedly we can find a sequence $t_1, t_2, \ldots$, such that

$$t_f{}^*(\theta_1) > t_1 > t_2 > \cdots > 0 \tag{10}$$

(note: strict inequality) *and* for each k, $k = 1, 2, \ldots, y$ is an interior point of $\mathcal{Q}_{\theta_2}(t_k)$, since y is an interior point of $\mathcal{Q}_{\theta_2}(t_f{}^*(\theta_1))$. It follows from (10) that

$$\inf\{t_k : t_k \text{ in } (10)\} = \inf\{t_k : y$$

is an interior point of

$$\mathcal{Q}_{\theta_2}(t_k)\} < t_f{}^*(\theta_1) \quad \text{and} \quad y \in Z \tag{11}$$

On the other hand, it is obvious that

$$\inf\{t : y \quad \text{is an interior point of} \quad \mathcal{Q}_{\theta_2}(t), t \geqslant t_0\}$$

and

$$y \in Z$$

$$\leqslant \inf\{t_k : y \quad \text{is an interior point of} \quad \mathcal{Q}_{\theta_2}(t_k)\}$$

and

$$y \in Z \tag{12}$$

since we have the relation

$$\{t : y \quad \text{interior point of} \quad \mathcal{Q}_{\theta_2}(t), t \geqslant t_0\}$$

and

$$y \in Z$$

$$\supseteq \{t_k : y \quad \text{interior point of} \quad \mathcal{Q}_{\theta_2}(t_k)\}$$

and

$$y \in A$$

Furthermore, since Z may contain more than one point y, clearly

$$\exists y \quad \text{interior point of} \quad \mathcal{Q}_{\theta_2}(t) \quad \text{and} \quad y \in Z$$

$$\Rightarrow \mathcal{Q}_{\theta_2}(t) \cap Z \neq \phi$$

which implies

$$\{ t : y \quad \text{interior of} \quad \mathcal{Q}_{\theta_2}(t) \} \subseteq \{ t : \mathcal{Q}_{\theta_2}(t) \cap Z \neq \phi \}$$

and

$$y \in Z$$

and consequently

$$\inf \{ t : \mathcal{Q}_{\theta_2}(t) \cap Z \neq \phi \} \leqslant \inf \{ t : y \text{ interior of} \quad \mathcal{Q}_{\theta_2}(t) \}$$

and

$$y \in Z \tag{13}$$

Combining (11), (12) and (13), and by definition of $t_f^*(\theta_2) \triangleq \inf\{ t : \mathcal{Q}_{\theta_2}(t) \cap Z \neq \phi \}$, we conclude that $t_f^*(\theta_2) < t_f^*(\theta_1)$

Thus we have shown that $(\theta_2 < \theta_1)$ implies $t_f^*(\theta_2) \leqslant t_f^*(\theta_1)$, which means that in the time-optimal control problem, if the bound $\mu_C^{-1}(\theta)$ of the control magnitude is increased, the corresponding minimal time may be reduced or at least equal to the original minimal time. This indeed is a rather reasonable property of the time-optimal control problem for normal systems. Since t_f^* is a non-decreasing function of θ, and since $[\sup_{v \in V_\theta} \mu_T(t_f)] = \mu_T(t_f^*(\theta))$ which is a non-increasing function of θ as a consequence, we have

$$\left[\sup_{v \in V_\theta} \mu_T(t_f) \right] \wedge \theta = \begin{cases} \theta, & \text{if } \theta \leqslant \theta^* \\ \mu_T(t_f^*(\theta)), & \text{if } \theta^* < \theta \end{cases} \tag{14}$$

where θ^* is the solution to the equation $\mu_T(t_f^*(\theta)) = \theta$. It follows immediately that θ^* maximizes the function $[\sup_{v \in V_\theta} \mu_T(t_f)] \wedge \theta$.

Note that since the solution θ^* in the above equation is unique, we have a unique solution θ^* to step (i). In step (ii), the time-optimal control y^* which maximizes $\mu_T(t_f)$ (i.e., which minimizes $t_f(\theta^*)$) over V_θ^* is also unique for a normal system as we stated above. Hence we can summarize our results in the following statement.

Proposition *For a normal linear system with a fixed target set, the optimal control v^* for the fuzzy control problem in subcase (D) has a unique solution in bang-bang form that can be determined from step (ii) using the parameter θ^* obtained by the previous proposition. Finally, it is interesting to note that v^* obeys the principle of optimally.*

Proof Let v^* denote the optimal control for the fuzzy control problem in subcase (D), $v^* = (u^*, t_f^*)$ where t_f^* and u^* are, respectively, the minimal time and time-optimal control obtained in steps (i) and (ii) by the third proposition. Let $t_1 \in (t_0, t_f^*)$, and let $v_1^* = (u_1^*, \tau_f^*)$ be the optimal fuzzy control for the same problem starting in initial state $x(t_1; u^*)$ at time t_1 reached on application of the first part of u^* from t_0 to t_1. Form a new control $v_n = (u_n, t_n)$ where $t_n = t_f^* + \tau_f^*$ and

$$u_n(t) \triangleq \begin{cases} u^*(t), & \text{for } t_0 \leqslant t \leqslant t_1 \, . \\ u_1^*(t), & \text{for } t_1 < t \leqslant t_1 + \tau_1^* \end{cases} \tag{15}$$

Then if $|u_1^*(t)| > |u^*(t)|$, independently of τ_f^*, the new control (u_n, t_n) is inferior to the original optimal fuzzy control (u^*, t_f^*) since

$$\inf_t \mu_C(u_n(t)) < \inf_t \mu_C(u^*(t))$$

which implies $\mu_J(u_n, t_n) < \mu_J(u^*, t_f^*)$. Now if $|u_1^*(t)| = |u^*(t)|$, the new control v_n must be identical to v^* by the uniqueness of v^* in step (ii) since $\mu_C(u^*(t)) = \mu_C(u_1^*(t)) = \theta^*$ is the same for both u^* and u_1^*. If $|u_1^*(t)| < |u^*(t)|$, then $\theta_1^* \triangleq \mu_C(u_1^*(t)) \geqslant \theta^* = \mu_C(u^*(t))$, and since t_f^* is a non-decreasing function of θ as we showed in the proof of the previous proposition, it follows that

$$\tau_f^* \geqslant (t_f^* - t_1) \tag{16}$$

which in turn implies $\mu_T(t_1 + \tau_f^*) \leqslant \mu_T(\tau_f^*)$ and finally

$$\mu_J(u_n, t_n) \leqslant \mu_J(u^*, t_f^*)$$

It also implies that (v^*, τ_f^*) is not optimal even for the second part starting at time t_1, in view of (16). In other words, it is not possible at any time $t_1 \in (t_0, t_f^*)$ to find a new control (u_1^*, τ_f^*) such that both conditions

$$|u_1^*| \leqslant |u^*|$$

$$\tau_f^* \leqslant (t_f^* - t_1)$$

are satisfied. Thus we conclude that the overall performance $\mu_J(u^*, t_f^*)$ using the optimal fuzzy control (u^*, t_f^*) computed at time t_0 in initial state x^0 is *not* improved by applying a newly computed optimal fuzzy control (u_1^*, τ_f^*) starting at any time $t_1 \in (t_0, t_f^*)$ in initial state $x(t_1, u^*)$ reached by the system using the first part of the original optimal fuzzy control $(u^*(\tau))$ for τ from t_0 to t_1. This is essentially the principle of optimality.

REFERENCES

1. Bellman, R. and Zadeh, L. A., "Decision Making in a Fuzzy Environment," *Man. Sci.* **17**, No. 4 (1970), B141–156.

2. Chang, S. S. L., (1969). "Fuzzy Dynamical Programming and Decision Making Process," *Third Ann. Princeton Conf. on Infor. Sci. Systems*, March, 1969.
3. Fung, L. W. and Fu, K. S., "An Axiomatic Approach to Rational Decision-Making Based on Fuzzy Sets," in *Fuzzy Sets and Their Applications to Cognitive and Decision Processes* (L. A. Zadeh *et al.*, eds.), Academic Press, N.Y., 1975.
4. Hermes, H. and LaSalle, J. P., *Functional Analysis and Time Optimal Control*. Academic Press, N.Y., 1969.
5. Johnson, C. D., "Optimal Control with Chebyshev Minimax Performance Index," *J. Basic Engineering* (1967), 251–262.
6. Neustadt, L. W., "Minimum Effort Control Systems," *J. SIAM Control*, Ser. A, 1, No. 1 (1962), 16–31.
7. Zadeh, L. A., "Fuzzy Set," *Inform. and Control*, 8(1965).

SOLUTIONS IN COMPOSITE FUZZY RELATION EQUATIONS: APPLICATION TO MEDICAL DIAGNOSIS IN BROUWERIAN LOGIC

Elie Sanchez

We begin the paper with a statement from Goguen [4]:

> The importance of relations is almost self-evident. Science is, in a sense, the discovery of relations between observables.... Difficulties arise in the so-called "soft" sciences because the relations involved do not appear to be "hard," as they are say, in classical physics. A thoroughgoing application of probability theory has relieved many difficulties, but it is clear that others remain. We suggest that further difficulties might be cleared up through a systematic exploitation of fuzziness.

In this paper, we first review previous results from a method for the solution of the sup-min fuzzy relation equations that gives a greatest element of the set of solutions, if it exists. When there is no solution, we then look at the corresponding inequalities.

Our purpose is to find the minimal solutions, thus we introduce a composite fuzzy relation in the finite case, and then we describe the set of all solutions. Lastly, an application to medical diagnosis assistance in terms of Brouwerian logic is proposed.

PRELIMINARY DEFINITIONS AND RESULTS OF FUZZY SETS AND FUZZY RELATIONS

If L is a *lattice* and if x and y are elements of L, the *"meet"* or *greatest lower bound* (glb) of x and y is denoted $x \wedge y$: the *"join"* or *least upper bound* (lub) of x and y is denoted $x \vee y$. For the partial order relation on L we use the symbol $\leqslant$.

Let us recall some useful definitions of lattice theory [1]. A lattice L is *complete* when each of its subsets X has a lub, denoted by $\sup X$ or $\bigvee X$, and a glb, denoted by $\inf X$ or $\bigwedge X$, in L. A *Brouwerian lattice* is a lattice L in which, for any given elements a and b, the set of all $x \in L$ such that

$a \wedge x \leqslant b$ contains a *greatest element*, denoted $a \alpha b$, the *relative pseudo-complement* of a in b. We can now assume the following definition of a fuzzy set.

Definition Let L be a fixed complete Brouwerian lattice, and E be a nonempty set, a *fuzzy set A* of E is a function $A: E \rightarrow L$. The class of all the fuzzy sets of E is denoted by $\mathcal{L}(E)$.

We note that if L is taken to be the closed interval $[0,1]$ of the real line, then L is then a complete lattice in which $x \wedge y$ is simply the smaller and $x \vee y$ the larger of x and y. Moreover, if for any elements a and b in $[0,1]$ we define $c = a \alpha b$ by $c = 1$ if $a \leqslant b$ and $c = b$ if $a > b$, then c is the relative pseudo-complement of a in b, so that $[0,1]$ is a Brouwerian lattice. Fuzzy sets defined above are then *Zadeh's membership functions*.

However, any *Boolean lattice* is easily verified to be a Brouwerian lattice with $a \alpha b$ defined $a' \vee b$, where a' denotes the *complement* of a. If L is the Boolean lattice consisting of only the points 0 and 1, then a fuzzy set according to the above definitions is just the *characteristic function* defining a subset A of a set E.

Completeness of a lattice is needed here in order to be able to define the composition of fuzzy relations.

Let us recall usual definitions in fuzzy sets theory:

(1) The fuzzy set $A \in \mathcal{L}(E)$ is *contained* in the fuzzy set $B \in \mathcal{L}(E)$ (written $A \subseteq B$) whenever $A(x) \leqslant B(x)$ for all $x \in E$.

(2) The fuzzy sets A and $B \in \mathcal{L}(E)$ are equal (written $A = B$) whenever $A \subseteq B$ and $B \subseteq A$, i.e., $A(x) = B(x)$ for all $x \in E$.

(3) A *fuzzy relation* between two nonempty sets X and Y is a fuzzy set R of $X \times Y$, i.e., an element of $\mathcal{L}(X \times Y)$.

(4) Let $R \in \mathcal{L}(X \times Y)$ be a fuzzy relation, the fuzzy relation R^{-1}, the *inverse* or *transpose* of R, is defined by $R^{-1} \in \mathcal{L}(Y \times X)$ and $R^{-1}(y,x) = R(x,y)$ for all $(y,x) \in Y \times X$.

(5) Let $Q \in \mathcal{L}(X \times Y)$ and $R \in \mathcal{L}(Y \times Z)$ be two fuzzy relations, we define $T = R \circ Q \in \mathcal{L}(X \times Z)$, the $\circ$-*composite fuzzy relation* of R and Q, by $(R \circ Q)(x,z) = \bigvee_y [Q(x,y) \wedge R(y,z)]$ where $y \in Y$, for all $(x,z) \in X \times Z$.
This composition stands for a *Boolean matrix product* when L is a complete Boolean lattice.

(6) If R_1 and $R_2 \in \mathcal{L}(Y \times Z)$ and if $R_1 \subseteq R_2$, one verifies that $R_1 \circ Q \subseteq R_2 \circ Q$ where $Q \in \mathcal{L}(X \times Y)$.

We need now introduce the following new composition. Let $Q \in \mathcal{L}(X \times$

Y) and $R \in \mathcal{L}(Y \times Z)$ be two fuzzy relations, we define $T = Q \ \alpha \ R$, $T \in \mathcal{L}(X \times Z)$, the α *-composite fuzzy relation* of Q and R, by

$$(Q \ \alpha \ R)(x,z) = \bigwedge_y \left[Q(x,y)) \ \alpha \ R(y,z) \right]$$

where $y \in Y$, for all $(x,z) \in X \times Z$. According to the Brouwerian structure of the lattice L, for each $y \in Y, Q(x,y) \ \alpha \ R(y,z)$ is the relative pseudo-complement of $Q(x,y)$ in $R(y,z)$.

Let us point out the following properties of the α operation.

With $a,b \in L, c = a \ \alpha \ b$ is the greatest element in L such that $a \wedge c \leqslant b$. In fact,

$$a \wedge (a \ \alpha \ b) \leqslant b \tag{1}$$

With $a,b,d \in L$, it is easy to verify that

$$a \ \alpha \ (b \vee d) \geqslant a \ \alpha \ b \quad (\text{or} \geqslant a \ \alpha \ d) \tag{2}$$

$$a \ \alpha \ (a \wedge b) \geqslant b \tag{3}$$

The following theorems have been proved previously [6, 7].

Theorem *For every pair of fuzzy relations $Q \in \mathcal{L}(X \times Y)$ and $R \in \mathcal{L}(Y \times Z)$, we have*

$$R \subseteq Q^{-1} \ \alpha \ (R \circ Q) \tag{4}$$

Theorem *For every pair of fuzzy relations $Q \in \mathcal{L}(X \times Y)$ and $R \in \mathcal{L}(Y \times Z)$, we have*

$$Q \subseteq \left(R \ \alpha \ (R \circ Q)^{-1} \right)^{-1} \tag{5}$$

Theorem *For every pair of fuzzy relations $Q \in \mathcal{L}(X \times Y)$ and $T \in \mathcal{L}(X \times Z)$, we have*

$$(Q^{-1} \ \alpha \ T) \circ Q \subseteq T \tag{6}$$

Theorem *For every pair of fuzzy relations $R \in \mathcal{L}(Y \times Z)$ and $T \in \mathcal{L}(X \times Z)$, we have*

$$R \circ (R \ \alpha \ T^{-1})^{-1} \subseteq T \tag{7}$$

We deduced two fundamental theorems for existence and determination of solutions of $\circ$-composite fuzzy relational equations.

Theorem *Let $Q \in \mathcal{L}(X \times Y)$ and $T \in \mathcal{L}(X \times Z)$ be two fuzzy relations, $\mathcal{X}$ be the set of fuzzy relations $R \in \mathcal{L}(Y \times Z)$ such that $R \circ Q = T$, then*

$$\mathcal{X} = \{\text{fuzzy}\, R \in \mathcal{L}(Y \times Z) | R \circ Q = T\} \neq \emptyset, \text{ if and only if,}$$

$Q^{-1} \alpha T \in \mathcal{X}$; and it then is the greatest element in $\mathcal{X}$.

Theorem *Let $R \in \mathcal{L}(Y \times Z)$ and $T \in \mathcal{L}(X \times Z)$ be two fuzzy relations, $\mathcal{X}$ be the set of fuzzy relations $Q \in \mathcal{L}(X \times Y)$ such that $R \circ Q = T$, then*

$$\mathcal{X} = \{\text{fuzzy}\, Q \in \mathcal{L}(X \times Y) | R \circ Q = T\} \neq \emptyset, \text{ if and only if,}$$

$(R \alpha T^{-1})^{-1} \in \mathcal{X}$; and it then is the greatest element in $\mathcal{X}$.

The following weaker theorems are also easy to handle.

Theorem *Let $Q \in \mathcal{L}(X \times Y)$ and $T \in \mathcal{L}(X \times Z)$ be two fuzzy relations, if $\mathcal{X} = \{\text{fuzzy}\ R \in \mathcal{L}(Y \times Z) | R \circ Q = T\} \neq \emptyset$, then $T(x,z) \leqslant \bigvee_y Q(x,y)$ for all $(x,z) \in X \times Z$.*

Theorem *Let $R \in \mathcal{L}(Y \times Z)$ and $T \in \mathcal{L}(X \times Z)$ be two fuzzy relations, if $\mathcal{X} = \{\text{fuzzy}\, Q \in \mathcal{L}(X \times Y) | R \circ Q = T\} \neq \emptyset$, then $T(x,z) \leqslant \bigvee_y R(y,z)$ for all $(x,z) \in X \times Z$.*

These results provided a means of solving sup-min fuzzy relations equations and the fundamental fifth and sixth theorems are a generalization of known results in Boolean relations, or matrix, equations.

To solve inf-max fuzzy relations equations, we need to choose the fixed lattice L, in the definition of a fuzzy set, to be complete and *dually Brouwerian*, i.e., for any given elements a and b in L, the set of all $x \in L$, such that $a \vee x \geqslant b$ contains a least element, denoted $a \epsilon b$. When $L = [0,1]$, $c = a \epsilon b = b$ if $a < b$ and $c = a \epsilon b = 0$ if $a \geqslant b$. Theorems that correspond to the above theorems can easily be proved for these conditions.

Zadeh [9] has shown the study of relations to be equivalent to the general theory of *systems*. If we think of $R \in \mathcal{L}(Y \times Z)$ as a system, X being a set containing only a single point, i.e., $Q \in \mathcal{L}(Y)$ and $T \in \mathcal{L}(Z)$, $R \circ Q = T$ describes the effect of the system R between the fuzzy *input* Q and the *fuzzy output* T. Knowing Q and T the above results give, when it exists, the "greatest" system R that verifies $R \circ Q = T$ or $R(Q) = T$.

Given now two fuzzy relations $Q \in \mathcal{L}(X \times Y)$ and $T \in \mathcal{L}(X \times Z)$, when no $R \in \mathcal{L}(Y \times Z)$ such that $R \circ Q = T$ exist, the fuzzy relation $Q^{-1}@T$ of the fifth theorem is shown, in the following section, to be the greatest fuzzy relation in $\mathcal{L}(Y \times Z)$ such that $R \circ Q \subseteq T$. In the study of systems, $Q^{-1}@T$ is the "best" system that approaches the output T, given the input Q.

FUZZY RELATION INEQUATIONS

The results of this section are stated according to the definitions of the preceding section. The α operation enjoys the following property:

(i) If b and $d \in L$ and if $b \leqslant d$, then $a \alpha b \leqslant a \alpha d$, for all $a \in L$.

Let us assume $a \alpha d < a \alpha b$. From (1) we have $a \wedge (a \alpha b) \leqslant b$, but $b \leqslant d$, then $a \wedge (a \alpha b) \leqslant d$. According to $a \alpha d < a \alpha b$, $a \alpha d$ is not the greatest element of the set of all $x \in L$ such that $a \wedge x \leqslant d$, so necessarily $a \alpha b \leqslant a \alpha d$.

The $\textcircled{a}$-composition enjoys the following property

(ii) If R_1 and $R_2 \in \mathcal{L}(Y \times Z)$ and if $R_1 \subseteq R_2$, then $Q \textcircled{a} R_1 \subseteq Q \textcircled{a} R_2$, for all $Q \in \mathcal{L}(X \times Y)$.

$$(Q \textcircled{a} R_1)(x,z) = \bigwedge_y \left[Q(x,y) \alpha R_1(y,z) \right]$$

where $y \in Y$, for all $(x,z) \in X \times Z$.

Given $(x,y) \in X \times Z$, the hypothesis implies $R_1(y,z) \leqslant R_2(y,z)$ for all $y \in Y$. From (i), we have $Q(x,y) \alpha R_1(y,z) \leqslant Q(x,y) \alpha R_2(y,z)$ for all $y \in Y$, which implies $(Q \textcircled{a} R_1)(x,z) \leqslant (Q \textcircled{a} R_2)(x,z)$ and $Q \textcircled{a} R_1 \subseteq Q \textcircled{a} R_2$ for all $Q \in \mathcal{L}(X \times Y)$.

Theorem *For every pair of fuzzy relations $Q \in \mathcal{L}(X \times Y)$ and $T \in \mathcal{L}(X \times Z)$, the set of all fuzzy relations $R \in \mathcal{L}(Y \times Z)$ such that $R \circ Q \subseteq T$ contains a greatest element $Q^{-1} \textcircled{a} T$.*

Let

$$\mathcal{X}^* = \{ \text{fuzzy } R \in \mathcal{L}(Y \times Z) | R \circ Q \subseteq T \}$$

$\mathcal{X}^* \neq \varnothing$ because the null relation **0**, defined by $\mathbf{0}(y,z) = 0$ for all $(y,z) \in Y \times Z$, belongs to $\mathcal{X}^*$.

Let $R \subseteq \mathcal{X}^*$: $R \circ Q \subseteq T$; from (ii) we have $Q^{-1} \textcircled{a}(R \circ Q) \subseteq Q^{-1} \textcircled{a} T$, but from the first Theorem we have $R \subseteq Q^{-1} \textcircled{a}(R \circ Q)$, then $R \subseteq Q^{-1} \textcircled{a} T$. If we prove that $Q^{-1} \textcircled{a} T \in \mathcal{X}^*$, then $Q^{-1} \textcircled{a} T$ will be the greatest element in $\mathcal{X}^*$. This result is just given by the third Theorem.

Theorem *For every pair of fuzzy relations $R \in \mathcal{L}(Y \times Z)$ and $T \in \mathcal{L}(X \times Z)$, the set of all fuzzy relations $Q \in \mathcal{L}(X \times Y)$ such that $R \circ Q \subseteq T$ contains a greatest element $(R \textcircled{a} T^{-1})^{-1}$.*

The proof is analogous to the proof of the previous theorem, we point out that $U \subseteq V$ if and only if $U^{-1} \subseteq V^{-1}$, using (ii) and the second and fourth theorems.

Similar results can be obtained with the inf-max fuzzy relation inequalities when L is dually Brouwerian, as one can easily verify.

Our purpose is now to describe, for the *finite case*, all the solutions of $R \circ Q = T$ with respect to system theory and medical applications in the field of *diagnosis assistance*.

We change our notations according to the usual terminology, $R \in \mathcal{L}(Y \times Z)$, $Q \in \mathcal{L}(X \times Y)$ and $T \in \mathcal{L}(X \times Z)$ will be replaced by $R \in \mathcal{L}(X \times Y)$, $A \in \mathcal{L}(X)$ and $B \in \mathcal{L}(Y)$, respectively; $R \circ A = B$ will replace $R \circ Q = T$.

The preceding results will carry over, because of isomorphisms between fuzzy relations in $\mathcal{L}(X \times Y)$, when X is a set consisting of a single point for example, and fuzzy sets in $\mathcal{L}(Y)$. In system theory, speaking of fuzzy inputs, this single point determines a class of inputs.

Moreover, the following results are stated with $L = [0, 1]$, so that fuzzy sets are now Zadeh's membership functions (recall that $[0, 1]$ is a complete Brouwerian lattice).

σ-FUZZY RELATIONS

We begin this section with a definition.

Definition If $a \in [0, 1], b \in [0, 1]$, we define $c = a \sigma b \in [0, 1]$ by

(i) $a \sigma b = 0$, if $a < b$ $a \sigma b = b$, if $a \geqslant b$

It is easy to verify that

(ii) $a \sigma b \leqslant b$ and $a \sigma b \leqslant a$, so that:
(iii) $a \sigma b \leqslant a \wedge b$
(iv) $a \wedge (a \sigma b) = a \sigma b$
(v) $a \vee (a \sigma b) = a$

Let us point out that σ is different from ϵ, the dual operator of α: If $a \in [0, 1]$ and $b \in [0, 1]$, then

$$a \epsilon b = b, \quad \text{if } a < b \qquad a \epsilon b = 0, \quad \text{if } a \geqslant b$$

Let us focus our attention on the restriction of the σ and $\wedge$ (min) operator to the Boolean case with $L = \{0, 1\}$:

a	b	$a \sigma b$	$a \wedge b$
0	0	0	0
0	1	0	0
1	0	0	0
1	1	1	1

In the Boolean case with $L = \{0,1\}$, we have $a\,\sigma\,b = a\wedge b = a\cdot b$, where $(\cdot)$ denotes the Boolean product. When $L = [0,1]$, if $0 < a < b$, we have $a\,\sigma\,b = 0$ and $a\wedge b = a, a \neq 0$, moreover $a\,\sigma\,b \leqslant a\wedge b$. One can already think that this σ operator will produce minimization properties.

Definition Let $A \in \mathcal{L}(X)$ and $B \in \mathcal{L}(Y)$ be two fuzzy sets, we define the fuzzy relation $A\textcircled{$\sigma$}B \in \mathcal{L}(X \times Y)$ by

$$(A\textcircled{σ}B)(x,y) = A(x)\,\sigma\,B(y), \qquad \text{for all } (x,y) \in X \times Y \qquad (8)$$

Given the fuzzy sets $A \in \mathcal{L}(X)$ and $B \in \mathcal{L}(Y)$, we define

$$\mathcal{R} = \{\text{fuzzy } R \in \mathcal{L}(X \times Y) | R\circ A = B\} \quad \text{and} \quad \text{a map } \Gamma : Y \to P(X) \qquad (9)$$

where $P(X)$ consists of all the subsets of X, by

$$\Gamma(y) = \{x \in X | A(x) \geqslant B(y)\}, \qquad \text{for all } y \in Y \qquad (10)$$

Lemma *If $\mathcal{R} \neq \varnothing$, then $\Gamma(y) \neq \varnothing$ for all $y \in Y$.*

Let us assume $\mathcal{R} \neq \varnothing$. From the seventh theorem we have $B(y) \leqslant \bigvee_x A(x)$, for all $y \in Y$.

If there exists $y \in Y$ such that $\Gamma(y) = \varnothing$, from (10) we have $A(x) < B(y)$ for all $x \in X$, then $\bigvee_x A(x) < B(y)$ (finite case).

Theorem *If $\Gamma(y) \neq \varnothing$ for all $y \in Y$, then $A\textcircled{$\sigma$}B \in \mathcal{R}$.*

$$[(A\textcircled{σ}B)\circ A](y) = \bigvee_x [A(x)\wedge(A(x)\,\sigma\,B(y))] \qquad \text{for all } y \in Y$$

$$= \bigvee_x (A(x)\,\sigma\,B(y)) \qquad \text{from } (iv)$$

$$= \left[\bigvee_{x\in\Gamma(y)} (A(x)\,\sigma\,B(y))\right] \vee \left[\bigvee_{x\notin\Gamma(y)} (A(x)\,\sigma\,B(y))\right]$$

$$= \left[\bigvee_{x\in\Gamma(y)} B(y)\right]\vee 0 \qquad \text{from } (10) \text{ and } (i)$$

$$= \bigvee_{x\in\Gamma(y)} B(y) \qquad \text{because } \Gamma(y) \neq \varnothing$$

$$= B(y)$$

$(A\textcircled{$\sigma$}B)\circ A = B$ and $A\textcircled{$\sigma$}B \in \mathcal{R}$.

Notation Let us denote by

$|E|$ the *cardinality*, or number of elements (finite case) of a set E.

Theorem $\mathcal{R}$ *has a least element* $*R$, *if and only if, for all* $y \in Y$, *we have either* $|\Gamma(y)| = 1$, *either* $B(y) = 0$; *moreover, when it exists,* $*R = A\textcircled{\sigma}B$.

$\mathcal{R}$, $\Gamma(y)$ and $|\Gamma(y)|$ are defined in (9), (10), and the notation. Let $*R \in \mathcal{L}(X \times Y)$ be the least element of $\mathcal{R}$ and let us assume that there exists $y_0 \in Y$ such that $|\Gamma(y_0)| \neq 1$, our purpose is to prove that $B(y_0) = 0$.

From the Lemma, we have $\Gamma(y_0) \neq \varnothing$ or $|\Gamma(y_0)| \neq 0$, then $|\Gamma(y_0)| \neq 1$, if and only if, $|\Gamma(y_0)| > 1$. So let x_{01} and $x_{02} \in \Gamma(y_0)$, $x_{01} \neq x_{02}$, and define R_1 and $R_2 \in \mathcal{L}(X \times Y)$ by

$$\begin{cases} R_1(x_{01}, y_0) = B(y_0) \\ R_1(x, y_0) = 0 & \text{for all } x \in X - \{x_{01}\} \\ R_1(x, y) = *R(x, y) & \text{for all } (x, y) \in X \times (Y - \{y_0\}) \end{cases}$$

$$\begin{cases} R_2(x_{02}, y_0) = B(y_0) \\ R_2(x, y_0) = 0 & \text{for all } x \in X - \{x_{02}\} \\ R_2(x, y) = *R(x, y) & \text{for all } (x, y) \in X \times (Y - \{y_0\}). \end{cases}$$

One easily verifies that $R_1 \circ A = B$ and $R_2 \circ A = B$, i.e., R_1 and $R_2 \in \mathcal{R}$. Since $*R$ is the least element of $\mathcal{R}$, we have $*R \subseteq R_1$ and $*R \subseteq R_2$, then[1] $*R \subseteq R_1 \cap R_2$. However, $x_{01} \neq x_{02}$ implies $(R_1 \cap R_2)(x, y_0) = 0$ for all $x \in X$, then $*R(x, y_0) = 0$ for all $x \in X$.

$$B(y_0) = (*R \circ A)(y_0) = \bigvee_x (A(x) \wedge *R(x, y_0)) = 0$$

Let us now assume that for all $y \in Y$. we have either $|\Gamma(y)| = 1$, either $B(y) = 0$, our purpose is to prove that $A\textcircled{\sigma}B$ is the least element of $\mathcal{R}$. We define $Y_1 = \{y \in Y$ such that $|\Gamma(y)| = 1\}$ and $Y_2 = \{y \in Y$ such that $B(y) = 0\}$, Y_2 being the complement of Y_1 in Y. For all $y \in Y_1$, $|\Gamma(y)| = 1$ then there exists a unique point $x_y \in X$ such that $A(x_y) \geqslant B(y)$. For all $y \in Y_1$,

$$\begin{cases} (A\textcircled{\sigma}B)(x_y, y) = B(y) \\ (A\textcircled{\sigma}B)(x, y) = 0 & \text{for all } x \in X - \{x_y\} \end{cases}$$

and for all $(x, y) \in X \times Y_2$, $(A\textcircled{\sigma}B)(x, y) = 0$. We can easily verify that $(A\textcircled{\sigma}B) \circ A = B$, i.e. $A\textcircled{\sigma}B \in \mathcal{L}$.

Let $R \in \mathcal{R}$, and let us prove that $A\textcircled{\sigma}B \subseteq R$, so that $A\textcircled{\sigma}B$ will be the least element in $\mathcal{R}$. For all $(x, y) \in X \times Y_2$, $(A\textcircled{\sigma}B)(x, y) = 0$ and $0 \leqslant R(x, y)$. When $y \in Y_1$, for all $x \in X - \{x_y\}$, $(A\textcircled{\sigma}B)(x, y) = 0$ and $0 \leqslant$

---

[1] We recall that if A and $B \in \mathcal{L}(X)$, $(A \cap B)(x) = A(x) \wedge B(x)$ for all $x \in X$.

$R(x,y)$; if $x = x_y$, $(A \widehat{\odot} B)(x_y,y) = B(y)$; let us assume $R(x_y,y) <$ $(A \widehat{\odot} B)(x_y,y)$, i.e., $R(x_y,y) < B(y)$, but $y \in Y_1$, then $A(x_y) \geqslant B(y)$ and we deduce that $R(x_y,y) < A(x_y)$.

$$B(y) = \bigvee_x (A(x) \wedge R(x,y))$$

$$B(y) = (A(x_y) \wedge R(x_y,y)) \vee \left[\bigvee_{x \neq x_y} (A(x) \wedge R(x,y)) \right]$$

$$= R(x_y,y) \vee \left[\bigvee_{\substack{x \\ x \neq x_y}} (A(x) \wedge R(x,y)) \right]$$

$$\leqslant R(x_y,y) \vee \left[\bigvee_{\substack{x \\ x \neq x_y}} A(x) \right]$$

But for all $x \in X - \{x_y\}$, $A(x) < B(y)$, and according to $R(x_y,y) < B(y)$, we have $B(y) < B(y)$ which is impossible. Then $(A \widehat{\odot} B)(x_y,y) \leqslant R(x_y,y)$.

Let us recall that $R_m \in \mathcal{L}(X \times Y)$ is a minimal element of $\mathcal{R}$, if and only if, $R_m \in \mathcal{R}$ and if $R \in \mathcal{R}$, $R \subseteq R_m$, then $R = R_m$.

Theorem *If $\mathcal{R} \neq \emptyset$, then $\mathcal{R}$ has minimal elements. In this case, every minimal element R_i in $\mathcal{R}$ is defined by: For all $y \in Y$, the only possible element $R_i(x,y) \neq 0$ is just $R_i(x_i,y) = B(y)$ for $x_i \in \Gamma(y)$.*

If $\mathcal{R} = \emptyset$, it is evident that $\mathcal{R}$ cannot have a minimal element, because a minimal element of $\mathcal{R}$ must belong to $\mathcal{R}$. To determine a minimal element R_i in $\mathcal{R}$, it is sufficient to determine it by defining for all $y \in Y$ the fuzzy set $R_i(y) \in \mathcal{L}(X)$ by

$$R_i(y)(x) = R_i(x,y), \qquad \text{for all } x \in X \tag{11}$$

Let y be a fixed element in Y; according to the lemma we have $\Gamma(y) \neq \emptyset$. For all $x_i \in \Gamma(y)$, we define the fuzzy set $R_i(y) \in \mathcal{L}(X)$ by

$$\begin{aligned} R_i(y)(x_i) &= B(y) \\ R_i(y)(x) &= 0 \text{ for all } x \in X - \{x_i\} \end{aligned} \tag{12}$$

We can easily verify that $R_i \in \mathcal{R}$.

Let $R \in \mathcal{R}$, $R \subseteq R_i$, and let us prove that $R = R_i$. For all $x \in X - \{x_i\}, R_i(x,y) = R_i(y)(x) = 0$, but $R \subseteq R_i$ implies $R(x,y) = 0$ then $R_i(x,y) =$

$R(x,y)=0$ for all $x \in X - \{x_i\}$. We note that $R \in \mathcal{R}$, i.e., $R \circ A = B$ and thus

$$B(y) = \bigvee_x (A(x) \wedge R(x,y))$$

$$B(y) = (A(x_i) \wedge R(x_i,y)) \vee \left[\bigvee_{\substack{x \\ x \neq x_i}} (A(x) \wedge R(x,y)) \right]$$

$$B(y) = (A(x_i) \wedge R(x_i,y)) \vee 0$$

$$B(y) \leqslant R(x_i,y)$$

Since $R \subseteq R_i$, we have $B(y) \leqslant R(x_i,y) \leqslant R_i(x_i,y)$, but $R_i(x_i,y) = R_i(y)(x_i) = B(y)$, then $B(y) = R(x_i,y) = R_i(x_i,y)$.

Let us prove now that every minimal in $\mathcal{R}$, is of R_i type defined above in (11) and (12). Let R_m be a minimal element in $\mathcal{R}$; y be a fixed element in Y; and $B(y) = \bigvee_x (A(x) \wedge R_m(x,y))$. For all $x \notin \Gamma(y)$, according to (10), we have $A(x) \wedge R_m(x,y) \leqslant A(x) < B(y)$, then $\bigvee_{x \notin \Gamma(y)} (A(x) \wedge R_m(x,y)) < B(y)$ which implies that $R_m(x,y) = 0$ for all $x \notin \Gamma(y)$, because R_m is a minimal element, $0 \leqslant R_m(x,y) \leqslant 1$, and we cannot reach $B(y)$, with the elements in the complement of $\Gamma(y)$, in the max-min composition. Hence, we have

$$B(y) = \bigvee_{x_i \in \Gamma(y)} (A(x_i) \wedge R_m(x_i,y)), \qquad \Gamma(y) \neq \varnothing \text{ because } R_m \in \mathcal{R}$$

$$B(y) \leqslant \bigvee_{x_i \in \Gamma(y)} R_m(x_i,y). \tag{13}$$

Let us assume that for all $x_i \in \Gamma(y), R_m(x_i,y) < R_i(x_i,y)$, R_i being a minimal element defined in (11) and (12). According to (12) we should have, for all $x_i \in \Gamma(y), R_m(x_i,y) < B(y)$ which is inconsistent with (13), hence $\exists x_i \in \Gamma(y)$ such that $R_m(x_i,y) \geqslant R_i(x_i,y)$.

Moreover, for all $x \in X - \{x_i\}, R_i(x,y) = 0$ according to (11) and (12). So $R_i \subseteq R_m$, but R_m being minimal we conclude that $R_m = R_i$.

Corollary *If $\mathcal{R} \neq \varnothing$, then the union[2] of all minimal elements in $\mathcal{R}$ is equal to $A \textcircled{o} B$.*

Let us denote $^*R \in \mathcal{L}(X \times Y)$ the union of all minimal elements in $\mathcal{R}$: $^*R = \cup R_i$. From (11) and (12), we deduce that for all $y \in Y$

$$\begin{cases} ^*R(x,y) = B(y) & \text{if } x \in \Gamma(y) \\ ^*R(x,y) = 0 & \text{if } x \notin \Gamma(y) \end{cases}$$

[2]We recall that the union of two fuzzy sets A and $B \in \mathcal{L}(X)$ is defined by $(A \cup B)(x) = A(x) \vee B(x)$ for all $x \in X$.

and from the definition of $\Gamma(y)$ in (10), we have for all $y \in Y$,

$$\begin{cases} *R\,(x,y) = B\,(y) & \text{if } A\,(x) \geqslant B\,(y) \\ *R\,(x,y) = 0 & \text{if } A\,(x) < B\,(y) \end{cases}$$

from (i) and (8), we then deduce $*R = A\widehat{\sigma}B$

Theorem *If $\mathfrak{R} \neq \varnothing$, for all $R \in \mathfrak{L}(X \times Y)$ such that $A\widehat{\sigma}B \subseteq R \subseteq A\widehat{\alpha}B$ we have $R \in \mathfrak{R}$.*

From the first theorem of this section we have $A\widehat{\sigma}B \in \mathfrak{R}$. This result could be deduced from the corollary, $A\widehat{\sigma}B = *R = \cup R_i$, where the R_i stand for the minimal elements in $\mathfrak{R}$. $*R \circ A = (\cup R_i) \circ A = \cup (R_i \circ A)$, see [4]; but for every minimal element R_i we have $R_i \circ A = B$, hence $*R \circ A = B$. Moreover, $A\widehat{\alpha}B$ is the greatest element in $\mathfrak{R}$, see the fundamental theorem about solutions in the first section, and the change of notations at the end of the previous section, hence $A\widehat{\alpha}B \in \mathfrak{R}$. From $A\widehat{\sigma}B \subseteq R \subseteq A\widehat{\alpha}B$ we deduce that

$$(A\widehat{\sigma}B) \circ A \subseteq R \circ A \subseteq (A\widehat{\alpha}B) \circ A$$

that is, $B \subseteq R \circ A \subseteq B$, hence $R \circ A = B$.

MEDICAL DIAGNOSIS AND BROUWERIAN LOGIC

In [1], we find the following definition and theorem.

Definition A *Brouwerian logic* is a propositional calculus that is a lattice with 0 and I, in which

$$(P \to Q) = I \quad \text{if and only if} \quad P \leqslant Q \tag{13}$$

$$P \to (Q \to R) = (P \wedge Q) \to R, \quad \text{for all } P, Q, R \tag{14}$$

Theorem *A Brouwerian logic L is a Brouwerian lattice with*[3] *$P\alpha Q$ relabelled as $P \to Q$.*

Relation (13) is evident in a Brouwerian lattice with I, let us now prove the following theorem corresponding to (14).

Theorem *Let L be a Brouwerian lattice. If a, b, and $c \in L$, we have*

$$(a \wedge b)\alpha c = a\alpha(b\alpha c) = b\alpha(a\alpha c) \tag{15}$$

[3]Birkhoff uses the notation $Q{:}P$ instead of $P\alpha Q$.

Let $p = a\alpha(b\alpha c)$ and $q = (a\wedge b)\alpha c$. Changing b into $b\alpha c$ in (1), we have $a\wedge p \leqslant b\alpha c$. Then $a\wedge b\wedge p \leqslant b\wedge(b\alpha c)$, but changing a into b and b into c in (1), we have $b\wedge(b\alpha c)\leqslant c$. Hence,

$$(a\wedge b)\wedge p \leqslant c$$

From the definition of q, we deduce $p \leqslant q$.

Changing a into b and b into $a\wedge q$ in (3), we have

$$a\wedge q \leqslant b\alpha(b\wedge(a\wedge q)) \tag{16}$$

From the definition of q, we have $(a\wedge b)\wedge q \leqslant c$ and from property (i) in the third section we deduce

$$b\alpha(a\wedge b\wedge q)\leqslant b\alpha c$$

From (16), we deduce

$$a\wedge q \leqslant b\alpha c$$

and from the definition of p, we deduce that $q \leqslant p$.

We have proved that $a\alpha(b\alpha c)=(a\wedge b)\alpha c$, but $a\wedge b = b\wedge a$; hence, $a\alpha(b\alpha c)=(b\wedge a)\alpha c = b\alpha(a\alpha c)$.

Let $\mathcal{S}$ be a set of *symptoms*, $\mathcal{D}$ be a set of *diagnosis*, $\mathcal{P}$ be a set of *patients*. Let us assume we are given $Q\in\mathcal{L}(\mathcal{P}\times\mathcal{S})$, a fuzzy relation between the patients and the symptoms in $\mathcal{S}$, and $T\in\mathcal{L}(\mathcal{P}\times\mathcal{D})$, the fuzzy relation between the same patients and the diagnosis in $\mathcal{D}$; the range of these fuzzy relations is assumed to be a Brouwerian lattice[4]; so they can be membership relations according to Zadeh's fuzzy relations definition of course.

To express the *medical knowledge* observed from Q and T, we suggest a determination of the greatest fuzzy relation $R\in\mathcal{L}(\mathcal{S}\times\mathcal{D})$ between the symptoms and diagnosis such that

$$R(s,d)\rightarrow[Q(p,s)\rightarrow T(p,d)] \tag{17}$$

for all $s\in\mathcal{S}, d\in\mathcal{D}, p\in\mathcal{P}$.

From (14), we have (17) for all $s\in\mathcal{S}, d\in\mathcal{D}, p\in\mathcal{P}$, if and only if,

$$[R(s,d)\wedge Q(p,s)]\rightarrow T(p,d) \tag{18}$$

From (13), we have $(18) = I$ for all $s\in\mathcal{S}, d\in\mathcal{D}, p\in\mathcal{P}$, if and only if,

$$R(s,d)\wedge Q(p,s)\leqslant T(p,d) \tag{19}$$

---

[4]*Completeness* is not needed in the finite case.

Hence, for all $(p,d) \in \mathscr{P} \times \mathscr{D}$,

$$\bigvee_s \left[R(s,d) \wedge Q(p,s) \right] \leqslant T(p,d)$$

For all $(p,d) \in \mathscr{P} \times \mathscr{D}$,

$$(R \circ Q)(p,d) \leqslant T(p,d)$$

$$R \circ Q \subseteq T \tag{20}$$

From the first theorem of the third section, the greatest R such that $R \circ Q \subseteq T$ is equal to $\check{R} = Q^{-1}\textcircled{a}T$, which gives the medical knowledge associated to Q and T.

Given, now, a patient q with a known fuzzy set of symptoms $Q_q(s)$ for all $s \in \mathscr{S}$. According to the proposed model, the composition $\check{R} \circ Q_q = T_q$ expresses the "nearest" fuzzy set of diagnosis presented by q.

These techniques can be performed by a digital computer taking into account a great number of patients. When a fuzzy set of diagnosis is made for a patient, if the physician is not completely satisfied with the given results he/she can verify the accuracy of the fuzzy set of symptoms presented by the patient, or introduce a new knowledge in the fuzzy relation of medical knowledge. This fuzzy model can be enlarged by the study of fuzzy entropy of the fuzzy relations, see [2,3].

CONCLUSION

We quote from K. Levin:

> Rien n'est aussi pratique qu'une bonne theorie.

Since Zadeh's pioneer work, much research into previously unrelated branches of sciences have been brought together and developed together into new fields of research. The author plans to investigate new medical aspects of fuzzy relations at some future time.

REFERENCES

1. Birkhoff, G. (1967). *Lattice Theory* (3rd ed.), Am. Math. Soc. Coll. Publ., Vol XXV, Providence, R. I.
2. De Luca, A., and Termini, S. (1972). "A Definition of a Nonprobabilistic Entropy in the Setting of Fuzzy Sets Theory," *Infor. Control* **20**, 301–312.
3. De Luca, A., and Termini, S. (1974). "Entropy of *L*-Fuzzy Sets", *Infor. Control* **24**, 55–73.

4. Goguen, J. A. (1967). "*L*-Fuzzy Sets", *J. Math. Anal. Appl.* **18**, 145–174.
5. Kaufmann, A. (1973–1975). "Introduction a la théorie des Sous-ensembles Flous" Tome I. Elements théoriques de base; Tome II. Langages, sémantique et logique; Tome III. Classification et reconnaissance des formes-Automates. Machines de Turing—Problèmes multi-critères-Systèmes. Masson, Paris.
6. Sanchez, E. (1974) "Equations de Relations Floues" Thèse Biologie Humaine, Faculté de Médecine de Marseille.
7. Sanchez, E. (1976). "Resolution of composite fuzzy relation equations," *Infor. Control* **30**, No. 1, 38–48.
8. Zadeh, L.A. (1965). "Fuzzy Sets," *Infor. Control* **8**, 338–353.
9. Zadeh, L.A., and Desoer, C.A. (1963). *Linear System Theory*, McGraw-Hill, N.Y.

FUZZY-THEORETICAL DIMENSIONALITY REDUCTION METHOD OF MULTIDIMENSIONAL QUANTITY

16

Masasumi Kokawa, Moriya Oda, and Kahei Nakamura

Decision making in our multidimensional society today has become very important. The process of human decision-making is usually accompanied by the property of "fuzziness." In order to formulate the human decision-making process, we have reported on a human decision-making model [1], a fuzzy process of memory behavior [2], fuzzy-theoretical and concept-formational approaches to inference [3], hint effect in a decision-making process [4], and so on. In a continuation of the authors series of studies, this paper focuses its attention on a fuzzy-theoretical dimensionality reduction method of multidimensional quantity. At first, two kinds of dimensionality reduction methods that introduce a fuzzy function with its fuzziness are proposed. One is a dimensionality reduction method by the linear model method (the least squares method), and the order is by the typical-dimension method. Secondly, in order to examine the appropriateness of the proposed methods, the estimation problem of an arrangement rule of playing cards is taken up, and the fuzzy-theoretical relation between the total inference curve of card arrangement and the inference curve of each of the dimensions (number, suit, or color) of card arrangement is studied. Finally, in order to point out the applicability of the dimensionality reduction methods to the ranking problem, the evaluation test of human character is described, and the fuzzy-theoretical relation between the total human evaluation and the evaluation of each of the dimensions (health, fortune, figure or heart) is studied. The relation between the methods proposed in the paper and the method of factor analysis is as follows. The method of factor analysis clusters at first many factors into a few groups, and next represents each group with its principal factor. In the method of factor analysis, an interpretation of the *factors* or *correlation coefficients* has an important role [5]. On the other hand, in our methods proposed in the paper the *dimensionality reduction mechanism* in factor evaluation has an important role.

Acknowledgment: We gratefully acknowledge the helpful suggestions and criticisms of Mr. S. Watanabe and other members of our laboratory.

FUZZY-THEORETICAL DIMENSIONALITY REDUCTION METHOD

In this paper, two kinds of dimensionality reduction methods introducing a fuzzy function with its fuzziness are proposed. One is a dimensionality reduction method by the linear model method, and the other one is by the typical-dimension method.

Dimensionality Reduction Method by the Linear Model Method

The dimensionality reduction method by the linear model method (Method (i)) is as follows. The fuzzy function $f_F(x)$ with fuzziness of an event x, which is multidimensional, is approximated by the linear model of fuzzy functions $f._F(x)$'s with fuzziness of all dimensions of the multidimensional event. We will call this function the approximate fuzzy function $F_F(x)$ of the event. The relative degree of the subject's evaluation for each dimension is calculated by the application of the least squares method to both the fuzzy function $f_F(x)$ with fuzziness of the event and the approximate fuzzy function $F_F(x)$.

The fuzzy function with fuzziness of an event[1] is defined

$$f._F(x) \cong f.(x) - \omega.(x)/K \tag{1}$$

where K is a positive constant which satisfies $f._F(x) \geqslant 0$, and $\omega.(x)$ is the ambiguity (fuzziness) of the fuzzy function $f.(x)$ of a dimension of the event, in Fig. 1 the difference between the maximum and the minimum

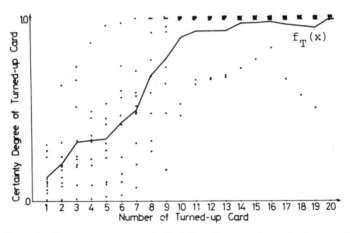

Figure 1. Averaged process and its deviation of concept formation in test 1-T.

values at each trial can be considered as the fuzziness of the averaged value of the fuzzy function [3]. Equation (1) shows that the value of the fuzzy function $f.(x_i)$ is corrected by its fuzziness $\omega.(x_i)$ (see Appendix A).

A more concrete explanation of the method is as follows. Firstly, fuzzy functions[1] $f(x), f_1(x), f_2(x), \ldots, f_m(x)$ are obtained through the experiments. Secondly, fuzzy functions with fuzziness $f_F(x), f_{1F}(x), f_{2F}(x), \ldots, f_{mF}(x)$ are obtained by (1). Finally, the weights (the relative degree of the subject's evaluation) $a_1, a_2, \ldots, a_m$ of each dimension are obtained, which satisfy

$$\min \sum_{i=1}^{n} e_i^2 = \min \sum_{i=1}^{n} \left[f_F(x_i) - F_F(x_i) \right]^2 \tag{2}$$

where

$$F_F(x) = a_1 f_{1F}(x) + a_2 f_{2F}(x) + \cdots + a_m f_{mF}(x) \tag{3}$$

Dimensionality Reduction Method by the Typical-Dimension Method

The dimensionality reduction method by the typical-dimension method (ii) is the one that a typical dimension only in the decision-making process is selected as a representative dimension of the whole dimensions. The value of the fuzzy function of the representative dimension of the event is the closest value to the value of the fuzzy function of the multidimensional event itself. By means of the method, we can see which dimension of the event is most representative, and which is the value of the representative dimension among the fuzzy functions of possible dimensions, the maximum, the minimum, the medium, and so on.

A more concrete explanation of the method is that the fuzzy function $f_{jF}(x_i)$ with fuzziness is selected for every trial i, where it satisfies

$$\min |e_i| = \min_{j} \left| f_F(x_i) - f_{jF}(x_i) \right|, \qquad i = 1, 2, \ldots, n,$$

$$\times j = 1, 2, \ldots, m \tag{4}$$

Equation (4) yields the typical (representative) dimension j at the trial i. In other words, a summative evaluation value of the multidimensional event is represented by an evaluation value of the typical dimension of the event. In order to prove appropriateness and applicability of the two kinds of fuzzy-theoretical dimensionality reduction methods proposed in this paper, two kinds of fuzzy-theoretical experiments and results are described in later sections.

---

[1]Let $f(x)$ be the fuzzy function of the multidimensional event x, and $f_j(x)$ be that of the dimension j of the event x.

ESTIMATION PROBLEM OF ARRANGEMENT RULE
OF PLAYING CARDS

Fuzzy-Theoretical Experiments

In this work, playing cards are used as the experimental material. The card arrangements total three and are constructed symmetrically as much as possible (arrangements 1, 2, and 3, Fig. 2). Ten subjects participated in the test (five males and five females, faculty members and graduate students, aged 20 to 26 years).

The experiments were carried out according to the following procedure. For each subject and each case (cases N, S, C, and T) of arrangements 1, 2 and 3 (where case N means the case which fixes our eyes on the *number* dimension of card arrangement, case S on the *suit* dimension, case C on the *color* dimension, and case T on the *total* dimensions) the method followed was:

(1) The experimenter selects one of the twelve test arrangements (three kinds × four cases) of the cards ($4 \times 13 = 52$ cards).
(2) At first, all cards are arranged wrongside up.
(3) The experimenter asks the subject to tell the name of the card and

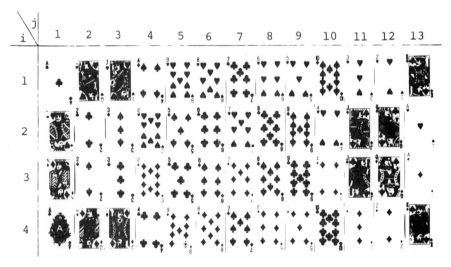

Figure 2. Example of card arrangement (arrangement 3-T).

to write its certainty degree on the test form when the card is pointed to.[2]

(4) The subject then tells the experimenter the name of the selected card, and writes its certainty degree on the test form (Fig. 1), and then turns the card up. (The turned-up card is then kept face-side up.)

(5) Procedures (3) and (4) are repeated until the subject can guess correctly the selected card with a certainty degree of 1.0.

When a subject turns up and sees a card, he/she pictures a covert rule of the card arrangement by himself/herself; that is, he/she forms a hypothetical concept of the card arrangement. Then, based on the hypothetical concept he/she will write the certainty degree of another card that will next be pointed to. The hypothetical concept of the card arrangement is considered to be a composition of multi-dimensional concepts (number, suit, and color) of the arranged cards. Therefore, comparing the results (f_N, f_S, and f_C) of cases N, S, and C with that (f_T) of case T, we can study the fuzzy-theoretical dimensionality reduction method of the multi-dimensional quantity (*cf.*, the next section).

Table 1 shows the test form and an entry example, i.e., the result of arrangement 1, case T, and subject T.I. For instance, let us consider the first trial in Table 1. The location of the card pointed to first is the "cell" in the third row and the fifth column. The subject's answer is that the card is " ♣5," while the real card is actually " ♦5." Therefore, the answer is

Table 1
Test Form and Entry Example

Test: Card Arrangement(_1_)-Case(_T_)
Date:_2_month_8_day_1974_year
Subject: sex(_male_, f̶e̶m̶a̶l̶e̶), age(_20_yrs.), name(_T.I._)

Trial Order	1	2	3	4	5	6	⋯	14	⋯	40
Location of Pointed Card (i,j)	3,5	4,11	1,4	1,2	2,4	2,5	⋯	4,7	⋯	1,11
Answered Card by Subject	♣5	♥J	♥4	♣10	♥10	♥5	⋯	♣7		
Real Card	♦5	♣3	♣10	♦10	♦4	♣5	⋯	♣7	⋯	♥3
Correctness of* Answered Card	×	×	×	×	×	×	⋯	○		

*∘means a correct answer and x a wrong answer.

[2]The order of the location of the chosen card is decided by the pseudo-random numbers to prevent the experimenter's subjective decision (See Table 1).

wrong. At the fourteenth trial the covert rule of the card arrangement is completely found in the test example of Table 1.

Experimental Results

Tables 2 through 4 show the results obtained through the methods (i) and (ii) described in the first section. Table 2 shows the results by method (i) and tells us that the dimension with the greatest numeral in the row cells represents mainly the evaluation of the multidimensional quantity.

Table 2
Coefficients of Dimensions by Method (i)

	$K = \infty$			$K = 3$		
		Coefficient of Dimension				
Arrangement	a_1 (number)	a_2 (suit)	a_3 (color)	a_1 (number)	a_2 (suit)	a_3 (color)
1	-0.143	1.12	0.00941	-0.433	0.623	0.721
2	-0.00574	0.829	0.146	0.144	0.450	0.341
3	0.165	0.984	-0.128	0.731	0.374	-0.0519

Table 3, the results by method (ii), tells us that the typical dimension shows a transition process among the periods of S-dimension, C-dimension, and N-dimension.[3] We should also notice a confused period of N, S, and C-dimension in the transition process. In other words, the transition process of the typical dimension changes from S-dimension period→ confused period of N, S, and C-dimension→C-dimension period→ confused period of N, S, and C-dimension→N-dimension period.

The value of the fuzzy function of one of the three dimensions varies among three values of the maximum(A), the median(E), and the minimum(I), in the following process: I-period→confused period of A, E, and I (or E-period)→A-period). This phenomenon is one of the typical examples where the human evaluation in the estimation process develops gradually from a pessimistic evaluation (minimum-depending decision) to an optimistic evaluation (maximum-depending decision).

Table 4 shows the range of error and the mean value of the absolute error which are obtained by method (i), where those by method (ii) are omitted. The mean values of the absolute errors are 8.07% or less (method (i), $K = \infty$), 10.23% or less (method (i), $K = 3$), 5.00% or less (method (ii), $K = \infty$), and 9.21% or less (method (ii), $K = 3$). The mean value of absolute

---

[3]The period of S-dimension, C-dimension, or N-dimension means that the certainty degree of the arrangement rule of playing cards is mainly dependent on the certainty degree of the *suit* arrangement, the *color* arrangement, or the *number* arrangement, respectively.

Table 3
Transition Process of Typical Dimension and Order of its Evaluation Value by Method (ii)

Test		Trial Order	1	2	3	4	5	6	7	8	9	10	11	12	13	14	15	16	17	18	19	20	21	22	23	24	25	26	27	28	29	30	31
1	K=∞		N	S	S	S	S	S	S	S	S	S	C	S	S	S	N,S,C	C	⌐	N,S,C	→N,S,C ✱												
			I	I	I	I	I	I	I	I	I	I	E	I	I	I		I		I													
	K=3		S	S	S	S	S	S	S	S	S	S	C	S	S	S	N,S,C	C	⌐	N,S,C	→N,S,C ✱												
			E	I	I	I	I	I	I	I	I	I	E	I	I	I		I		I													
2	K=∞		N	S	S	S	S	C	S	C	C	C	C	S	N	S	C	C	C	C	⌐	N,S	→N,S,C ✱										
			E	I	I	I	I	E	I	I	I	I	I	E	A	I	I	I	I	A		A	A	A									
	K=3		S	S	S	S	C	S	C	S	C	S	S	S	N	S	S	C	C	C	⌐	N,S	→N,S,C ✱										
			E	I	I	I	E	I	I	I	E	E	E	E	A	E	I	I	I	A		A	A	A									
3	K=∞		S	S	S	S	S	S	N	S	N	S	C	S	C	N	S	C	C	C	N	C	N	N	N	N	N	N	N	N	N	N,S,C ✱	
			I	I	I	I	I	I	A	A	A	A	A	A	E	I	A	I	I	A	A	A	A	A	A	A	A	A	A	A	A		
	K=3		S	S	S	S	C	S	S	S	C	N	S,C	S	C	N	S	S	C	C	N	N	N	N	N	N	N,S	N	N	N,C	N,S,C ✱		
			E	I	I	I	I	E	E	A	A	E	A	A	E	I	A	I	I	A	A	A	A	A	A	A	A	A	A	A	A		

Note: N, number dimension; S, suit dimension; C, color dimension; and * means the termination of experiment.

242 / *Kokawa, Oda, and Nakamura*

Table 4
Range of Error and Mean Value of Absolute Error by Method (i)

Arrangement	$K = \infty$ Range of error	Error (%) Mean value of |letter|	$K = 3$ Range of error	mean value of |error|
1	$0.54 \leqslant e < 22.53$	8.07	$-15.23 \leqslant e < 14.52$	6.84
2	$-11.11 \leqslant e < 9.73$	4.57	$-28.40 \leqslant e < 30.28$	10.23
3	$-10.69 \leqslant e < 19.67$	5.59	$-23.52 \leqslant e < 22.18$	9.05

errors by method (ii) is less than that of method (i), therefore we can consider that the subject makes his/her decision-making mainly through the typical-dimension method (method (ii)) in the estimation problem of an arrangement rule of the cards. The fact is also confirmed in the oral test made later by subjects (see Appendix B).

EVALUATION TEST OF HUMAN CHARACTER

Fuzzy-Theoretical Experiments

This experiment also uses playing cards as the experimental material. In this experiment, we consider for simplicity four kinds of evaluation dimensions $X_j, j = 1, 2, \ldots, 4$, which are concerned with human character, i.e., X_1: health (represented by ♠), X_2: fortune (♦), X_3: figure (♣), and X_4: heart (♥). The value $x_{jk}, k = 1, 2, \ldots, 13$, of the dimension X_j has thirteen kinds, i.e., $A, 2, \ldots, 10, J, Q, K$. The experiment consists of three cases, case 1 ($\sum_{j=1}^4 x_{jk} = 16$), Case 2 ($\sum_{j=1}^4 x_{jk} = 28$), and Case 3 ($\sum_{j=1}^4 x_{jk} = 40$), where A, J, Q, and K correspond to 1, 11, 12, and 13, respectively. Seven different sets are prepared for each case (Fig. 3). Each set is a combination of four kinds of cards, and any card is used only once in the sets. The sums of the numerals of seven cards in any dimension are $\sum_{k=1}^7 x_{jk} = 28$ (case 1), 49 (case 2), and 70 (case 3). Both the difference among $\max_k X_{jk}$ and the difference among $\min_k X_{jk}$ are equal to or less than one for each case.

Experiments are executed for each of the subjects (thirty in total, fifteen males and fifteen females including faculty members and graduate students, aged 20 to 30) and each case according to the following procedure:

(1) The experimenter instructs the subject that the set {♠A, ♦A, ♣A, ♥A} represents a person with the lowest evaluation value, 0.0; while the set {♠K, ♦K, ♣K, ♥K} represents a person with the highest evaluation value, 1.0.

(2) The experimenter shows the seven sets simultaneously to the subject.

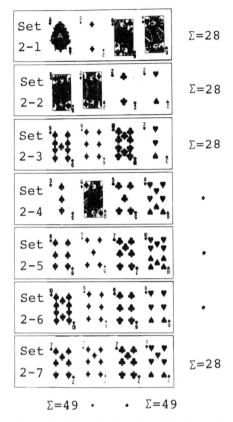

Figure 3. Example of card sets 2-*i* of case 2.

(3) The subject draws a circular form on the test form around the evaluation value of each set and the ranking order of each set, where the position and width of the drawn circular form mean the evaluation value and its fuzziness, respectively (Fig. 4).[4]

Experimental Results

Figure 5 shows the relation between the rank and frequency of each set in case 2 by the thirty subjects. Figure 5 shows that the highest ranked set, set 5, and the lowest ranked set, set 2, have a high frequency, while the middle ranked set, set 6, has a low but bimodal frequency. Other cases show the similar results, but are omitted here.

[4]This entry method by ellipse is a newly developed experimental method to abstract the fuzziness of an event.

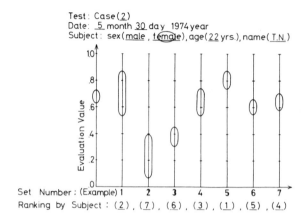

Figure 4. Test form and entry example.

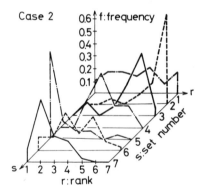

Figure 5. Relation between rank and frequency of each set in case 2.

Figure 6 shows that both the mean of the evaluation value (center of the circular form in Fig. 4) and the mean of its fuzziness (width of circular form) for the fifteen male and the fifteen female subjects. In other words, this figure shows the values of $f(x_i)$ and $\omega(x_i)$, studied in the first section. In Fig. 6, the means of fuzziness by male and female subjects are nearly equal in each of the sets.

Figure 7 shows the relation between the evaluation value and its frequency of each set in case 3 by the fifteen male subjects. In Fig. 7, the data of the total evaluation value is processed by an interval of 0.01. This figure shows another expression of the evaluation value $f(x_i)$ and its fuzziness $\omega(x_i)$ (Fig. 7).

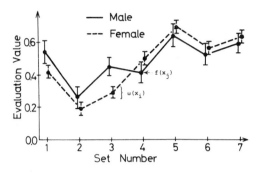

Figure 6. Mean of evaluation values and its fuzziness of each set in case 2.

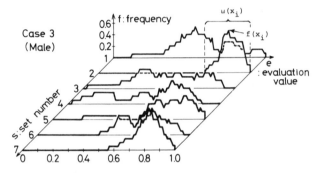

Figure 7. Relation between evaluation value and its frequency of each set (case 3, fifteen male subjects).

Table 5 shows the weight coefficients of each dimension which are obtained by method (i). Table 5 tells us that the priority order of the weights is on the whole from "heart" (top priority) to "health", "figure", and finally "fortune" (end priority).

Table 6 shows the range of error and the mean value of the absolute error which are obtained by method (i). As shown in the table, the mean value of the absolute errors is about 10% or less (10.41% or less when $K = \infty$, or 10.63% or less when $K = 3$), which lies within the allowable domain in the human decision-making process.

Table 7 shows the results that are obtained from method (ii), $K = 3$. Table 7 illustrates the typical dimension with the highest frequency for male subjects is "health", "figure", and "fortune" for cases 1, 2, and 3, respectively. On the other hand, the typical dimension for female subjects is always "heart" for each case. The mean value of the absolute errors obtained by method (ii) is about 11% or less (11.69% or less when $K = \infty$

Table 5
Coefficients of Dimensions by Method (i)

		$K = \infty$				$K = 3$			
					Coefficient of Dimension				
		a_1 (health) X_1	a_2 (fortune) X_2	a_3 (figure) X_3	a_4 (heart) X_4	a_1 (health) X_1	a_2 (fortune) X_2	a_3 (figure) X_3	a_4 (heart) X_4
Case	Subject								
1	Male	0.275	−0.000262	0.334	0.343	0.270	−0.0299	0.329	0.312
	Female	0.298	−0.0676	0.117	0.627	0.301	−0.0705	0.121	0.623
	Total	0.285	−0.0397	0.221	0.491	0.282	−0.0561	0.223	0.472
2	Male	0.249	0.00463	0.203	0.438	0.238	0.00427	0.215	0.406
	Female	0.255	0.0423	−0.118	0.681	0.250	0.0441	−0.109	0.665
	Total	0.256	0.0208	0.0433	0.556	0.243	0.0253	0.0586	0.526
3	Male	0.270	−0.128	0.433	0.360	0.272	−0.145	0.426	0.352
	Female	0.340	−0.0586	0.0818	0.527	0.339	−0.0590	0.0816	0.526
	Total	0.306	−0.102	0.261	0.442	0.308	−0.123	0.263	0.444

Table 6
Range of Error and Mean Value of Absolute Error by Method (i)

		$K = \infty$		$K = 3$	
			Error (%)		
Case	Subject	Range of error	Mean value of |error|	Range of error	Mean value of|error|
1	Male	$-7.72 < e < 7.44$	5.03	$-9.89 < e < 5.86$	5.33
	Female	$-9.00 < e < 7.52$	5.51	$-9.02 < e < 7.66$	5.51
	Total	$-8.58 < e < 7.73$	5.42	$-9.66 < e < 6.92$	5.57
2	Male	$-10.85 < e < 10.48$	5.85	$-12.52 < e < 8.34$	6.30
	Female	$-16.65 < e < 18.72$	10.41	$-17.23 < e < 18.29$	10.63
	Total	$-13.83 < e < 13.85$	7.83	$-15.07 < e < 12.43$	8.31
3	Male	$-9.85 < e < 5.68$	3.81	$-11.38 < e < 3.92$	3.58
	Female	$-8.58 < e < 2.64$	2.45	$-8.72 < e < 2.50$	2.34
	Total	$-9.28 < e < 3.06$	2.65	$-10.38 < e < 2.15$	2.42

and 11.14% or less when $K = 3$), which also lies within the allowable domain in the human decision-making process.

Our combined and important result is that the decision-making is done mainly by the linear model method in the evaluation test of a human character, because the mean value of the absolute errors obtained by method (i) is less than that by method (ii) (see Appendix C). This fact is checked up by the oral test made later by subjects (see Appendix B).

CONCLUSION

This article presents two kinds of fuzzy-theoretical dimensionality reduction methods of the multidimensional quantity in the human decision-

Table 7
Typical Dimension and its Order by Method (ii), $K = 3$

Case	Subject	1	2	3	4	5	6	7
				Set Number				
1	Male	A	D	D	B	C	A	A
		3	2	4	2	2	2	1
	Female	B	D	D	B	C	D	A,C
		2	2	4	2	2	1	1,2
	Total	B	D	D	B	C	D	A
		2	2	4	2	2	1	1
2	Male	B	C,D	B	C	C	B	C
		3	3,4	3	3	2	2	1
	Female	B	C,D	D	D	D	B	B
		3	3,4	4	2	1	2	1
	Total	B	D	B	C	C	B	B,C
		3	3	3	3	2	2	1,2
3	Male	A	C	B	D	B	B	C,D
		3	2	3	3	3	3	1,2
	Female	D	A,C	B	D	B	D	A,B,C,D
		4	2,3	3	3	3	4	1,2,3,4
	Total	D	A	B	D	B	B	A,B,C,D
		4	3	3	3	3	3	1,2,3,4

Note: A—health, B—fortune, C—figure, D—heart. 1—maximum value in four cards, 2—second value in four cards, 3—third value in four cards, 4—minimum value in four cards.

making process. The two kinds of methods introduce a fuzzy function with its fuzziness. Appropriateness and applicability of the two methods are proved through the two kinds of fuzzy-theoretical experiments. The two kinds of methods can be applicable to such decision-making problems as which car to buy, which house to buy, how to evaluate a student's performance (evalaution in education), and so on.

Appendix A

Equation (1) is composed in the way to satisfy the following conditions:

(1) $f.(x_i) \geqslant f.(x_j)$ and $\omega.(x_i) = \omega.(x_j) \Leftrightarrow f._F(x_i) \geqslant f._F(x_j)$

For example, in the problem of comparing the case having the value of the fuzzy function $f.(x_i) = 0.8$ and its fuzziness $\omega.(x_i) = 0.4$ with the case having $f.(x_j) = 0.4$ and $\omega.(x_j) = 0.4$, it is generally agreed that the former has a better evaluation value. This fact means that there is an order relation between $f._F(x_i)$ and $f._F(x_j)$ based only on the size of $f.(x)$ when $f.(x_i) \neq f.(x_j)$ and $\omega.(x_i) = \omega.(x_j)$.

(2) $f.(x_i) = f.(x_j)$ and $\omega.(x_i) \leqslant \omega.(x_j) \Leftrightarrow f._F(x_i) \geqslant f._F(x_j)$.

(3) If $f.(x_i) \geqslant f.(x_j)$ and $\omega.(x_i) \geqslant \omega.(x_j)$, e.g., $f.(x_i) = 0.5, f.(x_j) = 0.45, \omega.(x_i) = 0.6$ and $\omega.(x_j) = 0.05$, then an order relation between $f._F(x_i)$ and $f._F(x_j)$ depends on the valuational basis of a valuer. In this case, the order relation is realized by the appropriate selection of K in (1).

(4) The evaluation of the value of $f._F(x_i)$ is more dependent on the value of $f.(x_i)$ than that of $\omega.(x_i)$.

Appendix B

In interviews after the experiments of the estimation problem of an arrangement rule of playing cards, almost all subjects answered that the estimation value of the card itself was represented by the estimation value of one specific dimension of the card; in other words, the weighted sum method of the estimation values and their weights of all dimensions was not adopted, since it seemed very troublesome under the situation of vague estimation of any dimension. The above reasoning suggests to us a consideration that the decision-making in the arrangement rule estimation problem is performed mainly by the typical-dimension method.

On the other hand, in the evaluation test of the human character, they answered that the value of total evaluation was represented by the combined value which is composed of the weighted multidimensional evaluation values.

According to this fact and Appendix C, in the human character evaluation test, the decision-making is mainly performed by the linear model method.

Appendix C

The reason why the linear model is used as the total evaluation model in the problems taken up in this paper is that for two kinds of problems taken up in the paper, the error obtained by using the linear model is almost 10% or less. Generally speaking, this amount of error is always recognized in the human decision-making process. Even if the error can be reduced to 1% or less by using the nonlinear model, it is only a mathematical fitting, since the original data has not such preciseness. Therefore, the linear model is sufficient for our purpose.

REFERENCES

1. M. Kokawa, K. Nakamura and M. Oda, "Experimental Approach to Fuzzy Simulation of Memorizing, Forgetting and Inference Process" (L.A. Zadeh *et al.*, eds.), *Fuzzy Sets and Their Applications to Cognitive and Decision Processes*. Academic Press, N.Y., 1975.
2. M. Kokawa, K. Nakamura and M. Oda, "Fuzzy Process of Memory Behavior," *Trans. Soc. of Instr. Control Eng.* **10**, No. 3. (1974), 385–386.
3. M. Kokawa, K. Nakamura and M. Oda, "Fuzzy Theoretical and Concept Formational Approaches to Memory and Inference Experiments," *Trans. Inst. Elec. and Comm. Eng. Japan* **57-D**, No. 8 (1974), 487–493.
4. M. Kokawa, K. Nakamura and M. Oda, "Hint Effect and a Jump of Logic in a Decision Process", *Trans. Inst. Elec. Comm. Eng. Japan* **58-D**, No. 5, (May 1975), 256–263.
5. B. Yasumoto and M. Honda, "An Introduction to Factor Analysis," *Math. Sci.* No. 132 (1974), 74–79.

ANALYSIS OF FUZZY SYSTEMS 17

Ramesh Jain

Imprecisely defined terms and ill-defined variables are frequently encountered in most of humanistic and present day complex systems. In the absence of any suitable tool to deal with these variables, it is a common practice to apply tools used for the analysis of mechanistic systems to the analysis of humanistic systems. However, these tools cannot be used for the representation of ill-defined or imprecise variables, and hence also for the analysis of humanistic systems. The problem of the representation of imprecisely-defined variables in precise terms was solved by Zadeh [13]. Zadeh introduced the concept of fuzzy sets and showed that this concept may be very useful in analyzing economic, urban, social, biological, and other human-oriented systems [13, 14, 3, 15, 16, 6].

Many workers have used the concept of fuzzy sets for the analysis of different types of systems [2, 5, 1, 7, 12, 8, 10]. However, most of these applications have been concerned either with decision-making in the presence of fuzzy variables or, with the execution of an imprecisely-defined course of action. Methods have been proposed for quantitative representation of fuzzy terms [15, 16], and for decision-making in fuzzy environment [3, 16, 1]. In these applications, fuzzy sets are used to consider the ill-defined nature of certain variables. These applications illustrate the fact that fuzzy sets may be effectively used to consider the impreciseness of variables, analogous to statistics that consider the uncertainty of variables. By using this type of reasoning, we may represent quantitatively, terms such as, 'tall', 'not tall,' 'very tall,' 'very very tall,' 'not very tall,' etc., and make decisions faced with these imprecisely-defined terms. These and similar terms are frequently employed by human beings and are understood by them without any difficulty. Fuzzy sets enable us to represent precisely these terms and to decide the best course of action in the given situation where variables have impreciseness, and cannot be handled using the tools of statistics.

Another field in which fuzzy sets is finding applications is automata theory. The human brain has the ability to execute imprecise instructions. In our daily life, most instructions have impreciseness yet we do not encounter any difficulty in performing the various fairly complex tasks. At present, we cannot expect machines to perform any task of comparable

251

complexity. This is due to the fact that most problems cannot be formulated exactly and their solutions, too, do not need to be very precise. If we introduce, in machines, the capability of following an imprecise course of action, then we may expect machines to perform such tasks. Methods have been proposed for executing fuzzy programs [14,9,4,11]. Using these methods, one may program a computer to execute programs that do not have a precisely-defined course of action.

In this paper, we outline a method for the analysis of systems in which variables are fuzzy. We shall refer to fuzzy systems as those systems in which information in at least one part of the system is fuzzy. This fuzziness may be due either to the ill-defined parameters of the system or to ill-defined input. In the analysis of systems, we have to use algebraic operations and compute the response of the system for the indicated input. If a system is fuzzy then one may have to consider operations such as 'small + large,' 'small/large.' At present the algebraic operations for fuzzy quantities are not defined precisely. A method for performing algebraic operations for fuzzy quantities is presented and used to analyze linear memoryless fuzzy systems. Next, a method for the convolution of fuzzy variables is discussed and is used for analyzing linear fuzzy systems having a memory. It is observed that these mathematical operations may cause tremendous increase in the data handled. This large amount of data may be restrictive in the application of these methods to practical systems. Two methods are proposed to reduce this data considerably. Using these methods it is hoped that we may be in a position to analyze fairly complex humanistic systems.

We shall denote a fuzzy variable A^f by

$$A^f = \left\{ (f_A(A_1),A_1),(f_A(A_2),A_2),\ldots,(f_A(A_n),A_n) \right\}$$
$$= \left\{ (f_A(A_i),A_i) \right\}, \quad i=1,\ldots,n \tag{1}$$

where $f_A(A_i)$ represents the grade of membership of A_i in A^f. We consider f_A to represent the membership function $f_A : U \to [0,1]$, where U is the universe of discourse. The set $A \subset U$, given by

$$A = \{ A_1,A_2,\ldots,A_n \} \tag{2}$$

is called the support of the fuzzy set A^f and is the set of points of U at which $f_A(A_i)$ is positive.

ALGEBRAIC OPERATIONS

The algebraic operations are well-defined for non-fuzzy quantities. It is well-known how to perform the operations of addition, subtraction, multiplication, or division for non-fuzzy variables. However, for fuzzy variables these operations have not been defined precisely. We do not know how to add 'small' and 'large' or how to divide 'small' by 'large.' It is intuitively obvious that 'small' and 'large' are not well-defined variables and hence using conventional methods we may not perform the algebraic operations for these variables. Since in humanistic systems, we have to deal with such fuzzy variables, we should have some method of performing these operations. The following method of performing algebraic operations for fuzzy variables may be very helpful in analyzing fuzzy systems.

Let us consider two fuzzy quantities, represented by

$$A^f = \{(f_A(A_i), A_i)\}, \qquad i = 1, \ldots, m \tag{3}$$

and

$$B^f = \{(f_B(B_j), B_j)\}, \qquad j = 1, \ldots, n \tag{4}$$

The sets A^f and B^f have A and B, respectively, as their supports. It is intuitively clear that the sum of these fuzzy quantities will not be, in general, a non-fuzzy quantity. Thus, if

$$S^f = A^f + B^f \tag{5}$$

then

$$S^f = \{(f_S(S_k), S_k)\}, \qquad k = 1, 2, \ldots, p \tag{6}$$

The support S of S^f depends on A and B. Since A^f represents all elements of A, though with different grades of membership, and similarly B^f represents all elements of B, we cannot add any element $A_i \in A$ and $B_j \in B$ and say that this is the sum of A^f and B^f. We should consider the sum of each element of A with each element of B separately and assign a suitable grade of membership to these sums. In other words, the set S^f should be formed by considering each element of space $A \times B$ and assigning them suitable grades of membership. Thus in (6), we have

$$p = m \cdot n$$

$$S_k = S_{ij} = A_i + B_j, \qquad A_i \in A, B_j \in B \tag{8}$$

$$f_S(S_k) = f_S(S_{ij}) = f_A(A_i) \wedge f_B(B_j) \tag{9}$$

where $a \wedge b$ denotes minimum of a and b.

Thus, we see that the number of elements in S^f is $m \cdot n$. However, in many cases it is possible that a particular element S^* may appear in S^f more than once, that is,

$$S_i = S_j = \cdots = S^* \tag{10}$$

This is due to the possibility of the same result S^* when different pairs (A_i, B_j), with $A_i \in A, B_j \in B$, are added. The grades of membership of these equal elements in S^f may be same or different. It is obvious that as S^* appears more than once with different grades of membership, the membership of S^* in S^f should be considered on the basis of the membership of all elements satisfying (10). One of the possible ways of considering the membership of such multimembership elements is to assign the grade of membership to account for all equivalent elements. We may do this by assigning the grade of membership

$$f_S(S^*) = \oplus_i f_S(S_i) \qquad \forall S_i = S^* \tag{11}$$

where

$$f(a) \oplus f(b) = f(a) + f(b) - f(a) \cdot f(b) \tag{12}$$

and $\oplus_i f(a_i)$ is the serial operation given in (12) for all values of i.

This grade of membership takes into account the membership of all the elements which are equal. The resultant membership of S^* is increased depending on the elements satisfying (10) and hence seems to represent this element in S^f with the correct grade of membership.

In S^f, there may be many multimembership elements. We should reduce all such terms to unimembership elements by assigning the resultant grade of membership, given by (11). Thus, though the number of elements in S^f is originally p, we may reduce this number by coverting all multimembership elements to unimembership elements, using above procedure. This procedure is illustrated in the first example (below).

So far, we have been discussing the operation of addition for fuzzy quantities. The discussion is valid for other algebraic operations as well. In general, if we denote by $\circ$ any algebraic operation (whether addition, subtraction, multiplication or division), then

$$C^f = A^f \circ B^f \tag{13}$$

such that

$$C^f = \left\{ \left(f_C(C_{ij}), C_{ij} \right) \right\} \tag{14}$$

where

$$C_{ij} = A_i \circ B_j, \quad A_i \in A, B_j \in B \tag{15}$$

and

$$f_C(C_{ij}) = f_A(A_i) \bigwedge f_B(B_j) \tag{16}$$

Example Let us assume that in a certain system when we say that a particular quantity is 'small', we mean that this quantity is represented by

$$\text{small} = \left\{ (0.7, 2), (0.8, 3), (1, 4), (0.8, 5) \right\}$$

Similarly, by 'large' we mean

$$\text{'large'} = \{(0.8, 8), (0.9, 9), (1, 10), (0.9, 11), (0.8, 12)\}$$

If we are interested in finding the result of adding 'small' to 'large', then we apply the method outlined above. Thus,

$$\text{'small'} + \text{'large'} = \{(0.7, 2), (0.8, 3), (1, 4), (0.8, 5)\} +$$
$$\{(0.8, 8), (0.9, 9), (1, 10), (0.9, 11), (0.8, 12)\}$$

Using (14), (15), and (16) we get

$$\text{'small'} + \text{'large'} = \{(0.7, 10), (0.7, 11), (0.7, 12), (0.7, 13), (0.7, 14),$$
$$(0.8, 11), (0.8, 12), (0.8, 13), (0.8, 14), (0.8, 15),$$
$$(0.8, 12), (0.9, 13), (1, 14), (0.9, 15), (0.8, 16),$$
$$(0.8, 13), (0.8, 14), (0.8, 15), (0.8, 16), (0.8, 17)\}$$

We observe that the elements 11, 12, 13, 14, 15, and 16 appear as multimembership terms and hence we apply (10)–(12) to convert these terms to unimembership terms. Thus,

$$\text{'small'} + \text{'large'} = \{(0.7, 10), (\oplus[0.7, 0.8], 11),$$
$$(\oplus[0.7, 0.8, 0.8], 12), (\oplus[0.7, 0.8, 0.9, 0.8], 13)$$
$$(\oplus[0.7, 0.8, 1, 0.8], 14), (\oplus[0.8, 0.9, 0.8], 15),$$
$$(\oplus[0.8, 0.8], 16), (0.8, 17)\}$$
$$= \{(0.7, 10), (0.94, 11), (0.988, 12), (0.9988, 13),$$
$$(1, 14), (0.996, 15), (0.8, 17)\}$$

The above result looks intuitively sound as on addition of 'small' to 'large' the result is more than 'large', as is clear on considering the supports of these quantities.

ANALYSIS OF LINEAR–MEMORYLESS FUZZY SYSTEMS

We shall refer to as fuzzy systems, those systems in which information in at least one part of the system is fuzzy. The given system may be either an open loop system as shown in Fig. 1, or a closed loop system as shown in Fig. 2. It is well known that a closed loop system of Fig. 2 may be represented in the form of an open loop system of Fig. 1, by using the

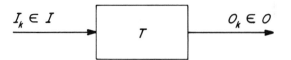

Figure 1. Open loop system.

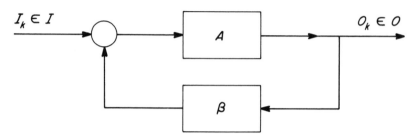

Figure 2. Feedback system.

relation

$$T = \frac{A}{1 - A\beta} \tag{17}$$

where T is the over-all transfer characteristic of the system, and A and β are forward path and feedback transfer functions, respectively. Now, let us consider the open loop system of Fig. 1. The transfer characteristic T of the system represents the mapping of the input space I into the output space O and is such that

$$O_k = I_k \cdot T; \qquad I_k \in I, O_k \in O \tag{18}$$

We assume, in this section, that this system is memoryless, and hence the output at any instant depends only on the input at that instant. It is obvious that if the input to the system is non-fuzzy and the system is also non-fuzzy, then the output will also be non-fuzzy. However, if the input and/or the system is fuzzy, then the output will also be fuzzy. Thus, if

$$I^f(t) = \left\{ \left(f_I(I_j), I_j \right) \right\} \tag{19}$$

is the input at instant t and

$$T^f = \left\{ \left(f_T(T_i), T_i \right) \right\} \tag{20}$$

is the transfer characteristic, then the output of the system is

$$O^f(t) = I^f(t) \cdot T^f \tag{21}$$

We may represent this output as

$$O^f(t) = \left\{ \left(f_O(O_{ij}), O_{ij} \right) \right\} \qquad (22)$$

where

$$O_{ij} = I_j \cdot T_i \qquad (23)$$

and

$$f_O(O_{ij}) = f_T(T_i) \bigwedge f_I(I_j), \qquad T_i \in T, I_j \in I(t) \qquad (24)$$

However, if only one of the two independent quantities is fuzzy then these expressions are slightly different. In this case

$$O^f(t) = \left\{ \left(f_O(O_i), O_i \right) \right\} \qquad (25)$$

Here if T is non-fuzzy and input is fuzzy, then

$$O_i = T \cdot I_i, \qquad I_i \in I(t) \qquad (26)$$

$$f_O(O_i) = f_I(I_i) \qquad (27)$$

and if input is non-fuzzy with the fuzzy T, then

$$O_i = I \cdot T_i, \qquad T_i \in T \qquad (28)$$

$$f_O(O_i) = f_T(T_i) \qquad (29)$$

Using the above relations, we are in a position to determine the response of a fuzzy system in which the input and/or the transfer characteristic is fuzzy.

The analysis of the closed loop memoryless system may be carried out using the above relations. However, in this case we first have to evaluate T using (17). The fuzziness of T depends on the nature of A and β. If both A and β are non-fuzzy then T will also be non-fuzzy. However, if A and/or β is fuzzy, then T is also fuzzy. First, let us consider

$$A^f = \left\{ \left(f_A(A_i), A_i \right) \right\} \qquad (30)$$

$$\beta^f = \left\{ \left(f_\beta(\beta_j), \beta_j \right) \right\} \qquad (31)$$

Then the transfer characteristic of this system is

$$T^f = \left\{ \left(f_T(T_{ij}), T_{ij} \right) \right\} \qquad (32)$$

where

$$T_{ij} = A_i / (1 - A_i \beta_j) \qquad (33)$$

$$f_T(T_{ij}) = f_A(A_i) \oplus f_\beta(\beta_j) \qquad (34)$$

From this general relation, we may get the expression for T^f when only one, either A or β, is fuzzy. When A is non-fuzzy, we have

$$T^f = \{(f_T(T_i), T_i)\} \tag{35}$$

where

$$T_i = A/(1 - A\beta_i) \tag{36}$$

$$f_T(T_i) = f_\beta(\beta_i) \tag{37}$$

Similarly, if A is fuzzy but β is non-fuzzy, then

$$T^f = \{(f_T(T_i), T_i)\} \tag{35}$$

where

$$T_i = A_i/(1 - A_i\beta) \tag{36}$$

$$f_T(T_i) = f_A(A_i) \tag{37}$$

Thus, we may analyse a fuzzy feedback system by first deriving T^f for a given A^f (or A) and β^f (or β), and then using the method of analysis of open loop fuzzy systems. This is illustrated by considering the following simple example.

Example   Let us consider a system in which

$$A^f = \{(0.7, 50), (0.9, 60), (0.6, 70)\}$$
$$\beta^f = \{(0.8, 9), (0.9, 1)\}$$
$$I^f = \{(0.5, 4), (1, 5), (0.5, 6)\}$$

For this system with negative feedback, using the expression developed, we get

$$
\begin{aligned}
T^f = \quad & \{(0.7, 50/46), (0.8, 60/55), (0.6, 70/64), (0.7, 50/51), \\
& (0.9, 60/61), (0.6, 70/71)\}
\end{aligned}
$$

The output O^f for a given input I^f is

$$
\begin{aligned}
O^f = \quad & \{(0.5, 100/23), (0.5, 240/55), (0.5, 70/16), (0.5, 200/51), \\
& (0.5, 240/61), (0.5, 280/71), (0.7, 250/46), (0.8, 60/11), \\
& (0.6, 350/60), (0.7, 250/51), (0.9, 300/61), (0.6, 350/71), \\
& (0.5, 150/23), (0.5, 360/55), (0.5, 210/32), (0.5, 300/51), \\
& (0.5, 360/61), (0.5, 420/71)\}
\end{aligned}
$$

If we are interested in the result having accuracy up to the first digit after the decimal point, then

$$O^f = \{(\oplus[0.5,0.5,0.5],4.3),(\oplus[0.5,0.5,0.5],3.9),$$

$$(\oplus[0.7,0.8,0.6],5.4),(\oplus[0.7,0.9,0.6],4.9),$$

$$(\oplus[0.5,0.5,0.5,],6.5),(\oplus[0.5,0.5,0.5],5.9)\}$$

$$= \{(0.875,4.3),(0.875,3.9),(0.988,4.9),(0.976,5.4),$$

$$(0.875,6.5),(0.875,5.9)\}$$

CONVOLUTION OF FUZZY VARIABLES

In this paper, we consider the convolution of discrete variables and hence the convolution of variables $A(n)$ and $B(n)$ given by

$$C(m) = \sum_{k=0}^{m} A(k) \cdot B(m-k) \qquad (38)$$

Here $A(n)$ and $B(n)$ are sequences. In non-fuzzy cases (38) is easily solved. However, if any one (or both) of these sequences is fuzzy, then the result is also fuzzy. Before we consider convolution of such fuzzy variables, let us consider two different types of fuzziness, which may be present in the case of sequences.

CASE 1 (Fuzzy Sequence) There may be many known sequences $A_i(k)$, but it may not be precisely known which particular sequence is preferred. In other words, when we say that $A(k)$ is a fuzzy sequence, it is meant that $A^f(k)$ is

$$A^f(k) = \{(f_A(A_i(k)),A_i(k))\} \qquad (39)$$

where $A_i(k)$ is a well-defined non-fuzzy sequence and $f_A(A_i(k))$ is the grade of membership of the $A_i(k)$ in the $A^f(k)$.

CASE 2 (Fuzzy at Each Instant) In some situations, the variable A has a fuzzy value at each instant. It is not well-defined at any instant. This situation is different from the first one. In a fuzzy sequence, only the information about the sequence is not precisely defined, whereas, in this case there is no non-fuzzy sequence. The sequence which is fuzzy at each instant is represented by

$$A^f(O) = \left\{ \left(f_{A_o}(A_i), A_i \right) \right\}$$
$$A^f(1) = \left\{ \left(f_{A_1}(A_i), A_i \right) \right\}$$
$$\vdots$$
$$A^f(k) = \left\{ \left(f_{A_k}(A_i), A_i \right) \right\} \tag{40}$$
$$\vdots$$
$$A^f(n) = \left\{ \left(f_{A_n}(A_i), A_i \right) \right\}$$

where $A^f(k)$ gives the value at the kth instant.

It is clear that this case is entirely different from the first case where the variable is following a non-fuzzy sequence with a given grade of membership. Whereas, if the variable is fuzzy at each instant, it is represented by a fuzzy set at each instant.

Now let us consider that we have two sequences of variables which are fuzzy. These two variables may be the input and weighting function of a given system. Let us assume that these variables are $A^f(k)$ and $B^f(k)$. The convolution of these two will yield the result at the nth instant to be

$$C^f(n) = \sum_{k=0}^{n} A^f(k) \cdot B^f(n-k) \tag{41}$$

Now the result of convolution $C^f(n)$ will depend on the nature of $A^f(k)$ and $B^f(k)$. We consider various possibilities.

(i) *One sequence is fuzzy*: Let only $A^f(k)$ be fuzzy, and the $B(k)$ be non-fuzzy variables. Then

$$C^f(n) = \sum_{k=0}^{n} A^f(k) \cdot B(n-k) \tag{42}$$

which may be written as

$$C^f(n) = \left\{ \left(f_{C_n}(C_i(n)), C_i(n) \right) \right\} \tag{43}$$

Now $A^f(k)$ may be a fuzzy sequence or may be fuzzy at each instant. If $A^f(k)$ is a fuzzy sequence, then in (43).

$$C_i(n) = \sum_{k=0}^{n} A_i(k) \cdot B(n-k) \tag{44}$$

and

$$f_{Cn}\left(C_i(n)\right) = f_A(A_i) \tag{45}$$

In this case if the fuzzy sequence has m elements, then the result $C^f(n)$ will also have m elements.

The convolution in case of the variable which is fuzzy at each instant is obtained by first expanding $C^f(n)$ as

$$C^f(n) = A^f(O) \cdot B(n) + A^f(1) \cdot B(n-1) + \cdots + A^f(n) \cdot B(O)$$
$$= C_0^f + C_1^f + \cdots + C_n^f \tag{46}$$

The ith term C_i^f in the right-hand side of (46) may have m_i terms due to m_i terms of $A^f(i)$. For getting $C^f(n)$ we have to add all the terms of RHS. Since each term of RHS is fuzzy and has m_i elements, the result of the summation is to have m_c elements given by

$$m_c = m_0 \cdot m_1 \cdot m_2 \cdots \cdots m_n \tag{47}$$

The element $C_i(n)$ and its grade of membership $f_C(C_i(n))$ are determined by solving (46).

(ii) *Both sequences are fuzzy*: Now we consider that the sequence of the variable B is also fuzzy and the fuzziness in this is also such that we have either a fuzzy sequence given by

$$B^f(k) = \left\{ \left(f_B(B_i(k)), B_i(k) \right) \right\} \tag{48}$$

or is fuzzy at each instant such that

$$B^f(0) = \left\{ \left(f_{B_0}(B_i), B_i \right) \right\}$$
$$B^f(1) = \left\{ \left(f_{B_1}(B_i), B_i \right) \right\}$$
$$\vdots$$
$$B^f(n) = \left\{ \left(f_{B_n}(B_i), B_i \right) \right\} \tag{49}$$

The number of elements, in the support of $B^f(k)$ (given by (48) is assumed to be P and in $B^f(i)$ (of (49)) is assumed to be P_i.

Now when both sequences are fuzzy, we may have any of the following three situations.

(i) *Both variables are fuzzy sequences*: In this case, the result of the convolution may be represented as

$$C^f(n) = \left\{ \left(f_{Cn}(C_{ij}), C_{ij} \right) \right\} \tag{50}$$

where

$$C_{ij} = \sum_{k=0}^{n} A_i(k) \cdot B_j(n-k), \qquad A_i(k) \in A(k), B_j(k) \in B(k) \qquad (51)$$

$$f_{Cn} = f_A(A_i(k)) \bigwedge f_B(B_j(k)) \qquad (52)$$

Now, since each sequence $A_i(k) \in A(k)$, is to be convolved with each sequence $B_j(k)$ to yield one element of $C^f(n)$, the total number of elements in $C^f(n)$ is given by

$$m_C = m \cdot P \qquad (53)$$

where m and P are number of elements in support sets $A(k)$ and $B(k)$, respectively.

(ii) *One variable is a fuzzy sequence; other is fuzzy at each instant*: Let us assume that $A^f(k)$ is fuzzy at each instant and $B^f(k)$ is a fuzzy sequence. In (46), $A^f(k)$ was considered to be fuzzy at each instant and $B(k)$ was non-fuzzy. Now let us consider $B_i(k) \in B(k)$ (the support of $B^f(k)$) and using (46) to get the result for this sequence as

$$C^{if}(n) = \sum_{k=0}^{n} A^f(k) \cdot B_i(n-k) \qquad (54)$$

The result $C^{if}(n)$ is a fuzzy set with the number of elements given by (47). Since $B^f(k)$ is a fuzzy sequence having P elements, we will have to consider each sequence and use (54) to get the result due to this sequence. Moreover, since each sequence $B_i(k)$ has different grade of membership in $B^f(k)$, the grade of memberships of the elements of $C^{if}(n)$ in $C^f(n)$ should be decided by considering the grades of membership of elements from (54) and from the grade of membership for $B_i(k)$. Thus, if

$$C^{if}(n) = \left\{ \left(f_{C_{in}}(C_j), C_j \right) \right\} \qquad (55)$$

then

$$C^f(n) = \left\{ \left(f_{C_n}(C_k), C_k \right) \right\} \qquad (56)$$

where

$$f_{O_n}(C_k) = f_{Cin}(C_k) \bigwedge f_B(B_i(k)), \qquad C_k \in C^i(n) \qquad (57)$$

where $C^i(n)$ is the support of $C^{if}(n)$.

Now, since there are P elements in set $B^f(k)$ and each of these sequences combines with $A^f(k)$ to yield $C^{if}(n)$, the total number of elements in $C^f(n)$ will be

$$m_C = P \cdot m_0 \cdot m_1 \cdots \cdot m_n \qquad (58)$$

(iii) *Both variables fuzzy at each instant*: We express the convolution as

$$C^f(n) = \sum_{k=0}^{n} A^f(k) \cdot B^f(n-k)$$

$$= A^f(0) \cdot B^f(n) + A^f(1) B^f(n-1) + \cdots + A^f(n) B^f(0) \tag{59}$$

The term $A^f(i) \cdot B^f(n-1)$ is the product of two fuzzy sets having m_i and P_{n-1} elements. The result of this product has $m_i \cdot P_{n-1}$ elements. Now on considering first two terms of RHS, we find that these have $m_0 \cdot P_n$ and $m_1 \cdot P_{n-1}$ elements. When we add these terms, the sum has $m_0 \cdot m_1 \cdot P_{n-1} \cdot P_n$ elements. Thus, the set $C^f(n)$ has m_c elements, given by

$$m_c = m_0 \cdot m_1 \cdots \cdot m_n \cdot P_0 \cdot P_1 \cdots \cdot P_n \tag{60}$$

ANALYSIS OF LINEAR FUZZY SYSTEMS

In an earlier section we considered the analysis of linear, memoryless fuzzy systems. Considering several different situations, we derived the relations for output in terms of given input and transfer characteristic. It is well-known that if the system has a memory, then the output at any time is not the product of input and transfer characteristic, but is given by the convolutation of the input and the transfer characteristic. Thus, if we denote convolution by * then for Fig. 1

$$O(t) = I(t) * T \tag{61}$$

For fuzzy systems, this is

$$O^f(t) = I^f(t) * T^f \tag{62}$$

The closed loop system of Fig. 2 may be reduced to that of Fig. 1, by using

$$T^f = A^f / (1 - A^f * \beta^f) \tag{63}$$

Using the fuzzy convolution, we may analyze fuzzy systems with a memory by replacing the product by convolution in the expressions derived for the analysis of memoryless systems. Thus, the modification of the method for the analysis of memoryless systems to the method of analysis of fuzzy systems with memory is straightforward. However, we have to consider that the number of elements in a fuzzy set may become very large due to all these operations. We have seen that each operation results in increased number of terms, and hence we have to devise some method to reduce this growing dimension of a fuzzy variable. This problem is discused in next section.

DIMENSION REDUCTION

Let us consider a simple case of convolution. If the set $A^f(k)$ is fuzzy at each instant having only 4 elements in each $A^f(i)$ and $B(k)$ is non-fuzzy, then the number of terms in the result $C^f(n)$ will be 4^{n+1}. Assuming $B(k)$ to be an impulse response of the system having memory up to $t = 4T$, and $A^f(k)$ to be the input to the system, the output at any instant will be a fuzzy set having 4^5 terms. If we consider also that the impulse response is fuzzy at each instant with 4 members in each term, then the output is a fuzzy set having $4^5, 4^5$ terms. If these sets have more terms, or we have the system whose impulse response decays more slowly, then the output fuzzy set has more terms.

In large systems, the number of elements may be much higher than this number, and hence there is certainly a need for a method of reduction of data. Here we propose the following two methods for the reduction of data without going into details about the effects of this method.

Method A

The first method is based on the present democratic set up of electing a fixed number of representatives from a vast number of citizens of a country. In this set up, it is well known that, the person who gets the highest number of votes from a certain area, having a fixed number of voters, is elected to represent that area.

Suppose, we have fuzzy set S^f given by

$$S^f = \left\{ \left(f_S(S_i), S_i \right) \right\} \tag{64}$$

and having N elements in its support S. It is desired to reduce this set to have P elements, where $P < N$. For this problem a simple approach is to partition the support set S into P disjoint subsets S_i^*, and then to select from each subset S_i^* an element $S_j \in S_i^*$ having the highest grade of membership among the elements of S_i^* to represent the set S_i^*. Then the P elements thus selected should be retained to represent S^f and all others should be neglected.

Formally, we partition S such that

$$S = S_1^* \cup S_2^* \cup \cdots \cup S_p^* \tag{65}$$

where

$$S_i^* \cap S_j^* = \varnothing, \qquad i \neq j \tag{66}$$

and

$$N = \sum_{i=1}^{p} N_i \tag{67}$$

where N_i is number of elements in S_i^*.
Now the reduced set S_r^f is

$$S_r^f = \left\{ \left(f_S(S_j), S_j \right) \right\}, \qquad j = 1, 2, \ldots, p \tag{68}$$

where

$$f_S(S_j) = \bigvee {}_k f_S(S_k), \qquad S_k \in S_j^*, \forall S_j^* \tag{69}$$

and S_j is that element of set S_j^* whose grade of membership is given by (69).

Method B

In some cases one may be more interested in the extremal values. In such cases, first the elements of the set S should be arranged in ascending order of their values. Let this ordered set be

$$S^a = \left\{ S^1, S^2, S^3, \ldots, S^N \right\} \tag{70}$$

Since in this case the extremal values are of more interest, the elements S^2 and S^N are natural candidates for inclusion in the reduced set. The remaining $P-2$ elements are the elements having highest grades of memberships in $P-2$ fuzzy sets having as their support disjoint subsets $\{ S^2, S^3, \ldots, S^{k+1} \}, \ldots, S^{k+2}, \ldots, S^{2k+1} \}, \ldots, \{ S^{(P-3)k+2}, \ldots, S^{N-1} \}$, with their grades of membership the same as in the set S. The value of k is

$$k = \left[(N-2)/(P-2) \right] \tag{71}$$

where $[x]$ denotes the least integer higher than x.
A simple example is considered to illustrate the fuzzy convolution and the reduction technique.

Example   We consider both variables to be fuzzy at each instant having the values as given below.

$$A^f(0) = \left\{ (0.8, 4), (0.9, 5), (0.6, 6) \right\}$$
$$A^f(1) = \left\{ (0.6, 9), (0.9, 10), (0.7, 11) \right\}$$
$$A^f(2) = \left\{ (0.9, 20), (0.7, 22), (0.6, 23) \right\}$$

and

$$B^f(0) = \{(0.95, 1), (0.9, 0.9)\}$$
$$B^f(1) = \{(0.9, 0.9), (0.8, 0.8)\}$$
$$B^f(2) = \{(0.7, 0.3), (0.75, 0.25)\}$$

If no reduction is applied, then $C^f(2)$ will have $3.3, 3.2, 2.2 = 216$ elements. Even in this oversimplified case, it sounds ridiculous to say that the result of convolution is a fuzzy set having 216 elements. Moreover, this clearly demonstrates that in fuzzy systems data to be handled will become prohibitively large. Now, let it be desired that the output should not contain more than three elements. For achieving this, at each step we apply the reduction technique and keep the result of any step restricted to two elements. Thus,

$$C^f(2) = A^f(0) \cdot B^f(2) + A^f(1) \cdot B^f(1) + A^f(2) \cdot B^f(0)$$

We consider $A^f(0) \cdot B^f(2)$ and illustrate the reduction procedure.

$$A^f(0) \cdot B^f(2) = \{(0.8, 4), (0.9, 5), (0.6, 6)\}, \{(0.7, 0.3), (0.75, 0.25)\}$$
$$= \{(0.7, 1.2), (0.75, 1), (0.7, 1.5), (0.75, 1.25), (0.6, 1.8), (0.6, 1.5)\}$$

Since '1.5' appears with grades of membership 0.7 and 0.6, we assign the resulting grade of membership to this element, which is

$$f(1.5) = 0.7 \oplus 0.6 = 0.88$$

Substituting this and selecting two terms after arranging in ascending values of elements, we get

$$S_1^f = A^f(0)B^f(2)$$
$$= \{(0.75, 1), (0.7, 1.2), (0.75, 1.25), (0.88, 1.5), (0.6, 1.8)\}$$

Hence

$$S_1^{f_r} = \{(0.75, 1.25), (0.88, 1.5)\}$$

Here, we have assumed that in case of multi-maximum-grade of membership terms, we select a term having the highest value among these terms as the representative term. Similarly, we obtain

$$S_2^{f_r} = \{(0.8, 8), (0.9, 9)\}$$
$$S_3^{f_r} = \{(0.9, 20), (0.7, 22)\}$$

Hence the result is

$$C^f(2) = \{(0.75, 1.25), (0.88, 1.5)\} + \{(0.8, 8), (0.9, 9)\} + \{(0.9, 20), (0.7, 22)\}$$
$$= \{(0.75, 9.25), (0.75, 10.25), (0.8, 9.5), (0.88, 10.5)\}$$
$$+ \{(0.9, 20), (0.7, 22)\}$$

Applying the reduction technique to the first term, we get

$$C^f(2) = \{(0.8, 9.5), (0.88, 10.5)\} + \{(0.9, 20), (0.7, 22)\}$$
$$= \{(0.8, 29.5), (0.7, 31.5), (0.88, 30.5), (0.7, 32.5)\}$$

Again applying the reduction technique, the result is

$$C^f(2) = \{(0.88, 30.5), (0.7, 32.5)\}$$

Using the second method for reduction, we get

$$C^f(2) = \{(0.6, 26.2), (0.6, 32.5)\}$$

Thus, applying the reduction method at each stage of the computation, we may keep the number of elements in a fuzzy set always within a useful limit.

CONCLUSION

In this paper, a method is presented for the analysis of those systems that are too complex to be analyzed using conventional techniques. Such systems may be analyzed using the concept of fuzzy sets. A technique, for performing algebraic operations with fuzzy quantities is proposed. This technique is used in developing a method for the convolution of fuzzy variables. Using these operations, we are in a position then to analyze fuzzy systems, with or without memory, and with or without feedback. Again using this method, we may then analyze humanistic systems involving fuzzy variables.

REFERENCES

1. A. D. Allen, "A Method for Evaluating Technical Journals on the Basis of Published Comments through Fuzzy Implications. A Survey of the Major IEEE Transactions," *IEEE Trans. Systems, Man and Cybernetics* **SMC-3**, No. 4, (1973) 422–425.
2. R. E. Bellman, R. Kalaba, and L. A. Zadeh, "Abstraction and Pattern Classification," *J. Math. Anal. Appl.* **13** (1966), 1–7.
3. R. E. Bellman and L. A. Zadeh, "Decision-Making in a Fuzzy Environment," *Mgmt. Sci.* **17**, No. 4 (1970) B-141–B-164.

4. S. K. Chang, "On the Execution of Fuzzy Programs Using Finite State Machines," *IEEE Trans. Computers* **C-2**, No. 3 (1972), 241–253.
5. S. K. Chang, "Automated Interpretation and Editing of Fuzzy Line Drawings," *Proc. Spring Joint Comp. Conf.* (1971) 393–399.
6. S. S. L. Chang and L. A. Zadeh, "Fuzzy Mapping and Control," *IEEE Trans. on Systems, Man and Cybernetics* **SMC-2**, No. 1 (1972), 30–35.
7. B. Gluss, "Fuzzy Multistage Decision Making and Terminal Regulators and their Relationship to Nonfuzzy Quadratic State and Terminal Regulators," *Int. J. Control* **17**, No. 1 (1973), 177–192.
8. A. Kandel, "On the Properties of Switching Function," *J. Cybernetics* **4**, No. 1 (1974), 119–126.
9. R. C. T. Lee, "Fuzzy Logic and the Resolution Principle," *J. Asso. Comput. Mach* **19** (1972), 109–118.
10. E. H. Mamdani, and A. Assilian, "An Experiment in Linguistic Systhesis with a Fuzzy Logic Controller," *Int. J. Man-Mach. Studies* **7** (1975), 1–13.
11. E. Santos, "Fuzzy Algorithms," *Info. Control* **17** (1970), 326–339.
12. S. Tamura, S. Niguchi, and K. Tanaka, "Pattern Classification Based on Fuzzy Relations," *IEEE Trans. Systems, Man and Cybernetics* **SMC-1**, No. 1 (1971), 61–66.
13. L. A. Zadeh, "Fuzzy Sets," *Info. Control* **8** (1965), 338–353.
14. L. A. Zadeh, "Fuzzy Algorithms," *Info. Control* **12** (1968), 94–102.
15. L. A. Zadeh, "Quantitative Fuzzy Semantics," *Infor. Sci.* **3** (1971), 159–176.
16. L. A. Zadeh, "Outline of a New Approach to the Analysis of Complex Systems and Decision Processes," *IEEE Trans. on Systems, Man and Cybernetics* **SMC-3**, No. 1 (1973), 28–44.

PART THREE
APPLICATIONS

INDICES OF PARTITION FUZZINESS AND DETECTION OF CLUSTERS IN LARGE DATA SETS

18

J. C. Dunn

Let X be a set of n vectors in d-dimensional Euclidean space, and let $u(\cdot) = \{u_1(\cdot), \ldots, u_k(\cdot)\}$ be a fuzzy k-partition of X, as in [9,6], i.e.,

$$0 \leqslant u_i(x) \leqslant 1, \qquad 1 \leqslant i \leqslant k$$

$$\sum_{i=1}^{k} u_i(x) = 1$$

for all $x \in X$. To each such k-partition $u(\cdot)$ and each set of k "prototype" vectors $v_1, \ldots, v_k$ in R^d assign the number

$$J\left(u(\cdot); v_1, \ldots, v_k\right) = \sum_{i=1}^{k} \sum_{x \in X} \left(u_i(x)\right)^{\omega} \|x - v_i\|^2$$

where $\|\cdot\|$ is the standard norm in R^d and ω is a fixed real exponent greater than or equal to 1. If X consists of k "well-separated" clusters, then the characteristic functions and the centroids of these clusters closely approximate the partition-prototype set $\{u^*(\cdot); v_1^*, \ldots, v_k^*\}$ which globally minimizes J [7]. On the other hand, if k clusters are not present in X, then even those partitions that locally minimize J are likely to exhibit substantial fuzziness. This suggests the following heuristic for deciding whether a clustering structure is present in X for any value of k, and if so, at which value of k it is most conspicuous [8,2]: For each fixed k, compute as many locally minimizing k-partitions $u^*(\cdot)$ for J as is feasible and give special consideration to those which are least fuzzy, as measured by some suitable scalar index.

The iterative algorithm derived in [6] for $\omega = 1$ and 2, and extended to general real $\omega > 1$ in [2] provides a simple and effective means of approximating extremal partitions for J. As $\omega \to 1$, this algorithm behaves more and more like the classical Isodota process [1] and is equivalent to this process for $\omega = 1$. For ω near 1, extremal partitions $u^*(\cdot)$ for J exhibit little fuzziness (i.e., the membership functions in $u^*(\cdot)$ are very nearly Boolean) irrespective of clustering structure in X. At the other extreme, for large values of ω extremal partitions tend to be very fuzzy regardless of whether clusters are present in X. For present purposes, the choice $\omega = 2$ seems a good compromise, and all further considerations are limited to this special case.

Ruspini [9] proposes the following scalar measure of partition fuzziness, called the partition entropy,

$$H(k; u(\cdot)) = -\frac{1}{n \log_a(k)} \sum_{i=1}^{k} \sum_{x \in X} u_i(x) \log_a(u_i(x)) \tag{1}$$

Bezdek [4] compares the index (1) to another coefficient that measures the overlap in the membership functions of $u^*(\cdot)$, namely

$$F(k; u(\cdot)) = \frac{1}{n} \sum_{i=1}^{k} \sum_{x \in X} u_i(\cdot)^2 \tag{2}$$

It is shown [2] that $1 - F$ is the average content of pairwise fuzzy intersections of the membership functions in $u(\cdot)$. Moreover,

$$\frac{1}{k} \leqslant F(k; u(\cdot)) \leqslant 1 \tag{3}$$

with the upper value assumed on any ordinary partition of X and the lower value assumed on the "maximally equivocal" partition

$$u_i(x) = \frac{1}{k}, \qquad 1 \leqslant i \leqslant k \tag{4}$$

for all $x \in X$. Finally,

$$0 \leqslant H(k; u(\cdot)) \leqslant 1 \tag{5}$$

with the lower value assumed on ordinary partitions and the upper value assumed on (4). Thus, increasing values of F or decreasing values of H indicate decreasing fuzziness in $u(\cdot)$. Accordingly, either of these indices may be incorporated into the heuristic procedure outlined above; as in e.g., [3,5] compute a set $\mathcal{E}_k$ of extremal k-partitions for J, compute $\underline{H}(k) = \min_{u^*(\cdot)\mathcal{E}_k} H(k; u^*(\cdot))$ or $\bar{F}(k) = \max_{u^*(\cdot)\mathcal{E}_k} F(k; u(\cdot))$ and the associated k-partition, and plot $\underline{H}(k)$ or $\bar{F}(k)$ vs. k. Further experiments of this kind are described later on.

One shortcoming of earlier investigations has been the failure to establish suitable "benchmark" values for the indices $\underline{H}$ and $\bar{F}$. Thus, how small must $\underline{H}$ be before one is justified in inferring that X consists of k well-separated clusters? That the endpoints of the intervals (3) or (5) are not always appropriate reference values can be seen by considering what happens as $k \to n$. When $k = n$, the optimal fuzzy k-partition $u^*(\cdot)$ always consists of the $k = n$ characteristic functions of the singleton sets $\{x_i\}, 1 \leqslant i \leqslant n$, consequently, $H = 0$ and $F = 1$ for $u^*(\cdot)$. However, the fact that n vectors can be partitioned into n well-separated "clusters" is hardly suprising or of any interest. As k approaches n, a similar situation prevails. But when $k \ll n$, values of $\bar{F}$ near 1 or $\underline{H}$ near 0 are of much greater significance. This suggests that $\bar{F}$ and $\underline{H}$ should be weighted or normalized in some way to compensate for the inherent tendancy of optimal partitions for J to become less fuzzy as k increases.

With these observations in mind, consider a set X_0 of $n = \nu^d$ vectors uniformly distributed in a hypercubical lattice in R^d. By any reasonable interpretation, this set is cluster-free at every level k, with the trivial exception of $k = n$, and, in fact, the separation index α defined in [7] is $\leqslant 1$ for all ordinary k-partitions of X_0 for $2 \leqslant k < n$. Accordingly, it would seem that $\underline{H}_0(k)$ and $\bar{F}_0(k)$ might serve as useful benchmark values for the indices $\underline{H}$ and $\bar{F}$; to be more specific, if X is any other set of $n = \nu^d$ vectors in R^d it seems plausible that X will consist of k clusters if $\underline{H}(k)$ is small compared to $\underline{H}_0(k)$ or $1 - \bar{F}(k)$ is small compared with $1 - \bar{F}_0(k)$. It is therefore of some interest to see how the curves $\underline{H}_0(k)$ and $\bar{F}_0(k)$ look for the reference set X_0.[1]

In Figs. 1 and 2, approximate $\underline{H}_0$ and $\bar{F}_0$ curves are displayed for a 9-point square lattice ($\nu = 3, d = 2$) and a 27 point cubical lattice ($\nu = 3$ and $d = 3$), respectively. These curves were generated by computing the smallest value of H and the largest value of F on the finite set $\mathcal{E}_k$ of $\leqslant 3$ distinct approximate extremal k-partitions obtained by running out up to 30 iterations of the fuzzy partitioning algorithm in [6] from each of 3 different sets of k initial prototype vectors; each initial prototype set was formed by taking the first k vectors from some random permutation $x_{\phi_1}, \ldots, x_{\phi_n}$ of the labeling originally furnished with X_0. The most striking aspect of these diagrams is the nearly linear charceter of the H_0 curve. At present, it is not known whether $\underline{H}_0(k)$ is always approximately equal to $1 - (k/n)$; if this should prove to be true for all reference hypercubes ν^d vectors in R^d, and more generally for all "homogeneously distributed" sets of n vectors, then one can eliminate the expense of computing H_0 and simply take

$$\underline{\tilde{H}}(k) = \frac{\underline{H}(k)}{1 - (k/n)} \qquad (6)$$

as a suitable normalized entropy parameter. In any event, this parameter is computed in the numerical experiments described below and serves as a reliable indicator of clustering structure.

---

[1]The position, orientation, and size of X relative to X_0 is of no consequence since the indices $\underline{H}$ and $\bar{F}$ are invariant under Euclidean similarity transformations, e.g., shifts, rotations, and homothetic scale changes.

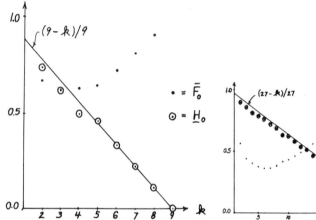

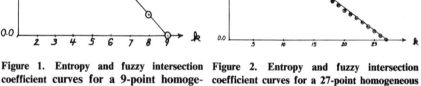

Figure 1. Entropy and fuzzy intersection coefficient curves for a 9-point homogeneous square in R^2.

Figure 2. Entropy and fuzzy intersection coefficient curves for a 27-point homogeneous cube in R^3.

EXPERIMENTS

In all of the experiments described below, the graphs of $\underline{H}$, $\overline{F}$, and $\tilde{H}$ were constructed by the procedure described in the previous section for the homogeneous square and cube. All the data sets in R^2 are drawn to scale.

(A) In Fig. 3, 9 vectors in R^2 are arranged into two well-separated clusters. The corresponding graphs of $\underline{H}$, $\overline{F}$, and $\tilde{H}$ are shown in Fig. 3. A dip in the graph of $\underline{H}$ and a peak in the graph of $\overline{F}$ suggest that clustering structure is most conspicuous at $k = 2$, however, this is shown even more clearly in the graph of the normalized entropy parameter $\tilde{H}$, which attains its absolute minimum value of 0.16 at $k = 2$. For this data set, the fuzzy partitioning algorithm converged rapidly[2] to the same extremal 2-partition $u_1{}^*(\cdot), u_2{}^*(\cdot)$ (Table 1 and Fig. 3) from all three distinct initial prototype sets; the membership functions in this partition closely ap-

[2]Five iterations.

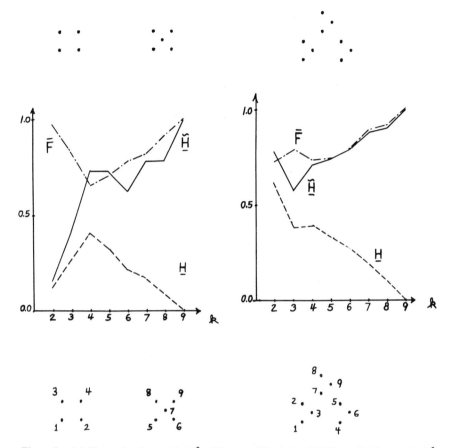

Figure 3. (a) Nine point data set in R^2, with 2 clusters; (b) entropy and fuzzy intersection coefficient curves for the data set in (a); (c) labeling for the data set in (a).

Figure 4. (a) Nine-point data set in R^2, with 3 clusters; (b) entropy and fuzzy intersection coefficient curves for the data set in (a); (c) labeling for the data set in (a).

proximate the characteristic functions of the two clusters and the corresponding extremal prototypes coincide almost exactly with the cluster centroids.

(B) In Fig. 4, 9 vectors in R^2 are arranged into three loose clusters. This structure is again clearly reflected in the graphs of H, $\bar{F}$, and $\tilde{H}$ in Fig. 4, and particularly in the normalized entropy graph. For $k = 3$, all the initial prototype sets are quickly mapped into the same limiting 3-partition by the fuzzy partitioning algorithm (Table 2 and Fig. 4); the membership functions in this partition roughly approximate the characteristic functions of

Table 1
**Limiting 2-Partition for Data Set
in Figure 3(C)**

x	$u_1^*(x)$	$u_2^*(x)$
1	0.984	0.016
2	0.976	0.024
3	0.984	0.016
4	0.976	0.024
5	0.024	0.976
6	0.016	0.984
7	0.000	1.000
8	0.024	0.976
9	0.016	0.984

Table 2
Limiting 3-Partition for Data Set in Figure 4(C)

x	$u_1^*(x)$	$u_2^*(x)$	$u_3^*(x)$
1	0.051	0.045	0.904
2	0.050	0.100	0.850
3	0.030	0.030	0.940
4	0.888	0.047	0.065
5	0.785	0.144	0.071
6	0.959	0.023	0.018
7	0.100	0.751	0.149
8	0.041	0.910	0.049
9	0.031	0.947	0.022

the clusters and the extremal prototypes closely approximate the cluster centroids.

(C) In Fig. 5, 140 vectors in R^2 are arranged in such a way that well-separated clusters are present at levels $k = 3$ and $k = 6$, with the most conspicuous clustering at $k = 3$. Figure 5 shows the graphs of H and $\bar{F}$ for $2 \leqslant k \leqslant 8$; in this range, $k \ll n = 140$, consequently the difference between entropy and normalized entropy is not significant. Again, these curves clearly reflect the data set's clustering structure. For $k = 3$, the fuzzy partitioning algorithm quickly converges from all starting prototype sets to the same limiting partition and prototypes, which coincide almost exactly with the cluster characteristic functions and centroids, respectively.

(D) In Fig. 6, 50 "noise" points are added to the data set (C). The principal effect is an upward displacement of the H curve and a downward displacement of the $\bar{F}$ curve, with enough distortion of the latter to produce a (misleading) shift in attention from $k = 6$ to $k = 7$ (compare Figs. 5 and 6). At $k = 3$, all starting prototype sets are quickly mapped onto the same limiting partition. Each vector in a cluster has a very high level of membership ($\geqslant 0.960$) in precisely one of the fuzzy subsets in the limiting

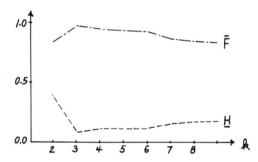

Figure 5. (a) 140 point data set in R^2, with 3 clusters; (b) entropy and fuzzy intersection coefficient curves for the data set in (b).

partition, whereas noise points have divided membership. The limiting prototypes coincide almost exactly with cluster centroids.

(E)   In Fig. 7, the data set (D) has been rearranged so that clustering is now more conspicuous at $k = 6$. The effect of this change is apparent in the H and $\bar{F}$ curves in Fig. 7, especially in the entropy curve. For $k = 6$, all initial prototype sets are again quickly mapped onto the same limiting partition; cluster vectors have essentially undivided membership in the subsets of this partition and noise points have divided membership. The limiting prototypes coincide almost exactly with the cluster centroids.

(F)   In Figs. 8 and 9, five sample data "signals" in the topmost row are corrupted with additive zero mean Gaussian white noise (next five rows). Sampling is done at nine equally spaced points to produce data sets of twenty five vectors in R^9. The value of the standard deviation σ of the noise is 0.1 in Fig. 8 and 0.6 in Fig. 9; with respect to the minimum

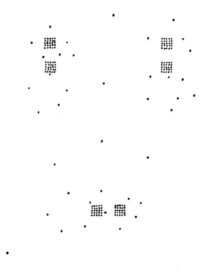

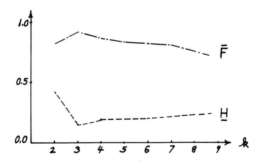

Figure 6. (a) **190 point data set in** R^2, **with 3 clusters and noise; (b) entropy and fuzzy intersection coefficient curves for the data set in (a).**

distance between signal pairs (Tables 3 and 4), these values of σ correspond to signal-to-noise (S/N) ratios of 1.4 and 0.23, respectively. Calculations were also performed for $\sigma = 0.025$, 0.2, and 0.4 (S/N = 5.6, 0.70, and 0.35). The corresponding graphs for H, $\bar{F}$, and $\tilde{H}$ for all cases are shown in Fig. 10. At the low end of the noise range (S/N = 5.6), these curves indicate that the most conspicuous clustering occurs at $k = 5$ (which suggests that five different underlying signals are present in the data set of twenty five sample functions). For this value of k, all starting prototype

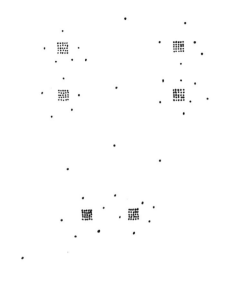

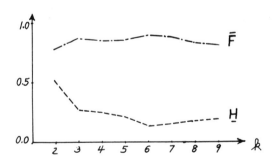

Figure 7. (a) 190 point data set in R^2, with 6 clusters and noise; (b) entropy and fuzzy intersection coefficient curves for the data set in (a).

sets are quickly mapped into the same limiting fuzzy 5-partition which correctly identifies five clusters, each consisting of five sample functions derived from one of the five different signals; the corresponding limiting prototypes coincide almost exactly with the original signals. When S/N is decreased to $\leqslant 1.4$, the distinction between signals 2 and 3 becomes blurred and the H, $\bar{F}$, and $\tilde{H}$ curves now indicate four clusters in the data set. Again, all starting prototype sets are rapidly mapped onto the same limiting 4-partition which identifies four clusters consisting of the sample functions generated by signals 1, 2 and 3, 4, 5 (i.e., the signal classes 2 and 3

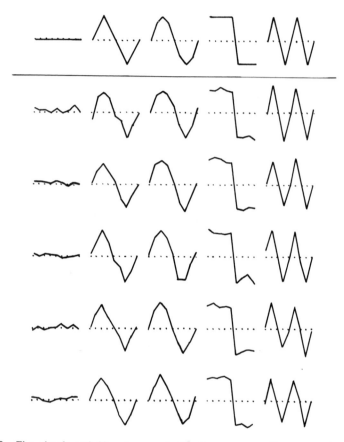

Figure 8. **Five signals and 25 noisy sample functions corresponding to a noise standard deviation = 0.1 (S/N = 1.4).**

are now merged); the corresponding limiting prototypes are shown in Fig. 11. Essentially the same observations apply to S/N = 0.70, however at the very low signal-to-noise ratios 0.35 and 0.23, the curves for H and $\overline{F}$, and especially $\overline{H}$, indicate that no significant clusters are present in the data set at *any* level k; nevertheless, in the former case the limiting partition for $k = 4$ (where $\underline{H}$ attains its global minimum) does correctly identify four clusters consisting of the sample functions generated by signals 1, 2 and 3,4,5., and the corresponding prototypes still resemble the underlying signals (Fig. 11).

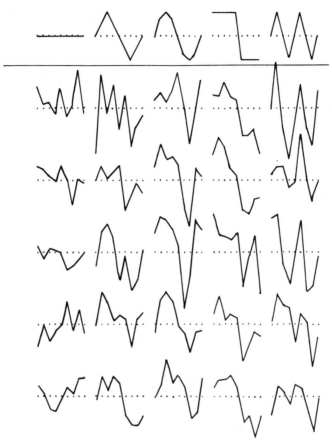

Figure 9. Five signals and 25 noisy sample functions corresponding to a noise standard deviation = 0.6 (S/N = 0.23).

Table 3
Sample Data Signals in R^9

Signal No.		Components								
null signal)	1	0.0	0.0	0.0	0.0	0.0	0.0	0.0	0.0	0.0
(saw tooth)	2	0.0	0.5	1.0	0.5	0.0	−0.5	−1.0	−0.5	0.0
(sine)	3	0.0	0.7	1.0	0.7	0.0	−0.7	−1.0	−0.7	0.0
(square)	4	1.0	1.0	1.0	1.0	1.0	−1.0	−1.0	−1.0	−1.0
(sawtooth)	5	0.0	1.0	0.0	−1.0	0.0	1.0	0.0	−1.0	0.0

Table 4
RMS Distances Between Signals in Table 3

Signal No.	1	2	3	4	5
1	0.00	0.58	0.67	1.0	0.67
2		0.00	0.14	0.67	0.88
3			0.00	0.61	0.94
4				0.00	1.2
5					0.0

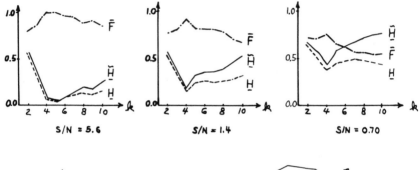

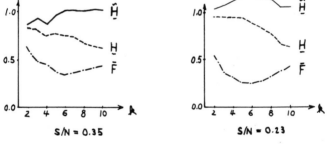

Figure 10.   Entropy and fuzzy intersection coefficient curves for the signal detection problem.

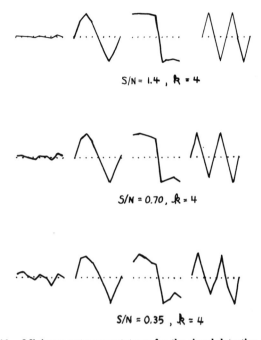

Figure 11.   Minimum entropy prototypes for the signal detection problem.

REFERENCES

1. G. H. Ball, and D. J. Hall, "ISODATA, an Iterative Method of Multivariate Analysis and Pattern Classification," *Behav. Sci.* **12** (1967).
2. J. C. Bezdek, "Fuzzy Mathematics in Pattern Classification," PhD Thesis, Cornell University, N. Y., 1973.
3. J. C. Bezdek, "Cluster Validity with Fuzzy Sets," *J. Cybern.* **3** (July–Sept. 1973), 3.
4. J. C. Bezdek, "Mathematical Models for Systematics and Taxonomy," *Eighth Inter. Conf. on Numerical Taxonomy*, Lisbon, 1974.
5. J. C. Bezdek, "Numerical Taxonomy with Fuzzy Sets," *J. Math. Biol.* **1** (1974).
6. J. C. Dunn, "A Fuzzy Relative of the ISODATA Process and its Use in Detecting Compact Well-Separated Clusters," *J. Cybern.* **3** (July–Sept. 1973), 3.
7. J. C. Dunn, "Well Separated Clusters and Optimal Fuzzy Partitions," *J. Cybern.* **4** (Jan.–Mar. 1974) 1.
8. J. C. Dunn, "Some Recent Investigations of a New Fuzzy Partitioning Technique and its Application to Pattern Classification Problems," *J. Cybern.* **4** (April–June 1974), 2.
9. E. H. Ruspini, "A New Approach to Clustering," *Inf. Contr.* **15** (1969).

FUZZY LOGIC CONTROL OF A HEAT
EXCHANGER PROCESS

19

J.-J. Østergaard

The first approach to fuzzy logic was presented by Zadeh [6,5] about twelve years ago. Since then investigations have been carried on concerning the application of the theory to a wide variety of problems such as information processing, control, pattern recognition, and system identification.

Certain complex industrial plants, e.g., a cement kiln, can be controlled with better results by an experienced operator than by conventional automatic controllers. The control strategies employed by an operator can often be formulated as a number of rules that are simple to carry out manually but difficult to implement by using conventional algorithms. This difficulty is because human beings use qualitative rather than quantitative terms when describing various decisions to be taken as a function of different states of the process. It is this qualitative or fuzzy nature of man's way of making decisions that has encouraged control engineers to try to apply fuzzy logic to process control.

At the Electric Power Engineering Department, this work with fuzzy logic controllers was started in the spring of 1975 in the form of a master thesis [3]. This work emphasized the practical application of fuzzy logic to the control of physical processes, and the application of the programming language APL to formulate fuzzy algorithms. The present investigation should be looked on as a continuation of this earlier work; the main change being that the APL-programmed controller has been implemented directly using the concept of shared variables.

The next section gives a brief description of fuzzy set theory relevant to writing fuzzy algorithms. The article is not intended to be a detailed introduction to the theory, but rather an attempt is made to give the

Acknowledgment: The project which was completed in three months, was supported financially by the Danish Technical-Scientific Research Council and was carried out at the Electric Power Engineering Department, in close cooperation with the Automatic Control Group and the System Science Group. Financial support given by the Danish Technical-Scientific Research Council is gratefully appreciated, and also the staff assistance. Civilingeniør J. A. Richter, who enabled APL to share variables with a physical process and thus made it possible to complete the project in three months, is especially thanked.

background necessary for understanding how the actual fuzzy controller is dimensioned and implemented by means of APL.

The final section describes the control problem used to study the practical applicability of fuzzy logic to process control. The actual fuzzy controller is discussed, and it is shown how a pure linguistic formulation of the control scheme is translated into an APL-program. Finally, the characteristics of the fuzzy controller are illustrated by some experimental results.

BASIC CONCEPTS OF FUZZY LOGIC IN APL-NOTATION

The purpose of this chapter is to make the report self-contained by introducing the theory of fuzzy logic in a similar way as done by Zadeh [6]. The dissimilarities between Zadeh's presentation of the theory and the one given in this chapter are that here we use the notation of APL language, and use examples taken from the field of control problems to illustrate the theory. Therefore, some basic knowledge about the APL programming language and the terminology of control theory are required to read this article.

The general DDC-control problem considered is illustrated in Fig. 1. The problem consists in dimensioning a control algorithm based on the error vector $e = (e_1, e_2, \ldots, e_p)$ that generates an output vector $u = (u_1, u_2, \ldots, u_r)$ to the process so that the output vector $y = (y_1, y_2, \ldots, y_p)$ of the process is close to or eventually equal to the setpoint vector $r = (r_1, r_2, \ldots, r_p)$. In other words, we want to control the process by means of an algorithm of the following general form

$$u[(k+1)T] = f\big(u[kT], u[(k-1)T], \ldots, u[0],$$
$$\times e[(k+1)T], e[kT], \ldots, e[0]\big) \qquad (1)$$

where $k = 1, 2, \ldots$, and T is the sampling time.

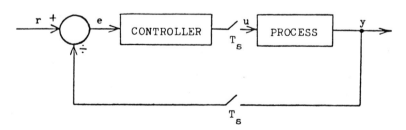

Figure 1. DDC-control system.

The next subsection gives a brief summary of the theory of fuzzy sets relevant for the present application, and the following subsection describes a special type of fuzzy algorithms called fuzzy decisional algorithms. This type of algorithm is used when applying fuzzy logic to process control.

Fuzzy Set Theory in APL-Notation

A fuzzy subset A of a universe of discourse V is characterized by a membership function μ_A which associates to each element v of V a number $\mu_A(v)$ in the interval $[0, 1]$.

In connection with the control problem defined in the preceding section, the universe of discourse V is always some interval or some discrete points in the space of real numbers. As will be discussed in greater detail later on in this chapter, it is suitable to scale the considered problem so that V is the interval $[-1, 1]$ or a number of discrete points in that interval. And furthermore, in the attempt to dimension a controller it is natural to consider a fuzzy variable called 'magnitude,' i.e.

$$v \triangleq \text{MAGNITUDE} \tag{2}$$

where the symbol $\triangleq$ stands for "equal to by definition."

The values of the fuzzy variable 'magnitude' may be expressed by fuzzy subsets of the type: 'large positive,' 'small positive,' and 'medium negative,' where for example the fuzzy subset of V labeled 'large positive' may be characterized by the membership function μ_{LPOS} given by the following APL-function called LPOS

$$
\begin{aligned}
&\nabla \quad \text{MYLPOS} \leftarrow \text{LPOS } V \\
[1] \quad &\quad \text{MYLPOS} \leftarrow 1 - * - (0.5 + |1 - V)*2.5 \\
&\nabla
\end{aligned}
$$

This membership function is shown graphically in Fig. 2. The value $\mu_{\text{LPOS}}(v_1)$ of the membership function corresponding to the element v_1 in the interval $[-1, 1]$ represents the grade of membership of v_1 in the fuzzy subset 'large positive.' In agreement with the everyday meaning of the phrase 'large positive,' Fig. 2 shows that the element v_2 has a larger grade of membership in the fuzzy subset 'large positive' than the element v_1.

Representing a fuzzy subset A by an APL-function is suitable in cases where the calculations require only a single value of the membership function μ_A corresponding to a single value of v. As will be seen later, the calculations are, however, very often carried out with the fuzzy subset represented by its membership function as a whole. In this case, we represent A by a number of discrete values of μ_A. These values are conveniently generated by dividing the interval $[-1, 1]$ into N subintervals

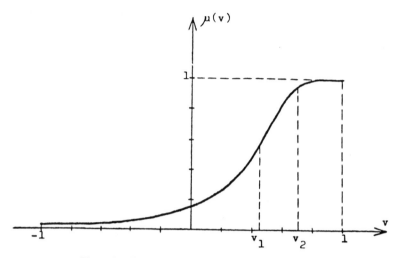

Figure 2. Graphical representation of 'large positive.'

$[v_i, v_{i+1}]$, $i = 1, 2, \ldots, N$ of equal length, and then calculating $\mu_A(v_i)$. After this, the fuzzy subset A is characterized by a vector of $N+1$ elements with the ith element equal to $\mu_A(v_i)$. For example, the fuzzy subset labeled 'large positive' is characterized by the membership function LPOS listed above and may be approximated by a vector VLPOS of 21 elements given by

VLPOS

0.031 0.035 0.040 0.046 0.053 0.062 0.073 0.088 0.106 0.130 0.162
0.205 0.266 0.350 0.470 0.632 0.826 0.972 0.999 1.000 1.000

So far we have seen that with the universe of discourse V equal to the interval $[-1, 1]$ or some discrete points of that interval, we can express values of the fuzzy variable 'magnitude' by means of fuzzy subsets of V characterized by either APL-functions or APL-vectors.

Some basic operators relating to fuzzy subsets used in this application are summarized:

(1) The union of fuzzy subsets A and B both of V is [6] denoted by $A + B$ and corresponds to the connective 'or.' By using the APL-language, this operator can be implemented by means of the function 'or' given by

$$\nabla \text{ OR } [\square] \nabla$$
$$\nabla \quad Z \leftarrow X \text{ OR } Y$$
$$[1] \quad Z \leftarrow X \lceil Y$$
$$\nabla$$

where X and Y are vectors of equal dimension approximating the membership functions μ_A and μ_B, respectively, or X and Y stand for explicit results of APL-functions corresponding with μ_A or μ_B.

(2) The intersection of A and B is [6] denoted by $A \times B$ and corresponds with the connective AND. This operator is in APL carried out by the function AND defined by

$$\nabla \text{ AND } [\square] \nabla$$
$$\nabla \quad Z \leftarrow X \text{ AND } Y$$
$$[1] \qquad Z \leftarrow X \mathbf{L} Y$$
$$\nabla$$

where X and Y can have the same meaning as described above.

(3) The complement of a fuzzy subset A is denoted by $\neg A$ and corresponds to negation—NOT, which using APL is implemented by

$$\nabla \text{ NOT } [\square] \nabla$$
$$\nabla \quad Z \leftarrow \text{NOT } X$$
$$[1] \qquad Z \leftarrow 1 - X$$
$$\nabla$$

where X is the explicit result of the APL-function corresponding with μ_A or X is the vector approximating μ_A.

To illustrate the introduced subjects we will consider the fuzzy subsets 'medium positive' and 'small positive' both of the interval $[-1, 1]$ and characterized by the membership functions MPOS and SPOS given, respectively, by

$$\nabla \quad \text{MYPOS} \leftarrow \text{MPOS } V$$
$$[1] \qquad \text{MYMPOS} \leftarrow 1 - * - (0.25 + |0.7 - V - 1E^-4) * 2.5$$
$$\nabla$$

$$\nabla \quad \text{MYSPOS} \leftarrow \text{SPOS } V$$
$$[1] \qquad \text{MYSPOS} \leftarrow 1 - * - (0.25 + |0.4 - V - 1E^-4) * 2.5$$
$$\nabla$$

The membership functions MPOS and SPOS are shown in Fig. 3, while Fig. 4 shows the membership function corresponding with the fuzzy subset labeled 'medium positive and not small positive.' Assume that we have only one setpoint for a given process. Considering this setpoint we have the

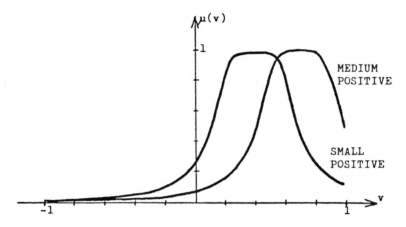

Figure 3. Graphical representation of 'medium positive' and 'small positive.'

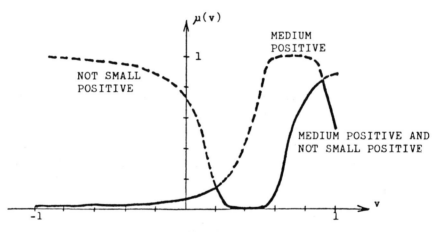

Figure 4. Graphical representation of the fuzzy subset labeled 'medium positive' and 'not small positive.'

universe of discourse

$$U: 0.1 \quad 0.5 \quad 0.7 \quad 1.0 \tag{3}$$

where U is the magnitude of setpoint.

In addition, it is assumed that the response time of the process depends on the working point which, for example, leads to the following universe of discourse

$$V: 0.1 \quad 0.3 \quad 0.5 \quad 0.7 \quad 0.9 \quad 1.0 \tag{4}$$

where V is the response time.

The working point of the process is given by the setpoint and we want to express the relation between U and V. This relation is denoted by R and is represented by a fuzzy subset of the Cartesian product $U \times V$ ($U \times V$ is the collection of ordered pairs (u,v)). R is characterized by a bivariate membership function $\mu_R(u,v)$ and may be represented as a relation matrix, which in this case is of dimension two. We assume the following relation matrix

	0.1	0.3	0.5	0.7	0.9	1.0
0.1	0.1	0.4	0.6	0.8	0.9	1.0
0.5	0.5	0.7	0.9	1.0	0.8	0.7
0.7	0.8	1.0	0.7	0.5	0.2	0.1
1.0	0.7	0.6	0.4	0.3	0.4	0.4

in which the (i,j)th element is the value of $\mu_R(u,v)$ for the ith value of u and the jth value of v. For example, element number $(2,2)$ shows that with the setpoint value 0.5, we have a response time which for grade 0.7 equals 0.3.

A fuzzy relation R from U to V can be visualized as a fuzzy graph, since given R and a fuzzy subset x of U we can find the fuzzy subset y of V which is induced by x. This induced fuzzy subset is given by the compositional rule of inference [6]

$$y = x \circ R$$

which is defined by

$$x \circ R = x\lceil . \lfloor R \quad \text{or} \quad x\lceil . \times R$$

An illustration of how to use the compositional rule of inference, the relation matrix given above is considered. It is assumed that the setpoint is described as

LARGE OR MEDIUM AND NOT SMALL,

where the fuzzy subset of U labeled 'large,' 'medium,' and 'small' are characterized by the following membership functions

$$\mu_{\text{LARGE}} = 0 \quad 0.3 \quad 0.7 \quad 1.0 \tag{5}$$

$$\mu_{\text{MEDIUM}} = 0.2 \quad 0.7 \quad 1.0 \quad 0.8 \tag{6}$$

$$\mu_{\text{SMALL}} = 0.7 \quad 1.0 \quad 0.6 \quad 0.3 \tag{7}$$

Then the actual setpoint is given by the membership function

$$\left(\mu_{\text{LARGE}} \lceil \mu_{\text{MEDIUM}} \right) \lfloor 1 - \mu_{\text{SMALL}}$$

which results in

$$0.2 \quad 0 \quad 0.4 \quad 0.7$$

This response time induced by this setpoint is computed as

$$(0.2 \quad 0 \quad 0.4 \quad 0.7) \lceil \cdot \lfloor \begin{bmatrix} 0.1 & 0.4 & 0.6 & 0.8 & 0.9 & 1.0 \\ 0.5 & 0.7 & 0.9 & 1.0 & 0.8 & 0.7 \\ 0.8 & 1.0 & 0.7 & 0.5 & 0.2 & 0.1 \\ 0.7 & 0.6 & 0.4 & 0.3 & 0.4 & 0.4 \end{bmatrix}$$

which equals

$$0.7 \quad 0.6 \quad 0.4 \quad 0.4 \quad 0.4 \quad 0.4$$

This shows that given a 'large or medium and not small' setpoint value, the process responds rather quickly because the greatest values of the membership function correspond to small values of the response time.

Linguistic Hedges

Linguistic hedges are used to generate new fuzzy sets from what may be called primary terms. Primary terms are labels of specified fuzzy subsets of the universe of discourse, e.g., 'large,' 'medium,' and 'small.' As an example, we consider the natural hedge 'very,' which together with the primary terms generates new fuzzy subsets of the universe of discourse, e.g., 'very large' and 'very small.'

Fuzzy Algorithms

The type of algorithms that are used in this application of fuzzy logic are classified as fuzzy decisional algorithms [6], which serve to provide an approximate description of a strategy or decision rule. Control algorithms are built up of expressions of the following form

$$\text{IF } A \text{ THEN } B \text{ ELSE } C \tag{8}$$

where, in general, A and (B and C) are fuzzy subsets of possibly different universes U and V, respectively. Such statements are defined as follows

$$\text{IF } A \text{ THEN } B \text{ ELSE } C = (A \circ. \lfloor B) \lceil (1 - A) \circ. \lfloor C$$

or if we use multiplication instead of the minimum operator

$$= (A \circ. \times B) \lceil (1 - A) \circ. \times C$$

As a simple illustration of (8), suppose we have the following statement

$$\text{IF LARGE } x \text{ THEN MEDIUM } y \text{ ELSE SMALL } y, \tag{9}$$

with the universe of discourse U given in (3) and the fuzzy subsets 'large,' 'medium,' and 'small' characterized by the membership functions given in (5) to (7). Then the considered statement results in the following relation matrix using the min-operator

$$(0 \quad 0.3 \quad 0.7 \quad 1.0)\circ.\lfloor (0.2 \quad 0.7 \quad 1.0 \quad 0.8)$$

$$\lceil (1 \quad 0.7 \quad 0.3 \quad 0.0)\circ.\lfloor (0.7 \quad 1.0 \quad 0.6 \quad 0.3)$$

which results in

$$\begin{bmatrix} 0.7 & 1.0 & 0.6 & 0.3 \\ 0.7 & 0.7 & 0.6 & 0.3 \\ 0.3 & 0.7 & 0.7 & 0.7 \\ 0.2 & 0.1 & 1.0 & 0.8 \end{bmatrix}$$

Now it is possible to compute y expressed by its membership function if, e.g., x is given as 'very large.' This computation is carried out by using the compositional rule of inference, interpreted, e.g., as the max-min-product, i.e.,

$$y = (0 \quad 0.09 \quad 0.49 \quad 1.0)\lceil .\lfloor \begin{bmatrix} 0.7 & 1.0 & 0.6 & 0.3 \\ 0.7 & 0.7 & 0.6 & 0.3 \\ 0.3 & 0.7 & 0.7 & 0.7 \\ 0.2 & 0.1 & 1.0 & 0.8 \end{bmatrix}$$

$$y = 0.3 \quad 0.49 \quad 1.0 \quad 0.8$$

In the present application of the statement (8), the antecedent A depends on the error variable e and/or the change in the error, and thus appears as input to the controller, whereas the consequents B and C are outputs from the control algorithm. Because the error signal at each sampling instant and the change in error between successive samplings are represented by numbers rather than by linguistic variables it is natural to choose the quantity A to be non-fuzzy, i.e., represented by a scalar. This imply that the relation matrix corresponding with each rule of the control algorithm need not to be calculated and stored. To illustrate this, we consider the rule (9), and assume that x is represented by the number 0.75. The grade of membership of this value in the fuzzy subset 'large' is then found as the explicit result of an APL-function that represents the membership function of 'large' of a given universe of discourse. If we assume that 0.75 has a grade of membership in 'large' equal to 0.8, the rule (9) implies the following

$$y = 0.8\circ.\lfloor (0.2 \quad 0.7 \quad 1.0 \quad 0.8)\lceil (1 - 0.8)\circ.\lfloor (0.7 \quad 1.0 \quad 0.6 \quad 0.3)$$

that is

$$y = 0.2 \quad 0.7 \quad 0.8 \quad 0.8$$

To outline the details how expressions of the form (8) have been implemented in APL we first state that an error value and a change of an error value can be positive as well as negative. This means that it is

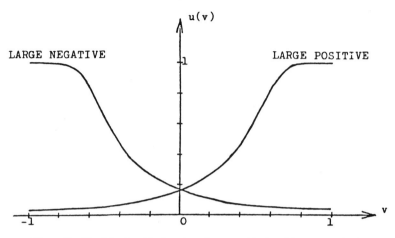

Figure 5. The Membership functions 'large positive' and 'large negative.'

necessary to work with, for instance, 'large positive' and 'large negative' values of the linguistic variable 'magnitude.' In the present application all variables are scaled to be placed in the interval $[-1, 1]$, and the membership functions corresponding to 'large positive' and 'large negative' have been chosen symmetrically as shown in Fig. 5.

The values of the linguistic variable 'magnitude' concerning the error values and the change in the error values are characterized by means of composite terms using the primary terms listed in Table 1.

Table 1

Fuzzy Subset	Expression
'large positive' x	$1 - \exp\left[-\left(\dfrac{0.5}{\text{abs}(1-x)} \right)^{2.5} \right]$
'medium positive' x	$1 - \exp\left[-\left(\dfrac{0.25}{\text{abs}(0.7-x)} \right)^{2.5} \right]$
'small positive' x	$1 - \exp\left[-\left(\dfrac{0.25}{\text{abs}(0.4-x)} \right)^{2.5} \right]$
'zero positive' x	$\exp[-5\,\text{abs}(x-0.05)]$
'zero negative' x	$\exp[-5\,\text{abs}(x+0.05)]$
'small negative' x	$1 - \exp\left[-\left(\dfrac{0.25}{\text{abs}(-0.4-x)} \right)^{2.5} \right]$
'medium negative' x	$1 - \exp\left[-\left(\dfrac{0.25}{\text{abs}(-0.7-x)} \right)^{2.5} \right]$
'large negative' x	$1 - \exp\left[-\left(\dfrac{0.5}{\text{abs}(-1-x)} \right)^{2.5} \right]$

The membership function corresponding with one of the fuzzy subsets of the interval $[-1,1]$ given in Table 1 has been implemented in APL by using two functions. For example, the grade of membership of an error value 'E1' in 'medium positive' and 'small negative' is evaluated, respectively, by

$$\text{MEDIUM POSITV E1}$$

$$\text{SMALL NEGATV E1}$$

where the functions 'medium,' 'small,' 'positv,' and 'negatv' are listed below:

$$\nabla \text{ MEDIUM } [\square]\nabla$$

	∇ $Z \leftarrow \text{MEDIUM } X$
[1]	$\rightarrow \text{VEC} \times \iota 2 < \rho X$
[2]	$Z \leftarrow 1 - * - \left(0.25 \div |(X[1] \times 0.7) - X[2] - 1E^-4\right) * 2.5$
[3]	$\rightarrow 0$
[4]	$\text{VEC:} \rightarrow \text{POS} \times \iota X[1] = 1$
[5]	$Z \leftarrow \text{MNEG}$
[6]	$\rightarrow 0$
[7]	$\text{POS: } Z \leftarrow \text{MPOS}$
	∇

$$\nabla \text{ SMALL } [\square]\nabla$$

	∇ $Z \leftarrow \text{SMALL } X$
[1]	$\rightarrow \text{VEC} \times \iota 2 < \rho X$
[2]	$Z \leftarrow 1 - * - \left(0.25 \div |(X[1] \times 0.4) - X[2] - 1E^-4\right) * 2.5$
[3]	$\rightarrow 0$
[4]	$\text{VEC:} \rightarrow \text{POS} \times \iota X[1] = 1$
[5]	$Z \leftarrow \text{SNEG}$
[6]	$\rightarrow 0$
[7]	$\text{POS: } Z \leftarrow \text{SPOS}$
	∇

$$\nabla \text{ POSITV } [\square]\nabla$$

	∇ $Z \leftarrow \text{POSITV } X$
[1]	$Z \leftarrow 1, X$
	∇

$$\nabla \text{ NEGATV } [\Box]\nabla$$
$$\nabla \quad Z \leftarrow \text{NEGATV } X$$
$$[1] \qquad Z \leftarrow {}^-1, X$$
$$\nabla$$

The above listed APL-functions show that the first element to be the explicit result of 'positv' or 'negatv' that is simply used to select the right expression from Table 1. Furthermore, if the argument to 'positv' or 'negatv' is a vector $E2$, it is seen to be the result of

MEDIUM POSITV E2

which equals MPOS, a global vector resulting from the execution of the function 'diskr' listed below.

$$\nabla \text{ DISKR } [\Box]\nabla$$

$$\nabla \quad \text{DISKR } X; D$$

$[1]$ $\qquad D \leftarrow ((\iota X + 1) - (X + 2) \div 2) \div 10$

$[2]$ $\qquad \text{LPOS} \leftarrow 1 - * - (0.5 \div |1 - D - 1E^-4) * 2.5$

$[3]$ $\qquad \text{MPOS} \leftarrow 1 - * - (0.25 \div |0.7 - D - 1E^-4) * 2.5$

$[4]$ $\qquad \text{SPOS} \leftarrow 1 - * - (0.25 \div |0.4 - D - 1E^-4) * 2.5$

$[5]$ $\qquad \text{ZPOS} \leftarrow * - 5 \times |{}^-0.05 + D$

$[6]$ $\qquad \text{ZNEG} \leftarrow * - 5 \times |0.05 + D$

$[7]$ $\qquad \text{SNEG} \leftarrow 1 - * - (0.25 \div |{}^-0.4 - D - 1E^-4) * 2.5$

$[8]$ $\qquad \text{MNEG} \leftarrow 1 - * - (0.25 \div |{}^-0.7 - D - 1E^-4) * 2.5$

$[9]$ $\qquad \text{LNEG} \leftarrow 1 - * - (0.5 \div |{}^-1 - D - 1E^-4) * 2.5$

$[10]$ $\qquad \text{ANY} \leftarrow (X + 1)\rho 1$

$$\nabla$$

The argument of the function 'diskr' is the number of subintervals by which the universe of discourse $[-1, 1]$ is divided to approximate the membership functions by vectors. Thus, if the calculation requires the fuzzy subset as a whole, we can either execute 'positv' or 'negatv' with a vector argument or directly use one of the global variables resulting from 'diskr.'

Until now, an example has been described to evaluate the antecedent A and the consequents B and C using APL-language. Next, we show how the total statement (8) has been implemented by means of the functions 'else,' 'then,' and 'if,' listed below:

$$\nabla \text{ELSE} \, [\Box] \nabla$$

$\nabla \quad Z \leftarrow B \text{ ELSE } C$

$[1] \qquad Z \leftarrow \text{UEND}, (\rho B), (\rho C), B, C$

∇

$$\nabla \text{ THEN } [\Box] \nabla$$

$\nabla \quad Z \leftarrow A \text{ THEN } B; B1; C$

$[1] \qquad \rightarrow \text{ELSE} \times 1((,B)[1]) = \text{UEND}$

$[2] \qquad Z \leftarrow (A \circ . \times B) \lceil (1-A) \circ . \times 1 - B$

$[3] \qquad \rightarrow 0$

$[4] \qquad \text{ELSE: } B1 \leftarrow B[3 + 1B[2]]$

$[5] \qquad C \leftarrow B[3 + B[2] + 1B[3]]$

$[6] \qquad Z \leftarrow (A \circ . \times B1) \lceil (1-A) \circ . \times C$

∇

$$\nabla \text{ IF } [\Box] \nabla$$

$\nabla \quad Z \leftarrow \text{IF } X$

$[1] \qquad Z \leftarrow X$

∇

From these listings it is seen that the value of the fuzzy decisional expression (8) is calculated by means of the following APL-statement

$$V \leftarrow \text{IF } A \text{ THEN } B \text{ ELSE } C$$

where the function 'else' has the effect of producing an argument to 'then' from which B and C can be found again. In addition, the function 'else' uses an arbitrary global variable called 'uend' which is used in 'then' to tell that we are not dealing with an expression of the form

$$V \leftarrow \text{IF } A \text{ THEN } B$$

which is interpreted as

$$V \leftarrow \text{IF } A \text{ THEN } B \text{ ELSE NOT } B$$

The function 'then' splits up its right argument in the B and C vectors, and we calculate

$$(A \circ . \times B) \lceil (1-A) \circ . \times C \quad .$$

if the first element of the right argument is equal to 'uend.' Otherwise the function 'then' results in

$$(A \circ . \times B) \lceil (1 - A) \circ . \times 1 - B$$

The function 'if' is a dummy function that returns its argument which is the explicit result from the function 'then.'

To summarize what have been stated about APL-implementation of (8), the following example is considered

WCH←IF (SMALL POSITV TCOE) THEN SPOS ELSE WCH

WCH←IF (MEDIUM NEGATV TCOE) THEN MNEG ELSE WCH

These two statements are taken from the fuzzy controller described in the next section. The variable 'wch' is output from the controller and denotes the change to be given the setpoint of the power W. 'tcoe' is input to the algorithm and denotes the error of the temperature 'tco' which is to be controlled by the delivered power W.

The first statement shows that the power W is given a small positive change if the error 'tcoe' is small positive, else the power is changed as given by the previous values of 'wch.' On the other hand, as shown in the second statement, if we have a medium negative 'tcoe,' the power is given a medium negative change and else W is changed in accordance with the previous rules.

Having gone through the control algorithm with given values of the errors and changes in errors, the outputs of the algorithm are given as membership functions approximated by vectors. Each output vector represents a change $\Delta u_i[kT]$ of one of the control variables u_i of the process. However, it is not possible to transmit these vectors directly to the process, which means that it is necessary to decide a way of transforming an output vector into a scalar Δu_i so that the new value of u_i is given by

$$u_i[(k+1)T] = u_i[kT] + \Delta u_i[kT]$$

Figure 6 shows a possible fuzzy subset of an output variable resulting from a control algorithm. A number of different ways of transforming such a fuzzy subset into a scalar have been suggested [5]. One way consists of simply choosing the greatest element which in Fig. 6 is indicated by a. Another way is characterized by choosing the element v_i with a probability proportional to the grade of membership $\mu(v_i)$. And the final example, which is used in this application, consists in finding the point v_j between -1 and 1 which imply that the area A_1 equals the area A_2. This point is found by means of the function 'storst' listed below:

$$\nabla \text{ STORST } [\square] \nabla$$
$$\nabla \quad \text{RES←DEFMG STORST FUZMG}$$
$$[1] \quad \text{RES←}(+/\text{FUZMG}\times\text{DEFMG}) \div +/\text{FUZMG}$$
$$\nabla$$

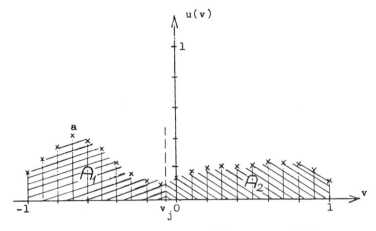

Figure 6. Membership function of fuzzy output variable.

The left argument of the function 'storst' is a vector with the elements v_j, and the right argument is the fuzzy subset which is to be transformed into a scalar.

FUZZY LOGIC CONTROL OF HEAT EXCHANGER PROCESS

This section presents some of the results obtained from performing fuzzy logic control of a heat exchanger process. No mathematical model has been established and used as basis for dimensioning and tuning the fuzzy controller. Only a rough idea about the relations between the input and output variables of the process is necessary when formulating the controller.

The control problem considered has been solved by using two different algorithms both implemented on the IBM/1800 of the department. The first algorithm is a conventional digital PI-controller, which has been implemented for the purpose of comparing it with the second algorithm which is the fuzzy controller.

The first subsection gives a brief review of the heat exchanger process that has been used as a practical object for investigating the applicability of fuzzy logic to process control. This section gives also a description of the defined control problem and a few examples are presented concerning the performance of the PI-controller in relation to this problem.

The following subsection gives a description of how the fuzzy controller has been formulated. First, the pure verbal formulation is presented and next it is shown how this formulation has been transformed into a fuzzy controller formulated in APL. Furthermore, this section gives a short description of the principles used for implementing the APL-programmed controller directly.

The final subsection presents some experimental results.

Description of Heat Exchanger Process

Figure 7 shows a diagram of the heat exchanger process as it appears in the present application. The hot water circuit of the heat exchanger is a closed circuit in which water is circulated by a centrifugal pump driven by a small thyristor controlled ac motor. The flow rate FH in this circuit is one of the two input variables of the process. The setpoint for FH is output

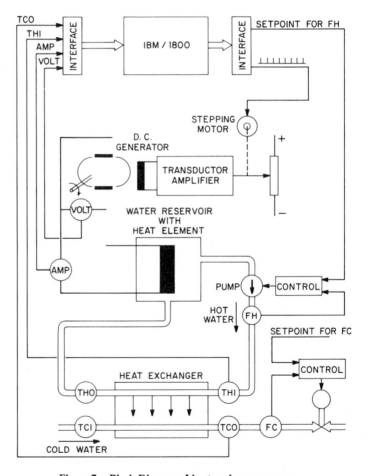

Figure 7. Block Diagram of heat exchanger process.

from the controller and is sent out on digital output to an external D/A-converter. After this, the setpoint is input to an analog PI-controller.

The second input variable of the process is the power W consumed for heating the hot water. The power is delivered by a dc generator and controlled through the field winding current of the generator by means of a transductor amplifier and a stepping motor.

The cold water flow rate FC is taken from an ordinary tap and controlled by a motor-actuated valve in step-by-step control loop based on flow measurements by means of a magnetic flow transducer. The setpoint for FC is not delivered from the computer but adjusted manually and considered a disturbance on the process.

The control problem, which has been used to study the practical applicability of fuzzy logic to process control, consists in adjusting the hot water flow rate FH and the delivered power W so that the cold water outlet temperature TCO and the hot water inlet temperature THI take on setpoint values TCOS and THIS, respectively. Consequently, the problem concerns what might be called a setpoint control problem with two input and two output variables.

Because of the strong coupling between especially the power W and both the two outputs and because of the very nonlinear process, the problem is sufficiently complicated to indicate whether a fuzzy logic controller is likely to be of any use in practice or not.

The steady state relationship between the two input variables FH and W and the output variables TCO and THI can be found by considering

$$W = C_V \text{FH}(\text{THI} - \text{THO}) \tag{9}$$

$$W = C_K \text{FC}(\text{TCO} - \text{TCI}) \tag{10}$$

where C_V and C_K are the heat capacities of the hot water and the cold water, respectively. These expressions assume that all of the heating power delivered to the heat element is conveyed to the cold fluid through the heat exchanger.

From (10) we get directly

$$\text{TCO} = \text{TCI} + \frac{W}{C_K \text{FC}}, \tag{11}$$

which shows that the output variable TCO depends only on one of the input variables, namely, W.

In order to find THI as function of the input variables W and FH, the general expression of heat transfer from one fluid to another through a barrier is considered

$$W = \text{AUT}_m, \tag{12}$$

where A is the barrier surface area; U the heat transfer coefficient of barrier; and T_m the mean temperature difference of fluids.

Under normal circumstances expression (12) can be approximated by

$$W = AU \frac{THI + THO - TCI - TCO}{2} \tag{13}$$

which yields the following expression of THO (the hot water outlet temperature)

$$THO = \frac{2W}{AU} + TCI + TCO - THI \tag{14}$$

or by using (11)

$$THO = \frac{2W}{AU} + 2TCI - THI + \frac{W}{C_K FC} \tag{15}$$

which yields the following expression of THI

$$THI = TCI + \left(\frac{1}{2C_V FH} + \frac{1}{2C_K FC} + \frac{1}{AU} \right) W \tag{16}$$

The following is a list of some important dimensions and parameters related to the applied heat exchanger process:

Hot water reservoir: Volume (V) about 25 l.
Heat element: Power (W) max. 4.5 kW at 220 V dc.
Heat exchanger: Alfa-Laval, type P01,
UA-value: 150–300 W/°C.
Hot water circuit: Closed loop of water circulated by small thyristor controlled centrifugal pump with capacity: 1.5–5.0 l/min.
Temperatures (THI, THO): 30–50 °C.
Cold water circuit: Water drawn from tap and controlled by motor-actuated valve.
Inlet temperature (TCI): 10–20 °C
Outlet temperature (TCO): 25–35 °C
Flow rate (FC): 1.25–3.0 l/min.
Temperature measurements: 4 NTC thermistors with amplifiers of own make.
Flow measurements: Magnetic flow meters (own make).

As pointed out in connection with (11), the output variable TCO depends on only one of the two input variables, namely the delivered power W. In contrast to this the hot water outlet temperature THI is a function of W as well as of the hot water flow rate FH. These facts indicate that the most straightforward way of solving the defined control

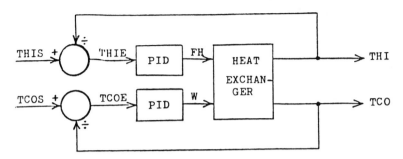

Figure 8.   Control schematic of heat exchanger process using two separated PID-control loops.

problem is by letting TCO be controlled by means of the power W alone, and then trying to control THI by means of the hot water flow rate FH. This simple control strategy involving two separated loops with conventional digital PID-controllers is shown schematically in Fig. 8.

   The dynamic characteristics of the heat exchanger process can roughly be described by stating that the time constants from W to THI and TCO, called TWTHI and TWTCO, respectively, are about

$$TWTHI = 12.0 \text{ min.} \qquad TWTCO = 7.5 \text{ min.} \qquad (17)$$

The response time of THI following a change of the hot water flow rate FH can be characterized by the time constant TFHTHI, which equals

$$TFHTHI = 15.0 \text{ min.} \qquad (18)$$

These time constants are, of course, very approximate and depend to some extent on the actual working point of the process. With this background, the sampling time in the TCO-loop has been choosen equal to 2 min., while the sampling time in the control loop of THI equals 3.5 min.

   The control scheme with the two digital PID-controllers have been implemented on the IBM/1800 of the Department by using the macro-programming language PROMAC [1]. The block diagram of this control program is shown in Fig. 9, where the PID-controllers are the KOMP-blocks with the numbers 46 and 12.

   In order to form a good standard of reference for the fuzzy logic controller, the described PID-control scheme has been given a good deal of work with the object of perfecting the algorithms. In the trial and error method used, both fast response and small overshoot as well as zero steady state error have been considered important characteristics.

   Figures 10 and 11 show typical transients of the heat exchanger process. In Fig. 10, the process has been in a steady state before the controller is activated at time 0. The steady state is characterized by the cold water flow

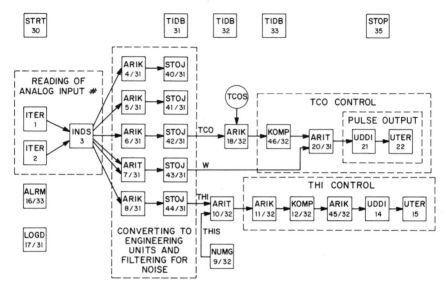

Figure 9.   PROMAC block diagram of PID-control scheme for heat exchanger process.

rate FC being equal to 2.2 1/min., FH being equal to 3.0 1-min., and *W* being equal to 2.0 kW, which implies that TCO is equal to about 24 °C and THI equal to about 32.0 °C. The setpoint value TCOS of the cold water outlet temperature has been chosen equal to 30.0 °C, while the setpoint THIS of THI equals 43.0 °C.

Figure 11 illustrates the behavior of the controllers when the process is subjected to disturbances. The initial state where the output variables TCO and THI are on their setpoint values is disturbed by changing the cold water flow rate from 2.2 1/min. to 1.9 1/min. After some time the process has reached a new steady state with the error between TCO and TCOS approximately equal to zero, whereas THI has not reached THIS because FH cannot be smaller than 1.5 1/min. This steady state is again disturbed by changing FC back to 2.2 1/min., which as seen from the curves is a value where both TCO and THI can reach their setpoint values.

Description of Fuzzy Logic Controller

The basic principles outlined in the previous section on how to apply fuzzy logic to process control are used in this subsection to dimension a fuzzy controller for the heat exchanger process described in the preceding subsection. The problem consists of writing a fuzzy decisional algorithm based on the error signals TCOE and THIE, and on the changes in errors

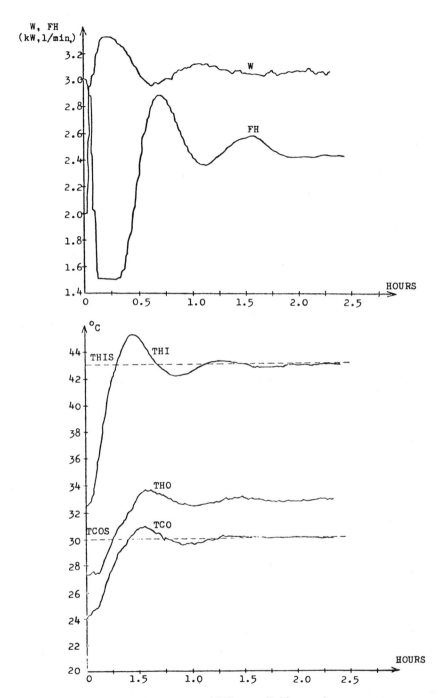

Figure 10. Transient response of PID-controlled heat exchanger process.

305

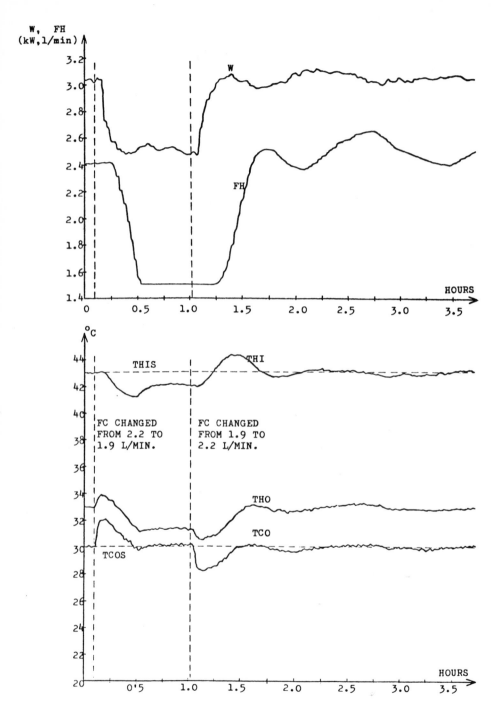

Figure 11. Transient responses of PID-controlled heat exchanger process subjected to disturbances.

306

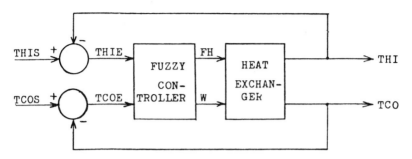

Figure 12. Control schematic with fuzzy controller.

TCOEC and THIEC to adjust the input variables W and FH so that the cold water outlet temperature TCO and the hot water inlet temperature THI approach their setpoint values. The configuration of the considered control problem is shown in Fig. 12.

As pointed out in the previous section, it is natural when dimensioning a controller to work with a fuzzy variable called 'magnitude.' In other words, we want to adjust the power W and the hot water flow rate FH on the basis of the magnitude of TCOE, THIE, TCOEC, and THIEC. The values of the variable 'magnitude' are characterized by means of fuzzy subsets composed of terms taken from the table of primary terms listed in Table 1. These fuzzy subsets are of a universe of discourse that is equal to the interval $[-1,1]$, which means that the actual values of TCOE, THIE, TCOEC, and THIEC have to be scaled.

In this application, TCOE and THIE are considered large positive if they are greater than about 5.0 °C. A temperature error is medium positive if it is about 3.5 °C, and small positive if it is about 2.0 °C. TCOE and THIE are decided to be zero positive if they are about 0.25 °C. For negative values of a temperature error the symmetrical points are chosen to characterize the actual value. For example, a temperature error is medium negative if it is about -3.5 °C. In consequence, the measured value of, for example, TCOE is first limited to the interval $[-5,5]$ and then divided by 5 after which we can use the membership functions listed in Table 1 to characterize the measured value.

In general, the changes TCOEC and THIEC of the temperature errors between successive samples also must be scaled. However, in connection with the heat exchanger process, it was found appropriate to work directly with the actual values of TCOEC and THIEC, and simply limit the calculated changes to be situated in the interval $[-1,1]$.

Verbal formulation of the fuzzy controller: After these introductory remarks about the scaling of the entering variables a pure verbal formulation is given of a possible strategy to control the heat exchanger process. The strategy is described without using quantitative terms but rather as far as possible by using phrases which in the previous sections have been used to characterize the fuzzy variable 'magnitude.'

First, we consider how to control the cold water outlet temperature TCO. As seen from (11), it is reasonable to control TCO mainly by means of the power W. Because increasing the power W results in a larger cold water outlet temperature TCO, the power W is given a positive change WCH if the error TCOE is positive and a negative change WCH if TCOE is negative. The magnitude of the positive or negative change WCH depends on the magnitude of the positive or negative error TCOE so that WCH, for example, is large positive if TCOE is large positive. This very simple scheme for adjusting W, which simply expresses that W is given a change WCH that in some measure is proportional to the error TCOE, is not the only rule used for controlling TCO.

In order to reduce the overshot, the change TCOEC of the error TCOE between successive samples is also considered. If TCO is close to the setpoint TCOS and at the same time is changing rather fast so that TCOEC is large or medium positive it is reasonable to stop this fast approach of or remove away from TCOS by giving W a medium negative change. This situation occurs when TCO is approaching TCOS rather fast from values of TCO that are less than TCOS. In the opposite case where TCOEC is large or medium negative and TCO again is close to TCOS, the power W is given by a medium positive adjustment.

By combining this set of rules it has been attempted to increase or decrease the power W so that TCO approaches its setpoint reasonably fast at the same time as it has been tried to reduce the overshot.

However, not only the input variable W is used to control TCO but also the hot water flow rate FH enters this control loop. The steady state value of TCO does not depend on FH, but under dynamic states following a stepwise change of FH the cold water outlet temperature TCO increases or decreases depending on whether FH has increased or decreased. Therefore, in order to reduce the response time of the TCO-control loop FH is given a medium positive change FHC if TCOE is large or medium positive. This adjustment of FH, however, is only proved reasonable if we also require that THIE is not large or medium positive. In the opposite case, characterized by a large or medium negative TCOE, and not a large or medium negative THIE, the hot water flow rate FH is given a medium negative change FHC.

Next it is described how the control strategy of THI has been formulated. THI is controlled solely by means of FH by following the basic strategy that states that FH is increased if THI is larger than THIS, and FH is decreased if FH is less than THIS.

The hot water inlet temperature THI is a function of both FH and *W*. In fact, for the considered variation range of FH and *W*, THI depends much stronger on *W* than on FH. This means that in most cases the registered THI-variation is caused by adjustments of the power *W*. This, of course, is very unfavourable, and has necessitated that before applying the basic strategy, outlined above, for changing FH, the fuzzy algorithm investigates whether THI is changing very smoothly or not. Only if the variation of THI is very smooth, i.e. only if THIEC is small or zero positive or small or zero negative, it is found worthwhile to try to control THI by means of FH.

APL-formulation of fuzzy controller: The pure verbal control strategy presented in the above paragraphs is in this section translated into APL-language. By the verbal formulation of the controller, we endeavored to use phrases that previously have been given an APL-formulated fuzzy interpretation. This, of course, very much facilitates the work inherent in writing the APL-program. For example, one of the rules for controlling the cold water outlet temperature TCO states that the hot water flow rate FH is given a medium positive change FHC if TCOE is large or medium positive and THIE is not large or medium positive. This rule is very simple to translate into a sequence of APL-statements, e.g., the following

T1←(LARGE POSITV TCOE) OR (MEDIUM POSITV TCOE)

T2←(LARGE POSITV THIE) OR (MEDIUM POSITV THIE)

FHC←IF (T1 AND NOT T2) THEN MPOS ELSE FHC

In a similar way we can translate directly almost all the described rules in the above paragraphs into APL-statements, which results in the APL-function listed in Table 2.

The error values TCOE and THIE and the change in error values TCOEC and THIEC used in the function FUZZ2 are the scaled values, i.e., they are situated in the interval [−1.1].

The first seven statements implement the rules for adjusting FH in connection with the TCO-control loop, and as seen these statements are almost self-documenting. The only term not previously explained is the variable ANY. This variable is generated by the function DISKR described in the previous section from which it is seen that ANY is a vector with all elements equal to one. Consequently, the vector ANY is simply used to indicate no change in the considered variable.

Table 2

∇ FUZZ2 [□] ∇
  ∇ FUZZ2; T1; T2; T3
[1]   T2←(LARGE NEGATV TCOE) OR (MEDIUM NEGATV TCOE)
[2]   T3←(LARGE NEGATV THIE) OR (MEDIUM NEGATV THIE)
[3]   FHC←IF(T2 AND NOT T3) THEN MNEG ELSE ANY
[4]   T1←(LARGE POSITV TCOE) OR (MEDIUM POSITV TCOE)
[5]   T2←(LARGE POSITV THIE) OR (MEDIUM POSITV THIE)
[6]   FHC←IF(T1 AND NOT T2) THEN MPOS ELSE FHC
[7]   FH←FH + (DEFMG STORST FHC) ÷ 2
[8]   T1←(ZERO POSITV TCOE) OR SMALL POSITV TCOE
[9]   T1←T1 OR ZERO NEGATV TCOE
[10]   T1←T1 AND (LARGE POSITV TCOEC) OR MEDIUM POSITV TCOEC
[11]   WCH←IF T1 THEN MNEG ELSE ANY
[12]   T1←(ZERO NEGATV TCOE) OR SMALL NEGATV TCOE
[13]   T1←T1 OR ZERO POSITV TCOE
[14]   T1←T1 AND (LARGE NEGATV TCOEC) OR MEDIUM NEGATV TCOEC
[15]   WCH←IF T1 THEN MPOS ELSE WCH
[16]   T1←(LARGE POSITV TCOEC) OR MEDIUM POSITV TCOEC
[17]   T1←T1 OR (LARGE NEGATV TCOEC) OR MEDIUM NEGATV TCOEC
[18]   WCH←IF((ZERO NEGATV TCOE) AND NOT T1) THEN ZNEG ELSE WCH
[19]   WCH←IF ((ZERO POSITV TCOE) AND NOT T1) THEN ZPOS ELSE WCH
[20]   WCH←IF((SMALL NEGATV TCOE) AND NOT T1) THEN SNEG ELSE WCH
[21]   WCH←IF((SMALL POSITV TCOE) AND NOT T1) THEN SPOS ELSE WCH
[22]   WCH←IF(MEDIUM NEGATV TCOE) THEN MNEG ELSE WCH
[23]   WCH←IF(MEDIUM POSITV TCOE) THEN MPOS ELSE WCH
[24]   WCH←IF(LARGE NEGATV TCOE) THEN LNEG ELSE WCH
[25]   WCH←IF(LARGE POSITV TCOE) THEN LPOS ELSE WCH
[26]   W←W + (DEFMG STORST WCH) × 250
[27]   T2←(SMALL NEGATV THIE) OR (ZERO NEGATV THIE)
[28]   FHC←IF T2 THEN SPOS ELSE ANY
[29]   T1←(SMALL POSITV THIE) OR (ZERO POSITV THIE)
[30]   FHC←IF(VERY T1) THEN SNEG ELSE FHC
[31]   T1←(LARGE NEGATV THIE) OR (MEDIUM NEGATV THIE)
[32]   FHC←IF T1 THEN MPOS ELSE FHC
[33]   T1←(LARGE POSITV THIE) OR (MEDIUM POSITV THIE)
[34]   FHC←IF T1 THEN MNEG ELSE FHC
[35]   T1←(SMALL POSITV THIEC) OR (SMALL NEGATV THIEC)
[36]   T2←(ZERO POSITV THIEC) OR (ZERO NEGATV THIEC)
[37]   FHC←IF(NOT T1 OR T2) THEN ANY ELSE FHC
[38]   FH←FH + (DEFMG STORST FHC) ÷ 6.5
[39]   FH←((FH∘⌈(1.5,5))∘⌊(1.5,5))[1;2]
  ∇

In statement [7], we calculate the new setpoint for FH resulting from the TCO-control loop by adding the transformed vector representation of FHC divided by two to the old value of FH. By this we have introduced a new parameter in the controller, namely the factor by which the transformed value of the output from the controller is multiplied. The explicit result of the function STORST is always a scalar between -1 and 1, which means that the result must be converted into a suitable magnitude depending on the magnitude and the variation range of the actual variable.

Statements [8] to [26] are the sequence that calculate the new setpoint for the power W. From statement [26] it is seen that the conversion factor in this case equals 250, which implies that a large positive change of the power results in a change that equals about 250 W.

Statements [27] to [38] implement the THI-control loop which results in a new value of FH. The conversion factor for FHC is in this case, chosen equal to $1/6.5$.

The final statement of the fuzzy control algorithm considers the capacity of the centrifugal pump by which the hot water is circulated. The capacity of the pump limits the flow rate FH to be situated in the interval from 1.5 to 5.0 l/min.

How APL share variables with PROMAC: Although it is not the object of this article to describe in detail the software that enables an APL-program to communicate, i.e., share variables, with a physical process the basic principles are reviewed briefly. (Details about this subject will be published later by J. A. Richter.)

The IBM/1800 used in this investigation has 56k 16-bit words of memory and a multiprogramming operating system (MPX), which occupies about 17k of memory. The rest of the memory is divided into five partitions: three areas (AREA1, AREA2, and AREA3) that in principle are reserved process programs, a partition called variable core (VCORE) which is used as a batch processing partition, and finally a small communication area called COMMON/INSKEL/ which permits different programs to exchange information.

The macro program PROMAC executes in AREA1 while the APL-system is running in AREA2, and these two programs share data placed in COMMON/INSKEL/.

At runtime the function of the complex of control programs can be described by the following sequence of actions

(1) The PROMAC program, which is shown in block diagram form in Fig. 13, collects data, e.g., the temperature error TCOE, from the heat exchanger process with a given sampling rate. These data are placed in certain locations in COMMON/INSKEL/. In addition,

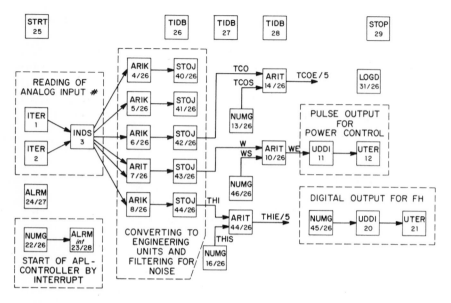

Figure 13. PROMAC block diagram of program that share variables with the APL-programmed fuzzy controller.

the PROMAC-program fetches data from COMMON/INSKEL/, e.g., the setpoint for the hot water flow rate FH, and transmits the relevant data to the process.

(2) With a given sampling time established by the time control block number 28, PROMAC generates a programmed interrupt by means of block number 22.

(3) The generated interrupt on a specified interrupt level is serviced by a sign-on program which activates the APL-system. The sign-on program is a true copy of the terminal session that an APL-user normally would apply when executing the functions that enter the chosen control algorithm. In addition, the sign-on program defines the absolute addresses in COMMON/INSKEL/ by which the signed-on APL-program is to communicate. That is, the programmer must specify the addresses from where the APL-program can find the necessary input for the control algorithm and specify the absolute addresses into which the APL-controller stores its output variables.

(4) The APL-system is activated by a PROMAC-generated interrupt, the APL-system fetches the specified variables from COMMON-/INSKEL/, executes the fuzzy control-algorithm, and stores

setpoint values for the power W and the hot water flow rate FH in COMMON/INSKEL/. Finally, the APL-system SAVE's the active work space and performs an automatic sign-off.

Thus, implementing an APL-programmed controller online consists of three essential ingredients:

(1) A PROMAC-program that collects data from the physical process and transmits data back to the process;

(2) APL-functions that do the processing of the chosen control algorithm;

(3) An interrupt-activated program that defines the terminal session and establishes the communication addresses between APL and PROMAC.

Experimental Results

This section presents some results obtained with the fuzzy controller discussed in the previous subsections. The behavior of the controller is illustrated by means of four examples depicted in Figs. 14 and 15. Common to these examples is the sampling time, i.e., the time interval established by the time control block number 28 in the PROMAC-program, which has been chosen equal to 2.5 min.

(1) The first example (Fig. 14) is characterized by the initial values of the power W and the hot water flow rate FH being equal to 2.0 kW and 1.7 l/min., respectively, while the cold water flow rate FC has been adjusted to 2.2 l/min. These values imply THI equal to 34.5 °C, THO equal to 27 °C, and TCO equal to 25 °C. The setpoint values of THI and TCO are as in connection with the PI-controllers chosen equal to 43 °C and 30 °C, respectively. The transients depicted in Fig. 14 show that the controller results in a reasonably small transient period, small overshoot, and zero steady state error for TCO and almost the same for THI.

(2) In the second example (Fig. 15) the output temperatures THI and TCO are very close to their setpoint values when the process is disturbed by increasing FC from 2.2 to 2.8 l/min. Figure 15 shows that THI is almost unaffected while TCO decreases very suddenly after which the controller brings it back to the setpoint value.

(3) The first part of the third example (Fig. 16) is almost equivalent to the case presented in Fig. 14. After the temperatures have reached the setpoint values, the second part of Fig. 16 shows the transients followed by a change of the setpoint TCOS from 30 °C to 33 °C.

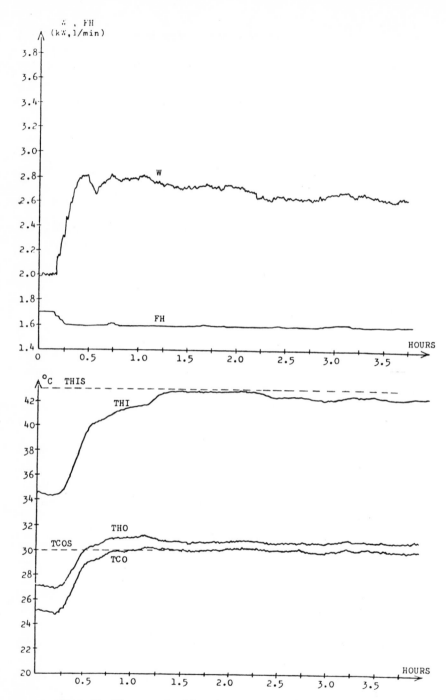

Figure 14.   First example of fuzzy logic control of heat exchanger process.

314

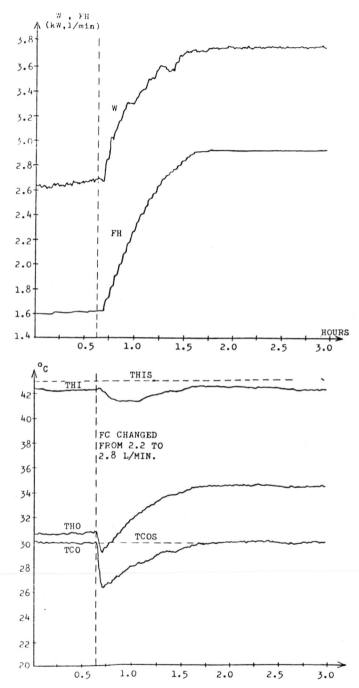

Figure 15. Second example of fuzzy logic control of heat exchanger process.

315

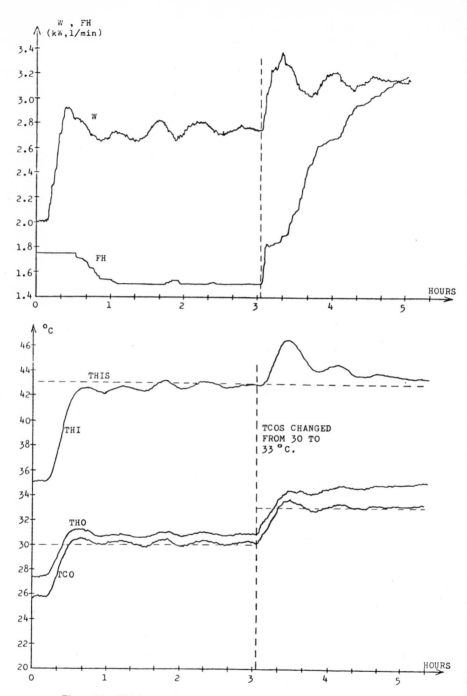

Figure 16. Third example of fuzzy logic control of heat exchanger process.

316

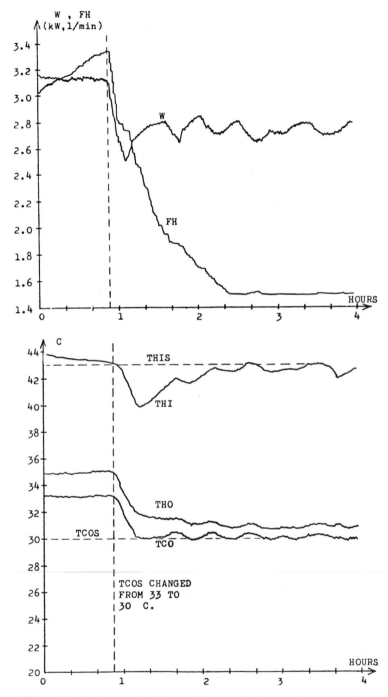

Figure 17. Fourth example of fuzzy logic control of heat exchanger process.

317

(4) The last example (Fig. 17) is, in fact, a continuation of the case shown in Fig. 16. The setpoint having increased TCOS to 33 °C, and having reached steady state conditions, Fig. 17 shows the transients that follow when TCOS again is decreased to 30 °C.

CONCLUSION

The present article presents the results obtained from a case study with the two main objectives:

(1) Firstly, the project is meant to be a contribution to the practical applicability of fuzzy logic to process control.
(2) Secondly, the project is to evaluate further the usefulness of applying APL programming language to formulate fuzzy logic algorithms. In addition, an important part of the case study is the investigation of the advantages of implementing directly the APL-programmed controller.

To satisfy the first object a control problem is defined for a small heat exchanger process, and a fuzzy logic control algorithm is dimensioned to solve that problem. The heat exchanger process has two input variables, namely the power delivered to an electric heat element and the flow rate of the heated water. The process has two output variables which are the cold water outlet temperature and the hot water inlet temperature, and the concrete control problem consists of adjusting the two input variables so that the two output temperatures take on chosen setpoint values.

Because of the strong coupling between the power and the two output temperatures, and because of the very nonlinear process, the defined control problem is considered complicated enough to reveal whether a fuzzy controller is likely to be of any practical applicability. In order to have some sort of standard of reference by which the fuzzy controller is compared, the chosen control problem is also solved by using conventional digital PI-controllers.

By comparing the experimental results obtained from the two different control strategies it can be stated that in this case the characteristics of the fuzzy controller are as good as those of the PI-controllers. This is, in fact, a very promising conclusion with respect to the applicability of fuzzy logic to process control. The application of fuzzy logic to control of physical processes is at the present moment found at a very early level of research, and the actual controller has been dimensioned in a very straightforward way, in a very short time, and, in fact, on the basis of only the basic knowledge of fuzzy logic theory. It is on this background that the obtained results are considered promising, and under all circumstances the project encourages further investigation on the subject.

The background of the present project in relation to applying APL when formulating fuzzy algorithms is based on Molzen's work [3]. In this work, it is pointed out that APL is a very suitable language when the various computational rules defined for fuzzy sets are to be performed by a computer. This fact has been further underlined by the present work from where it is seen that a fuzzy algorithm when written in APL results in a very legible program.

The procedure used [3] to investigate the practical applicability of an APL-programmed fuzzy controller can be described by the following sequence of steps:

(1) The inputs of the control algorithm, i.e., the error values of the considered control scheme, are discretized.

(2) The control algorithm is then executed with all possible combinations of the discrete values of the input variables. This results in a decision table which for all values of errors gives the corresponding values of the output variables of the algorithm.

(3) The decision table is implemented on the computer and the control characteristics are observed.

(4) If the controller does not satisfy the stated demands, suitable modifications are made in the original APL-program, and steps (1) through (4) are repeated.

The main problem of this procedure is related to step (2) and concerns the very large computing time required to calculate the decision tables. In connection with specific rather simple control problems with two input and two output variables and with one of the input variables discretized into 7 levels and the other into 9 levels, step (2) implies that two decision tables of dimension 7×9 must be calculated. On the IBM/1800 this calculation takes about 7 hours. With this background, it is obvious that it would be very desirable to implement the APL-programmed controller directly, and thus save the very time needed in the calculation of the decision tables.

Richter has enabled the APL-system on the IBM/1800 to share variables with a physical process, and by this the tuning of the APL-programmed controller is very much facilitated.

However, the characteristics of the developed online APL-version puts rather strong restrictions on the control problems treated. The execution time of the APL-algorithms is large compared with the execution time of, e.g., an equivalent FORTRAN-routine. This is due to the fact that the configuration of the IBM/1800 requires that the APL-system perform a lot of time-consuming disk operations. For example, the algorithm presented in this report takes about 45 seconds to execute, which, of course, implies that only processes with rather large time constants can be controlled by an online APL-algorithm.

A general conclusion of the present work is related to the application of a high-level language to solve control problems. When dealing with control strategies of a certain complexity, which is often one of the justifications for employing computer control, it is found very important that the design and tuning phases are supported by as high a programming language as possible. By using, e.g., APL in the phases where the controller is dimensioned and tested it is possible to concentrate mainly on the problems related to the control characteristics of the written programs. In this way, the control engineer need not be a computer specialist on the machine instruction level. Under all circumstances, the amount of time required to solve a given control problem is remarkably reduced by using a high-level language.

For the sake of justice, it is pointed out that certain problems, e.g., in cases where the control actions must be very fast, require more effective code than normally produced by a high-level language. In these cases, the programmer is forced to use assembly language.

REFERENCES

1. L. P. Holmblad, "Promac/1800. A Real-Time Macroprogramming Language for On-Line Process Control," Electric Power Engineering Dept., Tech. U. Denmark, May 1972.
2. E. H. Mamdani, "Application of Fuzzy Algorithms for Control of Simple Dynamic Plant," *Proc. IEE*, **121**, no. 12 (Dec. 1974), 1585–1588.
3. N. Molzen, "Fuzzy Logic Control," (in Danish), Master Thesis, Electric Power Engineering Dept., Tech. U. Denmark, 1975.
4. J. A. Richter, "APL\1800—A Programming Language for IBM 1800," Electric Power Engineering Dept., Publication No. 7305, Tech. U. Denmark, July 1973.
5. L. A. Zadeh, "Fuzzy Algorithms," *Infor. Control*, **19** (1968), 94–102.
6. L. A. Zadeh, "Outline of a New Approach to the Analyses of Complex Systems and Decision Processes," *IEEE Trans. Systems, Man, and Cybernetics*, No. 1 (January 1973), 28–44.

THE APPLICATION
OF FUZZY CONTROL SYSTEMS
TO INDUSTRIAL PROCESSES

20

P. J. King and E. H. Mamdani

Complex industrial processes such as batch chemical reactors, blast furnaces, cement kilns and basic oxygen steelmaking are difficult to control automatically. This difficulty is due to their nonlinear, time varying behavior and the poor quality of available measurements. In such cases, automatic control is applied to those subsidiary variables that can be measured and controlled, for example, temperatures, pressures and flows. The over-all process control objectives, such as the quality and quantity of product produced, has in the past been left in the hands of the human operator.

In some modern plants with process control computers, plant models have been used to calculate the required controller settings automating the higher level control functions. The plant models whether they are based on physical and chemical relationships or parameter estimation methods are approximations to the real process and may require a large amount of computer time. Some successful applications have been reported, but difficulties have been experienced where processes operate over a wide range of conditions and suffer from stochastic disturbances.

An alternative approach to the control of complex processes is to investigate the control strategies employed by the human operator. In many cases, the process operator can control a complex process more effectively than an automatic system; when he experiences difficulty this can often be attributed to the rate or manner of information display or the depth to which he may evaluate decisions.

The operator usually expresses his control strategy linguistically as a set of heuristic decision rules. It is difficult to convert this qualitative control strategy into a quantitative controller design due to the imprecise nature of the rules. Therefore means of implementing the human operators control rules directly as an automatic control system is of interest. Zadeh's development of fuzzy sets [3] and fuzzy algorithms [4] provides a means of expressing linguistic rules in a form suitable for processing in using a computer. In this paper are reported some case studies on pilot-scale processes in which heuristic strategies using fuzzy statements are applied to the control of dynamic processes.

CONTROL SYSTEMS

The structure of the control system is shown in Fig. 1; the heuristic decision rules replace a conventional feedback controller in the error channel. The calculation of the control action is composed of the following four stages:

(1) calculate the present error;
(2) assign the error value to a fuzzy variable such as 'positive big';
(3) evaluate the decision rules using the compositional rule of inference; and
(4) calculate the deterministic input required to regulate the process.

The exact form of the decision rules and the variables used in them depends on the process under control and the heuristics employed. In general, the process operator uses error E and rate of change of error CE to calculate a change in the value of the process input CU, and the decision rules are designed to have the same effect. This approach also corresponds to the versatile proportional plus integral controller used frequently in the process industry.

The error value and the change of error values calculated are quantized into a number of points corresponding to the elements of a universe of discourse, and the values are then assigned as grades of membership in seven fuzzy subsets as follows:

(1) PB is 'positive big;'
(2) PM is 'positive medium';
(3) PS is 'positive small';
(4) PO is 'positive nil';
(5) NO is 'negative nil';
(6) NS is 'negative small';
(7) NM is 'negative medium'; and
(8) NB is 'negative big'.

The relationship between measured error or change in error value and grade of membership are defined by look-up tables of the form given in Table 1. These basic subsets may then be used with the three basic operators of union, intersection and complement to compute such values

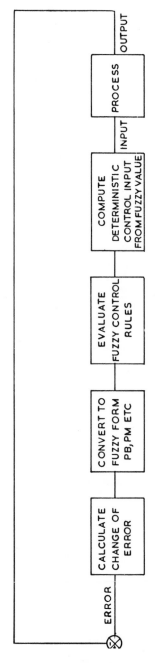

Figure 1. Control system using fuzzy rules.

323

Table 1
Look-up Table Relating Fuzzy Subsets to Quantized Error Values

	−6	−5	−4	−3	−2	−1	−0	+0	+1	+2	+3	+4	+5	+6
PB	0	0	0	0	0	0	0	0	0	0	0.1	0.4	0.8	1.0
PM	0	0	0	0	0	0	0	0	0	0.2	0.7	1.0	0.7	0.2
PS	0	0	0	0	0	0	0	0.3	0.8	1.0	0.5	0.1	0	0
PO	0	0	0	0	0	0	0	1.0	0.6	0.1	0	0	0	0
NO	0	0	0	0	0.1	0.6	1.0	0	0	0	0	0	0	0
NS	0	0	0.1	0.5	1.0	0.8	0.3	0	0	0	0	0	0	0
NM	0.2	0.7	1.0	0.7	0.2	0	0	0	0	0	0	0	0	0
NB	1.0	0.8	0.4	0.1	0	0	0	0	0	0	0	0	0	0

as 'not positive big or medium.' Hedges may also be used but to avoid complications these were not implemented in this study.

The decision rules are implemented as a set of fuzzy conditional statements of the form,

$$\text{If } E \text{ is NB then } CU \text{ is PB}$$

This expression is evaluated using the compositional rule of inference for a particular value of error E as described by Zadeh [5]. The result is a value for change of input CU for any given value of error E. In most cases the rules are more complex than the above example. For the system using change of error CE and error E the rules are of the form

$$\text{If } E \text{ is PB or PM then if } CE \text{ is NS then } CU \text{ is NM}$$

but the same methods of evaluation still apply.

Several rules are required to define completely a control system; the results of evaluating each rule are combined using the union operator max to give an over-all fuzzy value for the control action. For example,

$$\text{If } A_1 \text{ then (if } B_1 \text{ then } C_1)$$

or

$$\text{If } A_2 \text{ then } \quad \text{(if } B_2 \text{ then } C_2)$$

$$\vdots \qquad\qquad \vdots$$

So given values of measurements A_1' and B', etc. the individual rules results are C_1', C_2', etc., and these are combined to give the over-all resulting control action

$$C' = \max(C_1', C_2', \text{ etc.})$$

Hence, more than one rule may contribute to the computation of a control action.

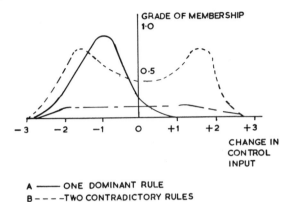

A ——— ONE DOMINANT RULE
B — — — TWO CONTRADICTORY RULES
C — · ——— · NO SATISFACTORY RULE

Figure 2. **Change in control input calculated by fuzzy rules: (a) one dominant rule; (b) two contradictory rules; and (c) no satisfactory rule.**

The result of evaluating the fuzzy rules for a particular set of input values is a fuzzy set of grades of membership for all possible control actions. In order to take a deterministic action one of these values must be chosen, the choice procedure depending on the grades of membership and the particular application. In this work, the control value with the largest grade of membership was selected, except in the cases where several control actions had the same (largest) grade of membership. In these cases where more than one peak or a flat peak is obtained the value midway between the two peaks or in the center of the plateau was selected. Typical results are shown in Fig. 2 as curves of grade of membership versus control action. The shape of these curves can be used to assess the quality of the control rules used, Fig. 2(a) shows a single strong peak indicating one dominant control rule in this region. Fig. 2(c) shows a fuzzy result that indicates an absence of a good set of rules, while Fig. 2(b) with two peaks shows that at least two strong and contradictory rules are present. In both these latter cases some modification of the control rules may be necessary to obtain good control.

The rules are evaluated at regular intervals in the same way as a conventional digital control system. The choice of sampling interval depends on the process being controlled and should be selected so that at least five significant control actions are made during the process settling time.

Control of Boiler and Steam Engine

Mamdani and Assilian [1, 2] conducted an application study on a small boiler steam engine combination. The heat input to the boiler was used to control the boiler pressure and the steam engine speed was controlled by adjusting the throttle opening at the input of the engine cylinder.

The process dynamics could be approximated by two first order lags in series, with time constants and gains varying depending on the operating conditions. The rules were evaluated with a 10 sec. sampling interval.

Operating experience and technical knowledge of the process was used to specify two sets of heuristic fuzzy control rules for the two feedback loops. The look-up tables used to specify the fuzzy subsets for values are all similar in form to Table 1; the number of quantization levels used was 14 for error, 13 for change of error, 15 for heat input change and 5 for throttle input change. Details of the rules used are given in the Appendix.

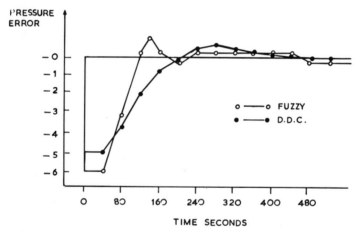

Figure 3. Pressure control responses for D.D.C. and fuzzy control systems applied to a small boiler and steam engine.

The fuzzy control rules were implemented on a PDP-8 computer and used to control the plant and a conventional digital controller was also used to control the two loops. The control results obtained for the pressure loop are shown in Fig. 3, the digital controllers were difficult to adjust as the process is highly nonlinear and good control could not be achieved at different operating conditions with the same controller settings. The fuzzy control system was much less sensitive to process parameter changes and gave good control at all operating points, in many cases better than the conventional control system results. This can largely be attributed to the nonlinear nature of the heuristic rules, which could be used to give a rapid response and a small amount of overshoot.

Temperature Control of Stirred Tank

The results obtained using fuzzy control of the steam engine were much better than expected, so a second application study on the temperature control of a stirred vessel, part of a batch reactor process, is currently being conducted. The process consists of an 80-gallon stirred tank that can be heated by a steam heating coil and is cooled by recirculating tank fluid through an external heat exchanger. The vessel temperature is controlled by changing the steam or recirculating flows.

The dynamics of the stirred tank can be approximated for small changes in temperature by an integrator with different gains for heating and cooling and a pure time delay of 1 min. for heating and 0.6 min. for cooling. Initial control experiments were conducted using the pressure control rules developed on the steam engine, while the process dynamics differs considerably it was thought that similar heuristic rules would be effective, if the values used to define the fuzzy subsets of magnitude were suitably adjusted.

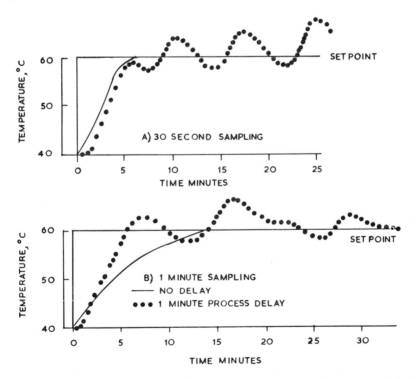

Figure 4. Simulated responses of stirred tank to set point changes with and without delay.

The results obtained by simulating these control rules in the simple process model are shown in Fig. 4 for set point changes. Two different sampling intervals were used to evaluate the rules, 30 sec. and 1 min.; in both cases when delays were included the temperature oscillated about the desired value. If the delay was removed from the process model, however, good control responses were obtained. In the case with a 1-min. sampling interval the process finally settled to a steady value; this result was confirmed in practice as the results in Fig. 5 show the response of the process with a 1 min. sampling time interval to set point changes.

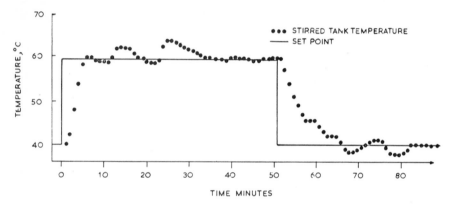

Figure 5. **Response of stirred tank temperature to set point changes with a 1-min. sampling interval.**

The input quantization levels for the fuzzy subsets of value can be adjusted to improve the system response. However, more detailed simulations over a wide range of quantization values show that the delay is the cause of the instability. The steam engine had negligible pure time delays, and the rules formulated using error and change of error values were adequate. However, when delays are present, the rules must also account for the control inputs applied to the process that have not yet been observed as a change in the process output. For systems with pure time delays the control rules have to include a fuzzy model of the system to predict the future output of the system, or, in other words, previous values of control input have to be included in the rules. New rules to control the whole of the reactor process are being formulated along these lines, but results are not yet available.

CONCLUSIONS

The results obtained so far show that processes can be c   ed effectively using heuristic rules based on fuzzy statements. To obt good control the fuzzy rules must be correctly formulated to take account of time delays when they occur; this conclusion is similar to that arrived at for conventional controllers when delays are present.

The designer requires some knowledge of the process in formulating the rules, for instance knowledge of process delays and speed and magnitude of response, but only approximate values are required and can usually be obtained by operating the process. The fuzzy control system described is inherently nonlinear and phase plane plots showing the system quantization levels, the rules used in each area and the magnitude of control action have been used to advantage as a design aid.

The approach described here is not proposed as an alternative to conventional control in situations where this is effective; however, in complex systems the use of fuzzy algorithms for control may be a nontrivial alternative approach. The fuzzy measurements required can be obtained from instruments or directly from the human operator, and there is considerable scope for man–machine interaction due to the fuzzy nature of the algorithms.

In the most complex situations, control is often based not on one variable but on a combination of variables or events that the human operator recognizes as significant. Before control rules can be formulated these patterns must be identified as significant measured variables. While the approach described does not resolve this problem, the use of fuzzy concepts is of use in this situation.

APPENDIX: STEAM ENGINE CONTROL RULES

Pressure Control Algorithm

Let PE be the pressure error; CPE the change in pressure error; HC the heat input change.

If PE = NB *then if* CPE = *not* (NB *or* NB) *then* HC = PB
If PE = (NB *or* NM) *then if* CPE = NS *then* HC = PM
If PE = NS *then if* CPE = PS *or* NO *then* HC = PM
If PE = NO *then if* CPE = (PB *or* PM) *then* HC = PM
If PE = NO *then if* CPE = (NB *or* NM) *then* HC = NM
If PE = PO *or* NO *then if* CPE = NO *then* HC = NO
If PE = PO *then if* CPE = (NB *or* NM) *then* HC = PM
If PE = PO *then if* CPE = (PB *or* PM) *then* HC = NM
If PE = PS *then if* CPE = (PS *or* NO) *then* HC = NM
If PE = (PB *or* PM) *then if* CPE = NS *then* HC = NM
If PE = PB *then if* CPE = *not* (NB *or* NM) *then* HC = NB

If PE = NO *then if* CPE = PS *then* HC = PS
If PE = NO *then if* CPE = NS *then* HC = NS
If PE = PO *then if* CPE = NS *then* HC = PS
If PE = PO *then if* CPE = PS *then* HC = NS

Speed Control Algorithm

Let SE be the speed error; CSE the change in speed error; and TC the change in throttle opening.

If SE = NB *then if* CSE = *not* (NB *or* NM) *then* TC = PB
If SE = NM *then if* CSE = (PB *or* PM *or* PS) *then* TC = PS
If SE = NS *then if* CSE = PB *or* PM *then* TC = PS
If SE = NO *then if* CSE = PB *then* TC = PS
If SE = PO *or* NO *then if* CSE = (PS *or* NS *or* NO) *then* TC = NO
If SE = PO *then if* CSE = PB *then* TC = NS
If SE = PS *then if* CSE = PB *or* PM *then* TC = NS
If SE = PM *then if* CSE = PB *or* PM *or* PS *then* TC = NS
If SE = PB *then if* CSE = *not* (NB *or* NM) *then* TC = NB

REFERENCES

1. S. Assilian and E.H. Mamdani. "Artificial Intelligence in the Control of Real Dynamic Systems," Electrical Engineering Dept. Report, Queen Mary College, London, August 1974.
2. E.H. Mamdani, "Application of Fuzzy Algorithms for the Control of a Dynamic Plant," *Proc. IEE* **121**, No 12 (1974), 1585–1588.
3. L.A. Zadeh, "Fuzzy Sets," *Info. Control* **8** (1965), 338–353.
4. L.A. Zadeh, "Fuzzy Algorithms," *Info. Control* **12** (1968), 94–102.
5. L.A. Zadeh, "Outline of a New Approach to the Analysis of Complex Systems and Decision Processes," *IEEE Trans. Systems, Man Cybernetics* **SMC. 3** (January 1973), 1.

PROFILE TRANSFORMATION ALGEBRA AND GROUP CONSENSUS FORMATION THROUGH FUZZY SETS

21

Rammohan K. Ragade

Large system planning and design is an activity in which individuals, designers, planners, and various interest groups interact with distributed databanks of related information. Such interaction is purposeful. It creates an information environment in which the above agents engage in a group *purposeful information processing activity* (pipa). At the outset of any such activity *a priori* assumptions, notions, biases, etc., can be identified.

These are identified in this paper as constituting a *profile* of an entity X with which the pipa. is concerned. Further, various situations of pipa. are examined where profiles are processed by the group according to given protocol and communication structures.

The study of small group communication is in itself not new. Cathcart and Samovar [4] provide a useful summary of the modern concerns of this area. These groups may be in an organized problem-solving model [19] or in an informal social exchange mode. A multidimensional framework is considered [17]. Complexities of small groups range from intrapersonal, interpersonal or social networks of behavior.

Communication today is considered as occurring in a contextual (environmental) mode; this viewpoint has been advanced by Watzlawik *et al.* (1967), who developed the metacommunication theory, which seeks to incorporate aspects of relativity and indeterminancy. Organizational theorists, such as Bavelas [2], have studied communications in a task-oriented small group. Such studies are relevant to planning and design problems [13], retrieval [5], and conferencing [25].

The analysis of communication content [9] has been discussed from several viewpoints. However, it relates only to the encoding and decoding of a message in one given transaction, the concerns are not aimed at

Acknowledgment: Research partly supported by grants from the National Council of Canada and University of Waterloo. Thanks to Profs. H. J. Zimmerman, L. A. Zadeh, and M. M. Gupta for their interest in this work.

transformational aspects of content in problem-solving situations except for [21]. In information-retrieval a framework [12] has been developed in which people are viewed as information processors. The information-retrieval system is designed to meet the needs of these information processors who have various user needs for documents, topics, etc., which is often in some interaction problem-solving network. Lucas *et al.* [15] review six frameworks for information systems. As they point out these are best suited for a class of specific problem-solving purposes. Since information-systems exist to aid decision-makers, their usefulness (and that of the databases which are integrated into the system) depends on the communication system devised for the context. In the larger societal contexts, there are other societal issues of privacy and a potential of change in social information processing for better or for worse [11].

The methods presented in this paper may provide a way of understanding and evaluating any information-processing system with human beings as part of it, such as conferencing and opinion forming systems as the Delphi system (see [20], [7], [10], [25]).

In the next section, the constituents of purposeful information processing systems are discussed; in the following section some of the operations in an algebra of profiles are developed based on fuzzy set theory [27]. The next section deals with the transformational aspects of profiles, some memory related aspects are outlined in the following section. The next section deals with the communication and decision-making structures that lead to a purposeful information processing activity; and the final section examines some consensus formation models.

COMPONENTS FOR PURPOSEFUL
INFORMATION PROCESSING SYSTEMS

Each profile handling agent, be it a computer database, or be it a human designer or planner, is seen as having

(i)   a collection of 'relevant' files termed 'relevant memory' or 'memory';
(ii)   a set of procedures by which to process and report.

These files are descriptions in a certain property space P^i associated with the agent. In other words, each agent characterizes any *entity* by a *profile* in the property space P^i. A similar term used only for data processing operations is a *record*.

The values of a given property q_j^i range from 100% (1) indicating complete possession of it to 0% (0) indicating absence. Thus, these values can be interpreted as the grades of membership in a fuzzy subset F^i of P^i [28]. The membership vector ξ^i will be used henceforth when F^i is meant. These profiles may be generated by semantic differential techniques [23].

Thus, a pipa occurs in a system with four major components—people, computers, information stores (databases or libraries) and communication links. Each activity is concerned with three major ingredients—people, a context of purposes (topics) and procedures of profiles (documents) [12].

An example of profiles generated is in evaluation of perceptions of a system design, product or organization. Lozar [14] uses a semantic differential technique to determine the image of work stations and rooms. This, in turn, enables a design team to evaluate the physical environment so generated, for organizational effectiveness. Suppose the property space P by which a user characterizes a physical environment is made of the following (partial) list

$$q_1: \quad \text{roominess}$$
$$q_2: \quad \text{clean}$$
$$q_3: \quad \text{light}$$
$$q_4: \quad \text{chaotic}$$
$$q_5: \quad \text{exciting}$$
$$q_6: \quad \text{casual}$$
$$q_7: \quad \text{interesting}$$

Then a (fuzzy) profile may be identified by the vector $\xi = (0.55, 0.9, 0.7, 0.6, 0.7, 0.8, 0.65)$ which is interpreted as the environment being slightly more roomy than average, extremely clean, has about 70% illumination of an open area with glass all around, quite chaotic, very exciting, very very casual, quite very interesting. The hedge associated with each property and the degrees in ξ may be seen as the perception of the user reported via the semantic differential technique.

Purposeful information processing takes place when such profiles, which are gathered by a briefing team, a design team and an execution team, are evaluated and processed by a steering group together with a project manager and the leaders of subteams possibly interacting within a management information system environment.

n-ARY OPERATIONS ON PROFILES

Profiles of opinions may be considered as "representational pictures." Profiles may be subjected to unary, binary, ternary or in general *n*-ary operations. These form the basis for creating an algebra of profiles. Hence, processing of profiles is similar to (representational) picture processing.

Likewise a purposeful information processing activity by a group, may be looked on as group picture processing. Only profiles that are represented as a fuzzy subset are considered here. Some of the unary, binary and ternary operations are listed below [27, 28, 29, 30].

Unary

(a) *Complementation*: Since the set of all fuzzy subsets forms a complemented lattice, a number of complements are possible.

   (i)   *negation* $(-)$ of ξ is defined as $\neg\,\xi_i = 1 - \xi_i$
   (ii) *union complement* $(\sim\vee)$ of ξ is defined as

$$(\sim\vee)\xi_i = 1 \qquad \text{if } \xi_i < 1$$
$$= \alpha, \text{otherwise}, \quad \alpha < 1$$

   (iii) *intersection complement* $(\sim\wedge)$ of ξ is defined as

$$(\sim\wedge)\xi_i = 0 \qquad \text{if } \xi_i > 0$$
$$= \alpha \text{ otherwise}, \quad \text{where } 0 < \alpha$$

(b) *concentration* (CON) of a profile ξ^1 defined as

$$\text{CON}\,\xi_i^1 = \left(\xi_i^1\right)^2$$

(c) *dilation* (DIL) of a profile ξ^1 is defined as

$$\text{DIL}\,\xi_i^1 = \left(\xi_i^1\right)^{0.5}$$

(d) *contrast intensification* (INT) of a profile ξ^1 is defined as

   (i)

$$\text{INT}_a\xi_i^1 = 2\left(\xi_i^2\right)^2 \qquad \text{for } 0 \leqslant \xi_i^1 < 0.5$$
$$= \neg\,2\left(\neg\,\xi_i^1\right)^2 \qquad \text{for } 0.5 \leqslant \sigma_i^1 \leqslant 1$$

   Concentrating a profile reduces the grade of membership, dilating a profile increases the grade while INT increases the grade above 0.5 and reduces below 0.5.

   (ii) By combining CON and DIL, INT_b may also be defined alternatively as a compound unary operator.

$$\text{INT}_b\xi_i^1 = \text{CON}\,\xi_i^1 \qquad \text{for } \xi_i^1 < 0.5$$
$$= \text{DIL}\,\xi_i^1 \qquad \text{for } \xi_i^1 \geqslant 0.5$$

These may now be illustrated in terms of the following example.

Example Let

$$\xi = \begin{vmatrix} 1 \\ 0.8 \\ 0.4 \end{vmatrix}$$

Then

$$\neg \xi = \begin{vmatrix} 0 \\ 0.2 \\ 0.6 \end{vmatrix} \qquad (\sim \vee)\xi = \begin{vmatrix} \alpha \\ 1 \\ 1 \end{vmatrix} \qquad (\sim \wedge)\xi = \begin{vmatrix} 1 \\ \alpha \\ \alpha \end{vmatrix}$$

$$\text{CON}\xi = \begin{vmatrix} 1 \\ 0.64 \\ 0.16 \end{vmatrix} \qquad \text{DIL}\xi = \begin{vmatrix} 1 \\ 0.892 \\ 0.637 \end{vmatrix}$$

$$\text{INT}_a\xi = \begin{vmatrix} 1 \\ 0.92 \\ 0.32 \end{vmatrix} \qquad \text{INT}_b\xi = \begin{vmatrix} 1 \\ 0.892 \\ 0.36 \end{vmatrix}$$

Binary

To understand binary (and more generally n-ary) operations consider profiles ξ^1 and ξ^3 received by individual 2, who can form their

(a) *union* $\xi^1 \vee \xi^3$, such that

$$(\xi^1 \vee \xi^3)_i = \max(\xi_i^1, \xi_i^3)$$

(b) *intersection* $\xi^1 \wedge \xi^3$ defined as

$$(\xi_1^1 \wedge \xi_3^1)_i = \min(\xi_1^1, \xi^3)$$

(c) *product* $\xi^{1\cdot}\xi^3$ obtained by

$$(\xi^{1\cdot}\xi^3)_i = \xi_i^1 \xi_i^3$$

(d) *linear combination* for $0 \leqslant \alpha \leqslant 1$

$$\alpha \cdot \xi^1 + (1 - \alpha) \cdot \xi^3$$

(e) *Concatenation* $\xi^1 ¢ \, \xi^3$, where the two profiles are adjoined.

(f) they are *equal* if and only if

$$\xi_i^1 = \xi_i^3, \qquad \text{for all } i$$

(Equality is to be seen as a selection operator [6].)

(g) ξ^1 is a subset of ξ^3 if and only if

$$\xi_i^1 \leqslant \xi_i^3, \qquad \text{for all } i$$

This is then written as $\xi^1 \subseteq \xi^3$

The first three operations can be shown to be associative and commutative, so also is (f). Operators (e) and (g) are associative but not commutative.

(h)   The Cartesian product of two fuzzy subsets ξ^1 and ξ^3 is defined as the *outerproduct* of their membership vectors. Thus,

$$\xi^1 \times \xi^3 \triangleq \theta^{13} = \left[\theta_{ij}^{13} = \xi_i^1 \min \xi_j^3 \right] \triangleq \left[\min\left(\xi_i^1, \xi_j^3\right) \right]$$

θ^{13} is a matrix. In this case it is a square matrix. However, one can also define the '×' product for fuzzy subsets of different universes.

Example

$$\xi^1 = \begin{vmatrix} 1 \\ 0.8 \\ 0.5 \end{vmatrix} \qquad \xi^3 = \begin{vmatrix} 0.4 \\ 0.2 \\ 1 \end{vmatrix}$$

Now each of the above operators can be applied to ξ^1 and ξ^3.

$$\xi^1 \bigvee \xi^3 = \begin{vmatrix} 1 \\ 0.8 \\ 1 \end{vmatrix} \qquad \xi^1 \bigwedge \xi^3 = \begin{vmatrix} 0.4 \\ 0.2 \\ 0.5 \end{vmatrix} \qquad \xi^1 \cdot \xi^3 = \begin{vmatrix} 0.4 \\ 0.16 \\ 0.5 \end{vmatrix}$$

$$\alpha\xi^1 + (1-\alpha)\xi^3 = \begin{vmatrix} \alpha + 0.4(1-\alpha) \\ 0.8\alpha + 0.2(1-\alpha) \\ 0.5\alpha + (1-\alpha) \end{vmatrix} = \begin{vmatrix} 0.4 + 0.6\alpha \\ 0.2 + 0.6\alpha \\ 1 - 0.5\alpha \end{vmatrix}$$

$$\xi^1 \not\subset \xi^3 = \begin{vmatrix} 1 \\ 0.8 \\ 0.5 \\ 0.4 \\ 0.2 \\ 1 \end{vmatrix}$$

ξ^1 is not a subset of ξ^3 nor vice-versa. A subset of ξ^1 would be

$$\begin{vmatrix} 0.6 \\ 0.5 \\ 0.2 \end{vmatrix}$$

$$\xi^1 \times \xi^3 = \begin{vmatrix} (1 \wedge 0.4) & (1 \wedge 0.2) & (1 \wedge 1) \\ (0.8 \wedge 0.4) & (0.8 \wedge 0.2) & (0.8 \wedge 1) \\ (0.5 \wedge 0.4) & (0.5 \wedge 0.2) & (0.5 \wedge 1) \end{vmatrix} = \begin{vmatrix} 0.4 & 0.2 & 1 \\ 0.4 & 0.2 & 0.8 \\ 0.4 & 0.2 & 0.5 \end{vmatrix}$$

Ternary

In fuzzy inference statements a ternary operator of the type "If ξ^1 then ξ^2 else ξ^3" is needed. This is written as $\xi^2 \leftarrow \xi^1 \rightarrow \xi^3$ and may be defined in two ways:

(a) $\xi^2 \leftarrow \xi^1 \rightarrow \xi^3 \triangleq (\xi^1 \times \xi^2) \vee (\neg \xi^1 \times \xi^3)$
(b) $\xi^2 \leftarrow \xi^1 \rightarrow \xi^3 \triangleq (\xi^1 \times \xi^2) \vee ((\sim \vee) \xi^1 \times \xi^3)$

With *negation* ($\neg$) and *union complement* ($\sim \vee$).
Let

$$\xi^1 = \begin{vmatrix} 1 \\ 0.8 \\ 0.5 \end{vmatrix} \qquad \xi^2 = \begin{vmatrix} 0.3 \\ 1 \\ 0.4 \end{vmatrix} \qquad \xi^3 = \begin{vmatrix} 0.4 \\ 0.2 \\ 1 \end{vmatrix}$$

Hence

$$\neg \xi^1 = \begin{vmatrix} 0 \\ 0.2 \\ 0.5 \end{vmatrix} \qquad (\sim \vee) \xi^1 = \begin{vmatrix} 0.99 \\ 1 \\ 1 \end{vmatrix} = \begin{vmatrix} 0.3 & 1 & 0.4 \\ 0.3 & 0.8 & 0.4 \\ 0.4 & 0.5 & 0.5 \end{vmatrix}$$

and with *union complement* ($\sim \vee$)

$$\xi^2 \leftarrow \xi^1 \rightarrow \xi^3 = \begin{vmatrix} 0.3 & 1 & 0.4 \\ 0.3 & 0.8 & 0.4 \\ 0.3 & 0.5 & 0.4 \end{vmatrix} \vee \begin{vmatrix} 0.4 & 0.2 & 0.99 \\ 0.4 & 0.2 & 1 \\ 0.4 & 0.2 & 1 \end{vmatrix} = \begin{vmatrix} 0.4 & 1 & 0.99 \\ 0.4 & 0.8 & 1 \\ 0.4 & 0.5 & 1 \end{vmatrix}$$

TRANSFORMATIONS RELATED TO INCOMING PROFILES AT A NODE

Two property spaces P^1 and P^2 may be related to each other through transformations. Let T^{12}; $P^2 \rightarrow P^1$ and T^{21}: $P^1 \rightarrow P^2$ denote transformation matrices. The jth column of T^{12} is the profile of $q_j^2 \in P^2$ in P^1. Similarly the jth column of T^{21} is the profile of $q_j^1 \in P^1$ in P^2. Thus, a profile of an entity X in P^1 say ξ^1 gets transformed through T^{21} to $\hat{\xi}^1$. We may write this in equation form as

$$\hat{\xi}^1 = T^{21} * \xi^1 \tag{1}$$

where the composition $*$ may be defined in four ways ($t_{ij} \in T^{21}$)

(a) as the *(average) sum of products*

$$\left(\hat{\xi}_i^1 = \frac{1}{n_1} \sum_j t_{ij} \cdot \xi_j^1 \right) \tag{2}$$

(b)   as the *maximum of products*

$$\left(\hat{\xi}_i^{\,1} = \max_j t_{ij} \cdot \xi_j^{\,1}\right) \tag{3}$$

(c)   as the *maximum of minimums*

$$\left(\hat{\xi}_i^{\,1} = \max_j \left(t_{ij} \min \xi_j^{\,1}\right)\right) \tag{4}$$

(d)   as the *(average) sum of minimums*

$$\hat{\xi}_i^{\,1} = \frac{1}{n_1} \sum_j \left(t_{ij} \min \xi_j^{\,1}\right) \tag{5}$$

Note the average sum-min and sum-prod operations can be easily generalized to weighted sum-min and weighted sum-prod operations.

Since the profiles are fuzzy subsets, the average of minimums or of products defined above lead to proper fuzzy subsets. It is very likely that human processing uses all four in various combinations. For the purposes of this paper, it is assumed that one of these transformations exist. The profiles generated by the four definitions have the following property.

Theorem   *Profile transformations under the four composition rules above are termed, respectively, sum-prod, max-prod, max-min, and sum-min, and have the property that*

$$\hat{\xi}^1 \,(\text{sum-prod}) \subseteq \hat{\xi}^1 \,(\text{sum-min}) \subseteq \hat{\xi}^1 \,(\text{max-min}) \tag{6}$$

$$\hat{\xi}^1 \,(\text{sum-prod}) \subseteq \hat{\xi}^1 \,(\text{max-prod}) \subseteq \hat{\xi}^1 \,(\text{max-min}) \tag{7}$$

Proof

$$t_{ij} \cdot \xi_j^{\,1} \leqslant \xi_j^{\,1} \qquad \text{for any } i$$

$$\leqslant t_{ij}, \qquad \text{for any } j$$

Hence,

$$t_{ij} \cdot \xi_j^{\,1} \leqslant \left(\xi_j^{\,1} \min t_{ij}\right)$$

Thus,

$$\sum_j t_{ij} \cdot \xi_j^{\,1} \leqslant \sum_j \xi_j^{\,1} \min t_{ij}$$

Hence

$$\hat{\xi}^1 \,(\text{sum-prod}) \subseteq \hat{\xi}^1 \,(\text{sum-min}) \tag{8}$$

Again for any i,

$$t_{ij} \min \xi_j^1 \leqslant \max_j t_{ij} \min \xi_j^1, \qquad \text{for all } j$$

Thus,

$$\sum_j t_{ij} \min \xi_j^1 \leqslant \sum_j \max_j t_{ij} \min \xi_j^1$$

$$\leqslant n_1 \max_j t_{ij} \min \xi_j^1$$

Hence,

$$\hat{\xi}^1 (\text{sum-min}) \subseteq \hat{\xi}^1 (\text{max-min}) \tag{9}$$

Relations (8) and (9) together form relation (6). Similarly, for any i,

$$t_{ij} \cdot \xi_j^1 \leqslant \max_j t_{ij} \cdot \xi_j^1, \qquad \text{for all } j$$

Hence

$$\sum_j t_{ij} \cdot \xi_j^1 \leqslant \sum_j \max_j t_{ij} \cdot \xi_j^1 = n_1 \max_j t_{ij} \cdot \xi_j^1$$

Thus,

$$\hat{\xi}^1 (\text{sum-prod}) \subseteq \hat{\xi}^1 (\text{max-prod}) \tag{10}$$

Finally, for any i, since

$$t_{ij} \cdot \xi_j^1 \leqslant \left(\xi_j^1 \min t_{ij} \right)$$

$$\max_j t_{ij} \cdot \xi_j^1 \leqslant \max \left(\xi_{1j}^1 \min t_{ij} \right)$$

Thus,

$$\hat{\xi}^1 (\text{max-prod}) \subseteq \hat{\xi}^1 (\text{max-min}) \tag{11}$$

Relations (10) and (11) together yield relation (7).

Thus, profile transformations have their upper bound formed from the max-min composition and their lower bound from the sum-prod composition. In purposeful information processing, these two bounding compositions, yield solution bounds for group processing.

Example Let one design team use the attributes

$$P^1 = \{ \text{exciting, casual, exposed} \}$$

and another team use

$$P^2 = \{\text{chaotic, interesting, distracting, accessible}\}$$

Let the perception by the second team of the first be given by

$$T^{21} = \begin{vmatrix} 1 & 0.5 & 0.6 \\ 0.5 & 0.3 & 1 \\ 0.5 & 1 & 0.5 \\ 0.3 & 0.6 & 1 \end{vmatrix}$$

Then an opinion profile say ξ^1 which is 100% exciting, 70% casual and 50% exposed, may be transformed by T^{21} under the four rules of composition. Thus,

$$\xi^1 = \begin{vmatrix} 1 \\ 0.7 \\ 0.5 \end{vmatrix}$$

$$\hat{\xi}^1_{\text{(sum-prod)}} = \frac{1}{3} \begin{vmatrix} 1 & 0.5 & 0.6 \\ 0.5 & 0.3 & 1 \\ 0.5 & 1 & 0.5 \\ 0.3 & 0.6 & 1 \end{vmatrix} * \begin{vmatrix} 1 \\ 0.7 \\ 0.5 \end{vmatrix} = \begin{vmatrix} 0.55 \\ 0.403 \\ 0.483 \\ 0.406 \end{vmatrix}$$

$$\hat{\xi}^1_{\text{(max-prod)}} = \begin{vmatrix} 1 \\ 0.5 \\ 0.7 \\ 0.5 \end{vmatrix} \qquad \hat{\xi}^1_{\text{(max-min)}} = \begin{vmatrix} 1 \\ 0.5 \\ 0.7 \\ 0.6 \end{vmatrix} \qquad \hat{\xi}^1_{\text{(sum-min)}} = \begin{vmatrix} 0.667 \\ 0.433 \\ 0.567 \\ 0.467 \end{vmatrix}$$

Theorem *The property space P^1 covers P^2 under compositions (b) and (c), i.e., the max compositions, if for each i there exists a j such that $t_{ij} = 1$.*

Proof Let

$$\xi^1 = \begin{vmatrix} 1 \\ 1 \\ . \\ . \\ 1 \end{vmatrix}$$

That is, the membership of each property is 1. Then since for each i there exists a j such that $t_{ij} = 1$, it follows that for this j

$$t_{ij} \cdot \xi_j^1 = 1$$

and

$$t_{ij} \min \xi_j^1 = 1$$

Hence under the max compositions (b) and (c),

$$\hat{\xi}^1 = \begin{Vmatrix} 1 \\ \cdot \\ \cdot \\ \cdot \\ 1 \end{Vmatrix}$$

That is, the membership of each property for the transformed profile is 1. Hence the theorem.

Thus, a reduction in covering properties occurs when P^1 does not cover P^2 under compositions (b) and (c). This is an important observation for the consensus formation model later.

These are some of the transformations and operations on profiles. In this manner it is possible to create an algebra of transformations of profiles. Since a node in a pipa network is a potentially decision node, functions are formed here. These node-related processes are discussed next.

MEMORY AND MEMORY PROCESSES AT A NODE

A node is a processing unit at which incoming profiles are operated on by a procedure either given from outside or decided on at the node. A procedure consists of various memory operations of the type discussed in the earlier section plus the operations of processing which may be of three types:

(1) Internal: such as storing, keying, classifying, indexing, summarizing, updating, bundling, glumping.
(2) Accepting: profiles from other nodes, weighing transforming, profiles from environment, decoding.
(3) Dispatching: to other nodes, profiles of valuations, decisions, queries, requests, opinions, summaries, etc., encoding.

Each of the above processing types may be complex enough to require (possibly fuzzy) algorithms.

A node is also considered as a decision node. That is, an information processing agent may be identified with it. Thus the interaction in a pipa between agents is the transformations of profiles under a given purpose.

In the simplest of interaction, it may consist of a file of last dispatched profile(s), a weighing scheme for incoming profiles, and a procedure to update the last dispatched profile. Such a scheme is the one considered in interaction between planners [1]. They begin with initial attitudes to a plan, which are modified by interaction. Later in this paper a similar scheme in the context of (fuzzy) profile transformation is considered.

The memory processes themselves are considered as constituting a collection of files. The following processes with respect to records and files have been previously recorded [16]:

(1) Entering values on to a record.
(2) Sorting according to a predetermined sequence.
(3) Merging of two or more files.
(4) Deleting a record.
(5) Changing values in a record.
(6) Changing output formats of records.
(7) Changing medium of file storage.
(8) Searching.
(9) Selection, extraction, abstraction, etc.

Information processing tasks [24] are related primarily to record-based procedures of libraries. In consensus formation in the framework considered here, these are related to a weighted agreement procedure. These are discussed in the next section.

COMMUNICATION AND DECISION MAKING STRUCTURES

Communication Structures

In group processing, many combinatorial possibilities exist. A given processing network may result from many factors, externally imposed or internally evolved. In the study of the network itself, one examines the dynamics of message flow and the limitations imposed on message transmission by the intervening media between two communicators [17]. These may be related to the type of message channels, delays, evaluative messages, etc. The simplest situation of a dyadic processing is that of man–computer problem-solving interaction of teacher–learner interaction, shared data processing between two central processing units, and so forth. Information retrieval problems are dyadic in nature for a single user.

For more than two processing nodes (n-ads or poly-ads), it is rare that a node is in communication with every other node, particularly when $n \geqslant 4$. Environmental, contextual and task constraints result in less than a completely connected network. When a structure is externally imposed such as in planning, design and decision-making, often informal channels develop spontaneously. Group processing takes place in both the formal and

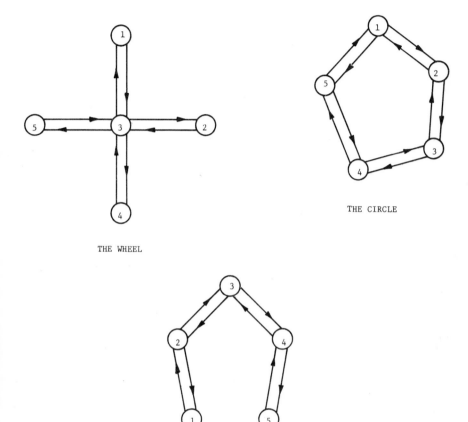

Figure 1. Some common processing structures.

informal structures. Figure 1 (adapted from [17]) illustrates some commonly discussed structures.

In the wheel networks only one node communicates with all others, regardless of group size. The circle allows a node to communicate with two adjacent nodes. The chain is the circle minus one link. The extreme members are isolated. Other structures such as the pinwheel as illustrated in Fig. 2 are discussed. Performance results are varied in each type. It is seen that the nature of the task determines the performance of processing (Shaw, 1971).

In any processing network formal and/or informal one may identify a so called "communication structure." This consists of

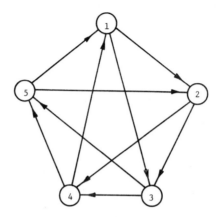

Figure 2. Pinwheel communication structure.

(1) schemes by which an agent i (associated with node i) weighs incoming profiles from other nodes;
(2) directed channels between nodes;
(3) limitations on these channels;
(4) delays on profile transmission;
(5) transformational matrices between nodes for the property spaces of each node identified with the processing context;
(6) protocol of communication, i.e., who communicates, at what times and under what conditions and to whom.
(7) memory associated with the nodes.

Consensus formation [10] and design conflict resolution [1] are two purposeful information processing activities of a group. Bishop Oglesby and Willeke [1970] investigated seven alternative freeway planning systems for consensus designs (see [10]). These seven are termed:

(1) strategy of information
(2) information with feedback
(3) coordinator's strategy
(4) community advocacy planning, the ombudsman
(5) arbitrative planning: a hearing officer
(6) the coordinator catalyst
(7) plural planning

Strategies (1), (2) and (3) are like one-way chains. Strategies (4) and (5) are like the wheel. Strategy (6) is like the pinwheel. Consensus formation may therefore be examined in any of these structures.

Nodal Decision Rules

An agent i at node i has transformed profiles denoted $\Phi^{kj}(k)$ incoming a stage k from node j, where

$$\Phi^{ij}(k) = T^{ij} * \xi^j(k) \tag{12}$$

and $\xi^j(k)$ is the profile at node j at stage k. In the simplest of consideration, this agent may follow six rules of forming a profile for the next state.

(a) *max-min consensus*: The agent chooses to transform $\xi^i(k)$ by accepting any agreed improvement in the $\Phi^{ij}(k)$'s. Thus

$$\xi^j(k+1) = \xi^i(k) \vee \left(\bigwedge_{j \neq i} \Phi^{ij}(k) \right) \tag{13}$$

(b) *min-max consensus*: Here the agent chooses to transform $\xi^i(k)$ by rejecting any improvement.

$$\xi^i(k+1) = \xi^i(k) \wedge \left(\bigvee_{j \neq i} \Phi^{ij}(k) \right) \tag{14}$$

Thus in (a) an optimistic-pessimistic viewpoint is advanced by agent i, while in (b) a pessimistic-optimistic viewpoint is chosen.

(c) *Commonality or min-min consensus*: Here only common agreements are acceptable to agent i. Thus

$$\xi^i(k+1) = \xi^i(k) \wedge \left(\bigwedge_{j \neq i} \Phi^{ij}(k) \right) \tag{15}$$

(d) *Pseudo-linear-maximum consensus*: The rule is

$$\xi^i(k+1) = \alpha \xi^i(k) + (1-\alpha) \left(\bigvee_{j \neq i} \Phi^{ij}(k) \right) \qquad 0 \leqslant \alpha \leqslant 1 \tag{16}$$

(e) *Pseudo-linear-minimum consensus*: This is the opposite of (d).

$$\xi^i(k+1) = \alpha \xi^i(k) + (1-\alpha) \left(\bigwedge_{j \neq i} \Phi^{ij}(k) \right) \qquad 0 \leqslant \alpha \gg 1 \tag{17}$$

(f) *Weighted consensus*: In this case the agent decides to combine profiles linearly by a scheme of weights.

$$\xi^i(k+1) = \alpha_i \xi^i(k) + \sum_{j \neq i} \alpha_{ij} \Phi^{ij}(k) \tag{18}$$

A model of fuzzy-concept communication has been proposed [22] that investigates the transformations of concepts from individual i to individual j in an agreement analysis framework, which is based on Newcombe's model of communication [18]. As may be seen the transformations and models considered in this paper generalizes and includes the results of that paper.

The incoming profiles may be 'treated' before combining as above, i.e., these may be 'sharpened' (i.e., concentrated), blurred (i.e., diluted). For example, a sharpened commonality consensus may be written as

$$\xi^i(k+1) = \xi^i(k) \wedge \left(\bigwedge_{j \neq i} \text{CON}\left(\phi^{ij}(k)\right) \right) \tag{19}$$

A profile $\phi^{ij}(k)$ may be *split* into two parts $\zeta^{ij}(k)$ and $\eta^{ij}(k)$ such that for some reordering shecme ρ of the property spaces

$$\rho\left(\phi^{ij}(k)\right) = \zeta^{ij}(k) \, \varsigma \eta^{ij}(k) \tag{20}$$

The split parts are transformed according to different schemes. One may be transformed according to a max-min consensus and the other a pseudo-linear consensus. The agent can choose to concentrate or dilate or complem,ent a split part.

On a different level a 'valuation scheme' may be set up by i for incoming profiles. A valuation scheme for the qth coordinate of a profile $\varphi^{ij}q(k)$ is defined as a function

$$\nu^{ij}q(k) : V_q \rho[0,1] \tag{21}$$

where V_q is the set of permissible values of property q. For fuzzy profiles $V_q \equiv [0,1]$. For example if q is the property "crowded" and a value is 'mildly crowded' with an associated membership 0.5, the valuation of q is 1 whereas if it is extremely crowded (membership 1), not crowded at all (membership 0) the valuation of q is 0. The entropy function for fuzzy sets of de Luca and Termini [1973] is such a valuation scheme. Such valuation schemes aid in deciding which parts have to be concentrated or dilated. Valuation schemes also lead to "payoff" functions at nodes and hence to a game theoretic formulation of consensus formation.

CONSENSUS FORMATION MODELS

A group of n experts and/or databases may perceive an entity X in terms of n-property spaces $P^1 \ldots P^n$ and associated *a priori* profiles of opinions $\xi^1(0), \ldots, \xi^n(0)$. Interactions between these have the following assumptions:

(i)　Profile transformation matrices between nodes are given. The matrix T^{ij} is a fuzzy relation between P^i and P^j. The kth column of T^{ij} is the profile of property $q_k \in P^j$, in P^i, i.e., it is a fuzzy subset of P^2. T^{ij} is also termed the cross-perception matrix.

(ii) Each node assigns a probability measure ω_{ij}, termed weight, of importance to incoming profiles to a node.

(iii) T^{ij}'s and ω_{ij}'s are assumed constant.

(iv) Profiles are dispatched at each stage.

(v) These are transformed according to the six rules of transformation given in (13)–(18).

A general formulation of the consensus formation model is developed. This takes into account the possibility of different agents following different schemes. The formulation leads to a fuzzy automaton model of group consensus. It intends to bring out a unifying framework for analysis. As will be seen later in the example, there seem to be some similarities with Markŏv models described in the literature. These are somewhat superficial and possibly misleading.

For the above purpose, form a property space Π, which is obtained by concatenating $P^1 \ldots P^n$, i.e.,

$$\Pi = P^1 \phi P^2 \phi \ldots \phi P^n \tag{22}$$

Similarly form a fuzzy subset $\Psi(k)$ of Π by concatenating $\xi^1(k), \ldots, \xi^n(k)$, i.e.,

$$\Psi(k) = \xi^1(k)\phi\, \xi^2(k)\phi \ldots \phi\, \xi^n(k) \tag{23}$$

By suitably defining a transformation operator K^*, one may write

$$\Psi(k+1) = K^*\Psi(k) \tag{24}$$

Properties of consensus formation in the given communication structure may be investigated by studying the operator K^*. The operator K^* has the structure

$$K^* = \begin{bmatrix} \omega_{11}I_1 & \omega_{12}T^{12} & \cdots & \omega_{1n}T^{1n} \\ \omega_{21}T^{21} & \omega_{22}I_2 & \cdots & \omega_{2n}T^{2n} \\ \cdot & & & \\ \cdot & & \cdots & \\ \omega_{n1}T^{n1} & \omega_{n2}T^{n2} & \cdots & \omega_{nn}T_n \end{bmatrix} \tag{25}$$

Where $T^{ij} = 0$ if j is incomprehensible to i for every property pair (q_i, q_j) such that $q_i \in P^i$ and $q_j \in P^j$ and ω_{ij}'s and $*$ depend on the consensus formation choice for agent i.

Further modifications may be introduced. At each node, the incoming profiles are concentrated dilated, intensified or valuated. Let the unary operator on the incoming profile $\Phi^{ij}(k)$ be denoted by $\tau^{ij}\otimes$. The operator

K^* is then modified to K'^* and has the structure

$$
K'^* = \begin{bmatrix}
\omega_{11}I_1 & \omega_{12}T^{12}\otimes T^{12} & \cdots & \omega_{1n}T^{1n}\otimes T^{1n} \\
\omega_{21}T^{21}\otimes T^{21} & \omega_{22}I_2 & \cdots & \omega_{2n}T^{2n}\otimes T^{2n} \\
\vdots & & \cdots & \vdots \\
\omega_{n1}T^{n1}\otimes T^{n1} & \omega_{n2}T^{n2}\otimes T^{n2} & \cdots & \omega_{nn}I_n
\end{bmatrix}
$$

Thus by examining K^* or K'^* for different structures an understanding of consensus formation may be obtained. It may be noted that certain forms of fixed point theorems are applicable. In the next paragraphs, sixteen basic consensus models are examined for a non-null consensus.

Assume that all agents choose the same transformation rules if the six profile transformations in (13)–(18) are combined with the four transformation operators; thus twenty-four possibilities exist as may be examined in Fig. 3. Of these, six always lead to null consensus, i.e., the profiles at stage infinity are zero vectors. These are the possibilities formed by

Node profile formation rules (12)–(17)	Transformation Operators			
	max-min	max-prod	sum-min	sum-prod
max-min	I	II	III	IV
min-max	V	VI	VII	VIII
min-min or commonality	IX	X	XI	XII
pseudo-linear max	XIII	XIV	XV	XVI
pseudo-linear min	XVII	XVIII	XIX	XX
Weighted	XXI	XXII	XXIII	XXIV

Figure 3.   Twenty-four major consensus formation models.

combining the pseudo-linear and/or the weighted consensus formation with the sum product of sum-min operators. This observation may be summarized as in the following theorem.

Theorem   *Models XV, XVI, XIX, XX, XXIII, XXIV (Fig. 3) invariably lead to null consensus.*

Proof For any node i the profile at stage k for each of the models is given by

$$\text{XV:} \quad \xi^{i}(k+1) = \omega_{i}\xi^{i}(k) + (1-\omega_{i})\left(\bigvee_{j\neq i} T^{ij} \text{ (sum-min)}\xi^{j}(k)\right)$$

$$\text{XVI:} \quad \xi^{i}(k+1) = \omega_{i}\xi^{i}(k) + (1-\omega_{i})\left(\bigvee_{j\neq i} T^{ij} \text{ (sum-prod)}\xi^{j}(k)\right)$$

Similarly for models XIX and XX the '$\bigvee$' operation above is replaced by '$\bigwedge$'.

$$\text{XXIII:}\xi^{i}(k+1) = \omega_{ii}\xi^{i}(k) + \sum_{j\neq i} \omega_{ij} T^{ij} \text{ (sum-min) } \xi^{j}(k)$$

$$\text{XXIV:} \quad \xi^{i}(k+1) = \omega_{ii}\xi^{i}(k) + \sum_{j\neq i} \omega_{ij} T^{ij} \text{ (sum-prod) } \xi^{j}(k)$$

By the theorem in the second section, it is sufficient to prove that models XV and XIX, and XXIII have null consensus, since the result for the others follows. Let $\xi_{t}^{i}(0)=1$, for all i and t. That is, the initial profiles are the property spaces. Thus, the tth element

$$\left(T^{ij} \text{ (sum-min) } \xi^{j}(0)\right)_{t} = \frac{1}{n_{j}} \sum_{j} (T^{ij})_{ts} \cdot \xi_{s}^{j}(0)$$

$$= \frac{1}{n_{j}} \sum_{s} (T^{ij})_{ts}$$

$$= 1 \qquad \text{if for all } s\, (T^{ij})_{ts} = 1$$

$$< 1 \qquad \text{otherwise}$$

Thus, in general, T^{ij} (sum-min) $\xi^{j}(0)$ are vectors with not all 1's. Let the tth element be denoted β_{tj}. Then

$$\omega_{i}\xi_{t}^{i}(0) + (1-\omega_{i}) \bigvee_{j\neq i} \beta_{tj} < 1 \qquad \exists j \text{ st } \omega_{ij} < 1$$

$$= 1 \qquad \forall j \, \beta_{tj} = 1$$

Similarly

$$\omega_{i}\xi_{t}^{i}(0) + \sum_{j\neq i} \omega_{ij}\beta_{tj} < 1 \qquad \text{if } \exists j \text{ st } \beta_{tj} = 1$$

$$= 1 \qquad \forall j \, \beta_{tj} = 1$$

$\beta_{tj}=1$ only for the trivial case with $(T_{ij})_{st}=1$ for all s,t. Hence, for all other cases we have

$$\xi^{i}(1) \subset \xi^{i}(0) \qquad \text{for models XV and XIX and XXIII}$$

By the same reasoning

$$\xi^i(2)\subset\xi^i(1) \qquad \text{for the same models}$$

Let

$$\lim_{k\to\infty}\xi^i(k)=\xi^i(\infty)$$

Then

$$\xi^i(\infty)\subset\xi^i(k) \qquad \text{for all } k$$

Now to prove $\xi^i(\infty)=0$: For any $\epsilon>0$ let M be such that for some $s=s'$, $\xi_s^1(M)=\epsilon$ and for $s\neq s'$ $\xi_s^i(M)<\epsilon$. Then for $M+1$, $\xi_s^i(M+1)<\epsilon$. Hence

$$\lim\epsilon\to 0,\ 0\leqslant\xi_s^i(M+1)\leqslant\epsilon.$$

Thus, it is shown that models XV and XIX and XXIII have zero consensus. Some of these models are examined in the next example.

Example Consider the communication structure shown in Fig. 4. The initial profiles are

$$\xi^1=\begin{vmatrix}1.0\\0.5\\0.2\\0.0\end{vmatrix} \quad \xi^2=\begin{vmatrix}0.3\\0.6\\1.0\\0.2\\0.9\end{vmatrix} \quad \xi^3=\begin{vmatrix}0.5\\1.0\\0.8\end{vmatrix} \quad \xi^4=\begin{vmatrix}0.2\\0.6\\1.0\\0.8\end{vmatrix} \quad \xi^5=\begin{vmatrix}0.6\\1.0\\0.5\\0.3\end{vmatrix}$$

The transformation matrices are given as

$$T^{13}=\begin{vmatrix}1.0 & 0.5 & 0.6\\0.7 & 1.0 & 0.3\\0.6 & 0.4 & 1.0\\1.0 & 0.2 & 0.7\end{vmatrix} \qquad T^{31}=\begin{vmatrix}1.0 & 0.7 & 0.6 & 1.0\\0.5 & 1.0 & 0.4 & 0.2\\0.6 & 0.3 & 1.0 & 0.7\end{vmatrix}$$

$$T^{12}=\begin{vmatrix}1.0 & 0.8 & 1.0 & 0.4 & 0.5\\0.6 & 1.0 & 0.2 & 0.9 & 0.9\\0.2 & 0.1 & 0.1 & 1.0 & 0.5\\0.1 & 0.5 & 1.0 & 0.6 & 1.0\end{vmatrix} \qquad T^{21}=\begin{vmatrix}1.0 & 0.7 & 0.3 & 0.2\\0.9 & 1.0 & 0.2 & 0.7\\1.0 & 0.4 & 0.3 & 0.8\\0.3 & 0.8 & 1 & 0.3\\0.5 & 0.8 & 1 & 0.9\end{vmatrix}$$

$$T^{23}=\begin{vmatrix}1.0 & 0.5 & 0.8\\0.4 & 1.0 & 0.2\\0.7 & 0.6 & 1.0\\0.1 & 0.2 & 1.0\\0.1 & 1.0 & 0.6\end{vmatrix} \qquad T^{32}=\begin{vmatrix}1.0 & 0.4 & 0.3 & 0.6 & 0.8\\0.5 & 1.0 & 0.6 & 0.2 & 1.0\\0.9 & 0.2 & 1.0 & 1.0 & 0.7\end{vmatrix}$$

$$T^{34} = \begin{vmatrix} 1.0 & 1.0 & 0 & 0 \\ 0 & 0.5 & 1.0 & 0 \\ 0.5 & 0 & 0 & 1.0 \end{vmatrix} \qquad T^{42} = \begin{vmatrix} 1.0 & 0.2 & 0.3 \\ 1.0 & 0.5 & 0.7 \\ 0.1 & 1.0 & 0.2 \\ 0.5 & 0.6 & 1 \end{vmatrix}$$

$$T^{25} = \begin{vmatrix} 1 & 0 & 0 & 0 \\ 0 & 1 & 0 & 0 \\ 0 & 0 & 0.8 & 0 \\ 0 & 0 & 1 & 0.5 \\ 0 & 0 & 0.6 & 1 \end{vmatrix} \qquad T^{52} = \begin{vmatrix} 1.0 & 0.1 & 1.0 & 0.2 & 0 \\ 0.5 & 1.0 & 0.3 & 0.3 & 0 \\ 0.6 & 0.2 & 1.0 & 1.0 & 0.6 \\ 0.1 & 0.3 & 0.4 & 0.5 & 1.0 \end{vmatrix}$$

The weighting scheme is given by the W matrix

$$W = [\omega_{ij}] = \begin{vmatrix} 0.6 & 0.2 & 0.2 & 0 & 0 \\ 0.2 & 0.5 & 0.2 & 0 & 0.1 \\ 0.2 & 0.1 & 0.6 & 1 & 0 \\ 0 & 0 & 0.4 & 0.6 & 0 \\ 0 & 0.3 & 0 & 0 & 0.7 \end{vmatrix}$$

In this example it is assumed that incoming profiles at a node are transformed according to the max-min composition. Thus, only the six models of weighted, pseudo-linear minimum, pseudo-linear maximum, minimin, min-max and max-min consensus formation are investigated. Twenty iterations are chosen for convenience. If there is a stable profile

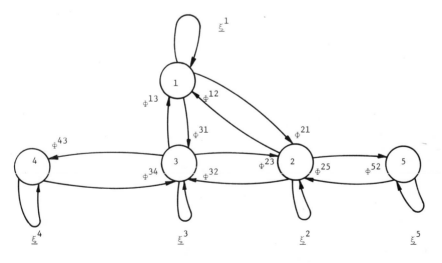

Figure 4. Flow diagram for the example,

then it is likely to stabilize by 20 iterations. In Table 1 the sequence of transformations under the weighted consensus formation rule is displayed. As may be seen the consensus stabilizes with membership values for the properties between 77% and 83%. In Table 2, the consensus of the universes of discourse are examined. That is, if the initial memberships are all 100% then after stabilization, the universe is "reduced" only for $q_3 \in P^2$, under the three rules weighted, pseudo-linear, minimum and min-min. For the other cases no "reduction" of the universe occurs. In Table 3 the stabilized profiles at iteration 20 are given for each of the six rules. It may be observed that the pseudo-linear-max rule yields the universes as the consensus. The max-min and min-max rules yield normalized profiles generally. The weighted and pseudo-linear rules tend to even out the profiles. In all cases, the stabilized consensus are subsets of their stabilized consensus of the universes.

Table 1
Profile Transformations for Example Under Weighted Consensus Formation

	Iterations						
Profiles	0	1	2	3	4	5	20
$\xi^1 1$	1	0.92	0.86	.83	.81	.80	.7964
2	0.5	.62	.70	.76	.79	.80	.8227
3	0.2	.38	.48	.55	.61	.65	.7712
4	0	.34	.53	.63	.69	.73	.8006
$\xi^2 1$	0.3	.57	.70	.75	.77	.77	.7931
2	0.6	.78	.84	.84	.84	.83	.8228
3	1.0	.91	.86	.83	.80	.79	.7806
4	0.2	.41	.55	.64	.70	.73	.7814
5	0.9	.8	.76	.75	.75	.76	.8099
$\xi^3 1$	0.5	.64	.71	.74	.75	.76	.7960
2	1.0	.89	.84	.82	.82	.82	.8227
3	0.8	.78	.76	.74	.73	.73	.7700
$\xi^4 1$	0.2	0.32	.45	.55	.63	.68	.7928
2	0.6	0.64	.66	.68	.70	.72	.7928
3	1.0	1.0	.96	.91	.87	.85	.8227
4	0.8	0.8	.79	.78	.76	.75	.7642
$\xi^5 1$	0.6	.72	.78	.80	.81	.81	.7900
2	1.0	.88	.85	.85	.84	.84	.8229
3	0.5	.65	.73	.77	.78	.79	.7777
4	0.3	.48	.58	.63	.67	.69	.8069

Table 2
Consensus of Universe of Discourse in Three Cases at Iteration 20

Profiles	Weighted Consensus	Pseudo Linear Minimum	Min- Min.
$\xi^1 1$	1	1	1
2	1	1	1
3	1	1	1
4	1	1	1
$\xi^2 1$	1	1	1
2	1	1	1
3	.96	.8	.8
4	1	1	1
5	1	1	1
$\xi^3 1$	1	1	1
2	1	1	1
3	1	1	1
$\xi^4 1$	1	1	1
2	1	1	1
3	1	1	1
4	1	1	1
$\xi^5 1$	1	1	1
2	1	1	1
3	1	1	1
4	1	1	1

Theorem *Under any consensus formation rule the consensus at infinity is always a subset of the universal consensus at infinity.*

Proof This should follow immediately from the subset properties at each stage.

In the above major models, cross-combinations were not examined. It may in fact reflect various experts' predisposition in a conferencing situation such as the Delphi method. This section is concluded by noting that the "reduction" of the universe observed in the example may be avoided by requiring the T^{ij} matrices to conform to an earlier theorem (the second theorem of the second section).

Consensus formation guided by "payoff" or evaluative considerations are discussed in [31]. In such models the tendencies of null consensus may be arrested.

Table 3
Transformed Profiles in Example for Different Cases at Iteration 20

Profiles	Weighted Min.	Pseudo Linear Min.	Pseudo Linear Max.	Min- Min.	Min- Max.	Max- Min.
$\xi^1 1$	.7964	.6247	1	.8	1	1
2	.8227	.66	.9999	.5	.5	.9
3	.7712	.6154	.9998	.2	.2	.8
4	.8006	.6247	.9999	0	0	.7
$\xi^2 1$	.7931	.6247	.9999	.3	.3	.8
2	.8228	.6600	.9999	.5	.6	.9
3	.7806	.6247	.9999	.5	1	1
4	.7814	.6156	.9999	.2	.2	.8
5	.8099	.6000	.9999	.5	.9	.9
$\xi^3 1$	.7960	.6247	1	.5	.5	.7
2	.8227	.6600	.9999	.5	1	1
3	.7700	.6156	.9997	.5	.8	.8
$\xi^4 1$	.7928	.6246	.9997	.2	.2	.7
2	.7928	.6247	1	.5	.6	.7
3	.8227	.6600	.9998	.5	1	1
4	.7642	.6156	.9996	.5	.8	.8
$\xi^5 1$	.7900	.6251	.9995	.5	.6	1
2	.8229	.6606	.9995	.5	.6	1
3	.7777	.6250	.9996	.5	.5	1
4	.8069	.5999	.9993	13	13	.9

CONCLUSION

An algebraic approach for investigating purposeful information processing activity based on fuzzy set theory has been proposed. In particular, the approach is well-suited for analyzing consensus-formulation systems, in planning and decision-making. A number of questions may be raised, regarding the properties of the transformational matrices and their effect in such sequential systems. As may be noted, the problems of intervening memory at processing nodes adds further complexity to the analysis.

REFERENCES

1. Batty, M. (1974), "Social Power in Plan Generation", *Town Planning Review*, Vol. 45, No. 3, p. 290–310.

2. Bavelas, Alex (1950), "Communication Patterns in Task Oriented Groups", *Journal of the Acoustical Society of America*, Vol. 22, p. 725–730.
3. Bishop, A. B., Oglesby, C. H., and Willeke, G. E. (1970), "Community Attitudes Towards Freeway Planning: A Study of California's Planning Procedures", *Highway Research Record*, No. 305, p. 42–43.
4. Cathcart, R. S., and Samovar, L. A. (1974), *Small Group Communication: A Reader*, Second Edition, Dubuque, Iowa, Wm. C. Brown, Publishers.
5. Churchman, C. W. (1971), *Design of Inquiring Systems*, New York, Basic Books.
6. Codasyl Development Committee (1962), "An Information Algebra Phase 1. Report", *Communications of the ACM*, Vol. 5, No. 4, April.
7. Dalkey, N. C. (1972), *Studies in the Quality of Life Delphi and Decision Making*, Lexington, Mass., Health Publishers.
8. DeLuca and S. Termini (1972), "A Definition of a Non-Probabilistic Entropy in a Setting of Fuzzy Sets Theory", *Information and Control* Vol. 20, p. 301–312.
9. George Gerbner, et. al. (ed.) (1969), *The Analysis of Communication Content*, New York, John Wiley and Sons Ltd.
10. van Gigch, John P. (1974), *Applied General Systems Theory*, New York, Harper and Row, Chapters 13–15.
11. Gotlieb, C. C., and Borodin, A. (1973), *Social Issues in Computing*, New York, Academic Press.
12. Kochen, M. (1974), *Principles of Information Retrieval*, New York, John Wiley and Sons Ltd.
13. Lindblom, C. E. (1968), *The Policy Making Process*, Englewood Cliffs, N. J., Prentice Hall, Inc.
14. Lozar, C. C. (1976), "Evaluation of Research Work Stations and Office Environment for Improved Performance", *Proceeding of the CIB W-65 Symposium on Organization and Management of Construction*, May 19–20, 1976.
15. Lucas, H. C., Clowes, K. W., and Kaplan, R. B. (1974), "Frameworks for Information Systems", Vol. 12, No. 3, p. 245–260.
16. Meadows, C. T. (1973), *The Analysis of Information Systems*, Los Angeles, Melville Publishing Company.
17. Mortensen, C. D. (1972), *Communication: The Study of Human Interaction*, New York, McGraw-Hill Book Company.
18. Newcomb, T. M. (1953), "An Approach to the Study of Communicative Acts" *Psychological Review*, Vol. 60, p. 393–404.
19. Newell, A. and Sinon, H. A. (1972), *Human Problem Solving*, Englewood Cliffs, N. J., Prentice Hall.
20. Pill Juri (1971), "The Delphi Method: Substance, Context, A critique and an annotated bibliography", *Socio-Economic Planning Sciences*, Vol. 5, No. 1, pp. 27–71.
21. Psathas, G., "Analyzing Dyadic Interaction", in Ref. 9.
22. Ragade, R. K. (1973), "On Some Aspects of Fuzziness in Communication: Fuzzy Concept Communication", December 1973, Systems Research and Planning, Bell Northern Research, Ottawa, Canada.

23. Snider, J. G. and Osgood, C. E. (1969), *Semantic Differential Technique* A source book, Chicago, Aldine Publishing.
24. Thomas, P. A. (1971), *Task Analysis of Library Operations*, London, Aslib.
25. Turoff, M. (1971), "Delphi Conferencing: Computer Based Conferencing with Anonymity Washington, D. C.," Executive office of the President, Office of Emergency Preparedness, Office of the Assistant Director for Resource Analysis.
26. Vickery, B. C. (1973), *Information Systems*, London, Butterworths.
27. Zadeh, L. A. (1965), "Fuzzy Sets", *Information and Control*, Vol. 8, p. 338.
28. Zadeh, L. A. (1971), "Quantitative-Fuzzy Semantics", *Information and Control*, Vol. 3, p. 159.
29. Zadeh, L. A. (1972), "A fuzzy-set theoretic interpretation of hedges" Memo Dept. of Electrical Engineering and Computer Science, University of California, Berkeley.
30. Zadeh, L. A. (1973), "Outline of a New Approach to the Analysis of Complex Systems and Decision Processes", *IEEE Trans. on System Science and Cybernetic*, Vol. SMC-3, No. 1.
31. Ragade, R. K. (1976) "A Differential Game Formulation of Fuzzy Consensus." Paper presented at TIMS/ORSA joint national meeting in Miami Beach Florida, Nov. 3–5, 1976.

USE OF FUZZY FORMALISM IN PROBLEMS WITH VARIOUS DEGREES OF SUBJECTIVITY

22

Lucas Pun

This paper presents two subjects:

(1) practical applications of fuzzy formalism;
(2) comparative analysis of such applications in systems of varying degrees of subjectivity.

The Research Group in Integrated Automation (GRAI) (Bordeaux, France, created in 1971) has developed successively several projects in the following three types of systems:

(1) industrial processes, the characteristics of which are completely and objectively defined;
(2) production management systems, (which is semi-subjective);
(3) didactical system, (which is completely subjective).

In reality, subjectivity is not the guiding concept for choosing a particular project area. The choice came naturally for a new research group interested in automatic control that was able:

(1) to continue the process control, although no longer in the chemical products, iron and steel, paper, etc., fields, but more oriented toward fruit and food problems.
(2) to start to work in management control problems, which constitute today's (treatable) control problems;
(3) to search for didactical control problems, which are tomorrow's (treatable) control problems.

In each of these fields, two projects are analyzed. In each case, the general control problem is first briefly formulated. Then, attempts are made to answer the following two questions in order:

(1) Is the fuzzy formalism really needed?
(2) If yes, what becomes the control process and what becomes the decision processes?

The necessity of fuzzy formalism, in fact, mainly concerns the formulation of the control problem. This can be stated in the following way: In a control problem, the fuzzy formalism can be considered to be needed, if without using fuzzy formalism the control problem could not be clearly specified. This applies to all the elements of the control, that is:

(1) the state variables or the control variables, either because they cannot be known quantitatively, or because one ignores what are their dimension spaces;
(2) the system structure or parameters, either because the basic formulation problem cannot be solved, or because the identification costs are too high;
(3) the control conditions, namely, the criteria and the constraints, either because they are too complex, or because one cannot decide clearly what their importance is with respect to the objective of the control.

Once the fuzzy formalism is judged needed and introduced, two questions arise concerning the resolution aspect of the problem:

(1) either the conventional control methods are sufficient, with perhaps some easy extrapolation;
(2) or they are not sufficient, and then new operators and new control methods must be found.

INDUSTRIAL PROCESSES

Optimal Control of Olive Oil Manufacturing Process

The process consists of two main parts (Fig. 1): transformation of the olives into olive paste after washing, grinding and malaxation and transformation of the olive paste into olive oil by pressing or by centrifugation. The optimization criteria are to obtain the maximum quantity of the best quality olive oil. Two control loops are used: a predictive control that adjusts the washing-grinding, malaxation-condition according to the characteristics of the input olives and a feedback control that adjusts the pressing conditions according to the characteristics of the olive oil and the olive paste.

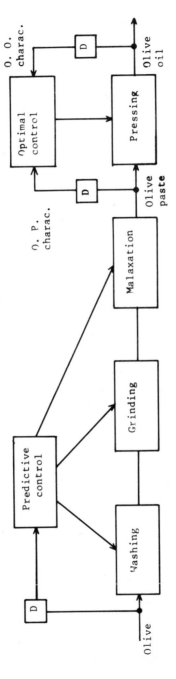

Figure 1. Optimal control of the olive oil manufacturing process.

The fuzzy formalism analysis is useful in two places. Firstly, to take into account the classification of the olive oil quality, generally defined subjectively. Secondly, to reduce the large number of olive characteristics by a suitable grouping so that the number of corresponding control laws remains reasonable.

Ordinarily, the quality of an olive oil is determined (just like wines) by a panel of professional testers according to its acidity content, its impurities, and its flavor; the oil is then judged to belong to one of eight classes $C = (C_1, C_2, \ldots, C_8)$.

In order for automatic control to be possible, an automatic quality analyzer has been developed [2] that measures and analyzes two objective characteristics:

(1) the impurity E (converted into the 2700 Å-ray extinguishing rate).
(2) the acidity A.

For the fuzzy formalism, let $A = (a_1, \ldots, a_6)$ be the set of 6 objectively measured classes of acidity-degree; $E = (e_1, \ldots, e_5)$, the set of 5 objectively measured classes of impurity; $D = (d_1, \ldots, d_{30})$ be the set of 30 couples of (a_i, e_j) elements, $i = 1$ to 6, $j = 1$ to 5; and $P = (p_1, \ldots, p_8)$ be the set of 8 ordered partitions of d elements. The fuzzy application begins with the conversion of the d-elements into the p-elements. The grouping of the 30 d-elements into 8 p-ordered classes is subjective, and then the correspondence between the sets C and P is bijective.

During the online control, the output of the quality analyzer is used for two purposes:

(1) to determine the pressure vs. time program;
(2) to control electrovalves that force the oil into the container corresponding to its respective quality.

Apparently, once the subjectivity of the quality judgment is done, and in a sense eliminated by a fuzzy conversion, the design of the control system becomes conventional, i.e.,

(1) modelization and identification of various transfer laws;
(2) formulation of the optimal control functions and adjustment of these functions to correspond to the various olive, input characteristics.

In reality, practical economical considerations require another use of fuzzy formalism.

In fact, the relevant outputs of the press are oil and water flow rates, the input of the press is the pressure program $p(t)$. Theoretical formulization shows that the input–output relations are two sets of partial derivative equations. Identification of the parameters requires implementation of very costly measuring devices, and is not economically justifiable.

The oil quality is influenced by many characteristics of the input olives, such as maturity, origin, atmospherical conditions, size, nut-hardness, stocking conditions, etc. Ideally, one must find a specific control function for each of the combinations of these parameters. Obviously, this is not economically justifiable. It is therefore necessary to decompose the set of characteristics into unrelated subsets so that a fewer number of control-function classes are needed. This can be viewed as a fuzzy classification problem [5, 16]. Combined experimental and simulation studies are required to get the minimal number of subsets of control functions. This, also, can be viewed as a fuzzy algorithm and mapping problem [17, 8]. Each experimentation represents a point fuzzy-mapped in the decision space. The problem is to search for the optimum set of these points.

Optimal Control of Plum-Drying Tunnels

Plums placed on various hurdles of a wagon, are dried in wind tunnels; each tunnel may contain from 4 to 14 wagons. Hot air is *blown* into the tunnel from one side, and recycled at the other side. The control variables are the heating energy level, the blowing speed, and the flow rates of the recycled air and the fresh air. The plums must be dried so that their humidity content reaches approximately 24% without exploding their skins and without losing their sweet flavor. Without optimization, the over-all drying time is 24 to 30 hours, so that the wagons move at a rate of 2 to 7 hours per unit. The main optimization criterion is to decrease the over-all drying time; a minor criterion is to minimize the energy consumption.

The optimization scheme is depicted in Fig. 2. On the basis of laboratory experimentations, ideal programs of the tunnel temperature gradient, the plum inner temperature gradient and the plum water-loss gradient are found, corresponding to an over-all drying time of less than 15 hours. The actual shapes of these gradients are evaluated on the basis of a limited number of measurements, and by the help of a partial differential equation model. Optimal policies are defined according to the differences of the gradients. This is a typical control problem with incomplete information about the input parameters, and with an unsufficient number of control variables.

The fuzzy formalism is the following. Let $P = (p_1, \ldots, p_8)$ be the set of 8 noncorrelated plum characteristics (maturity, size, ground nature, weather,

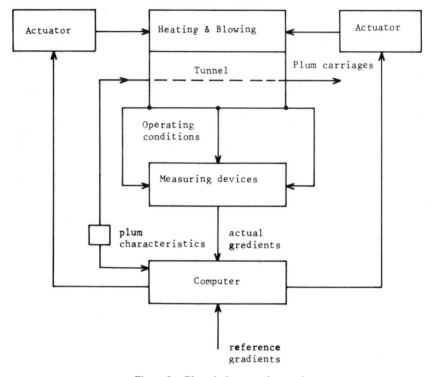

Figure 2. Plum-drying tunnel control.

etc...); $G = (G_1, G_2, G_3)$, the three sets of gradient solutions; $S = (s_1, \ldots, s_m)$, the set of m objectively determinable characteristics; $U = (U_1, U_2, U_3, U_4)$, the four sets of control variables; and $C = (c_1, c_2, \ldots, c_m)$, the set of m elements, each of which is a 4-tuple of u-elements.

The decisions C are then connected to the situatións by three application $\Gamma_1, \Gamma_2, \Gamma_3$.

$$(P, G) \xrightarrow{\Gamma_1} S, \qquad\qquad \Gamma_1 \text{ bijective} \qquad (1)$$

$$U \xrightarrow{\Gamma_2} C, \qquad\qquad \Gamma_2 \text{ injective} \qquad (2)$$

$$C \xrightarrow{\Gamma_3} S, \qquad\qquad \Gamma_3 \text{ bijective} \qquad (3)$$

In this formalization, the sets P, G, Γ_1, Γ_2, Γ_3, are fuzzy sets.

The actual gradients are obtained by solving a set of partial differential equations, while knowing only a small number of the limiting conditions. On the other hand, it is impossible to control three complete gradients (even descretized) by only 4 control variables. Therefore, there is no sense in using analytical optimization algorithms. The control solutions are determined by simulation and then tabulated in the memories of the computer. The online control procedure follows (1), (2), and (3). The mapping Γ_1 between the sets P, G and S is again, as in the olive oil problem, a fuzzy algorithm mapping.

PRODUCTION MANAGEMENT SYSTEMS

The activities of GRAI in this field can be divided into two directions:

(1) analysis of fundamental functions of production management towards its automatic control [11, 12, 13, 14];
(2) research work on precise problems in connection with local industries.

The following examples are extracted from the practical research works falling into the second category.

COMPATIBILITY ANALYSIS
OF LONG-TERM PREDICTIVE PLANNING

In mechanical construction industries, with the long term predictive planning, that is, 1 to 3 years, with a further adjustment period of 3 months to 1 year, can be established on the one hand, on the basis of commercial data, and on the other hand, on adopted production policies (Fig. 3).

The planning is established in terms of the quantities to be produced and the corresponding due dates (for each product). The detailed scheduling for the external purchasing and the internal manufacturing are made only after the short-term planning has been determined. The resource compatibility must be analyzed, however, at this step for various known critical factors. External to the system, this concerns some kinds of rare raw materials, or items that are subcontracted and need a long time for their actual realization. Internal to the system, this concerns some machines or some workshops that might present bottle-neck delays.

In order for the compatibility analysis to be processed automatically, it is necessary to formalize all the data and all the operators. Two categories of parameters must be formalized by using fuzzy sets; these are

(1) external resource parameters: quantities and corresponding ranges of delivery delays;
(2) internal resource parameters: quantities of products, machine loads and their computing accuracy.

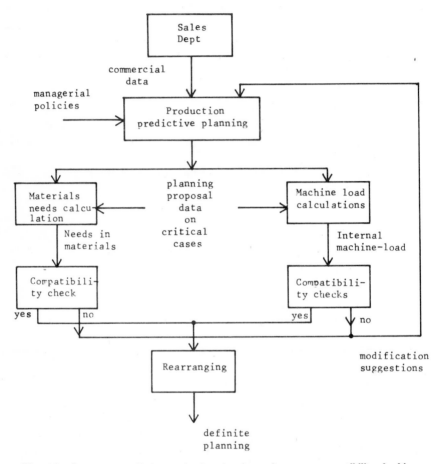

Figure 3.   Long-term predictive production planning and resource-compatibility checking.

For the first case, the use of fuzzy sets is natural. In most practical circumstances, the delivery delays caused by suppliers or subcontractors cannot be determined by objective statistics. Generally, however, the possible ranges of these delivery delays can be estimated, for a given quantity, with a certain degree of probability by using subjective knowledge. For example, for a given material, for various quantities $(q_1, q_2, \ldots, q_m)$, the set of delivery, delay ranges $(d_1, d_2, \ldots, d_m)$ can be determined. Note that the fuzzy formalism can be applied either to the delays, or to the quantities.

In the second case, the use of fuzzy sets is artificial. The reason being to avoid lengthy calculations for obtaining load diagrams of the machines. In fact, if these diagrams are to be calculated exactly, it is necessary

(1) to decompose the products into their elements according to their nomenclatures;
(2) to determine the machine operations for each element;
(3) to adopt a scheduling for machining all the elements.

These are very long and, in fact, unnecessary calculations at the prediction level. Some simplifying computing methods must therefore be adopted: leading each to a class of calculating errors. These errors somehow play the role of probabilities of the first case. The machine-load diagrams are therefore estimated subjective values.

Once the fuzzy sets of the previously mentioned parameters are defined, it becomes possible to automate completely the processing of the decision loops. Curiously, we see that the parameter fuzzy formalism leads in these cases to the definition of two new complex logical operators (multioperators), one of them operates on the binary basis, and the other one on the n-ary basis. We shall illustrate these points by indicating the complete formalism regarding the two subfunctions of the external resource compatibility analysis.

The first subfunction computes the calculation of the quantities of critical materials needed. The outputs are $E = (e_1, e_2, \ldots, e_m)$, the name of the critical items; $Q = (q_1, q_2, \ldots, q_m)$, the needed quantities; and $D = (d_1, d_2, \ldots, d_m)$, the needed due dates. The inputs are δ_0, the predicted date; $P = (p_1, p_2, \ldots, p_n)$, the final products to be manufactured; $C = (c_1, c_2, \ldots, c_n)$, the planned quantities; $\Delta = (\delta_1, \delta_2, \ldots, \delta_n)$, the planned due dates. The parameters are the nomenclature of the final products. Let $D^m = (d_1^m, d_0^m, \ldots, d_n^m)$ be the ranges of the needed purchasing delays for elements to be mounted on the final products; $D^a = (d_1^a, d_2^a, \ldots, d_n^a)$, the ranges of the needed purchasing delays for the elements to be assembled; $D^u = (d_1^u, d_2^u, \ldots, d_n^u)$, the ranges of the needed purchasing delays of the elements to be machined. The constraints are $D \leqslant \Delta - \delta_0$. The operations are to determine E and Q by decomposing the nomenclatures of the P-elements at the successive levels of mounting, assembling and machining; and also according to C. Then, to determine D, according to D^m, D^a and D^u.

The second subfunction is to analyze the external compatibility. The outputs are $\Gamma = (\gamma_1, \gamma_2, \ldots, \gamma_m)$, the binary variables and the compatibility of the critical elements. Let $\gamma_t = U_i \gamma_i$ be the over-all compatibility binary, where

$$\gamma_i = 1, \quad \text{due date compatible}$$

$$\gamma_i = 0, \quad \text{due date noncompatible}$$

and $S = (s_1, s_2, \ldots, s_m)$ are the n-ary variables representing suggestions for decreasing the quantities or the delays. The inputs are the previously defined sets E, Q, D. The parameters (resource characteristics of the suppliers or of the subcontractors) are given by $F_{ik} = (q_{ik}', d_{ik}')$, for a given element e_i with $i = 1, 2, \ldots, m$; $k = 1, 2, \ldots, k$. Also, $Q_i' = (q_{i1}', q_{i2}', \ldots, q_{ik}')$ $Q' = (Q_1', Q_2', \ldots, Q_m')$ $\quad D_i' = (d_{i1}', d_{i2}', \ldots, d_{ik}')$ $\quad D' = (D_1', D_2', \ldots, D_m')$ where the primal problem is q_{ik}', given, and d_{ik}', estimated; and the dual problem is q_{ik}', estimated, and d_{ik}' given (the estimated q_{ik}' or d_{ik}' are fuzzy sets determined for a given probability). The operations are first the compatibility analysis:

(1) Choose $e_i = e_1 \in E$;
(2) Compare $q_1 \in Q$ to all $q_{1k}' \in Q'$, stop at $k = g$, so that $q_{1g}' = q_1$;
(3) Compare d_{ig}' and d_1, determine γ_1 so that

$$\gamma_1 = 1, \qquad \text{if } d_1 \leqslant d_{1g}'$$
$$\gamma_1 = 0, \qquad \text{if } d_1 > d_{ig}'$$

(4) Vary $i = 2, \ldots, m$ and determine the set $\Gamma = (\gamma_1, \gamma_2, \ldots, \gamma_m)$;
(5) Determine $\gamma_t = \overset{m}{\underset{1}{\bigcup}} \gamma_i$.

Formally, all these operations can be summarized into a single operator, which can be called "compatibilizer" C so that

$$\Gamma_t = \bigcup_{i=1}^{m} \gamma_i = \bigcup_{i=1}^{m} (q_i, d_i) C (q_{ik}', d_{ik}'), \qquad k = 1, 2, \ldots, K \tag{4}$$

Secondly, the calculations of the suggestions are performed as:

(1) Start the calculations if $\Gamma_t = 0$;
(2) Compare d_i to the set of elements $d_{ik}' \in D_i'$, stop at a particular value f of k, if

$$d_{if}' = d_i$$

(3) Calculate $S_i = q_i - q_{if}$;
(3) Vary $i = 1, 2, \ldots, m$ in order to determine the complete set

$$S = (s_1, s_2, \ldots, s_m)$$

Formally, all these operations can be summarized into a single operator, which can be designated by the name "suggeror" with the symbol s so that

$$s_i = (q_u, d_i) s (q_{ik}', d_{ik}'), \qquad k = 1, 2, \ldots, K \tag{5}$$

Let us note that in cases where there are several articles, and for each article, there are several potential suppliers (or subcontractors), it is possible to devise an automatic procedure for finding the optimal suggestion set S by using the generalized Hamming distance. For this, we note that

(1) for each candidate set S_i, one calculates the Hamming distance $d_i(S_i, S_0)$ with respect to the zero set S_0;
(2) one defines a search domain $\mathcal{D}$ around the required due date D, (such a domain needs not to be very large);
(3) one prospects all the candidate solutions S_i, and computes the corresponding Hamming distances;
(4) the optimal solution S is given by the smallest Hamming distance.

There is no need for a sophisticated optimization procedure. An enumerative search of all the S-candidates suffices, since the domain $\mathcal{D}$ around D is small.

The same type of procedure can be extended to take into account a more complex situation including cost consideration. While the satisfaction of the delays is a "must," that of the minimum cost is a "wish." In the early prediction stage, delays and costs generally are not fixed on a contractual basis. Subjective evaluations are therefore needed. Formally, instead of mapping evaluated delays, one can map combinations of delays and costs for given amounts of items and given suppliers. The minimum cost solution can be determined by a similar procedure.

Optimal Scheduling in Cutting Workshop *J* for Dress-Making in the Clothing Industry

The industrial manufacturing of dresses comprises two main processes, the cutting process and the finishing process [9]. The cutting process is formed by two lines of operations (Fig. 4), one for the main fabric and the other for the lining. Several operations are effectuated on each line, such as cutting, mending, thermopasting, in the work-stations 1, 2, 3, etc. The outputs of the two lines are assembled for each cloth in the station A, where various ornaments are added and the whole sent to the finishing process. The inputing orders are characterized by the fabric of the dress, the model, the color, the size, etc. The process is characterized by various known processing times that differ from one dress to another, and from one station to another. The problem is how to schedule the imputing orders so that

(1) over-all pass time θ is minimal;

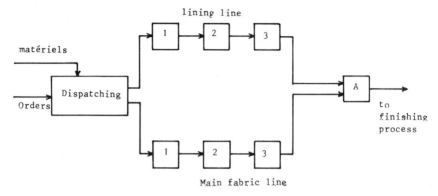

Figure 4. Cutting process in the cloth industry.

(2) there is minimum waiting queue before the work stations;
(3) there is synchronisation at *A* of the lines for the same dress.

Analyzing the problem under a control point of view, it is possible to define some of the control elements, but not all of them. The control criterion is triple. Let θ_t be the pass time of the main line: θ_1 be the pass time of the lining line; N_ω be the vector the components of which are the lengths of the various waiting queues. Then the control criteria are

$$1° \quad \min \theta = \max(\theta_t, \theta_1)$$
$$2° \quad \min \delta\theta = \theta_t - \theta_1 \tag{6}$$
$$3° \quad \min N_\omega$$

The parameters of the system are the various operating times of the work stations, these times depend on the kinds of dresses to be manufactured, but they are known. The difficulty is now to define the control variables *u* and the state variables *x* and also the relations between (u, x) and $(\theta_1, \theta_t, N_\omega)$. At the input of the system, we find the sequence of the orders. The succession order of this sequence certainly influences the values of the criteria, but we ignore how it does the influences. Therefore, we need to define relevant characteristics of the sequences and to find the relations between them and the criteria. The first point leads to the use of fuzzy sets, and the second to a way of solving the control problem.

Two sets of relevant characteristics are chosen, colors and sizes. The elements of the size set are ordered; the elements of the color set are not. In fact, the elements themselves of these sets do not influence the values of the criteria. The latters depends on the successive orders of the elements. On the basis of these considerations, two fuzzy sets are defined for each given collection of dresses. Let $(V_1, V_2, \ldots, V_m)$ be the designation of the set of dresses. According to the knowledge of the various operating times, the set is rearranged. At the first instance, they are rearranged according to the color succession that causes the least cleaning time of the work station. This gives for instance, for 7 cloths:

$$Y_1 = (V_3, V_2, V_5, V_7, V_1, V_4, V_6) \tag{7}$$

A set C is then created from Y_1 so that

$$C = (C_1, C_2, C_3, C_4, C_5, C_6, C_7) \tag{8}$$
$$C_1 = V_3, C_2 = V_2, \ldots, C_7 = V_6$$

At the second instance, the dresses are ordered according to the size succession that causes the least cutting time. This gives for instance

$$Y_2 = (V_5, V_1, V_6, V_4, V_3, V_7, V_2) \tag{9}$$

which is converted into a new set S so that

$$S = (s_1, s_2, s_3, s_4, s_5, s_6, s_7)$$
$$s_1 = V_5, s_2 = V_1, s_3 = V_6, \ldots, s_7 = V_2 \tag{10}$$

Let M be the total number of kinds of dresses in a given collection; $R = (r_i)$, $i = 1$ to M, the set of M numbers of dresses of each kind to be produced; $X = (x_1)$, $i = 1$ to M, the M choices of numbers with the constraint $x_i r_i$, all i; and $U = (u_1, u_2, \ldots, u_p)$, the set of sequences of M values of x, with $p = M$. The optimal control problem is formulated as follows:

$$\min J = N\,(u, \theta_t, \theta_1, M)$$
$$\text{with constraints } |\theta| < \theta_M; \ |\delta\theta| < \epsilon \tag{11}$$

and so that the M elements of the optimal solution u occupy geometrically one of the three privilege configurations in the test-matrix TM (Fig. 5): with (1) an uninterrupted column F_1; (2) an uninterrupted line F_2; and (3) a connex figure F_3, as close as possible to the upper left corner.

For solving this nonconventional problem, a certain number of methods are under experimentation, such as

(1) heuristic experimentations and determination of rationals from the results;
(2) integer linear and nonlinear programming with fuzzy boundries of feasible space.

Results of the first approach are given elsewhere [6].

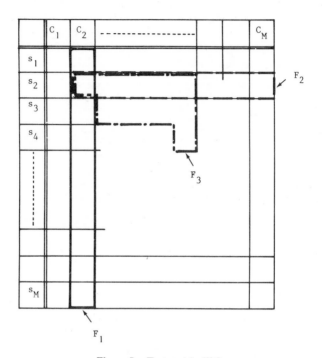

Figure 5. Test matrix TM.

DIDACTICAL SYSTEMS

Game-data logger

There are two problems—a pedagogical problem and a control problem. The pedagogical problem is to teach young children of 5 to 8 years old what is the *recurrence* concept by playing a game called "Hanoi Tower." The control problem (or rather the analysis problem) is to develop equipment that helps analyze the learning processes of these children. The equipment must operate automatically, since the moves in the play may be relatively fast.

The "Hanoi Tower" game is as follows. On a plate (Fig. 6) there are three vertical sticks A B C. On stick A, there are n discs (D_1, D_2, ,..., D_n), the diameters of which decrease with n. The game consists of displacing the pile of n discs from A to the stick C, so that the order of the pile remains the same. The rules of the play are:

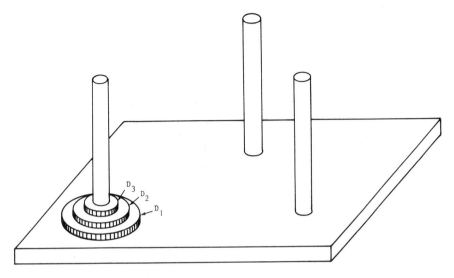

Figure 6. Pedagogical Game "Hanoi Tower."

(1) only one disc for each move, a move is achieved when the disc is on the stick;

(2) no disc, on any stick, can be placed above another one of smaller diameter.

It can be shown that, regardless the value of n, the problem always has a solution, and this solution bears the form of recurrent relations. In effect, if it is possible to displace p disc from A to C by a sequence S_{AC} of moves, it is possible to displace p discs from A to B by a sequence S_{AB}, or from B to C by a sequence S_{BC}. If there are $p+1$ discs on A, the solution $S_{AC}(p+1)$ can be obtained by the following manipulations

(1) use $S_{AB}(p)$;

(2) put the last disc $(p+1)$th from A to C;

(3) use $S_{BC}(p)$.

Since $S_{AC}(p=1)$, $S_{AC}(p=2)$, $S_{AC}(p=3)$ are easily found, the sequences $S_{AC}(p)$ for higher values of p can be learnt by recurrent relations.

The learning process L consists of a sequence of decision strategies used by the learner. Knowledge of the learner's behavior B can be made by considering the following decisions. Let d_1 be the execution of a short term strategy; d_2, the elaboration of a new strategy; d_3, the return back after an unsuccessful move, so that B is a sequence of decisions d_1, d_2, d_3. The main purposes of the L analysis for an n-disc problem is to find:

(1) how the learner dominates strategy structures of the modules, the orders of which are smaller than n;
(2) how the learner builds the n-modules from the preceding ones.

Unfortunately, the decisions d_1, d_2, d_3 are of subjective nature, and therefore cannot be measured directly. A subjective-to-objective conversion, of a fuzzy conversion is necessary to make the analysis possible. The objective dimensions adopted are the following. Let $C = (c_1, c_2, \ldots)$ be the set of stick-state configurations formed by the relative positions of the discs on the sticks after each move and $\theta = (\theta_1, \theta_2, \ldots)$ the set of time intervals between two decisions or between two disc-takeoffs. The fuzzy conversion is therefore defined as an application $\Gamma\Gamma = (C, \theta) \rightarrow B$.

At the present time, the development of the automatic data logger is achieved. The apparatus consists mainly of two parts:

(1) the game itself (sticks and discs);
(2) the logger that converts the C and θ data automatically into electrically coded signals, and records these signals on a paper tape.

A number of such experiments were conducted in primary schools. The research work under way has two aims:

(1) to establish formally the elements of Γ;
(2) to find the L-models according to the characteristics of the B-sequences.

OPTIMAL MANAGEMENT OF DIDACTICAL SYSTEMS

By adopting an enormous simplification, the management of a didactical system can be schematically represented by a set of four subsystems [7]. Let A be the structurer of the knowledge; B, the transmitter; C, the assimilator; and D, the coordinator (Fig. 7).

The subsystems A, B, and C are characterized by their individual parameters, their initial conditions, and eventual perturbations. The optimal management problem is posed to the coordinator in the following way: "Knowing the states of A, B, C of the generated and transmitted knowledge, and of the assimilation, under given constraints and pedagogical criteria, what kind of actions must suggest the coordinator:

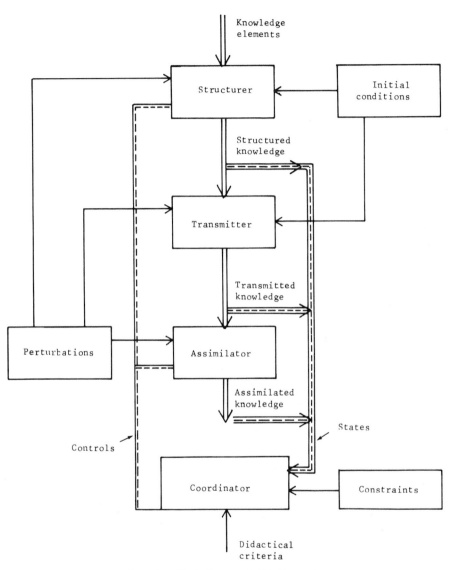

Figure 7. Block diagram of didactical systems.

(1) to modify the structure of the knowledge,
(2) to modify the transmission media,
(3) to influence the assimilator (learner) so that the didactical system operates optimally according to the predetermined criteria."

Such a formulation does not lead to any possibility of formalization if the criteria were not better defined. In order to avoid empty philosophical discussions, we do not use any cultural or humanistic considerations. The kind of criteria we adopt is of a technical nature such as

(1) speed of assimilation
(2) degree of assimilation
(3) over-all learning time.

In principle, these types of criteria can be evaluated on the basis of some objective measurements.

Using the conventional optimal control formalism, a rough fuzzy formalism can be implemented in the following way. Let $Y = (y_1, y_2, ...)$ be the set of measurable quantities, such as the speed of assimilating concepts, the speed of solving simple problems, the speed of solving complex problems, etc.. Let $X = (x_1, x_2, ...)$ be the set of significant characteristics of the assimilator, such as creativity, fatigue, serenity, and capacity of concentration. Let $U = (U^g, U^t, U^a)$ be the set of the three subsets of control characteristics; $U^g = (u_1^g, u_2^g, ...)$ the subset of control characteristics related to the knowledge generator, such as the various strategies for structuring the knowledge; $U^t = (u_1^t, u_2^t, ...)$, the subset of control characteristics related to the knowledge transmission media, such as the various ways of implementing the transmission media; $U^a = (u_1^a, u_2^a, ...)$ be the subset of control characteristics related to the ambiance in which the assimilator is put, such as being alone or in a group, relaxation possibilities, conversational possibilities, etc.. Under such a formulation, the elements of the sets Y, U^g, and U^t are the objective elements, those of the set X are the subjective elements and those of the subset U^a are semi-objective elements.

Let J denote the criterion, C the constraints, and the various conditions u_0, x_0. The optimal control problem is then to optimize $J = J(u, y)$, u, U, $C(u, x) = 0$, $U(t = 0) = U_0$, and

$$x(t = 0) = x_0. \tag{12}$$

At the present time, this formalization permits the location of the following three types of research problems:

(1) validation research, consisting of finding significant practical elements of the sets X, Y, U;

(2) modelization and identification, consisting of finding the applications

$$\Gamma_1 : X \to Y \qquad (13)$$

$$\Gamma_2 : U \to X \qquad (14)$$

(3) optimization, consisting of finding $u \in U$ solving the preceding optimal problem.

CONCLUSION

Fuzzy formalism is useful in all the three types of complex systems studied here, regardless of whether their characteristics can be defined objectively or not. In the case of the industrial processes, however, the reason for its use does not seem intrinsic. In the olive oil case, the reason is the subjective human appreciation. In the plum-drying case, it is a question of approximation. (See Table 1 that summarises all the results).

Table 1
Fuzzy Experience in Various Typical Applications

Example	Application Point of the Fuzzy Formalism	Control Problem
(1) Olive oil quality analyzer	Quality characteristics state variables transfer laws	Objective optimization problem
(2) Plum drying tunnel	Perturbations States Control laws	Fuzzy modelization problem Fuzzy optimization
(3) Predictive planning	Parameters Operators	Objective analysis
(4) Cutting workshop scheduling	System parameters Control variables Control laws	Heuristic optimization
(5) Game data logger	States Learning strategies	Fuzzy analysis
(6) Optimal didactical systems	State Measurement of the state Control of the state	Identification of the relations Heuristic optimization

The application points of fuzzy formalism cover every element of a control system:

the state signal in cases (1), (2), (5), (6);
the control signal in case (2), (4);
the system parameters in cases (3), (4);
the control laws in cases (2), (4), (5), (6);
the measurement laws in cases (1), (5).

In studying production management systems and the didactical systems, it seems evident that the need for fuzzy formalism is due to the presence of human beings. The effect of such a presence is shown, however, in two distinct ways

(1) internally, such as the operating times of the workers in case (4), or learning behavior in cases (5) and (6);
(2) externally, such as the fuzzy control laws in cases (4), (5), and (6) that are to be implemented by human beings under uncertain conditions.

Formally, the sets of fuzzy signals are well-defined; they are generally sets of ordered numerical values. The sets of fuzzy algorithms (or operators) are not defined so clearly. They are formally

(1) the logical operators in case (3);
(2) the correspondance matrix in case (4);
(3) undetermined in case (6).

When fuzzy formalism is applied to more than signals, the subjectiveness is converted into the objectiveness (cases (1), (2), (3)) and the control problem becomes a conventional, completely objective problem. When fuzzy formalism is applied to system laws, the control problem becomes generally very difficult (cases (2), (4), (6)). Unlike ordinary objective control situations, the modelization problem and the optimization problem seem to be intimately correlated, so that a solution to one seems very much dependent on how the other problem is considered.

In this respect, the subjectiveness of the system introduces, however, some nuances:

(1) In case (2), the various characteristics of the plums can be defined univoquely, after suitable experimentations, the corresponding optimal control laws can also be determined univoquely.

(2) In case (4), there are one state space (operating times) and several control spaces (color succession, size succession), once the control laws are identified objectively, the optimization problem is defined univoquely and objectively.

(3) In case (6), let Γ_3 be the application leading to optimal control

u:

$$\Gamma_3 : (\text{eq.}(21)) \to u \qquad (24)$$

since both the assimilator and the coordinator are two-sided subjective elements, the determination of Γ_1, Γ_2, and Γ_3 depends one on the other.

Finally, fuzzy formalism is a useful tool for treating decision-processes in systems where the characteristics are determined subjectively. In partially subjective situations, an objective methodology may be found and implemented leading to optimal decisions. In completely subjective situations, a common agreement (consensus) of an operating basis must be defined *a priori*.

REFERENCES

1. A. Almar, "Régulation et Optimisation Multicritère du Fonctionnement d'un Atelier de Coupe dans l'Industrie de Vêtement," Thèse de Docteur de Spécialité, U. Bordeaux, Nov. 1975.
2. M. Blazquez and Kimbatsa, "Analyseur Automatique de la Qualité de l'Huile d'Olive," *Grasas y aceites, 26,* No. 4, (July 1975).
3. J. Boebion and L. Pun, "A Series–Parallel Multicriteria Model for a Scheduling Problem in a Dress-making Industry," Conf. Multicriteria Decision-Making, Jouy-en-Josas, May 1975.
4. C. Bourcy, "Étude de la Saisie des Données dans les Jeux Pédagogiques et Réalisation d'un Appareil pour le Jeu "Tour d' Hanoi." Thèse de Docteur de Spécialité, Bordeaux, Sept. 1974.
5. S. S. L. Chang, "On Fuzzy Algorithm and Mapping," *IFAC Sixth Congr. Special Interest Session on Fuzzy Decisions,* Boston, Mass., 1975.
6. E. Diday and G. Govaert, "Apprentissage et Mesures de Ressemblances."
7. J. C. Eyheraguibel, J. Grislain, and L. Pun, "Sur Quelques Aspects de la Gestion Scientifique des Systèmes Didactiques," Revue de Pédagogie INRDP, No. 33, Oct. 1975.
8. A. Kaufmann, *Introduction à la Théorie des Sous-Ensembles Flous,* Masson & Cie, Paris, vol. 1, 1973 and vol. 2, 1975.
9. L. Latecoere, "Contribution à l'Étude d'un Système d'Ordonnancement Adaptatif dans une Industrie Textile," Thèse de Docteur de Spécialité, U. Bordeaux, Feb. 1974.
10. L. Latecoere, J. Boebion and L. Pun, "Model Adaptive Scheduling for Solving Perturbations in the Dress-Making Industry," Third Inter. Conf. Prod. Manag., Amherst, Mass., Aug. 1975.

11. L. Pun, "Formulation et Formalisation des Problèmes de Gestion Automatique de Production," *Colloque PAC,* Bordeaux, Nov. 1973.
12. L. Pun, "Couplage Entre les Problèmes et les Méthodes de la Gestion de Production Automatisée," *J. AFCET* (June 4, 1974).
13. L. Pun, "Formalisme Flou dans les Problèmes de Gestion Automatisée de Production," Production Management Seminar, Eur. Inst. Adv. Studies Manag. Brussels, Sept. 1974.
14. L. Pun, "Analyse Détaillée des Fonctions de Gestion de Production en Vue d'une Informatisation Automatisée," Séminaire ADEPA, Paris, Nov. 1974.
15. L. Pun and G. Doumeingts, "Fuzzy Decision Process for Solving Production Management Problem in the Industry of Mechanical Construction," Third Inter. Conf. Prod. Manag., Amherst, Mass., Aug. 1975.
16. R. Tanaka, "Learning in Fuzzy Machines Execution of Fuzzy Programs," *Symp. Comp.* Oriented Learning Process, Bonas, France, Aug. 1974.
17. L. A. Zadeh, "Fuzzy Sets," *Inf. Control* **8** (June 1965), 338–353.
18. L. A. Zadeh, "Fuzzy Algorithms," *Inf. Control* **12** (1968), 94–102.

FUZZY CLUSTER OF DEMAND WITHIN A REGIONAL SERVICE SYSTEM

23

D. Carlucci and F. Donati

The distribution process of the users of a given service within a whole system of service centers has been largely studied and several mathematical models have been proposed. Mainly these models can be classified in deterministic such as [5,6] or in probabilistic such as [7,8,9,10,11]. In the first case, the human decision in the service center choice is modeled in terms of some optimality criterion. In the second one, it is modeled in terms of some probability distribution.

Now it is difficult to accept humans operating strictly in terms of minimization of a mathematical cost function. At the same time introducing an uncertainty by the assumption that humans are taking their decisions in a random way seems to be rather extraneous to human nature.

The concept of fuzziness introduced by Zadeh [1,3,4] seems more suited to express uncertainty in human behavior. In this context, the problem seems to be better stated in terms of a fuzzy model rather than of deterministic or probabilistic ones.

The main line of the work developed here is as follows. Given a set of users and a set of service centers distributed over a given region, a fuzzy mathematical model is proposed to forsee the clustering of the user in the subsets of the customers of the same service center. The problem is developed by modeling by a fuzzy algorithm of the human-decision process, under the following assumptions:

(1) In the considered region, attraction centers and corresponding influence areas are defined and known for the concerns of the main basic services (work, shopping, school,...). Moreover, we assume that this configuration is not influenced by the network of considered service centers. In any case, we assume that the considered service centers are not located in all the mentioned attraction centers. So that the problem of evaluating the influence areas for our service center is not trivial.

Acknowledgment: Research in part supported by Casa di Risparmio di Torino; Dr. V. Lisanti proposed for the problem, for which the authors are grateful.

(2) Each user is assumed to be a regular customer of some service center.

(3) Different levels of service are considered, where higher levels indicate more specialized services, less frequently demanded. So centers and users are classified in levels, with the following qualifications. Any center offers at the same time all the services of a level lower than its one. Any customer demands the services up to his own level.

(4) All the service centers of the same level offer equivalent services (the same goods at the same prices).

The mathematical model is derived by translating into a fuzzy algorithm the following considerations:

> Customers choose among all the available service centers some which are "comfortably located," "not much crowded," and "corresponding to their demand."
>
> In order to be comfortably located a center may be located close to the customer's residence or work place or shopping center or, moreover, in any other place where the customer needs to go usually. Of course, service centers located along the way from the residence to the mentioned attraction centers are a little less comfortable. Locations where the customer has to go on purpose have to be considered uncomfortable; moreover the further they are far from his residence the more uncomfortable they are.
>
> A center is considered crowded when its mean queue time is long.
>
> A customer would like all his demands of any level to be satisfied by the same center; anyway, whenever he is more comfortable, he chooses different centers for the different levels of his demand, particularly by considering that his demand of lower level services is more frequent.

The idea of a center-comfortable location can be expressed by associating to each user a fuzzy set of the centers comfortably located. Given an admissible distribution of the customers within the whole service center system, the idea of "crowding" is quantified by the definition of a fuzzy set of the not crowded centers.

In order to model the user decision-process, let us ignore at the beginning the preference of the user to present all his demand of any level to the same center. Then let us consider a user which needs services of a given level l. His decision is modeled by the product of the fuzzy set of the comfortably located centers by the fuzzy set of the not crowded centers, when only centers which offer services of the specified level are considered. In other words, the decision is expressed for each user and for each level of his demand by a fuzzy set over the center set.

Then, the preference of the user to present all his demands to the same center, when it does not result in too much uncomfort, is considered as follows. A center which offers services only up to a certain level l is excluded from the l-level decision fuzzy set of a user who also has demands for services of a higher level if there exists a higher level center that presents a larger membership value.

These considerations are expressed in a more rigorous form in the next section. There, assuming that the fuzzy sets of the comfortably located centers and that of the not crowded ones are given, the fuzzy clustering model is introduced.

The above mentioned fuzzy sets definitions appear, then, very important. They, indeed, summarize all our knowledge on the geographical and economic configuration of the region, together with an evaluation of the influence of the local usages and customs in the clustering process.

The definition of the above fuzzy sets is discussed in the next sections.

FUZZY CLUSTERING MODEL

The services are classified in k levels. A customer of level $l \leqslant k$ demands for service up to the level l. A center of level 1 offers services up to the level l.

Users are partitioned into a class X of n subsets x, where each subset $x \in X$ contains all the users who live in the same compact geographical area (i.e., borough, village, ...).

Each subset x is characterized by a k-dimensional vector $D(x)$ whose lth-components gives the number of the users belonging to x whose highest demand level is l.

The set of the service centers is denoted by Y and is assumed to contain m elements y. The set Y is subdivided into k disjoint subsets $Y_l(l = 1, 2, ..., k)$ according to the highest level of the offered service. Each center y is characterized by a k-dimensional vector $C(y)$ whose lth-component gives the number of customers who demand services at the level l from y.

Then, a function $\mu_y(C(y))$ is given for each $y \in Y$ which gives the membership value of y in the fuzzy set $A \subset Y$ of the "not crowded" centers. Then, according to the different service level, the fuzzy set A is partitioned into the fuzzy subsets $A_l(l = 1, 2, ..., k)$.

Let B denote the fuzzy set contained in $X \times Y$ whose elements (x,y) represent a supply center y comfortably located with respect to the demand center x. Let $\mu(x,y)$ be the membership function of B.

For any fixed $x \in X$, $\mu(x,y)$ defines over Y the fuzzy set B_x of the centers y comfortably located with respect to x.

Let us now consider a customer of level l ($1 \leqslant l \leqslant k$) belonging to x. For each level $j \leqslant l$ of his demand, his decision is modeled by the following fuzzy sets S_{xlj} with membership $\mu_{xlj}(y)$.

$$S_{xll} = B_x \left(A_k \cup A_{k-1} \cup \cdots \cup A_l \right)$$

$$S_{xl(l-1)} = S_{xll} \cup \left(B_x A_{l-1} \right)_\alpha; \qquad \alpha = \max \mu_{xll}(y) \qquad (1)$$

$$S_{xlj} = S_{sl(j+1)} \cup \left(B_x A_j \right)_\alpha; \qquad \alpha = \max \mu_{xl(j+1)}(y)$$

where AB denotes the algebraic product of the fuzzy sets A and B ($\mu(y) = \mu_a(y) \cdot \mu_b(y)$), $A \cup B$ denotes the union of the fuzzy sets A and B ($\mu(y) = \max(\mu_a(y), \mu_b(y))$); and $(A)_\alpha$ denotes the fuzzy set defined by the membership $\mu(y)$ such that

$$\mu(y) = \mu_a(y), \quad \text{if } \mu_a(y) \geqslant \alpha$$

$$\mu(y) = 0, \qquad \text{if } \mu_a(y) < \alpha$$

Then we assume that customers of level l belonging to x apply to y for services of level J ($J \leqslant l$) with a probability $P_{jl}(x,y)$ proportional to $\mu_{xlj}(y)$[2].

$$p_{jl}(x,y) = \frac{\mu_{xlj}(y)}{\displaystyle\sum_{i=1}^{m} \mu_{xli}(y_i)} \qquad (2)$$

Assuming, now, by definition $p_{jl}(x,y) = 0$ when $j > l$, let $P(x,y)$ be the $k \times k$ matrix consisting of the elements $p_{jl}(x,y)$. The vector obtained by the product

$$P(x,y) \cdot D(x) \qquad (3)$$

expresses the expected value of customers x of whom apply to y for each service level. Then the expected value $C(y)$ of all customers applying to y results by summation of (3) when x runs over X is

$$C(y) = \sum_{i=1}^{n} P(x_i, y) D(x_i) \qquad (4)$$

The relations (1) through (4) allow us to obtain the solution of the clustering problem. Anyway, it is not easy to get a general closed solution. Indeed, (1) requires that the vector $C(y)$ be known in order for it to be possible to compute the membership function of A. On the contrary $C(y)$ is obtained by (4) only at the end of the computation process. The solution can be obtained by the following iterative procedure.

Assume an initial tentative value $C_0(y)$ of the distribution of customers among all the centers y, developing the computations from (1) to (4), a new customer distribution $C_0'(y)$ is obtained. If $C_0(y)$ is equal to $C_0'(y)$ then it represents a problem solution. On the contrary, a new tentative value can be defined as follows

$$C_1(y) = C_0(y) + G[C_0'(y) - C_0(y)]$$ (5)

When a suitable small value of G is given the convergence could be proved in the assumption that infinitesimal variations of the tentative value of $C(y)$ do not produce finite variations of the resulting value $C'(y)$.

FUZZY SET OF COMFORTABLY LOCATED CENTERS

In this section, some motivation will be given in order to illustrate that the idea of a comfortable location can be expressed by a fuzzy set. As it will be pointed out later, the definition of this fuzzy set is based on a study of the local usages and customs in addition to a process of objective data about the viability (transport service) of the region, and the location of the attraction centers for the main basic services.

Considering a demand center x and a supply center y, on the basis of objective data the mean trip cost (transport expenses and time capitalization) for operation can be evaluated.

About this evaluation we only remark the necessity of taking into account the fact that y may be an attraction center of x for basic services. In such a case, the mean trip cost has to be evaluated by discounting those trips that might be motivated by higher priority needs.

Similarly, the fact has to be considered that y might be along the trips from x to one of its main attraction center. Also, in this case, a discount of the mean trip cost has to be introduced.

Let $c(x,y)$ be the mean trip cost for operation paid by a user x who was a customer of y. The membership $\mu(x,y)$ of the fuzzy set B is defined as a function of $c(x,y)$ depending on some parameters that have to be evaluated by considering both the local usages and customs and the business amount of the considered service.

The authors consider suitable the following function

$$\mu(x,y) = e^{-\left(\frac{c(x,y)}{c_0}\right)^\beta}$$ (6)

which is illustrated by Fig. 1.

The parameter c_0 states the cost value at which the membership value is equal to 0.367. This parameter allows us mainly to take into account the service business amount. It is, indeed, a scale factor.

The parameter β influences the transition rate of the membership from 1 to 0. It allows us to consider the local usages and customs. In fact, large

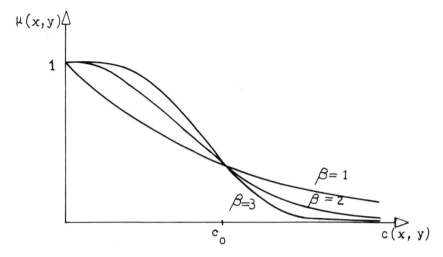

Figure 1. Membership of centers comfortably located with respect to x versus the cost.

values of β in (6) correspond to a general agreement among people to consider as not uncomfortable trips of relatively large costs.

FUZZY SET OF NOT CROWDED CENTERS

Here the concept of crowding is used to express the disease of being in a waiting line. In order to model such a disease in terms of a fuzzy set, also in this case as in that previously considered, two factors have to be considered. One is the mean waiting time which can be objectively evaluated; the other is the people impatience which is dependent on local usage and customs.

Given the vector $C(y)$ of the customers of the supply center y and knowing the center capacity, the mean waiting time can be evaluated. Let $c_w(y)$ be the capitalization of the mean waiting time of y. The membership of the fuzzy set A can be defined by a function similar to (6):

$$\mu_y(C(y)) = e^{-\left(\frac{c_w(y)}{c_{w0}}\right)^{\beta_w}} \tag{7}$$

The meaning of the parameters c_{w0} and β_w is the same as in (6), but, of course, different values are used.

CONCLUSION

The clustering model proposed has two main aspects of novelty. The first is to have modeled the human behavior by a fuzzy process. The other consists of the fact that the crowding of service centers is considered. The capacities of the service centers are taken into account and are never overcrowded.

REFERENCES

1. R. E. Bellman and L. A. Zadeh, "Decision-making in a fuzzy environment," *Man. Sci.* **17** (Dec. 1970), B-141-B-164.
2. B. J. L. Berry and W. Garrison, "Recent Developments of Central Place Theory," *Papers Proc. Regional Sci. Assoc.* **4**, 1958.
3. L. Curry, "The Geography of Service Centers within Towns: the Elements of an Operation Approach," *Proc. I.G.U. Symp. Urban Geography*, Lund, 1962.
4. L. Curry, "Central Places in the Random Spatial Economy," *J. Reg. Sci.* **7** (1967), 217–235.
5. M. F. Dacey, "A Probability Model for Central Place Location," *Ann. Assoc. Geogr.* **56** (1966), 550–568.
6. W. L. Garrison, B. Berry, D. F. Marble, J. D. Nystuen, and R. L. Morril, "Studies of Highways Developments and Geographic Change," U. Wash. Press, Seattle, Wash., 1959.
7. G. Olsson, "Distance and Human Interaction," Regional Sciences Research Institute, Philadelphia, Penn., 1965.
8. G. Olsson, "Central Place Systems, Spatial Interaction and Stochastic Processess," *Reg. Sci. Assoc. Papers Proc.* **18** (1966), 13–45.
9. L. A. Zadeh, "Fuzzy Sets," *Infor. Control*, **8** (1965), 338–353.
10. L. A. Zadeh, "Fuzzy Algorithms," *Infor. Control* **12** (1968), 94–102.
11. L. A. Zadeh, "Outline of a New Approach to the Analysis of Complex Systems and Decision Processes," *IEEE Trans. on Systems, Man and Cybernetics*, **1** (1973), 28–44.

FUZZY DECISON-MAKING IN PROSTHETIC DEVICES 24

George N. Saridis and Harry E. Stephanou

Decision-making in a fuzzy environment has recently attracted considerable attention. Several authors [1,3,13,14] have presented the theoretical formulation of the problem and have developed the appropriate mathematics to deal with it. The formulation of a fuzzy automaton as a multilevel decision-maker has also been proposed and investigated by several researchers [3,12,14]. Therefore, there is no question about the theoretical value of fuzzy decision-making, but its practical applications are rather scarce.

The recent investigation of Zadeh [5] has successfully associated linguistic methods to fuzzy decision-making, while the work of Fung and Fu has suggested possible control applications of fuzzy automata. Projecting the above ideas, one may construct an advanced control system as a three-level decision-maker that would accept qualitative commands, interpret them linguistically, then convey them to a fuzzy automaton that would coordinate the essential primitives of the desired motion to be executed by self-organizing control subsystems [9].

Such a controller should have direct applications to systems and must demonstrate exceptional "intelligence" in order to perform composite tasks defined by qualitative commands like speech or signals from a nervous system. An interesting application of such an intelligent controller is proposed in the next section to drive a prosthetic device for upper-extremity amputees.

Fuzzy and linguistic decision-making is proposed for the hierarchical computer control of a powered prosthesis to replace the upper limb of scapulothoracic amputees. The device under consideration has seven degrees of freedom (Fig. 1):

Shoulder flexion-extension	Wrist rotation
Shoulder abduction-adduction	Wrist flexion-extension
Humeral rotation	Hand prehension
Elbow flexion-extension	

Acknowledgment: Supported by NSF grant no. ENG 74-17586.

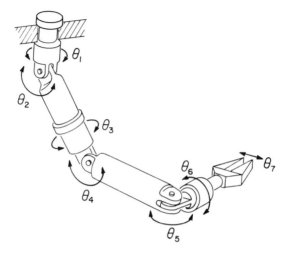

Figure 1. Seven degree of freedom prosthetic arm.

Investigation of such a device has been performed by researchers using rather heuristic approaches [6].

The Lagrange equations of motion were used to simulate the arm dynamics on the digital computer. The intricacy of the model precludes any variational approach. Instead, self-organizing control [10] represents an attractive alternative because it circumvents many problems arising from the complexity of the model and provides the system with a learning capability, which is a valuable feature in a behavior related problem.

The system input consists of a command emanating from the brain. The transmission of the command through nervous activity, speech, electromyographic signals, and its recognition by the prosthesis are beyond the scope of this article. However, because of the close relation of the command to mental activity, a linguistic description is appropriate. Furthermore, by the very essence of human behavior, the command and the resulting feedback signals can only be evaluated in a fuzzy way. A three-level hierarchical controller for a p-degree of freedom generalized bionic arm is depicted in Fig. 2.

DYNAMIC MODEL OF BIONIC ARM

The motion of the arm can be described by the position of the wrist and the orientation of the hand. The first four joints, corresponding to $\theta_1, \theta_2, \theta_3, \theta_4$ are involved in the former, while the last three joints are involved in the latter. The positioning of the wrist is the major control problem, while the

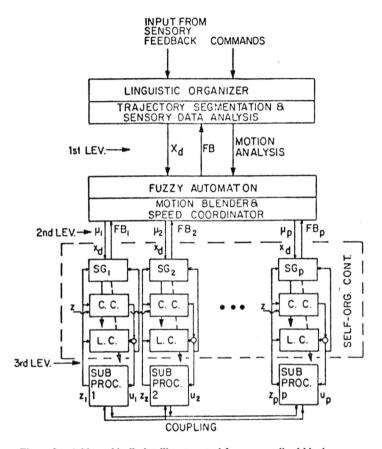

Figure 2. A hierarchically intelligent control for a generalized bionic arm.

proper orientation of the hand is decided by the higher decision levels in the hierarchy. A simplified representation of the arm assumes point masses, infinitesimal limb thickness, and ideal joints.

The dynamic model may be derived from Lagrange's equation of classical mechanics:

$$\frac{d}{dt}\frac{\partial E_k}{\partial \theta_i} - \frac{\partial E_i}{\partial \dot{\theta}_i} + \frac{\partial E_p}{\partial \theta_i} = T_i, \qquad i = 1,\ldots,4 \tag{1}$$

where T_i is the input torque applied to the ith joint; E_k and E_p denote the kinetic and potential energy of the system, respectively.

Substitution of the appropriate expressions for the energy terms results in the following set of ordinary differential equations

$$\ddot{\theta} = D^{-1}(H+T) \tag{2}$$

where $\theta = [\theta_1 \theta_2 \theta_3 \theta_4]^T$, the 4×4 matrix D and the 4×1 vector H are nonlinear functions of θ and $\dot{\theta}$. Let $F = D^{-1}H$, and $U = D^{-1}T$, then

$$\ddot{\theta} = F + U \tag{3}$$

Thus, the arm model is linear in U, and an input quantity is obtained from the actual input T by a nonlinear transformation. The basic principle underlying the hierarchical approach to the control problem is the decomposition of the four joint processes into four subprocesses, each corresponding to one mechanical degree of freedom. Thus, the equation of motion of the ith subsystem is

$$\ddot{\theta}_i = f_i + u_i \tag{4}$$

where $F = [f_1 f_2 f_3 f_4]^T$, and $U = [u_1 u_2 u_3 u_4]^T$. Rewriting (4) for a stochastic enviornment,

$$\dot{x}_i = A_i x_i + B_i(f_i + u_i + \eta_i) \tag{5}$$

$$z_i = C_i x_i + \nu_i, \, i = 1, \ldots, 4,$$

where

$$x_i = \begin{bmatrix} \theta_i \\ \dot{\theta}_i \end{bmatrix}, \qquad A_i = \begin{bmatrix} 0 & 1 \\ 0 & 0 \end{bmatrix}, \qquad B_i = \begin{bmatrix} 0 \\ 1 \end{bmatrix} \tag{6}$$

z_i is the output of the ith subsystem, η_i and ν_i are uncorrelated zero mean Gaussian white noise processes with convariance matrices ψ_i and Ξ_i, respectively, and C_i is a constant 2×2 diagonal matrix since the arm is equipped with feedback potentiometers and tachometers. For simplicity, it can be assumed that $C_i = I$, the identity matrix. f_i represents the gravity influence and the coupling terms from other subsystems through reaction torques, Coriolis forces, etc... If the ith subprocess was isolated from those force fields, f_i would be zero, and (5) would be linear in x_i

$$\dot{x}_i = A_i x_i + B_i(u_i + \eta_i) \tag{7}$$

The ith subsystem can now be interpreted as a double-integral plant representing a single-axis attitude control problem.

SELF-ORGANIZING CONTROL LEVEL

The objective of the control level is the application of direct control inputs to the joint actuators. Since the model developed in the previous section is based on partial knowledge of the system dynamics a performance adaptive control algorithm with the following control structure is used

$$u_i = L_i\left(x_i - x_i^d\right) + N_i f_i = u_{Li} + u_{Ni} \tag{8}$$

where the first part is the optimal control (L.C.) for the uncoupled subsystem while the second term (C.C.) represents a nonlinear term depending on the coupling with the other subsystems.

A performance criterion for the proper mechanical function of the system may be defined as

$$J(a) = \sum_{i=1}^{4} \mu_i J(\alpha_i) \tag{9}$$

$$J_i(\alpha_i) = \lim_{\tau \to \infty} \frac{1}{\tau} E \int_0^{\tau} \left[\|z_i(t) - x_i^d(\tau)\|_{Q_i(\alpha_i)}^2 + \mu_{Li}^2(t) \right] dt \tag{10}$$

where $x_i^d(\tau)$ is the vector of desired terminal states, $a = [\alpha_1 \alpha_2 \alpha_3 \alpha_4]^T$ is a vector of adjustable coefficients relative to the speed of response of the subprocesses

$$\mu_i = \begin{cases} 1 & \text{if } x_i(0) \neq x_i^d(\tau) \\ 0 & \text{otherwise} \end{cases}$$

since no cost is associated to a joint whose angular position is fixed during the motion of the arm, $Q_i(\alpha_i)$ are diagonal matrices pertaining to the damping and speed of response of the subprocesses, and

$$Q_i(\alpha_i) = \begin{bmatrix} \alpha_i^2 & 0 \\ 0 & 2\alpha_i \end{bmatrix}$$

for a critically damped response.

Infinite duration was assumed for simplicity of implementation, and this conjecture was verified experimentally. This quadratic term u_{Li}^2 penalizes acceleration, thus producing smooth, anthropomorphic motion, and makes the solution easy to implement.

The expanding subinterval algorithm [10] is used to yield the asymptotically optimal coefficients L_i and N_i. This online learning process sequentially improves the subgoal

$$J(a,k) = \sum_{i=1}^{4} \mu_i J_i(\alpha_i, k) \tag{11}$$

$$J_i(\alpha_i, k) = \frac{1}{\tau_k} \int_{t_{k-1}}^{t_k} \left[\|z_i(t) - x_i^d(\tau)\|_{Q_i(\alpha_i)}^2 + u_{Li}^2(t) \right] dt \quad i = 1, \dots, 4 \tag{12}$$

where the length of the interval $\tau_k = t_k - t_{k-1}$, $k = 1, 2, \ldots$ satisfies the conditions

$$\tau_{k-1} \leqslant \tau_k \quad \forall_k, \quad \text{and} \quad \lim_{k \to \infty} \tau_k = \infty \tag{13}$$

The higher levels are interfaced with the individual self-organizing controls through the adjustable relative speed coefficients α_i, the blending coefficients μ_i and the desired final states $x_i^d(\tau)$.

From the previous discussion, it is obvious that the third level self-organizing controls are designed for precision control of the mechanical subprocesses at hand but they do not exhibit higher quality intelligent functions, like intelligent decision-making for motion coordination, direction and goal accomplishment. With their limited capabilities they resemble more the reflexes of a biological system. The higher intelligent functions are hierarchically distributed to the higher levels of the controls, which are described next.

FUZZY AUTOMATON AS CONTROL COORDINATOR

Principle of Minimum Interaction

The self-organizing control level described in the previous section deals with the optimization of each joint motion with respect to a kinematic criterion that produces low acceleration trajectories. The proposed control structure can be given a physiological interpretation in terms of the principle of minimum interaction formulated by Gelfand and Tsetlin [4]. This principle, which is speculative, is an attempt to establish a "mathematical theory of complex control systems in which this principle would play the same role as the variational principles in analytical mechanics." Briefly stated, the minimum interaction principle says that "at each moment the subsystem solves its individual, particular problem—it minimizes its interaction with the environment. Consequently the complexity of the subsystem does not depend on the complexity of the whole system." As a direct consequence of the application of this principle to the prosthetic system, each joint motion has a trajectory similar to the one that would be produced by the corresponding subsystem if it were isolated from its environment.

Minimum Energy Criterion for Coordination

The purpose of the coordination level in the hierarchy is to account for the dynamic coupling between each subsystem and its environment. The interaction occurs in the form of reaction and Coriolis torques, and the gravity effect. The coordination problem deals with the over-all minimization of a dynamic criterion, specifically a minimum energy criterion, an important factor in view of the necessity for the patient to carry an energy source or storage device.

The coordination decision-making problem may now be formulated as follows: for every control pattern $\Gamma_0 = [\theta \; \dot{\theta} \; \theta^d \; \dot{\theta}^d]^T$ (that is, for every set of initial and desired states), select the coordination vector a^* among a finite predetermined set $\{a_1, \ldots, a_N\}$ that minimizes energy consumption,

$$\min_{a_1, \ldots, a_N} K(a) = K(a^*) \tag{14}$$

where

$$K(a) = \sum_{i=1}^{4} \mu_i \int_0^T |\dot{\theta}_i(t) T_i(t)| \, dt \tag{15}$$

Pattern Classification Approach to Coordination Problem

In pattern recognition terminology, the coordination problem consists in the partitioning of the control pattern Γ_0 feature space into coordination classes $C_1, \ldots, C_N$, where the coordination class C_i is associated with the coordination vector a_i. In view of the high degree of dynamic coupling between joints 2 and 4, we demonstrate the feasibility of the proposed coordination scheme by restricting our attention to two degree of freedom motions involving displacements along θ_2 and θ_4. The general case is presented in [11].

Preliminary simulation studies indicate that for a very large percentage of control patterns, the choice of the coordination vector a is independent of the velocity components in Γ_0. A simpler feature vector $\Gamma_1 = [\theta_2 \theta_4 \theta_2^d \theta_4^d]$ can therefore be used with negligible loss in classification accuracy.

In the absence of sufficient *a priori* knowledge about the solution of the coordination problem, several sets of hyperplanes are tried for the partition of the feature space. In order to simplify the description of each set of hyperplanes, it is convenient to quantize each component of Γ_1 as indicated in Table 1. Let N_1, N_2, M_1, M_2 denote the number of the quantization level of the variables θ_2, θ_4, θ_2^d, and θ_4^d, respectively, and let the coordination vector a be selected from the set $a = \{a_1, a_2, a_3\}$, where $a_1 = [\alpha_0, \alpha_0]^T$, $a_2 = [\alpha_0, 2\alpha_0]^T$, $a_3 = [2\alpha_0, \alpha_3]^T$. The term α_0 is a constant factor pertaining to the speed of response, and determined by the organization level. Eight sets of hyperplanes are heuristically constructed to partition the feature space into C_1, C_2, and C_3 as described in Tables 2, 3, 4 and 5. Sets no. 5, 6, 7 and 8 are defined by interchanging C_2 and C_3 in sets no. 1, 2, 3, and 4, respectively.

Table 1
Feature Space Quantization

Quantization Level	$\theta_2, \theta_2{}^d$	$\theta_4, \theta_4{}^d$
1	$-\dfrac{\pi}{2}$ to $-\dfrac{\pi}{6}$	0 to $\dfrac{\pi}{3}$
2	$-\dfrac{\pi}{6}$ to $\dfrac{\pi}{6}$	$\dfrac{\pi}{3}$ to $\dfrac{2\pi}{3}$
3	$\dfrac{\pi}{6}$ to $\dfrac{\pi}{2}$	$\dfrac{2\pi}{3}$ to π

Table 2
Hyperplanes—Set No. 1

N_2 ＼ M_2	1	2	3
1	C_1	C_3	C_3
2	C_2	C_1	C_3
3	C_2	C_2	C_1

Table 3
Hyperplanes—Set No. 2

N_1 ＼ M_1	1	2	3
1	C_1	C_3	C_3
2	C_2	C_1	C_3
3	C_2	C_2	C_1

Table 4
Hyperplanes—Set No. 3

N_1 ＼ N_2	1	2	3
1	C_3	C_3	C_2
2	C_3	C_2	C_2
3	C_2	C_2	C_2

Table 5
Hyperplanes—Set No. 4

N_1 ＼ N_2	1	2	3
1	C_2	C_2	C_2
2	C_3	C_2	C_2
3	C_3	C_3	C_2

Fuzzy Automaton as a Learning Model

Several sets of hyperplanes resulting in different partitions of the feature space have been considered in the previous section. In order to determine the "best" set, let us define R_k^j as the average performance cost associated with the jth set of hyperplanes $j = 1, \ldots, 8$ at the kth step of learning. The term R_k^j can then be computed by the following recursive relation:

$$R_{k+1}^j = \frac{k-1}{k} R_k^j + \frac{1}{k} \frac{1}{t_{k+1} - t_k} \int_{t_k}^{t_{k+1}} \left(\sum_{i=1}^4 |\dot{\theta}_i(t) T_i(t)| \right) dt \qquad (16)$$

Since the desired angular positions θ_2^d and θ_4^d are determined in the organization level from fuzzy commands, it is desirable to establish a fuzzy partition of the feature space by associating a membership function with each set of hyperplanes. A fuzzy automaton similar to that developed by Wee and Fu [12] can then be used to reinforce the grade of membership of each set of hyperplanes so as to minimize criterion (16). The automaton has eight states $q_1, \ldots, q_8$, one for each set of hyperplanes, so on convergence of this learning process, the set of hyperplanes with maximum grade of membership is selected.

Let $f_j(k)$, $j = 1, \ldots, 8$ denote the grade of membership for the fuzzy automaton to be in state q_j at the kth learning step. Define the fuzzy transition matrix by

$$f_{ij}(k) = f\{ q(k) = q_i, q(k+1) = q_j \} \qquad (17)$$

Then, with probability $\frac{1}{2}$, the automaton operates between

$$f_j(k+1) = \max_m \min[f_m(k), f_{mj}(k)] \qquad (18)$$

and

$$f_j(k+1) = \min_m \max[f_m(k), f_{mj}(k)] \qquad (19)$$

To simplify the problem, let

$$f_{mj}(k) = f_{jj}(k-1), \qquad \forall m \neq j \qquad (20)$$

$$f_{jj}(k) = \epsilon_j f_{jj}(k-1) + (1 - \epsilon_j) \lambda_j(k) \qquad (21)$$

where

$$0 < \epsilon_j < 1, \qquad 0 < \lambda_j \leqslant 1, \qquad j = 1, \ldots, 8 \qquad (22)$$

$$\lambda_j(k) = 1 - \frac{R_k^j}{\phi}, \qquad j = 1, \ldots, N; \qquad k = 1, 2, \ldots, \qquad (23)$$

$$\phi \geqslant \max_{j,k} R_K^j \qquad (24)$$

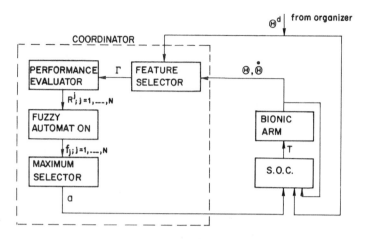

Figure 3. Structure of the coordinator.

The convergence of the above algorithm is proved in [12]. As

$$k \to \infty, \quad \lambda_j(k) \to \lambda_j, \quad f_{mj}(k) \to \lambda_j, \quad f_j(k) \to \lambda_j \qquad (25)$$

The structure of the coordination level, including the learning automaton, is indicated in Fig. 3. An alternative approach to the coordination problem, based on syntactic pattern classification is presented in [11].

LINGUISTIC METHODS FOR TASK ORGANIZATION

Based on the previous discussion given a command and a terminal state, the fuzzy automaton can be trained to produce the proper compound motion for the arm, which represents a level of control more intelligent than the self-organizing. However, the commands generated from the "brain" of the human operator are more in the form of compound tasks, such as "pick up a glass of water to drink" Therefore, an intelligent control system is needed to interface the brain with the fuzzy automaton and translate the above qualitative command to a sequence of compound motions of the area that will accomplish the task.

A machine which would produce decisions and functions of such a high level of intelligence must be an advanced digital computer, capable of processing qualitative information of high content, but also of a fuzzy nature in the sense that high precision in execution is not required. A natural system for this type of information processing is the linguistic methods approach that has been developed in the current literature for artificial intelligence, pattern recognition, scene analysis and other functions [2]. Such methods process strings of words with logic instruction for the task accomplishment so that they obey a certain predetermined grammar and syntax in a similar manner as it is done with natural languages. In particular, stochastic grammars developed by Fu for syntactic pattern recognition or fuzzy grammars proposed by Zadeh [5] are most desirable for generation of the command strings appropriate to organize the motion of the arm. A block diagram representation of the organization level is indicated in Fig. 4. Since a detailed description of this level is outside the scope of this paper, the interested reader is referred to [11]. The electromagnetic signals emanating from voluntary movement in the patient's remaining musculature are coded in binary words. Command strings, or sentences, are formed by the concatenation of several words following the production syntax rules of a context-free grammar in Chomsky normal form. The Cocke-Younger-Kasami parsing algorithm is used to verify the syntactic validity of each command. The interpretation of the command parse is performed by an automaton that extracts information about the desired position of the arm. The command variables thus obtained are x^d, y^d, z^d, θ_p^d, θ_r^d, α_0, i.e., the Cartesian coordinates of the desired wrist position, the desired pitch and roll angles of the hand and a factor pertaining to the desired speed of response, respectively. The final processing stage maps the first five command variables into a set of actuator angles $\theta_1^d, \ldots, \theta_6^d$.

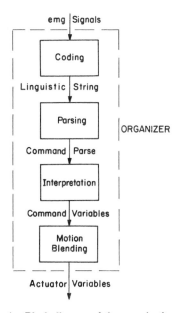

Figure 4. Block diagram of the organization level.

SIMULATION AND RESULTS

The arm model was simulated on a CDC 6500 digital computer. The learning behavior of the self-organizing control level is illustrated in Fig. 5, and shows the decrease of the kinematic cost as the number of iterations increases. Four trajectories taken at different stages of the learning process are shown in Fig. 6. Figure 7 depicts the phase plane trajectories for three different coordination vectors a_1, a_2, and a_3 applied to the same control pattern. The given control pattern is classified in coordination class C_3 since

$$\min_{a_1, a_2, a_3} K(a_i) = K(a_3).$$

Figure 8 shows the convergence of the grades of membership of some sets of hyperplanes, for $\epsilon_i = 0.8$. Set no. 1 has the highest grade of membership.

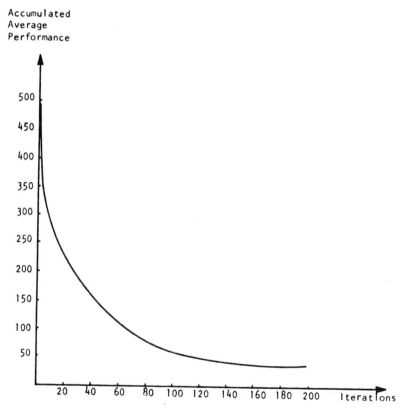

Figure 5.   Learning behavior of the self-organizing controller.

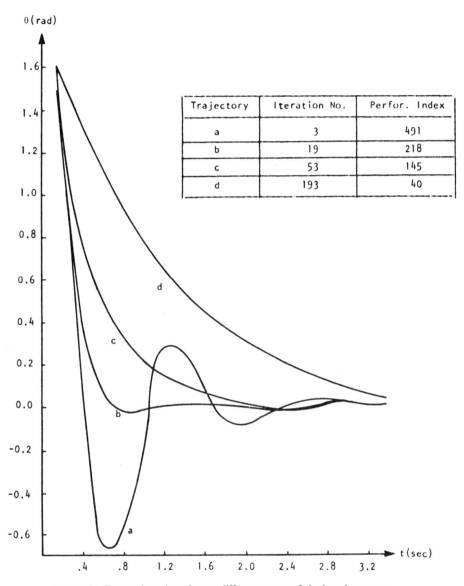

Figure 6. Four trajectories taken at different stages of the learning process.

CONCLUSION

The feasibility of the application of a hierarchical multilevel controller, using a combination of linguistics, fuzzy automata, and self-organizing

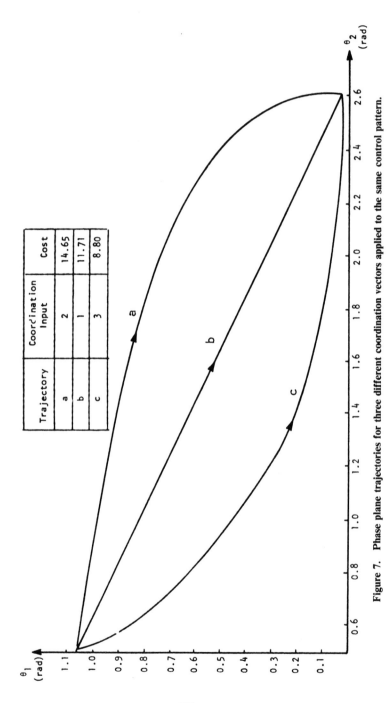

Trajectory	Coordination Input	Cost
a	2	14.65
b	1	11.71
c	3	8.80

Figure 7. Phase plane trajectories for three different coordination vectors applied to the same control pattern.

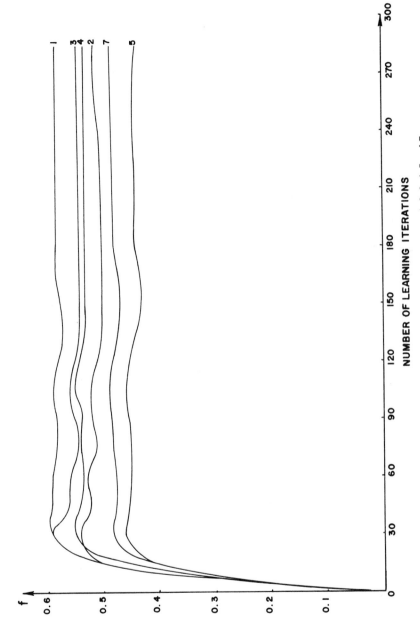

Figure 8. Grades of membership vs k for hyperplane sets 1, 2, 3, 4, 5 and 7.

401

control systems, has been demonstrated. Simulation studies are now completed and the hardware realization of the project is in the planning stage. This should eventually lead to the application of fuzzy decision-making to highly sophisticated machines like robots, manipulators or other prosthetic devices that may effectively help handicapped people to perform normal functions.

REFERENCES

1. Chang, S. S. L., and Zadeh, L. A., "On Fuzzy Mapping and Control," *IEEE Trans. Systems, Man, and Cybernetics*, **SMC 2** (Jan. 1972), 30–34.

2. Fu, K. S., *Syntactic Methods in Pattern Recognition*, Academic Press, N.Y., 1974.

3. Fung, L. N., and Fu, K. S., "Characterization of a Class of Fuzzy Optimal Control Problems," *Proc. Eighth Princeton Conf. on Info. Sci. Systems*, March, 1974.

4. Gelfand, I. M., and Tsetlin, M. L., "Mathematical Modeling of Mechanisms of the Central Nervous System," *Models of Structural-Functional Organization of Certain Biological Systems*, Gelfand *et al.* (Eds.), MIT Press, Cambridge, 1971.

5. Lee, E. T., and Zadeh, L. A., "Note on Fuzzy Languages," *Infor. Sci.* **1**, No. 6 (Oct. 1969), 421–434.

6. Lyman, J., Freedy, A., and Zadaca, H., "*Studies and Development of Heuristic End-Point Control for Artificial Upper Limbs*," UCLA Biotechnology Lab. Tech. Rep. No. 54, Oct. 1974.

7. Mendel, J. M., and Zapalac, J. J., "The Application of Techniques of Artificial Intelligence to Control System Design," *Advances in Control Systems: Theory and Applications*, Leondes, C. T. (Ed.), Academic Press, N.Y., 1968.

8. Mesarovic, M. D., Macko, D., and Takahara, Y., *Theory of Hierarchical Multilevel Systems*, Academic Press, N.Y., 1970.

9. Saridis, G. N., *Self-Organizing Control of Stochastic Systems*, Marcel-Dekker, N.Y., 1977.

10. Saridis, G. N., "On a Class of Performance adaptive Self-Organizing Systems," in *Pattern Recognition and Machine Learning*, Fu, K. S. (Ed.), Plenum Press, N.Y., 1971.

11. Saridis, G. N., and Stephanou, H. E., "Hierarchical Intelligent Control of a Prosthetic Arm," TR-EE 76-8, Purdue U., West Lafayette, Indiana.

12. Wee, W. G., Fu, K. S., "A Formulation of Fuzzy Automata and its Application as a Model of Learning Systems," *IEEE Trans. Systems Sci. Cybernetics* **SSC5** (July 1969), 215–223.

13. Zadeh, L. A., "Fuzzy Sets," *Info. Control* **8** (June 1965).

14. Zadeh, L. A., Tanaka, K., Fu, K. S., and Shimura, M., "*Fuzzy Sets and Their Applications*," Academic Press, N.Y., 1975.

THE FUZZY DECADE: A BIBLIOGRAPHY OF FUZZY SYSTEMS AND CLOSELY RELATED TOPICS

B.R. Gaines and L.J. Kohout

INTRODUCTION

This bibliography originated from personal attempts to come to grips with the literature explosion on fuzzy systems. It rapidly became apparent that: (a) there was much more work in progress than any individual involved in the area realized; (b) there was a substantial duplication of effort in some areas and neglect of others; (c) that the rate of growth of the literature was being sustained at a very high level (now known to be 40% a year). Thus, apart from the intellectual challenge, it seemed particularly worthwhile to attempt to publish a complete and comprehensive bibliography with the objective of consolidating a massive new area of study and increasing the awareness of those working in the area of its ramifications and extent.

This paper is the first normal publication of the bibliography. An earlier draft was distributed worldwide to over 200 research workers in some 20 countries, and many corrections and additions have been received. Undoubtedly there are more to be made—we have aimed in the "fuzzy" references for completeness before all else and have included working papers whose date may be dubious and references in which details of publication are unknown—in some cases our classification may be incorrect. Additional items, updates and corrections are still coming in and we welcome them. The bibliography is maintained, analyzed and formated on a computer, and updates, tabulations and printouts are swift and simple. We shall probably be forced to stop maintaining it at some time if the current growth rate of publications is maintained, but there will be at least one further publication of updates and analyses.

We are grateful to our colleagues, Willis Bandler and Václav Pinkava, for their help and suggestions. We also wish to thank Joe Goguen, Lotfi Zadeh, Abe Kandel, and Hans Zimmerman.

The papers are listed in alphabetical sequence of authors names. We know that some users will prefer alternative arrangements, e.g., chronological order or sub-division by classification, but the name order seemed generally most useful. The year of publication follows the name and classificatory keywords are in bold face at the end of each reference so that it is relatively easy to scan the bibliography on other bases. We found it very difficult to decide whether or not to split the bibliography into classified sections—some 1100 references in a single sequence is not readily searched or assimilated. However, we finally left it as a single list because we felt classification, even if completely accurate, would make it too easy to skip whole sections, in particular the non-**FUZ** references are a selection intended to link fuzzy system theory to the main body of mathematics, philosophy and system science. They are relevant to the future development of fuzzy system theory, not only building in its own right, but also contributing to parallel developments in other fields.

The organization of this preamble is aimed primarily at helping those with particular interests to find their way around the bibliography. It notes some of the key references in the main areas of development of fuzzy system theory. However, it is assumed that the majority of papers classified as **FUZ** will indicate through their title and associated keywords their place in the literature—we have not attempted an exhaustive annotation of these. On the other hand, whereas the "fuzzy" part of the bibliography aims at completeness, the "related topics" are very much a personal selection, references that we have found useful in coming to understand the role of fuzzy systems theory and its relationship to other fields of study. To be generally useful, this part of the bibliography needs more annotation than the "fuzzy" part, and we have indicated for each non-**FUZ** paper the reason for its inclusion.

This paper is, and is intended to be, a tribute to one man, Lotfi Zadeh, who initiated the area of study and has been a consistent driving force behind its further development and application. Many of us who saw his original papers in 1965 did not realize their significance until many years later. We were even somewhat disappointed in the change of direction that they represented, from hard system science (in which Zadeh had been a major pioneer) to a deliberate acceptance of imprecision in any real system applications. What was not clear at that time is that an ontology that denies the existence of this imprecision itself introduces such major artifacts that it is not just unreal but definitely false and positively misleading. Zadeh saw this as a fatal flaw in classical system science at the same time as the majority of us were looking for new peaks to conquer with the tools that had been so successful in the past. In retrospect one can see that, in many cases, it was the tools that were building the peaks, not conquering them!

SURVEY OF LITERATURE

We will first give a brief overview of fuzzy system theory and the related topics, and then cover each of them in a separate section. The compartments are not generally self-contained and there is considerable overlap between them.

In his earliest papers Zadeh (1965a) makes clear his *semantic* interest in fuzzy set theory. It is a tool for reasoning with the *inherently imprecise concepts* of systems engineering, and the tool is based on, and expected to model, *human linguistic reasoning* with such concepts. Thus the attempts by philosphers, logicians and scientists, to come to terms with, and represent, *vagueness, imprecision*, and so on, are clearly relevant. So are the more recent attempts by linguists to comprehend actual usage of terms representing and modifying *vague concepts*. Human linguistic reasoning seems to make less of a distinction between inductive and deductive reasoning than does logic, and *inductive generalization* in vague reasoning leads naturally to some contact with studies of *automated induction*. This in turn is closely related to what may be seen as the classical tool for studying systems about which our knowledge is imprecise, namely *probability theory*. In particular, *logical studies of probability* appear to have strong links with the mathematical foundations of fuzzy logic, and *subjective studies of probability* are relevant to the problems of human decision-making and the source of the numerical values in fuzzy reasoning.

Fuzzy set theory may be regarded either as a foundation for, or as founded upon, a system of logic. The first point of view emphasizes the direct links with classical *multivalued logics* (MVLs), and the second highlights those studies of the *foundations of set theory* that have used nonclassical logics, again particularly multivalued logics. One MVL in particular stands out as closely related to Zadeh's development and that is Lukasiewicz's infinite-valued logic (here abbreviated as L_1). However, there are also important links with other nonclassical logics, particularly *modal logics*. These in turn are closely linked with topological structures, and fuzzy system theory has links with both conventional topology and nonstandard systems, e.g., without points or with generalized closures, that may be regarded as precursors of *fuzzy topologies*. Many other mathematical structures may also be studied using fuzzy, rather than classical sets, leading to *fuzzy graphs, groups, algebras, automata*, etc.

These two directions of fuzzy system theory, the one oriented to human linguistic reasoning and the other to formal logic and mathematics, come together again in a wide range of applications. We have not attempted to gather background references for these applications because they are so diverse and the individual fuzzy applications papers generally have good bibliographies of the relevant non-fuzzy approaches.

Introductory Papers

The newcomer to fuzzy systems theory will probably be appalled by the sheer volume of literature now extant. However, there are a few key references which make it fairly easy to get into the central literature very rapidly and at a reasonable depth. The danger is only in assuming, for research purposes, that this central core fairly represents the current state of the art. There is now a complex, derivative literature: many problems are being explored at secondary, or even tertiary, levels. Many of the obvious avenues of exploration arising out of Zadeh's papers have now *beęn* explored and re-explored. This applies particularly to the technicalities and foundations of fuzzy reasoning—it is dangerous to rush into print with a "new" set of connectives or a variant fuzzy logic. Even some applications areas, notably pattern-recognition, clustering, decision-making and control, have been explored on a fairly wide front—it is certainly dangerous to rush out a note rediscovering and eulogizing the potential application of fuzzy system theory to a particular problem area. Such notes exist in great abundance and what is needed are solid application studies demonstrating actual results. Many such studies do also now exist, particularly in pattern-recognition, simulation and control engineering. Finally, the anti-fuzzy reaction, arguing that the concepts are misconceived or the approach wrong, has itself become antiquated, if only because each recipient of the fresh revelation does not realize how many others actively engaged in the field have been through the same process of critical reactive, appreciation, and constructive redevelopment. This is not to say that all or part of the literature is completely right, but there is now a wide variety of evidence to show that the concepts and approaches are certainly not completely wrong!

As in most areas of study, the best introduction is to go straight back to the source, and Zadeh (1965a) is still worth thorough reading. Zadeh (1973a) has served a great many workers as a general introduction to the area, and Bellman and Zadeh (1976), the latest paper, is particularly important for its new results on fuzzy reasoning and truth. Bellman and Zadeh (1970) has many interesting speculative remarks about fuzzy multistage decision-making, and Zadeh (1971d, 1975d) develop interesting technical concepts of fuzzy similarity relations, and fuzzy restrictions, respectively. Zadeh (1972c) is probably the most complete exposition of his analysis of *linguistic hedges*, and Zadeh (1975b) is a very clear and concise account of the syntax and semantics of multiterm hedges. Zadeh (1972b) links this work to studies of formal languages. Zadeh himself has written no book as yet on fuzzy system system theory, but the sum total of his papers forms a massive work encompassing a wide variety of topics. The collection is important not only for its technical content but also for expressing the motivation behind the developments in a more powerful form than in books or papers by other authors.

Other key introductory papers are Lakoff (1973c), which gives a linguist's view of Zadeh's analysis of fuzzy hedges (for some later comments see the conversation with Lakoff in Parrett 1974). These papers were published three times: in a conference proceedings, a journal (as referenced here), and in a book (Hockney, et al., 1975); the book also contains some comments by Van Fraassen (1975). Goguen (1969b) has some interesting remarks about, and variants of, Zadeh's approach including the first analyses of some paradoxes and fuzzy quantifiers. Goguen (1974b) presents axioms for the category of fuzzy sets and relates them directly to a phenomenal analysis of human concept processing. The book of the 1974 joint USA-Japan conference at Berkeley (Zadeh, et al., 1975) is a particularly useful introduction to the wide range of fuzzy system studies. The book by Negoiță and Ralescu (1975a) is a compact introduction to many technical aspects of fuzzy systems and their literature, while the series of three volumes by Kaufmann (1973, 1975a, b) is remarkable for its coverage at this early stage. No one should be fooled by the book format, however, into feeling that it is possible to put forward a definitive version of fuzzy system theory at present—the area is still developing rapidly and these books are research compendia rather than textbooks.

Apart from those so far mentioned, there is a noticeable lack of expository and survey papers in the literature—perhaps the former because Zadeh has done such a good job, and the latter because the literature explosion has been so rapid and recent! Gusev and Smirnova (1973) is worth reading and the report by Gupta and Mamdani (1976) of the 1975 Boston IFAC round table discussion is a useful survey of some current trends. Aizermann's (1975) paper for that discussion is particularly interesting for its strong motivation of fuzzy systems theory from an independent and eminent source.

Philosphy and Logic of Imprecision and Vagueness

Hacking (1975b) remarks in his book on the *emergence of probability* that, "Europe began to understand concepts of randomness, probability, chance and expectation precisely at that point in its history when theological views of divine foreknowledge were being reinforced by the amazing success of mechanistic models...This specific mode of determinism is essential to the formation of concepts of chance and probability."

It is reasonable to speculate that interest in the philosphy and logic of vagueness only really originated when the program of *precisiation* in science had gone so far and succeeded so well, i.e., in the twentieth century. Certainly most of the literature is concerned with the eradication of imprecision, not with the study of *inherent imprecision* in its own right. Russell (1923) and the series of publications by Black (1937, 1963, 1968, 1970) are most often quoted as studies of vague reasoning sympathetic to the direction of development of fuzzy system theory, and Machina (1972, 1976) provides an up-to-date account of recent developments.

Mehlberg (1958) analyzes the effect of inherent imprecision on meta-theories of scientific knowledge, truth, verification, etc. The so-called Popper-Carnap "controversy" (Popper, 1963, 1972a, 1976b; Carnap, 1963, 1964; Michalos, 1971) is in fact a far deeper and more multifaceted dialogue than that presented by most commentators, and both authors have much to say on inherent imprecision—the first chapter ("on explication") of Carnap's (1950) *Logical Foundations of Probability* presents a clear exposition of the process of precisiation in science, and section 7 of Popper's (1976b) autobiography presents the dangers of attempting to carry it too far. A miniature version of the controversy in the context of fuzzy system theory can be found in the Kalman-Zadeh discussion at the end of Zadeh (1974a).

The transition from the philosophy of imprecision to an appropriate logic of imprecise reasoning is the subject of all too few papers. Körner (1957, 1959, 1966, 1970, 1971, 1976a) has made it a subject of extensive study over many years, and his logical proposals have been developed technically by Cleave (1970, 1974, 1976). Körner (1976a) has the very appropriate subtitle, "A Study of Practical Reasoning", and is worth thorough reading. There are many background developments in logic also, some emanating from Łukasiewicz's (Borkowski, 1970) 3-valued logic, L_3, of future contingents which are neither true nor false, e.g., work on *truth-gaps* and *supervaluations* (Van Fraassen, 1968; Wilson, 1975). Susan Haack (1974, 1975) gives particularly clear and perceptive accounts of a range of such "deviant logics" and relates them both to the underlying requirements and to classical developments.

It is interesting to note that the 3-valued logic used by Körner was first studied by Kleene (1938, 1952) and Rescher (1969, pp. 34–35) in connection with the recursiveness of arithmetic functions. The meaning of the third value is not true or false but indeterminate, or indeterminable by certain specified decision procedures, i.e., by an effective algorithm. A recent technical paper on this logic is Martin (1975). Another independent development of the same logic has been motivated by work on computerized "automated systems for generating interesting hypotheses from experimental data", the GUHA method (Chytil, 1969; Hájek, 1968;

Havránek, 1971) which is a generalization of Hájek, *et al.* (1966). The 3-valued system was first announced in 1969 and is reported in detail in Hájek, et al. (1971). H.B. Curry noted in 1970 that the logic used was that of Kleene. The motivation for the third value in this case is to express the *absence of information on some objects and properties.*

The GUHA method is a special instance of a more general family of (infinite-valued) systems, ALIOS based on work of Hájek and his school (Hájek, 1973b–d, 1974a–b, 1975; Hájek and Harmancová, 1973; Hájek and Havránek, 1976; Havránek, 1974, 1975a, b; Pudlák 1975a, b). A prime thesis of the ALIOS method is that (Hájek, 1975): *"There are formal systems different from the predicate calculus that are appropriate for hypothesis formation (inductive generalization) and have a satisfactory mathematical theory".*

The authors define an *observational structure* as a relational system mapped into rational numbers, and theoretical statements are represented in a real-valued Σ-modal structure. It appears that the theory is sufficiently general to include both stochastic and fuzzy models. The best survey papers are Hájek (1975) and Havránek (1975); other key papers are Hájek (1973, 1974). Pudlák (1975) provides a link to computational complexity and Hájek (1975) to semisets.

The recent issue of Synthese (1975, **30**(3/4)) devoted to vague reasoning had a particularly stimulating and wide ranging series of papers by Adams and Levine (uncertainties from premise to conclusion), Arbib and Manes (fuzzy systems), Carlstrom (vague quantifiers), Dummett (Wang's paradox), Fine (vagueness and truth), Wright (vague predicates) and Zadeh (fuzzy logic). These papers covered both the philosophy and the logic of inexact reasoning and relating technical developments to classical logics, probability theory, and fuzzy system theory; the issue is worth acquisition as a reference work in its own right. Earlier significant papers on imprecise reasoning include: Verma (1970) on *vagueness and excluded middle*; Khatchadourian (1965) on *vagueness, meaning and absurdity;* Axinn & Axinn on *ignorance relations*; Kerridge (1961) on *inaccuracy and inference* in a classical framework; Simon (1967) on *the logic of heuristic decision making*; Morton (1975) on *complex individuals and multigrade relations*; Morgan (1975) on *similarity as a theory of graded equality;* Sober (1975) on *simplicity*; Wiredu (1975) on *truth as a logical constant*; Rescher & Manor (1970) on *inference from inconsistent premises*, Adams (1965) on *inexact measurement*; and the book by Krantz, *et al.* (1971) on *foundations of measurement.*

One important paper on vague reasoning that is not generally accessible because it exists only in Polish is Kubiński's (1958) analysis of *vague terms.* Kubiński classifies vagueness in terms of pragmatic, semantic and syntactic definitions, and, in the appendix, analyzes some of the ancient paradoxes. His logical system is based on *quasi-ontologies* that are generalizations of Lesniewski's *ontology* originally developed as an alternative to set theory for the foundations of mathematics (Luschei 1962; Fraenkel, *et al.*, 1973).

According to Kubiński's syntactic definition, a nonindividual term b is vague if there exists an individual term a such that neither the expression: (1) "a is b", nor the expression (2) "a is non-b" are theses of definite systems called quasi-ontologies. The sense of the functor "is" used in (1) and (2) above is determined by an axiom of Lesniewski's ontology. The meaning of "non" in (2) is determined by a special axiom—it neither term-negation of ontology nor the negation of classical logic.

The system on which the work is based is defined by the following syntactic forms:

A1: $\forall x \forall y \big[\, \epsilon xy \equiv \exists z (\epsilon zx) \wedge \forall v \forall w (\epsilon vx \wedge \epsilon wx \rightarrow \epsilon vw) \wedge \forall u (\epsilon ux \rightarrow \epsilon uy) \big]$

A2: $\forall x \forall y \big[\, \epsilon xy \rightarrow (\epsilon xNy)' \big]$

D1: $\forall x \forall y \forall z (\epsilon xAyz \equiv \epsilon xy \vee \epsilon xz)$

D2: $\forall x \forall y \forall z (\epsilon xKyz \equiv \epsilon xy \wedge \epsilon xz)$

A3: $\forall x \forall y \forall z \big[(\epsilon xNAyz \equiv \epsilon xNy \wedge \epsilon xNz)$

$$\wedge (\epsilon xNKyz \equiv \epsilon xNy \vee \epsilon xNz) \wedge (\epsilon xNNy \equiv \epsilon xy) \big]$$

A1 is an axiom of ontology and D1, D2 are definitions of conjunction and alternation. It should be noted that the functors $\{\wedge, \vee, \rightarrow, '\}$ belong to a different semantic category from that of the functors $\{A, K, N\}$, the former are "expression-generating" while the latter are "name-generating".

Kubiński's semantic definition of vague terms involves the concept of a *fringe*. The fringe of a term "a" is the set of all objects which are denoted neither by "a" nor by "non-a". A term is vague if and only if its fringe is non-empty. The following are the semantical axioms for the system: Let U be a set of individuals and Z a set with the following two properties: (1)$a_1, a_2, \ldots$ belong to Z; (2) if x and y belong to z then so do Axy, Kxy and Nx.

Let f be a function whose domain is Z and whose range is subsets of U, then

(a) $fAxy = fx \cup fy$

(b) $fKxy = fx \cap fy$

(c) $fNNx = fx$

(d) $fNAxy = fNx \cap fNy$

(e) $fNKxy = fNx \cup fNy$

(f) $fx \cap fNx = \varnothing$

Z is called the "name space" and the elements of the set fx are called the designates of the name x. The set Bx is the *fringe* of the name "x" (where *x* is a member of the name space *Z*) if and only if *Bx* is equal to the set difference, $U - (fx + fNx)$. The name "*x*" belonging to *Z* is *vague* (nieostra —not sharp, not crisp) if and only if the fringe *Bx* is not empty, and it is *crisp* (ostry—sharp) otherwise.

Kubiński (1960) introduces some new primitive functors into his system, with the intuitive meanings: *x* is undoubtedly *y*; *x* is rather *y* than *z*; *x* is rather *y* than non-*y*; *x* is *y* and *z* to the same degree. Neustupný (1966) outlines the application of this system to questions of linguistic vagueness.

Kubiński's work is important as a formalization of vagueness within the framework of Lesniewski's ontology, and it is interesting to compare it with similar attempts within the framework of set theory. Whereas Black (1937, 1963) approaches vagueness from the point of view of pragmatics and Kubiński through syntax and *extensional* semantics, Materna (1972) chooses an *intensional* approach, modifying Tichý's (1969) explication in the terms of Turing machines. He also gives an intentional definition of "fringe" that satisfies the axioms of Kubiński. Other papers relevant to Kubiński's work are Przełecki (1958) who discusses the connections between meaningfulness and vagueness of theoretical terms and Wojcicki (1966) who applies model theory to the analysis of *empirical meaningfulness* (significance) and investigates some of its properties.

That vagueness is an important issue in linguistics has been shown by the *Prague Linguistic Circle* (Vachek 1966a) whose writings since the late twenties have consistently emphasized the role of vagueness in language (Skalička 1935) under the heading of the relation of *center and periphery*. It has been proposed that vagueness might be an important *language universal*, and an impressive volume of evidence for this has been built up by analysis of actual language at phonological, grammatical, and other levels (see Daneš, 1966, for a survey and references). Neustupný succintly reviewed and summarized the problem of vagueness in a lecture given to the linguistic association in Prague in 1964 (Neustupný, 1966) adumbrating the similarities and distinctions between the work of the Circle and the philosophical and logical theories of vagueness of Black, Quine and Kubiński. He also outlined the implications of this issue for the structure of logical theories of language and mathematical linguistics.

Basic methodological issues concerning the dynamics of language raised by Mathesius (1911) that influenced the whole development of the views of the Prague Linguistic Circle strikingly resemble many of the methodological problems raised by contemporary system theory. Thus it is not surprising that the approach of the Circle is particularly attractive in terms of the 'linguistic' approach to systems advanced by Zadeh:

(1)   They regard language as a *semantic system*, where the *linguistic sign* and *communication* are two fundamental concepts.

(2) Their approach is based on *functional* structuralism concerned with problems of (synchronic) structural stability as well as with the dynamics of temporal (diachronic) changes and evolution in language.

(3) Prominence has been given to methodological problems of the segmentation of language and to the identification of units of language at various levels of the *structural hierarchy*. The combination of structuralism with a 'functional' point of view means that language is evaluated not only with respect to the linguistic system as a whole but also with respect to the ultimate function it fullfills in the larger setting of extra-linguistic reality.

Prague linguists distinguished and analysed separately vagueness appearing on several different functional levels, e.g., in a phonological system or on the structural grammar level (Vachek, 1964a; Daneš and Vachek, 1964). For example, in terms of grammar, "...one is faced with a phenomenon strikingly parallel to the one noted above in the discussion on phonological problems in language.... One meets here again what might be termed the 'fuzzy points' of the system..." (Daneš and Vachek, 1964). Vaneck (1964a, b) points out that "research in generative grammar has failed to cope with the problem of the 'fuzzy points' of the system of language; the problem of paramount importance for dynamics of the synchrony of language". Vachek (1964b) is criticized by Chomsky and Halle (1965), but Vachek (1966a) replies to this criticism, "N. Chomsky's and M. Halle's reaction to this paper misses exactly this most important point of 'fuzzy points', and so in no way invalidates our arguments".

Travaux Linguistiques de Prague devotes its second volume (1966) to a series of articles concerned with *problems of center and periphery*. The date of the editorial, June 1965, indicates that the collection went to the printers that year and hence could not have contained any reflections on Zadeh's pioneering paper. This issue contains a list of terms by which vagueness is referenced by various linguists, Nestupný's (1966) paper, and an exposition of the concepts of vagueness of the Prague Circle in terms of Kubiński's logic.

In conclusion, it is illuminating to compare the views of the Prague Linguistic Circle, a group of linguists primarily concerned with the structural stability of language, with those of the eminent control theorist, Aizerman (1975), on the need for a new approach to handle problems of stability in control engineering:

> Unsolved problems...of structural stability, absolute stability, etc. In such areas we do not have answers...a mathematics which should be based on a different system of axioms, a different set of rules of

inference, and above all, a different concept of precision. (Aizerman 1975)

A final remark should justify the fact that the above arguments do not attempt to formalize the present theses. It will have been noted that the theses are, for the great part, concerned with problems of a diachronistic, though strictly structural, character. And it is commonly admited that mathematical science has not yet developed a formal apparatus capable of expressing what is happening within a changing structure. There can be no doubt, however, that one day such apparatus will be available. Perhaps one of the justifications of these modest lines may be to urge the necessity of working out such apparatus. (Vachek 1966a)

Paradoxes

In the same way that much of our understanding of human behavior comes from study of its pathology, so do the *paradoxes* of formal reasoning act to clarify its structure and mold the form of associated research. Patterns of reasoning that lead to contradictory or counter-intuitive results indicate a flaw in the logic, its application, or in our interpretation of it. Russell's discovery of a paradox in Frege's *Foundations of Arithmetic* (Van Heijenoort, 1967) may be seen as the prime source of the major research on axiomatic set theory. The paradox takes many forms (Kleene, 1952; Martin, 1970; Chiara, 1973; Post, 1973; Parsons, 1974). Hughes and Brecht (1976) is a particularly useful source book of interesting variants.

Many attempts to circumvent Russell's paradox involve legislating to remove the constructs leading to problems (e.g., of a set being a member of itself) but some nonstandard analyses regard it as a logical problem arising from the law of the excluded middle (LEM) and change the logic to a 3-valued one that does not give rise to the paradox (Shaw-Kwei, 1954; Skolem, 1960; Skyrms, 1970). Varela (1975, 1976a, b) has put forward a very interesting approach extending G.S. Brown's (1969) *calculus of indications* to allow the paradoxical self-referential concepts (Smullyan, 1957) but use them in a way similar to Asenjo's (1966) *calculus of antinomies* to generate new truth values. He argues that living organisms use self-reference and it is inappropriate to attempt to avoid it, yet in order to avoid certain unwanted consequences the self-referential loops should be separate in the calculus—hence the third value assignment. This introduction of new truth values is a general procedure that can be used to staticize certain aspects of a dynamical system giving a new MVL. It is a homomorphism on the fine structure of the consequence-closure system and the main danger comes from this being inadequately known (e.g., in human and animal behavior) so that the MVL generated is misleading.

Pinkava (1965, 1976b) analyzes some paradoxes listed in Kleene (1952) and shows that, in general:

(1) self-reference is relevant only to a certain type of paradox;
(2) when it is relevant it is only the *necessary*, not a sufficient, condition, i.e., there may exist self-referential systems without paradoxes.

Further he shows that a paradox can be generated in a self-referential system if, for example, the following additional conditions are satisfied:

(1) the problem is representable by a certain form of propositional function;
(2) non-logical constants appearing in this representation have to come from a certain *critical* subset of all constants.

Pinkava's approach makes it possible to view the interaction of paradoxes and self-reference as a problem of stability in Tarski's general calculus of systems (Tarski 1956, pp. 30–37, 60–109, 342–383). The approach is constructive allowing paradoxes with specified structures to be generated. Sadovskiĭ (1974) has analyzed various General Systems theories and come to the conclusion that such paradoxes appear in the foundations of the subject and require urgent attention. Mackie's (1973) book on *Truth, Probability and Paradox* is particularly interesting in bringing these three topics together.

The analysis of Russell's paradox in fuzzy logic takes a similar route to that of Varela (Hendry, 1972; Gaines, 1976g) and resolves it by allocating a new truth-value to the paradoxical case. This can be extended to allow the continuum of truth values in fuzzy logic to be generated from the higher-order "paradoxical" expressions of an axiomatic system (Gaines, 1976g).

Another class of paradoxes that has been widely studied in terms of fuzzy reasoning are those concerned with the application of conventional logic to vague predicates. The problems that arise were noted by Greek philosophers and go under the names of *sorites* (the heap that remains one even if an item is removed), *falakros* (the bald man that remains one even if grows one more hair), and so on (Cargile, 1969; Weiss, 1973, 1976). Because they are concerned with vagueness as such, these paradoxes provide a good test of systems of fuzzy reasoning and their avoidance has been studied by Goguen (1969b), Lake (1974b), Gaines (1976g), and others. Weiss (1973, 1976) gives an interesting alternative analysis of these paradoxes, as does Sanford (1975b).

Many-Valued Logics

Although Zadeh (1965a) proposes a theory of fuzzy *sets*, set theory is itself dependent on the underlying logic and his proposal may be viewed as using an MVL as an alternative to the 2-valued classical logical calculus. In later papers Zadeh (1975b) suggests that this MVL is in fact the infinite-valued logic, $Ł_1$, first studied by Łukasiewicz (Borkowski, 1970; Borkowski and Slupecki, 1958; Rescher, 1969). The literature on MVLs is very extensive (Rescher, 1969; Wolf, 1975) but their development has been somewhat erratic. The introduction of more than two truth values leads to philosophical problems of interpretation (Zinovev, 1963; Haack, 1974), for example in Tarski's theory of truth (Tarski, 1956; Blackburn, 1975; Evans and McDowell, 1976; McKay and Merrill, 1976), and, while 3-valued logics have been given reasonable interpretations (e.g., Putnam, 1957; Segerberg, 1967; Borkowski, 1970; Evenden, 1974), the problem of doing so for infinite values has never been satisfactorily resolved. Hence much of the literature is concerned with uninterpreted MVLs used for technical purposes such as demonstrating the independence of logical axioms. Dana Scott's (1976) paper, "Does many-valued logic have any use?", and the ensuing discussion by Smiley and Cleave (Körner 1976b) is particularly interesting for its remarks on the important work of Giles (see section entitled "Probability Theory"), Körner and Hájek (section entitled Philosophy and Logic of Imprecision and Vagueness).

Zadeh's application of fuzzy system theory to imprecise reasoning does seem to provide a reasonable interpretation of logics such as L_1, and recently Bellman and Zadeh (1976), Maydole (1975) and Gaines (1976g) have argued strongly for there being a reasonable theory of truth in terms of infinite-valued MVLs. Even at a fundamental level this should not be unexpected since Tarski's theory is based on a general theory of consequence that does not require the 0–1 valuation.

Rescher's (1969) book is the best overall introduction to MVLs, being reasonably nontechnical, covering the most interesting cases and having an excellent review of the literature. Ackermann's (1967) short book is more concerned with the axiomatic form of $Ł_1$ and enables the logic to be compared with the classical propositional calculus (PC). He points out the absence of a key deduction theorem from $Ł_1$ which makes Fitch-style (Hackstaff, 1966) *natural deduction* impossible, and hence the patterns of reasoning in $Ł_1$ markedly differ from those of PC. Rosser and Turquette's (1952) book is another useful reference, although concerned primarily with the axiomatization of finite-valued MVLs, and the older review papers by Frink (1938) and Salomaa (1959) are still worth reading. Epstein, *et al.* (1974) is a recent note on applications of MVLs in computer science, and

Kitahashi (1975) surveys Japanese work. Pinkava (1975), Kohout (1974) and Kohout and Pinkava (1976) give a very useful construction for arbitrary complete families of MVLs.

It is not possible here to do more than highlight a few papers with significant results related to L_1, such as those of Wajsberg (1967), Rosser and Turquette (1945), Rose (1950, 1951a, b, 1952, 1953, 1958) Rose and Rosser (1958), C.C. Chang (1958a, 1959), Meredith (1958), Rosser (1960), Jobe (1962), Schock (1964a, b, 1965), Turquette (1963), Marek and Traczyk (1969), Georgescu and Vraciu (1970), Georgescu (1971a–d) and Grigolia (1975). Dummett (1959) links MVLs with the intuitionistic propositional calculus (IPC) and proves a key tautology of truth-functional MVLs. Morgan (1976a) provides a very interesting interpretation of many-valued intuitionistic logics. Dienes (1949) has an interesting discussion of MVL implication, as do Webb (1936), and Salomaa (1959). Turquette (1954), Prior (1955a), and Schuh (1973) compare it with *strict implication* in modal logic and Woodruff (1974) gives a translation of $Ł_3$ into S5. Segerberg (1967) is one of a series of papers going back to antiquity which discusses many-valued *modal* logics, a topic also deeply studied by Łukasiewicz (Borkowski, 1970; Borkowski and Slupecki, 1958), although Dugundji (1940) has shown that no finite-valued MVL can be characteristic of the Lewis-Langford modal logics.

The most important area of development for $Ł_1$, however, is to extend it to a predicate calculus with quantifiers. Rescher (1969) discusses the introduction of quantifiers in MVLs and Mostowski (1957), Borkowski (1958) and Rescher (1964) give some interesting possibilities. Studies of axiomatic predicate calculi built on $Ł_1$ include: McNaughton (1951), Mostowski (1961), Scarpellini (1962), Hay (1963), Belluce and Chang (1963), and Belluce (1964). Scott's (1974) Tarski Symposium paper is particularly worth reading, and Maydole's (1972) thesis contains a wealth of material. The series of papers in German by Klaua and its continuation by Gottwald is also a major contribution. In the context of fuzzy logics, Goguen (1967) introduces fuzzy quantifiers and Giles (1975, 1976b, c) and Gaines (1976g) both consider quantified forms of $Ł_1$.

Papers giving special semantics for MVLs, such as Kripke-style *possible worlds* (Synder, 1971; Lewis, 1973), are also of interest, such as those of Bertolini (1971), and Urquhart (1973), and related studies of other logics (Nagai, 1973; Ohnishi and Matsumoto, 1957). The problems of making deductions in a nonstandard logic give computer-based theorem-proving systems special significance and, apart from the general literature (Chang and Lee, 1973), papers by Ehrenfeucht and Orlowska (1967) and Orlowska (1967, 1973) that consider MVLs are particularly worth studying. The recent special issue of *IEEE Transactions on Computers* (C–25, August

1976) on *automated theorem proving* is a useful source, and Morgan's (1976b) paper in it on *nonclassical logics* is particularly relevant. It should be noted that many theorem provers for classical predicate calculi rely on LEM and need radical change for MVLs.

Other Non-Standard Logics

Those attempting to break out of the framework of classical formal reasoning can gain much by studying the motivations and attempts of others to do so, for example, with *intuitionistic logics, strict implication, relevance logics*, and general *modal logics*. In addition there is also a variety of technical links between these topics and fuzzy system theory.

Kneale and Kneale (1962) is a scholarly but readable general history. Prior's (1962) textbook is an excellent introduction using Polish notation (which is essential to many key references), while Hughes and Creswell (1968) has an excellent introduction to classical propositional and predicate calculi in *Principia* notation as well as its survey of the Lewis-Langford modal systems. Mostowski's (1966) survey of *thirty years of foundational studies* gives a feel both for the intuitionistic propositional calculus and for the task of developing nonstandard systems, and Prior's (1967) book on tense logics has some historical background again giving a feel for the problems involved. His many other books and papers are an excellent introduction to both the techniques and the motivations behind many logical developments (e.g., Prior, 1953, 1954, 1955a, b, 1957, 1962, 1967, 1971). The same can be said for Rescher's (1968) collection and for Von Wright's (1957) collection. Tharp (1975) gives some motivation for, and constraints upon, nonstandard approaches. McCall (1967) is an excellent introduction to the key work in Polish logic between the wars, and Łukasiewicz's collected works (Borkowski, 1970) are clearly mandatory reading!

As well as the use of numeric quantifiers in MVLs mentioned in the previous section, there have also been developed models of the linguistic usage of vague numeric terms such as *some, any, almost all*, etc. (Altham, 1971; Adams, 1974). Such "modalities" are included amongst the very extensive list discussed in White's (1975) book on *modal thinking*, and Creswell (1973) develops a reasonably full model of language within a modal framework. Snyder (1971) is a very clear introduction to modal logic, its history, technicalities and proof techniques. Lewis (1973) shows how the model-theoretic, possible worlds, semantics of Kripke and Hintikka allows a formal model to be established of the *counterfactual conditional*, and hence of much practical reasoning. A contrasting approach to modal logics, based on the *intension* of predicates rather than their extensions (Carnap, 1947), is taken by Gallin (1975). Schotch (1975) discusses *fuzzy modal logics*, a topic worthy of much further study.

The studies of *strict implication* (Barcan, 1946; Marcus, 1953; Hacking, 1963; Lemmon, *et al.*, 1969) motivating the development of the modal logics of possibility and necessity are of particular interest because they are in turn motivated by practical problems of reasoning about causality. Indeed all studies of implication that attempt to place upon it constraints corresponding to *reasonableness* in human reasoning are very interesting in the context of imprecise reasoning. For example Goddard and Routley (1973) have investigated contraints of *significance and content*, and have much incidental material on MVLs also. Anderson and Belnap's (1975) book on *entailment* has a fascinating presentation and wide-ranging reviews of attempts to impose relevance and necessity on logical implication so that it more closely models entailment in reasoning. The notion of *relevance* (Belnap, 1960; Anderson and Belnap, 1962, 1975) is important in any logical system and its introduction in $Ł_1$ could well follow the lines they suggest for more classical logic.

Foundations of Set Theory

Zadeh's proposal of $Ł_1$ as a logic on which to found a set theory was based on informal pragmatic arguments applying to engineering applications. There has been a parallel, and apparently independent, development of the same structure based on purely formal arguments concerned with removing the paradoxes from naive set theory already discussed. This is reviewed in Gaines (1976g) and involves a sequence of papers commencing with Shirai (1937), but coming to full fruition with Shaw-Kwei (1954), Skolem (1957), 1960), C. C. Chang (1963a, b, 1965), and Fenstad (1964). The initial avoidance of the paradoxes of Russell and of Curry (1942) (a variant not involving negation) involved 3-valued logics (Prior, 1955b) but higher order paradoxes were found that forced infinite-valued logics. The current state of the art is best summarized by Maydole (1972, 1975) who has developed a technique for generating paradoxes that eliminates the standard predicate calculus, intuitionistic and modal (strict implication) variants, etc. leaving only a few infinite-valued MVLs as possible paradox-free foundations.

There have also been various developments within the framework of fuzzy set theory: Goguen (1974b) gives a Lawvere-style axiomatization of the category of fuzzy sets based on his thesis (1968); Lake (1974a) suggests a von Neumann style axiomatization that encompasses both Zadeh's fuzzy sets and Rado's multisets; Netto (1970) develops a theory in which fuzzy classes are taken as primitives using the first-order predicate calculus with equality; Chapin (1971) announced a ZF-like axiomatization of fuzzy set theory and has now developed it in some detail (Chapin, 1974, 1975). The models involve a set-valued membership function as a primitive and contain classical ZF set theory, Zadeh's fuzzy set theory, and various generalizations of them. Chapin also notes that Zadeh's fuzzy set theory is not contained in J. G. Brown's (1969) lattice-theoretic generalization.

Another important series of papers on MVL foundations for set theory are those of Klaua (1965, 1966a, b, 1967a, b, 1968, 1969a, b, 1970, 1972, 1973) in which he develops variants based upon both Łukasiewicz finite-, and infinite-valued, logics, and used them as a foundation for MVL-based mathematics. Klaua's set theory is developed cumulatively as a theory of types, which suggests that the prime motivation was not the parodoxes of the axiom of comprehension (although he quotes Skolem's work). His principal connectives are:

$$\tilde{}_w s = 1 - s,$$

$$s \bigwedge{}_w t = \min\{s, t\}, \qquad s \bigvee{}_w t = \max\{s, t\},$$

$$s \rightarrow_w t = \min\{1, 1 - (s - t)\}, \quad s \leftrightarrow_w t = 1 - |s - t|,$$

$$s \bigwedge{}^w t = \max\{0, s + t - 1\}, \quad s \bigvee{}^w t = \min\{1, s + t\}.$$

Klaua's work has been continued by some of his former students, notably Gottwald (1969, 1971a, b, 1973, 1974, 1975a, b, 1976a–c) who in his Habilitationschrift (1975a) investigates in great detail the features of various finite variants. He finds that direct, many-valued analogies may be found for the following axioms: (i) empty set; (ii) pairing; (iii) union; (iv) power-set; (v) substitution; (vi) choice; (vii) infinity. The axiom of extension is valid only in a weaker form. The possibility of a many-valued analogy of the classical axiom of choice that suggests the existence of a choice-set is still open. An example is given which shows that a many-valued analogy of the axiom of choice (in this formulation) does not hold in constructive sets.

A rather different motivation for a deviant set theory arises in the context of the Popper-Carnap "controversy" discussed earlier. Both Popper and Carnap aim at quantifying the process of precisiation and its evaluation by introducing various measures upon it, and both their approaches seem completely plausible and self-consistent. Indeed in recent years Carnap (1963) has gone so far as to say that there is no mutual incompatibility in their views and that Popper exagerates the difference. Yet recent developments have indicated that there may be a fundamental source of conflict between the approaches in the underlying logic and set theory. For example, Hájek and Harmancová (1973) show that one of

Carnap's measures of subjective probability is not viable in terms of classical set theory but it exists if the weaker structure of *semisets* is used instead (Vopěnka and Hájek, 1972; Hájek, 1967, 1973a).

Similarly, Popper's development of a verisimilitude measure (in terms of knowledge or a theory being only partially true and having some falsity content) is based (Popper, 1972a, pp. 330–335) on Tarski's metalogical theory of consequence (Tarski, 1956, pp. 30–37, 60–109). However, Miller (1974) and Tichý (1974) show independently that Popper's definition of verisimilitude is empty if the Tarski calculus of systems is restricted to classical logic. Miller and Tichý both infer that Popper's intuition is wrong and that they should find a new definition, perhaps less general. Hence, Popper abandons his most general definition (but not his intuitive views) and all three start a new search for a less general but better definition (disagreeing as to what it should be) (Popper, 1976a; Tichý, 1976). It is interesting to note that Popper, as a philosopher, would probably reject any non-classical logic as a foundation for reasoning, but nevertheless his general theory of verisimilitude is closely connected with fuzzy system theory (Kohout, 1976c). Rather than search for a new definition, it may be better to assume that Popper's original approach was correct and that it is classical logic that is at variance with a real-world epistemology where imprecision and vagueness, as Popper (1976b) has noted himself, cannot be avoided (or perhaps *should* not be avoided).

Jaśkowski (1969) (who, independently of Gentzen, developed the first system of natural deduction in classical logic) analyses the role of contradiction in logical inference in the process of precisiation of theories, and discusses the limitations of classical logic. He surveys the suitability of various non-standard logics for inference from contradictory data, and develops a new system for this purpose.

It appears that metalogical and epistemological studies into the structure of fuzzy systems will become of increasing importance, and we have included in the bibliography a selection of key papers for this purpose. On the algebraic side are Birkhoff (1948), C. C. Chang (1958b), Halmos (1962), Epstein and Horn (1974, 1975a, b), Rasiowa (1974), Rasiowa and Sikorski (1970) and L. Rieger (1967). The approach based on residuated lattices (L. Rieger, 1949a, b; Blyth and Janowitz, 1972; Epstein and Horn, 1975a, b) links algebra to topology. And on the topological side are Čech (1966, 1968), Lemmon (1966a, b), McKinsey (1941, 1945), McKinsey and Tarski (1944, 1948), Pospišil (1937, 1939a, b, 1941a–d), Rasiowa and Sikorski (1970), Stone (1937–38), Tarski (1956), Rieger (1949a), and Takeuti and Zaring (1973). Some more general nonstandard systems necessitate the use of generalized topologies, e.g. Tarski's (1956, pp. 60–109) calculus of consequence is based on an MIU-topology, and the basic work here is

Čech's 1937 paper which has recently become available in English translation (Čech, 1968). Kohout (1975) surveys the work triggered by this paper. Hempel (1937) is particularly interesting in a fuzzy systems context because of its use of order relations to define a topology. Study of ordered algebraic structures leads naturally to *semirings* (Aczel, 1948; Arbib, 1970) which play a key role in fuzzy automata (Gaines and Kohout, 1975a,b) where important links between semirings and fuzzy languages are Schutzenberger (1962), Wechler and Dimitrov (1974), and Negoiță and Ralescu (1975a). All of these concepts integrate together under the auspices of *category theory* (Bunge, 1966; Banaschewska and Bruns, 1967; Banaschewska, 1968; Goguen, 1968, 1969a; Arbib and Manes, 1974, 1975a,b; Manes, 1976). See particularly Goguen's (1974b) work on categories of fuzzy concepts; MacLane's (1971, p. 94) note of adjoint properties in Boolean algebras, and the related developments of connections between category theory and logic (Lawvere, 1972; Lawvere, *et al.*, 1975).

Probability Theory

Many of the early writers on fuzzy system theory emphasized that although it used truth values in the interval [0, 1] it was in no way related to probability theory. However, probability theory has many aspects (Hamlin, 1959; Rubin, 1969; Stalnaker, 1970; Stalnaker and Thomason, 1970; Wolniewicz, 1970; Hart, 1972; T. L. Fine, 1973; Hacking, 1975a,b; L. J. Cohen, 1975; Pollock, 1975; Mathie and Rathie, 1975), and the lack of correspondence with any one of them was probably exaggerated because an obvious initial reaction from any audience to a [0, 1] system of vagueness was "oh, this is some form of probability theory." In fact, although there are clearly significant differences, there are also both formal and practical links between fuzzy system theory and probability theory (Gaines, 1976c,d,h). Because it is not truth-functional, the treatment of probability theory as a *logical calculus* (probability logic, PL) has never been fully developed although, for example, both Łukasiewicz (Borkowski, 1970, pp. 16–63) and Popper (1927b) have proposed such calculi (some notes on early developments will be found in Rescher, 1969, pp. 187–188). Popper's theory was developed in the late thirties and since that time he has repeatedly emphasized that the Boolean model is only one of many possible. More recently an interesting *non-Boolean* model of probability has been proposed by Novák (1968).

Carnap's (1950) studies of the logical foundations of probability in the context of confirmation theory (Bar-Hillel, 1964; Foster and Martin, 1966; Swinburne, 1973) have also triggered off several studies of probability systems over logical languages (Gaiffman, 1964; Adams, 1966; Scott and Krauss, 1966; Fenstad, 1967). There are also important links between probability theory and modal logic (Rescher, 1963; Danielson, 1967; Miura, 1972).

Giles (1974a–c, 1975, 1976a–c) in a series of papers has given a very attractive exposition of a formal calculus that encompases both probability logic and $Ł_1$, and gives an interesting interpretation of it in terms of a *dialogue model*—his initial area of application was quantum physics. Gaines (1976c, d, h) has given a construction for a non-truth-functional *basic probability logic* whose connectives are the same for PL and $Ł_1$, and which reduces to PL when LEM is added but to $Ł_1$ when strong truth-functionality is required. This logic again has an interesting interpretation in terms of the responses of a population and serves to link fuzzy logics with both frequentist and subjective approaches to probability. It is interesting to compare the analyses of Giles and Gaines with the related studies of Watanabe (1969, 1975) (again initiated in quantum physics), and the purely algebraic expositions of Epstein and Horn (1974, 1975a, b).

Watanabe (1975) emphasizes that under some circumstances both probabilistic and fuzzy approaches may be inadequate, e.g., when there is a strong interaction between observer and observed. DeLuca and Termini (1971) have stressed that in this situation the valuation-lattice is nondistributive, and there are also quantum-mechanical situations where noncommutativity is essential so that various lattice-like structures are of interest but with weaker properties. Jordan (1952) and Kotas (1963) give some background and corresponding algebraic structures are developed in Jordan (1962), Gerhardts (1965, 1969), and Beran (1974). Prugovecki's (1973, 1974, 1975, 1976a, b) is important in combining probabilistic and fuzzy structures in the context of quantum mechanics. Zadeh (1968b) and Loginov (1966) suggest other combinations, and the work on fuzzy measures of R. E. Smith (1970) and Sugeno (1972a, b, 1973, 1974, 1975a–d) establishes other important relationships in the context of non-additive measure theory.

Studies of human decision making have tended to assume a probabilistic norm, probably based on a Bayesian approach. Re-analysis of such experiments as those of Edwards, *et al.*, (1968) in terms of fuzzy reasoning might provide some new insights into the results obtained since these indicate a poorer performance by humans than the Bayesian model would predict. Indeed there is much to be gained by closer liaison between work on human decision making and *subjective probability* (Smith, 1961, 1965; Edwards, 1962; Good, 1962; Von Wright, 1962; Villegas, 1964; Aczel and Pfanzagl, 1966; Shuford, *et al.*, 1966; Winkler and Murphy, 1968; Menges, 1970, 1974; Savage, 1971; Winkler, 1974; Shuford and Brown, 1975;

Hogarth, 1975; Vickers, 1975), and work on fuzzy reasoning. In this context Pearl's (1975c) recent analysis of subjective probability, and related papers on modeling and approximation (Pearl, 1974, 1975a–e, 1976a, b; Leal and Pearl, 1976) are particularly interesting.

Whereas studies of subjective probability are largely concerned with isolated decisions, there have also been developed complete logics of human decision making, preference, belief, etc. Some of these are within a framework of probability theory (Hintikka and Suppes, 1970; Grofman and Hyman, 1973), but others are based on systems of modal logic (Rescher, 1967; Von Wright, 1957, 1963a, b, 1972). There are direct relationships between modal and probability logics already mentioned, and it would seem worthwhile to examine the comparable relationships with fuzzy logics for decision-making.

The studies of both logical probability/confirmation, and subjective probability/information, converge naturally in the analysis of *inductive reasoning* (De Finetti, 1972; Levi, 1967; Kyburg, 1970), and the literature discussing the relationship between inductive and deductive logics (Dilman, 1973; Dummett, 1973; Haack, 1976) or attempting to vindicate induction (Stove, 1973; Katz, 1962) is also relevant in a fuzzy context. There are important practical studies that link inductive reasoning to variable-valued logics (Michalski, 1974, 1975; Chilausky, *et al.*, 1976; Larsen, 1976) and a far-reaching series of studies previously discussed initiated by Hájek in Czechoslovakia that link it to MVLs including fuzzy logics. The GUHA schemes of Hájek find practical realization in algorithms such as those of Klir (1975, 1976), Klir and Uttenhove (1976a, b) and Gaines (1975b, 1976e, f) for determination of system structure from behavior, and these also serve to provide other links between various aspects of probability theory and fuzzy system theory.

There are now also a range of applications studies contrasting probabilistic and fuzzy systems: Baas and Kwakernaak (1975) re-analyse using fuzzy reasoning the problems analysed by Kahne (1975) on a probabilistic basis; Gaines (1975a) re-analyses the fuzzy control strategies of Mamdani and Assilian (1975) using a probability logic; Shortliffe and Buchanan's (1975) critique of Bayesian methods in medical inference is particularly interesting, although it only mentions fuzzy reasoning in passing; Shortliffe's book (1976) contains a wealth of theoretical material and practical results on inductive reasoning with inexact data.

Fuzzification of Mathematical Systems

If one takes the viewpoint that fuzzy sets are an alternative to classical sets then it is possible to consider the *fuzzification* (Goguen, 1967) of a wide variety of mathematical structures by taking the underlying sets to be fuzzy. This has been done for many specific structures, e.g., logics (Lee and Chang, 1971; Gaines, 1976d; Pinkava, 1976a); relations; (Goguen, 1967, Dijkman and Lowen, 1976); functions (Goguen, 1967; Davio and Thayse, 1973); graphs (Longo, 1975; Rosenfeld, 1975); groups (Rosenfeld, 1971); automata (Nasu and Honda, 1968; Santos, 1968a, b, 1969a, b, 1972a, b, 1975a, 1976a ; Santos and Wee, 1968; Mizumoto, *et al.*, 1969; Mizumoto and Tanaka, 1976; Bertoni, 1973); grammars (Mizumoto, 1971; Mizumoto, *et al.*, 1971, 1972a, b, d, 1973a, b; DePalma and Yau, 1975; Santos, 1975c); languages (Lee and Zadeh, 1969, 1970; Mizumoto, *et al.*, 1970; Santos, 1974; Thomason and Marinos, 1974; Hodda and Nasu, 1975; Rajasethupady and Lakshmivarahan, 1974; Lashmivarahan and Rajasethupady, 1974); algorithms (Zadeh, 1968a; Santos, 1970); programs (C. L. Chang, 1975; Santos, 1975c 1976b); and so on.

In his 1967 paper Goguen uses a category-theoretic approach to fuzzification which may be seen as encompassing all these specific structures, and Goguen (1974b) gives a Lawvere-style axiomatization of the category of fuzzy sets and hence, with specific extensions, of all such fuzzified structures. This approach is developed extensively and tutorially by Negoita and Ralescu (1975a) in their book, and is a key element in the important papers by Sols and Meseguer on fuzzified algebraic and topological systems (Sols, 1975a–c; Meseguer and Sols, 1974, 1975a, b) and by Arbib and Manes (1974, 1975a, b) on fuzzy automata. For those concerned with the theory of fuzzified structures, categories are important tools in avoiding duplication of the same results in a differing terminology and in transferring mathematical techniques from one area to another.

The structures obtained by fuzzification are not uniquely defined, being generally uninteresting unless some link is hypothesized between the fuzzy set operations and the other structural operations—this generally comes down to specifying what interaction rules for classical sets are to be preserved with fuzzy sets, and then determining what happens to other rules. This variety of possible approaches means that, for example, the *fuzzy topologies* of one author are not necessarily those of another.

Zadeh's original motivation in introducing fuzzy sets was systems theoretical and one would expect fuzzy topologies over these sets to have a key role paralleling that of crisp topologies in conventional system theory. As one would expect the 'deep' results in this area have been obtained by those, such as Goguen, Sols and Meseguer, cited above, using the category-theoretic approach. There are also key works in the 'non-fuzzy' literature on *generalized topologies* and *topologies without points* which are directly applicable to fuzzified topologies.

The majority of other papers on fuzzy topologies seem to stem from C. L. Chang's (1968) definition of a fuzzy topology as a family of open sets that preserves this property under arbitrary unions and finite intersections. Further development of the properties of such topologies appears in Hutton (1974, 1975), Hutton and Reilly (1974), Lowen (1974a, b, 1975, 1976a–d), M. D. Weiss (1975), Wong (1973, 1974a, b, 1975, 1976), Warren (1974b, c), Ganter, *et al.*, 1975, and Meseguer and Sols, 1975b. Other results on fuzzy topologies appear also in papers on the optimization of dynamical systems (Nazaroff, 1973; Warren, 1974a).

In these papers, a closed set is defined as the complement of an open set (using Zadeh's $1 - x$ complementation). However, since the lattice of all subsets of a fuzzy set is not complemented, this leads to a relationship between open and closed sets which is different from that of a standard crisp topology. Not all authors seem to realize the implications of this difference which creates a demand for increased mathematical rigour if one is to obtain meaningful and correct results. On the other hand, some authors who do fully realize the difference seem to 'infer' from it that fuzzy topologies defined on closed sets are of little significance (Goguen, 1974a; Negoita and Ralescu, 1975a).

The results of Michálek (1975) indicate that fuzzy topologies defined on families of closed sets are at least as important as those based on open set definition. He defines a topological structure in which the closed sets are fuzzified. This corresponds to fuzzification of a Fréchet topological space (ABU-topology[1]), generalized Fréchet convergence space (AB-topology) and Čech closure space (IM-topology), which includes the former cases as special instances. This approach leads to some interesting results which are expressible in the terms of probability theory (probabilistic Menger topological spaces—see Kramosil and Michálek, 1975) but which, it appears, have not been studied or proved in the probability context. Kramosil and Michálek (1975) define a fuzzy metric space by fuzzifying the metric and prove a theorem on the equivalence of their fuzzy topology to some stochastic metric topological spaces.

The lattice of fuzzy subsets is distributive (Negoita and Ralescu, 1975a, p. 15) and hence fuzzy topologies are closely related to a generalization of crisp topologies that has been surveyed and studied by Koutský (1947, 1952) who examined many general mappings on an arbitrary lattice as closure operators of topologies "*without points*" (Meseguer and Sols,

---

[1]Each letter designates an axiom according to the Čech-Koutský classification of generalized topologies and topologies without points, e.g. that defined by the Kuratowski closure axioms is designated as an AIOU-topology. For a list of the axioms see Kohout (1975, pp. 26–27).

1975b). Papers concerning such generalized topologies contain important results for fuzzy topologies (Foradori, 1933; Terasaka, 1937; Nakamura, 1941; Monteiro and Ribeiro, 1942; Chittenden, 1941; Koutský, 1947, 1952; Beran, 1974; Sikorski, 1964; D. Papert Strauss, 1968; Dowlker and Papert, 1966, etc.). The set of fuzzy subsets may also be described as a Morgan algebra, so that papers on Morgan and quasi-Boolean algebras are also relevant to fuzzy topologies (Moisil, 1935; Kalman, 1958; Henkin, 1963; State, 1971; Petrescu, 1971; Maronna, 1964; Bialnicki-Birula, 1957; Rasiowa, 1974).

Certain categories of generalized topologies which have been studied in great depth by Čech and his school (1966, 1968) admit not only generalized crisp topologies but also fuzzy and other lattice topologies as their realizations. The wealth of results contained in these works remains yet to be fully explored in the context of fuzzy topologies. Goguen (1974a) defines a class of fuzzy topologies based on the open set approach. In categorical terms, he investigates one of the possible duals to the category of IM-topologies and proves a Tychonov theorem. This theorem in its classical version plays an important role in meta-mathematics of mathematical proofs (Łoś and Ryll-Nardzewski, 1951). It would be interesting to examine the role of Goguen's version of the theorem in the meta-mathematics of fuzzy systems. It is also interesting to compare Goguen's results with Sikorski's on 5-additive closure algebras (for the list of references see Sikorski, 1964).

The previous discussion illustrates well the need to delimit carefully what part of a mathematical structure is to be fuzzified. For example, the distinction between the fuzzification of objects (or a family of subsets of objects) and the fuzzification of morphisms is a key one. The majority of modern algebraic techniques and theories are modelled on, or are extensions of, the theory of equivalence relations and congruences (as exemplifed by the work of Dubreil and Dubreil-Jacotin, 1937, or Ore, 1942). Yet in order to make the distinction between the fuzzification of morphisms and objects, it is often necessary to work with the objects directly.

A similar distinction appears in the structural theory of automata as exemplified by the remark of Hartmanis & Stearns (1966):

> The mathematical foundations of this structure theory rest on an algebraization of the concept of 'information' in a machine and supply the algebraic formalism necessary to study problems about the flow of this information in machines as they operate. The formal techniques and results are very closely related to modern algebra. Many of its results show considerable similarity with results in universal algebra, and some can be derived directly from such considerations. Nevertheless, the engineering motivation demands that this theory go its own

way and raises many problems which require new mathematical techniques to be invented that have no counterpart in the development of algebra

Analogous remarks can be made for fuzzy systems, but Hartmanis and Stearns' "error" of assuming that their techniques had no counterpart in the development of algebra should not be repeated. The extensive work of Borůvka (1937, 1938, 1939, 1941, 1974) and his school is based on the development of modern algebra through the theory of decompositions in sets. It is probable that any successful attempt at general fuzzification of mathematical systems will also invoke semantic distinctions that are not necessary in the standard textbook approach to algebra and will find a more appropriate basis in Borůvka's approach. Similar remarks apply to the work of Čech and his school, already cited, where finer semantic distinctions are made than are generally necessary for crisp structures. Apart from the material on generalized topologies, the sections of his book on non-topological constructs are also very relevant to fuzzification.

Clearly the key papers on fuzzification cited in this section are based on a full awareness of these distinctions, but there are others in which the results are superficial or incorrect because implicit results on crisp structures have been carried over when they no longer hold and may even be contradictory. When a mathematical structure is fuzzified, *all* the standard assumptions and results about its properties need explicit verification.

Note that the term, *fuzzy* has also been used in a sense distinct from that of Zadeh in the context of *tolerance spaces* (having a nontransitive neighborhood relation). However, this work is also of interest in terms of imprecision and we have included some references (Arbib, 1967; Poston, 1971a, b; Roberts, 1973; DalCin, 1975a, b).

Some Application Areas

We cannot detail the wide range of application studies using fuzzy system theory—the papers are in the bibliography with key words indicating the main application areas. In particular, *Pattern recognition* (**PAT**) and *Decision-making* (**DEC**) are two such obvious and extensive application areas that it is best to glance through looking for these keys. However, certain applications are of special interest or importance and we shall briefly outline those not already discussed.

Zadeh has emphasized throughout his work the direct relationship of fuzzy system theory to *human linguistic reasoning* with imprecise concepts. This is probably a very important factor in the wide general interest in this work, a breadth of interest never aroused by the work on formal logic which will probably, in the long term, be seen to provide the formal foundations for Zadeh's development. While the logical progress through, "this [induction] is formally impossible—however, people do it successfully —let's copy the behavior patterns of people," is almost a tautology for engineers, the resultant models of human linguistic behavior are also potentially of interest to linguists. One of the key early papers on fuzzy reasoning is that by George Lakoff (1973) already referenced, who has contributed to developments in linguistics on a far wider front but continues to emphasize the importance of fuzzy systems theory for linguistics (Parrett, 1974).

The interaction between linguistics and fuzzy systems theory, like that between linguistics and artificial intelligence, is a difficult one to specify. There is much common ground but very different attitudes to the treasures it contains. For the linguist, comprehension of actual language structures is vital, whereas for the system theorist such structures are only a stimulus, a bionic model. A good feel for the motivations and directions of current linguistic research can be gained from the conversations of Parrett (1974). Other useful collections on modern linguistics are Fillmore & Langendoen (1971), and the series of four volumes on *Syntax and Semantics* (Kimball, 1972, 1973, 1975; Cole and Morgan, 1975) which contains articles on such topics as *hedges* (Fraser, 1975; Lysvag, 1975) and *possible and must* (Karttunen, 1972). The study of language as a persuasive medium is clearly central to reasoning and often goes under the term *rhetoric*—a useful recent textbook with many examples is Simons (1976). Lewis' account of *convention* in inter-person communication is particularly important in establishing how precisiation occurs in a community. A particularly interesting non-fuzzy development that uses order relationships clearly related to fuzzy logic is Wilks (1975) *preference semantics*. A fascinating example of a linguist actually using fuzzy system theory to analyze actual textual material are Rieger's (1974, 1975, 1976a, b) studies of 18th century German student lyric poetry. Reddy (1972) has given a fuzzy-sets model of reference and metaphor in English.

Similar considerations to those above apply to the interface between fuzzy system theory and *human psychology*. There are system-theory oriented experiments on what fuzzy functions people use (MacVicar-Whelan, 1974; Kochen and Badre, 1974; Kochen and Dreyfuss-Raimi, 1974; Dreyfuss, *et al.*, 1975; Damerau, 1975; Rodder, 1975); psychological experiments on human linguistic usage that throw light on reasoning with imprecise concepts (Sheppard, 1954; Osgood, *et al.*, 1964); and psychological models of human behavior based on fuzzy systems theory (Hersh, 1976; Hersh and Caramazza, 1975, 1976; Hersh and Spiering, 1976). There are also fuzzy system theoretic studies of cognition and memory (Kokawa, *et al.*, 1972, 1973, 1974a, b, 1975a, b; Slack, 1976a, b).

Fuzzy system theory has had little impact on the literature of *artificial intelligence* (AI) as yet. Kling (1973a, b, 1974) and LeFaivre (1974a, b, 1976) give extensions to the AI programming language, PLANNER, to allow the use of fuzzy logic. R. C. T. Lee (1972) has made a preliminary study of resolution theorem proving for a fuzzified form of predicate calculus (quantified variant standard sequence, *not* quantified L_1). Winograd (1974) has criticized the role of fuzzy hedges in imprecise reasoning in AI. The only actual operational studies appear to be those of the "Fuzzy Robot Users Group" at UCLA (Goguen, 1976) who have implemented a robot environment similar to Winograd's blocks but allowing fuzzy specifications (Shaket, 1975) and fuzzy hints (Goguen, 1975b, 1976).

The *social sciences* provide some particularly attractive applications for fuzzy systems theory, although not as many yet as might be expected given the need for a methodology capable of dealing with inherent imprecision (Menges and Skala, 1974; Gottinger, 1973). Wenstop (1975a, b, 1976) provides the most convincing examples of what can be done in his fuzzy linguistic simulation of interpersonal dynamics in organizations. Gale's (1972, 1974a, b, 1975a, b) studies of conflict resolution in regional geography are another substantial body of results. Drosselmeyer and Wonneberger (1975) report application in the parochial field, Esogbue (1975) to modeling cancer research appropriation, and Van Velthoven (1974a, b, 1975a–c) to criminal investigation and personnel management. Economic applications have also been reported (Hatten, *et al.*, 1975, Stoica and Scarlat, 1975a) and it is interesting to refer back to some of Shackle's (1949, 1961) pioneering studies of economic decision-making.

Biology and medicine now also provide a range of interesting application studies such as Butnariu's (1975) neural models, Malvache's (1975) of visual perception, and Kohout's (1976c) of hierarchical movement structures. Adey (1972) reports use of fuzzy clustering for chimpanzee EEG analysis (Larsen, *et al.*, 1972). Albin (1975) has achieved considerable success in ECG diagnosis (Bremermann, 1971) and a variety of comparable applications have been reported (Fujisake, 1971; Kalmanson and Stegall, 1973; Sanchez, 1975; Wechsler, 1975; Woodbury and Clive, 1974). Certainly the direct application of Bayesian techniques to medical diagnosis has proved of limited value, and fuzzy system theory is providing an attractive alternative approach. It is interesting to compare it with other new methodologies such as Atkin's (1974) *q*-analysis, which are also having impact on automated diagnosis (see Sept. 1976 special issue of *International Journal of Man-Machine Studies* on *q*-analysis).

Control engineering provides a good test for fuzzy system theory since it was an area central to Zadeh's interests prior to 1965, and it is generally thought of as a *hard* area, perhaps less appropriate to fuzzification. However, control of complex industrial plant has been one of the key areas of successful application commencing with the work of Mamdani and Assilian (Assilian, 1974; Mamdani, 1974; Mamdani and Assilian, 1975). They were initially comparing learning algorithms for adaptive control of a nonlinear, multidimensional plant (a physical steam engine), but found that many learning schemes failed to even begin to converge on a reasonable time scale (running out of steam!). A fuzzy linguistic method was developed to *prime* the learning controller with an initial policy to speed adaption—the verbal statements of engineers were transcribed as fuzzy rules and used under fuzzy logic to form a control policy. The performance of these fuzzy linguistic controllers was so good in their own right, however, that they became central to a range of studies in their own right: Carter and Hague (1976) *sinter plant*; Jensen (1976) and Ostergaard (1976) *heat exchanger*; Kickert (1974, 1975a–c); Kickert and Nauta Lemke (1975) *water baths*; King and Mamdani (1975, 1976); Mamdani (1976a, b); Marks (1975a, 1975b); Procyk (1974, 1976a, b); Rutherford (1976) and Rutherford and Bloore (1975) *sinter plant*; Sinha and Wright (1975) *heat exchanger*; and Tong (1976a–c). Recently Mamdani has noted that the instructions for manual operation of a lime kiln are essentially fuzzy linguistic rules (Perry and Waddell 1972), and has shown that fuzzy control policies may be learned automatically by a controller with *fuzzy linguistic adaptive strategies* (Mamdani, 1976a, 1976b; Mamdani and Baakilini, 1975; Mamdani and Procyk, 1976; Procyk, 1976b).

There are many more application areas represented in the bibliography, e.g., Kandel's work on switching logic, Negoita's on information retrieval, Bezdek's on numerical taxonomy, Dunn's on fuzzy clustering, etc. Most of these are also now well represented and cross-referenced in the main literature, and are relatively easy to access. Further development of fuzzy systems theory clearly depends on the growth and strengthening of these, and the many other, applications areas mentioned. Formal logic, philosophy, mathematics, and like disciplines, always seem to follow the sources of excitement, and arrive at the party just in time to tidy up. It is in these diverse application areas that the excitement has to be generated and maintained.

THE BIBLIOGRAPHY AND ITS CLASSIFICATION

The bibliography contains 1164 references in total of which 763 are classified as fuzzy (**FUZ**). Table 1 gives a list and explanation of the 31 keywords used in classifying papers. We aimed at a set comprehensive enough to be useful, but small enough to be remembered in browsing through.

Table 1
Keywords

FUZ	Fuzzy System Theory	**SYS**	System Theory
MVLOG	Many-Valued Logic	**GAME**	Game Theory
MLOG	Modal Logic	**DEC**	Decision-Making
SWLOG	Switching Logic	**PAT**	Pattern Recognition
LOG	General Formal Logic	**PROB**	Probability Theory
INDUCT	Inductive Logic and Systems	**CON**	Control
VAG	Philosophy of Vagueness	**LMACH**	Learning Machines and
TRUTH	Philosophy of Truth		Artificial Intelligence
PARA	Analysis of Paradoxes	**AUT**	Automata
CAT	Category Theory	**LANG**	Formal Languages
SET	Set Theory	**LING**	Linguistics
TOP	Topology	**PSYCH**	Psychology
LAT	Lattice Theory	**SS**	Social Sciences
SEMR	Semirings	**MED**	Medical Sciences
TOL	Tolerance Spaces	**BIO**	Biological Sciences
IMEAS	Inexact Measurement	**INFR**	Information Retrieval

Table 2
Distribution of Additional
Keywords in Papers
Classified as Fuzzy

FUZ	763 (*total*)	**LMACH**	22
AUT	65	**INFR**	18
PAT	55	**CAT**	15
SS	49	**MED**	13
LING	49	**SYS**	11
CON	46	**BIO**	10
PROB	45	**LAT**	10
DEC	45	**INDUCT**	8
MVLOG	38	**GAME**	7
SWLOG	36	**PARA**	7
LANG	32	**TOL**	4
LOG	32	**SEMR**	3
TOP	29	**IMEAS**	1
PSYCH	27	**TRUTH**	1
VAG	24	**MLOG**	1
SET	23		

Table 3
Distribution of Year of Publication
of Papers Classified as Fuzzy

1965	2
1966	4
1967	4
1968	12
1969	22
1970	25
1971	42
1972	58
1973	88
1974	136
1975	227
1976	143 (*incomplete*)
	total 763

Table 2 shows the distribution of the keywords over the papers classified as fuzzy, and hence gives some indication of the main interactions with other fields. Table 3 shows the distribution of year of publication over the papers classified as fuzzy, and hence gives some indication of the rate of growth of the literature. Note that the figure for 1976 is not meaningful since (from experience of the 1975 figures a year ago) a very large number of 1976 references have not yet been sent to us.

Comparable tables are not given for the bibliography as a whole since the non-fuzzy references have been very much a personal selection and do not give a comprehensive picture of any specific field.

Ackermann, R. (1967) *Introduction to Many Valued Logics*, Routledge & Kegan Paul, London, **MVLOG**

Aczel, M. J. (1948) Sur les operations definies pour les nombres reels, *Bull. Soc. Math. Francaise*, *76*, 59–64, **PROB,SEMR**

Aczel, J., & Pfanzagl, J. (1966) Remarks on the measurement of subjective probability and information, *Metrika*, *5*, 91–105, **PROB**

Adámek, J., & Wechler, W. (1976) Minimization of R-fuzzy automata, in *Studien zur Algebra und ihre Anwendungen*, Akad.-Verl., Berlin, **FUZ,AUT**

Adams, E. W. (1965) Elements of a theory of inexact measurement, *Philos. Sci.*, *32*, 205–228, **VAG,IMEAS**

Adams, E. W. (1966) Probability and the logic of conditionals, in Hintikka, J., & Suppes, P. (eds.), *Aspects of Inductive Logic*, North-Holland, Amsterdam, 265–316, **PROB,LOG**

Adams, E. W. (1974) The logic of "almost all", *J. Philos. Logic*, *3*, 3–17, **LOG, MLOG**

Adams, E. W., & Levine, H. P. (1975) On the uncertainties transmitted from premises to conclusions in deductive inferences, *Synthese*, *30*, 429–460, **VAG, LOG**

Adavič, P. N., Borisov, A. N., & Golender, V. E. (1968) An adaptive algorithm for recognition of fuzzy patterns, in D. S. Kristinkov, J. J. Osis, L. A. Rastrigin (eds.), *Kibernetika i Diagnostika*, *2*, 13–18, (in Russian) Zinatne, Riga, U. S. S. R., **FUZ,PAT**

Adey, W. R. (1972) Organization of brain tissue: is the brain a noisy processor?, *Int. J. Neurology*, *3*, 271–284, **FUZ,BIO**

Aida, S. (1975) Informatics in "Eco-technology", in *Summary of Papers on General Fuzzy Problems*, The Working Group on Fuzzy Systems, Tokyo, Japan, Nov., 1–4, **FUZ**

Aizermann, M. A. (1975) Fuzzy sets, fuzzy proofs and some unsolved problems in the theory of automatic control, *Special Interest Discussion Session on Fuzzy Automata and Decision Processes*, 6th IFAC World Congress, Boston, Mass., USA, Aug., **FUZ,CON**

Albin, M. (1975) Fuzzy sets and their application to medical diagnosis, *PhD thesis*, Department of Mathematics, University of California, Berkeley, California, **FUZ,MED**

Allen, A. D. (1973) A method of evaluating technical journals on the basis of published comments through fuzzy implications: a survey of the major IEEE transactions, *IEEE Trans. Syst. Man Cybern.*, *SMC-3*, 422–425, **FUZ,INFR**

Allen, A. D. (1974) Measuring the empirical properties of sets, *IEEE Trans. Syst. Man Cybern.*, *SMC-4*, 66–73, **FUZ**

Altham, J. E. (1971) *The Logic of Plurality*, Methuen, London, **LOG**

Anderson, A. R., & Belnap, N. D. (1962) The pure calculus of entailment, *J. Symbolic Logic*, *27*, 19–25, **LOG**

Anderson, A. R., & Belnap, N. D. (1975) *Entailment*, Princeton University Press, New Jersey, **LOG**

Arbib, M. A. (1967) Tolerance automata, *Kybernetika (Prague)*, *3*, 223–233, **TOL,AUT**

Arbib, M. A. (1970) Semiring languages, Electrical Engineering Department, Stanford University, California, USA, **SEMR,FUZ,LANG**

Arbib, M. A. (1975) From automata theory to brain theory, *Int. J. Man-Machine Studies*, *7*, 279–295, **AUT,BIO**

Arbib, M. A., & Manes, E. G. (1974) Fuzzy morphisms in automata theory, *Proc. First International Symposium on Category Theory Applied to Computation and Control*, 98–105, **FUZ,AUT**

Arbib, M. A., & Manes, E. G. (1975a) A category-theoretic approach to systems in a fuzzy world, *Synthese*, *30*, 381–406, **FUZ,AUT,SYS**

Arbib, M. A., & Manes, E. G. (1975b) Fuzzy machines in a category, *Bulletin Australian Math. Soc.*, *13*, 169–210, **FUZ,CAT,AUT**

Arigoni, A. O. (1976) Membership characteristic function of fuzzy elements fundamental theoretical basis, *3rd Eur. Meeting Cybern. Syst. Res.*, *Vienna* **FUZ**

Asai, K., & Kitajima, S. (1971) Learning control of multimodal systems by fuzzy automata, in Fu, K. S. (ed.), *Pattern recognition and machine learning*, Plenum Press, New York, 195–203, **FUZ,AUT,LMACH**

Asai, K., & Kitjima, S. (1971) A method for optimizing control of multimodal systems using fuzzy automata, *Inform. Sci.*, *3*, 343–353, **FUZ,AUT,LMACH**

Asai, K., & Kitajima, S. (1972) Optimizing control using fuzzy automata, *Automatica*, *8*, 101–104, **FUZ,CON**

Asai, K., & Tanaka, H. (1975) Applications of fuzzy sets theory to decision-making and control, *J. JAACE*, *19*, 235–242, **FUZ,DEC,CON**

Asai, K., Tanaka, H., & Okuda, T. (1975) Decision making and its goal in a fuzzy environment, in Zadeh, L. A., Fu, K. S., Tanaka, K., & Shimura, M. (eds.), *Fuzzy Sets and Their Applications to Cognitive and Decision Processes*, Academic Press, New York, 257–277, **FUZ,DEC**

Asenjo, F. G. (1966) A calculus for antinomies, *Notre Dame J. Formal Logic*, *7*, 103–105, **LOG,PARA**

Assilian, S. (1974) Artificial intelligence in the control of real dynamic systems, *PhD thesis*, Queen Mary College, University of London, **FUZ,LMACH,CON**

Atkin, R. H. (1974) *Mathematical Structure in Human Affairs*, Heinemann, London, **SS,LOG,PAT**

Aubin, J. P. (1974a) Theorie de jeaux, *Comp. Rond. Acad. Sci. (Paris)*, *279*, A-891, **FUZ,GAME**

Aubin, J. P. (1974b) Theorie de jeaux, *Comp. Rond. Acad. Sci. (Paris)*, *279*, A-963, **FUZ,GAME**

Aubin, J. P. (1974c) Fuzzy games, *MRC Technical Summary Report 1480*, Mathematical Research Center, University of Wisconsin-Madison, Madison, USA, **FUZ,GAME**

434 / *Gaines and Kohout*

Aubin, J. P. (1976) Fuzzy core and equilibria of games defined in strategic form, in Ho, Y. C., & Mitter, S. K. (eds.), *Directions in Large-Scale Systems*, Plenum Press, New York, 371–388, **FUZ,GAME**

Axinn, A., & Axinn, D. (1976) Notes on the logic of ignorance relations, *Amer. Philos. Quart.*, *13*, 135–143, **LOG,VAG**

Baas, S. M., & Kwakernaak, H. (1975) Rating and ranking of multiple-aspect alternatives using fuzzy sets, *Memorandum Nr. 73*, Department of Applied Mathematics, Twente University of Technology, Enschede, The Netherlands, April, **FUZ,DEC**

Banaschewska, B., & Bruns, G. (1967) Categorical characterization of the Mac-Neville completion, *Archiv der Mathematik*, 369–377, **CAT**

Banaschewska, B. (1968) Injective hulls in the category of distributive lattices, *Journal für die Reine und Angewandte Mathematik*, 102–109, **CAT,LAT**

Bang, S. Y., & Yeh, R. T. (1974) Toward a theory of relational data structure, *SELTR-1*, University of Austin, Texas, USA, **FUZ**

Barcan, R. C. (1946) A functional calculus of first order based on strict implication, *J. Symbolic Logic*, *11*, 1–16, **MLOG**

Bar-Hillel, Y. (1964) *Language and Information*, Addison-Wesley, Reading, Mass., USA, **LING,INDUCT,PROB**

Barnev, P., Dimitrov, V., & Stanchev, P. (1974) Fuzzy system approach to decision-making based on public opinion investigation through questionnaires, *IFAC Symposium on Stochastic Control*, Budapest, Sep., **FUZ,DEC**

Becker, J. M. (1973) A structural design process, *PhD thesis*, Department of Civil Engineering, University of California, Berkeley, California, USA, **FUZ**

Bellman, R. E. (1970) Humor and Paradox, in Mendel, W. M. (ed.), *A Celebration of Laughter*, Mara Books, Los Angeles, California, 35–45, **FUZ,PARA**

Bellman, R. E. (1971) Law and mathematics, *Technical Report 71–34*, University of Southern California, Los Angeles, USA, Sep., **FUZ**

Bellman, R. E. (1973) Mathematics and the human sciences, in Wilkinson, J., Bellman, R. E., & Garaudy, R. (eds.), *The Dynamic Programming of Human Systems*, MSS Information Corp., New York, USA, 11–18, **FUZ,SS**

Bellman, R. E. (1973) Retrospective futurology: some introspective comments, in Wilkinson, J., Bellman, R. E., & Garaudy, R. (eds.), *The Dynamic Programming of Human Systems*, MSS Information Corp., New York, USA, 35–37, **FUZ**

Bellman, R. E. (1974) Local logics, *Technical Report No. USC EE RB 74–9*, University of Southern California, Los Angeles, USA, **FUZ,LOG**

Bellman, R. E. (1975) Communication, ambiguity and understanding, *Math. Biosciences*, *26*, 347–356, **FUZ,VAG**

Bellman, R. E., & Giertz, M. (1973) On the analytic formalism of the theory of fuzzy sets, *Inform. Sci.*, *5*, 149–156, **FUZ**

Bellman, R. E., Kalaba, R., & Zadeh, L. A. (1966) Abstraction and pattern classification, *J. Math. Anal. & Appln.*, *13*, 1–7, **FUZ,PAT**

Bellman, R. E., & Marchi, E. (1973) Games of protocol: the city as a dynamic competetive process, *Technical Report RB73-36*, University of Southern California, Los Angeles, California, USA, **FUZ,SS**

Bellman, R. E., & Zadeh, L. A. (1970) Decision-making in a fuzzy environment,

Management Sci., *17*, 141–164, **FUZ,DEC**

Bellman, R. E., & Zadeh, L. A. (1976) Local and fuzzy logics, *ERL-M584*, Electronics Research Laboratory, College of Engineering, University of California, Berkeley, California, USA, May, **FUZ,LOG,VAG,LING**

Belluce, L. P. (1964) Further results on infinite valued predicate logic, *J. Symbolic Logic*, *29*, 69–78, **MVLOG**

Belluce, L. P., & Chang, C. C. (1963) A weak completeness theorem for infinite valued first-order logic, *J. Symbolic Logic*, *28*, 43–50, **MVLOG**

Belnap, N. D. (1960) Entailment and relevance, *J. Symbolic Logic*, *25*, 144–146, **LOG**

Beran, L. (1974) *Grupy a Svazy*, SNTL-Technical Publishers, Prague, (in Czech: Groups and Lattices) **SEMR,LAT,TOP**

Bertolini, F. (1971) Kripke models and many valued logics, *Symposia Mathematica*, 113–131, **MVLOG**

Bertoni, A. (1973) Complexity problems related to the approximation of probabilistic languages and events by deterministic machines, in Nivat, M. (ed.), *Automata, Languages and Programming*, North-Holland, Amsterdam, 507–516, **FUZ,PROB,AUT**

Bezdek, J. C. (1973) Fuzzy mathematics in pattern classification, *PhD thesis*, Center for Applied Mathematics, Cornell University, Ithaca, New York, USA, **FUZ,PAT**

Bezdek, J. C. (1974) Numerical taxonomy with fuzzy sets, *J. Math. Biology*, *1*, 57–71, **PAT,FUZ**

Bezdek, J. C. (1974) Cluster validity with fuzzy sets, *J. Cybernetics*, *3*, 58–73, **PAT,FUZ**

Bezdek, J. C. (1975) Mathematical models for systematics and taxonomy, in Estabrook, G. (ed.), *Proceedings 8th Annual International Conference on Numerical Taxonomy*, Freeman, San Francisco, **PAT,FUZ**

Bezdek, J. C. (1976) A physical interpretation of fuzzy ISODATA, *IEEE Trans. Syst. Man Cybern.*, *6*, 387–389, **PAT,FUZ**

Bezdek, J. C. (1976) Feature selection for binary data: medical diagnosis with fuzzy sets, *Proc. National Computer Conference*, AFIPS Press, Montvale, New Jersey, June, **PAT,FUZ,MED**

Bezdek, J. C., & Dunn, J. C. (1975) Optimal fuzzy partitions: a heuristic for estimating the parameters in a mixture of normal distributions, *IEEE Trans. Comp.*, *C-24*, 835–838, **PAT,FUZ**

Bialnicki-Birula, A. (1957) Remarks on quasi-Boolean algebras, *Bull. de l'Academie Polonaise des Sciences, ser. math., astr. & phys.*, *5*, 615–619, **LOG,TOP**

Birkhoff, G. (1948) *Lattice theory*, American Mathematical Society, Rhode Island, USA, **LAT**

Black, M. (1937) Vagueness: an exercise in logical analysis, *Philos. Sci.*, *4*, 427–455, **VAG**

Black, M. (1963) Reasoning with loose concepts, *Dialogue*, *2*, 325–373, **VAG**

Black, M. (1968) *The labyrinth of language*, Mentor Books, New York, USA, **VAG**

Black, M. (1970) *Margins of precision*, Cornell University Press, Ithaca, New York, USA, **VAG**

Blackburn, S. (ed.) (1975) *Meaning, Reference and Necessity*, Cambridge University

Press, **TRUTH,LOG**

Blin, J. M. (1974) Fuzzy relations in group decision theory, *J. Cybernetics, 4*, 17–22, **FUZ,SS**

Blin, J. M. (1975) Fuzzy relations in multiple-criteria decision making, Northwestern University, Jan., **FUZ,SS,DEC**

Blin, J. M., & Whinston, A. B. (1973) Fuzzy sets and social choice, *J. Cybernetics, 3*, 28–33, **FUZ,SS**

Blyth, T. S., & Janowitz, M. F. (1972) *Residuation Theory*, Pergamon Press, Oxford, **SEMR,LOG,TOP**

Borghi, O. (1972) On a theory of functional probability, Revista Un. Mat. Argentina, *26*, 90–106, **FUZ,PROB**

Borisov, A., & Erenstein, R. X. (1970) Comparison of some crisp and fuzzy algorithms of recognition, *Metody i Sredstva Texničeskoĭ Kibernetiki, 6*, Riga, (in Russian) **FUZ,PAT**

Borisov, A. N., & Osis, J. J. (1969) Search for the greatest divisibility of fuzzy sets, in D. S. Kristinkov, J. J. Osis, L. A. Rastrigin (eds.), *Kibernetika i Diagnostika, 3*, 79–88, (in Russian) Zinatne, Riga, U.S.S.R., **FUZ**

Borisov, A. N., & Osis, J. J. (1970) Methods for experimental estimation of membership functions of fuzzy sets, in D. S. Kristinkov, J. J. Osis, L. A. Rastrigin (eds.), *Kibernetika i Diagnostika, 4*, 125–134, (in Russian) Zinatne, Riga, U.S.S.R., **FUZ,PSYCH**

Borisov, A. N., & Kokle, E. A. (1970) Recognition of fuzzy patterns, in D. S. Kristinkov, J. J. Osis, L. A. Rastrigin (eds), *Kibernetika i Diagnostika, 4*, 135–147, (in Russian) Zinatne, Riga, U.S.S.R., **FUZ,PAT**

Borisov, A. N., Vulf, G. N., & Osis, J. J. (1972) Prediction of the state of a complex system using the theory of fuzzy sets, in D. S. Kristinkov, J. J. Osis, L. A. Rastrigin (eds.), *Kibernetika i Diagnostika, 4*, 79–84, (in Russian) Zinatne, Riga, U.S.S.R., **FUZ,PAT**

Borkowski, L. (1958) On proper quantifiers I, *Studia Logica, 8*, 65–128, **LOG,MV-LOG**

Borkowski, L. (ed.) (1970) *Jan Łukasiewicz Selected Works*, North-Holland, Amsterdam, **PROB,MVLOG**

Borkowski, L., & Slupecki, J. (1958) The logical works of Łukasiewicz, *Studia Logica, 8*, 7–50, **MVLOG,PROB**

Borůvka, O. (1937) Studies on multiplicative systems (semigroups), part 1, *Publications de la Faculté des Sciences de l'Université Masaryk, No. 245*, (in English) **LAT**

Borůvka, O. (1938) Studies on multiplicative systems (semigroups), part 2, *Publications de la Faculté des Sciences de l'Université Masaryk, No. 265*, 1–24, (in English) **LAT**

Borůvka, O. (1939) Theory of groupoids, *Publications de la Faculté des Sciences de l'Université Masaryk, No. 275*, (in Czech.) **LAT,TOP**

Borůvka, O. (1941) Über ketten von faktoroiden, *Mathematische Annalen, 118*, 41–64, **LAT,TOP**

Borůvka, O. (1974) *Foundations of the Theory of Groupoids and Groups*, VEB Deutscher Verlag der Wissenschaften, Berlin, **LAT,SEMR,TOP**

Bossel, H. H., & Hughes, B. B. (1973) Simulation of value-controlled decision-making, *Report SRC-11*, Systems Research Center, Case Western Reserve University, Cleveland, Ohio, USA, **FUZ,DEC**

Bremermann, H. J. (1971) Cybernetic functionals and fuzzy sets, in *IEEE Symposium on Systems Man and Cybernetics*, *71C46SMC*, 248–253, **FUZ,PAT**

Bremermann, H. J. (1974) Complexity of automata, brains and behaviour, in Conrad, M., Güttinger & DalCin, M. (eds.), *Physics and Mathematics of the Nervous System*, *Lecture Notes in Biomathematics*, *4*, Springer, 304–331, **FUZ,AUT**

Brown, G. S. (1969) *Laws of Form*, Allen & Unwin, London, **LOG**

Brown, J. G. (1969) Fuzzy sets on Boolean lattices, *Rep. 1957*, Ballistic Research Laboratories, Aberdeen, Maryland, Jan., **FUZ,LAT**

Brown, J. G. (1971) A note on fuzzy sets, *Inform. & Control*, *18*, 32–39, **FUZ,LAT**

Brunner, J. (1976) Überlick zur theorie und anwendung von fuzzy-mengen, *Vorträge aus dem Problemseminar Automaten und Algorithmentheorie*, April, Weissig, 3–15, **FUZ**

Brunner, J., & Wechler, W. (1976) The Behaviour of R-fuzzy automata, Mazurkiewicz, A. (ed.), *Lecture Noted in Computer Science*, *45*, Springer-Verlag, Berlin, 210–215, **FUZ,AUT**

Bunge, M. C. (1966) Categories of sets valued functors, *PhD thesis*, Department of Mathematics, University of California, **SET,CAT**

Butnariu, D. (1975) L-fuzzy automata description of a neural model, *Proceedings of 3rd International Congress of Cybernetics and Systems*, Bucharest, Rumania, Aug., **FUZ,AUT,BIO**

Capocelli, R. M., & De Luca, A. (1972) Measures of uncertainty in the context of fuzzy sets theory, in *Atti del Ile Congresso Nazionale di Cibernetica di Casciana Terme*, Pisa, Italy, **FUZ,DEC**

Capocelli, R. M., & De Luca, A. (1973) Fuzzy sets and decision theory, *Inform. & Control*, *23*, 446–473, **FUZ,DEC**

Cargile, J. (1969) The sorites paradox, *Brit. J. Philos. Sci.*, *20*, 193–202, **PARA**

Carnap, R. (1947) *Meaning and Necessity*, University of Chicago Press, **VAG,M-LOG**

Carnap, R. (1950) *Logical Foundations of Probability*, University of Chicago Press, **LOG,VAG,PROB**

Carnap, R. (1963) The philosopher replies, in Schilpp, P. A. (ed.), *The Philosophy of R. Carnap, The Library of Living Philosophers*, *11*, Open Court, La Salle, Illinois, USA, **LOG,PROB,INDUCT**

Carnap, R. (1964) *The Logical Syntax of Language*, Routledge & Kegan Paul, London, (1st ed. 1937) **LOG,PARA**

Carter, G. A., & Hague, M. J. (1973) Fuzzy control of raw mix permeability at a sinter plant, in Mamdani, E. H., & Gaines, B. R. (eds.), *Discrete Systems and Fuzzy Reasoning*, *EES-MMS-DSFR-73*, Queen Mary College, University of London, (workshop proceedings) **FUZ,CON**

Castonguay, C. (1972) *Meaning of existence in mathematics, Library of Exact Philosophy*, *9*, Springer-Verlag, Vienna, **FUZ,SET**

Carlucci, D., & Donati, F. (1975) A fuzzy cluster of the demand within a regional service system, in *Special Interest Discussion Session on Fuzzy Automata and Decision Processes*, 6th IFAC World Congress, Boston, Mass., USA, Aug., **FUZ**

Carlstrom, I. F. (1975) Truth and entailment for a vague quantifier, *Synthese, 30,* 461–495, **VAG,LOG**

Čech, E. (1937) Topologické prostory, *Časopis pro pěstování matematiky a fysiky, 66,* D225–D236, **TOP**

Čech, E. (1966) *Topological Spaces,* Academia, Prague, **TOP,SEMR,LAT,CAT,SET**

Čech, E. (1968) Topological spaces, in *Topological Papers of E. Čech,* Academia, Prague, 436–472, (trans. 1937 paper in Czech.) **TOP**

Chang, C. C. (1958a) Proof of an axiom of Łukasiewicz, *Trans. Amer. Math. Soc., 87,* 55–56, **MVLOG**

Chang, C. C. (1985b) Algebraic analyses of many valued logics, *Trans. Amer. Math. Soc., 88,* 467–490, **MVLOG**

Chang, C. C. (1959) A new proof of the completeness of the Łukasiewicz axioms, *Trans. Amer. Math. Soc., 93,* 74–80, **MVLO 66**

Chang, C. C. (1963a) The axiom of comprehension in infinite valued logic, *Math. Scand., 13,* 9–30, **SET,MVLOG**

Chang, C. C. (1963b) Logic with positive and negative truth values, *Acta Philosophica Fennica, 16,* 19–39, **MVLOG**

Chang, C. C. (1964) Infinite valued logic as a basis for set theory, in Bar-Hillel, Y. (ed.), *Proceedings of 1964 International Congress for Logic Methodology and Philosophy of Science,* North-Holland, Amsterdam, 93–100, **SET,MVLOG**

Chang, C. L. (1967) Fuzzy sets and pattern recognition, *PhD thesis,* University of California, Berkeley, California, USA, **FUZ,PAT**

Chang, C. L. (1968) Fuzzy topological spaces, *J. Math. Anal. & Appln., 24,* 182–190, **FUZ,TOP**

Chang, C. L. (1971) Fuzzy algebra, fuzzy functions and their application to function approximation. Division of Computer Research and Technology, National Institutes of Health, Bethesda, Maryland, USA, **FUZ**

Chang, C. L. (1975) Interpretation and execution of fuzzy programs, in Zadeh, L. A., Fu, K. S., Tanaka, K., & Shimura, M. (eds.), *Fuzzy Sets and Their Applications to Cognitive and Decision Processes,* Academic Press, New York, 191–218, **FUZ**

Chang, C. L., & Lee, R. C. T. (1973) *Symbolic Logic and Mechanical Theorem Proving,* Academic Press, New York, **LOG**

Chang, S. K. (1971) Automated interpretation and editing of fuzzy line drawings, *SJCC, 38,* 393–399, **FUZ**

Chang, S. K. (1971) Picture processing grammar and its applications, *Inform. Sci.,* 121–148, **FUZ**

Chang, S. K. (1971) Fuzzy programs–theory and applications, in *Proc. of Polytechnic Institute of Brooklyn Symposium on Computers and Automata,* 147, **FUZ**

Chang, S. K. (1972) On the execution of fuzzy programs using finite state machines, *IEEE Trans. Comp., C-21,* 214–253, **FUZ,AUT**

Chang, S. S. L. (1969) Fuzzy dynamic programming and the decision making process, in *Proc. 3rd Princeton Conference on Information Science and Systems,* 200–203, **FUZ,DEC**

Chang, S. S. L. (1972) Fuzzy mathematics, man, and his environment, *IEEE Trans. Syst. Man Cybern.*, *SMC-2*, 93–93, **FUZ**

Chang, S. S. L. (1975) On risk and decision-making in a fuzzy environment, in Zadeh, L. A., Fu, K. S., Tanaka, K., & Shimura, M. (eds.), *Fuzzy Sets and Their Applications to Cognitive and Decision Processes*, Academic Press, New York, 219–226, **FUZ,DEC**

Chang, S. S. L. (1975) On fuzzy algorithm and mapping, in *Special Interest Discussion Session on Fuzzy Automata and Decision Processes*, 6th IFAC World Congress, Boston, Mass., USA, Aug., **FUZ**

Chang, S. S. L., & Zadeh, L. A. (1972) On fuzzy mathematics and control, *IEEE Trans. Syst. Man Cybern.*, *SMC-2*, 30–34, **FUZ,CON,AUT**

Chapin, E. W. (1971) An axiomatization of the set theory of Zadeh, *Notices American Mathematical Society*, *687-02-4*, 753, **FUZ,LOG**

Chapin, E. W. (1974) Set-valued set theory: Part 1, *Notre Dame J. Formal Logic*, *15*, 619–634, **FUZ,SET,LOG**

Chapin, E. W. (1975) Set-valued set theory: Part 2, *Notre Dame J. Formal Logic*, *16*, 255–267, **FUZ,SET,LOG**

Chen, C. (1974) Realizability of communication nets: an application of the Zadeh criterion, *IEEE Trans. Circuits & Syst.*, *CAS-21*, 150–151, **FUZ**

Chiara, C. S. (1973) *Ontology and the Vicious Circle Principle*, Cornell University Press, Ithaca, New York, **PARA,SET**

Chilausky, R., Jacobsen, B., & Michalski, R. S. (1976) An application of variable-valued logic to inductive learning of plant disease diagnostic rules, *Proc. 6th Int. Symp. Multiple-Valued Logic*, *IEEE 76CH1111-4C*, 233–240, **MVLOG-,INDUCT,FUZ**

Chittenden, E. W. (1941) On the reduction of topological functions, in Wilder, R. L., & Ayres, W. L. (eds.), *Lectures in Topology*, University of Michigan Press, Ann Arbor, USA, 267–285,

Chomsky, N. & Halle, M. (1965) Some controversial questions in phonological theory, *J. Linguistics*, *1*, 97–138, **LING**

Chytil, M. (1969) On constituting of semantical models for GUHA-methods, *Československá Fysiologie*, *18*, 43–147, (in Czech) **LOG,INDUCT**

Cleave, J. P. (1970) The notion of validity in logical systems with inexact predicates, *Brit. J. Philos. Sci.*, *21*, 269–274, **VAG,LOG**

Cleave, J. P. (1974) The notion of logical consequence in the logic of inexact predicates, *Z. Math. Logik Grundlagen Math.*, *20*, 307–324, **VAG,LOG**

Cleave, J. P. (1976) Quasi-Boolean algebras, empirical continuity and three-valued logic, *Z. Math. Logik Grundlagen Math.*, **MVLOG,VAG**

Cohen, L. J. (1975) Probability–the one and the many, *Proc. Brit. Academy*, *61*, 3–28, **PROB**

Cohen, P. J. (1967) Non-Cantorian set theory, *Scientific American*, Dec., 104–116, **SET**

Cole, P., & Morgan, J. L. (eds.) (1975) *Syntax and Semantics Vol. 3*, Academic Press, New York, **LING**

Conche, B. (1973) Elements d'une methode de classification par utilisation d'un automate flou, *J.E.E.F.L.N.*, University of Paris-Dauphine, **FUZ,PAT**

Conche, B., Jouault, J. P., & Luan, P. M. (1973) Application des concepts flous a la programmation en languages quasi-naturels, *Seminaire Bernard Roy*, University of Paris-Dauphine, **FUZ,LING**

Cools, M., & Peteau, M. (1973) STIM 5: un programme de stimulation inventive utilisant la theorie des sous-ensembles flous, *IMAGO Discussion Paper*, Universitie Catholique de Louvain, Belgium, **FUZ,DEC**

Creswell, M. J. (1973) *Logics and Languages*, Methuen, London, **MLOG,LANG**

Curry, H. B. (1942) The inconsistency of certain formal logics, *J. Symbolic Logic, 7*, 115–117, **LOG,PARA**

DalCin, M. (1975a) Fuzzy-state automata, their stability and fault-tolerance, *Int. J. Comp. Inf. Sciences, 4*, 63–80, **FUZ,AUT,TOL**

DalCin, M. (1975b) Modification tolerance of fuzzy-state automata, *Int. J. Comp. Inf. Sciences, 4*, 81–93, **FUZ,TOL**

Daneš, F. (1966) The relation of centre and periphery as a language universal, *Travaux Linguistiques de Prague, 2*, 9–21, **LING,VAG**

Daneš, F. & Vachek, J. (1964) Prague studies in structural grammar today, *Travaux Linguistiques de Prague, 1*, 21–31, **LING,VAG**

Damerau, F. J. (1975) On fuzzy adjectives, *RC5340*, IBM Research Laboratory, Yorktown Heights, New York, USA, **FUZ,PSYCH**

Danielsson, S. (1967) Modal logic based on probability theory, *Theoria, 33*, 189–197, **LOG,PROB**

Davio, M., & Thayse, A. (1973) Representation of fuzzy functions, *Philips Research Reports, 28*, 93–106, **FUZ**

De Finetti, B. (1972) *Probability, Induction and Statistics*, John Wiley, London, **PROB,INDUCT**

De Kerf, J. (1974) Vage Verzamelingen, *Omega (Vereniging voor Wis- en Natuurkundigen Lovanienses), 2*, 2–18, **FUZ,VAG**

De Kerf, J. (1974) Vage Verzamelingen, *Ingenieurstijdingen 23e jaargang*, 581–589, **FUZ,VAG**

De Kerf, J. (1975) A bibliography on fuzzy sets, *J. Computational & Applied Mathematics, 1*, 205–212 **FUZ**

DeLuca, A., & Termini, S. (1971) Algorithmic aspects in complex systems analysis, *Scientia, 106*, 659–671, **FUZ**

DeLuca, A., & Termini, S. (1972) A definition of a nonprobabilistic entropy in the setting of fuzzy sets theory, *Inform. & Control, 20*, 301–312, **FUZ**

DeLuca, A., & Termini, S. (1972) Algebraic properties of fuzzy sets, *J. Math. Anal. & Appln., 40*, 373–386, **FUZ,LAT**

DeLuca, A., & Termini, S. (1974) Entropy of L-fuzzy sets, *Inform. & Control, 24*, 55–73, **FUZ**

DePalma, G. F., & Yau, S. S. (1975) Fractionally fuzzy grammars with application to pattern recognition, in Zadeh, L. A., Fu, K. S., Tanaka, K., & Shimura, M. (eds.), *Fuzzy Sets and Their Applications to Cognitive and Decision Processes*, Academic Press, New York, 329–351, **FUZ,LANG**

Diamond, P. (1975) Fuzzy chaos, Department of Mathematics, University of Queensland, Brisbane, Australia, **FUZ**

Diarra, N. (1975) A propos des ensembles flous, *PhD thesis*, Centre Pedagogique Superieur de l'Ecole Normale Superieur Bamako, Tunisia, Oct., **FUZ**

Dienes, Z. P. (1949) On an implication function in many-valued systems of logic, *J. Symbolic Logic*, *14*, 95–97, **MVLOG**

Dijkman, J. G., & Lowen, R. (1976) Fuzzy relations on countable sets, Technical Highschool Delft & Vrije Universiteit Brussel, **FUZ**

Dilman, I. (1973) *Induction and Deduction*, Basil Blackwell, Oxford, **INDUCT,LOG**

Dimitrov, V., Wechler, W., Drjankov, D., & Petrov, A. (1975) Computer execution of fuzzy algorithms, *Proc. Conf. Applns. Math. Models & Computers in Linguistics*, Varna, Bulgaria, May, (in Russian) **FUZ**

Dorris, A. L., & Sadosky, Th.L. (1973) A fuzzy set theoretic approach to decision making, *44th National Meeting of ORSA*, San Diego, California, USA, Nov., **FUZ,DEC**

Dowker, C. H. & Papert, D. (1966) Quotient frames and subspaces, *Proc. London Math. Soc.*, *16*, 275–296 **LAT,TOP**

Dowker, C. H. & Papert, D. (1967) On Urysohn's lemma, *General Topology and its Relations to Modern Analysis and Algebra 2* (Proc. of the Second Prague Topol. Symp. 1966), 111–114, Academia, Prague & Academic Press, New York, **LAT,TOP**

Dravecký, J., & Riečan, B. (1975) Measurability of functions with values in partially ordered spaces, *Časopis pro pěstování matematiky*, *100*, 27–35, **PROB**

Dreyfuss, G. R., Kochen, M., Robinson, J., & Badre, A. N. (1975) On the psycholinguistic reality of fuzzy sets in Grossman, R. E., San, L. J., & Vance, T. J. (eds.), *Functionalism*, University of Chicago Press, 135–149, **FUZ,PSYCH**

Drosselmeyer, E., & Wonneberger, R. (1975) Studies on a fuzzy system in the parochial field, *Special Interest Discussion Session on Fuzzy Automata and Decision Processes*, 6th IFAC World Congress, Boston, Mass., USA, Aug., **FUZ,SS**

Dubois, T. (1974) Une methode d'evaluation par les sous-ensembles flous appliquee a la simulation, *IMAGO Discussion Paper 13*, Universitie Catholique de Louvain, Belgium, **FUZ**

Dubreil, P., & Dubreil-Jacotin, L. (1937) Proprietes des relations d'equivalence, *Comp. Rend. Acad. Sci. (Paris)*, *205*, 704–706, **LAT,LOG**

Dugundju, J. (1940) Note on a property of matrices for Lewis and Langford's calculi of propositions, *J. Symbolic Logic*, *5*, 150–151, **MLOG**

Dummett, M. A. E. (1959) A propositional calculus with denumerable matrix, *J. Symbolic Logic*, *24*, 97–106, **MVLOG**

Dummett, M. A. E. (1973) The justification of deduction, *Proc. Brit. Acad.*, *59*, 3–34, **LOG**

Dummett, M. A. E. (1975) Wang's paradox, *Synthese*, *30*, 301–324, **PARA**

Dunn, J. C. (1973) A fuzzy relative of the ISODATA process and its use in detecting compact well-separated clusters, *J. Cybernetics*, *3*, 32–57, **FUZ,PAT**

Dunn, J. C. (1974) Some recent investigations of a new fuzzy partitioning algorithm and its application to pattern classification problems, *J. Cybernetics*, *4*, 1–15, **FUZ,PAT**

Dunn, J. C. (1974) Well-separated clusters and optimal fuzzy partitions, *J. Cybernetics*, *4*, 95–104, **FUZ,PAT**

Dunn, J. C. (1974) A graph theoretic analysis of pattern classification via Tamura's fuzzy relation, *SMC-3*, 310–313, **FUZ,PAT**

Dunn, J. C. (1975) Indices of partition fuzziness and the detection of clusters in large data sets, in *Special Interest Discussion Session on Fuzzy Automata and Decision Processes*, 6th IFAC World Congress, Boston, Mass., USA, Aug., **FUZ,PAT**

Dunn, J. C. (1975) Canonical forms of Tamura's fuzzy relation matrix: a scheme for visualizing cluster hierarchies, *Proceedings of Computer Graphics, Pattern Recognition and Data Structure Conference*, Beverly Hills, California, USA, May, **FUZ,PAT**

Dunst, A. J. (1971) Application of the fuzzy set theory, Jan., **FUZ**

Edwards, W. (1962) Subjective probabilities inferred from decisions, *Psychological Review*, *69*, 109–135, **PROB,PSYCH**

Edwards, W., Phillips, L. D., Hayes, W. L., & Goodman, B. C. (1968) Probabilistic information processing systems: design and evaluation, *IEEE Trans. Syst. Man Cybern.. SMC-4*, 248–265, **PSYCH,PROB**

Ehrenfeucht, A., & Orlowska, E. (1967) Mechanical proof procedure for propositional calculus, *Bull. Acad. Polonaise des Sciences (serie math., astr. et phys.)*, *15*, 25–30, **LOG**

El-Fattah, Y. M. (1976) Control of complex systems by fuzzy learning automata, in Mamdani, E. H., & Gaines, B. R. (eds.), *Discrete Systems and Fuzzy Reasoning*, *EES-MMS-DSFR-76*, Queen Mary College, University of London, (workshop proceedings) **FUZ,CON**

Elliott, J. L. (1976) Fuzzy kiviat graphs, *Proc. European Computing Congress (EUROCOMP 76)*, Online, London, Sep., **FUZ**

Ellis, C. A. (1971) Probabilistic tree automata, *Inform. & Control*, *19*, 401–416, **AUT,PROB,FUZ**

Endo, Y., & Tsukamoto, Y. (1973) Apportion models of tourists by fuzzy integrals, *Annual Conference Records of SICE, Japan*, **FUZ,SS**

Engel, A. B., & Buonomano, V. (1973) Towards a general theory of fuzzy sets I, Institute of Mathematics, University Estaduel de Campinas, Brazil, **FUZ**

Engel, A. B., & Buonomano, V. (1973) Towards a general theory of fuzzy sets II, Institute of Mathematics, University Estaduel de Campinas, Brazil, **FUZ**

Epstein, G. (1972) Multiple-valued signal processing with limiting, *Symposium on Multiple-Valued Logic Design*, Buffalo, New York, USA, **MVLOG**

Epstein, G., Frieder, G., & Rine, D. C. (1974) The development of multiple-valued logic as related to computer science, *Computer*, *7*, 20–32, **MVLOG**

Epstein, G., & Horn, A. (1974) P-algebras, an abstraction from Post algebras, *Algebra Universalis*, *4*, 195–206, **LOG**

Epstein, G., & Horn, A. (1975a) Chain based lattices, *Pacific J. Maths.*, *55*, 65–84, **LOG,LAT**

Epstein, G., & Horn, A. (1975b) Logics which are characterized by subresiduated lattices, *Tech. Rep. 24*, Indiana University Computer Science Department, Bloomington, Indiana, USA, **LOG,LAT**

Epstein, G., & Shapiro, S. C. (1975) The development of language and reasoning in the child as connected with mathematical linguistics and logic, *Tech. Rep.*, *41*, Oct., **LOG,PSYCH,LING**

Esogbue, A. O. (1975) On the application of fuzzy allocation theory to the modelling of cancer research appropriation process, *Proceedings of 3rd International Congress of Cybernetics and Systems*, Bucharest, Aug., **FUZ,SS**

Esogbue, A. O., & Ramesh, V. (1970) Dynamic programming and fuzzy allocation processes, *Technical Memorandum 202*, Operations Research Department, Case Western Reserve University, Cleveland, Ohio, USA, **FUZ**

Eto, H. (1975) Multivariate analysis of ambiguous opinions on opening the sports facilities of firms to the public, in *Summary of Papers on General Fuzzy Problems*, The Working Group on Fuzzy Systems, Tokyo, Japan, Nov., 5–9, **FUZ,SS**

Evans, G., & McDowell, J. (eds.) (1976) *Truth and Meaning*, Clarendon Press, Oxford, **TRUTH**

Evenden, J. (1974) Generalised logic, *Notre Dame J. Formal Logic*, *15*, 35–44, **LOG**

Ezoe, T. (1975) Cause picture method introduced into categorical analysis of multi-variable's data, in *Summary of Papers on General Fuzzy Problems*, The Working Group on Fuzzy Systems, Tokyo, Japan, Nov., 10–13, **FUZ**

Fellinger, W. L. (1974) Specifications for a fuzzy systems modelling language, *PhD thesis*, Oregon State University, Corvallis, **FUZ,LING**

Fenstad, J. E. (1964) On the consistency of the axiom of comprehension in the Łukasiewicz infinite valued logic, *Math. Scand.*, *14*, 65–74, **MVLOG,SET**

Fenstad, J. E. (1967) Representations of probabilities defined on first order languages, in Crossley, J. N. (ed.), *Sets models and recursion theory*, North Holland, 156–172, **PROB,LOG**

Fevrier, P. (1976) On the representation of measurements results by fuzzy sets, *3rd Eur. Meeting Cybern. Syst. Res., Vienna*, **FUZ,IMEAS**

Fillmore, C. J., & Langendoen, D. T. (eds.) (1971) *Studies in linguistic semantics*, Holt, Rinehart & Winston, New York, **LING**

Fine, K. (1975) Vagueness, truth and logic, *Synthese*, *30*, 265–300, **FUZ,VAG,LOG**

Fine, T. L. (1973) *Theories of Probability*, Academic Press, New York, **PROB,FUZ**

Flondor, P. (1975) Models for property assignment, *Seminar on Fuzzy Systems*, Department of Cybernetics, ASE, Bucharest, **FUZ,INFR**

Foradori, E. (1933) Stetigkait und kontinuität als teilbarkeitseigenschaften, *Monatschefte für Math. und Physik*, *40*, 161–180, **TOP**

Foster, M. H., & Martin, M. L. (eds.) (1966) *Probability, Confirmation and Simplicity*, Odyssey Press, New York, **PROB,INDUCT**

Fraenkel, A. A., Bar-Hillel, Y., & Levy, A. (1973) *Foundations of Set Theory*, North-Holland, Amsterdam, **SET,PARA,LOG**

Frank, M. J. (1970) Probabilistic topological spaces, Illinois Institute of Technology, Chicago, USA, Jan., **TOP,PROB,FUZ**

Fraser, B. (1975) Hedged Performatives, in Cole, P., & Morgan, J. L. (eds.), *Syntax and Semantics Vol. 3*, Academic Press, New York, 187–210, **LING**

Frink, O. (1938) New algebras of logic, *Amer. Math. Monthly*, *45*, 210–219, **MVLOG**

Fu, K. S. (1974) Pattern recognition and some socio-economic problems, Purdue University, West Lafayette, Indiana 47907, USA, **FUZ,PAT,SS**

Fu, K. S., & Li, T. J. (1969) Formulation of learning automata and games, *Inform.*

Sci., 1, 237–256, **FUZ,LMACH,GAME**

Fujisake, H. (1971) Fuzziness in medical sciences and its processing, *Proceedings of Symposium on Fuzziness in Systems and its Processing*, Professional Group of System Engineering of SICE, **FUZ,MED**

Fung, L. W., & Fu, K. S. (1973a) Decision making in a fuzzy environment, *TR-EE73-22*, School of Electrical Engineering, Purdue University, USA, **FUZ,DEC**

Fung, L. W., & Fu, K. S. (1973b) An axiomatic approach to rational decision-making based on fuzzy sets, *Electrical Engineering Report*, Purdue University, Lafayette, Indiana, USA, **FUZ,DEC**

Fung, L. W., & Fu, K. S. (1974a) The k'th optimal policy algorithm for decision making in fuzzy environments, in Eykhoff, P. (ed.), *Identification and System Parameter Estimation*, North Holland, 1025–1059, **FUZ,DEC**

Fung, L. W., & Fu, K. S. (1974b) Characterization of a class of fuzzy optimal control problems, *Proceedings of the 8'th Princeton Conference on Information Science and Systems*, **FUZ,CON**

Fung, L. W., & Fu, K. S. (1975) An axiomatic approach to rational decision making in a fuzzy environment, in Zadeh, L. A., Fu, K. S., Tanaka, K., & Shimura, M. (eds.), *Fuzzy Sets and Their Applications to Cognitive and Decision Processes*, Academic Press, New York, 227–256, **FUZ,DEC**

Furukawa, M., Nakamura, K., & Oda, M. (1972) Fuzzy models of human decision-making process, *Annual Conference Records of JAACE*, **FUZ,DEC**

Furukawa, M., Nakamura, K., & Oda, M. (1973) Fuzzy variant process of memories, *Annual Conference Records of SICE, Japan*, **FUZ,INFR**

Gaifman, H. (1964) Concerning measures in first order calculi, *Israel J. Math., 2*, 1–18, **PROB,LOG**

Gaines, B. R. (1975a) Stochastic and fuzzy logics, *Electronics Lett., 11* *188–189.* **FUZ,LOG,CON**

Gaines, B. R. (1975b) Approximate identification of automata, *Electronics Lett., 11*, 444–445, **PROB,INDUCT**

Gaines, B. R. (1975c) A calculus of possibility, eventuality and probability, *in EES-MMS-FUZ1-75*, Department of Electrical Engineering Science, University of Essex, Colchester, UK, **FUZ,PROB**

Gaines, B. R. (1975d) Control engineering and artificial intelligence, *Lecture Notes of BCS AISB Summer School*, Cambridge, UK, July, 52–60, **FUZ,CON**

Gaines, B. R. (1975e) Multivalued logics and fuzzy reasoning, *Lecture notes of BCS AISB Summer School*, Cambridge, UK, July, 100–112, **FUZ,MVLOG**

Gaines, B. R. (1976a) Why fuzzy reasoning?, in Mamdani, E. H., & Gaines, B. R. (eds.), *Discrete Systems and Fuzzy Reasoning, EES-MMS-DSFR-76*, Queen Mary College, University of London, (workshop proceedings) **FUZ,INDUCT**

Gaines, B. R. (1976b) Research notes on fuzzy reasoning, in Mamdani, E. H., & Gaines, B. R. (eds.), *Discrete Systems and Fuzzy Reasoning, EES-MMS-DSFR-76*, Queen Mary College, University of London, (workshop proceedings) **FUZ,LOG**

Gaines, B. R. (1976c) General fuzzy logics, *3rd Eur. Meeting Cybern. Syst. Res., Vienna*, **FUZ,MVLOG,PROB**

Gaines, B. R. (1976d) Fuzzy reasoning and the logics of uncertainty, *Proc. 6th Int.*

Symp. Multiple-Valued Logic, IEEE 76CH1111-4C, 179–188, **FUZ,MV-LOG,PROB**

Gaines, B. R. (1976e) Behaviour-structure transformations under uncertainty, *Int. J. Man-Machine Studies, 8,* 337–365, **PROB,INDUCT**

Gaines, B. R. (1976f) System identification, approximation and complexity, *Int. J. General Syst., (3),* **LOG,PROB,INDUCT**

Gaines, B. R. (1976g) Foundations of fuzzy reasoning, *Int. J. Man-Machine Studies, 8,* **FUZ,VAG,SET,MVLOG,PARA**

Gaines, B. R. (1976h) Fuzzy and stochastic probability logics, *EES-MMS-FUZ-76,* Department of Electrical Engineering Science, University of Essex, Colchester, UK, **FUZ,PROB,MVLOG**

Gaines, B. R. (1976i) V-fuzzy q-analysis, *EES-MMS-QFUZ-76,* Department of Electrical Engineering Science, University of Essex, Colchester, UK, **FUZ**

Gaines, B. R., & Kohout, L. J. (1975a) Possible automata, *Proc. 1975 Int. Symp. Multiple-Valued Logic, IEEE 75CH0959-7C,* 183–196, **FUZ,AUT,PROB**

Gaines, B. R., & Kohout, L. J. (1975b) The logic of automata, *Int. J. General Syst., 2,* 191–208, **FUZ,AUT,PROB**

Gaines, B. R., & Kohout, L. J. (1977) The fuzzy decade: a bibliography of fuzzy systems and closely related topics, *Int. J. Man-Machine Studies, 9,* 1–69, Jan. **FUZ**

Gale, S. (1972) Inexactness, fuzzy sets and the foundations of behavioral geography, *Geographical Analysis, 4,* 337–349, **FUZ,SS**

Gale, S. (1974a) A resolution of the regionalization problem and its implications for political geography and social justice, *WP3 Research on Metropolitan Change and Conflict Resolution,* Peace Science Department, University of Pennsylvania, **FUZ,SS**

Gale, S. (1974b) A prolegomenon to an interrogative theory of scientific enquiry, *WP9 Research on Metropolitan Change and Conflict Resolution,* Peace Science Department, University of Pennsylvania, **FUZ,SS**

Gale, S. (1975a) Boundaries, tolerance spaces and criteria for conflict resolution, *Journal of Peace Science,* **FUZ,SS**

Gale, S. (1975b) Conjectures on many-valued logic, regions, and criteria for conflict resolution, *Proc. 1975 Int. Symp. Multiple-Valued Logic, IEEE 75CH0959-7C,* 212–225, **FUZ,SS**

Gallin, D. (1975) *Intensional and Higher Order Modal Logic,* North-Holland, Amsterdam, **MLOG**

Ganter, T. E., Steinlage, R. C., & Warren, R. H. (1975) Compactness in fuzzy topological spaces, Dept. Mathematics, University of Dayton, Dayton, Ohio, USA, **FUZ,TOP**

Gearing, Ch.E. (1975) Generalized Bayesian posterior analysis with ambiguous information, *45th ORSA/TIMS Joint National Meeting,* Boston, Mass., USA, April, **FUZ,PROB**

Gentilhomme, Y. (1968) Les ensembles flous en linguistique, *Notes on Theoretical and Applied Linguistics, 5,* Bucharest, Rumania, **FUZ,LING**

Georgescu, G. (1971a) *n*-Valued complete Łukasiewicz algebras, *Rev. Roum. Math. Pures et Appl., 16,* 41–50, **MVLOG**

Georgescu, G. (1971b) The theta-valued Łukasiewicz algebras I, *Rev. Roum. Math.*

Pures et Appl., *16*, Bucharest, 195–209, **MVLOG**

Georgescu, G. (1971c) Algebres de Łukasiewicz de orden theta II, *Rev. Roum. Math. Pures et Appl.*, *16*, 363–369, **MVLOG**

Georgescu, G. (1971d) The theta-valued Łukasiewicz algebras III, *Rev. Roum. Math. Pures et Appl.*, *16*, 1365–1390, **MVLOG**

Georgescu, G., & Vraciu, C. (1970) On the characterization of centred Łukasiewicz algebras, *J. Algebra*, *16*, 486–495, **MVLOG**

Gerhardts, M. D. (1965) Zur Charakterisierung distributiver Scheifverbande, *Math. Annalen*, *161*, 231–240, **PROB**

Gerhardts, M. D. (1969) Schragverbande und Quasiordnungen, *Math. Annalen*, *181*, 65–73, **PROB**

Giles, R. (1974a) A nonclassical logic for physics, *Studia Logica*, *33*, **FUZ,LOG**

Giles, R. (1974b) A pragmatic approach to the formalization of empirical theories, *Proceedings of Conference on Formal Methods in the Methodology of Empirical Sciences*, Warsaw, June, **FUZ,LOG**

Giles, R. (1974c) Formal languages and the foundations of physics. *Proc. International Research Seminar on Abstract Representation in Mathematical Physics*, D. Reidel, London, Ontario, Dec., **FUZ,MVLOG**

Giles, R. (1975) Łukasiewicz logic and fuzzy set theory, *Proc. 1975 Int. Symp. Multiple-Valued Logic, IEEE 75CH0959-7C*, May, 197–211, **FUZ,MVLOG**

Giles, R. (1976a) A logic for subjective belief, in Harper, W., & Hooker, C. A. (eds.), *Foundations of Probability Theory, Statistical Inference, and Statistical Theories of Science*, *1*, D. Reidel, Dordrecht, Holland, 41–72, **FUZ,PROB, LOG**

Giles, R. (1976b) Formal languages and the foundations of physics and quantum mechanics, in Hooker, C. A. (ed.), *The Logico-Algebraic Approach to Quantum Mechnaics*, *2*, D. Reidel, Dordrecht, Holland, **FUZ,PROB,MVLOG**

Giles, R. (1976c) Łukasiewicz logic and fuzzy set theory, *Int. J. Man-Machine Studies*, *8*, 313–327, **FUZ,MVLOG**

Gitman, I. (1970) Organization of data: a model and computational algorithm that uses the notion of fuzzy sets, *PhD thesis*, McGill University, Montreal, Canada, **FUZ,PAT**

Gitman, I., & Levine, M. D. (1970) An algorithm for detecting unimodal fuzzy sets and its application as a clustering technique, *IEEE Trans. Comp.*, *C-19*, 583–593, **FUZ,PAT**

Gluss, B. (1973) Fuzzy multistage decision making, *Int. J. Control*, *17*, 177–192, **FUZ,DEC**

Goddard, L., & Routley, R. (1973) *The Logic of Significance and Content*, Scottish Academic Press, Edinburgh, **LOG**

Goguen, J. A. (1967) L-fuzzy sets, *J. Math. Anal. & Appln.*, *18*, 145–174, **FUZ**

Goguen, J. A. (1968) Categories of fuzzy sets: applications of non-Cantorian set theory, *PhD thesis*, Department of Mathematics, University of California, Berkeley, California, USA, **FUZ,CAT**

Goguen, J. A. (1969a) Categories of V-sets, *Bulletin of the American Mathematical Society*, *75*, 622–624, **FUZ,CAT**

Goguen, J. A. (1969b) The logic of inexact concepts, *Synthese*, *19*, 325–373, **FUZ,VAG**

Goguen, J. A. (1969c) Representing inexact concepts, *ICR quarterly report No. 20*, Institute for Computer Research, University of Chicago, **FUZ,VAG**

Goguen, J. A. (1970) Mathematical representation of hierarchically organizad system, in Attinger, E. O. (ed.), *Global system dynamics*, S. Karger, Berlin, 111–129, **FUZ**

Goguen, J. A. (1972) Hierarchical inexact data structures in artificial intelligence problems, *Proc. 5th Hawaii International Conference on Systems Sciences*, Honolulu, 345, **FUZ,VAG**

Goguen, J. A. (1973) Systems theory concepts in computer science, *Proc. 6th Hawaii International Conference on Systems Sciences*, Honolulu, 77–80, **FUZ**

Goguen, J. A. (1974a) The fuzzy Tychonoff theorem, *J. Math. Anal. & Appln.*, *43*, 734–742, **FUZ,TOP**

Goguen, J. A. (1974b) Concept representation in natural and artificial languages: axioms extensions and applications for fuzzy sets, *Int. J. Man-Machine Studies*, *6*, 513–561, **FUZ,CAT,VAG**

Goguen, J. A. (1975a) Objects, *Int. J. General Syst.*, *1*, 237–243, **FUZ,CAT**

Goguen, J. A. (1975b) On fuzzy robot planning, in Zadeh, L. A., Fu, K. S., Tanaka, K., & Shimura, M. (eds.), *Fuzzy Sets and Their Applications to Cognitive and Decision Processes*, Academic Press, New York, USA, 429–447, **FUZ,LMACH**

Goguen, J. A. (1976) Robust programming languages & the principle of maximal meaningfulness, *Milwaukee Symposium on Automatic Computation and Control*, 87–90, **FUZ,LMACH**

Good, I. J. (1962) Subjective probability as the measure of a non-measurable set, in Nagel, E., Suppes, P., & Tarski, A. (eds.), *Logic, Methodology and Philosophy of Science*, Stanford University Press, California, USA, 319–329, **PROB**

Goodman, J. S. (1974) From multiple balayage to fuzzy sets, Institute of Mathematics, University of Florence, Italy, **FUZ**

Gottinger, H. W. (1973) Towards a fuzzy reasoning in the behavioural science, *Cybernetica*, 113–135, **FUZ,SS**

Gottinger, H. W. (1975) A fuzzy algorithmic approach to the definition of complex or imprecise concepts, *Conference on Systems Theory*, University of Bielefeld, April, **FUZ**

Gottinger, H. W. (1976) Some basic issues connected with fuzzy analysis, in Bossel, H., Klaczko, S., & Muller, N. (eds.), *Systems Theory in the Social Sciences*, Birkhauser Verlag, Basel, 323–325, **FUZ**

Gottinger, H. W. (1976) Toward an algebraic theory of complexity and catastrophe, *3rd Eur. Meeting Cybern. Syst. Res., Vienna*, **FUZ,SYS**

Gottwald, S. (1969) Konstruktion von zahlbereichen und die grundlagen der inhaltstheorie in einer mehrwertigen mengenlehre, *PhD thesis*, University of Leipzig, **MVLOG,SET,FUZ**

Gottwald, S. (1971a) Elementare Inhalts- und Masstheorie in einer mehrwertigen Mengenlehre, *Math. Nachr.*, *50*, 27–68, **MVLOG,SET,FUZ**

Gottwald, S. (1971b) Zahlbereichskonstruktionen in einer mehrwertigen mengen-lehre, *Z. Math Logik Grundlagen Math.*, *17*, 145–188, **FUZ,MVLOG,SET**

Gottwald, S. (1973) Uber einbettungen in zahlenbereiche einer mehrwertigen Mengenlehre, *Math. Nachr.*, *56*, 43–46, **MVLOG,SET,FUZ**

Gottwald, L. (1974) Mehrwertige Anordnungsrelationen in klassischen Mengen,

Math. Nachr., *63*, 205–212, **MVLOG,SET,FUZ**

Gottwald, S. (1975a) Ein kumulatives System mehrwertiger Mengen, *Habilitationeschrift*, University of Leipzig, **FUZ,MVLOG,SET**

Gottwald, S. (1975b) A cumulative system of fuzzy sets, *Proc. 2nd Colloqu. Set Theory & Hierarchy Theory*, Bierutovice, Poland, Sep., **FUZ,SET,MVLOG**

Gottwald, S. (1976a) On the formalism of fuzzy logic, **FUZ,LOG**

Gottwald, S. (1976b) Fuzzy propositional logics, **FUZ,LOG**

Gottwald, S. (1976c) Untersuchungen zur mehrwertigen Mengenlehre, *Math. Nachr.*, *72*, 297–303; *74*, 329–336, **MVLOG,SET,FUZ**

Grattan-Guiness (1976) Fuzzy membership mapped onto interval and many-valued quantities, *Z. Math. Logik Grundlagen Math.*, *22*, 149–160, **FUZ**

Grigolia, R. (1975) On the algebras corresponding to the *n*-valued Łukasiewicz-Tarski logical systems, *Proc. 1975 Int. Symp. Multiple-Valued Logic, IEEE 75CH0959-7C*, 234–239, **MVLOG**

Grofman, B., & Hyman, G. (1973) Probability and logic in belief systems, *Theory & Decision*, *4*, 179–195, **PROB,PSYCH**

Gupta, M. M. (1974) Introduction to fuzzy control, *Proc. Computer, Electronics & Control Symp.*, Calgary, May, VI 3.1–3.8, **FUZ,CON**

Gupta, M. M. (1975) Fuzzy automata and decision processes: a decade, *6th Triennial IFAC World Congress*, Boston, Mass., USA, Aug., **FUZ**

Gupta, M. M. (1975) IFAC report: Round table discussion on the estimation and control in fuzzy environments, *Automatica*, *11*, 209–212, **FUZ,CON**

Gupta, M. M., & Mamdani, E. H. (1976) Second IFAC round table on fuzzy automata and decision processes, *Automatica*, *12*, 291–296, **FUZ**

Gupta, M. M., Nikiforuk, P. N., & Kanai, K. (1973) Decision and control in a fuzzy environment: a rationale, *Proc. 3rd IFAC Symp. Identification & System Parameter Estimation*, The Hague, June, 1048–1049, **FUZ,DEC,CON**

Gusev, L. A., & Smirnova, I. M. (1973) Fuzzy sets: theory and applications (a survey), *Automation & Remote Control*, *No. 5*, May, 66–85, **FUZ**

Haack, S. (1974) *Deviant Logic*, Cambridge University Press, **LOG**

Haack, S. (1975) "Alternative" in "alternative logic", in Blackburn, S. (ed.), *Meaning, Reference and Necessity*, Cambridge University Press, 32–55, **LOG**

Haack, S. (1976) The justification of deduction, *Mind*, *85*, 112–119, **LOG,INDUCT**

Hacking, I. (1963) What is strict implication?, *J. Symbolic Logic*, *28*, 51–71, **MLOG**

Hacking, I. (1975a) All kinds of possibility, *Philosophical Review*, *84*, 319–337, **PROB,MLOG**

Hacking, I. (1975b) *The Emergence of Probability*, Cambridge University Press, **PROB**

Hackstaff, H. H. (1966) *Systems of Formal Logic*, D. Reidel, Dordrecht, Holland, **LOG**

Hájek, P. (1967) Sets, semisets, models, in *Axiomatic Set Theory, Proc. Symp. Pure Math.*, *13*, Amer. Math. Soc., Rhode Island, USA, 67–81, **SET,LOG,LAT**

Hájek, P. (1968) Problém obecného pojetí metody GUHA, *Kybernetika (Prague)*, *6*, 505–515, (in Czech: The question of the general concept of GUHA-methods) **LOG,INDUCT**

Hájek, P. (1973a) Why semisets, *Commentationes Math. Univ. Carolinae*, *14*, 397–420, **SET,MVLOG,LAT**

Hájek, P. (1973b) Some logical problems of automated research, *Proc. Symp. Math. Found. Comp. Sci.*, High Tatras Czechoslovakia, **LOG,INDUCT**

Hájek, P. (1973c) Automatic listing of important observational statements I, *Kybernetika (Prague)*, *9*, 187–206, **LOG,INDUCT**

Hájek, P. (1973d) Automatic listing of important observational statements II, *Kybernetika (Prague)*, *9*, 251–271, **LOG,INDUCT**

Hájek, P. (1974a) Generalized quantifiers and finite sets, *Proc. Autumn School in Set Theory & Hierarchy Theory*, Wroclaw, Poland, **LOG,INDUCT**

Hájek, P. (1974b) Automatic listing of important observational statements III, *Kybernetika (Prague)*, *10*, 95–124, **LOG,INDUCT**

Hájek, P. (1975) On logics of discovery, in Bečvář, J. (ed.), *Mathematical Foundations of Computer Science 1975, Lecture Notes in Computer Science, 32*, Springer-Verlag, Berlin, 30–45, **LOG,INDUCT**

Hájek, P., Bendová, K., & Renc, Z. (1971) The GUHA method and the three valued logic, *Kybernetika (Prague)*, *7*, 421–435, **MVLOG,INDUCT**

Hájek, P., & Harmancová, D. (1973) On generalized credence functions, *Kybernetika (Prague)*, *9*, 343–356, **INDUCT,LOG,VAG**

Hájek, P., Havel, I., & Chytil, M. (1966) The GUHA method of automatic hypotheses determination, *Computing*, *1*, 293–308, **LOG,INDUCT**

Hájek, P., & Havránek, T. (1976) On generation of inductive hypotheses, **LOG,INDUCT**

Halmos, P. R. (1962) *Algebraic Logic*, Chelsea Publ. Co., New York, **LOG,LAT**

Hamacher, H. (1975) Uber logische verknupfungen unscharfer aussagen und dehren zugehorige bewertungsfunkticnen, *Rep.75/14*, Lehrstuhl für Unternehmensforschung, RWTH, Aachen, West Germany, **FUZ**

Hamacher, H. (1976) On logical connectives of fuzzy statements and their affiliated truth-functions, *3rd Eur. Meeting Cybern. Syst. Res.*, Vienna, **FUZ,LOG**

Hamblin, C. L. (1959) The modal "probably", *Mind, 68*, 234–240, **MLOG,PROB**

Hanakata, K. (1974) A methodology for interactive systems, in Fu, K. S., & Tou, J. T.(eds.), *Learning Systems and Intelligent Robots*, Plenum Press, New York, 317–324, **FUZ**

Hara, F. (1975) A dynamic model of collective human flow from big fires, in *Summary of Papers on General Fuzzy Problems*, The Working Group on Fuzzy Systems, Tokyo, Japan, Nov., 14–18, **FUZ,SS**

Haroche, C. (1975) Grammar, implicitness and ambiguity—foundations of inherent ambiguity of discourse, *Foundations of Language*, *13*, 215–236, (in French) **FUZ,LING**

Harris, J. I. (1974) Fuzzy implication—comments on a paper by Zadeh, *DOAE Research Working Paper*, Ministry of Defence, Byfleet, Surrey, UK, **FUZ**

Harris, J. I. (1974) Fuzzy sets: how to be imprecise precisely, *DOAE Research Working Paper*, Ministry of Defence, Byfleet, Surrey, UK, **FUZ**

Hart, W. D. (1972) Probability as a degree of possibility, *Notre Dame J. Formal Logic*, *13*, 286–288, **PROB**

Hatten, M. L., Whinston, A. B., & Fu, K. S. (1975) Fuzzy set and automata theory applied to economics, *Reprint Series No. 533*, Purdue University H. C. Krannert Graduate School, **FUZ,AUT,SS**

Havránek, T. (1971) The statistical modification and interpretation of the GUHA

METHOD, *Kybernetika (Prague)*, 7, 13–21, **LOG,PROB,INDUCT**

Havránek, T. (1974) Some aspects of automatic systems of statistical inference, *Proc. European Meeting of Statisticians*, Prague, **LOG,PROB,INDUCT**

Havránek, T. (1975a) The approximation problem in computational statistics, in Bečvář, J. (ed.), *Mathematical Foundations of Computer Science 1975, Lecture Notes in Computer Science, 32*, Springer-Verlag, Berlin, 260–265, **LOG,INDUCT**

Havránek, T. (1975b) Statistical quantifiers in observational calculi: an application in GUHA-methods, *Theory & Decision*, 6, 213–230, **LOG,PROB,INDUCT**

Hay, L. S. (1963) Axiomatization of the infinite-valued predicate calculus, *J. Symbolic Logic*, 28, 77–86, **MVLOG**

Hempel, C. G. (1937) A purely topological form of non-Aristotelian logic, *J. Symbolic Logic*, 2, 97–112, **MVLOG,TOP**

Hendry, W. L. (1972) Fuzzy sets and Russell's paradox, Los Alamos Scientific Laboratory, University of California, Los Alamos, New Mexico, USA, **FUZ,PARA**

Henkin, L. (1963) A class of non-normal models for classical sentential logic, *J. Symbolic Logic*, 28, 300, **LOG,TOP**

Hersh, H. M. (1976) Fuzzy reasoning: the integration of vague information, *PhD thesis*, The Johns Hopkins University, Baltimore, MD, USA, **PSYCH,FUZ, LING,VAG**

Hersh, H. M., & Caramazza, A. (1975) The quantification of vague concepts, *Psychometric Society Meeting*, Iowa City, USA, April, **PSYCH,FUZ,LING**

Hersh, H. M., & Caramazza, A. (1976) A fuzzy set approach to modifiers and vagueness in natural language, *J. Experimental Psychology*, 105, 254–276, **FUZ,PSYCH, LING**

Hersh, H. M., & Spiering, J. (1976) How old is old ?, *Eastern Psychological Association Meeting*, New York, April, **PSYCH,FUZ,LING**

Hintikka, J., & Suppes, P.(eds.) (1970) *Information and Inference*, D.Reidel, Holland, **PROB,LOG**

Hirai, H., Asai, K., & Kitajima, S. (1968) Fuzzy automata and its application to learning control systems, *Memoirs of the Faculty of Engineering, 10*, Osaka City University, 67–73, **FUZ,AUT,LMACH**

Hockney, D., Harper, W., & Freed, B. (1975) *Contemporary research in philosophical logic and linguistic semantics*, Reidel, Holland, **FUZ,LING,LOG**

Hogarth, R. M. (1975) Cognitive processes and the assessment of subjective probability distributions, *J. Amer. Statist. Assn.*, 70, 271–294, **PROB, PSYCH**

Honda, N. (1971) Fuzzy sets, *J. Inst. Electron. Comm. Eng. (Japan)*, 54, 1359–1363, **FUZ**

Honda, N. (1975) Applications of fuzzy sets theory to automata and linguistics, *J. JAACE, 19*, 249–254, **FUZ,AUT,LING**

Honda, N., & Aida, S. (1975) Enviromental index by faces method, in *Summary of Papers on General Fuzzy Problems*, The Working Group on Fuzzy Systems, Tokyo, Japan, Nov., 19–22, **FUZ**

Honda, N., & Nasu, M. (1975) Recognition of fuzzy languages, in Zadeh, L. A., Fu, K. S., Tanaka, K., & Shimura, M.(eds.), *Fuzzy Sets and Their Applications to Cognitive and Decision Processes*, Academic Press, New York, 279–299, **FUZ,LANG**

Honda, N., & Nasu, M. (1975) F-recognition of fuzzy languages, in *Special Interest Discussion Session on Fuzzy Automata and Decision Processes*, 6th IFAC World Congress, Boston, Mass., USA, Aug., **FUZ,LANG**

Hořejš, J. (1965) Classifications and their relationship to a measure, *Publications de la Faculté des Sciences de l'Université J.E. Purkyně, No. 168*, Brno, Czech., 475–493, **PROB,PAT**

Hormann, A. M. (1971) Machine-aided value judgements using fuzzy set techniques, *SP-3590*, System Development Corporation, Santa Monica, California, USA, **FUZ,DEC**

Hughes, G. E., & Creswell, M. J. (1968) *An introduction to modal logic*, Methuen, London, **MLOG**

Hughes, P., & Brecht, G. (1976) *Vicious Circles and Infinity*, Jonathan Cape, London, **PARA**

Hung, N. T. (1975) Information fonctionelle et ensembles flous, *Seminar on Questionnaires*, University of Paris 6, Paris, France, **FUZ**

Hutton, B. (1974) Uniformities on fuzzy topological spaces, Mathematics Institute, University of Warwick, Coventry, UK, **FUZ,TOP**

Hutton, B. (1975) Normality in fuzzy topological spaces, *J. Math. Anal. & Appln.*, *50*, 74–79, **FUZ,TOP**

Hutton, B., & Reilly, J. L. (1974) Separation axioms in fuzzy topological spaces, University of Auckland, New Zealand, March, **FUZ,TOP**

Ichikawa, A., Nakao, K., & Kobayashi, S. (1975) An analysis of social group behavior by means of a threshold element network model, in *Summary of Papers on General Fuzzy Problems*, The Working Group on Fuzzy Systems, Tokyo, Japan, Nov., 23–28, **FUZ,SS**

Idesawa, M. (1975) Automatic input of line drawing and generation of solid figure, in *Summary of Papers on General Fuzzy Problems*, The Working Group on Fuzzy Systems, Tokyo, Japan, Nov., 29–33, **FUZ**

Inagaki, Y., & Fukumura, T. (1975) On the description of fuzzy meaning of context-free language, in Zadeh, L. A., Fu, K. S., Tanaka, K., & Shimura, M.(eds.), *Fuzzy Sets and Their Applications to Cognitive and Decision Processes*, Academic Press, New York, 301–328, **FUZ,VAG,LANG**

Ishikawa, A., & Mieno, H. (1975) Design of a video information system and the fuzzy information theory, *EUROCOMP 75*, Brunel University, UK, 441–450,**FUZ**

Itzinger, O. (1974) Aspects of axiomatization of behaviour: towards an application of Rasch's measurement model to fuzzy logic, in Bruckman, G., Freschl, F., & Schmatterer, L.(eds.), *COMSTAT 1974 (Proc. Symp. Computational Statistics, University of Vienna)*, Physica-Verlag, 173–182, **FUZ,SS**

Jacobson, D. H. (1976) On fuzzy goals and maximizing decisions in stochastic optimal control, *J. Math. Anal. & Appln.*, **FUZ,CON**

Jahn, K. U. (1971) Aufbau einer 3-wertigen linearen Algebra und affinen Geometrie auf grundlage der Intervall-arithmetik, *PhD thesis*, University of Leipzig, **MVLOG,SET,FUZ**

Jahn, K. U. (1974) Eine Theorie der Gleichungsysteme mit Intervall-koeffizienten,

Z. Angew. Math. Mech., 54, 405–412, **MVLOG,SET,FUZ**

Jahn, K. U. (1975) Intervall-wertige Mengen, *Math. Nachr.*, 68, 115–132, **MVLOG,SET,FUZ**

Jahn, K. U. (1975) Eine auf der Intervall–zahlen fussende 3–wertige lineare Algebra, *Math. Nachr.*, 65, 105–116, **MVLOG,SET,FUZ**

Jahn, K. U. (1976), Anvendungen von fuzzy sets, *Vorträge aus dem Problemseminar Automata- und Algorithmen theorie*, April, Weissig, 30–43, **FUZ**

Jain, R. (1975) Outline of an approach for the analysis of fuzzy systems, in *Special Interest Discussion Session on Fuzzy Automata and Decision Processes*, 6th IFAC World Congress, Boston, Mass., USA, Aug., **FUZ**

Jain, R. (1975 Pattern classification using property sets, *Symposium on Circuits, Systems & Computers*, University of Calcutta, India, Feb., **FUZ,PAT**

Jain, R. (1976) Convolution of fuzzy variables, *JIETE, 22*, **FUZ**

Jain, R. (1976) Decision making with fuzzy knowledge about the state of the system, *National Systems Conference*, Roorke, India, Feb., **FUZ,DEC**

Jarvis, R. A. (1975) Optimization strategies in adaptive control: a selective survey, *IEEE Trans. Syst. Man Cybern., SMC–5*, 83–94, **FUZ,CON**

Jakubowski, R., & Kasprak, A. (1973) Application of fuzzy programs to the design of machining technology, *Bulletin of the Polish Academy of Science, 21(21)*, 17–22, **FUZ**

Jaśkowski, S. (1969) Propositional calculus for contradictory deductive systems, *Studia Logica, 24*, 143-159, (trans. of 1948 Polish paper) **LOG,VAG,PARA**

Jensen, J. H. (1976) Application for fuzzy logic control, No. 1, *No. 7607*, Electric Power Engineering Dept., Technical University of Denmark, Lyngby, June, **FUZ,CON**

Jobe, W. H. (1962) Functional completeness and canonical forms in many-valued logics, *J. Symbolic Logic, 28*, 409–421, **MVLOG**

Jordan, P. (1952) Algebraische Betrachtungen zur Theorie des Wirkungskvantum, *Math. Sem. Hamburg, 18*, 99–119, **SEMR,LOG,PROB**

Jordan, P. (1962) Halbgruppen von idempotenten und nichtkommutative Verbande, *J. Reine Angew, Math. 211*, 136–161, **SEMR,LOG**

Jouault, J. P., & Luan, P. M. (1975) Application des concepts flous a la programmation en languages quasi-naturels, Institut informatique d'entreprise, C.N.A.M., Paris, France, **FUZ,LING**

Kahne, S. (1975) A procedure for optimizing development decisions, *Automatica, 11*, 261–269, **PROB,DEC**

Kalman, J. A. (1958) Lattices with involution, *Trans. Amer. Math. Soc., 87*, 485–491, **LOG,TOP,LAT**

Kalmanson, D., & Stegall, F. (1973) Recherche cardio-vaculaire et theorie des ensembles flous, *La Nouvelle Presse Medicale, 41*, 2757–2760, **FUZ,MED**

Kandel, A. (1972a) Toward simplification of fuzzy functions, *CSR114*, Computer Science Dept., New Mexico Institute of Mining & Technology, Socorro, New Mexico, USA, June, **FUZ,SWLOG**

Kandel, A. (1972b) On coded grammars and fuzzy structures, *CSR118*, Computer Science Dept., New Mexico Institute of Mining & Technology, Socorro, New Mexico, USA, Sep., **FUZ,LANG**

Kandel, A. (1972c) A new algorithm for minimizing incompletely specified fuzzy functions, *CSR127*, Computer Science Dept., New Mexico Institute of Mining & Technology, Socorro, New Mexico, USA, Nov., **FUZ,SWLOG**

Kandel, A. (1973a) A new method for generating fuzzy prime implicants and an algorithm for the automatic minimization of inexact structures, *CSR126*, Computer Science Dept., New Mexico Institute of Mining & Technology, Socorro, New Mexico, USA, Oct., **FUZ,SWLOG**

Kandel, A. (1973b) Comment on an algorithm that generates fuzzy prime implicants by Lee and Chang, *Inform. & Control, 22,* 279–282, **FUZ,SWLOG**

Kandel, A. (1973c) Fuzzy chains: a new concept in decision-making under uncertainty, *Computer Science Report 123,* New Mexico Institute of Mining and Technology, Aug., **FUZ,SWLOG,DEC**

Kandel, A. (1973d) On minimization of fuzzy functions, *IEEE Trans. Comp., C–22,* 826–832, **FUZ,SWLOG**

Kandel, A. (1973e) On the analysis of fuzzy logic, *Proc. 6th Int. Conf. Syst. Sciences,* Honolulu, Hawaii, Jan., **FUZ,SWLOG**

Kandel, A. (1973f) Comments on "Minimization of fuzzy functions", *IEEE Trans. Comp., C–22,* 217, **FUZ,SWLOG**

Kandel, A. (1973g) Fuzzy functions and their application to the analysis of switching hazards, *Proc. 2nd Texas Conf. on Computing Systems,* Austin, Texas, USA, Nov., 42:1–6, **FUZ,SWLOG**

Kandel, A. (1974a) Synthesis of fuzzy logic with analog modules: preliminiminary developments, *Computers in Education Transaction (ASEE Div.), 6,* 71–79, **FUZ,SWLOG**

Kandel, A. (1974b) On fuzzy maps: some initial thoughts, *CSR131,* Computer Science Department, New Mexico Institute of Mining and Technology, Socorro, New Mexico, USA, **FUZ,SWLOG**

Kandel, A. (1974c) Simple disjunctive decompositions of fuzzy functions, *CSR132,* Computer Science Dept., New Mexico Institute of Mining & Technology, Socorro, New Mexico, USA, July, **FUZ,SWLOG**

Kandel, A. (1974d) On the theory of fuzzy matrices, *CSR135,* Computer Science Dept., New Mexico Institute of Mining & Technology, Socorro, New Mexico, USA, Oct., **FUZ**

Kandel, A. (1974e) Generation of the set representing all fuzzy prime implicants, *CSR136,* Computer Science Dept., New Mexico Institute of Mining & Technology, Socorro, New Mexico, USA, Oct., **FUZ,SWLOG**

Kandel, A. (1974f) On the enumeration of fuzzy functions, *12th Holiday Symb. "Developments in Ombinatorics",* New Mexico State University, Las Cruces, New Mexico, USA, Dec., **FUZ,SWLOG**

Kandel, A. (1974g) Application of fuzzy logic to the detection of static hazards in combinational switching systems, *Int. J. Comp. Inf. Sciences, 3,* 129–139, **FUZ,SWLOG**

Kandel, A. (1974h) On the properties of fuzzy switching functions, *J. Cybernetics, 4,* 119–126, **FUZ,SWLOG**

Kandel, A. (1974i) On the minimization of incompletely specified fuzzy functions, *Inform. & Control, 26,* 141–153, **FUZ,SWLOG**

Kandel, A. (1974j) Codes over languages, *IEEE Trans. Syst. Man Cybern.*, *SMC-4*, 135–138, **FUZ,LANG**

Kandel, A. (1974k) Fuzzy representation CNF minimization and their application to fuzzy transmission structures, *1974 Symposium on Multiple-Valued Logic, IEEE 74CHO845-8C*, 361–379, **FUZ,SWLOG**

Kandel, A. (1975a) A note on the simplification of fuzzy switching functions, *CSR139*, Computer Science Dept., New Mexico Institute of Mining & Technology, Socorro, New Mexico, USA, May, **FUZ,SWLOG**

Kandel, A. (1975b) Fuzzy hierarchical classifications of dynamic patterns, *NATO ASI Pattern Recognition & Classification*, France, Sep., **FUZ,PAT**

Kandel, A. (1975c) Properties of fuzzy matrices and their applications to hierarchical structures, *9th Asilomar Conf. Circuits, Systems & Computers*, Pacific Grove, California, USA, Nov., **FUZ,SYS**

Kandel, A. (1975d) Block decomposition of imprecise models, *9th Asilomar Conf. Circuits, Systems & Computers*, Pacific Grove, California, USA, Nov., **FUZ, SYS**

Kandel, A. (1976a) Inexact switching logic, *IEEE Trans. Syst. Man Cybern.*, *6*, 215–219, **FUZ,SWLOG**

Kandel, A. (1976b) Fuzzy maps and their application in the simplification of fuzzy switching function, *Porc. 6th Int. Symp. Multiple-Valued Logic, IEEE 76CH1111-4C*, May, **FUZ,SWLOG**

Kandel, A. (1976c) Fuzzy systems and their applications to simulations, *Proc. 9th Hawaii Int. Conf. Syst. Sci.*, Honolulu, Hawaii, Jan., **FUZ**

Kandel, A. (1976d) On the decomposition of fuzzy functions, *IEEE Trans. Comp.*, *c–25*, 1124–1130, **FUZ**

Kandel, A., & Davis, H. A. (1976) The first fuzzy decade (bibliography on fuzzy sets and their applications), *CSR140*, Computer Science Dept., New Mexico Institute of Mining & Technology, Socorro, New Mexico, USA, April, **FUZ**

Kandel, A., & Hughes, J. S. (1975) Applications of fuzzy algebra to hazard detection in combinational switching circuits, *CSR138*, Computer Science Dept., New Mexico Institute of Mining & Technology, Socorro, New Mexico, USA, April, **FUZ,SWLOG**

Kandel, A., & Lee, S. C. (1976) *Fuzzy Switching and Automata*, **FUZ,SWLOG,AUT**

Kandel, A., & Neff, T. P. (1977) Simplification of fuzzy switching functions, *Int. J. Comp. Inf. Sciences*, **FUZ,SWLOG**

Kandel, A., & Obenhauf, T. A. (1974) On fuzzy lattices, *CSR 128*, Computer Science Department, New Mexico Institute of Mining & Tech., Socorro, New Mexico, USA, **FUZ,LAT**

Kandel, A., & Rickman, S. M. (1975) Column table approach for the minimization of fuzzy functions, *CSR137*, Computer Science Dept., New Mexico Institute of Mining & Technology, Socorro, New Mexico, USA, March, **FUZ,SWLOG**

Kandel, A., & Yelowitz, L. (1974) Fuzzy chains, *IEEE Trans. Syst. Man Cybern.*, *SMC-4*, 472–475, **FUZ**

Karttunen, L. (1972) Possible and Must, in Kimball, J. P. (ed.), *Syntax and Semantics Vol. 1*, Seminar Press, New York, 1–20, **LING**

Katz, J. J. (1962) *The Problem of Induction and its Solution*, University of Chicago Press, Chicago, USA, **INDUCT,LOG**

Kaufmann, A. (1973) *Introduction a la Théorie des Sous-Ensembles Flous, 1: Elements Theoretiques de Base*, Masson et Cie, Paris, France, **FUZ**

Kaufmann, A. (1975a) *Introduction a la Théorie des Sous-ensembles Flous, 2: Applications a la Linguistique et a la Sémantique*, Masson et Cie, Paris, France, **FUZ**

Kaufmann, A. (1975b) *Introduction a la Théorie des Sous-Ensembles Flous, 3: Applications a la Classification et la Reconnaisance des Formes, aux Automates et aux Systemes, aux Choix des Critares*, Masson et Cie, Paris, France, **FUZ**

Kaufmann, A. (1975c) *Introduction to the Theory of Fuzzy Subsets Vol. 1*, Academic Press, New York, **FUZ**

Kaufmann, A. (1975d) Introduction to a fuzzy theory of the human operator, *Special Interest Discussion Session on Fuzzy Automata and Decision Processes*, 6th IFAC World Congress, Boston, Mass., USA, Aug., **FUZ,SS**

Kaufmann, A., Cools, M., & Dubois, T. (1973) Stimulation inventive dans un dialogue homme-machine utilisant la methode des morphologies et la theorie des sous-ensembles flous, *IMAGO Discussion Paper 6*, Université Catholique de Louvain, Belgium, **FUZ,SS**

Kaufmann, A., Cools, M., & Dubois, T. (1975) Exercises avec solutions sur la theorie des sous-ensembles flous, Masson et Cie, Paris, **FUZ**

Kaufmann, F. (1974) A survey of fuzzy sets theory and applications to languages automata and algorithms, in *US-Japan Seminar on Fuzzy Sets and Their Applications*, Berkeley, California, USA, **FUZ,AUT**

Kay, & McDaniel (1975) Color categories as fuzzy sets, *Working Paper No. 44*, University of California, Berkeley, California, **FUZ,PSYCH**

Kerridge, D. F. (1961) Inaccuracy and inference, *J. Roy. Statist. Soc. (ser. B)*, 184–194, **PROB,VAG**

Khatchadourian, H. (1965) Vagueness, meaning and absurdity, *Amer. Philos. Quart.*, 2, 119–129, **VAG**

Kickert, W. J. M. (1974) Application of fuzzy set theory to warm water control, *thesis*, Delft University of Technology, (in Dutch) **FUZ,CON**

Kickert, W. J. M. (1975a) Analysis of fuzzy logic controller, *Fuzzy Logic Working Group Rep. F/WK1/75*, Queen Mary College, University of London, UK, June, **FUZ,CON**

Kickert, W. J. M. (1975b) Off-line analysis of the fuzzy rules, *Fuzzy Logic Working Group Rep.*, Queen Mary College, University of London, UK, July, **FUZ,CON**

Kickert, W. J. M. (1975c) Further analysis and application of fuzzy logic, *Fuzzy Logic Working Group Rep. F/WK2/75*, Queen Mary College, University of London, UK, Aug., **FUZ,CON**

Kickert, W. J. M., & Koppelaar, H. (1976) Application of fuzzy set theory to syntactic pattern recognition of handwritten capitals, *IEEE Trans. Syst. Man Cybern.*, 6, 148–151, **FUZ,CON**

Kickert, W. J. M., & Van Nauta Lemke, H. R. (1976) Application of a fuzzy controller in a warm water plant, *Automatica*, 12, 301–308, **FUZ,CON**

Kim, H. H., Mizumoto, M., Toyoda, J., & Tanaka, K. (1974) Lattice grammars, *Systems, Computers, Controls, 5*, 1–9, (orig. TIECE 57-d, 253–260) **FUZ,LAT, LING**

Kimball, J. P. (ed.) (1972) *Syntax and Semantics Vol. 1*, Seminar Press, New York, **LING**

Kimball, J. P. (ed.) (1973) *Syntax and Semantics Vol. 2*, Seminar Press, New York, **LING**

Kimball, J. P. (ed.) (1975) *Syntax and Semantics Vol. 4*, Academic Press, New York, **LING**

King, P. J., & Mamdani, E. H. (1975) The application of fuzzy control systems to industrial processes, in *Special Interest Discussion Session on Fuzzy Automata and Decision Processes*, 6th IFAC World Congress, Boston, Mass., USA, Aug., **FUZ,CON**

King, P. J., & Mamdani, E. H. (1976) The application of fuzzy control systems to industrial processes, **FUZ,CON**

Kise, V. A., & Osis, J. J. (1969) Search methods for establishing of maximal separability of fuzzy sets, in D. S. Kritinkov, J. J. Osis, L. A. Rastrigin, (eds.), *Kibernetika i Diagnostika, 3*, 79–88, (in Russian) Zinatne, Riga, U.S.S.R. **FUZ,PAT**

Kitagawa, T. (1973) Three coordinate systems for information science approaches, *Inform. Sci., 15*, 159–169, **FUZ**

Kitagawa, T. (1973) Biorobots for simulation studies of learning and inteligent controls, in *US-Japan seminar on learning control and intelligent control*, Gainesville, Florida, USA, **FUZ,LMACH**

Kitagawa, T. (1975) Fuzziness in informative logics, in Zadeh, L. A., Fu, K. S., Tanaka, K., & Shimura, M. (eds.), *Fuzzy Sets and Their Applications to Cognitive and Decision Processes*, Academic Press, New York, 97–124, **FUZ**

Kitahashi, T. (1975) A survey of studies on applications of many-valued logic in Japan, *Proc. 1975 Int. Symp. Multiple-Valued Logic, IEEE 78CH0959-7C*, 462–467, **FUZ,MVLOG**

Kitajima, S., & Asai, K. (1970) Learning controls by fuzzy automata, *Journal of JAACE, 14*, 551–559, **FUZ,LMACH**

Kitajima, S., & Asai, K. (1972) Learning model of fuzzy automaton with state-dependent output (3), *Annual Joint Conference Records of JAACE*, **FUZ,LMACH**

Kitajima, S., & Asai, K. (1974) A method of learning control varying search domain by fuzzy automata, in Fu, K. S, & Tou, J. T. (eds.), *Learning Systems and Intelligent Robots*, Plenum Press, New York, 249–262, **FUZ,LMACH**

Klabbers, J. H.G. (1975) General system theory and social systems: a methodology for the social sciences, *Nederlands Tijdschrift voor de Psychologie, 30*, 493–514 **FUZ,SS**

Klaua, D. (1965) Uber einen Ansatz zur mehrwertigen Mengenlehre, *Monatsb. Deutsch. Akad. Wiss. (Berlin), 7*, 859–867, **SET,MVLOG**

Klaua, D. (1966a) Uber einen zweiten Ansatz zur mehrwertigen Mengenlehre, *Monatsb. Deutsch. Akad. Wiss. (Berlin), 8*, 161–177, **SET,MVLOG**

Klaua, D. (1966b) Grundbegriffe einer mehrwertigen Mengenlehre, *Monatsb. Deutsch. Akad. Wiss. (Berlin), 8*, 782–802, **SET,MVLOG**

Klaua, D. (1967a) Ein Anstaz zur mehrwertigen Mengenlehre, *Math. Nachr., 33,* 273–296, **SET,MVLOG**

Klaua, D. (1967b) Einbettung der klassischen Mengenlehre in die mehrwertige, *Monatsb. Deutsch. Akad. Wiss. (Berlin), 9,* 258–272, **SET,MVLOG**

Klaua, D. (1968) Partiell aefinlerte Mengen, *Monatsb. Deutsch. Akad. Wiss. (Berlin), 10,* 571–578, **SET,MVLOG**

Klaua, D. (1969a) Partielle Mengen und Zahlen, *Monatsb. Deutsch. Akad. Wiss. (Berlin), 11,* 585–599, **SET,MVLOG**

Klaua, D. (1969b) Partielle Mengen mit mehrwertigen Grundbeziehunger, *Monatsb. Deutsch. Akad. Wiss. (Berlin), 11,* 573–589, **SET,MVLOG**

Klaua, D. (1970) Stetige gleichmachtigkeiten kontinuierlich-wertiger Mengen, *Monatsb. Deutsch. Akad. Wiss. (Berlin), 12,* 749–758, **SET,MVLOG**

Klaua, D. (1972) Zum Kardinalzahlbegriff in der mehrwertigen Mengenlehre, in *Theory of Sets and Topology,* Deutscher Verlag der Wissenschaften, Berlin, 313–325, **MVLOG,SET,FUZ**

Klaua, D. (1973) Zur Arithmetik mehrwertigen Zahlen, *Math. Nachr., 57,* 275–306, **MVLOG,SET,FUZ**

Kleene, S. C. (1952) *Introduction to Metamathematics,* Van Nostrand, New York, **LOG,PARA,MVLOG**

Kling, R. (1973a) Fuzzy planner, *Tech. Rep. 168,* Computer Science Department, University of Wisconsin, **FUZ,LMACH**

Kling, R. (1973b) Fuzzy planner: reasoning with inexact concepts in a procedural, problem-solving language, *J. Cybernetics, 3,* 1–16, **FUZ,LMACH**

Kling, R. (1974) Fuzzy-PLANNER: Reasoning with inexact concepts in a procedural problem-solving language, *J. Cybernetics, 4,* 105–122, **FUZ,LMACH**

Klir, G. J. (1975a) Processing of fuzzy activities of neutral systems, in Trappl, R., & Pichler, F. R. (eds.), *Progress in Cybernetics and Systems Research, 1,* 21–24, **FUZ,SYS**

Klir, G. J. (1975b) On the representation of activity arrays, *Int. J. General Syst., 2,* 149–168, **FUZ**

Klir, G. J. (1976) Identification of generative structures in empirical data, *Int. J. General Syst., 3,* 89–104, **FUZ,SYS,INDUCT**

Klir, G. J., & Uttenhove, H. J. J. (1976a) Procedure of generating hypothetical structures in the structure identification problem, *3rd Eur. Meeting Cybern. Syst. Res., Vienna,* **FUZ,SYS,INDUCT**

Klir, G. J., & Uttenhove, H. J. J. (1976b) Computerized methodology for structure modelling, in Stenfert, H. E. (ed.), *Annals of Systems Research, 4,* Kroese, Leiden, Holland, **LOG,INDUCT**

Kneale, W., & Kneale, M. (1962) *The Development of Logic,* Clarendon Press, Oxford, **LOG**

Kochen, M. (1975) Applications of fuzzy sets in psychology, in Zadeh, L. A., Fu, K. S., Tanaka, K., & Shimura, M. (eds.), *Fuzzy Sets and Their Applications to Cognitive and Decision Processes,* Academic Press, New York, 395–408, **FUZ,PSYCH**

Kochen, M., & Badre, A. N. (1974) On the precision of adjectives which denote fuzzy sets, *J. Cybernetics, 4,* 49–59, **FUZ,PSYCH,LING**

Kochen, M., & Dreyfuss-Raimi, G. (1974) On the psycholinguistic reality of fuzzy sets: Effect of context and set, University of Michigan Mental Health Research Institute, Ann Arbor, USA, June, **FUZ,PSYCH,LING**

Koczy, L. T. (1975) R-fuzzy algebra as a generalized formulation of the intuitive logic, Department of Process Control, Technical University, Budapest, Hungary, **FUZ,LOG**

Koczy, L. T. (1976) Some questions of sigma-algebras of fuzzy objects of type N, *3rd Eur. Meeting Cybern. Syst. Res., Vienna*, **FUZ,PROB**

Koczy, L. T., & Hajnal, M. (1975) A new fuzzy calculus and its application as a pattern recognition technique, *Proceedings of 3rd International Congress of Cybernetics and Systems*, Bucharest, Rumania, Aug., **FUZ,PAT**

Kohout, L. J. (1974) The Pinkava many-valued complete logic systems and their applications in the design of many-valued switching circuits, *IEEE 74CH0845-8C, Proc. 1974 Int. Symp. Multiple-Valued Logic*, May, 261–284, **MVLOG,SWLOG,FUZ,PAT**

Kohout, L. J. (1975) Generalized topologies and their relevance to general systems, *Int. J. General Syst., 2*, 25–34, **LOG,TOP**

Kohout, L. J. (1976a) Automata and topology, in Mamdani, E. H., & Gaines, B. R. (eds.), *Discrete Systems and Fuzzy Reasoning, EES-MMS-DSFR-76*, Queen Mary College, University of London, (workshop proceedings) **FUZ,AUT,TOP**

Kohout, L. J. (1976b) Application of multi-valued logics to the study of human movement control and of movement disorders, *Proc. 6th Int. Symp. Multiple-Valued Logic, IEEE 76CH1111-4C*, 224–231, **MVLOG,BIO**

Kohout, L. J. (1976c) Representation of functional hierarchies of movement in the brain, *Int. J. Man-Machine Studies, 8*, 699–709, **FUZ,MVLOG,BIO**

Kohout, L. J., & Pinkava, V. (1976) The functional completeness of Pi-algebras and its relevance to biological modelling and to technological applications of many-valued logics, in Mamdani, E. H., & Gaines, B. R. (eds.), *Discrete Systems and Fuzzy Reasoning, EES-MMS-DSFR-76*, Queen Mary College, University of London, (workshop proceedings) **FUZ,MVLOG,BIO**

Kokawa, M., Nakamura, K., & Oda, M. (1972) A formulation of human decision-making process, *19*, Automatic Control Laboratory, Nagoya University, Japan, 3–10, **FUZ,DEC,PSYCH**

Kokawa, M., Nakamura, K., & Oda, M. (1973) Fuzzy expression of human experience-to-memory process, *Research Reports of Automatic Control Laboratory, 20*, Automatic Control Laboratory, Nagoya University, Japan, June, 27–33, **FUZ,PSYCH**

Kokawa, M., Nakamura, K., & Oda, M. (1974a) Fuzzy-theoretical approaches to forgetting processes and inference, *21*, Automatic Control Laboratory, Nagoya University, Japan, 1–10, **FUZ,PSYCH**

Kokawa, M., Nakamura, K., & Oda, M. (1974b) Fuzzy theoretical and concept formational approaches to memory and inference experiments, *Trans. Inst. Electron. Comm. Eng. (Japan), 57-d*, 487–493, **FUZ,PSYCH**

Kokawa, M., Nakamura, K., & Oda, M. (1975a) Hint effect and jump of logic in a decision process, *Trans. Inst. Electron. Comm. Eng. (Japan), 58-d*, **FUZ, DEC,PSYCH**

Kokawa, M., Nakamura, K., & Oda, M. (1975b) Experimental approach to fuzzy simulation of memorizing, forgetting and inference process, in Zadeh, L. A., Fu, K. S., Tanaka, K., & Shimura, M. (eds.), *Fuzzy Sets and Their Applications to Cognitive and Decision Processes*, Academic Press, New York, 409–428, **FUZ,PSYCH**

Kokawa, M., Oda, M., & Nakamura, K. (1975) Fuzzy theoretical dimensionality reduction mmethod of multi-dimensional quantity, in *Special Interest Discussion Session on Fuzzy Automata and Decision Processes*, 6th IFAC World Congress, Boston, Mass., USA, Aug., **FUZ**

Kolibiar, M. (1972) Distributive sublattices of a lattice, *Proc. Amer. Math. Soc., 34*, 359–364, **LAT**

Konrad, E., & Bollman, P. (1976) Fuzzy document retrieval, *3rd Eur. Meeting Cybern. Syst. Res., Vienna*, **FUZ,INFR**

Körner, S. (1957) Reference, vagueness and necessity, *Philos. Rev., 66*, July, **VAG,LOG,MVLOG**

Körner, S. (1959) *Conceptual Thinking*, New York, **LOG,VAG**

Körner, S. (1966) *Experience and Theory*, Routledge & Kegan Paul, London, **LOG,VAG**

Körner, S. (1970) *Categorical Frameworks*, Basil Blackwell, Oxford, **VAG,LOG**

Körner, S. (1971) *Fundamental Questions of Philosophy*, Penguin Books, **LOG, VAG,MVLOG,MLOG,INDUCT**

Körner, S. (1976a) *Experience and Conduct*, Cambridge University Press, **VAG, LOG**

Körner, S. (1976b) *Philosophy of Logic*, Basil Blackwell, Oxford, **LOG,VAG,FUZ**

Kotas, J. (1963) Axioms for Birkhoff-v.Neumann quantum logic, *Bull. de l'Academie Polonaise des Sciences, ser. math., astr. & phys., 11*, 629–632, **LOG**

Kotoh, K., & Hiramatsu, K. (1973) A representation of pattern classes using the fuzzy sets, *Systems, Computers, Controls*, 1–8, (orig. TIECE 56-d, 275–282) **FUZ,PAT**

Koutský, K. (1947) Sur les lattices topologiques, *Comptes Rendus (Paris), 225*, 659–661, **LAT,TOP**

Koutský, K. (1952) Théorie des lattices topologiques, *Publicationes de la Faculté des Sciences de l'Université Masaryk, No. 337*, Brno, Czechoslovakia, 133–171, **LAT,TOP**

Knopfmacher, K. (1975) On measures of fuzziness, *J. Math. Anal. & Appln., 49*, 529–534, **FUZ**

Kramosil, I. (1975) A probabilistic approach to automaton-environment systems, *Kybernetika (Prague), 11*, 173–206, **PROB,FUZ,INDUCT,LOG**

Kramosil, I., & Michálek, J. (1975) Fuzzy metrics and statistical metric spaces, *Kybernetika (Prague), 11*, 336–344, **FUZ,TOP,PROB**

Krantz, D. H., Luce, R. D., Suppes, P., & Tversky, A. (1971) *Foundations of Measurement*, Academic Press, New York, **PROB,IMEAS**

Krivine, J. L. (1974) Langages à valeurs reelles et applications, *Fundamenta Mathematicae, 81*, 213–253, **MVLOG,LANG**

Kubiński, T. (1958) Nazwy nieostre (vague terms), *Studia Logica, 7*, 115–179, **VAG,LOG**

Kubiński, T. (1959) Systemy pozornie sprzeczne, *Zeszyty naukowe Uniwersytetu Wroclawskiego, Seria B, Matematyka, Fizyka, Astronomia* (1959), 53–61, **VAG, LOG**

Kubiński, T. (1960) An Attempt to Bring Logic Nearer to Colloquial Language, *Studia Logica, 10*, 61–75, **VAG,LOG,LING**

Kyburg, H. E. (1970) *Probability and Inductive Logic*, MacMillan, London, **LOG,PROB**

Labov, W. (1973) The boundaries of words and their meanings, in Bailey, & Shuy (eds.), *New Ways of Analysing Variations in English*, Washington, Georgetown University Press, **FUZ,LING**

Lake, J. (1974a) Sets, fuzzy sets, multi-sets and functions, Department of Mathematics, Polytechnic of the South Bank, Borough Road, London, UK, **FUZ**

Lake, J. (1974b) Fuzzy sets and bald men, Department of Mathematics, Polytechnic of the South Bank, Borough Road, London, UK, **FUZ,PARA**

Lakoff, G. (1973a) Notes on what it would take to understand how one adverb works, *Monist, 57*, 328–343, **FUZ,LING**

Lakoff, G. (1973b) Pragmatics in natural logic, in Keenan, E. L. (ed.), *Formal Semantics of Natural Language*, Cambridge University Press, 253–286, **LING**

Lakoff, G. (1973c) Hedges: a study in meaning criteria and the logic of fuzzy concepts, *J. Philos. Logic, 2*, 458–508, **FUZ,LING**

Lakshmivarahan, S., & Rajasethupathy, K. S. (1974) Considerations for fuzzifying formal languages and synthesis of fuzzy grammars, Indian Institute of Technology, Madras, India, **FUZ,LANG**

Larsen, J. (1976) A multi-step formation of variable valued logic hypotheses, *Proc. 6th Int. Symp. Multiple-Valued Logic, IEEE 76CH1111-4C*, 157–163, **MVLOG,INDUCT,FUZ**

Larsen, L. E., Ruspini, E. H., McNew, J. J., Walter, D. O., & Adey, W. R. (1972) A test of sleep staging systems in the unrestrained chimpanzee, *Brain Research, 40*, 319–343, **FUZ,BIO**

Lawvere, F. W. (ed.) (1972) *Toposes, Algebraic Geometry and Logic*, Springer-Verlag, Berlin, **CAT,LOG**

Lawvere, F. W., Maurer, C., & Wraith, G. C. (eds.) (1975) *Model Theory and Topoi, Lecture Notes in Mathematics, 445*, Springer-Verlag, Berlin, **CAT,LOG**

Leal, A., & Pearl, J. (1976) A computer system for conversational elicitation of problem structures, *UCLA-ENG-7665*, School of Engineering & Applied Science, University of California, Los Angeles, USA, June, **PROB,DEC**

Lee, E. T. (1972a) Fuzzy languages and their relation to automata, *PhD thesis*, Department of Electrical Engineering and Computer Science, University of California, Berkeley, California, USA, **FUZ,AUT,LANG**

Lee, E. T. (1972b) Proximity measures for the classification of geometric figures, *J. Cybernetics, 2*, 43–59, **FUZ,PAT**

Lee, E. T. (1974) An application of fuzzy sets to the classification of geometric figures and chromosome images, in *US-Japan Seminar on Fuzzy Sets and Their Applications*, Berkeley, California, USA, **FUZ,PAT,MED**

Lee, E. T. (1975) Shape-oriented chromosome classification, *IEEE Trans. Syst. Man Cybern., SMC-5*, 629–632, **FUZ,PAT,MED**

Lee, E. T., & Chang, C. L. (1971) Some properties of fuzzy logic, *Inform. & Control,* *19,* 417–431, **FUZ,LOG,SWLOG**

Lee, E. T., & Zadeh, L. A. (1969) Notes on fuzzy languages, *Inform. Sci., 1,* 421–434, **FUZ,LANG**

Lee, E. T., & Zadeh, L. A. (1970) Fuzzy languages and their acceptance by automata, *4th Princeton Conference on Information Science and Systems,* 399, **FUZ,LANG**

Lee, R. C. T. (1972) Fuzzy logic and the resolution principle, *J. Assn. Comp. Mach., 19,* 109–119, **FUZ,LOG**

Lee, S. C., & Lee, E. T. (1970) Fuzzy neurons and automata, *Proceedings of 4th Princeton Conference on Information Science and Systems,* 381–385, **FUZ,BIO**

Lee, S. C., & Lee, E. T. (1974) Fuzzy sets and neural networks, *J. Cybernetics, 4,* 83–103, **FUZ,BIO**

Leenders, J. H. (1974) Vage verzamelingen: een kritische benandering, *Kwartaalschrift Wetenschappelijk Onderwijs Limburg (Belgium), 4,* 441–455, **FUZ,VAG**

LeFaivre, R. A. (1974a) Fuzzy problem solving, *Technical Report 37,* Madison Academy Computing Center, University of Wisconsin, USA, Aug., **FUZ,L-MACH**

LeFaivre, R. A. (1974b) The representation of fuzzy knowledge, *J. Cybernetics 4,* 57–66, **FUZ,LMACH**

LeFaivre, R. A. (1976) Procedural representation in fuzzy problem solving systems, *Proc. NCC,* **FUZ,LMACH**

Lemmon, E. J. (1966a) Algebraic semantics for modal logics I, *J. Symbolic Logic, 31,* 46–65, **MLOG**

Lemmon E. J. (1966b) Algebraic semantics for modal logics II, *J. Symbolic Logic, 31,* 191–218, **MLOG**

Lemmon, E. J., Meredith, C. A., Meredith, D., Prior, A. N., & Thomas, I. (1969) Calculi of pure strict implication, in Davis, J. W., Hockney, D. J., & Freed, W. K. (eds.), *Philosophical Logic,* D. Reidel, Dordrecht, Holland, 215–250, **MLOG**

Levi, I. (1967) *Gambling with Truth,* MIT Press, Cambridge, Mass., USA, **PROB-,DEC,LOG**

Lewis, D. K. (1969) *Convention: a Philosophical Study,* Harvard University Press, Cambridge, Mass., USA, **LING**

Lewis, D. K. (1973) *Counterfactuals,* Basil Blackwell, Oxford, **MLOG,LING**

Lientz, B. P. (1972) On time dependent fuzzy sets, *Inform. Sci., 4,* 367–376, **FUZ**

Loginov, V. I. (1966) Probability treatment of Zadeh membership functions and their use in pattern recognition, *Engineering Cybernetics,* 68–69, **FUZ,PROB**

Lombaerde, J. (1974) Mesures d'entropie en theorie des sous-ensembles flous, *IMAGO Discussion Paper IDP-12,* Centre Interfacultaire IMAGO, Universite Catholique de Louvain, Heverlee, Belgique, Jan., **FUZ,PROB**

Longo, G. (1975) Fuzzy sets, graphs and source coding, in Swirzynski, J. K. (ed.), *New Directions in Signal Processing in Communications and Control,* Noordhoff-Leyden, 27–33, **FUZ**

Los, J., & Ryll-Nardzewski, C. (1951) On the application of Tychnoff's theorem in mathematical proofs, *Fundamenta Mathematicae, 38,* 233–237, **LOG, TOP**

Lowen, R. (1974a) A theory of fuzzy topologies, *PhD thesis,* Free University of Brussels, Belgium, **FUZ, TOP**

Lowen, R. (1974b) Topologies flous, *C.R. Acad. des Sciences, (Paris) 278A,* 925–928, **FUZ, TOP**

Lowen, R. (1975) Convergence flous, *C.R. Acad. des Sciences, (Paris) 280,* 1181–1183, **FUZ, TOP**

Lowen, R. (1976a) Fuzzy topological spaces and fuzzy compactness, *J. Math. Anal. & Appln.,* **FUZ, TOP**

Lowen, R. (1976b) Initial and final fuzzy topologies and the fuzzy Tychnoff theorem, *J. Math. Anal. & Appln.,* **FUZ, TOP**

Lowen, R. (1976c) A comparison of different compactness notions in fuzzy topology, Vrije Universiteit Brussel, Brussels, Belgium, **FUZ, TOP**

Lowen, R. (1976d) Lattice convergence in fuzzy topological spaces, Vrije Universiteit Brussel, Brussels, Belgium, **FUZ, TOP**

Luschei, E. C. (1962) *The Logical Systems of Lesniewski,* North-Holland, Amsterdam, **VAG, LOG, LANG**

Lysvag, B. (1975) Verbs of hedging, in Kimball, J. P. (ed.), *Syntax and Semantics Vol. 4,* Academic Press, New York, 125–154, **LING**

Maarschalk, C. G. D. (1975) Exact and fuzzy concepts superimposed on the GST (a meta theory), *Proceedings of 3rd International Congress of Cybernetics and Systems,* Bucharest, Rumania, Aug., **FUZ, SYS**

Maarschalk, C. G. D. (1976) Methodology in systems thinking and systems language—an approach to formalized and conceptual systems, exact and fuzzy concepts and Systol (system oriented language), *3rd Eur. Meeting Cybern. Syst. Res., Vienna,* **FUZ, SYS**

Machina, K. F. (1972) Vague predicates, *Amer. Philos. Quart., 9,* 225–233, **VAG, FUZ**

Machina, K. F. (1976) Truth, belief and vagueness, *J. Philos. Logic, 5,* 47–77, **FUZ, VAG, TRUTH, MVLOG**

Mackie, J. L. (1973) *Truth, Probability and Paradox,* Clarendon Press, Oxford, **LOG, PROB, PARA**

MacLane, S. (1971) *Categories for the Working Mathematician,* Springer-Verlag, Berlin, **CAT, LOG, TOP**

MacVicar-Whelan, P. J. (1974) Fuzzy sets, the concept of height, and the hedge very, *Technical Memorandum 1,* Physics Department, Grand Valley State Colleges, Allendale, Michigan, USA, **FUZ, PSYCH, LING**

MacVicar-Whelan, P. J. (1975) Un modele de signification de termes quantifiant les dimensions: application a la taille humaine, *LAAS-SMA4 75.I.49,* Laboratoire d'Automatique et d'Analyse des Systemes, Toulouse, France, Dec., **FUZ, LING, PSYCH**

MacVicar-Whelan, P. J. (1976) Fuzzy sets for man-machine interaction, *Int. J. Man-Machine Studies, 8,* **FUZ, LING, PSYCH, CON**

Malvache, N. (1975) Analyse et identification des systemes visuel et manuel en vision frontale et peripherique chez l'homme, *PhD thesis,* Lille, France, April, **FUZ, BIO**

Malvache, N., Milbred, G., & Vidal, P. (1973) Perception visuelle: champ de vision laterale, modele de la fonction du regard; Rapport de synthese, *Contrat DRME No. 71-251*, Paris, France, **FUZ, BIO**

Malvache, N., & Vidal, P. (1974) Application des systemes flous a la modelisation des phenomenes de prise de decision et d'apprehension des informations visuelles chex l'homme, *A.T.P.-C.N.R.S 1K05*, Paris, **FUZ, BIO**

Malvache, N., & Willayes, D. (1974) Representation et minimisation de fonctions flous, Doc. Centre Universitie de Valenciennes, France, **FUZ**

Mamdani, E. H. (1974) Applications of fuzzy algorithms for control of simple dynamic plant, *Proc. IEE, 121*, 1585–1588, **FUZ, CON**

Mamdani, E. H. (1976a) Application of fuzzy logic to approximate reasoning using linguistic synthesis, *Proc. 6th Int. Symp. Multiple-Valued Logic, IEEE 76CH1111-4C*, May, 196–202, **FUZ, CON**

Mamdani, E. H. (1976b) Advances in the linguistic synthesis of fuzzy controllers, *Int. J. Man-Machine Studies, 8*, 669–678, **FUZ, CON**

Mamdani, E. H., & Assilian, S. (1975) An experiment in linguistic synthesis with a fuzzy logic controller, *Int. J. Man-Machine Studies, 7*, 1–13, **FUZ, CON**

Mamdani, E. H., & Baaklini, N. (1975) Prescriptive method for deriving control policy in a fuzzy-logic controller, *Electronics Lett., 11*, 625–626, **FUZ, CON**

Mamdani, E. H., & Gaines, B. R. (eds.) (1976) *Discrete Systems and Fuzzy Reasoning, EES-MMS-DSFR-76*, Queen Mary College, University of London, (workshop proceedings) **FUZ, CON, LING**

Mamdani, E. H., & Procyk, T. J. (1976) Application of fuzzy logic to controller design based on linguistic protocol, *3rd Eur. Meeting Cybern. Syst. Res.*, Vienna, **FUZ, CON**

Manes, E. G. (1976) *Algebraic Theories*, Springer-Verlag, **FUZ, SYS, AUT**

Marcus, Ruth Barcan, (1953) Strict implication, deducibility and the deduction theorem, *J. Symbolic Logic, 18*, 234–236, **MLOG**

Manek, W., & Traczyk, T. (1969) Generalized Łukasiewicz algebras, *Bull. de l'Academie Polonaise des Sciences, ser. math., astr. & phys., 17*, 789–792, **MVLOG**

Marinos, P. N. (1966) Fuzzy logic, *Tech. Memo. 66-3344-1*, Bell Telephone Labs., Holmdel, New Jersey, USA, Aug., **FUZ, SWLOG**

Marinos, P. N. (1969) Fuzzy logic and its application to switching systems, *IEEE Trans. Comp., C-18*, 343–348, **FUZ, SWLOG**

Marks, P. (1975a) FLCS: a control system for fuzzy logic, *MSc thesis*, Queen Mary College, London, Sep., **FUZ, CON**

Marks, P. (1975b) FLCS: a control system for fuzzy logic, *Fuzzy Logic Working Group Rep. 3*, Queen Mary College, University of London, UK, Nov., **FUZ, CON**

Maronna, R. (1964) A characterisation of the Morgan lattices, *Portugalia Mathematica, 23*, **LOG, TOP, LAT**

Martin, J. N. (1975) A syntactic characteristic of Kleene's strong connectives with two designated values, *Z. Math. Logik Grundlagen Math., 21*, 181–184, **MVLOG**

Martin, J. K., & Turksen, I. B. (1975) Formative evaluation of information need analysis, Dept. Industrial Engineering, University of Toronto, Canada, **FUZ, DEC**

Martin, R. L. (ed.) (1970) *The Paradox of the Liar,* Yale University Press, New Haven, **PARA, LOG**

Martin, T. (1976) Fuzzyalgorithmische schemata, *Vorträge aus dem Prolemseminar Automaten– und Algorithmentheorie,* April, Weissig, 44–51, **FUZ**

Materna, P. (1972) Intensional semantics of vague constants. An application of Tichý's concept of semantics, *Theory & Decision, 2,* 267–273, **VAG, LOG**

Mathai, A. M., & Rathie, P. N. (1975) *Basic Concepts in Information Theory and Statistics: Axiomatic foundation and applications,* Wiley Eastern Ltd., New Delhi, **PROB**

Mathesius, V. (1911) "O potenciálnosti jevů jazykových" (On the potentiality of the phenomena of Language) *Věstník Král., České společnosti nauk, třída filosoficko-historická* (Prague). English translation in *Prague School Reader in Linguistics,* Vachek, J. (ed.), Indiana University Press, Bloomington, 1964, **LING**

Maurer, W. D. (1974) Input-output correctness and fuzzy correctness, George Washington University, **FUZ**

Mauro, V., Bona, B., & Inaudi, D. (1976) A fuzzy approach to residential location theory, *3rd Eur. Meeting Cybern, Syst. Res. Vienna,* **FUZ, SS**

Maydole, R. E. (1972) Many-valued logic as a basis for set theory, *PhD thesis,* Boston University, Boston, Mass., **FUZ, MVLOG, SET**

Maydole, R. E. (1975) Paradoxes and Many-valued Set Theory, *J. Philos. Logic, 4,* 269–291, **FUZ, SET, LOG**

McCall, S. S. (ed.) (1967) *Polish Logic 1920–1939,* Clarendon Press, Oxford, **LOG, MVLOG**

McCawley (1975) Fuzzy logic and restricted quantifiers, University of Chicago, **FUZ, LOG**

McKay, A. F., & Merrill, D. D. (eds.) (1976) *Issues in the Philosophy of Language,* Yale University Press, New Haven, USA, **TRUTH, LOG**

McKinsey, J. C. C. (1941) A solution of the decision problem for the Lewis systems S2 and S4, with an application to topology, *J. Symbolic Logic, 6,* 117–134, **MLOG, TOP**

McKinsey, J. C. C. (1945) On the syntactical construction of systems of modal logic, *J. Symbolic Logic, 10,* 83–94, **MLOG**

McKinsey, J. C. C., & Tarski, A. (1944) The algebra of topology: *Annals Math., 45,* 141–191, **LOG, TOP**

McKinsey, J. C. C., & Tarski, A. (1948) Some theorems about the sentential calculi of Lewis and Heyting, *J. Symbolic Logic, 13,* 1–15, **LOG, MLOG**

McNaughton, R. (1951) A theorem about infinite-valued sentential logic, *J. Symbolic Logic, 16,* 1–13, **MVLOG**

Mehlberg, H. (1958) *The Reach of Science,* University of Toronto Press, **VAG**

Menges, G. (1970) On subjective probebility and related problems, *Theory & Decision, 1,* 40–60, **PROB**

Menges, G. (ed.) (1974) *Information, Inference and Decision,* Reidel, Dordrecht, Holland, **FUZ, DEC, SS**

Menges, G., & Kofler, E. (1976) Linear partial information as fuzziness, in Bossel,

H., Klaczko, S., & Muller, N. (eds.), *Systems Theory in the Social Sciences,* Birkhauser Verlag, Basel, 307–322, **FUZ**

Menges, G., & Skala, H. J. (1974) On the problem of vagueness in the social sciences, in Menges, G. (ed.), *Information, Inference and Decision,* D. Reidel, Dordrecht, Holland, 51–61, **FUZ, VAG, SS**

Meredith, C. A. (1958) The dependence of an axiom of Łukasiewicz, *Trans. Amer. Math. Soc., 87,* 54, **MVLOG**

Meseguer, J., & Sols, I. (1974) Automata in semimodule categories, *Proceedings of First International Symposium on Category Theory Applied to Computation and Control,* 196–202, **FUZ, AUT, CAT**

Meseguer, J., & Sols, I. (1975a) Fuzzy semantics in higher order logic and universal algebra, University of Zaragoza, Spain, **FUZ, LOG**

Meseguer, J., & Sols, I. (1975b) Topology in complete lattices and continuous fuzzy relations, University of Zaragoza, Spain, **FUZ, TOP**

Michalek, J. (1975) Fuzzy topologies, *Kybernetika (Prague), 11,* 345–354, **FUZ, TOP**

Michalos, A. C. (1971) *The Popper-Carnap Controversy*, M. Nijhoff, The Hague, **LOG, PROB**

Michalski, R. S. (1974) Learning by inductive inference, *Proc. NATO Advanced Study Institute Seminar on Computer Oriented Learning Processes,* Bonas, France, Aug., **FUZ, INDUCT, PAT**

Michalski, R. S. (1975) Variable-valued logic and its applications to pattern recognition and machine learning, in *Multiple-Valued Logic and Computer Science,* North-Holland, Amsterdam, **FUZ, PAT, INDUCT**

Miller, D. (1974) Popper's qualitative theory of verisimilitude, *Brit. J. Philos. Sci., 25,* 166–188, **INDUCT, VAG**

Miura, S. (1972) Probabilistic models of modal logics, *Bull. Nagoya Institute of Technology, 24,* 67–72, **LOG, PROB**

Mizumoto, M. (1971) Fuzzy automata and fuzzy grammars, *PhD thesis,* Faculty of Engineering Science, Osaka University, Osaka, Japan, **FUZ, AUT, LANG**

Mizumoto, M. (1971) Fuzzy sets theory, *11th Professional Group Meeting on Control Theory of SICE,* **FUZ**

Mizumoto, M., & Tanaka, K. (1976) Fuzzy-fuzzy automata, *Kybernetes, 5,* 107–112, **FUZ, AUT**

Mizumoto, M., & Tanaka, K. (1976) Various kinds of automata with weights, *J. Comp. Syst. Sci.,* **FUZ, AUT**

Mizumoto, M., Toyoda, J., & Tanaka, K. (1969) Some considerations on fuzzy automata, *J. Comp. Syst. Sci., 3,* 409–422, **FUZ, AUT**

Mizumoto, M., Toyoda, J., & Tanaka, K. (1970) Fuzzy languages, *Systems, Computers, Controls, 1,* 36, (orig. TIECE 53-c, 333–340) **FUZ, LANG**

Mizumoto, M., Toyoda, J., & Tanaka, K. (1971) N-fold fuzzy grammars, *Trans. Inst. Electron. Comm. Eng. (Japan), 54-c,* 856–857, **FUZ, LANG**

Mizumoto, M., Toyoda, J., & Tanaka, K. (1972a) General formulation of formal grammars, *Trans. Inst. Electron. Comm. Eng. (Japan), 54-c,* 600–605, **FUZ, LANG**

Mizumoto, M., Toyoda, J., & Tanaka, K. (1972b) General formulation of formal grammars, *Inform. Sci., 4,* 87–100, **FUZ, LANG**

Mizumoto, M., Toyoda, J., & Tanaka, K. (1972c) L-fuzzy logic, in *Research on*

Many-Valued Logic and its Applications, Kyoto University, Japan, **FUZ,LOG**

Mizumoto, M., Toyoda, J., & Tanaka, K. (1972d) Formal grammars with weights, *Trans. Inst. Electron. Comm. Eng. (Japan)*, *55-d*, 292–293, **FUZ,LANG**

Mizumoto, M., Toyoda, J., & Tanaka, K. (1973a) N-fold fuzzy grammars, *Inform. Sci.*, *5*, 25–43, **FUZ,LANG**

Mizumoto, M., Toyoda, J., & Tanaka, K. (1973b) Examples of formal grammars with weights, *Inf. Processing Lett.*, *2*, 74–78, **FUZ,LANG**

Moisil, G. C. (1935) Recherches sur l'algebre de la logique, Annales Sci. de l'Universite de Jassy, Roumania, *22*, 1–77,**LOG,TOP**

Moisil, G. C. (1971) Role of computers in the evolution of science, *Proceedings of International Conference on Science and Society*, Belgrade, Yugoslavia, 134–136, **FUZ**

Moisil, G. C. (1972a) La logique des concepts nuances, in *Essais sur les logiques non chrysippiennes*, Editions de l'Academie de la Republique Socialiste de Roumanie, Bucharest, 157–163, **FUZ,LOG**

Moisil, G. C. (1972b) Sur les algebres de Łukasiewicz θ-valentes, in *Essais sur les logiques non chrysipiennes*, Editions de l'Academie de la Republique Socialiste de Roumanie, Bucharest, 311–324,**FUZ,LOG**

Moisil, G. C. (1975) Lectures on fuzzy logic, Scientific & Encyclopaedic Editions, Bucharest, Rumania, (in Rumanian) **FUZ,LOG**

Molzen, N. (1975) Fuzzy logic control, *PhD thesis*, Technical University of Denmark, (in Danish) **FUZ,CON**

Monteiro, A. A., & Ribeiro, H. (1942) L'operation de fermeture et ses invariants dans les systemes partiellement ordonnes, *Portugaliae Mathematica, 3*, 171–184, **TOP**

Montes, C. G., Camacho, E. F., & Aracil, J. (1976) A fuzzy algorithm for nonlinear system identification, *3rd Eur. Meeting Cybern. Syst. Res., Vienna*, **FUZ**

Morgan, C. G. (1975) Similarity as a theory of graded equality for a class of many-valued predicate calculi, *Proc. 1975 Int. Symp. Multiple-Valued Logic, IEEE 75CH0959-7C*, 436–449, **MVLOG,VAG**

Morgan, C. G. (1976a) Many-valued propositional intuitionism, *Proc. 6th Int. Symp. Multiple-Valued Logic, IEEE 76CH1111-4C*, 150–156, **MVLOG,LOG**

Morgan, C. G. (1976b) Methods for automated theorem proving in non-classical logics, *IEEE Trans. Comp.*, *C-25*, 852–862, **LOG,MLOG,MVLOG,FUZ**

Morita, Y., & Iida, H. (1975) Measurement, information and human subjectivity described by an order relationship, in *Summary of Papers on General Fuzzy Problems*, The Working Group on Fuzzy Systems, Tokyo, Japan, Nov., 34–39, **FUZ,PSYCH**

Morozov, A. (1975) Some problems of decision theory, *Ekonomika i matematičeskie metody*, *11*, 252–262, (in Russian) **DEC,FUZ**

Morton, A. (1975) Complex individuals and multigrade relations, *Nous, 9*, 309–318, **VAG,LOG**

Mostowski, A. (1957) On a generalization of quantifiers, *Fundamenta Mathematicae, 44*, 12–36, **MVLOG**

Mostowski, A. (1961) Axiomatizability of some many valued predicate calculi, *Fundamenta Mathematicae, 50*, 165–190, **MVLOG**

Mostowski, A. (1966) *Thirty Years of Foundational Studies*, Basil Blackwell, Oxford, **LOG**

Mukaidono, M. (1972) On some properties of fuzzy logic, *Technical Report on Automation of IECE*, **FUZ,SWLOG**

Mukaidono, M. (1972) On the B-ternary logical function—a ternary logic with consideration of ambiguity, *Trans. Inst. Electron. Comm. Eng. (Japan)*, *55-d*, 355–362, **FUZ,SWLOG**

Muszynski, W., & Jacak, W. (1976) Conception of describing the behavior of the eventistic system by means of the formalism of fuzzy sets and relations' *3rd Eur. Meeting Cybern. Syst. Res.*, *Vienna*, **FUZ,SYS**

Nagai, S. (1973) On a semantics for non-classical logics, *Proc. Japan Acad.*, *49*, 337–340, **LOG,MLOG**

Nahmias, S. (1974) Discrete fuzzy random variables, University of Pittsburgh, USA, **FUZ,PROB**

Nakamura, M. (1941) Closure in general lattices, *Proc. Imper. Academy*, *17*, 5–6, Tokyo, **TOP**

Nakamura, K. (1975) A simulation model of pedestrian flow and its investigation, in *Summary of Papers on General Fuzzy Problems*, The Working Group on Fuzzy Systems, Tokyo, Japan, Nov., 40–45, **FUZ,SS**

Nakata, H., Mizumoto, M., Toyoda, J., & Tanaka, K. (1972) Some characteristics of N-fold fuzzy CF grammars, *Trans. Inst. Electron. Comm. Eng. (Japan)*, *55-d*, 287–288, **FUZ,LANG**

Nasu, M., & Honda, N. (1968) Fuzzy events realized by finite probabilistic automata, *Inform. & Control*, *12*, 284–303, **FUZ,AUT,LANF**

Nazaroff, G. J. (1973) Fuzzy topological polysystems, *J. Math. Anal. & Appln.*, *41*, 478–485, **FUZ,TOP**

Negoiţă, C. V. (1969) Informational retrieval systems, *PhD thesis*, Polytechnic Institute of Bucharest, (in Rumanian) **INFR,FUZ**

Negoiţă, C. V. (1970) On the strategies in automatic information systems, *6th Int. Congr. Cybernetic Systems*, Namur, Belgium, **INFR,FUZ**

Negoiţă, C. V. (1971) *Information Storage and Retrieval*, Editura Academiei, Bucharest, (in Rumanian) **INFR,FUZ**

Negoiţă, C. V. (1972) Linear and nonlinear information retrieval systems, Atlas Computer Laboratory, Didcot, UK, **INFR,FUZ**

Negoiţă, C. V. (1973) Linear and nonlinear information retrieval, *Studii si Cercetari de Documentare*, 21–57, **INFR,FUZ**

Negoiţă, C. V. (1973) On the decision process in information retrieval, *Studii si Cercetari de Documentare*, 369–381, **INFR,FUZ**

Negoiţă, C. V. (1973) On the notion of relevance in information retrieval, *Kybernetes*, *2*, 161–165, **FUZ,INFR**

Negoiţă, C. V. (1973) On the application of the fuzzy sets separation theorem for automatic classification in information retrieval systems, *Inform. Sci.*, *5*, 279–286, **FUZ,INFR**

Negoiţă, C. V. (1976) Fuzzy systems and management science, *3rd Eur. Meeting Cybern. Syst. Res.*, *Vienna*, **FUZ**

Negoiţă, C. V. (1976) Fuzzy models for social processes, in Bossel, H., Klaczko, S.,

& Muller, N. (eds.), *Systems Theory in the Social Sciences*, Birkhauser Verlag, Basel, 283–291, **FUZ,SS**

Negoiţă, C. V., & Flondor, P. (1976) On fuzziness in information retrieval, *Int. J. Man-Machine Studies, 8*, 711–716, **FUZ,INFR**

Negoiţă, C. V., & Ralescu, D. A. (1974) *Multini vagi applicabile lor*, Editura Technica, Bucharest, Rumania, **FUZ**

Negoiţă, C. V., & Ralescu, D. A. (1974) Inexactness in dynamic systems, *Economic Computation and Economic Cybernetics Studies and Research, 4*, 69–81, **FUZ**

Negoiţă, C. V., & Ralescu, D. A. (1974) Fuzzy systems and artificial intelligence, *Kybernetes, 3*, 173–178, **FUZ**

Negoiţă, C. V., & Ralescu, D. A. (1975a) *Applications of Fuzzy Sets to Systems Analysis*, Birkhauser Verlag, Basel, **FUZ**

Negoiţă, C. V., & Ralescu, D. A. (1975b) Representation theorems for fuzzy concepts, *Kybernetes, 4*, 169–174, **FUZ**

Negoiţă, C. V., & Ralescu, D. A. (1975c) Some results in fuzzy systems theory, *Proc. 3rd International Congress on Cybernetics and General Systems*, Bucharest, Rumania, Aug., **FUZ**

Negoiţă, C. V., & Ralescu, D. A. (1975d) Relations on monoids and minimal realization theory for dynamic systems; applications for fuzzy systems, *Proceedings of 3rd International Congress of Cybernetics and Systems*, Bucharest, Rumania, Aug., **FUZ,AUT**

Negoiţă, C. V., & Ralescu, D. A. (1976) Comment on a comment on an algorithm that generates fuzzy prime implicants by Lee and Chang, *Inform. & Control, 30*, 199–201, **FUZ,SWLOG**

Negoiţă, C. V., & Stefanescu, A. C. (1975) On the state equation of fuzzy systems, *Kybernetes, 4*, 231–214, **FUZ,AUT**

Negoiţă, C. V., & Sulariu, M. (1976) On fuzzy mathematical programming and tolerances in planning, *Economic Computation and Economic Cybernetics Studies and Research*, Bucharest, Rumania, **FUZ,SS**

Netto, A. B. (1970) Fuzzy classes, *Notices of the American Mathematical Society, 68T-H28*, 945, **FUZ,SET**

Neuhaus, N. J., & Spevack, M. (1975) Shakespeare dictionary—some preliminaries for a semantic description, *Computers and the Humanities, 9*, 263–270, **FUZ, LING**

Neustupný, J. V. (1966) On the analysis of linguistic vagueness, *Travaux Linguistiques de Prague, 2*, 39–51 **LING,VAG,LOG**

Nguyen, C-H. (1973) Generalized Post algebras and their application to some infinitary many-valued logics, *Dissertationes Mathematicae, 107*, Warsaw, **MVLOG**

Noguchi, Y. (1972) A pattern clustering method on the basis of association schemes, *Bulletin Electrotechnical Laboratory, 36*, 753–767, **FUZ,PAT**

Novák, J. (1968) On probability defined on certain classes of non-Boolean algebra, *Nachrichten der Österreichischen Mathematische Gesellschaft, 23*, 89–90, (No. 91) **PROB,LOG**

Nowakowska, M. (1976) Methodological problems of measurement of fuzzy concepts in social sciences, *Behavioral Sciences*, **FUZ,SS**

Nowakowska, M. (1976) Towards a formal theory of dialogues, *Semiotics, 18,* **FUZ,SS**

Nowakowska, M. (1976) Formal theory of actions and its application to social sciences, *3rd Eur. Meeting Cybern. Syst. Res., Vienna,* **FUZ,SS**

Nurmi, H. (1976) On fuzzy games, *3rd Eur. Meeting Cybern. Syst. Res., Vienna,* **FUZ,GAME**

Nurminen, M. I. (1976) About the fuzziness in the analysis of information systems, *3rd Eur. Meeting Cybern. Syst. Res., Vienna,* **FUZ**

Nurminen, M. I. (1976) Studies in systemeering on fuzziness in the analysis of information systems, Dissertation, Institue for Applied Mathematics, University of Turku, Finland, **FUZ,INFR,DEC**

Oden, G. C., & Anderson, N. H. (1974) Integration of semantic constraints, *J. Verbal Learnign & Behavior, 13,* 138–148, **FUZ,LING**

Ohnishi, M., & Matsumoto, K. (1957) Gentzen method in modal calculi, *Osaka Math. J., 9,* 113–130, **MLOG**

Okada, N., & Tamachi, T. (1974) Automated editing of fuzzy line drawings for picture description, *Trans. Inst. Electron. Comm. Eng. (Japan), 57-a,* 216–223, **FUZ**

Okuda, T., Tanaka, H., & Asai, K. (1974) Decision-making and information in fuzzy events, *Bulletin of University of Osaka Prefecture, 23A,* **FUZ,DEC**

Onicescu, O. (1971) *Principles de Logique et de Philosophie Mathematique,* Rumanian Academy of Science, Bucharest, **PROB,LOG**

Ore, O. (1942) Theory of equivalence relations, *Duke Math. J., 9,* 573–627, **LAT,LOG**

Orlowska, E. (1967) Mechanical proof procedure for the *n*-valued propositional calculus, *Bull. de l'Academie Polonaise des Sciences, ser. des sciences math., astr. et phys., 15,* 537–541, **MVLOG**

Orlowska, E. (1973) Theorem-proving systems, *Dissertationes Mathematicae, 103,* Warsaw, **LOG,MLOG,MVLOG**

Osgood, C. E., Suci, G. J., & Tannenbaum, P. H. (1964) *The Measurement of Meaning,* University of Illinois Press, **PSYCH,LING**

Osis, J. J. (1968) Fault detection in complex systems using theory of fuzzy sets, in D. S. Kristinkov, J. J. Osis, L. A. Ravtrigin (eds.), *Kibernetika i Diagnostika, 2,* 13–18, (in Russian) Zinatne, Riga, U.S.S.R., **FUZ**

Ostergaard, J. J. (1976) Fuzzy logic control of a heat exchanger process, *no. 7601,* Electric Power Engineering Dept., Technical University of Denmark, Lyngby, Jan., **FUZ,CON**

Otsuki, S. (1970) A model for learning and recognizing machine, *Information Processing, 11,* 664–671, **FUZ,LMACH**

Papert (-Strauss), D. (1968) Topological lattices, *Proc. Lond. Math. Soc., 18,* 217–230, **LAT,TOP**

Parret, H. (1974) *Discussing Language,* Mouton, The Hague, (see dialogue with G. Lakoff) **LING,FUZ**

Parsons, C. (1974) The liar paradox, *J. Philos. Logic, 3,* 381–412, **PARA, LOG,TRUTH**

Pask, G. (1975a) *The Cybernetics of Human Learning and Performance,* Hutchison,

London, **FUZ,PSYCH**

Pask, G. (1975b) *Conversation, Cognition and Learning*, Elsevier, Amsterdam, **FUZ,PSYCH,LING**

Pask, G. (ed.)(1976) Current scientific approaches to decision making in complex systems, System Research Ltd., Richmond, UK, April, **DEC,FUZ**

Paz, A. (1967) Fuzzy star functions, probabilistic automata and their approximation by nonprobabilistic automata, *J. Comp. Syst. Sci., 1,* 371–389, **FUZ,PROB,AUT**

Pearl, J. (1974) Problem presentation research, *UCLA-ENG-7404,* School of Engineering & Applied Science, University of California, Los Angles, USA, **PROB,DEC**

Pearl, J. (1975a) On the complexity of computing probabilistic assertions, *UCLA-ENG-7562,* School of Engineering & Applied Science, University of California, Los Angles, USA, July, **PROB,DEC**

Pearl, J. (1975b) On the complexity of inexact computations, *UCLA-ENG-PAPER-0775,* School of Engineering & Applied Science, University of California, Los Angeles, USA, July, **PROB,DEC**

Pearl, J. (1975c) An economic basis for certain methods of evaluating probabilistic forecasts, *UCLA-ENG-REP-7561,* School of Engineering & Applied Science, University of California, Los Angeles, USA, July, **PROB,DEC**

Pearl, J. (1975d) On the storage economy of inferential question-answering systems, *IEEE Trans. Syst. Man Cybern., SMC– 5,* 595–602, **PROB,DEC**

Pearl, J. (1975e) State complexity of imprecise causal models, *UCLA-ENG-REP-7560,* School of Engineering & Applied Science, University of California, Los Angeles, USA, Dec., **PROB,DEC**

Pearl J. (1976a) A note on the management of probability assessors, *UCLA-ENG-REP-7664,* School of Engineering & Applied Science, University of California, Los Angeles, USA, Feb., **PROB,DEC**

Pearl, J. (1976b) A framework for processing value judgments *UCLA-REP-7622,* School of Engineering & Applied Science, University of California, Los Angeles, USA, March, **PROB,DEC**

Perry, K. E., & Waddell, J. J. (1972) *The rotary cement kiln,* The Chemical Publishing Co., New York, **CON**

Peschel, M. (1975) Some remarks to "fuzzy systems" as a complement to the topic paper from L. A. Zadeh, Berlin, Feb., **FUZ**

Petrescu, I. (1971) Algebres de Morgan injectives, in Moisil, G. C. (ed.), *Logique, Automatique, Informatique,* Bucharest, 171–176, **LOG,TOP**

Pinkava, V. (1965) On the nature of some logical paradoxes, *Kybernetika (Prague), 1,* 111–121, (in Czech., Eng. summary) **PARA,LOG,AUT**

Pinkava, V. (1975) Some further properties of the Pi-logics, *Proc. 1975 Int. Symp. Multiple-Valued Logic, IEEE 75CH0959-7C,* 20–26, **MVLOG**

Pinkava, V. (1976a) "Fuzzification" of binary and finite multivalued logical calculi, *Int. J. Man-Machine Studies, 8* 717–730, **FUZ,LOG**

Pinkava, V. (1976b) On the nature of some logical paradoxes, *Int. J. Man-Machine Studies* (to appear). **LOG,PARA,AUT**

Pinkava, V., & Kohout, L. J. (1976) Enumerably infinite-valued functionally complete Pi-logic algebras, in Mamdani, E. H., & Gaines, B. R. (eds.), *Discrete Systems and Fuzzy Reasoning, EES-MMS-DSFR-76,* Queen Mary College, University of London, (workshop proceedings) **FUZ,MVLOG**

Pollock, J. L. (1975) Four kinds of conditionals, *Amer. Philos. Quart., 12,* 51–59, **LOG**

Ponsard, C. (1975) L'imprecision et son traitement en analyse economique, *Document de Travail IME,* University of Dijon, **FUZ,SS**

Ponsard, C. (1975) Contribution a une theorie des espaces economiques imprecis, *Document de Travail IME,* University of Dijon, **FUZ,SS**

Popper, K. R. (1963) *Conjectures and Refutations,* Routledge & Kegan Paul, London, **PROB,INDUCT,VAG,LOG**

Popper, K. R. (1972a) *Objective Knowledge,* Clarendon Press, Oxford, **PROB,IN-DUCT,VAG,LOG**

Popper, K. R. (1972b) *The Logic of Scientific Discovery,* Hutchison, London, (1st ed. 1959) **LOG,PROB,INDUCT**

Popper, K. R. (1976a) A note on verisimilitude, *Brit. J. Philos. Sci., 27,* 147–164, **INDUCT,VAG**

Popper, K. R. (1976b) *Unended Quest,* Fontana, London, **VAG**

Pospíšil, B. (1937) Remark on bicompact spaces, *Annals of Math., 38,* 845–846, **TOP,LOG**

Pospíšil, B. (1939a) On bicompact spaces, *Publications de la Faculté des Sciences de l'Université Masaryk, No. 270,* Brno, Czech., 3–16, **TOP,LOG**

Pospíšil, B. (1939b) Primideale in vollstandigen ringen, *Fundamenta Mathematicae, 33,* 66–74, (the whole vol. published in Dec. 1945) **TOP,LOG**

Pospíšil, B. (1940) Über die messbaren funktionen, *Mathematische Annalen, 117,* 327–355, **TOP,SEMR,PROB**

Pospíšil, B. (1941a) Eine bemerkung über vollstandige raume, *Časopis pro Pěstování Matematiky a Fysiky (Prague), 70,* 38–41, **TOP,SEMR,PROB**

Pospíšil, B. (1941b) Von den verteilungen auf Booleschen Ringen, *Mathematische Annalen, 118,* 32–40, **SEMR,PROB,TOP**

Pospíšil, B. (1941c) Eine bemerkung über stetige verteilung, *Časopis pro Pěstování Matematiky a Fysiky (Prague), 70,* 68–72, **SEMR,PROB,TOP,LAT**

Pospíšil, B. (1941d) Eine benerkung über funktionenfolgen, *Časopis pro Pěstování Matematiky a Fysiky, 70,* 119–121, **SEMR,PROB**

Post, J. F. (1973) Shades of the liar, *J. Philos. Logic, 2,* 370–386, **PARA,LOG**

Poston, T. (1971a) Fuzzy geometry, *PhD thesis,* University of Warwick, UK, **FUZ,TOL**

Poston, T. (1971b) Fuzzy geometry, *Manifold, 10,* University of Nottingham, **FUZ,TOL**

Preparata, F. P., & Yeh, R. T. (1970) A theory of continuously valued logic, *Tech. Rep. 89,* University of Texas, Austin, USA, June, **FUZ,MVLOG**

Preparata, F. P., & Yeh, R. T. (1971) On a theory of continuously valued logic, *Conference Record of 1971 Symposium on Theory & Applications of Multiple-Valued Logic Design,* 124–132, **FUZ,MVLOG**

Preparata, F. P., & Yeh, R. T. (1972) Continuously valued logic, *J. Comp. Syst. Sci., 6,* 397–418, **FUZ,MVLOG**

Prior, A. N. (1953) On propositions neither necessary nor impossible, *J. Symbolic Logic, 18,* 105–108, **MLOG,MVLOG**

Prior, A. N. (1954) The interpretation of two systems of modal logic, *J. Comp. Syst., 4,* 201–208, **MLOG,MVLOG**

Prior, A. N. (1955a) Many-valued and modal systems: an intuitive approach, *Philos. Rev., 64,* 626–630, **MLOG**

Prior, A. N. (1955b) Curry's paradox and 3-valued logic, *Australasian Journal of Philosophy, 33,* 177–182, **MVLOG,PARA**

Prior, A. N. (1957) *Time and Modality,* Clarendon Press, Oxford, **MLOG**

Prior, A. N. (1962) *Formal Logic,* Clarendon Press, Oxford, (2nd ed.) **LOG**

Prior, A. N. (1967) *Past, Present and Future,* Clarendon Press, Oxford, **MLOG**

Prior, A. N. (1971) *Objects of Thought,* Clarendon Press, Oxford, (edited by Geach & Kenny) **LOG,TRUTH,PARA**

Procyk, T. J. (1974) The control of systems possessing delay using fuzzy set theory, *Fuzzy Logic Working Group Rop.,* Queen Mary College, University of London, UK, Dec., **FUZ,CON**

Procyk, T. J. (1976a) Linguistic Representation of Fuzzy Variables, *Fuzzy Logic Working Group Rep. 3,* Queen Mary College, University of London, UK **FUZ,CON**

Procyk, T. J. (1976b) A fuzzy logic learning system for a single input single output plant, *Fuzzy Logic Working Group Rep. 3,* Queen Mary College, University of London, UK, **FUZ,CON,LMACH**

Prugovecki, E. (1973) A postulational framework for theories of simultaneous measurement of several observables, *Foundations of Physics, 3,* 3–18, **FUZ,PROB**

Prugovecki, E. (1974) Fuzzy sets in the theory of measurement of incompatible observables, *Foundations of Physics, 4,* 9–18, **FUZ,PROB**

Prugovecki, E. (1975) Mearurement in quantum mechanics as a stochastic process on spaces of fuzzy events, *Foundations of Physics, 5,* 557–571, **FUZ,PROB**

Prugovecki, E. (1976a) Probability measures on fuzzy events in phase space, *J. Math. Physics, 17,* 517–523, **FUZ,PROB**

Prugovecki, E. (1976b) Quantum two-particle scattering in fuzzy phase space, Department of Mathematics, University of Toronto, Canada, Jan., **FUZ,PROB**

Przełecki, M. (1958) W sprawie terminow nieostrych, *Studia Logica, 8,* **LOG,VAG**

Pudlák, P. (1975a) The observational predicate calculus and complexity of computations, *Commentationes Math. Universitatis Carolinae, 16,* 395–398, **INDUCT,LOG**

Pudlák, P. (1975b) Polynomially complete problems in the logic of automated discovery, Bečvář, J. (ed.), *Lecture Notes in Computer Science, 32,* Springer-Verlag, Berlin, 358–361, **LOG,INDUCT**

Pultr, A. (1976) Closed categories of L-fuzzy sets, *Vorträge aus dem Problemseminar Automaten- und Algorithmentheorie,* April, Weissig, **FUZ,SET,CAT**

Pun, L. (1975) Experience in the use of fuzzy formalism in problems with various degrees of subjectivity, in *Special Interest Discussion Session on Fuzzy Au-*

tomata and Decision Processes, 6th IFAC World Congress, Boston, Mass., USA, Aug., **FUZ**

Putnam, H. (1957) Three-valued logic, *Philos. Stud.*, 8, 73–80, **MVLOG**

Ragade, R. K. (1973) On some aspects of fuzziness in communication: I Fuzzy entropies, *W–002–73*, Systems Research and Planning, Bell-Northern Research, Ottawa, Canada, Nov., **FUZ**

Ragade, R. K. (1973) On some aspects of fuzziness in communication: II A note on fuzzy entropies associated with a fuzzy channel, *W–006–73*, Systems Research and Planning, Bell-Northern Research, Ottawa, Canada, Nov., **FUZ**

Ragade, R. K. (1973) On some aspects of fuzziness in communication: III Fuzzy concept communication, *W–005–73*, Systems Research and Planning, Bell-Northern Research, Ottawa, Canada, Dec., **FUZ**

Ragade, R. K. (1973) A multiattribute perception and classification of (visual) similarities, *S–001–73*, Systems Research and Planning, Bell-Northern Research, Ottawa, Canada, Nov., **FUZ**

Ragade, R. K. (1974) Incertitude characterization of the retriever-system communication process, *Proc. 37th Annual Meeting American Society Information Sciences*, Atlanta, Georgia, USA, Oct., **FUZ**

Ragade, R. K. (1974) Naive users and ill-formed problems in interactive systems, *Tech. Rep.*, Bell-Northern Research, Dec., **FUZ**

Ragade, R. K. (1975) Profile transformation algebra and group consensus formation through fuzzy set theory, *SES–75–1*, Department of Systems Design, University of Waterloo, Ontario, Canada, Jan., **FUZ**

Ragade, R. K. (1975) Benefit cost analysis under imprecise conditions, *1–S–040675*, Department of Systems Design, University of Waterloo, Ontario, Canada, June, **FUZ**

Ragade, R. K. (1976) Fuzzy sets in communication systems and consensus formation systems, *TIMS/ORSA Joint Meeting*, Philadelphia, USA, April, **FUZ**

Ragade, R. K. (1976) Fuzzy games in the analysis of options, *J. Cybernetics*, **FUZ,GAME**

Ragade, R. K. (1976) Fuzzy interpretive structural modelling, *J. Cybernetics*, **FUZ**

Ragade, R. K. (1976) Fuzzy set theory and the mathematical probability theory of Kolmogorov: some observations, *Int. Conf. Information Systems & Sciences*, Patras, Greece, **FUZ,PROB**

Ragade, R. K., Hipel, & Unny (1975) Non-quantitative methods in water resource management, *ASCE Speciality Conference on Water Resources Management*, July, **FUZ**

Rajasethupathy, K. S., & Lakshmivarahan, S. (1974) Connectedness in fuzzy topology, Department of Mathematics, Vivekanamdha College, Madras, India, **FUZ,TOP**

Rajeck, R. K. (1975) Benefit cost analysis under imprecise conditions, University of Waterloo, Ontario, Canada, June, **FUZ**

Ralescu, D. A. (1974) On fuzzy characters and subobjects, *Seminarul de Sisteme Fuzzy*, Dept. Economic Cybernetics, Academy of Economic Studies, Bucharest, **FUZ**

Ralescu, D. A. (1975) Decomposition theorems for fuzzy automata, *Seminarul de Sisteme Fuzzy,* Dept. Economic Cybernetics, Academy of Economic Studies, Bucharest, **FUZ, AUT**

Rasiowa, H. (1974) *An Algebraic Approach to Non-Classical Logics,* North-Holland, Amsterdam, **LOG, MVLOG**

Rasiowa, H., & Sikorski, R. (1970) *The Mathematics of Metamathematics,* Warsawa, Poland, **LOG, MVLOG**

Rauch, J. (1975) Ein beitrag zu der GUHA methode in der dreiwertigen logik, *Kybernetika (Prague), 11,* 101–113, **MVLOG, INDUCT**

Reisinger, L. (1974) On fuzzy thesauri, *Proc. Comp. Stat.,* Vienna, **FUZ, INFR**

Reddy, D. (1972) Reference and metaphor in human language, PhD thesis, Department of English, University of Chicago, **FUZ, LING**

Rescher, N. (1963) A probabilistic approach to modal logic, *Acta Philosophica Fennica, 16,* 215–226, **PROB, MVLOG**

Rescher, N. (1964) Quantifiers in many-valued logic, *Logique et Analyse, 7,* 181–184, **MVLOG**

Rescher, N. (1967) Semantic foundations for the logic of preference, in Rescher, N. (ed.), *The Logic of Decision and Action,* University of Pittsburgh Press, 37–79, **LOG, PROB**

Rescher, N. (1968) *Topics in philosophical logic,* D. Reidel, Holland, **LOG, MVLOG, MLOG**

Rescher, N. (1969) *Many-valued logic,* McGraw-Hill, New York, **MVLOG**

Rescher, N. (1973) *The Coherence Theory of Truth,* Clarendon Press, Oxford, **TRUTH, PROB**

Rescher, N. & Manor, R. (1970) On inference from inconsistent premises, *Theory & Decision, 1,* 179–217, **VAG, LOG**

Reiger, B. (1974) Eine "tolerante" lexikonstruktur. Zur abbildung naturlich-sprachlicher bedeutung auf "unscharfe" mengen in toleranzraumen, *Zeitschrift fur Literaturwissenschaft und Linguistik, 16,* 31–47, **FUZ, LING**

Rieger, B. (1975) On a tolerance topology model of natural language meaning, Germanic Institute, Tech. Hochschule, Aachen, Germany, **FUZ, LING**

Rieger, B. (1976a) Theorie der unscharfen mengen und empirische textanalyse, *Deutscher Germanistentag 76,* Dusseldorf, April, **FUZ, LING**

Rieger, B. (1976b) Fuzzy structural semantics. On a generative model of vague natural language meaning, *3rd Eur. Meeting Cybern. Syst. Res.,* Vienna, **FUZ, LING**

Reiger, L. (1949a) A note on topological representation of distributive lattices, *Časopis pro Pěstování Matematiky a Fysiky (Prague), 74,* 55–61.

Rieger, L. (1949b) On the lattice theory of Brouwerian propositional logic, *Acta Facultatis Rerum Naturalium Universitatis Carolinae (Prague), 189,* **LAT, LOG**

Rieger, L. (1967) *Algebraic Methods of Mathematical Logic,* Academia, Prague & Academic Press, New York, **LOG, LAT**

Roberts, F. S. (1973) Tolerance geometry, *Notre Dame J. Formal Logic, 14,* 68–76, **TOL**

Rodder, W. (1975) On "and" and "or" connectives in fuzzy set theory, *EURO I,*

Lehrstuhl fur Unternehmensforschung RWTH Aachen, Germany, **FUZ, LOG,PSYCH**

Rose, A. (1950) Completeness of Łukasiewicz-Tarski propositional calculus, *Mathematische Annalen, 122,* 296–298, **MVLOG**

Rose, A. (1951a) The degree of completeness of some Łukasiewicz-Tarski propositional calculi, *J. London Math. Soc., 26,* 47–49, **MVLOG**

Rose, A. (1951b) Axiom systems for 3-valued logic, *J. London Math. Soc., 26,* 50–58, **MVLOG**

Rose, A. (1952) The degree of completeness of the M-valued Łukasiewicz propositional calculus, *J. London Math. Soc., 27,* 92–102, **MVLOG**

Rose, A. (1953) The degree of completeness of the lamda-zero-valued Łukasiewicz propositional calculus, *J. London Math. Soc., 28,* 176–184, **MVLOG**

Rose, A. (1958) Many-valued logical machines, *Proc. Cambridge Philosophical Soc., 54,* 307–321, **MVLOG**

Rose, A., & Rosser, J. B. (1958) Fragments of many-valued statement calculi, *Trans. Amer. Math. Soc., 87,* 1–53, **MVLOG**

Rosen, R. (1974) Planning, management policies and strategies: four fuzzy concepts, *Int. J. General Syst., 1,* 245–252, **FUZ**

Rosenfeld, A. (1971) Fuzzy groups, *J. Math. Anal. & Appln., 35,* 512–517, **FUZ**

Rosenfeld, A., Hummel, R. A., & Zucker, S. W. (1976) Scene labeling by relaxation operations, *IEEE Tran. Syst., Man Cybern., SMC–6,* 420–433, **FUZ,PAT**

Rosenfeld, A. (1975) Fuzzy graphs, in Zadeh, L. A., Fu, K. S., Tanaka, K., & Shimura, M. (eds.), *Fuzzy Sets and Their Applications to Cognitive and Decision Processes,* Academic Press, New York, 77–95, **FUZ**

Rosser, J. B. (1960) Axiomatization of infinite valued logics, *Logique et Analyse, 3,* 137–153, **MVLOG**

Rosser, J. B., & Turquette, A. R. (1945) Axiom schemes for M-valued propositional calculi, *J. Symbolic Logic, 10,* 61–82, **MVLOG**

Rosser, J. B., & Turquette, A. R. (1952) *Many-Valued Logics,* North-Holland, Amsterdam, **MVLOG**

Rubin, H. (1969) A new approach to foundations of probability, in Bullof, J. J., Holyoke, T. C., & Haha, S. W. (eds.), *Foundations of Mathematics, Symposium Papers Commemorating the 60th Birthday of K. Godel,* Springer, New York, **PROB,LOG**

Ruspini, E. (1969) A new approach to clustering, *Inform. & Control, 15,* 22–32, **FUZ,PAT**

Ruspini, E. (1970) Numerical methods for fuzzy clustering, *Inform. Sci., 2,* 319–350, **FUZ,PAT**

Ruspini, E. H. (1972) Optimization in sample descriptions: data reduction and pattern recognition using fuzzy clustering, *IEEE Trans. Syst. Man Cybern., SMC–2,* 541, **FUZ,PAT**

Ruspini, E. H. (1973) New experimental results in fuzzy clustering, *Inform. Sci., 6,* 273–284, **FUZ,PAT**

Russell, B. (1923) Vagueness, *Australian Journal of Philosophy, 1,* 84–92, **VAG**

Rutherford, D. A. (1976) The implementation and evaluation of a fuzzy control algorithm for a sinter plant, in Mamdani, E. H., & Gaines, B. R. (eds.), *Discrete Systems and Fuzzy Reasoning, EES–MMS–DSFR–76,* Queen Mary College, University of London, (workshop proceedings), **FUZ, CON**

Rutherford, D. A., & Bloore, G. C. (1975) The implementation of fuzzy algorithms for control, Control Systems Centre, University of Manchester Institute of Science and Technology, Manchester, UK, **FUZ, CON**

Sadovskiĭ, V. N. (1974) *Osnovanija Obščeĭ Teorii Sistem,* Nauka, Moscow, (in Russian, On Foundations of General Systems Theories) **LOG, SYS**

Sagaama, S. (1976) Subjective probabilities, fuzzy sets and decision making, *3rd Eur. Meeting Cybern. Syst. Res., Vienna,* **FUZ, PROB**

Saito, T. (1975) Chronology analysis of a social conflict, in *Summary of Papers on on General Fuzzy Problems,* The Working Group on Fuzzy Systems, Tokyo, Japan, Nov., 46–48, **FUZ, SS**

Salomaa, A. (1959) On many-valued systems of logic, *Ajatus, 22,* 115–119, **MVLOG**

Sanchez, E. (1974) Equations de relations floues, *Thesis de doctorat en biologie humaine,* Faculté de Medecine de Marseille, France, July, **FUZ, MED**

Sanchez, E. (1975) Solutions in composite fuzzy relation equations. Application to medical diagnosis in Brouwerian logic, *Special Interest Discussion Group on Fuzzy Automata & Decision Processes,* 6th IFAC World Congress, Boston, Mass., USA, Aug., **FUZ, MED**

Sanchez, E. (1976) Resolution of composite fuzzy relation equations, *Inform. & Control, 30,* 38–47, **FUZ**

Sanchez, E. (1976) Eigen fuzzy sets, *National Computer Conference,* New York, June, **FUZ**

Sanchez, E., & Sambuc, R. (1976) Relations floues. Fonctions o-floues. Application a l'aide audiagnostic en pathologie thyroidienne, *IRIA Medical Data Processing Symposium,* Taylor & Francis, Toulouse, **FUZ, MED**

Sanford, D. H. (1975a) Borderline logic, *Amer. Philos. Quart., 12,* 29–39, **VAG, PARA, FUZ**

Sanford, D. H. (1975b) Infinity and Vagueness, *Philosophical Review, 84,* 520–535, **VAG, PARA**

Santos, E. S. (1968a) Maximin, minimax and composite sequential machines, *J. Math. Anal. & Appln., 24,* 246–259, **FUZ, AUT**

Santos, E. S. (1968b) Maximin automata, *Inform. & Control, 13,* 363–377, **FUZ, AUT**

Santos, E. S. (1969a) Maximin sequential chains, *J. Math. Anal. & Appln., 26,* 28–38, **FUZ, AUT**

Santos, E. S. (1969b) Maximin sequential-like machines and chains, *Mathematical Systems Theory, 3,* 300–309, **FUZ, AUT**

Santos, E. S. (1970) Fuzzy algorithms, *Inform. & Control, 17,* 326–339, **FUZ, AUT**

Santos, E. S. (1972a) Max-product machines, *J. Math. Anal. & Appln., 37,* 677–686, **FUZ, AUT**

Santos, E. S. (1972b) On reductions of maximin machines, *J. Math. Anal. & Appln., 40,* 60–78, **FUZ, AUT**

Santos, E. S. (1973) Fuzzy sequential functions, *J. Cybernetics, 3,* 15–31, **FUZ, AUT**

Santos, E. S. (1974) Context-free fuzzy languages, *Inform. & Control, 26,* 1–11,

FUZ, AUT, LANG
Santos, E. S. (1975a) Realization of fuzzy languages by probabilistic max-product and maximin automata, *Inform. Sci., 8,* 39–53, **FUZ, PROB, LANG, AUT**

Santos, E. S. (1975b) Max-product grammars and languages, *Inform. Sci., 9,* 1–23, **FUZ, AUT, LANG**

Santos, E. S. (1975c) Fuzzy programs, in *Special Interest Discussion Session on Fuzzy Automata and Decision Processes,* 6th IFAC World Congress, Boston, Mass., USA, Aug., **FUZ, AUT**

Santos, E. S. (1976a) Fuzzy automata and languages, *Inform. Sci., 10,* 193–197, **FUZ, AUT, LANG**

Santos, E. S. (1976b) Fuzzy and probabilistic programs, *Inform. Sci., 10,* 331–345 **FUZ, PROB, AUT**

Santos, E. S., & Wee, W. G. (1968) General formulation of sequential machines, *Inform. & Control, 12,* 5–10, **FUZ, AUT**

Saridis, G. N. (1974) Fuzzy notions in nonlinear system classification, *J. Cybernetics, 4,* 67–82, **FUZ, PAT**

Saridis, G. N. (1975) Fuzzy decision making in prosthetic devices and other applications, in *Special Interest Discussion Session on Fuzzy Automata and Decision Processes,* 6th IFAC World Congress, Boston, Mass., USA, Aug., **FUZ**

Sasama, H. (1975) Fuzzy set model for train composition in marshalling yard, in *Summary of Papers on General Fuzzy Problems,* The Working Group on Fuzzy Systems, Tokyo, Japan, Nov., 49–54, **FUZ**

Savage, L. J. (1971) Elicitation of personal probabilities and expectations, *J. Amer. Statist. Assn., 66,* 783–801, **PROB, PSYCH**

Scarpellini, B. (1962) Die nicht-axiomatisierbarkeit des unendlichwertigen praedikatenkalkuls von Łukasiewicz, *J. Symbolic Logic, 27,* 159–170, **MVLOG**

Schek, H. J. (1975) Tolerating fuzziness in keywords by similarity searches, *TR75 11.010,* IBM Heidelberg Scientific Center, Nov., **FUZ, INFR**

Schock, R. (1964a) On finitely many-valued logics, *Logique et Analyse, 28,* 43–58, **MVLOG**

Schock, R. (1964b) On denumerably many-valued logics, *Logique et Analyse, 28,* 190–195, **MVLOG**

Schock, R. (1965) Some theorems on the relative strengths of many-valued logics, *Logique et Analyse, 30,* 101–104, **MVLOG**

Schotch, P. K. (1975) Fuzzy modal logic, *Proc. 1975 Int. Symp. Multiple-Valued Logic, IEEE 75CH0959–7C,* May, 176–182, **FUZ, MVLOG**

Schuh, E. (1973) Many-valued logics and the Lewis paradoxes, *Notre Dame J. Formal Logic, 14,* 250–252, **MLOG, MVLOG, PROB**

Schutzenberger, M. P. (1962) On a theorem of R. Jungen, *Proc. American Mathematical Society, 13,* 885–890, **SEMR, LANG**

Schwartz, D. (1972) Mengenlehre über vorgegebenen algebraischen systemen, *Math. Nachr., 53,* 365–370, **MVLOG, SET, FUZ**

Schwede, G. (1976) N-variable fuzzy maps with application to disjunctive decomposition of fuzzy switching functions, *Proc. 6th Int. Symp. Multiple-Valued Logic, IEEE 76CH1111–4C,* May, 203–216, **FUZ, SWLOG**

Scott, D. (1974) Completeness and axiomatizability in many-valued logic, in Henkin, L. (ed.), *Proceedings of the Tarski Symposium,* American Mathematical Society, Rhode Island, USA, 412–435, **MVLOG**

Scott, D. (1976) Does many-valued logic have any use?, in Körner (1976b), 64–88, **MVLOG, FUZ**

Scott, D., & Krauss, P. (1966) Assigning probabilities to logical formulas, in Hintikka, J., & Suppes, P. (eds.), *Aspects of Inductive Logic,* 219–264, **PROB, LOG**

Segerberg, K. (1967) Some modal logics based on a three-valued logic, *Theoria, 33,* 53–71, **MLOG, MVLOG**

Serfati, M. (1974) Algebres de Boole avec une introduction à la theorie des graphes orientes et aux sous-ensembles flous, *Ed. C.D.U.,* Paris, **FUZ**

Seriwaza, M. (1973) A search technique of control rod pattern of smoothing care power distributions by fuzzy automaton, *Journal of Nuclear Science and Technology, 10,* **FUZ**

Shackle, G. L. S. (1949) *Expectation in Economics,* Cambridge University Press, Cambridge, UK, **SS, PROB**

Shackle, G. L. S. (1961) *Decision, Order and Time in Human Affairs,* Cambridge University Press, Cambridge, UK, (2nd ed. 1969) **SS, PROB**

Shaw-Kwei, Moh. (1954) Logical paradoxes for many-valued systems. *J. Symbolic Logic, 19,* 37–39, **MVLOG, PARA**

Sheppard, D. (1954) The adequacy of everyday quantitative expressions as measurements of qualities, *Brit. J. Psychol., 45,* 40–50, **VAG, PSYCH**

Shimura, M. (1972) Application of fuzzy functions to pattern classification, *Trans. Inst. Electron. Comm. Eng. (Japan), 55–d,* 218–225, **FUZ, PAT**

Shimura, M. (1973) Fuzzy sets concept in rank-ordering objects, *J. Math. Anal. & Appln., 43,* 717–733, **FUZ, PAT**

Shimura, M. (1975) Applications of fuzzy sets theory to pattern recognition, *J. JAACE, 19,* 243–248, **FUZ, PAT**

Shimura, M. (1975) An approach to pattern recognition and associative memories using fuzzy logic in Zadeh, L. A., Fu, K. S., Tanaka, K., & Shimura, M. (eds.), *Fuzzy Sets and Their Applications to Cognitive and Decision Processes,* Academic Press, New York, 449–476, **FUZ, PAT**

Shirai, T. (1937) On the pseudo-set, *Memoirs of the College of Science Kyoto Imperial University, 20A,* 153–156, **LOG, SET, PARA**

Shortliffe, E. H. (1976) *Computer-Based Medical Consultation: MYCIN,* Elsevier, New York, **MED, PROB, FUZ**

Shortliffe, E. H., & Buchanan, B. G. (1975) A model of inexact reasoning in medicine, *Math. Biosciences, 23,* 351–379, **MED, FUZ**

Shuford, E. H., Albert, A., & Massengill, H. E. (1966) Admissible probability measurement procedures, *Psychometrika, 31,* 125–145, **PROB**

Shuford, E. H., & Brown T. A. (1975) Elicitation of personal probabilities and their assessment, *Instructional Science, 4,* 137–188, **PROB, PSYCH**

Sikorski, R. (1964) *Boolean Algebras,* Springer-Verlag, Berlin **LAT, TOP**

Simon, H. A. (1967) The logic of heuristic decision making, in Rescher, N. (ed.),

The Logic of Decision and Action, University of Pittsburgh Press, 1–35, **LOG, INDUCT**

Simons, H. W. (1976) *Persuasion,* Addison-Wesley, Reading, Mass., USA, **LING, PSYCH**

Sinha, N. K., & Wright, J. D. (1975) Application of fuzzy control to a heat exchanger, in *Special Interest Discussion Session on Fuzzy Automata and Decision Processes,* 6th IFAC World Congress, Boston, Mass., USA, Aug., **FUZ, CON**

Siy, P. (1973) Fuzzy logic for handwritten character recognition, *PhD thesis,* Department of Electrical Engineering, University of Akron, Ohio, USA, June, **FUZ, PAT**

Siy, P., & Chen, C. S. (1972) Minimization of fuzzy functions, *IEEE Trans. Comp., C–21,* 100–102, **FUZ, SWLOG**

Siy, P., & Chen, C. S. (1974) Fuzzy logic for handwritten numerical character recognition, *IEEE Trans. Syst. Man Cybern., SMC–4,* 570–575, **FUZ, SW-LOG, PAT**

Shaket, E. (1975) Fuzzy semantics for a natural-like language defined over a world of blocks, MSc thesis, Computer Science Dept., UCLA, Los Angeles, Calif., USA, **FUZ, LMACH, LING**

Skala, H. J. (1974) On the problem of imprecision, Dordrecht, Netherlands, **FUZ, VAG**

Skala, H. J. (1975) *Non-Archimedean Utility Theory,* D. Reidel, Dordrecht, **FUZ, PROB**

Skala, H. J. (1976a) Fuzzy concepts: logic, motivation, application, in Bossel, H., Klaczko, S., & Muller, N. (eds.), *Systems Theory in the Social Sciences,* Birkhauser Verlag, Basel, 292–306, **FUZ, VAG**

Skala, H. J. (1976b) Not necessarily additive realizations of comparative probability relations, **FUZ, PROB**

Skalička, V. (1935) *Zur Ungarischen Grammatik,* Prague, **LING**

Skolem, Th. (1957) Bemerkungen zum komprehensionsaxiom, *Z. Math. Logik Grundlagen Math., 3,* 1–17, **SET, LOG**

Skolem, Th. (1960) A set theory based on a certain 3-valued logic, *Math. Scand., 8,* 127–136, **MVLOG, SET**

Skolem, Th. (1962) *Abstract Set Theory,* Notre Dame Press, Indiana, USA, **SET, LOG, MVLOG**

Skyrms, B. (1970) Return of the liar: three-valued logic and the concept of truth, *Amer. Philos. Quart., 7,* 153–161, **PARA, MVLOG, TRUTH**

Slack, J. M. V. (1976a) A fuzzy set-theoretic approach to semantic memory: a resolution to the set-theoretic versus network model controversy, in Mamdani, E. H., & Gaines, B. R. (eds.), *Discrete Systems and Fuzzy Reasoning, EES–MMS–DSFR–76,* Queen Mary College, University of London, (workshop proceedings) **FUZ, LING**

Slack, J. M. V. (1976b) Possible applications of the theory of fuzzy sets to the study of semantic memory in Mamdani, E. H., & Gaines, B. R. (eds.), *Discrete Systems and Fuzzy Reasoning, EES–MMS–DSFR–76,* Queen Mary College,

University of London, (workshop proceedings) **FUZ, LING**

Slupecki, J. (1958) Towards a generalized mereology of Lesniewski, *Studia Logica,* 131–154, **LOG, VAG**

Smith, C. A. B. (1961) Consistency in statistical inference and decision, *J. Roy. Statist. Soc. (ser. B), 23,* 1–37, **PROB**

Smith, C. A. B. (1965) Personal probability and statistical analysis, *J. Roy. Statist. Soc. (ser. A), 128,* 469–499, **PROB**

Smith, R. E. (1970) Measure theory on fuzzy sets, *PhD thesis,* University of Saskatchewan, Saskatoon, Canada, **FUZ, PROB**

Smullyan, R. M. (1957) Languages in which self-reference is possible, *J. Symbolic Logic, 22,* 55–67, **LOG, PARA**

Snyder, D. P. (1971) *Modal Logic,* Van Nostrand Reinhold, New York, **MLOG**

Sober, E. (1975) *Simplicity,* Clarendon Press, Oxford, **PROB, LOG, INDUCT**

Sobolewski, M. (1976) Classification system semantics in terms of fuzzy sets, *3rd Eur. Meeting Cybern. Syst. Res., Vienna,* **FUZ, PAT**

Sols, I. (1975a) Fuzzy universal algebra and applications, Department of Geometry, Faculty of Sciences, Zaragoza, Spain, **FUZ, LAT, CAT**

Sols, I. (1975b) Aportaciones a la teoria de topos, al algebra universal y a las mathematicas fuzzy, PhD thesis, Zaragoza, Spain, **FUZ, LAT, CAT**

Sols, I. (1975c) Unmarco unificato para la teoria de automatas, Department of Geometry, Faculty of Sciences, Zaragoza, Spain, **FUZ, LAT, CAT**

Sommer, G. (1976) A fuzzy programming approach to an air pollution regulation problem, *3rd Eur. Meeting Cybern. Syst. Res., Vienna,* **FUZ**

Stalnaker, R. (1970) Probability and conditionals, *Philos. Sci., 37,* 64–80, **LOG, PROB**

Stalnaker, R. C., & Thomason, R. H. (1970) A semantic analysis of conditional logic, *Theoria, 36,* 23–42, **LOG**

State, L. (1971) Quelques proprietes des algebres de Morgan, in Moisil, G. C. (ed.), *Logique, Automatique, Informatique,* Bucharest, 195–207, **LOG, TOP**

Stefanescu, A. C. (1975) Category SETf(L), *Seminarul de Teoria Sistemelor,* Dept. Economic Cybernetics, Academy of Economic Studies, Bucharest, **CAT, FUZ**

Stoica, M., & Scarlat, E. (1975a) Fuzzy algorithms in economic systems, *Economic Computation & Economic Cybernetic Studies & Research, 3,* Centre of Economic Computation & Economic Cybernetics, Bucharest, Roumania, 239–247, **FUZ, DEC**

Stoica, M., & Scarlat, E. (1975b) Fuzzy concepts in the control of production systems, *Proceedings of 3rd International Congress of Cybernetics and Systems,* Bucharest. Rumania, Aug., **FUZ, CON**

Stone, M. H. (1937–38) Topological representations of distributive lattices and Brouwerian logics, *Časopis pro pěstování matematiky a fysiky, 67, 1–25,* **LAT, LOG**

Stove, D. C. (1973) *Probability and Hume's Inductive Scepticism,* Clarendon Press, Oxford, **INDUCT, PROB, LOG**

Sugeno, M. (1971) On fuzzy nondeterministic problems, *Annual Conference Record of SICE,* **FUZ**

Sugeno, M. (1972a) Fuzzy measures and fuzzy integrals, *Transactions of SICE, 8,* 218–226, **FUZ, PROB**

Sugeno, M. (1972b) Evaluation of similarity of patterns by fuzzy integrals, *Annual Conference Records of SICE*, **FUZ, PAT**

Sugeno, M. (1973) Constructing fuzzy measure and grading similarity of patterns by fuzzy integrals, *Transaction SICE, 9,* 359–367, **FUZ, PROB**

Sugeno, M. (1974) Theory of fuzzy integrals and its applications, *PhD thesis,* Tokyo Institute of Technology, Tokyo, Japan, **FUZ, PROB**

Sugeno, M. (1975a) Theoretical developments of fuzzy sets, *J. JAACE, 19,* 229–234, **FUZ**

Sugeno, M. (1975b) Inverse operation of fuzzy integrals and conditional fuzzy measures, *Trans. SICE, 11,* 32–37, **FUZ**

Sugeno, M. (1975c) Fuzzy decision-making problems, *Trans. SICE, 11,* 709–714, **FUZ, DEC**

Sugeno, M. (1975d) Fuzzy measures and fuzzy integrals, in *Summary of Papers on General Fuzzy Problems,* The Working Group on Fuzzy Systems, Tokyo, Japan, Nov., 55–60, **FUZ, PROB**

Sugeno, M., & Terano, T. (1973) An approach to the identification of human characteristics by applying fuzzy integrals, *Proceedings of 3rd IFAC Symposium on Identification and System Parameter Estimation,* Hague, **FUZ, PAT**

Sugeno, M., & Terano, T. (1975) Analytical representation of fuzzy systems, in *Special Interest Discussion Session on Fuzzy Automata and Decision Processes, 6th* IFAC World Congress, Boston, Mass., USA, Aug., **FUZ**

Sugeno, M., & Terano, T. (1976) A model of learning based on fuzzy information, *3rd Eur. Meeting Cybern. Syst. Res.,* Vienna, **FUZ, PSYCH**

Sugeno, M., Tsukamoto, Y. & Terano, T. (1974) Subjective evaluation of fuzzy objects, *IFAC Symposium on Stochastic Control,* **FUZ, PSYCH**

Swinburne, R. (1973) *An Introduction to Confirmation Theory,* Methuen, London, **PROB, INDUCT**

Tahani, V. (1971) Fuzzy sets in information retrieval, *PhD thesis,* Department of Electrical Engineering and Computer Science, University of California, Berkeley, California, USA, **FUZ, INFR**

Takeuti, G., & Zaring, W. M. (1973) *Axiomatic Set Theory,* Springer-Verlag, Berlin, **SET, TOP, LOG**

Tamura, S. (1971) Fuzzy pattern classification, *Proceedings of a Symposium on Fuzziness in Systems and its Processing, Professional Group of System Engineering of SICE,* **FUZ, PAT**

Tamura, S., Higuchi, S., & Tanaka, K. (1971) Pattern classification based on fuzzy relations, *IEEE Trans. Syst. Man Cybern., SMC–1,* 61–66, **FUZ, PAT**

Tamura, S., & Tanaka, K. (1973) Learning of fuzzy formal language, *IEEE Trans. Syst. Man Cybern, SMC–3,* 98–102, **FUZ, LANG**

Tanaka, K. (1972) Analogy and fuzzy logic, *Mathematical Sciences,* **FUZ**

Tanaka, K. (1975) Fuzzy sets theory and its application, *Journal of JAACE, 19,* 227–228, **FUZ**

Tanaka, K., & Mizumoto, M. (1975) Fuzzy programs and their execution, in Zadeh, L. A., Fu, K. S., Tanaka, K., & Shimura, M. (eds.), *Fuzzy Sets and Their Applications to Cognitive and Decision Processes,* Academic Press, New York, 41–76, **FUZ, AUT**

Tanaka, K., Toyoda, J., Mizumoto, M., & Tsuji, H. (1970) Fuzzy automata theory and its application to automatic controls, *Journal of JAACE, 14,* 541–550, **FUZ, AUT**

Tanaka, K., Okuda, T., & Asai, K. (1972) On the fuzzy mathematical programming, *Annual Conference Records of SICE,* **FUZ**

Tanaka, K., Okuda, T., & Asai, K. (1973) Fuzzy mathematical programming, *Transactions of SICE, 9,* 109–115, **FUZ**

Tanaka, H., Okuda, T., & Asai, K. (1974) Decision-making and its goal in a fuzzy environment, *US-Japan Seminar on Fuzzy Sets and Their Applications,* Berkeley, California, USA, July, **FUZ, DEC**

Tanaka, H., Okuda, T., & Asai, K. (1976) A formulation of fuzzy decision problems and its application to an investment problem, *Kybernetes, 5,* 25–30, **FUZ, DEC**

Taranu, C. (1976) Fuzzy aspects in cost theory, *3rd Eur. Meeting Cybern, Syst. Res., Vienna,* **FUZ, DEC**

Tarski, A. (1956) *Logic, Semantics, Metamathematics,* Clarendon Press, Oxford, **LOG, TRUTH, TOP, MVLOG, LAT**

Tazakai, E. (1975) Heuristic synthesis in a class of systems by using fuzzy automata, in *Summary of Papers on General Fuzzy Problems,* The Working Group on Fuzzy Systems, Tokyo, Japan, Nov., 61–66, **FUZ**

Terano, T. (1971) Fuzziness and its concept, *Proceedings of a Symposium on Fuzziness in Systems and its Processing, Professional Group of System Engineering of SICE,* **FUZ**

Terano, T. (1972) Fuzziness of systems, Nikka-Giren Engineers, 21–25, **FUZ**

Terano, T., & Sugeno, M. (1975) Conditional fuzzy measures and their application, in Zadeh, L. A., Fu, K. S., Tanaka, K., & Shimura, M. (eds.), *Fuzzy Sets and Their Applications to Cognitive and Decision Processes,* Academic Press, New York, 151–170, **FUZ, PROB**

Terano, T., & Sugeno, M. (1975) Macroscopic optimization by using conditional measures, in *Summary of Papers on General Fuzzy Problems,* The Working Group on Fuzzy Systems, Tokyo, Japan, Nov., 67–72, **FUZ, PROB**

Terasaka, H. (1937) Theorie der topologischen verbande, *Proc. Imperial Academy, 13,* Tokyo, **TOP**

Tharp, L. (1975) Which logic is the right logic?, *Synthese, 31,* 1–21, **LOG**

Thomason, M. G. (1975) Finite fuzzy automata, regular fuzzy languages and pattern recognition, *Pattern Recognition, 5,* 383–390, **FUZ, AUT, LANG**

Thomason, M. G. (1974) The effect of logic operations on fuzzy logic distributions, *IEEE Trans. Syst. Man Cybern., SMC–4,* 309–310, **FUZ, SWLOG**

Thomason, M. G. (1974) Fuzzy syntax-directed translations, *J. Cybernetics, 4,* 87–94, **FUZ, LANG**

Thomason, M. G., & Marionos, P. N. (1974) Deterministic acceptors of regular fuzzy languages, *IEEE Trans. Syst. Man Cybern., SMC–4,* 228–230, **FUZ, LANG**

Tichý, P. (1969) Intension in terms of Turing machines, *Studia Logica, 24,* 7–25, **LOG, AUT, VAG**

Tichý, P. (1974) On Popper's definition of verisimilitude, *Brit. J. Philos. Sci., 25,* 155–160, **INDUCT, VAG**

Tichý, P. (1976) Verisimilitude redefined, *Brit. J. Philos. Sci., 27,* 25–42, **INDUCT, VAG**

Tong, R. M. (1976a) An assessment of a fuzzy control algorithm for a nonlinear multivariable plant, in Mamdani, E. H., & Gaines, B. R. (eds.), *Discrete Systems and Fuzzy Reasoning, EES-MMS-DSFR-76,* Queen Mary College, University of London, (workshop proceedings) **FUZ, CON**

Tong, R. M. (1976b) Some problems with the design and implementation of fuzzy controllers, *CUED/F-CAMS/TR127(1976),* Cambridge University Control Engineering Dept., **FUZ, CON**

Tong, R. M. (1976c) Analysis of fuzzy control algorithms using the relation matrix, *Int. J. Man-Machine Studies, 8,* **FUZ, CON**

Tsichritzis, D. (1969) Fuzzy properties and almost solvable problems, *Tech. Rep. 70,* Computer Science Laboratory, Department of Electrical Engineering, Princeton University, **FUZ**

Tsichritzis, D. (1969) Measures on countable sets, *Technical Report 8,* Department of Computer Science, University of Toronto, Canada, **FUZ, PROB**

Tsichritzis, D. (1969) Fuzzy computability, *Proc. Princeton Conf. Information Sciences & Systems,* 157–162, **FUZ**

Tsichritzis, D. (1971) Participation measures, *J. Math. Anal. & Appln., 36,* 60–72, **FUZ, PROB**

Tsichritzis, D. (1971) Approximation and complexity of functions on the integers, *Inform. Sci.,* 70–86, **FUZ**

Tsichritzis, D. (1973) A model for iterative computation, *Inform. Sci., 5,* 187–197, **FUZ**

Tsichritzis, D. (1973) Approximate logic, *Proc. Symp. Multivalued Logic,* May, **FUZ**

Tsuji, H., Mizumoto, M., Toyoda, J., & Tanaka, K. (1972) Interaction between random environments and fuzzy automata with variable structures, *Trans. Inst. Electron. Comm. Eng. (Japan), 55-d,* 143–144, **FUZ**

Tsuji, H., Mizumoto, M., Toyoda, J., & Tanaka, K. (1973) Linear fuzzy automaton, *Trans. Inst. Electron. Comm. Eng. (Japan), 56-a,* 256–257, **FUZ**

Tsukamoto, Y. (1975) A subjective evaluation on attractivity of sightseeing zones, in *Summary of Papers on General Fuzzy Problems,* The Working Group on Fuzzy Systems, Tokyo, Japan, Nov., 73–76, **FUZ, SS**

Tsukamoto, Y., & Iida, H. (1973) Evaluation models of fuzzy systems, *Annual Conference Records of SICE,* **FUZ**

Turksen, I. B., & Martin, J. K. (1976) Decision-information systems, a conceptual framework, 76–010, Department of Industrial Engineering, University of Toronto, Canada, **FUZ, DEC**

Turquette, A. R. (1954) Many-valued logics and systems of strict implication, *Philos. Rev., 63,* 365–379, **MVLOG**

Turquette, A. R. (1963) Independent axioms for infinite-valued logic, *J. Symbolic Logic, 28,* 217–221, **MVLOG**

Uhr, L. (1975) Toward integrated cognitive systems which must make fuzzy decisions about fuzzy problems, in Zadeh, L. A., Fu, K. S., Tanaka, K., & Shimura, M. (eds.), *Fuzzy Sets and Their Applications to Cognitive and Decision Processes,* Academic Press, New York, 353–393, **FUZ, PSYCH**

Urquhart, A. (1973) An interpretation of many-valued logic, *Z. Math. Logik Grundlagen Math., 19,* 111–114, **MVLOG**

Vachek, J. (1964a) Prague phonological studies today, *Travaux Linguistiques de Prague, 1,* 7–20, **LING, VAG**

Vachek, J. (1964b) On some basic principles of "classical" phonology, *Zeitschr. für Phonetik, Sprachwissenschaft u. Kommunikationsforschung (Berlin), 17,* 409–431, **LING, VAG**

Vachek, J. (1966a) On the integration of the peripheral elements into the system of language, *Travaux Linguistique de Prague, 2,* 23–37, **LING, VAG**

Vachek, J. (1966b) *The Linguistic School of Prague,* Indiana University Press, Bloomington, **LING**

Van Fraassen, B. C. (1968) Presuppositions, supervaluations and self-reference, *J. Philos., 65,* 136–152, **MVLOG, PARA**

Van Fraassen, B. C. (1974) Hidden variables in conditional logic, *Theoria, 40,* 176–190, **MLOG**

Van Fraassen, B. C. (1975) Comments: Lakoff's fuzzy propositional logic, in Hockney, D., Harper, W., & Freed, B. (eds.), *Contemporary research in philosophical logic and linguistic semantics,* Reidel, Holland, **FUZ, LOG**

Van Heijencort, J. (ed.) (1967) *From Frege to Godel: A Source Book in Mathematical Logic 1879-1937,* Harvard University Press, Cambridge, Mass., USA, **LOG, SET**

Van Velthoven, G. D. (1974a) Application of fuzzy sets theory to criminal investigation, *PhD thesis,* University of Louvain, Belgium, **FUZ, SS**

Van Velthoven, G. D. (1974b) Onderzoek naar toepasbaarheid van de theorie der vage verzamelingen op het parametrisch onderzoek inzake criminaliteit, Dec., **FUZ, SS**

Van Velthoven, G. D. (1975a) Application of fuzzy sets theory to criminal investigation, *Proc. First European Congress on Operations Research,* Brussels, Jan., **FUZ, SS**

Van Velthoven, G. D. (1975b) Fuzzy models in personnel management, *Proc. Third International Congress of Cybernetics and Systems,* Bucharest, Aug., 15, **FUZ, SS**

Van Velthoven, G. D. (1975c) Quelques applications de la taxonomie floue, *Seminaire sur la contribution des systemes flous a l'automatique: processus humain et industriel,* Centre d'automatique, Universite des Sciences et techniques de Lille, France, June, **FUZ, SS**

Varela, F. J. (1975) A calculus for self-reference, *Int. J. General Syst., 2,* 5–24, **LOG**

Varela, F. J. (1976a) The arithmetic of closure, *3rd Eur. Meeting Cybern, Syst. Res., Vienna,* April, **LOG, PARA**

Varela, F. J. (1976b) The extended calculus of indications interpreted as a three-valued logic, *Notre Dame J. Formal Logic, 17,* **LOG, PARA**

Verma, R. R. (1970) Vagueness and the principle of the excluded middle, *Mind, 79,* 66–77, **VAG**

Vickers, J. M. (1965) Some remarks on coherence and subjective probability, *Philos. Sci., 32,* 32–38, **PROB**

Villegas, C. (1964) On quantitative probability sigma-algebras, *Ann. Math. Statist.,* *35*, 1787–1796, **PROB**

Vincke, P. (1973) Une application de la theorie des graphes flous, *Cahiers du Centre d'Etudes de Recherche Operationelle, 15(3),* 375–395, **FUZ**

Vincke, P. (1973) La theorie des ensembles flous, *Memorie,* Faculte de Science, Universitie Libre de Bruxelles, Belgium, **FUZ**

Von Wright, G. H. (1957) *Logical Studies,* Routledge & Kegan Paul, London, **MLOG, DEC, TRUTH**

Von Wright, G. H. (1962) Remarks on the epistemology of subjective probability, in Nagel, E., Suppes, P., & Tarski, A. (eds.), *Logic, Methodology and Philosophy of Science,* Stanford University Press, California, USA, 330–339, **PROB, IN-DUCT**

Von Wright, G. H. (1963a) *The Logic of Preference,* Edinburgh University Press, **MLOG, DEC**

Von Wright, G. H. (1963b) *Norm and Action,* Routledge & Kegan Paul, London, **MLOG, DEC**

Von Wright, G. H. (1972) *An Essay in Deontic Logic and the General Theory of Action,* North-Holland, Amsterdam, **MLOG, DEC**

Vopěnka, P., & Hájek, P. (1972) *Theory of Semisets,* North-Holland, Amsterdam, **SET, MVLOG, LAT**

Vossen, P. H. (1974) Fuzzy set convolution with respect to a group operation, *Memo 1974.06.20,* Department of Psychology, Nijmegen University, Holland, **FUZ**

Vossen, P. H. (1974) Notes for a theory of fuzziness. The emergence of a basic concept in mathematics, science and technology, *SSRG-74-01,* Department of Psychology, Nijmegen University, Holland, **FUZ, VAG**

Vossen, P. H. (1975) Vertaling van voorwoord, voorbericht en inhoudsopgave van Kaufmann 1973, *Memo 75-08,* Department of Psychology, Nijmegen University, Holland, (in Dutch) **FUZ**

Vossen, P. H., & Klabbers, J. H. G. (1973) In vogelvlucht over algemene systemleer en vage verzamlingenleer, *SSRG-73-00,* Department of Psychology, Nijmegen University, Holland, (in Dutch) **FUZ, VAG**

Vossen, P. H., & Klabbers, J. H. G. (1974) A formal and experimental inquiry into the applicability of nonstandard set theory to the analysis of valuation processes in social systems, *SSRG 74-11,* Department of Psychology, Nijmegen University, Holland, **FUZ, SS**

Wajsberg, M. (1967) Axiomatization of the three-valued propositional calculus, in McCall, S. (ed.), *Polish Logic 1920-1939,* Clarendon Press, Oxford, 264–284, **MVLOG**

Warren, R. H. (1974a) Optimality in fuzzy topological polysystems, Applied Mathematics Research Laboratory, Wright-Patterson Air Force Base, Ohio, USA, **FUZ, TOP**

Warren, R. H. (1974b) Boundary of a fuzzy set, Applied Mathematics Research Laboratory, Wright-Patterson AFB, Ohio, USA, (prev. Closure operator and boundary operator for fuzzy topological spaces) **FUZ, TOP**

Warren, R. H. (1974c) Neighborhoods, bases and continuity in fuzzy topological spaces, Applied Mathematics Research Laboratory, Wright-Patterson AFB, Ohio, USA **FUZ,TOP**

Watanabe, S. (1969) Modified concepts of logic, probability and information based on generalized continuous characteristic function, *Inform. & Control, 15,* 1–21, **FUZ,PROB,LOG**

Watanabe, S. (1975) Creative learning and propensity automata, *IEEE Trans. Syst. Man Cybern., SMC-5,* 603–609, **FUZ,AUT,LMACH**

Webb, D. L. (1936) The algebra of n-valued logic, *Comptes Rendus des Seances de la Societe des Sciences et des Lettres de Varsovie, 29,* 153–168, **MVLOG**

Wechler, W. (1974) Analyse und synthes zeitvariabler R-fuzzy automaten, *ZKI Informationen (Akad. d. Wiss. de DDR), 1,* 32–366, **FUZ,AUT**

Wechler, W. (1975a) R-fuzzy grammars, in Bečvář, J. (ed.), *Mathematical Foundations of Computer Science, Lecture Notes in Computer Science, 32,* Springer-Verlag, Berlin, Germany, 450–456, **FUZ,LANG**

Wechler, W. (1975b) R-fuzzy automata with a time-variant structure, in Blikle, A. (ed.), *Mathematical Foundations of Computer Science, Lecture Notes in Computer Science, 28,* Springer-Verlag, Berlin, Germany, 73–76, **FUZ,AUT**

Wechler, W. (1975c) Zur verallgemeinergung des theorems von Kleene-Schutzenberger auf zeitvariable automaten, *J. EIK, 11,* 439–445, **FUZ,AUT**

Wechler, W. (1975d) Automaten uber inputkategorien, *J. EIK, 11,* 681–685, **FUZ,ZUT**

Wechler, W. (1975e) Gesteuerte R-fuzzy automaten, *ZKI-Informationen (Akad. d. Wiss. der DDR), 1,* 9–13, **FUZ,AUT**

Wechler, W. (1975f) The concept of fuzziness in the theory of automata, *Proceedings of 3rd International Congress of Cybernetics and Systems,* Bucharest, Rumania, Aug., **FUZ,AUT**

Wechler, W. (1976a) Zum verhalten gesteuerter R-fuzzy automaten, Tech. Univ. Dresden, Germany, **FUZ,AUT**

Wechler, W. (1976b) Hierarchy of n-rational languages, Tech. Univ. Dresden, Germany, **FUZ,LANG**

Wechler, W., & Agasandyan, G. A. (1974) Automata with a variable structure and metaregular languages, *Izv. Akad. Nauk SSSR Tehn. Kibernet., 1w,* 146–148, **FUZ,AUT,LANG**

Wechler, W., & Dimitrov, V. (1974) R-fuzzy automata, in *Information Processing 74, Proc. IFIP Congress,* North-Holland, Amsterdam, 657–660, **FUZ,AUT**

Wechsler, H. (1975) Applications of fuzzy logic to medical diagnosis, *Proc. 1975 Int. Symp. Multiple-Valued Logic, IEEE 75CH0959-7C,* May, **FUZ,MED**

Wee, W. G. (1967) On generalizations of adaptive algorithms and applications of the fuzzy sets concept to pattern classification, *PhD thesis,* Purdue University, Lafayette, USA, **FUZ,PAT**

Wee, W. G., & Fu, K. S. (1969) A formulation of fuzzy automata and its application as a model of learning systems, *IEEE Tran. Syst., Man Cybern., SMC-5,* 215–223, **FUZ,LMACH,AUT**

Weiss, M. D. (1975) Fixed points separation and induced topologies for fuzzy sets, *J. Math. Anal. & Appln., 50,* 142–150, **FUZ,TOP**

Weiss, S. E. (1973) The sorites antinomy: a study in the logic of vagueness and measurement, *PhD thesis,* University of North Carolina, Chapel Hill, **FUZ, VAG, PARA**

Weiss, S. E. (1976) The sorites fallacy: what difference does a peanut make?, *Synthese,* **FUZ, VAG, PARA**

Wenstop, F. (1975a) Application of linguistic variables in the analysis of organizations, *PhD thesis,* School of Business Administration, University of California, Berkeley, California, USA, **FUZ, SS**

Wenstop, F. (1975b) Evaluation of verbal organizational models, *NOAK 75,* Oslo, **FUZ, SS**

Wenstop, F. (1976) Deductive verbal models of organizations, *Int. J. Man-Machine Studies, 8,* 293–311, **FUZ, SS**

White, A. R. (1975) *Modal Thinking,* Basil Blackwell, Oxford, **MLOG, LING**

Wilkinson, J. (1973) Retrospective futurology, in Wilkinson, J., Bellman, R., & Garaudy, R. (eds.), *The Dynamic Programming of Human Systems,* MSS Information Corp., New York, USA, 19–33, **FUZ, SS**

Wilkinson, J. (1973) Archetypes, language, dynamic programming and fuzzy sets, in Wilkinson, J., Bellman, R., & Garaudy, R. (eds.), *The Dynamic Programming of Human Systems,* MSS Information Corp., New York, USA, 44–53, **FUZ, SS**

Wilkinson, J., Bellman, R., & Garaudy, R. (eds.) (1973) *The Dynamic Programming of Human Systems,* MSS Information Corp., New York, USA, **FUZ, SS**

Wilks, Y. (1975) Preference semantics, in Keenan, E. L. (ed.), *Formal Semantics of Natural Language,* C, 320–348, **LING**

Wilson, D. (1975) *Presuppositions and Non-Truth-Conditional Semantics,* Academic Press, London, **LOG, LING**

Winkler, R. L. (1974) Probabilistic prediction: some experimental results, *J. Amer. Statist. Assn., 66,* 625–688, **PROB**

Winkler, R. L., & Murphy, A. H. (1968) Good probability assessors, *J. Applied Meteorology, 7,* 751–758, **PROB**

Winograd, T. (1974) Lakoff on hedges, Artificial Intelligence Laboratory, Computer Science Dept., Stanford University, Stanford, California, USA, Sep., **FUZ, LING**

Wiredu, J. E. (1975) Truth as a logical constant, with an application to the principle of the excluded middle, *Philos. Quart.,* 305–317, **LOG, TRUTH**

Wojcicki, R. (1966) Semantical criteria of empirical meaningfulness, *Studia Logica, 19,* 75–107, **LOG, VAG**

Wolf, R. G. (1975) A critical survey of many-valued logics 1966-1974, *Proc. 1975 Int. Symp. Multiple-Valued Logic, IEEE 75CH0959-7C,* 468–474, **MVLOG**

Wolniewicz, B. (1970) Four notions of independence, *Theoria, 36,* 161–164, **LOG**

Wong, C. K. (1973) Covering properties of fuzzy topological spaces, *J. Math. Anal. & Appln., 43,* 697–704, **FUZ, TOP**

Wong, C. K. (1974a) Fuzzy topology: product and quotient theorems, *J. Math. Anal. & Appln., 45,* 512–521, **FUZ, TOP**

Wong, C. K. (1974b) Fuzzy points and local properties of fuzzy topology, *J. Math. Anal. & Appln., 46,* 316–328, **FUZ, TOP**

Wong, C. K. (1975) Fuzzy topology, in Zadeh, L. A., Fu, K. S., Tanaka, K., & Shimura, M. (eds.), *Fuzzy Sets and Their Applications to Cognitive and Decision Processes*, Academic Press, New York, 171–190, **FUZ,TOP**

Wong, C. K. (1976) Categories of fuzzy sets and fuzzy topological spaces, *J. Math. Anal. & Appln.*, *53*, 704–714, **FUZ,CAT,TOP**

Wong, G. A., & Sheng, D. C. (1975) On the learning behaviour of fuzzy automata, in Rose, J. (ed.), *Advances in Cybernetics and Systems*, *2*, Gordon & Breach, London, 885–896, **FUZ,LMACH**

Woodbury, M. A., & Clive, J. (1974) Clinical pure types as a fuzzy partition, *J. Cybernetics, 4*, No. 3, 111–121, **FUZ,MED**

Woodhead, R. G. (1972) On the theory of fuzzy sets to resolve ill-structured marine decision problems, Department of Naval Architecture and Shipbuilding, University of Newcastle upon Tyne, UK, **FUZ**

Woodruff, P. W. (1974) A modal interpretation of three-valued logic, *J. Philos. Logic, 3*, 433–439, **MVLOG,MLOG**

Wright, C. (1975) On the coherence of vague predicates, *Synthese, 30*, 325–365, **VAG,LOG**

Yager, R. R. (1976) Comparing fuzzy constraints, *Proc. 5th Northeast Aids Conf.*, Philadelphia, USA, **FUZ,DEC**

Yager, R. R. (1976) An eigenvalue method of obtaining subjective probabilities in decision analysis, **PROB,FUZ**

Yager, R. R. (1976) Multiple objective decision making using fuzzy sets, **FUZ,DEC**

Yager, R. R., & Basson, D. (1975) Decision making with fuzzy sets, *Decision Sciences 6*, 590–600, **FUZ,DEC**

Yeh, R. T. (1974) Toward an algebraic theory of fuzzy relational systems, *Proceedings of International Congress on Cybernetics*, Namur, **FUZ**

Yeh, R. T., & Bang, S. Y. (1975) Fuzzy relations, fuzzy graphs and their applications to clustering analysis, in Zadeh, L. A., Fu, K. S., Tanaka, K., & Shimura, M. (eds.), *Fuzzy Sets and Their Applications to Cognitive and Decision Processes*, Academic Press, New York, 125–149, **FUZ,PAT**

Zadeh, L. A. (1965a) Fuzzy sets, *Inform. & Control, 8*, 338–353, **FUZ**

Zadeh, L. A. (1965b) Fuzzy sets and systems, in Fox, J. (ed.), *System Theory*, Microwave Research Institute Symposia Series XV, Polytechnic Press, Brooklyn, New York, 29–37, **FUZ**

Zadeh, L. A. (1966) Shadows of fuzzy sets, *Problems in Transmission of Information*, *2*, 37–44, (in Russian) **FUZ**

Zadeh, L. A. (1968a) Fuzzy algorithms, *Inform. & Control, 12*, 94–102, **FUZ**

Zadeh, L. A. (1968b) Probability measures of fuzzy events, *J. Math. Anal. & Appln.*, *23*, 421–427, **FUZ,PROB**

Zadeh, L. A. (1969) Biological applications of the theory of fuzzy sets and systems, in Proctor, L. D. (ed.), *Biocybernetics of the Central Nervous System*, Little, Brown & Co., Boston, Mass., USA, 199–212, **FUZ**

Zadeh, L. A. (1971a) Towards a theory of fuzzy systems, in Kalman, R. E., & DeClaris, R. N. (eds.), *Aspects of Netwroks and Systems Theory*, Holt, Rinehart and Winston, New York, **FUZ**

Zadeh, L. A. (1971b) On fuzzy algorithms, *ERL-M325*, University of California,

Berkeley, California, USA, 469–490, **FUZ**

Zadeh, L. A. (1971c) Quantitative fuzzy semantics, *Inform. Sci., 3,* 159–176, **FUZ, LING**

Zadeh, L. A. (1971d) Similarity relations and fuzzy orderings, *Inform. Sci.,* 177–200, **FUZ**

Zadeh, L. A. (1971e) Human intelligence vs. machine intelligence, *Proceedings of International Conference on Science and Society,* Belgrade, Yugoslavia, 127–133, **FUZ, LING**

Zadeh, L. A. (1971f) Towards fuzziness in computer systems–fuzzy algorithms and languages, in Boulaye, G. (ed.), *Architecture and Design of Digital Computers,* Dunod, Paris, 9–18, **FUZ**

Zadeh, L. A. (1972a) A rationale for fuzzy control, *Journal of Dynamic Systems, Measurement and Control, G94,* 3–4, **FUZ**

Zadeh, L. A. (1972b) Fuzzy languages and their relation to human intelligence, *Proc. International Conference on Man and Computer,* S. Karger, Basel 130–165, **FUZ, LING**

Zadeh, L. A. (1972c) A fuzzy set interpretation of linguistic hedges, *J. Cybernetics, 2,* 4–34, **FUZ, LING**

Zadeh, L. A. (1973a) Outline of a new approach to the analysis of complex systems and decision processes, *IEEE Trans. Syst. Man Cybern., 2,* 28–44, **FUZ, LING**

Zadeh, L. A. (1973b) A system-theoretic view of behaviour modification, in Wheeler, H. (ed.), *Beyond the Punitive Society,* W. H. Freeman, San Francisco, 160–169, **FUZ**

Zadeh, L. A. (1974a) A new approach to system analysis, in Marois, M. (ed.), *Man and Computer,* North-Holland, Amsterdam, 55–94, **FUZ**

Zadeh, L. A. (1974b) Fuzzy logic and its application to approximate reasoning, in *Information Processing 74, Proc. IFIP Congress 74, 3,* North-Holland, Amsterdam, 591–594, **FUZ, LING**

Zadeh, L. A. (1974c) The concept of a linguistic variable and its application to approximate reasoning, in Fu, K. S., & Tou, J. T. (eds), *Learning Systems and Intelligent Robots,* Plenum Press, New York, 1–10, **FUZ, LING**

Zadeh, L. A. (1975a) Linguistic cybernetics in Rose, J. (ed.), *Advances in Cybernetics and Systems, 3,* Gordon & Breach, London 1607–1615, **FUZ, LING**

Zadeh, L. A. (1975b) Fuzzy logic and approximate reasoning, *Synthese, 30,* 407–428, **FUZ, LING**

Zadeh, L. A. (1975c) Calculus of fuzzy restrictions, in Zadeh, L. A., Fu, K. S., Tanaka, K., & Shimura, M. (eds.), *Fuzzy Sets and Their Applications to Cognitive and Decision Processes,* Academic Press, New York, 1–39, **FUZ, LING**

Zadeh, L. A. (1975d) A relational model for approximate reasoning, *IEEE International Conference on Cybernetics and Society,* San Francisco, USA, Sep., **FUZ, LING**

Zadeh, L. A. (1976a) The linguistic approach and its application to decision analysis, in Ho, Y. C., & Mitter, S. K. (eds.), *Directions in Large-Scale Systems,* Plenum Press, New York, **FUZ, LING**

Zadeh, L. A. (1976b) Semantic inference from fuzzy premisis, *Proc. 6th Int. Symp.*

Multiple-Valued Logic, IEEE 76CH1111-4C, May, 217–218, **FUZ,LING**

Zadeh, L. A. (1976c) A fuzzy-algorithmic approach to the definition of complex or imprecise concepts, *Int. J. Man-Machine Studies, 8,* 249–291, **FUZ,LING**

Zadeh, L. A. (1976d) A fuzzy algorithmic approach to the definition of complex or imprecise concepts, in Bossel, H., Klaczko, S., & Muller, N. (eds.), *Systems Theory in the Social Sciences,* Birkhauser Verlag, Basel, 202–282, **FUZ,LING**

Zadeh, L. A., Fu, K. S., Tanaka, K., & Shimura, M. (eds.) (1975) *Fuzzy Sets and Their Applications to Cognitive and Decision Processes,* Academic Press, New York, **FUZ**

Zeleny, M. (1976e) The theory of displaced ideal, in Zeleny, M. (ed.), *Multiple Criteria Decision Making Kyoto 1975, Lecture Notes in Economics & Mathematical Systems, 123,* Springer-Verlag, Berlin, 153–206, **FUZ,DEC**

Zimmermann, H. J. (1974) Optimization in fuzzy environments, *Technical Report,* Institute for Operations Research, Technical Hochschule, Aachen, Germany, **FUZ**

Zimmermann, H. J. (1975) Optimale entscheidungen bei unscharfen problembeschreibungen, Lehrstuhl fur Unternehmensforschung, RWTH, Aachen, Germany, **FUZ**

Zimmermann, H. J. (1975) Description and ecoptimization of fuzzy systems, *Int. J. General Syst., 2,* 209–215, **FUZ**

Zimmermann, H. J. (1975) The potential of fuzzy decision making in the private and public sector, *SOAK-75,* Lidingo, Sweden, **FUZ,DEC**

Zimmermann, H. J. (1975) Bibliography: theory and applications of fuzzy sets, Lehrstuhl fur Unternehmensforschung, RWTH, Aachen, Germany, Oct., **FUZ**

Zimmermann, H. J. (1975) Fuzzy decisions, fuzzy algorithms–a promising approach to problem solving, *NOAK75,* Oslo, Oct., **FUZ,DEC**

Zimmermann, H. J., & Gehring, H. (1975) Fuzzy information profile for information selection, 4th Inst. Congress, AFCET, Paris, France, **FUZ,INFR**

Zimmermann, H. J., & Rodder, W. (1975) Analyse, beschreibung und optimierung von unscharf formulierten problemen, Lehrstuhul fur Unternehmensforschung, RWTH, Aachen, Germany, **FUZ**

Zinovev, A. A. (1963) *Philosophical Problems of Many-valued Logic,* D. Reidel, Dordrecht, Holland, **MVLOG**

BIOGRAPHICAL INFORMATION ABOUT THE EDITORS AND CONTRIBUTING AUTHORS

DONATO CARLUCCI

Gruppo Informatica e Automatica, Instituto Elettrotecnico Nazionale galileo Ferraris, Politecnico di Torino, Torino, Italy
Donato Carlucci is an Associate Professor of Systems Theory. He received the Laurea degree in Electronic Engineering from the Politecnico of Torino, Italy in 1969. His current research interests are in control of uncertain systems, modeling and identification with applications to electric power systems and socioeconomic problems.

SHELDON S. L. CHANG

State University of New York, Stony Brook, New York 11794 (USA)
Sheldon Chang is a Professor of Engineering. He received the B.S. and M.S. degrees from Tsinghua University, China, and the Ph.D. degree from Purdue University in 1947. He is the author of *Synthesis of Optimum Control Systems* (McGraw Hill, 1961) and *Energy Conversion* (Prentice Hall, 1963) and over a hundred technical articles. He is a Fellow of the Institute of Electrical and Electronic Engineers and a member of the Econometric Society.

FRANCESCO DONATI

Gruppo Informatica e Automatica, Instituto Elettrotecnico Nazionale galileo Ferraris, Politecnico di Torino, Torino, Italy
Francisco Donati is a Professor at di Ruolo and Director of the Electric Machines Department of Politecnice di Torino. He received the Laurea degree in Electrical Engineering from Politecnico di Torino in 1960. His research interests include electric power systems, theory of control, modeling and identification of uncertain systems and their applications.

J. C. DUNN

Mathematics Department, North Carolina State University, Raleigh, North Carolina, 27607 (USA)
Joseph C. Dunn is an Associate Professor of Mathematics. He received the B.Aero.E. and the M.S. in applied mechanics from the Polytechnic Institute of New York and the Ph.D. in mathematics from Adelphi University. From 1959 to 1969 he was employed by the Grumman Aerospace Engineering Corporation, Bethpage, N.Y. During 1969–1976 he was with the faculty of the Department of Theoretical and Applied Mechanics, and the Center for Applied Mathematics, Cornell University. He is an active contributor to the mathematical literature on monotone operator theory and optimization, and pattern classification problems.

KING-SUN FU
Purdue University, West Lafayette, Indiana 47907 (USA)
King-Sun Fu is a Professor of Electrical Engineering. He received his Ph.D. degree in Electrical Engineering from the University of Illinois, Urbana. He is the author of *Sequential Methods in Pattern Recognition* and *Syntactic Methods in Pattern Recognition* (Academic Press, 1966; 1974). He is a recipient of a Guggenheim Foundation Fellowship.

LAI-W. FUNG
Purdue University, West Lafayette, Indiana 47907 (USA)
Lai-Wo Fung is an Assistant Professor in the school of Electrical Engineering, University of Tennessee, Knoxville. He received his B.S. degree in Electrical Engineering from Cornell University; the M.S. degree in Electrical Engineering from the State University of New York at Stony Brook; and the Ph.D. degree from Purdue University.

BRIAN R. GAINES (*Editor*)
University of Essex, Wivenhoe Park, Colchester CO43SQ England
Brian R. Gaines is Professor of Electrical Engineering and Chairman of the Electrical Engineering Science Department. He studied mathematics and psychology at Trinity College, Cambridge, where he obtained the BA, MA, and Ph.D. He is editor of the *International Journal of Man-Machine Studies* and is an associate editor of the IFAC Journal, *Automatica*, and the *International Journal of General Systems*. His interests lie in the area of stochastic computing, high-level language architectures, machine learning, human operator studies, adaptive control, commercial and medical applications of interactive computer, grammatical inference, and foundations of probability theory and the logics of uncertainty.

MADAN M. GUPTA (*Editor*)
University of Saskatchewan, Saskatoon, Sask., Canada S7N 0W0
Madan M. Gupta is a Professor in the College of Engineering. He studied at the University of Warwick where he obtained the Ph.D. in 1967 in Control Systems. He is active in teaching and research in the area of control systems and adaptive processes, signal processing, biomedical engineering, fuzzy automata, and socio-economic problems. He is an associate editor of the newly founded *International Journal of Fuzzy Sets and Systems*. He is a senior member of the Institute for Electrical and Electronic Engineers, U.S.A.

SADAKI HIROSE
Research Institute of Electrical Communications, Tohoku University, Sendai 980, Japan
Sadak Hirose is a student of the Graduate Course of Electrical Engineering, Faculty of Engineering, Tohoku University. He received the B.Elec.Eng. from Toyama University. His research interest includes the theory of automata and languages.

NAMIO HONDA
Nagoya University, Nagoya 464, Japan
Namio Honda is a Professor of the Faculty of Engineering. He received the

B.Elec.Eng. and Dr.Elec.Eng. degrees from Tohoku University in 1944 and 1959. His research interest includes the theory of automata and languages.

RAMESH JAIN
Indian Institute of Technology, Kharagpur 721302, India
Ramesh Jain is presently in West Germany on a DAAD fellowship where he will be working at the University of Hamburg. He obtained his B.Elec.Eng. degree at Nagpur and Ph.D. at I.I.T. Kharagpur. His research interests include digital control systems, pattern recognition and decision-making in a fuzzy environment.

A. KAUFMANN
2, allee du Chene, Corenc-Montfluery, 38700-La Tronche, France
Professor Kaufmann is the author of over fifty books on topics in applied mathematics, philosophy of science and other fields. He has written extensively on problems in operations research, mathematical programming, dynamic programming and combinations, and is the author of a five-volume treatise on the theory of fuzzy subsets and its applications. He was associated with the University of Grenoble for many years and is currently a faculty member of the University of Louvain and a consultant to Companie Internationale pour l'Informatique, Honeywell-Bull.

L. J. KOHOUT
University College Hospital Medical School, University of London
Professor Kohout is a lecturer at University College. He studied electrical engineering and computing at Czech Technological University of Prague (CVUT) and theoretical physics at Charles University, Prague. He was with the Institute of Physics, and later with the Institute of Astronomy, both of the Czechoslovak Academy of Science, and since 1969 he has been associated with the University of Essex.

PETER J. KING
Warren Spring Laboratory, P.O. Box 20, Gunnels Wood Road, Stevenage, Herts SG1 2BX, U.K.
Peter J. King is with the Control Engineering Division of Warren Spring Laboratory since 1969. He obtained a B.Sc. degree in Electrical Engineering from London University, and M.Sc. and Ph.D. degrees in Systems Engineering from the University of Surrey. His current research interest includes the application of automatic control techniques, fuzzy systems and man-machine interfaces.

MASASUMI KOKAWA
System Development Laboratory, Hitachi Ltd., 5030 Kokubunji, Tokyo 185, Japan
Masasumi Kokawa received his B.S., M.S. and Ph.D. degrees from Nagoya University in 1970, 1972 and 1975, respectively.

E. H. MAMDANI
Queen Mary College, University of London, London E14NS, England
E. H. Mamdani is a lecturer in the Department of Electrical and Electronics Engineering. He graduated from the College of Engineering, Poona, India, and the University of London. His research interests include pattern recognition, artificial intelligence and fuzzy systems.

KAHEI NAKAMURA
Nagoya University, Faculty of Engineering, Automatic Control Laboratory, Furo-Cho, Chikusa-Ku, Nagoya, Japan
Kahei Nakamura is a Professor in the Department of Information and Control Science, and Head of Automatic Control Laboratory. He received his B.D. (Electrical Engineering), Eng.D. (Control Engineering) degrees from Nagoya University. His research interests include system theory, control theory (discrete-time control, computer control, etc.), control strategy (optimizing control), adaptive and learning control, and artificial intelligence.

MASAKAZU NASU
Tohoku University, Sendai 980, Japan
Masakazu Nasu is an Associate Professor of the Research Institute of Electrical Communication. He received his B.Elec.Eng. degree from Kysushu Institute of Technology and Ph.D. degree from Tohoku University. His interest includes the theory of automata and languages.

MORIYA ODA
Nagoya University, Faculty of Engineering, Automatic Control Laboratory, Furo-Cho, Chikusa-Ku, Nagoya, Japan
Moriya Oda is an Associate Professor in the Department of Information and Control Engineering. He received his Ph.D. degree from Nagoya University. His research interests include control theory, artificial intelligence (learning, heuristics, concept formation), and instructional engineering (instructional system, fuzzy-theoretical systems approach to concept formation, structural learning).

J.-J. ØSTERGAARD
AELEROSEVEJ 7, DK 8541 Skødstrup, Denmark
J. J. Østergaard is in computer control of a glass-making machine. He received his M.Sc. and Ph.D. at the Electrical Power Engineering Department, Technical University in Denmark. His research interest is in the application of microcomputers, optimization methods and fuzzy logics.

LUCAS PUN
Laboratoire d'Electroniquee, 351, cours de la Liberation, F-33405-Talence, France
Lucas Pun is a Professor at the Bordeaux University No. 1, and is directing a Research Group in the area of automatic control. He obtained his B.E.E.&B.Math. at the Aurora University of Shanghai, his Diploma of Engineering from the Ecole Supérieure d'Electricité of Paris, his Dr.Ing. at the Grenoble University and his State-Doctor at the Toulouse University. His present interests are agriculture, management, and didactical system controls.

RAMMOHAN K. RAGADE
University of Louisville, Systems Science Center, Belknap Campus, Louisville, Kentucky 40208
Rammohan K. Ragade obtained his Ph.D. from the Indian Institute of Science, Kampur, India. He is currently Assistant Professor at the Systems Science Center. Prior to this, he was a member of the Systems Design Faculty, at the University of Waterloo, Canada. He worked with Bell Northern Research, Ottawa, Canada during 1973–74 on problems of communication and information systems design. It

was here that he developed an interest in the applications of fuzzy set theory. He has written a number of papers in fuzzy set theory applications, game theory, water resources management, control systems, communication and information systems and construction management. He is a member of TIMS, and Society for General Systems Research.

ELIE SANCHEZ
Laboratoire de Physique Medicale, Section Biomathematiques et Informatique Medicale, Faculte de Medecine, Marseille, France
Elie Sanchez is currently a "Chef de Travaux de Faculté-Assistant des Hôpitaux" at the Department of Biophysics, Section of Biomathematics, Statistics and Medical Informatics of the "Faculte de Medecine" in Marseille. He received a Ph.D. in mathematics (Boolean Logic) in 1972 from the "Faculte des Sciences de Marseille" and the Ph.D. in "Biologie Humaine" (Fuzzy Sets Theory) in 1974 from the "Faculté de Medecine de Marseille." He is mainly interested in theoretical aspects of composite fuzzy relations and to their application in medical diagnosis and system theory.

EUGENE S. SANTOS
Youngstown State University, Youngstown, Ohio 44503 (USA)
Eugene Santos is a Professor of Mathematics and Computer Science and the Supervisor for Computer Science. His current interests include automata, formal languages, and fuzzy sets.

GEORGE N. SARIDIS (*Editor*)
Purdue University, West Lafayette, Indiana 47907 (USA)
George N. Saridis is a Professor of Electrical Engineering. He is an elected member of the New York Academy of Science. His teaching and research interest is in the area of Systems Engineering. He is an author of *Self-Organizing Systems of Stochastic Systems* (Marcel Decker, 1976).

HARRY E. STEPHANOU
Purdue University, West Lafayette, Indiana 47907 (USA)
Harry E. Stephanou is a Ph.D. candidate in the School of Electrical Engineering. He received his B.E.E. degree from the American University of Beirut and the M.S.E. degree from Purdue University. His interest includes hierarchical control, learning systems, pattern recognition, and their application to biomedical and geophysical systems.

MICHIO SUGENO
Tokyo Institute of Technology, Oh-okayama, Meguro-ku, Tokyo 152, Japan
Michio Sugeno is a Research Associate in Control Engineering. He received the B.S. degree in Physics from the University of Tokyo, and the Ph.D. degree in control engineering from Tokyo Institute of Technology. His research interests include fuzzy mathematics and the application of fuzzy integrals to humanistic systems.

TOSHIRO TERANO
Tokyo Institute of Technology, Oh-okayama, Meguro-ku, Tokyo 152, Japan
Toshiro Terano is a Professor in the System Science Department. He is a graduate

of the University of Tokyo. His present research interests include modeling, optimization, and evaluation of very complex and fuzzy problems of social, environmental and biological systems.

LOTFI A. ZADEH
Computer Science and Electronics, University of California, Berkeley, California (USA)
Dr. Zadeh is a member of the Computer Science Division of the Department of Electrical Engineering and Computer Sciences. He served as chairman of the Department from 1963 to 1968. Prior to his development of the theory of fuzzy sets, Dr. Zadeh had written extensively on system theory and was one of the leading contributors to the state-space approach, the analysis of time-varying systems by Fourier techniques and various extensions of Wiener's theory.